THE CHICANO HERITAGE

This is a volume in the Arno Press collection

THE CHICANO HERITAGE

See last pages of this volume for a complete list of titles.

ASPECTS OF THE MEXICAN-AMERICAN EXPERIENCE

With an Introduction by Carlos E. Cortés

ARNO PRESS
A New York Times Company
New York — 1976

Editorial Supervision: LESLIE PARR

Reprint Edition 1976 by Arno Press Inc.

Within These Borders was reprinted by permission of the Friendship Press.

Within These Borders was reprinted from a copy in the State Historical Society of Wisconsin Library. The Vaquero was reprinted from a copy in the Princeton University Library. The Development of an Americanization Program was reprinted from a copy in the University of Illinois Library. First Regional Conference was reprinted from a copy in the University of Texas at Austin Library.

THE CHICANO HERITAGE
ISBN for complete set: 0-405-09480-9
See last pages of this volume for titles.

Manufactured in the United States of America

Publisher's Note: This anthology has been reprinted from the best available copies of articles and books.

Library of Congress Cataloging in Publication Data
Main entry under title:

Aspects of the Mexican-American experience.

(The Chicano heritage)
CONTENTS: Hill, M. E. The development of an Americanization program.--Scotford, J. R. Within these borders.--The survey, v. LXVI, no. 3, May 1, 1931. [etc.]
1. Mexican Americans--Addresses, essays, lectures.
I. Cortés, Carlos E. II. Series.
E184.M5A85 973'.04'6872 76-1473
ISBN 0-405-09534-1

ASPECTS OF THE MEXICAN-AMERICAN EXPERIENCE

Introduction

This anthology reflects the diversity of the Mexican-American experience and the variety of ways in which this experience has been perceived and interpreted. Spanning nearly four decades, the six selected publications provide perspectives on numerous topics of significance in the Chicano heritage.

The first selection, *The Development of an Americanization Program* by southern California educator Merton E. Hill, is one of the earliest published studies of educational issues relating to Mexican immigrants. In this 1928 study, Hill specifies his goal as that of developing an "Americanization" educational program based on a "melting pot" orientation and his perception of Mexican immigrants as culturally disadvantaged — common beliefs underlying educational efforts in the 1920's. Despite the limitations imposed by these value assumptions, the study is important both because it reflects one aspect of Americanization educational reform of that era and because of its extensive survey data on Mexican students and their families.

Published three years after Hill's study, the May 1, 1931, issue of *The Survey,* a New York-based magazine, was one of the first general circulation periodicals devoted entirely to Mexican Americans and Mexicans in the United States. Subjects include Mexican migration to and from the United States, Mexican labor in the U.S., vaqueros, and Hispano culture, while there are reproductions of art work of José Clemente Orozco, Diego Rivera, Georgia O'Keefe, and B.J.O. Nordfeldt. Among the contributors to this special issue are economists Ernesto Galarza and Paul Taylor, anthropologist Manuel Gamio, and novelist D.H. Lawrence.

The next publication is the report of an early conference on the education of Mexican Americans held at the University of Texas, Austin, in December, 1945. The thirty participants formed a series of panels which produced position statements on critical educational issues. The resulting conference summary provides an important view of the educational problems facing Mexican Americans and the solutions being considered by leading reformers in the mid-1940's.

Eight years after that conference came the publication of *Within These Borders* by John R. Scotford. A Congregational minister, staff member of the *Missionary Herald,* and editor of *Advance,* Scotford became particularly interested in the problems facing Mexican Americans. Written from the perspective of a sympathetic Protestant missionary to the Spanish-speaking people, this broad survey reflects concern for Mexican Americans and presents concrete ideas for bringing Protestantism to Chicanos and Puerto Ricans.

A survey — but of a different nature and with different goals — was conducted by International Research Associates of Mexico City and published in 1962 by Belden Associates of Dallas. This study of the Mexican-American market in Arizona, California, Colorado, New Mexico, and Texas (done in conjunction with a parallel study of the Black American market) won first prize for quantitative research in the annual Los Angeles Advertising Women Achievement Awards. Focusing on Mexican-American housewives in twelve urban concentrations, the survey provides revealing statistics on such subjects as income, credit use, occupations, vacation habits, education, media preferences, and ownership of homes, automobiles, radios, television sets, and appliances.

The final study in this anthology is *The Vaquero* by Arnold R. Rojas. A vaquero for fifty years, Rojas draws on oral tradition and his personal experience to give a panoramic view of this old and proud profession. Of particular interest are the many vaquero stories and recollections which Rojas recorded in conversations with other vaqueros.

The six selections in this anthology provide a glimpse at the Mexican American experience. Moreover, they indicate some of the ways in which observers — both Mexican Americans and Anglo-Americans — have viewed, recorded, and interpreted this experience.

CARLOS E. CORTÉS
Professor of History
Chairman, Chicano Studies
University of California, Riverside
June, 1976

CONTENTS

THE DEVELOPMENT OF AN AMERICANIZATION PROGRAM

MERTON E. HILL, Ed. D.

Published by
The Board of Trustees of the Chaffey Union High School
and the Chaffey Junior College
Ontario, California
in co-operation with the County Board of Education
of San Bernardino County

1928

PREFACE

The material presented in the six chapters is a portion of a thesis accepted for the degree of Doctor of Education by the University of California. There is additional material that has been secured from a survey of Americanization of San Bernardino County. This survey was conducted during the years 1927 and 1928. Many of the tables used in obtaining some of the conclusions of the thesis are omitted, for they are technical in nature and will not be of general interest.

The writer believes firmly that there are presented in the pages following a procedure and technique that will be of interest and of value to other school systems. It is hoped that a new interest will be aroused in the great work of the public school system in Americanization.

The writer wishes it clearly understood that he is making no attempt to prove the children or adults of any nation inferior in native capacity; he shows conclusively, however, that the Mexican children and adults have not had advantages equal to those of American children. There is an effort made to make possible such opportunities and advantages that all the children and all the adults shall have the school training that insures success, happiness, and worthy American citizenship.

IN APPRECIATION

Acknowledgment is made of the helpful co-operation of Miss Ida M. Collins, County Superintendent of Schools of San Bernardino County, her assistants, and the many teachers and principals who aided in submitting the reports.

INTRODUCTION

THE PROBLEM

One of the most momentous problems confronting the great Southwest today, is the assimilation of the Spanish-speaking peoples that are coming in ever increasing numbers into that land formerly owned by Mexico and since 1848 owned by the United States. The problem of developing, setting up, and carrying out an educational program that will lead ultimately to the "Americanization" of all aliens coming into a typical union high school district, is the subject of this thesis.

DEFINITION

For use in this thesis Americanization is hereby defined as the securing through instruction such reactions on the part of non-Americans that they will accept and practice those ideals, customs, methods of living, skills and knowledge that have come to be accepted as representative of the best in American life.

DIVISIONS OF THE PROBLEM

After tracing the history of the Americanization efforts put forth in the Chaffey Union High School District over a period of eight years, the following topics will be developed:

1. The effects of Mexican peon parentage upon pupil progress.
2. The educational status of Mexican peon parents.
3. The economic status of Mexican adults.
4. Establishing an index of ability of the average Mexican pupil.
5. Setting up a program of Americanization.

THE PROGRAM

The program to be presented is evolved from a study of the present status of non-Americans; it sets up those activities that will bring about the acceptance by aliens of American ideals, customs, methods of living, skills, and knowledge that will make them Americans in fact.

THE METHOD OF PROCEDURE

The problem involved in this thesis will be solved in the following manner:

1. The history of the Americanization movement in the Chaffey district will be reviewed in an introductory chapter.

2. The progress of foreign children will be compared with that of American children. In studying the facts relative to progress the age-grade reports of San Bernardino County for 1926-1927 will be

studied; also those of the elementary districts within the Chaffey Union High School District for 1927-1928 will be investigated.

3. In order to determine the extent of the Americanization problem a survey of enrollment in the elementary schools of San Bernardino County will be made. The numbers of pupils of different races enrolled on February 9, 1927. and enrolled during the months of September, October, November and December of the school year 1927-1928 will be tabulated. The October Census reports of 1927 will be surveyed and tables will be presented showing the numbers by races that are less than one year old, and the numbers that are found to dwell in San Bernardino County by ages one to seventeen. These tabulations will show the extent of the Americanization problem.

4. Case studies will next be made showing the educational and economic status of the Mexican adult population. Lists of questions will be presented to foreign children that will give facts relative to their parents. Other questions will be answered by foreign adults as they enroll in Americanization classes. Finally, questions will be submitted to Mexican adults by an attendance officer, by Americanization teachers, and by a Mexican adult employed for the purpose. The answers to these questions will be tabulated and such information as bears on the problem will be used.

5. Certain tests will be presented to large numbers of Mexican pupils and to American pupils of the same ages. The results of these tests will be tabulated to show the comparative abilities of Mexican and American pupils. These tests will be checked by comparing the standings of Mexican and American pupils with the standing of two hundred and one Mexican and American pupils of the same ages taken at random by two San Bernardino County Supervisors who have given certain Los Angeles City tests to the rural pupils of the county.

6. The subjective opinions of eighty-three teachers will be secured; these opinions will be presented by teachers who have had experience with both American and foreign pupils and are expected to throw light upon the comparative abilities of American and foreign pupils.

7. An index of ability of Mexican pupils will be determined by these studies; the ability index thus determined will be used to direct teachers in preparing new courses of study for Mexican pupils.

8. Finally, a program of Americanization will be set up; it will be shown that this program will be justified by the studies made. Every table, every figure, and all illustrations presented will point toward that line of procedure to be followed in the program of Americanization.

CHAPTER I

HISTORICAL BEGINNINGS

During the school year of 1919-1920 a program for adult education was established in the Chaffey Union High School District in western San Bernardino County, California. In addition to classes held at the central plant located at the extreme western limits of the district in Ontario, other classes were organized in the rural portions of the district, in some cases many miles from the Chaffey buildings. Groups of adults met with evening or afternoon high school extension teachers in elementary school buildings and were organized for instruction purposes along those lines of peculiar or of special interest to them. Opportunities to meet in classes were afforded the adults in from eight to ten rural centers, and the efforts of the administration to put across a rural educational program for adults met with increasing success.

As the Chaffey Union High School District is a large district, including ten elementary districts and covering approximately two hundred twenty-five square miles of territory, many problems early developed. The first was the problem of organization. The high school board owned no property in the rural districts, and consequently there were no buildings for class work conducted under the auspices of the high school. Happily there was worked out "An Association of School Trustees of the Chaffey Union High School District." This organization is composed of the five high school trustees, the thirty elementary trustees, the principals of the schools, and the county superintiendent of schools.

Through the medium of this organization arrangements were made to use elementary school buildings for the high school extension classes for adults.

It soon became evident that there was a real need for certain types of work that had not been foreseen. Mexican adults soon applied for admission to one of the rural evening schools that they might learn the English language. Many of these Mexicans lived in labor camps under conditions of ignorance and squalor. Some of them were working for the adults who were studying Spanish in the evening school. The Americans wanted Spanish that they might converse with their employees; the Mexicans wanted English in order to talk with their employers, and in order to transact the ordinary business affairs of community life. No suitable text-books were available at the time, and an effort was made to work out a vocabulary of the farm that might be usable in both English and Mexican

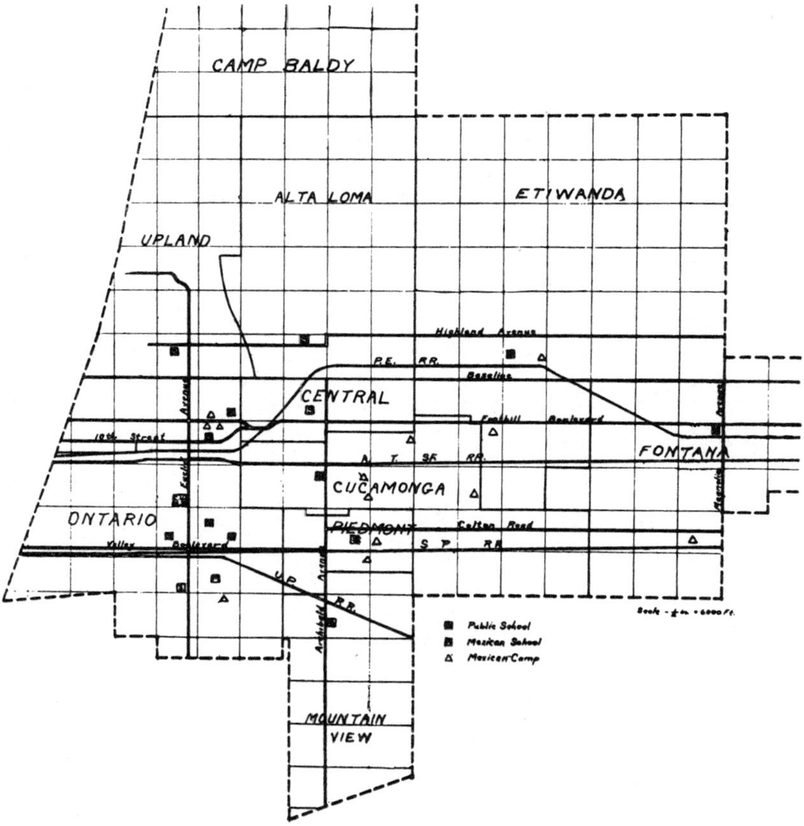

The Chaffey Union High School and Junior College District.

classes. The following vocabulary is typical of some of the earlier lessons attempted:

VERBS

to pick—recoger, pescar; to prune—podar; to put—poner; to remove—quitar.

NOUNS

box—cajon; branch—rama; clippers or pruning knife—pedadera; color—color; dust—polvo; lemon—limon; lemon tree—limonero; orange—naranja; orange tree—naranjo; orchard—huerto, pomar, verjel; sack—saco; row—file, hilera; sand—arena; shoot, sprout—retono, pimpollo; size—tomano; stem—tallo; peduncule; vine—vid, parra; vine branch—sarmiento; vine stock or stump—copa; vineyard—vina; wood, lumber—madera; firewood—lena; dead wood—ramas muertas, ramas secas.

ADJECTIVES, ADVERBS, PREPOSITIONS, ETC.

below—debajo de; colored—coloreado; dry—seco; large—grande; larger—mas grande; longer—mas largo; lower—inferior; shorter—mas corto; smaller—mas chico.

The experiment was interesting and was of value in pointing out one way of teaching Spanish to Americans and of teaching "American" to the Mexican adults; the early attempts, also, caused a concentration of effort to carry on further work among the foreign element in the community, and the creation of a program that developed into what is now called the Americanization of the foreigner.

While this work among the Mexicans was in its beginning stage at the Alta Loma evening school, a naturalization class was organized at the high school. This group wanted to become American citizens; they already understood English, hence the instruction for them consisted in the presentation of American history, geography, and government. This group had different needs from the first: they were American in most particulars, being chiefly English and Canadians; they wanted full participation in American life, and hence desired naturalization and the franchise. At the end of the school year a naturalization examiner was sent by the government; the men were publicly examined on the Constitution; they were given a talk by the examiner and were awarded certificates. These certificates were later accepted in lieu of the usual examination conducted by the Superior Court of the County before awarding the applicants their second papers.

These two types of classes, conducted to meet the needs of aliens within the district and first organized in 1920, led to a study of the very important problem of working out courses of study that might result in reaching the hundreds and perhaps thousands of men and women of foreign birth who were residents of the district, or who were being brought from time to time into the labor camps to maintain a necessary supply of labor, or that other group who had been coming in increasing numbers to develop new homes. As the work was continued many new problems arose; enlisting the interest of aliens in organized class work; the organization of classes of like-minded people; the working out of a definition and the thorough understanding of the term "Americanization"; the development or creation of courses of study that would function in the lives of the adult aliens; the securing of texts and the preparation of lessons to meet the actual needs of the adult foreigners; the securing of teachers with ability to teach the foreigner and who possessed that sympathetic understanding of the various types of foreigners so essential to success; the development of an educational program and the securing of the backing and co-operation of all educational agencies within the district; and finally the securing of the necessary funds to finance an educational program that would reach the great body of foreign adults within the districts. As these problems have been studied and partially solved, it has become apparent that within the district the problem of Americanization involves not only the adults, but their children; that any program neglecting a full consideration of the educational needs of the foreign children is destined to fall short of complete success. During an experience of eight years it has now become evident that these and other problems can be wholly or partially solved; special classrooms adapted to the needs of the foreign element must be provided in the high school plant, in the elementary school buildings, in Mexican camps. and in central buildings within certain camps; a travelling school room on a bus chassis has been provided; teachers must be trained for Americanization work; lessons must be prepared to meet the needs of both children and adults; budgetary provisions must secure sufficient amounts of money, and this money must be spent for the cause for which it has been apportioned; the public must be aroused to a realization of the great and immediate need of making provision for educational, vocational, and sanitation programs that will result in overcoming illiteracy, in eliminating unsanitary and unsightly labor camps, and in promoting the use of the English language, the right American customs, and the best possible standards of American life. As solutions, indicated above have been worked out, it has become perfectly clear that housing conditions, that the economic status of the family, and that the illiteracy of the vast majority of the adults have an important bearing upon the educational efforts that are being put forth both in elementary and secondary schools, and in the adult work of the evening high school. This additional problem will be taken up in a later chapter.

Aliens, like Americans, can be separated into at least two groups; there are those who feel a need for more training that they may succeed better in their occupational life, and they welcome every opportunity to increase their educational outlook; then there are those constituting the bulk of the alien group who are content "to leave well enough alone"; who do not wish to be disturbed, for are they not better off than they were in the country from which they came? Very often it is important to get the employer aroused before the alien can be placed in a class. or be given an impulse or a desire to take advantage of the instruction offered. For this reason it is very important to get the various welfare organizations of a community interested in the Americanization program. The employers of alien labor should be consulted about the matter. To illustrate this procedure several examples will be presented. There is located in the Chaffey Union High School District at Cucamonga the Lucas ranch of about four thousand acres; at this ranch Mexican laborers are employed the year round. In co-operation with Mr. Vincent G. Lucas of the firm, Lucas Co., Inc., a class for Mexicans was opened in the Mexican Camp. A "bunk house" was remodelled at high school expense; blackboards were put up, chairs, tables, and a sewing machine were introduced, and class work was organized in the afternoon for women and in the evening for men. Another illustration of procedure may be cited in Upland. The Citrus Associations have built three-roomed houses which are rented to the employees at ten dollars per month; these houses form the "Sonora Town", where dwell hundreds of Mexican families. Similar towns are now to be found in practically every citrus section. Consultations were held between the packing house managers and representatives of the Chaffey Union High School, and it was arranged that a well-located house in Sonora Town should be turned over—at no cost to the school authorities—to be fitted up as a school and community center for the Mexican adults and part-time students of the Mexican Camp. A conference was called of those interested in Mexican work, so that an intensive program of Americanization might be developed in this part of the district sponsored by many co-operating organizations. Those who were consulted and asked to join in this work were representatives of the Welfare work of Upland, the Presbyterian Church, the Catholic Church, the American Red Cross, and the Americanization Department of the Chaffey Union High School. A girl scout troop spent several afternoons and "tidied" up the rooms of the house, and the high school furnished

One of the Earlier Adult Classes.
Mexicans of the Lucas Ranch learning to read and write English, 1920.

One of the classes of Mexican women meeting at the home provided by the Upland Citrus Association.

the equipment. Then classes were opened for adults and for part-time pupils.

Such co-operation between school authorities and employers of labor is absolutely necessary in the development of a successful plan of Americanization. The California Fruit Growers' Exchange, the largest farmers' co-operative organization in the world, has interested itself in Americanization work. To illustrate what they have done it is only necessary to cite two or three instances. They have encouraged the placement of Americanization teachers in Mexican camps; they have prepared a text-book for aliens who are working in the citrus groves; this text-book has been used in class work, and is based on the actual needs of pickers and laborers in the groves; they have gone on as favoring no limit upon Mexican immigration and therefore should consistently foster an Americanization program amongst the Mexican people in the citrus areas of California.

The easiest places to conduct class work from the standpoint of teaching is in regular classrooms of the public schools. But it has been the experience of teachers and Americanization workers generally that comparatively few Mexicans will come to the public schools at night, unless the schools are located in close proximity to the Mexican camps. However, other aliens will come long distances, particularly those who wish to take out their naturalization papers. To illustrate this last statement it was announced at the Chaffey graduation exercises in 1926 that one member of the "naturalization class" had missed only one class session during the year, although he had travelled nineteen miles each way to each class session! The most successful Mexican classes are those located in the camps, or in those schools that are quite properly regarded as the "Mexican schools" of the district. Such classes have been maintained at public schools in the Chaffey Union High School District for the past seven years; hundreds of foreign adults have been in class attendance at public school centers in Ontario, Upland, Alta Loma, Cucamonga, Etiwanda, Fontana, Mountain View, and Piedmont. At one time there were representatives of fifteen nationalities in attendance at Americanization classes. During the school year 1926-1927 there were in attendance 470 foreign adults, and 251 part-time Mexicans sixteen years of age or over. This number was materially increased during the following year.

There are several ways in which the adults have been organized into classes. Announcement has been made to the school children and their parents are in this way invited to attend the classes. Employers have been notified of the opening of evening and afternoon classes for adults. Leaders among the Mexican or other foreign people have been invited to co-operate in the formation of classes; these leaders always have quite a following and help swell the enrollment in Americanization classes. Posters have been set up in the foreign quarters, printed both in English and in the language of the foreign group. Announcement is made through the papers, which can result in great aid to the cause of Americanization. To illustrate the importance of this, the Fontana Herald's efforts should be cited. In many issues the editor has printed word lists and citizenship lessons in Hungarian, Italian, Spanish, and English. He has promoted class work among the foreign element of his community, and has carried on through his paper Americanization work of the highest type.

A fourth way in which classes have been organized in Mexican centers is by means of a travelling school. In January, 1926, the Chaffey Union High School established such a travelling school for the labor camps of the district. An old bus body was renovated, put on a chassis. and worked over into a school room. Instead of the regular bus seats, folding chairs were used; a movable blackboard, a "drop" table, cabinets with several types of sanitary, Red Cross, and other equipment, a miniature bed, scales, and utensils of various types were introduced for class purposes. An electric gong was attached to the bus so that classes might be summoned when the school arrived in camp. This "new type" Americanization school has become very useful. Within the first two weeks after it began going to the camps fifty Mexican women and as many part-time Mexican girls were reached with class work; these had not had the advantage of Americanization work before. The little children of the camps came with their mothers, and began calling the bus "Escuelita", or little school, a name which has held. Since the establishment of this travelling school hundreds of adolescent girls and women have been reached in the labor camps. As many as twenty-six Mexicans have been seated at class work within the narrow walls of Escuelita.

One of the greatest difficulties in administering the work of Americanization is that of securing teachers who are willing and who actually like to teach aliens; and who are at the same time prepared adequately to teach. In the attempts made during the past eight years at Chaffey it has not been possible to secure teachers who have had experience with classes in the field; they have taken courses to teach foreign groups, and they have been able to visit teachers who have achieved success along this line. An additional aid to beginning teachers in this field is the collection of literature, lessons, and texts dealing with the instruction of foreigners. A fourth element in the preparation of teachers is their visitation of the foreign people in their homes, that they may become conversant with the needs of the people they are planning to teach; then they become encouraged to prepare lessons that will meet immediate needs; lessons that can be used by themselves and others.

Early in the history of Americanization work within the Chaffey Union High School District it became evident that there existed a strong impression that Americanization work among the Mexican people would be greatly handicapped due to a presumed native incapacity, or to a native inability on the part of the particular group of Mexicans residing in the district. In fact it has proven

"Escuelita"

An "Escuelita" Class.

difficult to teach successfully either Mexican adults or Mexican children; their lack of knowledge of the English language, and the lack of usable text-books present a problem that must be solved; the lack of knowledge of health and sanitation on the part of Mexican adults constitutes a problem the solution of which will decrease the death rate among Mexican infants; the difficulty in securing regular attendance on the part of Mexican pupils in the elementary schools, in the part-time department of the high school, and the slowness with which Mexican adults enroll in classes must be given attention in order that a program of Americanization will reach all who can profit by it. These are some of the problems that the experience of the last eight years has produced. These problems can be solved through scientific study, through trial programs, and through adapting procedure to meet the needs that arise. Chapter II presents a detailed study of the effects of Mexican peon parentage upon pupil progress in school.

CHAPTER II

THE EFFECTS OF MEXICAN PEON PARENTAGE UPON PUPIL PROGRESS

The field chosen for this investigation is San Bernardino County where all the reports regarding the distribution of children, both white and foreign, have been studied and analyzed. A more intensive study and analysis is made from various reports concerning pupils within the Chaffey Union High School District.

There are thirty-two different races appearing in the pupil population of San Bernardino County. The relative importance of the different racial groups can be determined by the enrollment in the public schools of the county during two successive years and by the late census enumeration of October, 1927. Table I, pages 17-19, presents the pupil population in the first eight grades in the county under date of February 9, 1927. There are sixty-five districts represented in this report with a total enrollment of 16,771 pupils. Twenty-one of these districts have enrolled only white children, while there are foreign children in forty-four districts. The enrollment of pupils other than whites is listed as follows:

Mexican	4.587 or 28⅛	of the entire pupil population.
Negro	113 or .7%	of the entire enrollment
Japanese	78 or .4%	of the entire enrollment
Other foreign groups	198 or 1.8%	of the entire enrollment

In order to learn more definitely regarding the relative numbers of foreign pupils the entire enrollment of pupils during the months of September, October, November, and December of 1927 have been considered. Table II, pages 20-22, sets forth clearly the numbers of foreign pupils present in the pupil population. Figure 1, page 23, shows graphically the proportions of foreign pupils, and it shows particularly the proportionate number of Mexican pupils in the first eight grades of the schools of the county. Table III, pages 24-25, presents an array of facts taken from the census enumeration of October, 1927. Figure 2, page 25, presents graphically the per cent of Mexicans, of whites, and of other foreign groups for each year of the census enumeration. Three out of every eight babies in San Bernardino County are Mexican. From twenty-five to twenty-eight out of every hundred pupils of the elementary schools are Mexican. This great proportion of foreign pupils would cause no serious alarm if they constitute no problem as to assimilation or as to education. Just what problems the foreign pupils present are shown by a study of retardation and of over-ageness of both white and foreign children.

TABLE I—AMERICANIZATION SURVEY

Schools of San Bernardino County

Districts	No. Whites Born U. S.	No. Whites Foreign Born	No. Mex. Born U. S.	No. Mex. Foreign Born	No. Negro Born U. S.	No. Negro Foreign Born	No. Japanese Born U. S.	No. Japanese Foreign Born	Others Born U. S.	Others Foreign Born	Totals
Alta Loma	64		28	4					4	3	103
Amboy			2	9							11
Apple Valley	19										19
Bagdad	8			1							9
Barstow	182	1	65	31							279
Big Bear Lake	31										31
Bloomington	253	6	40	11							310
Camp Baldy	16										16
Central	86		24	2			1				113
Chino	619	3	318	71			3				1014
Cima	3										3
City Creek	24						2				26
Colton	941	15	424	346	7		7		4	1	1745
Cram	50		65	4							119
Cucamonga	22	1	159	92							274
Daggett	12		5								17
Del Rosa	33		28	7					1		69
Etiwanda	91		30	15					14	6	156
Fairview	11		6	1							18
Fontana	404	23	65	31			2				525
Goffs	5		5	2							12

TABLE I—AMERICANIZATION SURVEY (Continued)

Districts	No. Whites Born U. S.	No. Whites Foreign Born	No. Mex. Born U. S.	No. Mex. Foreign Born	No. Negro Born U. S.	No. Negro Foreign Born	No. Japanese Born U. S.	No. Japanese Foreign Born	Others Born U. S.	Others Foreign Born	Totals
Greenleaf	42										42
Harper Lake	9										9
Hesperia	11			4							15
Highland	242										242
Hinkley	20		3	1							24
Hodge	24		1	4	2						31
Kelso	15		1	1							17
Kramer			2	2							4
Kramer Hills Emergency	5										5
Lake Arrowhead	22										22
Lanfair	9										9
L cerne	18										18
Ludlow	12		9	13					2		36
Midway	24										24
Mill	26				2						28
Minneola	3		5								8
Mission	94		47	4							145
Mojave	11		2	2							15
Morenga	5										5
Mountain View	46		15		3				39		103
Needles	315	2	151	66	22		8		21		585
Oak Glenn	6		2	1							9

TABLE I—AMERICANIZATION SURVEY (Continued)

Districts	No. Whites Born U. S.	No. Whites Foreign Born	No. Mex. Born U. S.	No. Mex. Foreign Born	No. Negro Born U. S.	No. Negro Foreign Born	No. Japanese Born U. S.	No. Japanese Foreign Born	Others Born U. S.	Others Foreign Born	Totals
Ontario	1893	39	160	58	14		2		1		2167
Oro Grande	49	3	42	23							117
Osdick	29	1									30
Pass	15										15
Phelan Union	10										10
Piedmont	23	25	29	26							105
Pioneer	19		1								20
Redlands	1404	27	281	58	12	1	8			1	1792
Rialto	216	7	31	4			6				264
San Bernardino	2880	18	885	350	37		16	3	80	15	4286
San Salvador	2		38	11							51
Summit	3		3	2							8
Sunrise	33										33
Terrace Union	70		13								83
Todd	10										10
Trona	40		8	6							54
Upland	536	18	117	83			14		2		770
Valley	8		4	5					3	1	21
Victor	219	5	66	40	10						340
Warm Springs	68						7				75
Yermo	45		2		2				1		50
Yucaipa	193		7	5							205
Total	11598	194	3198	1398	111	1	78	3	172	27	16771

TABLE II—AMERICANIZATION SURVEY

Schools of San Bernardino County

District	American	Mexican	Negro	Armenian	Austrian	Belgian	Canadian	Chinese	Czecho-Slovakian	Dutch	French	German	Hungarian	Indian	Italian	Japanese	Jew	Portuguese	Russian	Spanish	Swede	Swiss	Syrian	Other Races	Totals
Alta Loma......	76	26										3			3										108
Amboy	5	11												3											19
Apple Valley....	23																								23
Bagdad	7	5																							12
Barstow	205	126	1												3				2						337
Baxter																									
Big Bear	74																								74
Bloomington ..	334	57	1										1	1	9		1			6					410
Camp Baldy......	10																								10
Cedar Pines Pk.	10																								10
Central	80	14													7	2	1								104
Chino	904	383		5				1		8	19	2			36			10			3	11	4		1386
Cima	3	12									1									7					23
City Creek	25															5		1							31
City of S. B.......	3938	1495	57	6	4	1	1	1	1	2	6	5	16	6	63	31	10	1	1	35	4		2	43	*5729
Colton	913	757	6										3		7	7								12	1705
Cram	57	83																							140
Cucamonga	23	331													17										371
Daggett	19	4																							23
Del Rosa	41	43																							84
Etiwanda	74	38										1			34										147

* First six grades only.

TABLE II—AMERICANIZATION SURVEY (Continued)

District	American	Mexican	Negro	Armenian	Austrian	Belgian	Canadian	Chinese	Czecho-Slovakian	Dutch	French	German	Hungarian	Indian	Italian	Japanese	Jew	Portuguese	Russian	Spanish	Swede	Swiss	Syrian	Other Races	Totals
Fairview	9	9																							18
Fawnskin	15																								15
Fontana	477	105			12		9			1	3		16	2	11	2	1	2	2		3				646
Goffs	7	11																							18
Greenleaf	47	3																							50
Harper Lake	9																								9
Hesperia	16	4																							20
Highland	294									3			2												299
Hinkley	22	8																							30
Hodge	19																								19
Kelso	17	6																							23
Kramer		11																							11
Lake Arrowh'd	52																								52
Lanfair	11																								11
Lucerne	26																								26
Ludlow	21	21						1																	43
Midway	22																								22
Mill	42	2	11																						55
Minneola	4	12																							16
Mission	97	55																							152
Mojave	20																								20
Morenga																									
Mountain View	59	35	3			2						1			21	1						8			130
Needles	414	286	28					4						18		7									757

TABLE II—AMERICANIZATION SURVEY (Continued)

District	American	Mexican	Negro	Armenian	Austrian	Belgian	Canadian	Chinese	Czecho-Slovakian	Dutch	French	German	Hungarian	Indian	Italian	Japanese	Jew	Portuguese	Russian	Spanish	Swede	Swiss	Syrian	Other Races	Totals
Oak Glen	22	5																							27
Ontario	1911	320	11				18		1	2	5	5		3	31	2	1	18	3			1	3	11	2346
Oro Grande	63	85																							148
Osdick	35	8																							48
Pass	16																								16
Phelan Union..	12																								12
Piedmont		64									8				25			2		7					106
Pioneer	11	6																				1			18
Redlands	2836	383	30	5											2	8		26		7	1			3	3301
Rialto	297	39							2						3	11									352
Runn'g Springs	15	1																							16
San Salvador ..	3	68																							71
Summit	8	7																							15
Sunrise	46																								46
Terrace Union	70	14																							85
Todd	16																								16
Trona	50	17																							67
Union Joint																									
Upland	529	176	2												1	2									710
Valley	7	7																							14
Victor	244	110	13											5	3										375
Warm Spring..	75	1														6									82
Yermo	45	3	2												3										53
Yucaipa	219	14																							233

FIGURE 1

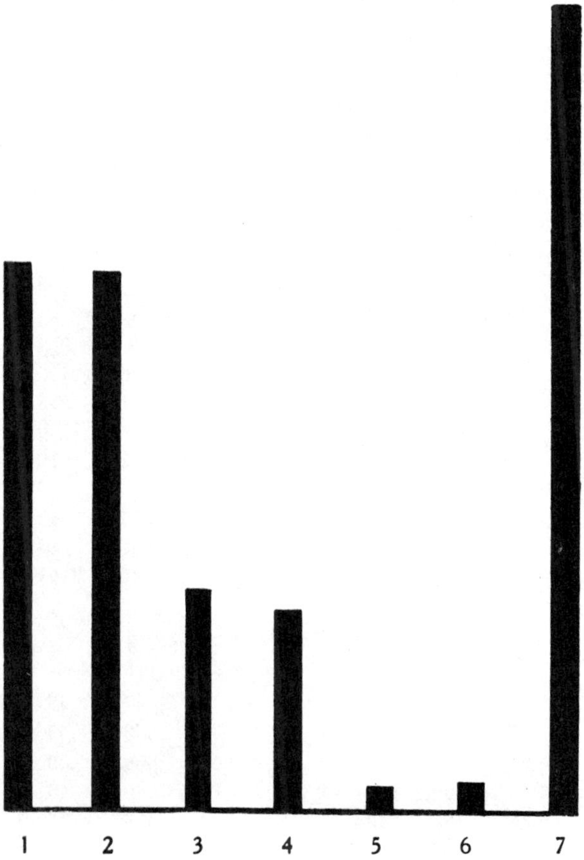

1. Number of white children enrolled in each 100 of grades 1-8, year 1926-1927.

2. Number of American (normal white) enrolled in each 100 of grades 1-8, Sept.-Dec., 1927.

3. Number of Mexican children enrolled in each 100 of grades 1-8, year 1926-1927.

4. Number of Mexican pupils enrolled in each 100 of pupil population, Sept.-Dec., 1927.

5. Number of all other foreign pupils enrolled in each 100 pupils of grades 1-8, 1926-1927.

6. Number of all other foreign pupils enrolled in each 100 pupils of grades 1-8, Sept.-Dec., 1927.

7. Figure representing 100 per cent.

TABLE III

Showing Age and Race of Minors

From the Census Report of October, 1927

In tabulating the minors the State Department of Education issued the following instructions: "Tabulate all minors according to age and race. . . . If parents are of different races, the race of the father is the race of the minor. excepting when one parent is white or Mexican. If either parent is white or Mexican, enter minor according to the race of the parent who is neither white nor Mexican. . . . If one parent is Mexican and the other is white, tally minor as Mexican."

RACE	Under 1 year	1	2	3	4	5	6	7	8
White	458	496	530	853	907	1363	1613	1623	1396
Black	2	5	1	9	7	15	15	13	14
Yellow	0	0	1	1	1	1	2	2	4
Red	17	9	8	10	10	10	10	8	6
Brown	3	0	3	2	3	3	8	1	1
Japanese	4	8	8	7	9	20	14	17	12
Mexican	307	307	300	351	384	382	533	488	454
TOTALS	791	825	851	1233	1321	1794	2195	2152	1887

RACE	% of Total	% of Total	% of Total	% of Total	% of Total	% of Total	% of Total	% of Total	% of Total
White	57.90	60.12	62.28	69.18	68.66	75.97	73.48	75.41	73.98
Black	.25	.60	.01	.73	.53	.83	.68	.60	.74
Yellow	.00	.00	.01	.08	.07	.06	.09	.09	.21
Red	2.15	1.09	.94	.81	.75	.55	.45	.37	.31
Brown	.38	.00	.35	.16	.22	.16	.36	.04	.05
Japanese	.50	.98	.94	.56	.68	1.11	.63	.79	.63
Mexican	38.81	37.21	35.25	28.46	29.06	21.29	24.28	22.67	24.06

TABLE III (Continued)

Showing Age and Race of Minors

From Census Report of October, 1927, San Bernardino County

RACE	9	10	11	12	13	14	15	16	17	Total
White	1290	1491	1618	1425	1513	1502	1312	1195	949	21714
Black	14	13	9	16	20	7	14	11	6	191
Yellow	0	0	2	0	0	2	3	3	4	26
Red	2	2	1	1	6	2	7	5	7	121
Brown	6	2	5	14	1	2	1	1	2	58
Japanese	11	6	9	8	11	8	5	4	2	163
Mexican	423	321	336	258	276	240	158	144	87	5759
Totals	1746	1835	1980	1722	1827	1763	1500	1363	1057	28032

TABLE III (Continued)

RACE	% of Total	% of Total	% of Total	% of Total	% of Total	% of Total	% of Total	% of Total	% of Total	% of Total
White	73.88	81.31	81.71	82.75	82.81	85.19	87.46	87.67	89.78	77.46
Black	.80	.71	.45	.93	1.09	.39	.93	.80	.57	.68
Yellow	.00	.00	.10	.00	.00	.21	.20	.22	.37	.09
Red	.11	.11	.05	.05	.32	.11	.46	.36	.66	.43
Brown	.34	.11	.25	.81	.05	.11	.06	.07	.19	.20
Japanese	.63	.33	.45	.46	.60	.45	.33	.30	.19	.58
Mexican	24.23	17.49	16.97	14.98	15.10	13.61	10.53	10.56	8.23	20.54

FIGURE 2

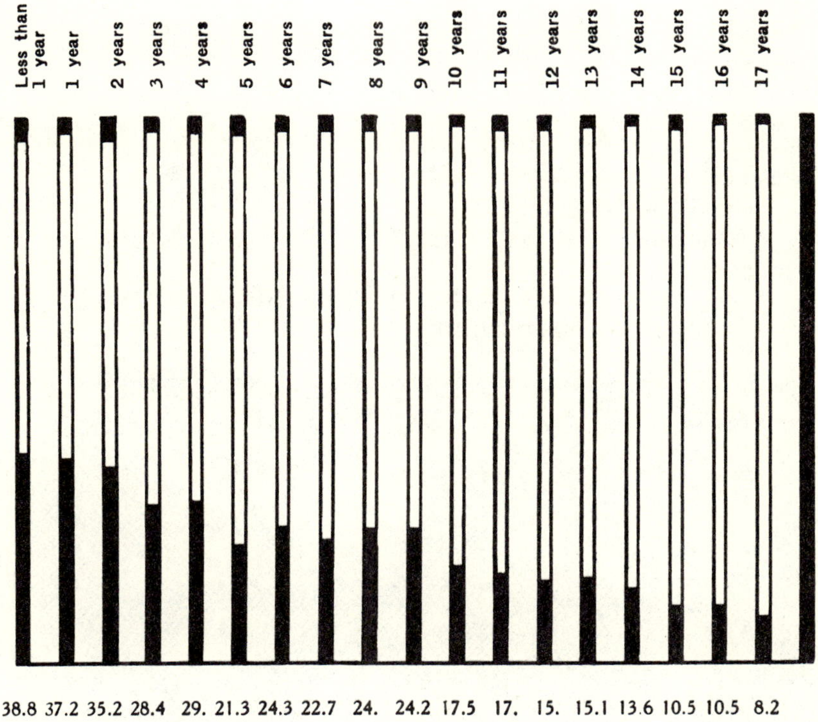

Lower black shows per cent of census population by age that is Mexican in San Bernardino County.

Upper black shows per cent of census population by age that is foreign other than Mexican.

White shows per cent of census population by age that is white.

Table IV presents illustrative facts showing over-ageness, or retardation among foreign pupils in certain districts within San Bernardino County. What obtains in one district is found to be true very largely in another. The number of foreign pupils, other than Mexican, is so small that the problem of retardation and over-ageness is almost exclusively a Mexican problem.

TABLE IV

City	Whites	% Ret.	Foreign	% Ret.	Mexicans
San Bernardino	3021	31	1360	86	1235
Ontario	1770	31	220	66.8	218
Upland	545	40	243	85	200
Fontana	429	59	96	84	98
Alta Loma	69	32	33	82	32
Camp Baldy	16	25	0	0	0
Central	86	39.5	27	77.7	26
Cucamonga	23	35	249	78	251
Etiwanda	91	27	65	75	45
Mountain View	53	45	62"	61	15"
Piedmont'"	0	....	105"'	78	57'"
Redlands	1295	31	347	58	339
27 Rural Districts	4391	....	944	70.1	914

' Tabulations were taken on different days; the Mexicans "come and go."

" Most of the foreign children in this district are Swiss.

'" Italians constitute the remainder of this foreign element.

A class of part-time girls brought in the Chaffey bus to the home economics department for instruction in home-making.

Quite a number of the Cucamonga, Fontana children classified as Mexican are undoubtedly Italian.

It has been supposed that the children of Mexican parentage do not progress as well in school as do their more fortunate American associates. This supposition is shown by an investigation of the facts as found in the age-grade sheets of San Bernardino County, dated March 1, 1927. These reports show a total of 16,121 pupils registered; of this number 4,902 are reported foreign. Under date of February 9, 1927, there were reported in these same schools 4.587 Mexican pupils; the age-grade sheets do not distinguish between Mexican and other foreign pupils, but separate sheets are studied

FIGURE 3

* Shows number of white children over-aged out of each 100 enrolled.
** Shows number of foreign children over-aged out of each 100 enrolled.

showing the age-grade situation regarding the white children and the age-grade situation regarding the foreign children. It might be argued that other foreign children might have an important bearing upon the situation; this matter will be presented separately.

Of the total group of white children numbering 11,219 cases, there were 3,735 children who were over-aged, or 33.28% of the total number of white children. Of the total group of foreign children numbering 4,902 there were 3,850 children who were over-aged, or 78.5% of the total number of foreign children. Figure 3 shows graphically this situation. It is noted that the foreign pupils are making only 42.4% as good progress through the schools as are the white children. Figures 3, 4, and 5 tell graphically the story of the comparative over-ageness of American and Mexican children.

FIGURE 4

Number of children of each 100 enrolled that are over-aged by one-half year.

Number of children of each 100 enrolled that are over-aged by one year.

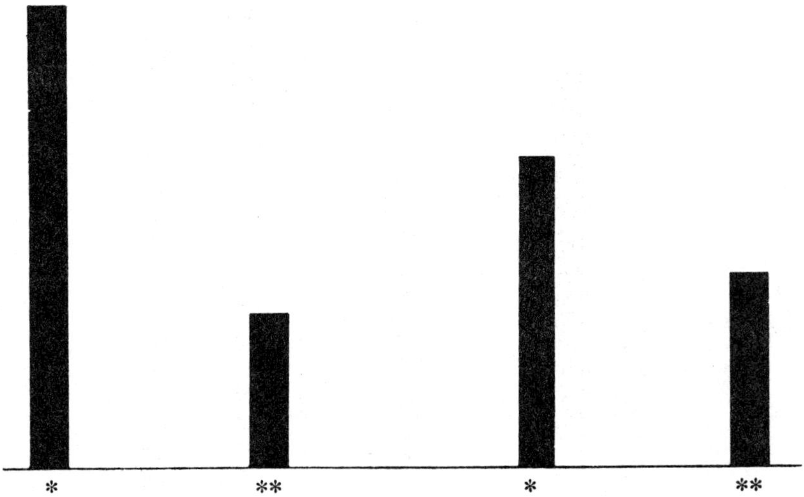

* American children.

** Foreign children.

FIGURE 5

Number of children of each 100 enrolled that are over-aged by more than one year.

* American children.

** Foreign children.

TABLE V

Table V presents facts relative to the proportion of Mexican pupils that are foreign born. A large majority of the Mexican pupils are American citizens by birth.

District	Total Mexicans	No. Foreign Born	% Foreign Born
Alta Loma	32	4	12.5
Central	26	2	7.7
Cucamonga	251	92	36
Etiwanda	45	15	33.3
Fontana	96	31	32.3
Mountain View	15	0	0
Ontario	218	58	26.6
Piedmont	57	28	50
Upland	200	83	41.5
TOTALS (Chaffey)	940	313	33.3
Redlands	339	58	14.1
Chino	389	71	18.2
Colton	770	346	45
San Bernardino	1235	350	28.3
All other districts	914	256	28.0

One of the Many Mexican Homes in One of the Poorer Camps.

Table VI presents the over-ageness by grades of white pupils in the schools of San Bernardino County. This is taken from the age-grade sheets in the reports of sixty-five districts to the County Superintendent of Schools, under date of March 1, 1927. Table VII presents, from the same source, the over-ageness by grades of foreign children in the schools; while Table VIII. page 44, presents the over-ageness by grades of both white and foreign children combined.

TABLE VI

Over-ageness by Grades of White Pupils in the Schools of San Bernardino County

Grade	Boys	Girls	Totals
L-1	45	32	77
H-1	157	89	246
L-2	63	41	104
H-2	202	127	329
L-3	76	38	114
H-3	240	158	398
L-4	69	36	105
H-4	282	190	472
L-5	69	68	137
H-5	282	191	473
L-6	80	40	120
H-6	294	230	524
L-7	36	29	65
H-7	144	119	263
L-8	26	13	39
H-8	160	109	269
TOTALS	2225	1510	3735

Out of a total white population of 11,219 only 3735 pupils were found to be over-aged. Of this number 1890, or 50.6% were above the fourth grade. The over-ageness of white children was found to be evenly distributed among all the grades.

TABLE VII

Over-ageness by Grades of Foreign Children in the Schools of San Bernardino County

Grade	Boys	Girls	Totals
L-1	493	364	857
H-1	269	223	491
L-2	93	89	182
H-2	217	229	446
L13	90	70	160
H-3	195	165	360
L-4	68	56	124
H-4	201	194	395
L-5	47	61	108
H-5	179	137	316
L-6	55	44	99
H-6	89	91	180
L-7	13	12	25
H-7	37	25	62
L-8	8	6	14
H-8	14	16	30
TOTALS	2068	1782	3850

Out of a total foreign pupil population of 4902 there were 3850, or 78.5% found to be over-aged; 834, or only 21.6% of the over-aged pupils found above the fourth grade, while 1348, or 35% of the over-aged pupils are found to be in the first grade; 2496, or 64.9% of the over-aged foreign pupils are found in the first three grades.

TABLE VIII

Over-ageness by Grades of White and Foreign Children combined:

Grade	Boys	Girls	Totals
L-1	538	396	934
H-1	426	312	738
L-2	156	130	286
H-2	419	356	775
L-3	166	108	274
H-3	435	323	758
L-4	137	92	229
H-4	483	384	867
L-5	116	129	245
H-5	461	328	789
L-6	135	84	219
H-6	383	321	704
L-7	49	41	90
H-7	181	144	325
L-8	34	19	53
H-8	174	125	299
TOTALS	4293	3292	7585

It is very clearly seen that the presence of foreign pupils causes a material increase of over-ageness within each class. It must be remembered that 94.7% of the foreign pupils enrolled are Mexicans.

Educate the mothers and give the children a chance.

Table IX presents the retardation by grades in the city schools of San Bernardino of the pupils listed as foreign:

TABLE IX

RETARDATION BY GRADES

City of San Bernardino, California

Grade	Number	Number Retarded	Per Cent Retarded	Number Repeating	Per Cent Repeating
L-1	355	270	76	93	26
H-1	133	108	81	7	5.2
L-2	124	114	91.9	96	77.4
H-2	114	103	90.3	3	2.6
L-3	107	102	95.3	41	38.3
H-3	88	75	85	5	5.6
L-4	75	68	90.6	11	14.6
H-4	95	85	89.4	14	14.7
L-5	69	62	90	18	26
H-5	63	58	92	2	3
L-6	63	59	93.6	3	4
H-6	74	66	89.2	7	9.4
Totals	1360	1170	86	300	22

L-Low: H-High.

NOTE: There are 792 out of 872 pupils above the first grade who are retarded, or 90.8%; 1235 of the 1360 foreign pupils shown in Table IX are Mexicans. In every grade the degree of over-ageness is very marked.

It is noted on page 26 that the tabulations were taken on different days, one on March 1, 1927, and the one regarding Mexican children on February 9, 1927. While there is a slight difference in totals due to the transient nature of the Mexican population, yet these differences are so small that they are insignificant. Of the entire pupil population 28% is Mexican, .7% is Negro, 4% is Japanese, while 1.8% belongs to other foreign groups. Of the entire population 69.1% is noted to be white. These figures are not significantly changed from the Census reports of October, 1927. From Table III, pages, 24-25, it is seen that 77.46% of the Census enumeration, ages under one to seventeen, of 28,032 children are listed as white; 20.54% as Mexican; .68% as black; .58% as Japanese; while the Red, Brown, and Yellow children comprise only .72% of the total. It is probably true that all Mexicans are not enumerated in the October Census, as Mexican parents are less likely to list their children with the authorities than are the white parents. It is clear that the Negro, Japanese, and other foreign pupils may be largely disregarded in considering the Americanization problem for San Bernardino County. Figure 2, page 25, shows graphically the relative position of white, Mexican, and all other foreign elements in the pupil population of San Bernardino County for the report dated February 9, 1927. The percentages have not been changed materially from the survey of September to December, 1927, as Table II, pages 20-22 indicate. There were 21,345 pupils enrolled; of this number 15,051 or 70.51% were classified as "American," 5,281 or 24.74% as Mexican, and 1,013, or 4.74% as belonging to 30 other races.

In the county as a whole it was found that 78.5% of all foreign children were over-aged, while only 33.28% of all white children were over-aged. Now in the city of San Bernardino 86% of the foreign children are over-aged; this takes into consideration 1360 children, 1235 of whom are Mexican. In Ontario 66.8% of the foreign children are over-aged; of these foreign children 218 of 220 are Mexican. Similarly from Table IV, page 26, it is clear that every district having foreign children shows a much higher percentage of over-ageness among foreign children than among white children. Those districts having the highest percentage of Mexican pupils, invariably show the greatest amount of over-ageness.

The table on page 34 shows not only the amount of over-ageness to be found among the foreign children, but also the amount of repeating. The table shows that there is less over-ageness and less repeating in the first grade. The longer the Mexican pupils remain the more certain they are to drop out of school. Although there are seventeen different nationalities represented in the population of the Chaffey Union High School District, the greatest problem confronting the schools is the Mexican problem. There are portions of the district where the schools show a great preponderance of Mexicans in their population. There are at least three schools that have no children other than Mexican in them. Two other schools show a Mexican population of fifty to ninety per cent. In San Bernardino County the school report of March 1, 1927 showed 16,765 pupils; of this number 4,587 or 28% of the entire pupil population is Mexican. The great majority of these children are from that type commonly called "Mexican Peon." When the term "Mexican Peon" is used it should be understood that the type of Mexican who is a worker is meant; he is one of that group descended either from the native Indians of Mexico, or from the native Indian stock mixed with a Spanish, or even with a Negro strain. The Mexican pupils enrolled in the elementary school, in high school, or in part-time continuation classes are usually from the laboring classes who are regarded as belonging to the peon group. Southern California is facing the great problem of the Americanization of an alien group; in certain sections this alien group is composed mostly of pupils and parents of the Mexican peon type. It is believed that the Americanization of these peoples is the most important problem facing Southern California today. There are a number of things to consider in an Americanization program. Adults must be educated, but there are those who think that real progress in Americanization can be made only through the proper education of the children. When they do not progress as well as they should, diagnosis should take place, there should be established a method of procedure leading to the removal of handicaps. Among the factors involved in pupil progress is that of parentage. It is the problem of this chapter to determine just what effects Mexican peon parentage may have upon pupil progress in elementary and in high schools.

There has been presented the proportion of Mexican children in our pupil population; there has been secured information from four sources; reports to the County Superintendent of Schools of San Bernardino County dated February 9, 1927, (see Table I, pages 17-19); the actual registration in the schools of San Bernardino County September-December, 1927 (see Table II, pages 20-22); and the Census Reports of Age and Race of Minors, dated October, 1927 (see Table III, pages 24-25); and the Age-grade reports of March 1, 1927.

Table X shows the enrollment by elementary districts within the Chaffey Union High School District under the date of February 9, 1927, while Table XI shows the enrollment by nationalities in the same schools from September to December, 1927.

TABLE X

Showing Enrollment in the Chaffey Union High School District

Grades 1-8 — March 1,1927

District	Total	Mexican
Alta Loma	102	32
Camp Baldy	16	0
Central (Cucamonga)	113	26
Cucamonga	272	251
Etiwanda	156	45
Fontana	525	96
Mountain View	115	15
Ontario	1990	218
Piedmont	105	57
Upland	788	200
Totals	4182	940

Per cent Mexican 22.47%

Table X show the enrollment of pupils on March 1, 1927. Table XI shows a similar enrollment during the months of September, October, November and December during the school year 1927-1928. The purpose of these tables is to show the composition of the pupil population of the Chaffey district.

TABLE XI

District	American	Mexican	Italian	Others	Total
Alta Loma	76	26	3	3	108
Camp Baldy	11	0	0	0	11
Central	81	14	7	3	105
Cucamonga	23	331	17	0	371
Etiwanda	74	38	34	1	147
Fontana	477	105	11	53	646
Mountain View	59	35	21	8	123
Ontario	1864	280	29	64	2237
Piedmont	0	64	25	17	106
Upland	529	176	0	14	719
Totals	3194	1069	147	163	4573

Per cent American	70.0
Per cent Mexican	23.3
Per cent Italian	3.2
Per cent other races	3.5

It is very clear from Tables X and XI that Mexican pupils constitute the greatest foreign element in the schools of the Chaffey district.

Tables XII, XIII and XIV present the facts relative to certain part-time and Americanization classes conducted in the Chaffey Union High School during the school year 1926-1927, while Table XV presents similar facts regarding classes conducted during the school year 1927-1928. These tables present in detail a striking proof that the Mexican pupils drop out of school very early and become an educational problem for the part-time and Americanization departments. During 1926-1927 there were only five Mexican pupils enrolled in the regular classes of Chaffey Union High School, yet there were two hundred fifty-nine enrolled in part-time classes; and during the school year 1927-1928 there were only fifteen Mexican pupils enrolled in regular classes at Chaffey, yet there have been three hundred sixty-six Mexican pupils enrolled in the Part-time classes. The tables show a very large number of Mexican pupils who have had no schooling before entering the part-time classes, while the average have had about two years in school either in the United States or in Mexico. Table VII presented clearly that the greatest amount of over-ageness is to be found among the foreign children in the lower grades, while the facts regarding the part-time pupils show that the Mexican pupils drop out of school early and must be enrolled in the part-time classes or they will get no further schooling.

TABLE XII

Part-time Girls

Ages	No.	Years in U. S.	No.	Years in School	No.	Nationality
15	5	1	3	0	13	38 Mexicans
16	35	2	1	Less than 1 year	2	41 Americans
17	26	3	0	1	1	1 Portuguese
18	8	4	2	2	2	1 Italian
19	4	5	2	3	2	—
20	2	6	2	4	3	81 Total
21	0	7	2	5	2	
22	1	8	1	6	5	
		9	2	7	6	
		10	1	8	12	
		11	1	9	22	
		12	3	10	6	
		13	0	11	5	
		14	2			
		15	2			
		Born in U. S.	55			
		Less than 1 year	2			

The part-time girls who have had the greatest number of years of schooling are the Americans. Half of the Mexican part-time girls have had less than three years' of schooling.

TABLE XIII

Part-time Boys

Ages	No.	Years in U. S.	No.	Years in School	No.	Nationality
15	5	Less than 1 year	2	0	11	72 Mexicans
16	33	1	6	1	3	42 Americans
17	48	2	1	2	9	6 Italians
18	17	3	6	3	8	1 Russian
19	11	4	2	4	7	—
20	3	5	4	5	10	121 Total
21	1	6	4	6	13	
22	3	7	2	7	9	
		8	5	8	13	
		9	4	9	21	
		10	3	10	9	
		11	6	11	2	
		12	1	12	4	
		13	3	Less than 1 yr.	2	
		14	0			
		15	2			
		16	2			
		17	3			
		18	2			
		Born in U. S.	63			

The part-time boys who have had the greatest number of years' of schooling are the Americans. Half of the Mexican part-time boys have had only four years' of schooling or less.

TABLE XIV

Americanization Classes Under Part-time Supervision (Women)

Ages	No.	Years in U. S.	No.	Years in School	No.	Nationality
14	1	Born in U. S.	21	0	40	149 Mexicans
15	2	Less than 1 year	11	Less than I year	11	7 Hungarians
16	10	1	6	1	18	1 Canadian
17	6	2	8	2	14	—
18	9	3	14	3	13	157 Total
19	10	4	12	4	21	
20	14	5	12	5	12	
21	5	6	11	6	11	
22	7	7	4	7	5	
23	5	8	2	8	9	
24	3	9	6	9	1	
25	6	10	18	10	2	
26	11	11	5			
27	1	12	7			
28	2	13	3			
29	1	14	2			
30	4	15	2			
31	3	16	3			
33	6	17	1			
34	3	20	2			
35	8	21	1			
36	7	24	1			
37	2	25	1			
38	2	26	1			
39	1	27	1			
40	9	30	2			
42	1					
44	3					
45	2					
46	1					
49	1					
51	1					
52	1					
53	2					
55	1					
59	1					
60	3					
65	1					
66	1					

This table shows that over half the Mexican women and older girls have had less than three years of schooling. Compare this fact with the summary, page 64; 304 Mexican women averaged 1.48 years of schooling each.

PART-TIME DEPARTMENT

Total enrollment February 3, 1928	481	
New students enrolled February 3-16	11	(American Girls)
	3	(American Boys)
	5	(Mexican Girls)
Total enrollment February 16	500	Students

Mexican girls	195	
Mexican boys	171	
	366	Mexican students
	134	American and other nationalilities
	500	Total

Mexican students 73.2%.

A group to be educated

TABLE XV

MEXICAN PART-TIME ATTENDANCE
CHAFFEY UNION HIGH SCHOOL

1927-28

MEN AND BOYS:

Yrs. Lived in U. S.	No. Students	Yrs. Attended School in U. S.	No. Students	In Mex.	No. Students	In Both Mex.-U. S.	No. Students
Less than 1 yr.	3	Less than 1 yr.	3				
1 "	13	1 "	2	1 yr.	6	1 yr.	1
2 "	9	2 "	2	2 "	3	2 "	..
3 "	6	3 "	5	3 "	12	3 "	3
4 "	8	4 "	14	4 "	7	4 "	2
5 "	5	5 "	16	5 "	5	5 "	..
6 "	7	6 "	22	6 "	1	6 "	1
7 "	4	7 "	10	7 "		7 "	..
8 "	5	8 "	6			8 "	1
9 "	5	9 "	4			9 "	..
10 "	2					10 "	1
11 "	3						
12 "	7						
13 "	9	Having no schooling.. 9					
14 "	5						
15 "	1						
16 "	4						
17 "	2						
18 "	1						
19 "	1						
Born in U. S.	39						
Total	139						

Sixty-four per cent of the Mexican part-time boys have had only four years of schooling or less.

TABLE XV (Continued)

WOMEN AND GIRLS:

Yrs. Lived in U. S.	No. Students	Yrs. Attended School in U. S.	No. Students	In Mex.	No. Students	In Both Mex.-U. S.	No. Students
Less than 1 yr.	3	Less than 1 yr.	2	Less than 1 yr.	3	Less than 1 yr.	3
1 "	10	1 "	4	1 "	2	1 "	2
2 "	5	2 "	8	2 "	8	2 "	3
3 "	4	3 "	7	3 "	10	3 "	0
4 "	5	4 "	10	4 "	4	4 "	5
5 "	6	5 "	17	5 "	4	5 "	6
6 "	8	6 "	23	6 "	2	6 "	1
7 "	4	7 "	6	7 "	0	7 "	1
8 "	5	8 "	9	8 "	0	8 "	1
9 "	6			9 "	1		
10 "	12						
11 "	9						
12 "	13						
13 "	6						
14 "	9						
15 "	9						
16 "	3						
17 "	3						
18 "	1						
19 "	1						
20 "	11						
21 "	2						
22 "	2						
23 "	0						
24 "	1						
25 "	0						

Having no schooling...... 26

Yrs. lived in U. S.	No. Stu.
26 years	0
27 years	1
Born in U. S.	29
Total	168

Men and boys	139
Women and girls	168
Grand Total	307

Fifty-five per cent of the Mexican part-time girls have had only four years of schooling or less.

FIGURE 6

Showing part-time enrollment by races in the part-time department of Chaffey Union High School during 1926-1927 and 1927-1928. The numbers are given in per cent of the total. See below and next page for legend.

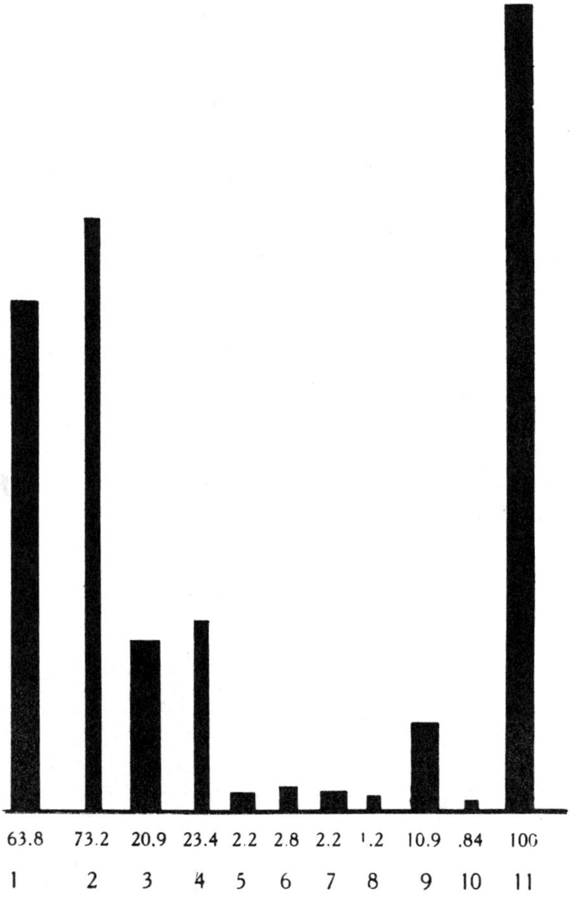

FROM ENROLLMENT OF 1926-1927, 1927-1928 PART-TIME DEPARTMENT, CHAFFEY UNION HIGH SCHOOL

1. Number of Mexicans enrolled in each 100 P-T pupils in 1926-1927.
2. Number of Mexicans enrolled in each 100 P-T pupils in 1927-1928.
3. Number of Americans enrolled in each 100 P-T pupils in 1926-1927.

4. Number of Americans enrolled in each 100 P-T pupils in 1927-1928.
5. Number of Italians enrolled in each 100 P-T pupils in 1926-1927.
6. Number of Italians enrolled in each 100 P-T pupils in 1927-1928.
7. Number of Hungarians enrolled in each 100 P-T pupils in 1926-1927.
8. Number of Hungarians enrolled in each 100 P-T pupils in 1927-1928.
9. Number of all other nationalities in 1926-1927.
10. Number of all other nationalities in 1927-1928.
11. Total enrollment.

Figures 4 and 5 show graphically the status of the Mexican part-time pupils in comparison with that of the American part-time pupils. The investigation of 241 part-time pupils enrolled during the year 1926-1927 shows that fifty-five of the number had spent less than one year in school; that sixty-four had spent from one to three years in school; and that the remainder, or 122, had spent from four to nine years in school. Figure 5 shows graphically this situation. The enrollment during 1927-1928 shows a similar situation. Out of the total of 307 part-time students whose educational status is known 137 have had three years or less of schooling.

There is no effort in this chapter to show that the American pupil has more native capacity than does the Mexican pupil; Chapter V will present an investigation regarding this problem; the purpose of the present chapter is to show that Mexican children do not progress as well in the schools as do the other pupils. A further study of enrollment by grades in Chaffey Union High School District during the months of September, October, November, and December, 1927, will show in what grades are found the greatest number of Mexican pupils, and in what grades there is the greatest dropping out. Table XI, page 37, and Table XVI, pages 47-50, show the enrollment by grades in the ten districts of the Chaffey Union High School District, while Table XVII, page 51, shows the numbers of Mexican pupils in each grade from the first to the twelfth, and then in the part-time classes at Chaffey. These facts are graphically presented in Figure 8.

FIGURE 7

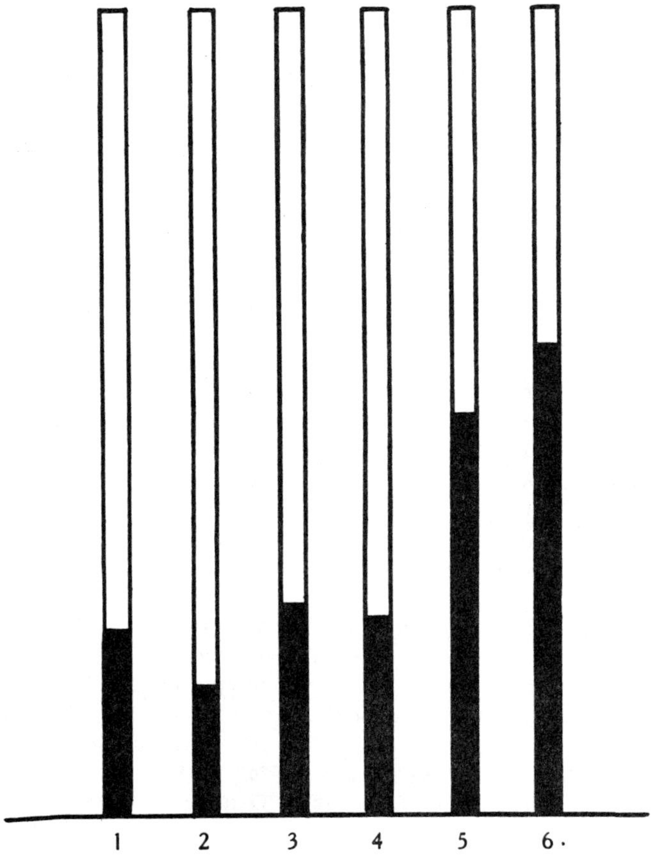

1. Illiterate, 1926-1927.

2. Illiterate, 1927-1928.

3. Number of Mexican part-time pupils out of each 100 that have had from one to three years of schooling—1926-1927.

4. Number of Mexican part-time pupils out of each 100 that have had from one to three years of schooling—1927-1928.

5. Number of Mexican part-time pupils out of each 100 that have had from four to nine years of schooling—1927-1928.

6. Number of Mexican part-time pupils out of each 100 that have had from four to nine years of schooling—1927-1928.

TABLE XVI

Enrollment—Elementary Schools
Chaffey Union High School District
September-December, 1927

Grade Alta Loma

	American	Mexican	Italian	Other	Over-aged	No. Amer. Over-aged	Per Cent	No. Mex. Over-aged	Per Cent
1	8	9			17	1	12.5	1	11.1
2	13	2			15	0	0.	1	50.
3	11	4			15	1	11.1	4	100.
4	9	7		2	16	0	0.	5	73.3
5	8	1	1			2	25.	1	100.
6	13	2	1			1	7.7	2	100.
7	7	0		1		0	0.		
8	7	1	1			0	0.	1	100.
Total	76	26	3	3	108	5	6.57	15	57.69

Grade Central

	American	Mexican	Italian	Other	Total	No. Amer. Over-aged	Per Cent	No. Mex. Over-aged	Per Cent
1	11	8	3	2	24	0	0.	2	25.
2	7	1	1	1	10	0	0.	0	0.
3	10	2	1		13	1	10.	1	50.
4	4	1	1	0	6	0	0.	1	100.
5	10	1			11	2	25.	1	100.
6	14	1	1		16	4	28.57	1	100.
7	15					5	33.3		
8	10					3	30.		
Total	81	14	7	3	105	15	19.75	6	42.85

Grade Camp Baldy

	American	Mexican	Italian	Other	Total	No. Amer. Over-aged	Per Cent	No. Mex. Over-aged	Per Cent
1	3					0	0.		
2	2					0	0.		
3	2					1	50.		
4	2					0	0.		
5	1					0	0.		
6	0								
7	1					0	0.		
Total	11					1	9.09		

TABLE XVI (Continued)
Enrollment—Elementary Schools
Chaffey Union High School District
September-December, 1927

Grade Piedmont

Grade	American	Mexican	Italian	Other	Total	No. Amer. Over-aged	Per Cent	No. Mex. Over-aged	Per Cent
1	0	22	5	1	28			3	13.61
2		11	3	4	18			7	63.63
3		13	3	1	17			9	69.23
4		8	7	5	20			4	50.
5		7	0	0	7			7	100.
6		1	4	3	8			1	100.
7		1	2	2	5			1	100.
8		1	1	1	3			1	100.
Total	0.	64	25	17	106			33	51.56

Grade Cucamonga

Grade	American	Mexican	Italian	Other	Total	No. Amer. Over-aged	Per Cent	No. Mex. Over-aged	Per Cent
1	2	192	6		200	2	100.	144	75.
2	4	51	4		59	2	50.	50	98.04
3	3	35	2		40	0	0.	35	100.
4	2	24	2		28	0	0.	24	100.
5	3	21			24	2	66.7	21	100.
6	4	7	1		12	1	25.	7	100.
7	1	0	2		3	1	100.		
8	4	1			5	1	25.	0	0.
Total	23	331	17		371	9	39.13	281	84.9

Grade Etiwanda

Grade	American	Mexican	Italian	Other	Total	No. Amer. Over-aged	Per Cent	No. Mex. Over-aged	Per Cent
1	12	18	10		40	1	8.33	4	22.22
2	11	9	2		22	0	0.	7	77.77
3	5	2	2		9	0	0.	2	100.
4	11	4	5		20	1	9.09	4	100.
5	10	1	5	1	17	0	0.	1	100.
6	11	1	2		14	2	18.18	0	0.
7	8	3	3		14	3	37.5	2	66.67
8	6	0	5		11	1	16.67		
Total	74	38	34	1	147	8	10.81	20	52.63

TABLE XVI (Continued)
Enrollment—Elementary Schools
Chaffey Union High School District *
September-December, 1927

Grade Fontana

Grade	American	Mexican	Italian	Other	Total	No. Amer. Over-aged	Per Cent	No. Mex. Over-aged	Per Cent
1	76	48	1	12	137	10	13.23	30	60.83
2	37	12	1	2	52	0	0.	11	91.67
3	48	11	1	7	67	4	8.33	9	81.81
4	55	19	1	8	83	14	25.45	18	94.73
5	55	10	3	12	80	20	36.36	9	90.
6	55	5	4	10	74	6	10.9	5	100.
7	72	0	0	1	73	14	19.44		
8	79	0	0	1	80	10	12.65		
Total	477	105	11	53	646	78	16.35	82	78.09

Grade Mt. View

Grade	American	Mexican	Italian	Other	Total	No. Amer. Over-aged	Per Cent	Over-aged No. Mex.	Per Cent
1	17	10	4	1	32	4	23.52	5	50.
2	5	8	4		17	0	0.	4	50.
3	3	5	3	1	12	1	33.33	5	100.
4	7	5	1	2	15	1	14.28	3	60.
5	13	5		2	20	4	30.77	3	60.
6	5	2	4		11	1	20.	0	0.
7	5	0	1	1	7	0	0.		
8	4		4	1	9	0	0.		
Total	59	35	21	8	123*	11	18.64	20	57.14

Grade Upland

Grade	American	Mexican	Italian	Other	Total	No. Amer. Over-aged	Per Cent	No. Mex. Over-aged	Total
1	67	62	0	2	131	1	1.49	41	66.12
2	73	31	0	2	106	5	6.85	19	61.29
3	65	26	0	1	92	6	9.23	18	69.23
4	77	21	0	2	100	14	18.18	20	95.23
5	75	21	0	4	100	15	20.	14	66.67
6	38	5	0	1	44	9	23.68	5	100.
7	59	9	0	1	69	9	15.25	8	88.88
8	75	1	0	1	77	20	26.67	1	100.
Total	529	176	0	14	719	79	14.93	126	71.59

*—Nine other foreign pupils not put in age-grade report.

TABLE XVI (Continued)

Enrollment—Elementary Schools

Chaffey Union High School District

September-December, 1927

Grade Ontario

	American	Mexican	Italian	Other	Total	No. Amer. Over-aged	Per Cent	No. Mex. Over-aged	Per Cent
1	258	129	6	9	402	11	4.2	43	33.33
2	238	41	3	8	290	26	10.9	36	87.8
3	230	38	4	4	276	29	12.6	31	81.5
4	246	19	2	7	274	47	19.1	15	78.9
5	236	27	1	8	272	55	23.3	22	81.4
6	206	9	4	14	233	40	19.4	9	100.
7	215	12	7	6	240	70	32.5	11	91.6
8	235	5	2	8	250	73	31.06	3	60.
Total	1854	280	29	64	2237	351	18.9	169	60.3

SUMMARY OF OVER-AGENESS IN TEN CHAFFEY DISTRICTS

American	Mexican	Over-Aged Americans	Over-Aged Mexicans
76	26	5	15
81	14	15	6
23	331	9	281
74	38	8	20
477	105	78	82
59	35	11	20
11	0	1	30
0	64	0	33
529	176	79	126
1864	280	351	126
3194	1069	557	752

Per cent Americans over-aged 17.4
Per cent Mexicans over-aged 70.3

A study of the age-grade situation in the elementary schools of the Chaffey District during 1927-1928 reveals the fact that there is four times as much over-ageness proportionately among Mexican pupils than among American pupils.

TABLE XVII

Enrollment of Mexican pupils by grades in the schools of the Chaffey Union High School District.

1	498	
2	166	
3	136	
4	108	
5	94	
6	33	
7	25	
8	9	Total Elementary
9	7	1069
10	4	
11	1	
12	2	
Part-time	366	
Total	1449	

Per cent of total enrollment of Mexican pupils by grades:

1	46.58
2	15.53
3	12.72
4	10.10
5	8.79
6	3.08
7	2.33
8	.84

This table sets forth clearly the fact that few Mexicans get beyond the fourth grade in school.

From the facts thus far presented it appears beyond the peradventure of a doubt that Mexican children are over-aged to a much greater extent than are American children. Figure 9 shows graphically the over-ageness of both American and foreign children by grades. The crossing of the two lines suggests the point where the foreign children begin dropping out, namely at the end of the third grade. This pictures graphically what the previous investigation shows: that the average amount of schooling that the Mexicans in our American schools have thus far received is less than three years. The Americanization program that should be set up should take cognizance of this, meet the situation, and provide the necessary remedies.

A further study was made to determine just how much Mexican children are over-aged as they are found in the grades of their schools. Fourteen-year-old white children are normally in the ninth grade. Where are the fourteen-year-old Mexican pupils found?

FIGURE 8

Showing location of Mexican pupils in the grades of the schools of the Chaffey Union High School District.

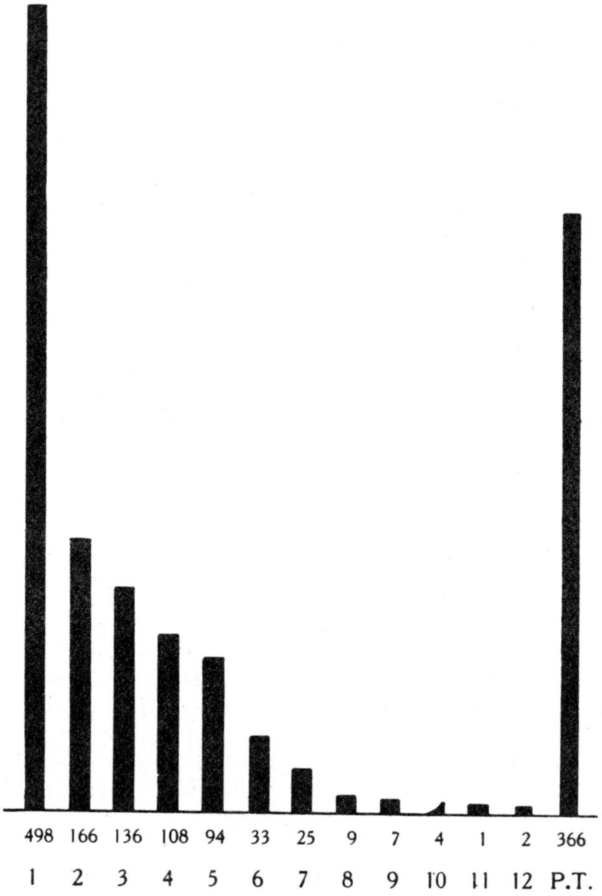

Thirty-one fourteen-year-old white children in a certain Spanish class at Chaffey total 283 years in grades represented, or an average of grade 9.129; twenty-three fourteen-year-old Mexican pupils at the Sultana School in Ontario total 120 years in grade represented, or an average grade of 5.217, a difference of 3.912. Similarly thirty-six fifteen-year-old white pupils represent grade 9.277; ten fifteen-year-old Mexican pupils represent grade 5.2, a difference of 4.077. This same situation was found in the County tests reported on page 157. The average reading grade placement of 101 Mexican children taken at random was 2.97, and of 100 American children of the same age was 7.12, a difference in grade placement of 4.15 years.

FIGURE 9

THE OVER-AGENESS OF AMERICAN AND FOREIGN PUPILS

Presented by Grades in the Elementary Schools of San Bernardino Co.

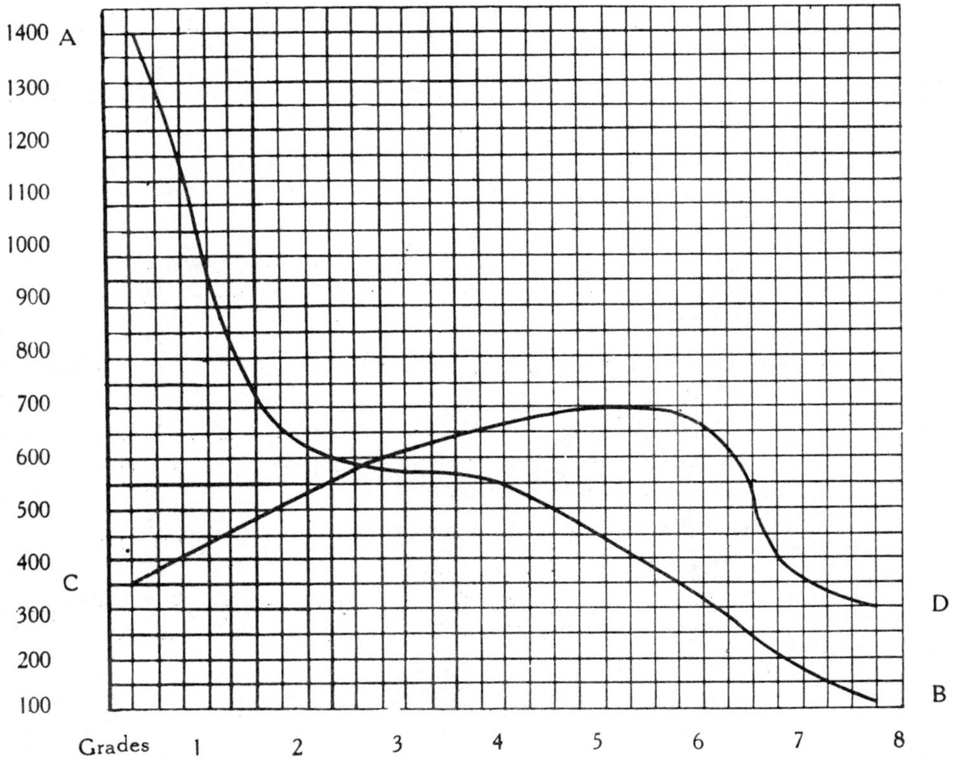

Line A B shows foreign children—90 per cent Mexicans.

Line C D shows white children,

SUMMARY

The facts, tables, and figures presented thus far agree in every particular with a statement that the children of Mexican peon parents do not exhibit that degree of progress that ought to be manifested by children in the public schools. These children are much behind the American children of the same age. The following facts stand out:

1. 69.1% of the pupils in the first eight grades of San Bernardino County were "white" children as reported February 9, 1927.
2. 70% of the pupils in the first eight grades of the County were reported as "normal American" in the survey of enrollment during September to December, 1927.
3. 28% of the pupils in the first eight grades of the County were Mexican as reported February 9, 1927.
4. 24.78% of the pupils in the first eight grades of the County were Mexican as reported in the survey of the enrollment during September to December, 1927.
5. There were pupils of thirty races other than American or Mexican reported in the survey of enrollment during September to December, 1927.
6. 2.9% of the pupils as reported February 9, 1927, were other than "white" or "Mexican."
7. 5.22% of the pupils as reported in the enrollment of pupils during September to December, 1927, belonged to thirty races other than American and Mexican.
8. The over-ageness of foreign children is almost exclusively the over-ageness of Mexican pupils.
9. In San Bernardino County as a whole 78.5% of the Mexican children are over-aged, while only 33.28% of the white children are over-aged.
10. In districts taken at random Mexican children are found to be over-aged to a much greater extent than American children, as for example: in San Bernardino City 86% of Mexican pupils of the first six grades are over-aged as against 31% of American pupils. In Ontario the figures are 66.8% to 31% in Upland, 85% to 40%; in Alta Loma, 82% to 32%; in Etiwanda, 85% to 27%; in Redlands, 58% to 31%; and in twenty-seven rural districts combined 70.1% of the Mexican children are retarded.

In considering older pupils,—those of high school age,—we find in the part-time enrollment the same story told in a different way, for here we see those who have not been in school, or those who have had little schooling. This situation is well portrayed by Figure 9, which tells us graphically what the part-time statistics have shown,—that the average number of years of schooling of the Mexican later adolescent is approximately three years. Again, the over-ageness by years as indicated in Figure 4 shows that there are more American than Mexican children who are over-aged by a half or by a whole year; but there are more than twice as many children among the Mexicans who are over-aged more than one year.

A question naturally arises: Is the over-ageness of Mexican children due to native inability to do the tasks commonly assigned children in the school, or are there home conditions that make the Mexican child under-nourished to such a degree that he is under par physically? Table XXXII sets forth conditions as found in seventeen Mexican camps by the Inspector from the California Commission of Immigration and Housing during April, 1926. These camps are all in the Chaffey Rural Districts.

These facts and figures show that the children of the Mexican peon laborers do not have a home environment that is conducive to good health, to good morals, or to educational advancement. Even if they might have abilities equal to those of American children the home conditions would prevent their progress. However, this last statement can be proved by our further investigation. Chapter III and Chapter IV will present the educational status and the economic status of Mexican peon parents.

Chapter II has presented many facts relative to the Americanization problem in San Bernardino County and in the Chaffey Union High School District. One-fourth of all elementary pupils are Mexicans; three-fourths of part-time pupils of high school age are Mexicans.

The Mexican pupils have made but forty-two per cent as good progress through the schools as have the American pupils.

The greatest numbers of Mexican pupils are found in the lower grades, more than forty-six per cent being found in the first grades within the Chaffey Union High School District.

About seventy per cent of the Mexican pupils are born in the United States and are therefore American citizens by birth.

There is such a small percentage of foreign pupils other than Mexican in the schools that the Americanization problem in the elementary schools is concerned with Mexicans almost exclusively.

Nearly all Mexican pupils leave school before completing an elementary school course. Nearly half leave school with less than three years of schooling.

All these facts point to the need of continuation classes for all Mexican boys and girls who drop out of school at the end of the compulsory age limit.

CHAPTER III

THE EDUCATIONAL STATUS OF MEXICAN PEON PARENTS

In Chapter II it has been clearly set forth that the children of Mexican peon parents have not advanced as far in school nor have they advanced as rapidly as have the children of white parents. The average thirteen, fourteen, and fifteen-year-old children represent those who have been held in their last years by the compulsory education law; those of these ages who are children of Mexican peon parents are normally four years behind the children of normal American parentage. As soon as the compulsory education law ceases to control the attendance, the children of Mexican peon parents drop out. This is shown very conclusively by reference to Table VII and Table VIII, pages 32, 33, showing the attendance of Mexican pupils, grade by grade, in the schools of the Chaffey Union High School District.

There are several very important reasons why this situation prevails. The educational status of the Mexican peon parent is very low and the average pupil of Mexican peon parentage has less ability to do the work commonly offered in our schools than has the normal American pupil. This chapter will present the evidence for such statements. The problem of Chapter IV is to determine the economic status of the Mexican peon parent and the problem of Chapter V is to determine the index of ability of the children of Mexican peon parentage. To determine the educational status of the Mexican peon parent is a comparatively simple matter. We can use the method of the United States Census Bureau and determine the percentage of illiteracy: it is possible to determine the amount of schooling the Mexican parents have had; and it is possible to submit to those attending afternoon or evening Americanization classes a simple test that will check their ability to do certain things required of those claiming any degree of schooling; in addition to these things an actual check has been made of several hundred men and women to determine just what educational status a fair sampling of the intelligence of the Mexican labor camps might produce. On pages 57, 58 is submitted a list of twenty-two questions that the children of Mexican parents have answered. On page 58 is submitted a list of questions that men and women in our Americanization classes have answered, and on pages 58, 59 is submitted a list of thirty-two questions that have been answered by scores of men and women. The information was secured by an attendance officer, a teacher of Americanization, and a young Mexican gentleman who was paid for securing the information by going from house to house. In securing answers there may have been some duplication of adults, but there were few if any.

A Young Mother Enrolled in a Chaffey Part-time Class

A copy of the questions submitted to the children of Mexican parents:

what do you think?

Cross out the wrong answer.

1.	Does your father speak English?	Yes	No
2.	Does your mother speak English?	Yes	No
3.	Can your father write English?	Yes	No
4.	Can your father write Spanish?	Yes	No
5.	Can your mother write English?	Yes	No
6.	Can your mother write Spanish?	Yes	No
7.	Can your father read English?	Yes	No
8.	Can your father read Spanish?	Yes	No
9.	Can your mother read English?	Yes	No

10. Can your mother read Spanish? Yes No
11. How many years has your father attended school in Mexico? .... In United States?.................... In....................? ....
12. How many years has your mother attended school in Mexico? .... In United States?.................... In....................? ....
13. Does your father attend evening school? Yes No
14. Does your mother attend afternoon or evening school? Yes No
15. Is your father an American citizen? Yes No
16. Is your mother an American citizen? Yes No
17. How many years has your father lived in United States?.............. Your mother?..............
18. Does your father wish to attend night school next year? Yes No
19. Does your mother wish to attend afternoon or evening school next year? Yes No
20. If your father has attended night school, what benefits has he received? (List below.)
21. If your mother has attended afternoon or evening school, what benefits has she received? List below.)
22. Do you expect to go back to Mexico? Yes No

Signed:..

A copy of the questions submitted by Americanization teachers to adult Mexicans:

1. How many years have you attended school in Mexico?.................. In United States?.................. In..................? ....
2. How many years have you attended Night School in Chaffey District?..................
3. How many years have you attended afternoon classes in Chaffey District?..................
4. Do you wish to attend classes next year?..................
5. What do you wish to study?....................................
6. Are you an American citizen?....................................
7. What benefits have you received from afternoon or evening school? (Give list.)
8. Do you expect to go back to Mexico?

Signed:..

A copy of the questionnaire submitted to Mexican adults by teachers, an attendance officer, and by a Mexican employed for the purpose:

ECONOMIC AND EDUCATIONAL FACTS

1. Name
2. Sex 3. Age
4. Where born

5. Years lived in U. S.
6. Married
7. Number of children living
8. Number of children dead
9. Number of years attended school in United States
10. Number of years attended school in................................
11. Can read Constitution in English
12. Can read "America" in Spanish
13. Number of books in the home
14. Takes what papers
15. Takes what magazines
16. Can speak English
17. Can write English
18. Can write Spanish
19. Kinds of work performed
20. Number days worked in 1927
21. Average wage per hour
22. Own home
23. Own other property
24. Bank account
25. What furniture in dwelling?
26. If American born, do you vote?
27. If foreign born, do you wish naturalization?
28. Do you wish to return to Mexico?
29. Number times moved in last two years
30. What rent do you pay?
31. Do you wish to attend a class to learn English?
32. Do you like to have your children in school?

The returns are tabulated in Tables XVIII, XIX, XX, and XXI, on pages 60-63. The returns may be a fair sampling of the general situation.

TABLE XVIII (A) MEN

Number Years Attended School	Number Cases Attended School in Mexico	Number Cases Attended School in United States	Number Cases Attended School in Both
0 years			89
Less than 1 year	2		
1 year	18	2	1
2 years	14	2	2
3 years	14	2	
4 years	16		
4½ years	1		
5 years	9	2	
6 years	11		2
8 years	4		
9 years		1	
10 years	1		
14 years	1		

Total years 347.5
Total number men 194
Average schooling .... 1.74 years each

Forty-five per cent of these men have had no schooling either in the United States or in Mexico; the medium is one year and the average is 1.74 years.

TABLE XVIII (B) WOMEN

Number Years Attended School	Number Cases Attended School in Mexico	Number Cases Attended School in United States	Number Cases Attended School in Both
0 years			100
Less than 1 year	4		
1 year	22	1	
2 years	24	3	
3 years	13	1	1
4 years	6		1
5 years	6	2	1
6 years	3	2	1
7 years	5	3	1
8 years		1	
10 years		1	

Total years 312
Total number women 202
Average schooling .... 1.54 years each

Practically half of these women have had no schooling, either in the United States or in Mexico; the medium is less than one year and the average is 1.54 years. These results are in agreement with the finding presented on pages 61, 62 and 63, and with the summary showing a high degree of illiteracy is presented on page 64.

TABLE XIX (A)

Report of 24 men in night school, taken at random:

Number Years Attended School	Number Cases
0 years	4
Less than 1 year	1
1 year	4
2 years	2
3 years	7
4 years	2
5 years	2
6 years	1
7 years	0
8 years	1
Total years	61
Average schooling	2.54 years each

Report of 35 women in Escuelita, taken at random:

Number Years Attended School	Number Cases Attended School in Mexico	Number Cases Attended School in United States	Number Cases Attended School in Both
0 years			8
Less than 1 year	1		1
1 year	4		1
2 years	5	2	
3 years	4	1	
4 years	1		
5 years	2		2
6 years	2		
9 years	1		
Total years		89	
Average schooling		2.54 years each	

TABLE XIX (B)

Report of 24 Mexican men in the Etiwanda Evening School:

Number Years Attended School	Schooling in Mex. Number Cases	Schooling in U. S Number Cases
0 years		4
Less than 1 year	1	
1 year	4	
2 years	1	1
3 years	7	
4 years	2	
5 years	0	2
6 years	1	
7 years	0	
8 years	1	
Total number years' schooling	61	
Average schooling	2.54 years each	

Report of 35 Mexican women who attended class in Escuelita:

Number Years Attended School	Number Cases Attended School in Mexico	Number Cases Attended School in United States	Number Cases Attended School in Both
0 years			8
Less than 1 year	1		1
1 year	4		1
2 years	5	2	
3 years	4	1	
4 years	1		
5 years	2	2	2
6 years	2		
7 years	0		
9 years	1		

Total number years' schooling..............89

Average number of years' schooling..............2.54 each

TABLE XX (A) MEN

Number Years Attended School	Number Cases Attended School in Mexico	Number Cases Attended School in United States	Number Cases Attended School in Both
0 years			66
Less than 1 year	3	5	1
1 year	5	10	
2 years	5	10	
3 years	4	7	2
4 years	5	6	
5 years	4	2	
6 years	2	3	1
7 years	1	2	
8 years	1	2	1
9 years		2	
10 years	1	1	

Total numbers years.............. 285

Total number men 152

Average schooling 1.87

TABLE XX (B) WOMEN

Number Years Attended School	Number Cases Attended School in Mexico	Number Cases Attended School in United States	Number Cases Attended School in Both
0 years			49
Less than 1 year	1	1	
1 year	3	3	
2 years	6	1	
3 years	1		
4 years	2		
5 years		1	1
6 years	2	2	
8 years		2	
9 years	1		
10 years		1	
Total number years			95
Total number women			77
Average schooling			1.233

TABLE XXI (A)

SPEAK ENGLISH

Men	No. Cases	Women	No. Cases
Yes	154	Yes	59
No	207	No	234

(B)

WRITE ENGLISH

Men	No. Cases	Women	No. Cases
Yes	73	Yes	41
No	282	No	245

(C)

READ ENGLISH

Men	No. Cases	Women	No. Cases
Yes	63	Yes	38
No	172	No	202

(D)

WRITE SPANISH

Men	No. Cases	Women	No. Cases
Yes	234	Yes	153
No	120	No	134

(E)

READ SPANISH

Men	No. Cases	Women	No. Cases
Yes	140	Yes	140
No	76	No	91

SUMMARY OF TABLES

Total number of men:	Total years of schooling:
194	3475.5
24	61.
152	285.
Total number 370	Total years of schooling....693.5

Average number of years of schooling per man 1.87

Total number of women:	Total years of schooling:
202	312
35	89
77	95
Total number 334	Total years of schooling....496.

Average number of years of schooling per woman 1.48

Total number of cases considered 704
Total years of schooling 1189.5
Average years of schooling per adult 1.67

ABSOLUTELY NO SCHOOLING

Number Men	Number Women
89	100
4	8
66	49
Total ....159 or 42%	Total ....157 or 47.7%

Using the definition of illiteracy as given by the United States Census Bureau as one who can not read or write any language, it is observed that the percentage of illiteracy among the Mexican peon parents is very high. In 1920 five per cent of the population of the United States, under ten years of age was illiterate; 3.3 per cent of the California population was illiterate, and here we find that one-third of the Mexican parents are absolutely illiterate, while the second third must be regarded as semi-illiterate. Consideration has just been given to the ability of Mexican parents to read, write, and speak English and read and write Spanish. The Tables XIX, XX, XXI set forth the years of schooling of a group of Mexican parents taken at random from the labor camps; 704 cases have been considered.

From these tables it is seen that 370 men have averaged 1.77 years of schooling, both in Mexico and United States, while 334 women have averaged 1.44 years of schooling both in Mexico and United States. It is also to be noted that 42 per cent of the men and 47.7 per cent of the women have been reported as having never attended school in either Mexico or the United States. It was said after the Great War that the United States was a nation of sixth-graders. The facts just reported show clearly that the Mexican peon laborers are a group of second-graders. It certainly can not be expected that the children of these parents would progress as well through the grades of our schools as do the normal American children. The educational status of the parents is a controlling factor of progress.

There is another way that the educational status of the parents can be judged. It is noted that questions thirteen, fourteen, and fifteen represent information regarding the number of books, papers, and magazines in the homes of the Mexicans. The returns of 146 cases show the following facts:

TABLE XXII (A)

Number of Books in the Home

MEN No. Books	MEN No. Cases	WOMEN No. Books	WOMEN No. Cases
0	47	0	24
1	5	1	2
2	10	2	7
3	5	3	3
4	7	4	3
5	2	5	1
6	2	7	1
7	2	12	3
10	3	15	1
12	3	16	1
15	2	30	1
16	2		
20	1		
25	1		
30	1		
40	1		
50	2		
100	1		

Number Papers Taken

MEN No. or Name	MEN No. Cases	WOMEN No. or Name	WOMEN No. Cases
0	63	0	27
El Dairio	4	Mexican papers	2
Mexican papers	9	Daily Report	2
La Opinion	13	La Opinion	5
La Epoca	2	San Bernardino Sun	8
La Prensa	1	L. A. Evening Express	1
L. A. Examiner	3	L. A. Examiner	1
L. A. Times	3	L. A. Times	1
L. A. Express	2		
San Bernardino Sun	7		
American papers	5		

Number Magazines

MEN No. or Name	MEN No. Cases	WOMEN No. or Name	WOMEN No. Cases
0	93	0	45
1	1	True Story	1
Household Journal	1		
Times Magazine	3		
Saturday Evening Post	1		
El Malcraido	1		
Cultura	1		
Gentleman	1		

SUMMARY

A study of the educational status of 704 Mexican adults shows that 42 per cent of the men and 47 per cent of the women have had no schooling.

The average number of years of schooling of the men is 1.87 years and of the women is 1.48 years.

Comparatively few Mexican adults can read, write, or even speak the English language.

Only 43 per cent of the men can speak English.

Only 20 per cent of the women can speak English.

Only 27 per cent of the men can read English.

Only 16 per cent of the women can read English.

Only 20 per cent of the men can write English.

Only 14 per cent of the women can write English.

These facts point very clearly to the necessity of an Americanization program for adults that will provide for teaching Mexicans to read, write and speak English.

It has been the experience of teachers that children coming from homes where books and magazines are available progress more rapidly through the schools than do others. The facts presented in the preceding tables show very clearly that the educational status of the Mexican adult is very low. This is an important factor in the retardation and elimination of Mexican pupils in the public schools. Chapter IV will present the economic status of the Mexican adult.

Children living under such conditions could not progress as well in school even if they possessed as much native ability as the normal American children.

CHAPTER IV

ECONOMIC STATUS OF MEXICAN PEON LABORERS

In Chapter III was presented the educational status of Mexican adults. It will be the purpose of Chapter IV to present the economic status. On preceding pages 58, 59 were presented a list of thirty-two questions submitted to Mexican adults. It was very difficult to get returns from every Mexican adult approached because many proved to be suspicious and did not like to fill out blanks when they could not read the language of the American. The economic facts presented were submitted by three types of individuals; an attendance officer whose duty it is to visit the Mexican homes in the interests of securing the attendance of part-time students; the teachers of Americanization who gradually gained the confidence of the Mexican adults, who have secured the filling out of quite a number of blanks; the third type who aided in the filling out of the blanks was a Mexican youth, twenty-two years of age, who went from home to home interviewing the Mexican adults. The figures presented will be at least conservative. Those men and women attending classes are of the best type and of the best economic condition. Questions 19, 20,

The investigations show that women like the members of this group have had little or no school opportunities; 47.7 per cent have had no schooling; the average is 1.48 years per woman.

21, 22, 23, 24, 25, 29, 30, 7, and 8 have considerable bearing on the economic status of the Mexican adults. Tables XXIII, XXIV, XXV, XXVI, XXVII, and XXXIII, which present the findings of 146 cases.

TABLE XXIII

NUMBER OF CHILDREN LIVING

Number Adult Men	Number Cases	Number Adult Women	Number Cases
0 children	19	0 children	2
1 child	9	1 child	8
2 children	7	2 children	4
3 children	6	3 children	7
4 children	11	4 children	5
5 children	8	5 children	7
6 children	18	6 children	8
7 children	6	7 children	2
8 children	7	8 children	3
9 children	3	9 children	1
10 children	2	19 children	1

This table shows that the medium size family for Mexican men has five children and for the women four children; the mode is six living children for both men and women. The average number of living children for the men is 4.9 and for the women is 4.2.

TABLE XXIV

NUMBER OF CHILDREN DEAD

Number Adult Men	Number Cases	Number Adult Women	Number Cases
0 children	28	0 children	13
1 child	23	1 child	11
2 children	11	2 children	6
3 children	11	3 children	8
4 children	2	4 children	1
5 children	7	5 children	3
6 children	2		
7 children	5		
8 children	1		
11 children	1		

This table shows that the average Mexican parent has buried two children. A considerable number of Mexican parents have buried three or more children. An Americanization program should aim to reduce infant mortality and should give much attention to health.

TABLE XXV KINDS OF WORK PERFORMED

Men Kinds of Work	Number Cases
Labor	54
Orange Picking	6
Lemon Picking	6
Ranch Work	15
Vineyard Work	2
Pool Room	1
Packing House	1
Cement Work	6
Pruner	2
Own Business	1
Barber	2
Store Keeper	2
Plasterer	1
Railroad Work	1

Women Kinds of Work	Number Cases
Housework	26
Cannery	4
Washing	1
Grape Picking	4
Pick Beans	1
Restaurant Work	2
Pick Cotton	1
Citrus Fruit	1

TABLE XXVI
NUMBER OF DAYS' WORK IN 1927

MEN

No of Days	No. Cases
60	1
90	1
100	1
125	1
156	1
175	4
150	3
180	4
200	20
208	6
224	2
225	1
234	2
240	2
250	9
260	3
275	2
280	1
300	12
303	1
313	1
315	1
318	1
330	1
360	1
365	1

WOMEN

No. of Days	No. Cases
30	1
60	1
365	25

This table shows that half the men were unemployed for 100 working days or more during the of the men were unem- year 1927. 73.5 percent ployed for 60 working days or more during 1927.

TABLE XXVII
AVERAGE WAGE PER HOUR

MEN

Wage	Number Cases
20c	1
25c	8
27½c	1
30c	2
33½c	13
35c	42
37c	1
38c	1
40c	15
42c	1
45c	8
50c	6
55c	2
62½c	1
65c	1
80c	2
Works for self	5

WOMEN

Wage	Number Cases
20c	1
25c	3
30c	1
35c	1
Do own housework	23

The average wage per hour for men is 38 cents, while that for women is 27 cents. When their families are considered, the men don't receive a wage sufficient for the economic or educational welfare of their children.

TABLE XXVIII
(A) OWN HOME

Men	Number Cases	Women	Number Cases
Yes	58*	Yes	34*
No	56	No	19

(B) OWN OTHER PROPERTY

Men	Number Cases	Women	Number Cases
Yes	30	Yes	5
No	85	No	47

(C) BANK ACCOUNT

Men	Number Cases	Women	Number Cases
Yes	14	Yes	2
No	98	No	48

*—In the larger camps the homes are owned by the employers. Practically none who live in these camps own property. This investigation shows that where the Mexicans are given an opportunity they gradually become owners of homes.

TABLE XXIX

WHAT FURNITURE IN DWELLING

MEN		WOMEN	
Amount	Number Cases	Amount	Number Cases
0	9	Very little	7
Very little	20	Ordinary	10
Ordinary	16	$10	1
$10	1	$20	1
$20	4	$25	1
$25	2	$30	1
$30	1	$35	1
$35	2	$50	1
$50	7	$60	1
$55	1	$75	1
$300	1	$100	10
$600	1	$150	1
$1000	1	$152	1
$1500 (business)	1	$200	3
Store Furniture	1	$250	3
		$300	1
		$350	3
		$1000	1

This table shows the lack of furniture in Mexican dwellings. An Americanization program should provide for teaching Mexican boys how to make inexpensive furniture.

TABLE XXX

TIMES MOVED IN LAST TWO YEARS

MEN		WOMEN	
No. Times	No. Cases	No. Times	No. Cases
0	57	0	23
1	15	1	5
2	17	2	14
3	8	3	2
4	4	4	3
12	1	12	1
15	1		

TABLE XXXI

RENTAL PAID

MEN Amount	Number Cases	WOMEN Amount	Number Cases
0	41	0	19
$ 1.50	1	$ 3.00	1
$ 3.00	3	$ 4.50	1
$ 4.00	3	$ 5.00	1
$ 5.00	9	$ 8.00	3
$ 6.00	4	$ 9.00	1
$ 6.50	1	$10.00	8
$ 7.00	3	$12.00	2
$ 8.00	3	$12.50	1
$ 8.50	1	$15.00	3
$ 9.00	1	$16.00	1
$10.00	7		
$11.00	2		
$12 00	3		
$12.50	1		
$14.00	1		
$15.00	3		
$16.00	1		
$35.00	1		
Works for board and room	1		

Such an Americanization program as has been set up will produce young women like those shown in the picture. One of the Mexican Chaffey Girl Scout troops at the girls' "Estate."

TABLE XXXII

Camps	Men	Women	Children	Total	Number Families	Number of Rooms to Family
No. 1	79	65	133	277	65	1
No. 2	2	3	3	8	3	1
No. 3	11	9	23	43	10	1
No. 4	6	7	20	33	10	1
No. 5	9	9	22	40	8	1
No. 6	18	16	30	54	15	1
No. 7	26	20	44	90	20	5 two-room houses 15 one-room houses
No. 8	51	20	24	95	20 for 17 families	3
No. 9	54	22	22	98	30 in 18 houses	3
No. 10	10	10	9	29	7 houses "all shacks"	tents, wagons, etc.
No. 11	24	21	34	79	21	15 two-room 1 three-room 5 one-room
No. 12	29	14	9	52	3 room bunk-house for 8 men 10 houses for 12 families.	
No. 13	15	5	3	23		
No. 14	15	13	32	60	9	1
No. 15	7	6	24	37	8	1
No. 16	41	17	29	87	18	2
No. 17	14	11	25	50	14	1 tent

In Table XXIII it is to be noted that 96 men report 348 living children, or an average of 3.7 children per father; while 48 women report 197 living children, or an average of 4.11 children per mother. Table XXXII shows the number of men, women, and children dwelling in seventeen labor camps of the Chaffey Union High School District as ascertained by representatives of the State Board of Health in a survey made in 1926. This report shows 486 children in 260 families, or an average of 1.87 children to the family. Table

XVII shows that the average wage for the men is 38½ cents per hour, while Table XXVI shows that only 28 out of 91 men reporting worked 300 days during 1927, while only 43 of the men worked as many as 250 days during the year. It is clear from these facts that children in the homes of Mexican parents can not have what are regarded as the necessities of life. A glance at the remaining tables will show that the Mexican home has little or no furniture; there are no books, or magazines, or newspapers, and Table XXXII shows crowded conditions where in many homes there are more than four people living in a single room. From these facts it is seen that the children of Mexican peon parents have little or nothing in the home that will aid them economically or educationally.

It is to be remembered that no effort is made to show the Mexican children are inferior in any way to the white, or American children. Chapter V, however, will take into consideration the relative ability of the Mexican children as compared with the ability of the normal American children to do the academic and the vocational work of the school. A further comparison will be made regarding those qualities that make for success in life.

SUMMARY

The facts revealed in this chapter clearly show that Mexican children come from homes where ignorance and poverty prevail. The Mexican children hear English spoken only in the classroom at school; they have no books, no magazines, and no newspapers in their homes; an educational background is lacking for them. The program of Americanization must take these things into consideration and supply in some way what the home conditions lack. The program must further provide a way for the adults to acquire information that should secure improved health conditions in the average Mexican home. A glance at the homes of many of the Mexicans should arouse the program-maker to the need of providing instruction for Mexican boys and for Mexican men that would make possible the improvement of the average Mexican home.

CHAPTER V

THE ABILITY INDEX OF THE MEXICAN PUPIL

That the pupil of Mexican peon parentage does not learn as quickly the lessons commonly required of American pupils is a proven fact. This fact, however, does not justify the statement that the native ability of these pupils is less than that of the normal American pupils. Other factors enter in that partially control the learning process. The low educational and economic status of the parents have been partially responsible for lack of progress through the schools of Mexican children. Lack of knowledge of the English language might be supposed to prevent progress, but a study of the over-ageness and retardation of foreign pupils other than Mexican reveals the fact that there is a small degree of over-ageness on the part of Italian and other foreign groups. The problem of Chapter V is to investigate the comparative abilities of children of different foreign groups and to determine an "index of ability" of Mexican children. It is proposed to obtain this index by obtaining information from four sources: The comparative scores of American and Mexican children of the same ages in different types of tests involving tasks commonly assigned pupils; the comparative scores of one hundred Mexican children and one hundred American children of the same ages in certain tests administered by two assistant superintendents of schools of San Bernardino County, the selections to be taken at random; the comparative progress of American and Mexican children through the schools of San Bernardino County; and the subjective opinions of eighty teachers who have had experience teaching American, Mexican and other foreign pupils.

In a preliminary study that was made a group of Americanization teachers responded to the following request: "Please write the nationalities in the order of their abilities to acquire English." Certain subjective opinions of value were presented: "Their ability to acquire English does not depend as much on the nationality as upon their previous schooling in their own language." "Other factors besides nationality enter into the problem of acquiring English—notably cultural background in one's own tongue." These statements are of value and are born out by investigation. There have been seventeen non-English speaking types of adults in Americanization classes at Chaffey and these peoples have been grouped on the basis of their apparent ability to acquire English as follows: German, Dutch, Swede, Danish, Swiss, Belgian, Russian, Japanese, Spanish, Italian. Hungarian, Polish, East Indian, Greek, Korean, Mexican, and Filipino. One teacher with experience with many foreign groups observes that "there is a wide gap between Europeans and the Mexican and Filipino."

It is of value to study the comparative individual abilities of many pupils as determined by the success with which they perform the tasks commonly assigned them at school. How well does the average Mexican pupil master the lessons assigned him? Can a comparison be made between the ability of Mexican children and that of American children? Can there be developed a technique that will make possible the determination of the comparative abilities of Mexican pupils to acquire those skills, those abilities, and that information required by the regular course of study?

A study is first made of the comparative abilities of Mexican pupils and American pupils to learn vocabulary lists; in each case the investigation sought to test the ability to learn both English and Spanish words. A list of words was selected that would be fair to both Mexican and American pupils of the same age, although it must be remembered that the Mexican pupils were four years behind the Americans in grade placement; to offset this possible advantage on the part of Americans it must be remembered that the Mexican pupils were somewhat familiar with two languages, the American pupils with but one. In the hands of each pupil was placed the following: "Allow ten minutes' time to memorize the following vocabulary, then have the pupils fill out the blanks on the accompanying sheets:

> Podar—to prunge; cajon—box; podadera—pruning knife; hilera—row; arena—sand; naranjo—orange tree; seco—dry; verjel—orchard; rama—branch; recoger—to pick; limon—lemon; saco—sack; tallo—stem; lumber—madera; polvo—dust; quitar—to remove.

After ten minutes of study the pupils were given a list of English words and were allowed ten minutes to fill in the blanks; then they were given a list of Spanish words and were allowed ten minutes to fill in the blanks. The pupils at the conclusion of ten minutes wrote their ages, grades, and signed their names.

From the papers turned in by pupils taking these and succeeding tests penmanship scores of Mexican pupils and of American pupils of the same age were secured; values were assigned by subjective opinion based upon experience with the Thorndike and Zaner scales, to the handwriting samples of a large number of pupils. Only children of ages thirteen, fourteen and fifteen were selected. The Mexican children averaged four years behind the American children in grade placement and consequently must be regarded as considerably below the American children in their capacity to do the academic work that the course of study provides for all pupils no matter what capacity they may have. It is to be observed that in each case the average score of American pupils is higher than the average score of Mexican pupils, but the results in favor of the American pupils are not significant when their respective abilities in penmanship are considered. The following average scores were obtained:

Age	American	Mexican
13	77.3	70.5
14	80.0	78.7
15	74.4	73.3
Average	77.23	74.16

The average score of the Mexican pupils divided by the average score of the American pupils results in the decimal .960, which is the comparative ability of the pupil of Mexican peon parents in one particular, that of handwriting or penmanship. This result is in accord with general observations regarding the handwriting of Mexican pupils who are known to take pains with their effort along manual lines. The decimal .960 represents the "index of ability" of Mexican pupils in one skill—that of handwriting.

The tables* just presented and teaching experience show that when American children who have had no knowledge of the Spanish language are given the vocabulary tests that the American children do not do as well as do the Mexican children. The American children are familiar with only one language, the Mexican children with two. But where the Mexican children of ages thirteen, fourteen, fifteen and sixteen were tested with children who were taking first year Spanish in the classes at Chaffey Union High School, it was

A Part-time Class of Mexican Girls

*—The tables are omitted.

found that the index of ability of Mexican children in the vocabulary tests was .832. Using the corrective decimal, .672 and the index of ability of the Mexican pupils becomes .559, when they are compared with children of the same age but of high school grade who are taking Spanish. Averaging the index, 1.256, found in the English-Spanish vocabulary test with the index, .927, found in the Spanish-English vocabularly test the true index for Mexican-American elementary children should be 1.09. Averaging this last index, 1.09, with the index, .559, found when high school pupils taking Spanish are involved the final vocabulary test reveals for Mexican pupils an index of .825. This is the index that will be used to determine the academic index of ability of Mexican pupils.

To determine the index of ability of Mexican pupils in arithmetic both Mexican and American children were given the following simple test and were allowed ten minutes to do the work:

7	4	6	9	8	7	6	7	8	564	78965
5	3	9	8	6	5	8	9	7	239	73546
4	7	6	7	3	7	5	8	4	847	26095
8	4	7	9	4	1	5	8	9	937	98898
7	5	8	7	6	9	8	7	5	407	52789
8	6	7	8	9	7	4	3	5	658	43796

SUMMARY OF SCORES IN ARITHMETIC TEST

Age	No. Cases Mexican	No. Cases American	No. Problems Mexican	No. Problems American	Av. Problems Mexican	Av. Problems American
6		1		2		2
7		2		5		2.5
8	5	26	31	147	6.2	5.65
9	6	52	37	334	6.16	6.42
10	11	34	92	255	8.36	7.5
11	18	83	139	688	7.72	8.29
12	20	71	142	610	7.1	8.59
13	16	55	126	456	7.875	8.29
14	15	23	132	233	8.8	10.13
15	10	10	78	81	7.8	8.1
16	6	2	49	12	8.166	6.
17		1		9		9.
Totals	107	360	826	2832		

The average number of problems worked by Mexicans is 7.7196. The average number of problems worked by Americans is 7.8666. Dividing 7.7196 by 7.8666 the index of .981 is obtained. To correct this index it is multiplied by the corrective decimal .672 and the true index of .659 is obtained. This is the arithmetic index that will be used to determine the academic index of ability of Mexican pupils.

Much of the work in academic departments is memory work. This is particularly true in the elementary schools. An effort was made to get the comparative abilities of Mexican and American children to memorize "America" in Spanish and a grammatical statement set to verse in English. Spanish was used for the purpose of giving the Mexican pupils every opportunity to use their own language in memory work. The standard Spanish version of America was used. It was typed and a copy was put in the hands of both Mexican and American children. After ten minutes of study the children wrote their ages and grades, signed their names, and turned in their papers. The total number of words memorized were counted.

SUMMARY OF SCORES, AMERICA IN SPANISH

Age	No. Cases Mexican	No. Cases American	No. Mem. Mexican	No. Mem. American	Av. Mex.	Ax. Amer.
9		4		26		6.5
10	2	21	45	149	22.5	7.095
11	11	30	204	263	18.545	8.766
12	12	30	258	249	21.5	8.3
13	11	20	170	516	15.454	25.8
14	25	51	882	1617	35.28	31.705
15	14	38	342	1370	24.428	36.05
16	3	24	49	841	16.333	35.041
17		6		239		39.833
Totals	78	224	1950	5270		

The average number of words memorized by Mexican pupils is 25. The average number of words memorized by American pupils is 23.52. Dividing 25 by 23.52, the index of ability to memorize Spanish poetry is found to be 1.06. The corrective index, .672, will be applied and the resultant index of .712 is obtained.

A copy of the English poem presented on the following page was put in the hands of both Mexican and American pupils.

MEMORIZATION OF ENGLISH POEM

Allow ten minutes' time to memorize; then have the children write immediately as much as they can remember without help. Have each pupil put on his paper at the top the following: Name, age, grade, and the number of minutes it took him to learn the selection, if less than ten.

"A noun's the name of anything;
As, school or garden, hoop or swing.

Adjectives tell the kind of noun;
As, great, small, pretty, white, or brown.
Three of these words we often see,
Called articles—a, an, and the.

Instead of nouns the pronouns stand;
John's head, his face, my arm, your hand.

Verbs tell of something being done;
As, read, write, spell, sing, jump, or run.

How things are done the adverbs tell;
As, slowly, quickly, ill, or well.
They also tell us where and when;
As, here, and there, and now, and then.

A preposition stands before
A noun; as, in or through, a door.

Conjunctions sentences unite;
As, kittens scratch and puppies bite.

The interjection shows surprise;
As, O, how pretty! Ah, how wise!"

DAVID B. TOWER and
BENJAMIN F. TWEED.

The pupils were given ten minutes to study the selection and were then required to write what they could remember. They gave their ages, grades and signed their names. The number of words correct was obtained for such pupil.

SUMMARY OF SCORES, MEMORIZATION OF ENGLISH SELECTION

Age	No. Cases Mexican	No. Cases American	No. Words Mexican	No. Words American	Average Mexican	Average American
9		4		197		49.25
10		28		1126		40.214
11	10	49	314	1569	31.4	32.02
12	9	40	235	1575	26.11	39.375
13	8	24	266	1161	33.25	48.375
14	19	15	774	703	40.736	46.866
15	9	11	459	848	51.	77.09
16	4	5	163	258	40.75	51.6
17	1	1	33	48	33.	48.
Totals	60	177	2244	7485		

The average number of words memorized by Mexican pupils is 37.4. The average number of words memorized by American pupils is 42.288. Dividing 37.4 by 42.288 the index of ability of Mexican pupils to memorize English selections is found to be .884. Using the corrective index of .672 the resultant index of .594 is obtained. This is the index that will be used in determining the index of ability of Mexican pupils from an academic standpoint.

To determine the final academic index of ability of Mexican pupils the four indices thus far obtained from the tests must be averaged.

Index obtained from vocabulary tests	.825
Index obtained from the arithmetic test	.659
Index obtained from memorization of the selection in Spanish	.712
Index obtained from memorization of the selection in English	.594
Average	.697

This composite academic index will be one of four to be used to determine the comparative ability of Mexican pupils to do the work required of pupils in the academic departments of our schools.

Another procedure in determining the index of ability of Mexican pupils has been to get the comparative scores of one hundred one Mexican pupils and one hundred American pupils of approximately the same ages as obtained in tests administered in the rural schools of San Bernardino County by Assistant Superintendent Gladys Potter who has charge of the "desert" schools, and by Assistant Superintendent Beulah Hartman who has charge of the schools west of the mountains. The tests chosen were the Los Angeles Elementary Reading Test, Form 1, and the Los Angeles Spelling Test. The children were selected at random, approximately half from the desert schools, and the remainder from the other schools. The comparative scores as obtained from these tests are tabulated and presented in Tables LIII (A) and LIII (B) on the four pages immediately following this page. The following facts should be considered:

Fifty-one Mexican pupils on the desert had an average grade placement of 3.74.

Fifty American pupils of approximately the same ages and living on the desert had an average grade placement of 6.97.

Fifty Mexican pupils west of the mountains had an average grade placement of 3.232.

Fifty American pupils of the same ages and living west of the mountains had an average grade placement of 7.96.

The average grade placement of the 101 Mexican pupils is 3.39.*

The average grade placement of the 100 American pupils is 7.49.*

Dividing 3.39 by 7.49 the index of ability as shown by the reading placement test is .452.

Forty-eight Mexican pupils on the desert had an average grade placement in spelling of 3.96, while 47 American pupils in the same locality and of approximamtely the same ages had a grade placement of 6.74.

Dividing 3.96 by 6.74 the index of ability as shown by the spelling placement is .587.

By averaging the two indices thus obtained, it is determined that the index of ability of Mexican pupils is .52. This is a second index that will be used to establish the academic index of ability of Mexican pupils.

*—The scores of 88 Mexican pupils and 95 American pupils are listed.

TABLE LIII-A

Comparative Scores*

In Reading and Spelling of 101 Pupils

Age	Grade	Reading Placement Mexican	Reading Placement American	Spelling Placement Mexican	Spelling Placement American
			5.0		4.1
9	5	3.5	3.8	4.9	4.1
10	4	1.5		1.0	
10	2	2.4		1.8	
11	3	2.2		2.8	
11	3	1.4		3.9	
11	4	4.3		3.1	
11	4	3.0		3.1	
11	4		7.7	4.9	5.9
11	5		4.8		5.4
11	6		4.0		3.8
11	5		7.4		6.4
11	6				
11	6		5.3		5.2
11	6		4.9		
11	7		6.8		7.8
12	3	1.6		1.5	
12	3	2.6		1.6	
12	5	2.5	4.5		3.4
12	3			1.5	
12	5	5.0	5.0	4.9	4.9
12	5		1.5	5.4	2.3
12	5	3.2		5.6	2.8
12	2	1.5		0.0	
12	2	1.5		0.0	
12	2	1.6		1.2	
12	5	5.3		4.9	
12	5			4.2	
12	5	3.5		4.2	
12	5	5.8		4.2	
12	6		5.6		4.7
12	6				4.2
12	6		6.6		8.9
12	6		6.1		6.8
12	7		7.4		10.3

*—From report of Mrs. Gladys Potter, Assistant Superintendent of Schools, San Bernardino County. The Los Angeles Elementary Reading Test, Form 1, was given. The scores are taken from pupils.

TABLE LIII-A (Continued)

Age	Grade	Reading Placement Mexican	Reading Placement American	Spelling Placement Mexican	Spelling Placement American
12	7		10.5		8.5
12	7		6.6		6.4
12	7		7.7		6.8
12	7		7.7		9.3
13	2	1.6		1.2	
13	3			1.8	
13	4	3.8		4.2	
13	5	6.1		5.4	
13	5	2.2		4.9	
13	5			4.7	
13	5			3.9	
13	5			3.2	
13	5	2.2		2.9	3.4
13	6	5.6	9.4	6.8	6.4
13	6		4.8		4.9
13	7	4.5	8.0	7.5	6.2
13	7		6.1		9.3
12	8		8.9		8.5
13	8		7.1		8.5
13	8		9.4		8.1
13	8		7.7		9.3
13	8		8.4		8.5
13	8		10.1		10.1
13	8		10.0		9.8
14	2			1.4	
14	3			1.6	
14	4			2.8	
14	6			5.2	
14	6	4.3		4.7	
14	7	5.6	6.1	9.3	
14	7	7.1	3.5	7.8	6.4
14	7	3.8	3.5		6.4
14	7	4.0		5.4	
14	8	11.5	9.4		6.8
14	8	7.7	7.7	8.5	7.9
14	8		7.7		8.5
14	8		7.4		6.4
14	8		9.4		5.4
14	8		9.4		10.6
14	8		7.4		
15	4			1.8	

TABLE LIII-A (Continued)

Age	Grade	Reading Placement Mexican	Reading Placement American	Spelling Placement Mexican	Spelling Placement American
15	4			3.8	
15	5	3.2		2.3	
15	5	4.5		5.9	
15	5	4.5		6.8	
15	6	3.8		3.6	
15	7		8.0		8.5
15	7				7.2
15	8				6.8
15	8		11.5		8.9
15	8		9.4		5.9
16	8			7.5	
17	8		4.8		6.4
Totals		138.4	314.0	190.1	317.1
Average		3.74	6.97	3.96	6.74

A Mexican Home

TABLE LIII-B
Comparative Scores*
In Reading of 100 Pupils

Age	Grade	Score Mexican	Score American	Grade Placement Mexican	Grade Placement American
12	6	18		4.3	
12	7		27		6.6
16	6	25		5.6	
16	8		31		7.7
14	6	19		4.5	
14	8		29		7.1
13	6	14		3.2	
13	8		32		8.0
14	7	26		6.3	
14	8		30		7.4
13	6	16		3.8	
13	7		35		9.4
14	7	27		6.6	
14	8		36		10.0
14	6	13		3.0	
14	8		33		8.4
14	7	7		1.8	
14	8		30		7.4
13	5	11		2.5	
13	8		25		6.1
13	5	6		1.7	
13	7		28		6.8
16	5	14		3.2	
16	8		39		11.5
15	5	9		2 0	
15	8		37		10.5
16	8	19		4.5	
16	8		36		10.0
15	6	11		2.5	
15	8		35		9.8
15	6	14		3.2	
15	8		37		10 5
15	6	8		1 9	
15	8		36		10.0
15	6	21		5.0	
15	8		39		11.5
15	6	15		3.5	
15	8		36		10.0

*—From report of Miss Beulah Hartman, Assistant Superintendent of Schools, San Bernardino County.

TABLE LIII-B (Continued)

Age	Grade	Score Mexican	Score American	Grade Placement Mexican	Grade Placement American
14	6	19		4.5	
14	8		36		10.0
16	5	14		3.2	
16	8		41		12.0
13	4	11		2.5	
13	8		29		7.1
14	4	10		2.2	
13	8		34		8.9
13	5	9		2.0	
13	8		31		7.7
15	8	24		5.8	
15	8		37		10.5
13	4	10		2.2	
12	4	14		3.2	
12	6		26		6.3
12	4	6		1.7	
12	6		36		10.0
10	4	3		1.2	
10	4		19		4.5
11	4	1		1.0	
11	5		23		5.3
11	4	13		3.0	
11	5		20		4.8
13	5	6		1.7	
13	8		31		7.7
12	5	13		3.0	
12	4		23		5.6
10	6	16		3.8	
10	6		22		5.3
12	6	16		3.8	
12	5		22		5.3
12	6	9		2.0	
12	6		31		7.7
13	6	12		2.8	
13	8		32		8.0
13	6	12		2.8	
13	6		25		6.1
12	6	21		5.6	
12	6		24		5.8
12	6	14		3.2	
12	8		36		10.0
15	6	12		2.8	
15	8		30		7.4

TABLE LIII-C (Continued)

		Score		Grade Placement	
Age	Grade	Mexican	American	Mexican	American
14	6	18		4.3	
14	8		30		7.4
15	8	19		4.5	
15	7		29		7.1
13	4	13		3.0	
13	8		34		8.9
11	4	11		2.5	
11	5		17		4.0
13	6	31		7.7	
13	8		32		8.0
12	6	21		5.0	
12	6		30		7.4
12	4	15		3.5	
12	6		34		8.9
11	5	20		4.8	
11	6		33		8.4
15	5	14		3.2	
15	7		30		7.4
Totals		720	1532	161.6	398.0
Average		14.4	30.62	3.232	7.96

Thus far the index of ability has been determined in two ways; simple tests have been given Mexican children and American children of the same ages. No test given had been standardized; the tests were given to test the comparative capacity of Mexican children to do the work required by present courses of study. The indices obtained from the vocabulary, arithmetic, and memorization tests were averaged and gave a composite index of approximately .70. A second index of ability of Mexican children was obtained from placement scores assigned to children by Mrs. Gladys Potter and Miss Beulah Hartman, assistant County Superintendents of Schools of San Bernardino County. They have given many tests to the pupils of the elementary schools. Cases were taken at random of one hundred one Mexican pupils and of one hundred American pupils of approximately the same ages. The Los Angeles Reading Test, Form 1, and the Spelling Test were used to derive the grade placement of the pupils. The information thus obtained shows again that the Mexican children are four years behind the American children in grade placement; the average placement of the one hundred one Mexican pupils was divided by the average placement of the one hundred American pupils; both reading and spelling placements were averaged, and a new index of ability of Mexican children of .52

was obtained. This is used to act as a check on other indices obtained and will partly determine the final

A third way that the index of ability of Mexican pupils can be determined is to compare the over-ageness of American pupils with that of Mexican pupils. This has been determined in San Bernardino County by the age-grade reports of March 1, 1927, and in the Chaffey Union High School District by the age-grade reports for the period September to December of the school year 1927 and 1928. In the Chaffey Union High School District the Mexican children are making only 24.7% as satisfactory progress as are the American children. In San Bernardino County 78.5% of the Mexican pupils were found to be retarded and over-aged, while only 33.28% of the white children were over-aged. Dividing 33.28 by 78.5 a new index of ability is found; this index of .421 represents the index of ability of Mexican pupils as determined by their actual progress through the schools of San Bernardino County. This is a third index that will be used to establish the index sought.

Thus far three indices have been obtained by investigating the comparative achievement of Mexican and American pupils as shown by their respective abilities to achieve in certain tests, and by their respective abilities to make progress in the schools. A final procedure has been to secure the subjective opinions of eighty-three teachers who have been having actual experience in teaching Mexican and other foreign pupils in practically all levels of attainment. A communication shown on the following page was addressed to

Teaching Mexican Women in Escuelita

these teachers. Their arithmetic opinions, although only subjective, have been tabulated in Tables LIV to LXI, inclusive, and make possible both a scholastic rating and a citizenship rating of the pupils of American, Mexican and other foreign races.

QUESTIONNAIRE TO TEACHERS OF FOREIGN GROUP

From your experience in teaching the foreign population you are well versed in the comparative abilities of Americans and foreigners.

In our Americanization work we are interested in determining an "Index of Ability" of various foreign groups. Will you kindly rate the following races in comparison with Americans? Please consider American ability as 1.00 and express the comparative abilities of the other races by decimals.

Races	Capacity to Do Academic Work	Capacity to Do Manual Work	Honesty	Initative	Dependability
American	1.00	1.00	1.00	1.00	1.00
Mexican					
Italian					
Japanese					
Spanish					
French					
Swiss					
German					
Negro					
Other					

Races	Industry	Determination	Energy	Loyalty	Conduct
American	1.00	1.00	1.00	1.00	1.00
Mexican					
Italian					
Japanese					
Spanish					
French					
Swiss					
German					
Negro					
Other					

TABLE LIV

MEXICAN

Capacity to do Academic Work		Capacity to do Manual Work	
Score	No. Cases	Score	No. Cases
1.00	9	1.50	2
.95	1	1.25	3
.90	8	1.10	2
.85	2	1.00	31
.80	6	.95	2
.75	12	.90	9
.70	3	.85	2
.65	2	.80	2
.60	4	.75	11
.55	1	.60	2
.50	18	.50	5
.40	3	.30	1
.25	2	.15	1
.15	1		73
.12	1		
	73		

TABLE LIV (Continued)

MEXICAN

Honesty		Dependability	
Score	No. Cases	Score	No. Cases
1.50	1	1.00	11
1.10	2	.90	2
1.00	19	.85	3
.95	1	.80	7
.90	5	.75	11
.85	5	.70	7
.80	5	.65	3
.75	12	.60	5
.70	5	.50	19
.65	1	.40	2
.60	6	.30	1
.50	15	.25	5
.30	1	.20	1
25	2	.15	1
	80	.10	1
		.05	1
			80

TABLE LIV (Continued)

MEXICAN

Initiative		Industry	
Score	No. Cases	Score	No. Cases
1.00	2	1.00	5
.90	4	.95	1
.80	2	.90	9
.75	16	.85	1
.70	6	.80	14
.65	3	.75	15
.60	9	.70	7
.55	1	.60	3
.50	17	.50	11
.40	3	.40	2
.30	2	.25	2
.25	9	.15	1
.15	1	.10	2
.10	3	.05	3
.01	1		—
	—		76
	79		

Mexican Home of An Ideal Type

TABLE LIV (Continued)

MEXICAN

Determination Score	No. Cases	Energy Score	No. Cases
1.00	3	1.00	3
.95	2	.90	8
.90	8	.85	6
.85	5	.80	5
.80	3	.75	15
.78	1	.70	8
.75	14	.65	1
.70	7	.60	4
.65	1	.50	16
.60	5	.45	1
.50	16	.40	2
.40	4	.30	1
.30	1	.25	1
.25	2	.15	1
.15	1	.10	1
.10	2	.05	3
.05	2		76
	77		

TABLE LIV (Continued)

MEXICAN

Loyalty Score	No. Cases	Conduct Score	No. Cases
1.25	2	1.50	1
1.00	24	1.05	1
.95	1	1.00	21
.90	9	.90	14
.85	3	.85	7
.80	5	.80	8
.78	1	.74	1
.75	11	.75	6
.70	5	.70	1
.65	1	.65	1
.60	2	.60	2
.50	8	.55	1
.30	1	.50	3
.15	1	.25	2
.10	1		
.05	1		78
	78		

SUMMARY OF TABLES SHOWING INDEX OF ABILITY

Representing Subjective Opinions of Eighty-three Teachers

	American	Mexican	No. Teachers Reporting	Italian	No. Teachers Reporting	Japanese	No. Teachers Reporting	Spanish	No. Teachers Reporting	French	No. Teachers Reporting	Swiss	No. Teachers Reporting	German	No. Teachers Reporting	Negro	No. Teachers Reporting
Capacity to Do Academic Work	1.000	.685	73	.802	35	1.030	28	.828	19	.906	9	.946	12	1.038	24	.580	20
Capacity to Do Manual Work	1.000	899	73	1.006	33	1.117	26	.926	17	.911	9	.968	11	1.022	23	.769	20
Honesty	1.000	.702	80	.911	36	.905	28	.884	19	.978	9	1.008	11	1.037	23	.558	19
Dependability	1.000	.649	80	.875	37	.855	29	.871	19	.970	9	.980	10	1.015	22	.661	19
Initative	1.000	.554	79	.826	37	.876	30	.783	19	.951	9	.925	10	.966	22	.590	19
Industry	1.000	.689	76	.909	36	1.035	30	.813	19	1.012	9	.953	11	1.041	22	.644	19
Determination	1.000	.640	77	.871	36	1.020	28	.798	18	1.052	9	.985	11	1.032	22	.641	18
Energy	1.000	.650	76	.891	36	.963	28	.851	17	.953	9	.970	11	1.003	20	.629	19
Loyalty	1.000	.804	78	.931	32	.894	23	.903	17	.963	9	1.031	9	.993	21	.786	19
Conduct	1.000	.808	78	.915	35	.979	25	.924	19	.956	9	1.100	11	.996	23	.747	19

SUMMARY

The summary of tables showing the comparative index of ability of children of different races is useful in several ways.

The comparisons between the Mexican and negro pupils shows that teachers consider them approximately on the same level. This is of value, for information regarding the development of negro education should prove useful in the development of Mexican education; as industrial education for negroes has proven most successful, so should it prove for the Mexican pupils.

The comparisons show again that the chief Americanization problems are concerned with the Mexicans.

Finally, the ten indices developed show where the Mexicans are weakest and where they are the strongest. These indices form a substantial basis for developing a new course of study to be advocated in the Americanization program.

This survey of the subjective opinions of teachers sets forth a fourth and final index of ability of Mexican pupils. It is interesting to know that the index, .685, is found by averaging the ratings of seventy-three teachers; but if the upper 25% and the lower 25% of ratings are eliminated the middle 50% average .685. This decimal represents very clearly the subjective opinions of a large number of experienced teachers and is entitled to be considered with the other indices obtained thus far. These have been derived to represent the comparative academic rating only. They represent further the comparative success of Mexican pupils in achieving what the present courses of study require. The indices should next be averaged to determine a composite index that represents clearly and fairly what we have sought.

Average index obtained from vocabulary, arithmetic, and memorization tests	.697
Average index obtained from the county tests	.52
Index obtained from the age-grade reports	.421
Index obtained from the subjective opinions of teachers	.685
Average	.58

This index shows that Mexican pupils can be expected to do the work that is of an academic type only 58% as well as the American pupils can do the work.

A study of the summary table on the previous page will show other useful indices. The scores represent those qualities, capacities, skills, and abilities that make most for success. The scores tabulated are valuable in directing attention to those activities most valuable in a program of Americanization.

To this point there have been shown the effects of Mexican peon parentage upon pupil progress in the elementary and high schools. There has been presented a survey of the educational and economic status of Mexican adults. It has been shown that the pupils of Mexican peon parentage do not progress as well in the schools as do the American pupils, and that they cannot be expected normally to be more than 58% as successful in pursuing academic courses. It has been shown that the education and Americanization of foreign pupils other than Mexican presents no serious problem neither in San Bernardino County nor in the Chaffey Union High School District. It has been clearly shown that Mexican pupils and Mexican adults do present a serious problem, both from the standpoint of education and of Americanization. It is therefore certain that any program of education and Americanization should be intensive as it may relate to the development of the Mexican. Chapter VI will present such a program.

CHAPTER VI

SETTING UP AN AMERICANIZATION PROGRAM

In the five preceding chapters it has been shown that:

1. Mexican children constitute one-fourth of the elementary pupil population of San Bernardino County, and nearly one-fourth of the pupil population of the elementary schools of the Chaffey Union High School District.

2. The Mexican population in San Bernardino County is on the increase, for three-eighths of the babies of San Bernardino County are Mexican.

3. The children of the thirty races other than American and Mexican composing the pupil population of San Bernardino County constitute no serious problem in educational administration.

4. The Mexican children are actually making only 42% as satisfactory progress through the schools as are the children of other races.

5. The Mexican pupils have only 58% as good ability to do the work of the schools as have the American pupils; yet they have 90% as good ability as have American pupils to do manual work, they show equal capacity in penmanship.

6. The Mexican adult peons are illiterate and ignorant; 42% of the men and 48% of the women have had no schooling; less than one-fifth of the adults can write English; less than one-fourth of the adults can read English; while less than one-fourth of the adults can speak English.

7. The economic status of the Mexican adults is low; there is a high infant death rate among Mexicans; the homes are unsanitary, crowded, and possess little or no furniture, books, or magazines; unemployment exists to a marked degree; while the average income of the Mexican parents is not sufficient to provide a satisfactory educational background for the children.

Because these are facts it is proposed in the program of Americanization to meet the conditions in the following way:

1. The important questions, considerations, and objectives pertinent to the program are selected.

2. An organization for carrying on the work is discussed.

3. The equipment needed for carrying out the program is determined.

4. A plan for creating courses of study to meet the needs of Mexican pupils and of Mexican adults is outlined.

5. A plan for co-operation between the Board of Supervisors and educational agencies is suggested.

The Right Sort of Mexican Homes

6. A new department of Mexican education is advocated.

7. The building and equipping of an industrial high school for Mexican adolescents and for Mexican adults is advocated in order to provide a partial solution of the problem of educating Mexican part-time pupils and Mexican adults.

8. A travelling school, "escuelita" is proposed.

The program here suggested will largely solve the Americanization problems by accomplishing the following:

1. The problems involved in Americanization will be recognized.

2. Separate courses of study will be developed for the education of Mexicans.

3. Equipment and buildings will be secured that will make possible carrying out the program.

4. Consistent effort will be made to enroll all Mexican adolescents and adults in classes that will be conducted to meet their actual needs and assure their educational and economic advancement.

The thirty races, other than American or Mexican, known to dwell in San Bernardino County present a comparatively slight Americanization problem. Their children can all be absorbed in the regular classes of the public schools. Table LXII shows that only 40.9% of the pupils of all races other than American or Mexican are over-aged; while Table LXIII shows that only 36.2% of the Italian pupils are over-aged. As 33.28% of all the white pupils of San Bernardino County were shown to be over-aged, the difference between this and the over-ageness of the pupils of other foreign races is insignificant.

TABLE LXII

Districts	Total all races other than American and Mexican	No. Over aged
Alta Loma	6	4
Camp Baldy	0	0
Central	9	2
Cucamonga	17	7
Etiwanda	35	10
Fontana	64	14
Mt. View	38	7
Ontario	117	28
Piedmont	42	25
Upland	14	2
Totals	242	99
		40.9% over-aged

TABLE LXIII

Districts	Italian	No. Over-aged
Alta Loma	3	3
Camp Baldy	0	0
Central	7	2
Cucamonga	17	7
Etiwanda	34	9
Fontana	11	1
Mt. View	21	5
Ontario	31	10
Piedmont	25	17
Upland	0	0
Total	149	54

Percent over-aged.. 36.2%

The comparative few adults should be enrolled in classes where English is taught when needed. Then there should be provided naturalization classes where American geography, the principles of American government, and American ideals are taught. The ultimate objective of these classes is full citizenship in the United States. Such classes have been maintained in the Chaffey Union High School for many years; the class work culminates each year in the awarding of citizenship certificates to those who are ready for their final papers at the annual commencement exercises of the Chaffey Union High School.

PROBLEMS

The greatest problem confronting Southern California today is that of dealing with the Mexican element that is forming year by year a larger proportion of the population. According to present tendencies the time is not far distant when every other child in the elementary schools will be Mexican. The Mexican families live in segregated districts of city and rural districts and import their native standards of living. How shall this element be taken care of? Can the Mexicans be raised to the American standards of life? Can American schooling figure in the upbringing of a race? What lessons should be taught and how much should be taught? What skills should be developed? Can the English language replace the Spanish as a medium of current use? Can the high infant death rate be overcome? Can sanitary methods be adopted to replace the less desirable methods that now prevail? Can Mexican adults be led to seek and secure naturalization? And finally, can the Mexican peon be assimilated into the American population as have the races of Europe? These are the problems involved everywhere, and an effective Americanization program must take them into account. The considerations involved are:

1. Mexican children can acquire both information and skill.
2. Mexican adults can learn the English language, can acquire useful information about our government, and can learn methods of sanitation.

"Educate All the Children of All the People"

3. Mexican parents should be taught as well as their children; teach both and prevent rifts in the home.

4. The regular course of study is developed to meet the needs of normal American children and does not meet the needs of Mexican children.

5. Mexican adults will not go to afternoon or evening schools very far from their homes; the school must be taken to them.

6. A new course of study must be created to meet the needs of the Mexican elementary pupils.

7. Separate courses must be set up for Mexican adolescents.

8. Courses must be developed for Mexican adults that will be based upon the actual needs and experiences of those adults.

9. An Americanization program will be justified from an economic standpoint.

10. Every inhabitant or dweller within the territory of the United States has an effect upon the success or failure of the American people; any racial group that numbers from one-fifth to one-fourth of our population has a tremendous effect upon the destiny of our country.

11. Raising the standards educationally, economically, and spiritually should be the aim of any system of education.

From these considerations it seems perfectly clear that there must be set up an Americanization program to take care of the foreign element of any community; it will be the purpose of this chapter to present an educational program for a typical union high school.

LESSON PLANS

The educators who are concerned with an Americanization program must set up clearly defined objectives as to what ought to be taught the Mexican peons. The latter will be required to use the English language. To meet this need language lessons should be developed by teachers and by boards of education to be adaptable to children, to adolescents, and to adults. Word or vocabulary lists should be worked out and developed into lesson units. Constant use of these words should be required in class work to accustom the Mexicans to their use. Simple arithmetic lessons leading to a mastery of the four fundamental processes should be developed. This should be done for the mere protection of the adults in their small business relations. Penmanship lessons should be developed, and the Mexican pupils and adults given an opportunity to learn our written language, for they appear to be adept in a certain manual dexterity that leads to proficiency in penmanship. Lessons in hygiene and health should be developed, together with lessons on pre-natal care and that of infants, that the high mortality amongst Mexican babies may be arrested. As the Mexicans are lovers of music and art, lessons should be developed so that they may become trained along these lines wherein they show great proficiency. As the average Mexican adult has had no training in the "home-owning virtues," it will be necessary to develop lessons regarding thrift, saving, and the value of keeping the money in the banks. As the Mexicans show considerable aptitude for hand work of any kind, courses should be developed that will aid them in becoming skilled workers with their hands. Girls should be trained to become domestic servants, and to do various kinds of handwork for which they can be paid adequately after they leave school.

TEACHING PROCEDURES

Such illustrative teaching procedures as the following have been determined by experience and through study of the problem:

1. Teach to all only the fundamental processes in arithmetic. Intensive drill in making change.
2. Make use of intensive drill in penmanship. Use old copybook methods. Teach thrift through successive copying of Poor Richard's sayings; teach both men and women to spend less than they earn.
3. Teach reading. Include such things as road signs, railroad signs, and advertisements; the buying and selling language of the stores; our best patriotic utterances. Teach the use of the newspaper, the magazine, and the Americanization text-books.
4. Teach every mother during the pre-natal period the care of babies: the preparation and use of clothing; the selection and preparation of wholesome food—food that will raise the energy index of the race.
5. Teach every boy how to make inexpensive furniture for the home. Plans should be drawn for cheap but strong chairs, tables, shelves and cabinets that will be taken and installed in the home. Boys should be taught to make use of discarded tin cans in the development of useful kitchen utensils.
6. Girls should be trained to become neat and efficient house servants.
7. The outstanding students, boys and girls alike, should be trained in leadership. To this end groups will be organized under their own leadership; the industrial high school will have its class officers and its student body officers. All will be trained in voting.
8. Teach boys and girls, men and women how to enjoy wholesome amusements; provide an extensive physical education program that will include health education; train the adolescents of both sexes in self-control. Above all, set up a program such that every Mexican boy and girl within the compulsory age limits, and every Mexican adult shall be organized into classes, arranged by groups according to their abilities and needs, and in spite of handicaps, taught and re-taught until they show the required proficiency to meet the ordinary needs of community life.

ORGANIZATION

In order to secure the objectives enumerated above it will be necessary to organize with the object of putting across the Americanization program. The city board of education and the union high school board, and the county school department should co-operate to develop the program. Under them, the superintendent and the principal should develop a group charged with the duty of putting across the program. This should be a department of Americanization with a head, assistant teachers, clerical aid, and an attendance officer. Committees of teachers, elementary, junior high and senior high should be set to work on courses. Community contacts should be made, so that county boards of education, county supervisors, welfare organizations, employers, companies employing large numbers of contract laborers, churches, women's clubs, D. A. R., and other patriotic organizations, chambers of commerce, and every agency concerned with the improvement of existing conditions will be co-operating in order to insure the success of the Americanization program. The head of the department should call meetings of representatives of all these groups and present the needs of the foreign people, and each organization should be led to interest itself and its members in the work and to do some stipulated share of the program. While this organization is somewhat satisfactory for a single district yet to reach the objectives there should be county-wide organizations and there should be instituted co-operative effort among the counties of that area most densely inhabited by Mexicans.

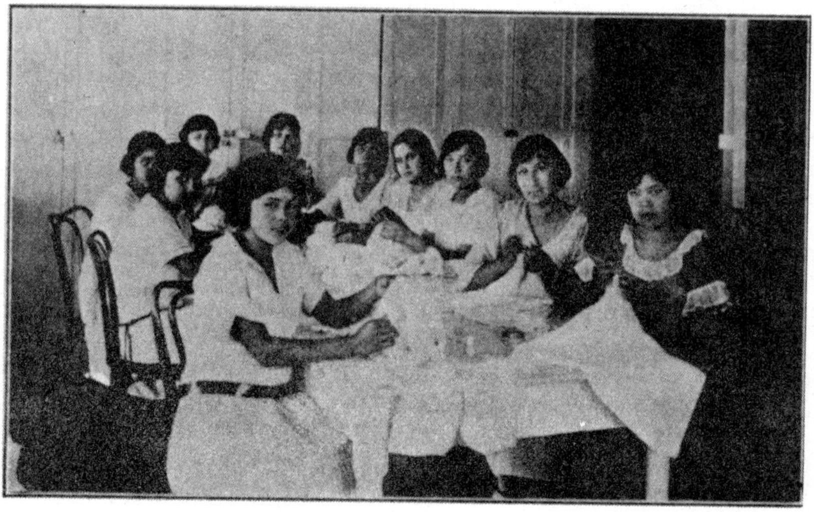

Teach the Young Women Household Duties

IMPORTANCE OF CO-OPERATION WITH THE BOARD OF SUPERVISORS

There is a great Americanization work that can be done by the Board of Supervisors. By ordinance they can clean up all the rural Mexican camps; by ordinance they can limit in the camps the number of persons living in single rooms; they can by ordinance require sanitary conditions that will insure a pure water supply and adequate sewage disposal; finally, the Board of Supervisors can establish a Bureau of Placement and Labor Investigation that will perform under the Supervisors' direction the following service:

1. Study labor conditions within the county.
2. Study the labor supply and demand.
3. Maintain monthly correspondence with the supervisors of other counties.
4. Publish monthly statements showing labor needs.
5. Advise restrictions of further influx of laborers when not needed.
6. Establish the closest possible co-operation with the County Department of Education in a continued study of the problems arising from the presence of so large a Mexican population.

A COUNTY SUPERVISOR OF MEXICAN EDUCATION

There should be established under the direction of the County Superintendent of Schools an assistant County Superintendent of Schools charged with the duty of studying the problems of the education of Mexicans and the supervision of teachers of Mexican children. The facts revealed in Chapter II show very clearly that the Mexican children are not progressing satisfactorily through the schools of the county. To meet this situation a new course of study should be developed for the Mexican pupils. The investigations in Chapter V show where should be placed the greatest stress in the new course of study. The index of ability of Mexican pupils to progress through the schools of San Bernardino County was shown to be .42, while his index of ability to do the academic work was shown to be .68, while the index showing his composite ability is .71. Yet his index of ability to do hand-work has been shown to be .90.* Therefore, it is clear that the new course of study should consider only the academic fundamentals of the English language, reading, and the fundamental processes in arithmetic and citizenship. Greater emphasis in the new course of study should be put upon music, art, and various forms of hand work. There should be developed a county-wide curriculum study that will result in the formation of ideals, objectives, and content matter of the new course of study. Finally, the investigations in Chapter V. show the rating of Mexi-

*—See page 78; the index of ability of Mexican pupils in penmanship is shown to be .96.

can pupils in eight traits or qualities that make for general success. There should be added thrift to these qualities for it is a well-known fact substantiated by the economic survey as portrayed in Chapter IV that the Mexican laborers are not possessed of thrift. The new course of study should consider these nine qualities and seek to develop the Mexican pupils along these lines. The investigations show that the Mexican pupils rate lowest (.55) in initiative; this being known, the course of study should deliberately make provisions for the development of Mexican pupils along this line. The investigations show that the Mexican pupils rate next lowest in energy. Perhaps it is the type of food they eat that causes this; perhaps physical conditions of their home life are conducive to this; if so, the teaching in schools will make possible a remedy. Similarly, the course of study should be so developed that it will seek to meet the actual needs of Mexican pupils.

SEGREGATION OF CLASSES ON AN ABILITY BASIS

There should be developed wherever numbers shall warrant a segregation of pupils on an ability basis. Pupils should not be put in Mexican classes because they are Mexicans; they should be put there because they can profit most by the instruction offered in such classes. There should always filter into all schools those Mexicans who can profit by the regular course of study.

COUNTY-WIDE ENFORCEMENT OF ATTENDANCE

There should be rigid county-wide enforcement of school attendance. Not a child should escape the schooling that the law requires and parents who do not comply with the law or who attempt to frustrate the law should be deported.

A PROGRAM OF ADULT EDUCATION

Finally, there should be established in the county at large an intensive program of adult education. Funds should be provided that would make it possible to teach every Mexican the English language, to teach every mother the care of infants, cleanliness, house sanitation, and economical house management including lessons in sewing, cooking, and thrift. The men should be trained in thrift, in gardening, and in the principles of the American government. In order to bring all the Mexican groups up to a higher level, parents and other adults must be taught as well as their children. This will prevent rifts in the family. Class instruction for all levels must be instituted; the program must exist for everyone; none should be allowed to escape the educational campaign.

EQUIPMENT

First of all there must be places to carry on the educational work with both parents and children. The best place is a public school. Experience shows that the Mexican children advance more rapidly when grouped by themselves. This is particularly true of their parents, and evening classes composed of Mexicans and other foreign groups soon lose the Mexican members. The school house in the Mexican section should be utilized for adult education; but the so-called Mexican school will not reach the greatest possible number. Community houses should be secured in all the larger camps.

These should be equipped at public expense and made available for class use, for clinical purposes and as recreation centers. Such a house was shown on page 11 and it has proven its value many times where the community house can not be made available, one of the larger houses of an enterprising Mexican can be used for class and clinic. A group meeting in such a house is shown on page 11. All Mexicans* not reached in any of the ways thus far suggested should be reached by the traveling school. Such an institution has already been described and photographs of it have been shown on uages 14 and 15.

What should be done in each individual district where the numbers warrant may be illustrated by the program being worked out in the Chaffey Union High School District. There has been established a new department to be known as the Department of Mexican Education. This step was taken because the survey of the district has shown fifteen hundred Mexicans in the schools in addition to the numbers of adults enrolled in the Americanization classes. This department numbers more than thirty teachers who have volunteered to do what they can to advance the cause of Mexican education. The purpose of this department is to make a scientific study of the Mexican. This study should trace the ethnological evolution of the modern Mexican; it should involve a study of the history of the Mexican people, and finally, it should involve a study of the racial extraction of the Mexican element of the population of San Bernardino County. The Department of Mexican Education should make a further study of the temperament of the race for this should be thoroughly understood in dealing with the people. There should be studied most carefully those qualities and abilities that are recognized as peculiar to the Mexican people, that educational effort in behalf of the Mexican may be applied to the maximum advantage. There should be studied the peculiar aptitudes of these good-natured and kindly people that they may be developed along the best possible lines. Their capacities to perform different types of service should be set forth that their employers may utilize them to the

*—Two hundred and seventy-seven adult Mexicans have been enrolled in the Americanization evening classes of Chaffey Union High School during 1927-1928. Many others have been enrolled in afternoon classes.

best interests of both employer and employed. Finally, this department and the separate department of Americanization should be charged with the creation of courses of study in the light of the investigations made, and there should be developed a continuous survey of the reaction of the Mexican pupils and adults to the educational effort put forth by the school system.

A committee should be developed and charged with the creation of courses of study (1) for each grade of the elementary and of the secondary school; (2) for part-time boys and girls who are in various levels of educational advancement; (3) for adults in the various levels of educational status. Such a committee is working in the Chaffey Union High School District and is composed of teachers of elementary, junior high, senior high, and of all teachers of the part-time and Americanization departments. To the committee was presented the following outline to direct their study and their work:

OUTLINE FOR CURRICULUM STUDY

Before the curriculum is put into its final form there are certain studies that should be made. I wish to express briefly my ideas regarding the curriculum:

ASSUMPTIONS:

1. The curriculum must be flexible, easily adaptable to individual and varying needs.
2. It must be readily adaptable to individual differences that appear within the group.
3. It should contain in the maximum degree opportunities for pupils to gain experience, for "experience educates."
4. The curriculum is for the pupils.
5. The curriculum should unfold from year to year, from group to group; the kindergarten should build on the foundations of the home, the elementary upon the kindergarten, the junior high upon the elementary, the senior high upon the junior high, and the college upon the senior high.

FUNCTION OF THE CURRICULUM

The function of the curriculum should be regarded from at least six viewpoints:

1. The preparation of pupils for
   (a) Their next step.
   (b) Life activities.
2. The holding of pupils in school longer by
   (a) Increasing their interest.
   (b) Showing them the worth-whileness of things.

3. Community development through
   (a) Aiding industry through investigation and research.
   (b) Preparation of workers through community activity.
4. Presentation of life activities, so that
   (a) Pupils may be directed wisely in the selection of their occupations and other activities.
   (b) Pupils may be given experience that will educate.
5. Exploration of the fields of knowledge.
6. Character building.

PROCEDURE

Before the final selection of the content of courses of study teachers should work out very carefully the following:

1. A brief but careful tabulation of those skills, abilities, attitudes, and types of knowledge possessed by pupils when they reach the given grade for which courses of study are being made.

2. A brief but careful tabulation of those skills, abilities, attitudes, and types of knowledge that should be acquired by pupils during the year for which the courses of study are being made.

3. Clearly defined and carefully worked out ideals and standards for (2) above.

Let Us Have More Camps Like These

4. The selection of that content, subject matter and those problems, and projects that will secure (2) and achieve (3).

After months of work the committee will make its report. The work is the result of .experience with try-out lessons prepared to meet the immediate needs of groups at different levels of attainments. Teachers of Mexican children, of Mexican adolescents, and of Mexican adults should be trained to adapt procedure for immediate needs. They must possess initiative, for they must be ready to change a course, or change a lesson when it is necessary to get results. Learning needful lessons by the Mexican learner is the goal.

In communities where there is sufficient Mexican population large enough to make such provision there should be developed industrial high schools for Mexican pupils and for Mexican adults. Figure 8, page 52, shows where the pupils are located grade by grade in the Chaffey Union High School District. This has warranted action by the Chaffey Board who on February 6, 1927, passed a resolution looking forward to the development of an industrial high school for Mexican pupils of the Chaffey district and of other portions of San Bernardino County should Mexican students desire to attend.

This school will mark the culmination of educational effort for Mexican advancement in the Chaffey district. The school will be located on a ten-acre campus. There will be a playground to be used as a recreational center for the Mexican population. It will be a health center and rooms will be provided for clinical use. There will be established a new type of room to be known as a "diagnosis" room. Pupils who at first do not fit into any program will be enrolled in the "diagnosis" room for observation. They will be given lessons within their range of intelligence and then will be transferred to one of the three groups attending the institution, for the facts portrayed in Tables XVIII to XXI, page 60-63, have set forth clearly the need for classes for three types, (1) those who have had no schooling; (2) those who have had a limited amount of elementary schooling; and (3) those who can profit by industrial or academic courses of junior and senior high school levels. Finally, there will be home-making and citizenship rooms provided for adults of the Mexican race. These rooms will be comfortably but simply equipped for social as well as instructional use, the ideal being the evolution eventuating in the Americanization Mexican.

The survey sets forth the probability that many of the Mexicans wish to return to Mexico. These returning patriots of Mexico will disseminate through every state in the great republic of Mexico a lasting friendship for America and they will introduce American methods and American ideals throughout the length and breadth of their nation.

Such a program as has been outlined will lead to an ultimate goal that is expressed with these words:—it should be books rather than bullets; teaching instead of crushing; friendship and not animosity; and the helping hand instead of the hindering foot. Such a co-operative spirit animating the inter-racial relations will make out of the United States-Mexican border a second international line similar to only one other found in the world, our northern, the Canadian-American international boundary.

The Americanization program that has been set up can be carried out under the law of the State of California. The law will not permit the segregation of Mexican pupils because of race, but it will permit the establishment of classes and schools on an ability basis; in the Americanization program set up provision is made for Mexican pupils of superior ability to attend the regular schools; but all others should attend those schools where they can secure the utmost advantage and progress the best.

The law provides for the attendance in part-time classes of all boys and girls of ages sixteen to eighteen who have not completed a high school course; it makes further provision for classes to accommodate foreign young people of ages eighteen to twenty-one; the law makes further provision for adult classes in any subject desired and encourages by special appropriations from the state and county funds for the carrying out of part-time and adult classes. Such a program as has been outlined will be very largely financed by state and county aid.*

*—See California School Law, Sections 1750-C, page 183; Act 7496, pages 352-340; Act 259, pages 241, 242.

SUPPLEMENT

Dr. Osborn, of Redlands University, through his class in Sociology, made a careful survey of Mexican adults and kindly consented to let the facts found by his class be used for comparative purposes. The author has read and tabulated the information obtained from Dr. Osborn's survey.

From Survey of 121 Adult Cases of Mexicans Living in Redlands

SCHOOL ATTENDANCE—MEN

No. Years Attended School	No. Cases in U. S.	No. Cases in Mexico	No. Yrs. Attended School in Both Men	Women
0	0	0	58	2
Less than 1 yr.	2	0	0	0
1	1	3	0	0
2	2	7		
3	2	5	1	
4	3	4	1	
5	0	2		
6	3	2	1	
7	1	1		
8	5	1		
9	1	0		
10	1	1		
15	1			

SCHOOL ATTENDANCE—WOMEN

0				3
1	1	3		
3		1		
4	1			
5	1			
6	1			
7	1			
8		1		

SUMMARY

There were others who gave indefinite answers, such as "Many," "Full time," and these results are not tabulated.

The average schooling of the Mexican adults of the Redlands district is 3.08 years.

On page 64 it was shown that the average school of Mexican adults in the Chaffey Union High School District was 1.67 years. The table just given on page 112 shows that the Redlands Mexican adults average a year and a half more schooling than do those of the Chaffey Union High School District. It must be noted that the Mexican children in the Redlands District show the best progress of any Mexican children in San Bernardino County. Table IV, page 26, shows that only 58 per cent of the Mexican children of the Redlands elementary schools are over-aged while 78.5 per cent of all the Mexican children of the schools of San Bernardino County are over-aged; and Table XVI, page 50, shows that 70.3 per cent of the Mexican children of the Chaffey Union High School District elementary schools are over-aged. This is convincing proof of the fact that the more schooling the parents receive the better progress their children will make.

The following table, showing the number of children living and dead in the Mexican homes of Redlands, shows that the death rate is lower in Redlands than in the Chaffey District. The greater amount of schooling of the Mexican parents of Redlands accounts for a lower death rate for Mexican babies in Redlands.

NUMBER CHILDREN LIVING

Men

Number Children	Number Cases
1	9
2	12
3	17
4	25
5	15
7	9
8	6
9	2
10	0
11	1
13	2
14	1

NUMBER CHILDREN DEAD

Men

Number Children	Number Cases
0	64
1	27
2	8
3	7
4	5
7	1
20	1

SUMMARY

Average number of children to the family, 5.45. Ninety-seven per cent of adults reported children.

READ CONSTITUTION IN ENGLISH

Men	No. Cases	Women	No. Cases
Yes	42	Yes	12
No	59	No	9

READ AMERICA IN SPANISH

Men	No. Cases	Women	No. Cases
Yes	77	Yes	15
No	25	No	5

NUMBER OF BOOKS IN THE HOME

Men		Women	
No. Books	No. Cases	No. Books	No. Cases
0	41	0	10
A few	36	A few	5
1	1	20	1
2	1	40	1
6	2	50	1
8	1	Many	1
10	1		
20	1		
40	2		
50	1		
Many	11		

NUMBERS OF PAPERS TAKEN

Men		Women	
No. or Name	No. Cases	No. or Name	No. Cases
0	52	0	12
1	13	1	3
San Bernardino Sun	2	Facts	2
Facts	6	Spanish papers	2
Spanish papers	17	L. A. Examiner	1
La Opinion	1		
L. A. Examiner	5		
L. A. Times	3		
Express	1		

NUMBER OF MAGAZINES TAKEN

Men: No. or Name	No. Cases	Women: No. or Name	No. Cases
0	86	0	16
1	7	1	1
2	1	Touring Topics	1
4	1	Ladies' Home Journal	1
13	2	Farm and Fireside	1
Literary Digest	1		
Touring Topics	1		
Ladies' Home Journal	2		
Farm and Fireside	1		

SPEAK ENGLISH

Men	No. Cases	Women	No. Cases
Yes	70	Yes	22
No	35	No	4

WRITE ENGLISH

Men	No. Cases	Women	No. Cases
Yes	35	Yes	12
No	69	No	13

WRITE SPANISH

Men	No. Cases	Women	No. Cases
Yes	66	Yes	19
No	35	No	6

KINDS OF WORK PERFORMED

Men: Kinds of Work	No. Cases	Men: Kinds of Work	No. Cases
Foreman	2	Fruit Work	2
Food Seller	1	Ranch Work	8
Picker	13	Gas Work	1
Restaurant Work	1	Gas Work	1
Laborer	22	Stone Mason	1
Barber	1	Hod Carrier	1
Cement Work	5		
Pipe Fitter	2		
Pruner	14	**Women**	
Railroad Work	1	Kinds of Work	No. Cases
Irrigation Work	3	Housework	4
Blacksmith	1	Restaurant Work	1
General Work	20	Packer	1
Council and Guard	1	Laborer	1
Trucker	1	Embroidery Work	1
Packer	1	Irrigation Work	1

NUMBER OF DAYS WORK IN 1927

Men		Women	
No. of Days	No. Cases	No. of Days	No. Cases
0	2	0	1
60	1	120	1
91	2	160	1
121	2	365	5
150	1		
182	26		
200	5		
242	4		
270	26		
365	30		

AVERAGE WAGE PER HOUR

Men		Women	
Wage	No. Cases	Wage	No. Cases
22c	2	30c	1
30c	1	35c c	1
33 1/3c	6	39c	1
35c	7	44½c	1
39c	15	47½c	1
40c	2	50c	2
44½c	14		
45c	2		
46c	1		
50c	36		
60c	1		
75c	1		

OWN HOME

Men	No. Cases	Women	No. Cases
Yes	58	Yes	18
No	44	No	8

OWN OTHER PROPERTY

Men	No. Cases	Women	No. Cases
Yes	9	Yes	3
No	91	No	19

BANK ACCOUNT

Men	No. Cases	Women	No. Cases
Yes	19	Yes	4
No	84	No	19

WHAT FURNITURE IN DWELLING

Men		Women	
Amount	No. Cases	Amount	No. Cases
Very little	8	Very little	3
Ordinary	56	Ordinary	4
Very good	2	Very good	1
One room	3	One room	1
Two rooms	9	Two rooms	2
Three rooms	5	Three rooms	1
Four rooms	13	Four rooms	6
Five rooms	1	Five rooms	1

IF AMERICAN BORN DO YOU VOTE?

Men	No. Cases	Women	No. Cases
Yes	6	Yes	2
No	19	No	4

IF FOREIGN BORN DO YOU WISH NATURALIZATION?

Men	No. Cases	Women	No. Cases
Yes	5	Yes	2
No	51	No	12

DO YOU WISH TO RETURN TO MEXICO?

Men	No. Cases	Women	No. Cases
Yes	22	Yes	3
No	59	No	16

NUMBER TIMES MOVED IN LAST TWO YEARS

Men	No. Cases	Women	No. Cases
0	66	0	20
1	12	3	2
2	9		
3	6		
4	5		
6	2		
8	1		

RENT PAID

Men	No. Cases	Women	No. Cases
0	27	0	6
$ 5.00	4	$6.00	2
6.00	4	7.00	1
7.00	2		
7.50	4		
8.00	1		
9.00	3		
10.00	6		
10.15	1		
12.00	9		
15.00	7		
16.00	1		
16.50	1		
18.00	1		
20.00	1		
40.00	1		

NUMBER OF ROOMS IN DWELLING AND NUMBER OF PEOPLE LIVING IN DWELLING

No. Rooms	No. People	No. Cases	No. Rooms	No. People	No. Cases
1	3	1	4	6	6
1	5	1	4	7	7
1	6	2	4	8	3
1	7	1	4	9	6
1	9	1	4	11	1
2	3	2	44	12	1
2	4	1	4	16	1
2	5	5	5	5	1
2	7	4	5	6	1
2	9	2	5	7	3
3	2	1	5	8	3
3	3	2	6	2	1
3	4	5	6	4	3
3	5	3	6	5	1
3	6	2	6	6	1
3	7	5	6	7	4
3	8	3	6	8	4
3	10	2	6	9	1
3	14	2	6	10	5
4	3	3	6	12	1
4	4	1	7	7	1
4	5	8	8	12	1

Average 1.77 people to a room.
Average .57 room per person.

DO YOU WISH TO ATTEND A CLASS TO LEARN ENGLISH?

Men	No. Cases	Women	No. Cases
Yes	15	Yes	5
No	43	No	3

WHAT ELSE DO YOU WISH TO LEARN?

Men	No. Cases	Women	No. Cases
Nothing	32	Nothing	4
Paint pictures	1	Take care of family	1
All good things	2		

DO YOU LIKE TO HAVE YOUR CHILDREN IN SCHOOL?

Men	No. Cases	Women	No. Cases
Yes	97	Yes	23
Don't care	3		

The facts presented in the preceding table show that it has paid Redlands to have Mexicans who have had better schooling advantages than have the Mexicans in other parts of San Bernardino County. Their children progress better in school than do the children of Mexicans living in other parts of the county; they have a lower death rate, they have a better economic status; they live under better conditions, and there is evidence that they are better prospective citizens than are the Mexicans in other parts of the County. All these facts justify the program set up in Chapter VI. Such a program should be set up for every district in the southwest that has a large number of Mexican children in the schools and Mexican adults in the labor camps.

MAY GRAPHIC

SURVEY

EXICANS IN OUR MIDST

Newest and Oldest
Settlers of the Southwest

MARY AUSTIN · PAUL S. TAYLOR · D. H. LAWRENCE
J. FRANK DOBIE · ADELINA OTERO · AMANDA CHASE · R. N. McLEAN
MANUEL GAMIO · WILLIAM TEMPLETON JOHNSON · MAX HANDMAN

DIEGO RIVERA · JOSE CLEMENTE OROZCO · GEORGIA O'KEEFFE

MAY 1, 1931

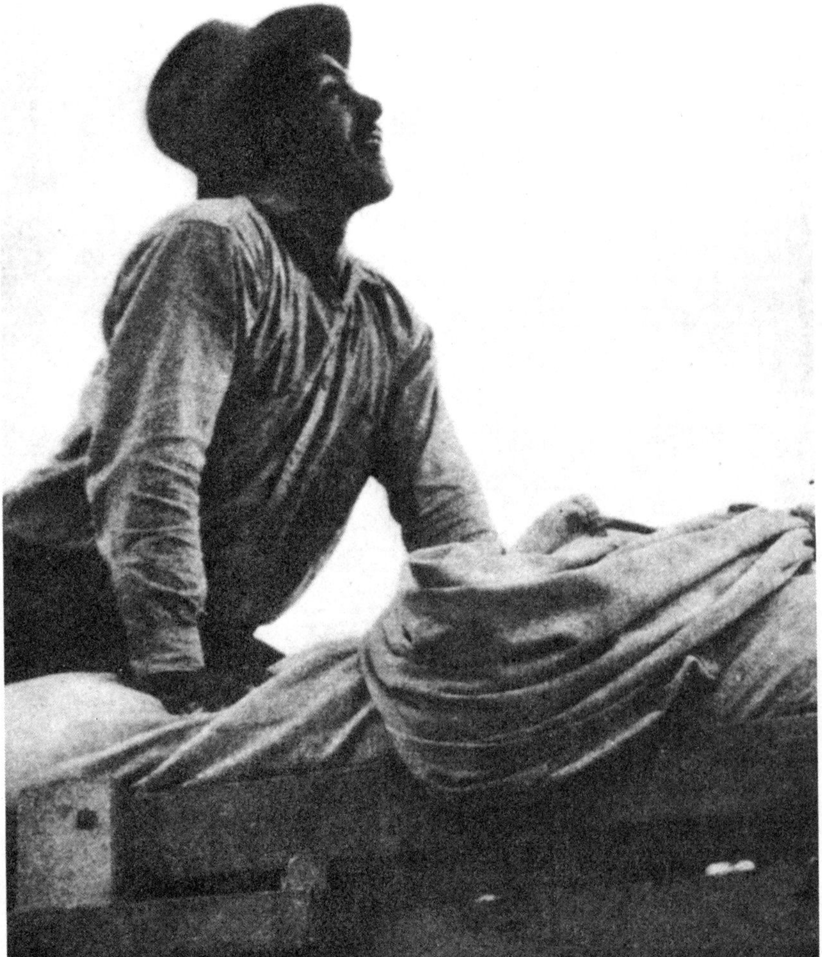

¿QUE TAL?
["How goes it?"]
Photographed for Survey Graphic by Ansel E. Adams

THE SURVEY

Graphic Number

Vol. LXVI, No. 3 May 1, 1931

CONTENTS

SURVEY ASSOCIATES, INC.

112 East 19th Street, New York

PUBLISHERS

THE SURVEY—Twice-a-month—$5.00 a year
SURVEY GRAPHIC—Monthly—$3.00 a year

The Gist of It

UP the railways, the irrigation ditches, the dusty roads of cotton lands the Mexicans came, and those who would turn to full length field studies of the regions canvassed in Professor Taylor's leading article (p. 135), will find them in his series of reports published by the University of California Press. In the midst of the depression, an ebb tide has set in and the jam in the border towns is appraised first-hand for Survey Graphic by Robert N. McLean, associate director of Spanish-speaking work of the Presbyterian Board of National Missions, who knows Mexicans through a constellation of neighborhood centers throughout the Southwest (p. 182). Mrs. Stephenson, an American journalist in Mexico City, similarly undertook a commission for us to follow them back to their home towns. Page 175.

Meanwhile Mary Austin envisions the horizons of our contacts with Spanish and Indian America, by way of the old trails by which New Mexico was settled three hundred years ago. Among the Colonials of that state we have harbingers of what this new-old element in American life may come to mean (p. 141). Mrs. Warren (Adelina Otero) brings us closer to her people (p. 149). And Frank Applegate, whose dusty Ford was known on every road in the mountain country round Santa Fe, interprets as no one else their arts and crafts. His winning book, Indian Stories from the Pueblos, was recently issued by Lippincott. Page 156.

THE author of Sons and Lovers, of the Plumed Serpent and Mornings in Mexico needs no introduction: by a rare stroke of fortune this manuscript was one of D. H. Lawrence's last writings and in "brushes of comets hair" he limns the great backdrop of the Indian spirit (page 153). The penetration of Spanish culture on the other hand, taking tangible shape in the architecture of the Southwest, is set forth by William Templeton Johnson, himself the architect of the Junipero Serro Museum at San Diego, which crystallizes it in enduring form. Page 158.

MAX HANDMAN, J. Frank Dobie and Robert H. Montgomery are outstanding members of the faculty group who have been making the University of Texas a center of social research. Mr. Dobie has made ranch life literature, his most recent book, Coronado's Children, The Southwest Press. Page 167. Mrs. Chase, the first home teacher appointed under the California law providing for instruction in citizenship for aliens, has worked for 15 years in a Los Angeles district principally inhabited by Mexicans. Her vivid story of Dona Soledad might well be dedicated to the suffrage movement. Page 161.

Manuel Gamio is a member of the Supreme Council of Social Protection and Prevention which carries out the provisions of the new penal code of Mexico. Author of Aspects of Mexican Civilization, of Mexican Immigration to the United States, his is the scientist's approach (p. 174) to the problems of migration and racial contact. Ernest Galarza speaks for the immigrant (p. 181); himself of Mexican birth, educated at Occidental College, Leland Stanford and Columbia, and for eight years spending his vacations in the beet fields, orchards and canneries of California. Chester Rowell speaks from a very different coign of vantage—regent of the University of California, member of state and national commissions. Page 180.

GEORGIA O'KEEFFE has added the desert crosses of New Mexico to the skyscrapers of New York as subjects for her luminous portrayal; Orozco's frescoes can be seen now at Pomona College and the New School of Social Research. Rivera is now in San Francisco painting his first frescoes "north of the Rio Grande"—and, who knows, may be off to Spain to interpret another Revolution.

THE SURVEY
GRAPHIC NUMBER

MAY 1, 1931

Volume LXVI
No. 3

Mexicans North of the Rio Grande

By PAUL S. TAYLOR

THE Mexicans are here—from California to Pennsylvania, from Texas to Minnesota. They are scattered on isolated sections along our western railroads in clusters of from two to five families; they are established in colonies in the agricultural West and Southwest which form, in places, from one to two thirds of the local population. They have penetrated the heart of industrial America; in the Calumet steel region on the southern shore of Lake Michigan they are numbered in thousands; in eastern industrial centers by hundreds. And they have made Los Angeles the second largest Mexican city in the world.

With the stoppage of European immigration and the increased labor demands of the war the trickle of Mexican immigrants enlarged to a stream which ran its course for a decade. In what follows, it should be understood that the statements about Mexicans refer to this whelming labor class migration, not to Mexicans, in general, nor to Mexican culture in Mexico. Variety and contradiction characterize the situations arising in different areas in the United States. There is hardly a statement I shall make, or an illustration I shall give but that its opposite has been observed, and a whole series of gradations in between.

TRADITIONALLY the growing of cotton connoted mud, mules and Negroes. Just so today the irrigation ditch stands for intensive agriculture, hand labor, and Mexicans. In Imperial Valley, California, they thin lettuce in the fall, and from December to March they cut it by hand for shipment so that the cities of the East may have fresh salads in mid-winter. From the middle of May to July, Mexicans with eyes keen to judge the ripeness of melons work under the hot sun at high speed, picking at fifteen cents a crate cantaloupes to be consumed by Chicago, New York or St. Louis. By mid-July the majority of the Mexican families have left for the grape harvest in the San Joaquin Valley.

In the Salt River Valley of Arizona, irrigated from the reservoir of the famous Roosevelt Dam, long staple Pima cotton has been grown on an increasing scale for the past fifteen years. Beginning in September some thousands of Mexican families annually are shipped in from California and Texas to pick cotton until January or February. In the spring many of these families drift away; others remain for the lettuce and vegetable harvest, and the cantaloupes which ripen just at the close of the season in Imperial Valley.

In the Winter Garden of south Texas, in November and December, Mexican men, women and children, on hands and knees, transplant Bermuda onions. With a short forked stick as a tool they make a hole, set the plant, and tamp it; they achieve incredible speed, and at from six to eight cents per acre row (157 feet), with plants three inches apart, they frequently earn $2 or even more a day. From January to March they cut spinach and carrots and tie them into bundles; in April and early May they pull onions, pile them into windrows, clip off the roots and tops with a sheep shears, grade and crate them.

In central, west and south Texas, the westward movement of cotton has been sus-

Now Is the Time to Take Stock

Mass immigration from Mexico has closed down. Hard times have tightened up an already rigid administrative restriction. What we have to reckon with are the fortunes of a permanent Mexican population, spreading fanwise from the Border throughout our South and central West. Like a human mitre, these men, women and children dovetail us to Spanish and Indian America, at the same time that our contacts south of the Border increase. Professor Taylor's studies under grant from the Social Science Research Council have taken him over the entire terrain of migration and settlement. No other man is so equipped to interpret the epic fact nor the challenge it lays on our capacity for understanding and on our ability to plan.

tained by Mexican labor. A line drawn from northwest of Corpus Christi on the Gulf, to San Antonio, thence northward through Austin to Dallas marks roughly the western fringe of the so-called black belt. West and south of this, Mexicans play the role in cotton traditionally played by Negroes. They are the tenant farmers—share-croppers on halves if they furnish only their labor and that of their families, with larger shares for themselves if they furnish teams, tools and seed. In this region there are white American

tenants too. They are in competition with the Mexicans for farms, and in the eyes of some landlords the lower living standards of the Mexicans are an asset in the competition. Said one proprietor of seven hundred acres of cotton land:

Left: Lettuce harvesters, Imperial Valley, California
Center: Track laborers, Arizona
Right: Transplanting onions with short forked stick, Winter Garden, Texas

I would rather have Mexican tenants than either Negroes or whites. You can't tell the whites so well what to do. They think they are on an equality with you and they want to live in a house about like you do. They are always wanting better clothes and more provisions. The Mexicans have bigger families and more labor to get out a big crop. If the Mexicans learn English they don't work so well; if they get educated a little they don't make such good farm hands.

A LARGE part, probably the majority, of the Mexican population is migratory. It is the most mobile element in our labor supply. It moves in seasonal cycles covering hundreds, even thousands of miles.

A Mexican family I met in south Texas during the onion harvest two years ago had come to the United States in 1920. Entering at Laredo, its working members began by grubbing brush to clear land near San Antonio. Shortly they set out (with the entire family, of course) for Belton, Texas. There they secured employment in a cotton-seed-oil factory where an uncle had preceded them. When work gave out they went to Fort Worth, and from there shipped to the beet fields near Billings, Montana. The next season they worked in sugar beets near Casper, Wyoming; wintered in Denver, and worked the following season in the beet fields of Colorado. In 1927 they "came out with $15 and an old car to Raton, New Mexico." When they got there they were broke; so they went to work in a local coal mine, and stayed for a year. In the fall of 1928 they drove to Texas, picked cotton until the season closed and followed the stream of laborers to the Winter Garden to try their luck at transplanting onions. The wanderings of individual Mexicans over a period of years may thus appear more or less erratic, but they usually follow one or another of the seasonal swirls.

The Southwest is the great reservoir of migratory Mexican labor. It winters there, or across the line in Mexico. Throughout the post-war years the pull of the labor market of Wyoming and Pennsylvania was felt on the *mesa central* of Mexico, six or eight hundred miles below the Rio Grande. On the river, El Paso, Laredo, and Nogales form a secondary tier of labor centers—gateways to the United States. Every spring from San Antonio, Fort Worth, Kansas City, Albuquerque, Phoenix, Los Angeles, and latterly from Chicago, St. Louis, Omaha, Denver, Sacramento, and in smaller numbers from a score of other cities, Mexicans are gathered up by *los enganchistas* and shipped out for a summer's work on the tracks at from 35 to 40 cents an hour in Nevada, Dakota, Kansas, Illinois, Ohio, or Pennsylvania. For with the spring the railroads resume maintenance and construction work. Skeleton section crews are augmented, and large extra gangs of fifty, sixty or more Mexican *solos* are organized for special projects. These men live in

the converted box-cars so familiar to all who travel, rolling from job to job, working in places remote or near, town or desert, strumming their guitars of an evening and singing their Mexican songs.

In May the sugar beets of the North need thinning—and the Mexicans of the Southwest are called upon to furnish their quota of hand laborers, as the German-Russians who preceded them are no longer immigrating. For this work families—families as large as possible—are wanted. They are transported by the train load to the Arkansas and South Platte Valleys and the Western Slope of Colorado, to Wyoming, Idaho, Montana, Nebraska, Dakota, Iowa, Minnesota, and Michigan. When they reach the beet fields they are scattered out on the farms, each family under contract to tend its allotted fields at from $23 to $25 an acre. A single Mexican tends ten acres or more in a season; families contract two, three, or more times ten acres, depending on the number of workers (men, women and children) there are in the family. In May and June beets are blocked and thinned. Time presses, and hours are long, perhaps twelve on the average. Women and children help although the Mexican man does not work them so long or so hard as the German-Russians. In July and August there is hoeing, and in September comes topping, lasting through October and into November. The beets are loosened by a machine lifter, pulled up by the tops by hand, piled in windrows; the tops are struck off by blows with a large knife, and the beets are hauled away to dumps for weighing and thence to the factory where they are made into sugar. In the winter the tide of beet workers, like that of the railroad laborers, recedes. But an increasing number stay on, responding to the stimulation of beet farmers or of sugar companies who offer houses rent free, or opportunities to build in colony tracts. In the Valley of the South Platte, in northeastern Colorado, the number of Mexican families so remaining rose in six years from 537 to 2084. Other families winter in increasing numbers in the cities of the North. Many drift into industry, particularly in Detroit.

Right: *Out from San Antonio*
Center: *Parked cars of the cotton pickers, Saturday shopping and holiday, Robstown, Texas*
Left: *On the way to the "Corpus" cotton patch*

The maturing cotton crop puts wheels under Mexican labor in Texas. They come down the Rio Grande in late June and July to Brownsville to chop and pick the first cotton of the season. In July and August seemingly most of the Mexicans of the state converge on Corpus Christi. Here on the flat Gulf coastal plain huge tracts of land have been planted to cotton; the young fields have been "chopped," i. e., thinned by hoeing to a proper stand of plants, by Mexicans, and now await the army of pickers which from far and near mobilizes at "Corpus." They used to come by train and by wagon; now they come by auto and truck, loaded with camp equipment. As the cotton season opens in other parts of the state, the Mexicans move on. Guided by the United States Employment Service, by the experience of other years, by correspondence with farmers, and by their own grapevine telegraph, they take to the highways by single families, groups of families, or by caravans led by *contratistas* who know enough English and have sufficient initiative and experience to take the lead in finding employment and making labor contracts for the others. The contractor weighs the cotton in the field, and as he is paid by the bale, the more pickers in his gang, the more he makes. At San Antonio the stream of pickers divides. Some work westward with the cotton to San Angelo and Sweetwater. Others make their way northward by stages to Taylor and Waco, thence west to Dallas and across west Texas even as far as Amarillo in the Panhandle. By the latter part of the year the cotton of the state is harvested, and the cycle of migration is closed by the return of the Mexicans to the places they call home.

A similar flow and ebb recurs annually in California. In May the Mexicans move northward from Imperial Valley. They "follow the fruit," thinning apricots and peaches, advancing as the season advances. They are joined by those who have delayed in order to harvest the cantaloupes, and together with thousands of Mexicans from all over southern California they surge northward to practically all the valleys of the state. Most of them ascend the ridge of the Tehachapi and pour over into the great Valley of California. In cars of all makes and all ages, used Fords predominating, with the entire family inside and the wash-tub and lantern tied on outside, they move along the highways, stopping in the hot sun by the roadside to repair blowouts, on grades to let the engine cool, or under eucalyptus trees to camp for the night.

Photographs by Ansel E. Adams

THE MIGRANT MEXICAN

In cars of all makes and all ages, with the entire family inside and the wash-tub and lantern tied outside, he moves along highways whose history reaches back to Padre and Conquistador

From June to August the Mexicans are busy thinning fruit; then picking fruit. They work in the San Joaquin Valley, around Bakersfield, Hanford, and Fresno, or they cross the Pacheco Pass to Hollister and Gilroy; they invade the Santa Clara Valley at the southern end of San Francisco Bay, and tongues of the flood pass on northward to the Napa Valley above the Bay, and up the Sacramento Valley into the northern interior of the state.

In late August the grape harvest, centering in Fresno, sucks into its vineyards Mexicans who have been dispersed in the fruit, together with fresh recruits from over the ridge to the south, some even from the states lying southeast of California. Mexicans, Japanese, Filipinos, "whites" from California, Texas and Oklahoma, a few Indians from the mountains, and Negroes, and still fewer Chinese and Hindus all enroll in the army of pickers which strips the vines. In the orchards under the fruit trees, down on the river banks, by the roadside or in the town park, in tents on the ranches

California and Arizona compete with the Old South, the Mexican peon with the Negro cotton picker

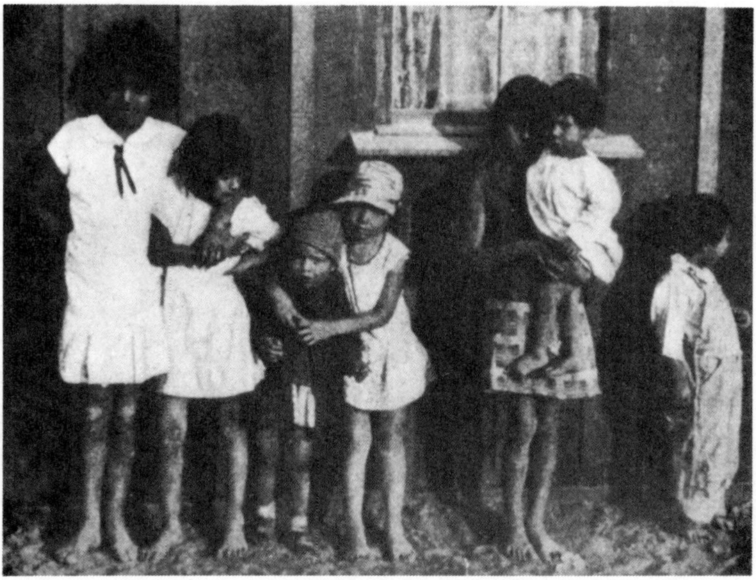

"Beyond the Tracks": children of a Mexican settlement. California leads in bringing education to them

of their employers, with or without tents elsewhere—sometimes as well without because of the heat—with or without water and sanitary facilities at hand, amid clouds of flies, you can see them preparing their *tortillas* and *frijoles* over open fire places or on portable stoves, and heating large galvanized iron tubs of water in which to do the family washing.

By the end of September, leaving a large nucleus to finish the grape harvest, the pickers begin to scatter. Many return to Los Angeles and southern California for urban employment, and for the walnut and citrus harvests; others return to Imperial Valley for the on-coming lettuce season or for cotton picking. The expansion of cotton in the San Joaquin Valley extends the season of employment in that region, and with the additional attractions of weather-proof housing and school facilities which are increasingly provided, operates to increase its year-round Mexican population. But most of the tide which moved across the Tehachapi recedes southward during the fall, and winters in southern California. In February, probably 80 per cent or more of the Mexican population of the state is found there.

THE American public has known that, since the war, Mexicans have been playing an important role in these hand labor operations of our modern agriculture, but it has been less generally realized that important nuclei of Mexican immigrants are found in the industrial centers of the Middle-west and the East. The largest employer of Mexican labor I came across in my field studies is located on the southern shore of Lake Michigan.

Here the Mexicans followed the immigrant European and even the migrant Negro. Most of them are still on the lowest rung of the ladder,[1] but appreciable numbers are rising to the ranks of the semi-skilled, some drawing wages of $6 and $7 a day. They show capacities seldom attributed to them by their agricultural employers. Mexicans entered the basic industries of the Chicago-Calumet region during and just after the war. With the economic slump of 1921 they almost disappeared from industrial payrolls in the North. A return movement set in strongly by 1923, stimulated by labor recruiting in the Southwest, and it is these recruits, in common with the general run of wage-earners in the northern centers, who have been caught in the present unemployment. Mexicans form a large proportion of track laborers of the Chicago-Calumet area; signs in Spanish advertising track work are general on Canal and Madison Streets and Mexicans are conspicuous among those sauntering by, or loitering before offices, who are fair game for the "man-catchers." They form an important element in the common labor supply of the steel mills, rising in one case to 30 per cent. To a less extent than in steel they are found in the packing industry. In considerable numbers Mexicans work in Michigan, not only in the beet fields, but in the automobile and other industries of that state. Small out-post colonies of two hundred, four hundred, or perhaps more each are scattered through the principal steel centers as far east as Ohio, Pennsylvania, New York and New Jersey.

THE story of Mexican labor in the United States might almost be told from the types of housing which characterize its settlements. I am not referring to the pathology of housing—all too often the laborers are poor, and their houses in accord with their purses; their families are large and their houses crowded—but I am speaking of the anatomy of housing.

Close along the border—not generally, but in some of the by-ways of south Texas, along the Rio Grande, in a place or two in Imperial Valley, one will find grass huts, which add the charm of the sub-tropical to an American landscape. Perhaps the house is made of mesquite, mud-plastered on the inside, its rough surface carrying the marks of the sweep of the hand of the *peon* and his wife who built it in two weeks time, ten years ago. It is roofed with grass or *tule* sewed to the rafters; the light, bark-covered timbers of the frame are bound together by strips of cactus which harden and hold like buckskin thongs. The floors are of dried mud, swept clean. Here are people migrating, and figuratively, like the turtle, carrying their distinctive culture pattern with them in the housing over their backs.

More widespread are the earth-brown adobes of El Paso Valley, New Mexico, and Arizona, almost indigenous to those parts of the Southwest, literally growing up out of the soil. Clusters of them have appeared farther north in the past few years, where the beet-workers—Mexicans from Old Mexico, and Spanish Americans from New Mexico—have erected them with their own hands in the Arkansas and South Platte Valleys of Colorado. There they stand in rows, out in the midst of the fields, mute, but eloquent evidence of the penetration of Indo-Spanish into North-European culture.

Thinning sugar beets, Colorado

Most of the housing of Mexican laborers, however, is not culturally so distinctive. Its class character is clearer, located in the poorest parts of town and crowded on small lots usually relieved by flowers in the yard. At the start, they may resort for building materials to flattened oil cans, cardboard cartons, lumber (*Cont. on p.* 197)

[1] Figures on wages and earnings refer to 1928 or 1929 when I was in the field; in many instances they doubtless have fallen since that time.

Mexicans and New Mexico

By MARY AUSTIN

Block Prints by Dorothy N. Stewart

MEXICAN immigration into what is now New Mexico began in the early part of 1598. Up to this time there had been only exploring parties and from the earliest times there must have been expeditions of trade across the invisible Border which had but one fixed point, the Ford of the Rio Grande near El Paso. Espejo, in the middle of the sixteenth century, reported finding knives and other articles of metal in the New Mexico pueblos, which could only have come from the Spanish settlements south of Chihuahua.

The first Mexicans who came to stay came with the first adventure of colonization, with the *Adelantado,* Don Juan de Oñate, who had married the granddaughter of Cortez and Montezuma and who with great pomp and ceremony took possession of the country in April of 1598 in the name of the King and all the Blessed Personages, under the patronage of the Seraphic Father San Francisco. They came as muleteers, as packers and camp attendants, as herdsmen and drivers of the vast baggage trains and droves of cattle of Oñate's *entrada.* They were themselves driven by much the same urge which sends their kinsmen across the Border today.

That first lot of immigrants with Oñate were chiefly Tlascalans, from the middle region, and natives from northern states picked up in passing. In Santa Fe when the men walk bare-headed in the procession on Corpus Christi day, you can still see in the skull shapes and features what tribes of old Mexico contributed to the new province, Aztecs, Tlascalans, Chihuahueños, Tarahumares. They came and went, with the settlers, with military detachments, with the great *conductas* of trade along the old Chihuahua trail, and they married freely with the native Indians of New Mexico.

OÑATE, when he had established his capital at Santa Fe, settled his Tlascalans across the river, where there was already the small Tewa pueblo of Analco; where now stands the ancient Church of San Miguel, probably the oldest religious foundation in the United States, close by the "oldest house," in what became known as the Barrio Analco. This was the first Mexican quarter north of the Border, and it retained that character until long after the American occupation. As late as the latter part of 1800 there were families living there who claimed a tradition of unbroken residence from pre-colonial times.

The course of settlement in New Mexico followed, in little, the history of settlement in Mexico, less violent, longer drawn out. There were successive influxes of colonists, scions of great Spanish families holding feudal grants, bringing with them, at first direct from their ancestral homes, small retinues of servants, useful craftsmen; there were respectable tradesmen to whom grants were made in commonalty *"villas real,"* for the founding of towns. Throughout the whole period of colonization small grants were freely made to individual settlers, civil servants, soldiers whose terms had expired, anybody who could muster a little political influence at home. There is reason to think that at first settlement was direct from Spain, but later the country filled slowly with disappointed gold seekers from the cities of Mexico, deracinated descendants of the Spanish-Mexican politicians. There was, however, enough uncontaminated Spanish blood to give the dominant Spanish tradition to the social life of the Colonies; at the same time there went on, at the lower levels of population, the fusions of Spanish peasants, Moorish slaves, Mexican and New Mexican Indians, which produced the peon class of old Mexico itself. There was, first of all as a factor in amalgamation, the Spanish practice of impressing pueblo labor to the service of the settlements when required, a factor which, even with the safeguards which the Church strove to throw about it, was the occasion of many admixtures. There was the practice of enslaving Indian captives taken in the raids of the nomadic tribes, Navajo, Ute, Comanche. And there were marriages of ex-service men to pueblo maidens which the Church encouraged, as well it might, for the Tewa and Keres women were comely, housewifely, modest and nominally Christian. They made on the whole as good wives as the hard-boiled *soldados* of the Army of the Americas could have hoped for at home.

Where permitted the invaders seem to have settled in the very towns of the Indians, and however much this might have been actuated by fear, fear of loneliness, of marauding nomads, or

"For better or worse," writes Mrs. Austin, "Spanish and Indian elements are indissolubly entered into the American future." Life-long student of Indian folkways that she is, instigator of the revival of Spanish and Indian arts at Santa Fe, Mrs. Austin interprets their portent against the background of the Colonials of New Mexico, whose history reaches back to before Plymouth Rock and the James River. She tells of arts and aptitudes and social organization, and we see Boulder Dam for example from a fresh angle against the communal life of the ancient Southwest.

by greed of the lands already cleared, ditches built, Missions established, there must have been at work secretly something of the *meztizo's* hunger to reestablish his inheritance by merging his half-caste condition in the pure blood. By degrees which are lost, or purposely blurred, many Indian towns were in the course of a hundred years or two completely absorbed. Abiquiu, which was for many years "coyote," that is to say a refuge for broken casts, Ranchos de Taos, half a dozen settlements from Isleta south, Cordoba, formerly San Antonio de Quimado, within recent years Pojoaque, have passed, and now Picuris and Sandia, are passing into the nondescript class which can not be distinguished by the stranger from the same class at present drifting across our borders from old Mexico.

In the Molino

Such distinctions as exist are largely the result of having lived in direct contact with modern American standards and ideas. And even that does not mean so much as we like popularly to suppose, for the Americanos, when they came, behaved as always toward cultures and aptitudes other than their own; despised the idealism they displaced, discredited its accomplishment, made of the New Mexican's unfamiliarity with our catch-as-catch-can economics, an excuse for fleecing him. For a generation or more they practiced against him all the impositions, both political and economic, which we publicly insist unfit him for our way of life. All these things fell most heavily on the class under discussion, the class of mixed blood and unclassified economic capacity. The small group of relatively uncontaminated Spanish have adjusted themselves not too disadvantageously to American life; the middle "business" class is slowly emerging from the long eclipse of an unprotested political alignment. It must be understood that the rest of this article concerns itself solely with the majority of Spanish speaking New Mexicans who are affiliated by inheritance and economic outlook with the immigrant Mexican of today.

THE manner of life in the Colonies was at first not distinguished except by its pioneer quality, from the social life of Spain. The great landed proprietors established themselves in the midst of their servants and artisans, in a manner as feudal as could be managed. There was an *hacienda* with its enclosed *patio* for the *patrón,* and contiguous to it, rooms and *patios* for the servants, two or three such, according to the estate, opening each into the other, and finally into walled enclosures for the domestic animals and the herdsmen. Often there was a *torreon* near the entrance for outlook and defense, pierced for the *arcabuceros.* In later times, when the raiding tribes had been subdued, about the middle of the eighteenth century, the house of the *haciendado* was two-storied, including *salas* for dancing, and extending itself by wings as the sons of the family brought their brides home. Every such estate was self contained, manufacturing its own utilities. Every landholder shared with every other the impressed labor of the Indians at ploughing, shearing and harvest, a type of labor which after the revolt of 1680 was handled cautiously. They shared too, according to their means, in the raids and reprisals which kept the settlements reasonably supplied with captive slaves, and in the semi-annual trade *conducta* to Chihuahua. On up to the time when goods began to come in from the East over the Santa Fe trail, trade caravans well supplied with packers and muleteers and armed escorts, went down across the Border with buffalo skins, hides, tallow, *serapes,* a coarse woolen cloth called yerga, cotton blankets from the pueblos, gold, silver, turquoise, horses; coming back with sugar, medicine, silk, fine linen, ladies' shawls, combs, crockery; whatever the country lacked. It was obligatory on any young man contemplating marriage to make at least one *conducta* for the purchase of the bride's trousseau and one raid to the Navajo country to supply her with a personal maid.

Many little towns in New Mexico sprang from the congregation of workers on the great *haciendas;* woodchoppers, *tortilla* makers, weavers, dyers, leather workers, saddle makers, blacksmiths, adobe makers, carpenters, sheep-herders, *vacqueros,* plowmen, and the host of house servants, as the leisurely way of the country required.

In the *villas reales,* the chartered towns, life was varied by the presence of civil and military officials, a small merchant class, and the parish church. Usually the great estates sustained private chapels, and visiting friars. In the towns which made themselves, insinuating themselves into the lands and the plazas of Indian pueblos too small for organized resistence, there were not infrequently *conventos* and schools, for the part that the missionary ardors of the Franciscans played in the colonizing of New Mexico must not be overlooked. These gave a feeling of spiritual security in a land overpoweringly vast and terrifyingly beautiful, to an agricultural, village type of emotionally insecure *meztizos.* Even in the purely rural districts, the land grants were so arranged as to bring the farm houses into reasonable communication. Out of such conditions and in this manner, slowly the valleys of the Rio Grande and the *cañadas,* the *cienegas* and *rincons* of the Sangre de Cristo mountains, filled with a population in which the laboring class was such as I have described.

Only one other item in their history, for the influence it may have had on later Americanization, is deserving of mention. New Mexico, holding directly from the Crown, never felt any great dependence upon Mexico, so far away, so little known. After Mexico declared her independence of Spain, an affair which echoed remotely in the isolated towns of the Sangre de Cristo, there was little intercommunication except what was involved in the payment of official salaries and the collection of taxes. About that time too, there began to be a thin thread of communication with the English speaking settlements along the Mississippi. The people of New Mexico never *felt* particularly Mexican, never liked to be called Mexicans; they like it now less than ever. They are "native New Mexicans," in fact and allegiance. They do not even like to be called Spanish-American. During the late war they found a new name for themselves. "We old American families," they said, "feel that we ought to be the first to come forward," which they did with promptitude and gallantry. It was about this time that the term Spanish-Colonial to describe the New Mexican pioneers and their works came into general use in the Southwest.

But we will have to go a little deeper than that to uncover the source and the manner of the native New Mexican acceptance of allegiance to the United States. Something of course is owed to their pioneer inheritance shared with all America; something to the Spanish genius for politics. But probably much more is owed to the Indian inheritance which makes it second nature to be directly, even emotionally, interested in the good of the whole, to be able to work better and more happily in groups than individually.

WHAT we have to deal with in the mixed populations of both old and New Mexico is an item that the American people can not face too soon and too completely, *the socio-political inheritance of communistic living.* Radicals who are enamored of communism, liberals who are disposed to give it—in Russia or other far off places—a fair trial, and conservatives who hold it anathema, all shirk a close up study of it as it is to be found next door, or even within our borders. They would all somehow prefer to think of it as a distant menace, or as a Utopian promise on the economic horizon, rather than what it is, a living factor in present day economic adjustments. From Central America, half way down the southern continent, and north into lower Colorado, among aboriginal American populations, economic communism has prevailed since a thousand years before the Conquest, perhaps longer.

As a constituent of economic form, based upon the indivisible utility of water for irrigation, communism came over into every pioneer settlement within the region described, and is a continuing factor—witness the Boulder Dam controversy—in all southwestern economic development. As a predisposing psychological factor it must be taken into account in dealing with Mexican-Indian labor. Such labor tends to think flock-mindedly, and to work better in a gang, cohering by a voluntary surrender of leadership, made visible in the person of the boss. And the same general pattern prevails in political realignments of these people. Party loyalty is instinctive; once they have accepted political leadership it is difficult to seduce them away from it. This is something our *Anglos*—the native term for the English speaking population—finds extremely irritating. Against this instinctive communal political bloc, neither spell-binding nor economic advantage is so potent as it is in the average American community. During the presidential election of 1928, although Spanish speaking New Mexico is ardently Catholic, it was necessary to play softly on that stop; it wasn't even to be hoped that religious prejudice would loosen the solidarity of party affiliations.

Americans unfamiliar with this habit of group-mindedness, call it corrupt. But it is not, in the sense that it can be bought and sold for money as political allegiance can be in New York or New Jersey or Illinois or any other center of hundred per cent Americanism. It is, in this respect, the most un-American trait of the group in question. That this tendency to flock-mindedness would expose them to political exploitation in our large industrial cities where Mexican immigrant labor is in demand, is probable. Yet it does not work that way altogether in New Mexico, for in an economic environment which they thoroughly understand, the group mind is likely to be thoroughly alive to its own interests as it is among Indians.

The Herd Fording

In as much as it permits of the utilization of large units of labor under competent direction, in a more compact manner than is possible where a greater degree of individualism prevails, I cannot see that the Mexican type of group-mindedness is wholly disadvantageous to an industrial civilization. Is it not an increasing need of our vast aggregations of mechanized industries that there should be self-cohering groups, cohorts of hands, accustomed to be handled as units, capable of being thrown, as an army is thrown, regiment by regiment into the breaches made by modern invention in the economic environment?

I believe that it is, and that if we could rid ourselves of several fetishistic ways of thinking to which our own civilization is committed—as for example the fetish of group-mindedness as somehow inferior to individualism; or of the necessity our industry is under to think of profits first rather than of community advantage—we should see it so.

There is another aspect of this type of communal mindedness which accounts for the least understood and—to the hundred per center—most affronting trait of the Mexican. I refer to the capacity of the individual mind steeped in two thousand years of communism, to find its satisfactions in communal rather than in the *individual expression of economic conquest.* I underline a phrase to mark so complete a reversal of our own practice that few Americans are capable of understanding it. For American Indian communism has accomplished for the tribes, what the Communist Party seems to be trying to do in Russia; it gives to everybody a share in the common gain and the common leisure, and succeeds in preventing the formation of a middle class. Under communism in Mexico, everyone had land and the opportunity to find self-expression in things *made.* There was no group who found, or tried to find, expression in the *possession of things.* Even yet, with all the three hundred years of Spanish oppression, Mexican cities are characterized, as were the ancient cities of Yucatan, by notable public buildings, by superb monuments, by magnificent communal festivals, and by shockingly inadequate private housing, by an almost total want of private accommodation. The children of communism have wantlessness for their inheritance. The Mexican peon, once his pride of race is appeased by temples and pageants and general civic ostentation, wraps his *serape* around him and lies down on the ground to sleep. He makes a few necessary utensils, and makes them beautifully, pots, fabrics, baskets. The people release themselves in songs and dancing, in the making of pottery and manners; but the satisfaction is in the making, not the owning.

Something of this state of holy poverty is in the corresponding class of unclassified labor in New Mexico, except that it has always been less colored here by the bitterness of oppression, than it is south of the Border. The New Mexican laborer has a good house, even as the New Mexican *puebleño,* his remote ancestor, had; well constructed walls, rooms commodious and of good proportion, and comfortable fireplaces. Such homes are almost invariably scrupulously clean. Both by Indian and Spanish inheritance, the worker's wife is industrious and orderly. Her underclothing is clean and more often than not exquisitely made, even when of the coarsest material. There are always beds, usually well supplied with bedding, even when not always slept in. In the remote mountain villages there still obtains the notion that it is a little effeminate for a man to remove his clothing and climb into bed every night. It has happened that I have more than once found a whole family sleeping contentedly on the floor around a clean piled bed, which is reserved for guests and sickness. When one is so ill that bed becomes a necessity, then it is time to send for the priest. But this condition is less prevalent now than it was ten years ago. One now finds the thrifty laborer's family not only supplied with complete bedroom sets, but with cook stoves as well.

In the towns where wages are better and shops more accessible, there will be phonographs, radios, second-hand cars, all the house furnishings that are found in workingmen's houses elsewhere. This is what I mean when I say that the chief distinction between unskilled labor in New and old Mexico, is that north of the Border, the worker's wantlessness has been to some extent mitigated by the American craving for the possession of things. To *own* things; whether or not the things are useful or beautiful, merely to have and to hold and to express one's ego in the measure of possession; that is the first step in the progression of American labor toward bourgeois security. In New Mexico one is able to see what has been paid for it.

The first thing that has happened is that there has been a lessened capacity for making things, individual products of the hand and the spirit working coordinately. I will come to that a little more in detail presently. The second item in the cost of Americanization, is that there is no gain in the private control of utilities that, by the old rule of communism, would naturally come under the head of public utility. There are few private, and no public baths; household water supplies are a hazard, open privies constitute a public nuisance, the simplest door stone is all that keeps the mud from the floor. There is no effort, either private or communal, toward efficiency in the use of natural resources. Several years ago there was a severe epidemic of influenza moving up and down the whole Spanish-Indian country, singularly fatal to these simple people who had established no immunity to it, and were defended by no policy of public health. One of the nurses, loaned by a neighboring state, complained to me that in the little mountain towns she had always the greatest difficulty in keeping her patients warm through the night. In vain she tried to have wood enough cut to keep the fireplace supplied for the dark hours, but nobody could be persuaded. Three or four times in the night she would have to rouse somebody to go out and cut two or three armfuls, and lie down, only to be called again and again. No one complained of this necessity; wood is always cut as needed and in no other fashion. Her American interpretation was that the people were careless and lazy. But that is not borne out by more intimate knowledge. Wood is a natural common possession; it is always accessible, as accessible as earth and water. In the old days, before the American arrived—and it was so in Mexico—when a man found a rich mineral vein, he called his neighbors who came with baskets and carried away what they could. That was how it was with the turquoise mines of the pueblos; they were the common possession of the town on whose land they were found. It has always been difficult for these native peoples to acquire any but a tribal sense of ownership and use in the earth, our mother. One does not store up the services of his mother to his private profit; he asks and receives.

MODERN Americanism which, in the Southwest at least, is much more communistic than many people will admit, has learned to make a common attack on natural resources by way of the intelligence; substituting the specialized intellection of the trained engineer for the old subconscious approach. The peon has not yet learned to make that approach, *consciously*. The thing that is going on in Mexico today is largely the attempt to approach the economic problem consciously, instead of subconsciously, *without altering its scope and direction;* to make the necessary transfer of emphasis from the old submerged sense of the good of the tribe to the enlightened scientific conviction of communal participation.

The question of what happens to Mexican labor visiting in the United States, is as vital to this problem as any other; it can not be considered apart from the discussion of what has happened to a similar class of labor which has been living in the United States.

And that brings us to the consideration of what can be done for peon labor by deliberate schooling. It was in the study of what is, and is not, being done with our Spanish speaking labor in the Southwest that I first began to be forcibly struck with a curious inconsistence of American practice. We seem always to have been urgently in pursuit of "cheap" labor, and always sedulously concerned in turning that labor as soon as we have it, into the most expensive article. The cost of labor to the country, is primarily the cost of producing a laborer. If we have to make at the same time a citizen of him, especially if we have to make a certain standardized type of citizen of him, the cost of his part in that making must be added to his wages. He is cheap to us so long as he is practically wantless, so long as he is satisfied to express himself in making and being, rather than in possessing; so long as he lives cheaply, and reproduces plentifully. At present the peon fulfills all those conditions. But if we teach him that the chief obligation of Americanization is keeping up with the Joneses, he is no longer cheap. A few years ago at Santa Fe you could get unskilled native labor for $2 a day. Now you pay the same man from $2.50 to $3; and for skilled native labor you pay from $6 to $9, only a dollar or two less than you pay for "white" skilled labor. The difference in the price is, by and large, the distinction in the quality of the labor. There *is* a distinction.

The distinction we have to deal with can't be stated in terms of intelligence tests. The testimony of school teachers is that up to the age of fifteen, or thereabouts, the native children are as "bright," learn as fast, and with apparently as much pleasure as any other children. It is at adolescence that the racial inheritance rises to bind them to the patterns of an older habit of thinking. And in this our educational system fails them, being based as it is on an educational fallacy which has not been seriously entertained by any expert educator for a generation. Our system goes on taking for granted that every public school child can and should take on the intellectual pattern of the orthodox university graduate. This is a pattern that was never learned by the ancestors of the children we are (*Continued on page* 187)

CHIMAYO

The Colonials

Etchings by B. J. O. Nordfeldt

THE descendants of the most ancient of immigrants to the U.S.A. are here interpreted by an artist whose heritage comes from a newer wave of immigration. Mr. Nordfeldt was born in Sweden, came to America at the age of thirteen, worked through from printer's devil on a Swedish newspaper in Chicago to the Art Institute where he studied by day and worked at night to win several years of study in France, England and Sweden. Back in New York he began to etch, while a later year or two in Italy, Spain and Tangier fixed his love for color. He has traveled from Provincetown to Brittany from Chicago to Paris, everywhere recording on canvas and on copper plate, places, people, the contemporary human scene. In Santa Fe he came into intimate contact with the Mexican Colonials, and from these contacts have come his surest etchings, his most vibrant paintings. "He chooses Mexican types as the vehicle for his theories in art and a strange thing happens; for all his modernist austerity, for all his holding himself to a problem, he gives us a primitive, emotional statement of those people that is sometimes intense with tragedy, always tense with life."

PETIA

WOMAN FROM CHIMAYÓ

ALVINO ORTEGA

MAN FROM ARROYA HONDO

PAULA MONTOYA

My People

By ADELINA OTERO

THE spell of my country? Perhaps it is the beauty of it all. To some it is the sunset of a fall afternoon, bathing a little community in its afterglow; turning the vivid yellow of the aspen trees to gold; the red-brown of the scrub oak to bronze; and dark, in the midst of these, the piñon trees. As the sun disappears behind the mountain in the west, its crimson glow is reflected on the snow-covered range in the east. My people watch this with reverence. *"Sangre de Cristo!"* (Blood of Christ) they call these mountains, so named by the early Franciscan missionaries.

Many persons believe New Mexico is a region of plains. But it is in the northern part, into the fertile valleys of the Rio Grande, back into the mountains and their canyons, that my work, as county superintendent of schools, takes me. Into Cundiyo, situated eight thousand feet high in the Sangre de Cristo range, reached by a difficult road down *arroyos* and up over mountains until it seems that we are to climb Baldy, ten thousand feet above us. Here is a typical mountain community, entirely occupied by Spanish-Americans, a gentle, industrious, and intelligent people, brown-eyed and suntanned. The houses are flat-roofed, and are plastered with adobe of a warm, brown color which conforms to the earth around. Wherever possible, space has been cleared for gardens and little farms fed by a stream of crystal water. In the background are the high pines. It is the fall of the year. The crops have been gathered from the mountain canyons. The men and women work together. Corn is husked and separated; the blue for *tortillas* and *atole,* the white for flour. Both will be taken to the water mill at Nambe to be ground. The yellow pumpkins are placed on the roofs; the *chili,* redder than any sunset, is hung in strings from the *vigas* to dry, and later will be ground into *chili molido.* Apples are sliced and placed on boards in the sun.

Since the road was bad, the school nurse and I left my car at Nambe, the Indian village, and hired an Indian boy to drive us in his wagon to Cundiyo. There are so many wood roads, it is easy to lose the way, as we were to learn when we started back. Darkness comes upon us suddenly in the high mountains, like a curtain lowered to cover our eyes from too much grandeur! But we were fortunate. A moon rose over the range, shedding its white light upon the countryside. A breeze stirred the pine trees that they might give forth a fragrance and refresh their guests in the canyons,—*El refresco de la noche!* Suddenly I heard a man singing. I looked back and noticed that he was following us on horseback. It was Teofilo, one of the school directors. I asked him,

"Teofilo, where are you going at this hour?"

"*Para* Santa Fe, Señora."

"To Santa Fe! It is thirty miles. You will not arrive there till late. Can I attend to your business for you?"

"No, Señora. No tenga pena." (Do not be worried.)

We drove on. Our Indian boy never saying a word; Teofilo just keeping us in sight. The moon, as it rose, gave us more and more light. At first the tall pines seemed like sentinels one is afraid to approach, but gradually they became more friendly and Teofilo began to sing:

Alli, en un bosque donde yo me hallo, solo se oye mi triste peñar. (In a forest where I find myself alone, I hear my sad thoughts.)

The melody of it, the pathos, *"Solo se oye mi triste peñar!"* The little Spanish community; the mountains; the moon; Teofilo's voice breaking the great silence. *La Hermosura de la noche!* We finally reached Nambe, and as I thanked and paid the Indian boy and got into my car, I noticed Teofilo was still following. He drew up to the car and addressed me.

"Are you all right, Doña Adelina?"

"Si, gracias."

"You will not have trouble with your car?"

"I think not."

"Well, then, *buenos noches, y Dio la cuide.* I shall return to Cundiyo. But, first would you be so kind as to mail this letter for me in Santa Fe?"

"But you are not going there yourself, then?"

Teofilo smiled, bowed, donned his hat, and rode off into the night. He had followed us for ten miles to see that we were not lost in the canyon! Yes, these are my people, my friends.

IN the little community we had left—the teacher had called the school directors to meet with me that day, and the children proceeded to recite their lessons. As I listened I was thinking how to encourage them to preserve the arts, the customs, and the traditions of this New Spain in an effort to

Not alone by grace of her deft ministrations as county superintendent of schools at Santa Fe throughout ten years can our author speak of "My People." When her mother, Doña Eloisa Luna became the bride of Don Manuel B. Otero, they united two of the most illustrious families from old Spain, whose holdings dated to 1695; leaders in the life of New and Old Mexico, judges, governors, captains under Cortez, the lines reaching back to noble houses of Castile and Aragon in the 13th century. The snapshot was taken during the last Santa Fe fiesta. The two Mexican musicians accompanied Mrs. Otero Warren in the Pasatiempo Parade.

save its charm, which is its very life. This is an American school, giving those little children the same reading, writing and arithmetic which is taught in the Far West, the Middle West, and the East. One of the fundamentals of our American education is to train children for life. My people's children have been working at the side of the father and the mother since they were old enough to work—the boy at the plow, herding the sheep, or in the tin shop; the girl a practical exponent of home economics, helping to keep the home and caring for the younger children. A practical effort, theirs, to keep the child in his surroundings. The idea is that the son will inherit the little farm, the sheep, or the tin shop. The girl will become a home maker—the desire and custom of the Spanish-speaking women. I have been lenient about school attendance in the fall of the year since they must bring their children into the work in order to save their crops. It is difficult to get farm hands, even if they could afford it (which they cannot), and as their neighbors are busy with their own farms, there is no alternative. I mention this in an effort to get across a vital point. While I recognize the wonderfully organized educational system of the United States, might it not be beneficial to modify requirements and curricula in other ways?

If we could, for example, in New Mexico include in our rural school curriculum the old arts such as dyeing, blanket-weaving, tin work, needle work, and wood-carving, employing experts in these lines from the community, and give credits in the schools for this work as we do for reading, writing and arithmetic, we might then perpetuate something of lasting educational value for the people. Do you ask why we can not do this now? Because a teacher who has been given her teacher's certificate is not usually expert in these lines, and without such a certificate our laws say that no one may be paid for teaching. Further, if no credits are allowed for these subjects, we will not be able to accredit the students for promotion or for graduation, according to the educational standards of the state. I might add, in passing, that we can not permit the children to speak Spanish in the classroom, and the teachers are instructed to keep the children from conversing in it on the playground, thereby conforming to the national system of education!

VIOLA By Kenneth M. Adams

But let me go back to the classroom where my twenty-six children from six to sixteen years were gathered. Having recited their lessons, I asked them what they would like to do next. They wanted to sing. It was their way of expressing pleasure at my being with them. (How often since then have I longed to express my joy in a similar way!) "We want to sing to you My Country 'Tis of Thee"—this to show me that they knew our national songs. Then a little chap, with eager brown eyes, asked: "May we sing *one* Spanish song?" And their voices rang out with real feeling in the rhythmical music of La Golondrina, which, according to a legend of our people, was sung by the king of Spain as he looked down on the Moorish siege of Granada:

> *Tambien yo estoy en la region perdido,*
> *O, Cielo santo, y sin poder volar.*
> (I also am in this region lost,
> O, blessed heaven, and unable to fly.)

Into this song went all the love of our natives for their ancestral land—a heritage from their Conquistador forebears. As Gabriela Mistral so beautifully expresses it: "*Una cancion es una respuesta que damos a la hermosura del mundo.*" (A song is a response which we give for the beauty of the world.)

THE Spaniards made their first stand against the Indian early in the 16th century, and from that time until the territorial division, we had practically reigned supreme over New Spain. With annexation to the American republic, we became a part of *e pluribus unum!* With a people whose traditions and customs had been established for some four hundred years, whose temperament is to live and let live, it has been somewhat difficult to acquiesce in the new order, expressed in this instance in the present educational system. The appeal which I make to my people is this: that since the American Occupation in 1846, we have been American citizens, members of *another* great nation, and it is to our best interests that we become educated according to the standards of that nation. It has, for us, its distinct advantages, its definite protection.

Education, in its first sense, is the "leading out" of knowledge and capacities. It requires great skill and a gift to do this without aggressive or hasty imposition of new and unfamiliar ideas. This is especially true in the case of those to whom the "old order changeth." In spite of the tremendous acreage of unsettled and uncultivated land, of sparse population, New Mexico is advancing educationally. Our children are getting their diplomas in reading, writing and arithmetic. Yet we are overlooking their expression of beauty in the native arts and crafts which would be, were these incorporated into the curriculum, a definite contribution to the cultural background of this country.

MY visit to Chupadero takes me to Tesuque, a small village about six miles north of Santa Fe. Here I leave my car, and climb into Macario Jimenez' wagon. He has placed a chair in the back for me and over the road we go. We climb one hill after another, into one canyon, and up over a mountain to Chupadero. The schoolhouse comes in sight. The American flag is flying from a pine tree which has been brought down from the mountains. The bark and branches have been carefully cut off, and as carefully our great flag, on a regulation pulley, has been raised to the very top of this one-time sentinel of the hills.

Macario drives me over another mountain pass to Rio

en Medio. On the top of this mountain, which is between the two communities, are more *descansos*, silhouetted against the blue sky. These are resting places where the people stop as they carry their dead to the grave. As we begin the ascent, I notice a procession going over the winding road. A wagon grinds its way ahead of a group of men. There are no women. The men are chanting. Macario tells me a young girl from Chupadero has died, and they are taking her to be buried in the church yard at Rio en Medio. The bell tolls in accompaniment to the chanting of the procession. *"Ese doble de campana, no es por el que se murio, sino para recordarme a mi que me he de morir mañana"* ("That tolling of the bell is not for the dead, but to remind me that I may die tomorrow"), says Macario softly as he watches them, with hat in hand. The coffin was a home-made one, covered with pink calico, a white strip making a cross on its lid. A man is driving the team sitting on the box seat, while a young man kneels at the coffin's head, holding a cross. The rest of the men, about a dozen in all, walk bare-headed behind the wagon. At the top of the mountain they halt and a *descanso* cross is erected. The procession winds on, taking the high road. The chanting dies out among the trees as they disappear into the mountains.

After examining the school at Rio en Medio, I visited Macario's home. His wife embraced me, as is the custom among my people, and then invited me to have dinner which had been especially prepared in my honor. It was a delicious repast: *Carne en arroz, frijoles con chile, tortillas, manzanas, secas hervidas, y café.* All of which on an American menu would have appeared as, meat cooked with rice, beans with chile, *tortillas* (which resemble American flap-jacks but are used as bread), and stewed dried apples. They have a small adobe house of five rooms, with rag rugs on the floor, a spotless home. One room was set aside as a *sanctuario*, or little chapel, where candles were burning that day in front of images of the saints and of Our Lord. The family meet together every evening, light the candles, and say evening prayers. A devout, religious people whose religion permeates each thought and action. As these people watch the snow on the Sangre de Cristo range, they feel that it is a sign from *Dios* that there will be water in the streams for their crops. "Why are we Catholics? Because we are Spanish," some of our people say.

On the long winter evenings I may see this same family sitting in front of an open fire-place; the father playing the guitar, the children the flute or the mouth harp, and the rest joining in with the sheer joy of singing:

Ay! ay, ay, ay canta y no llores,
Porque cantando se alegran, Cielito Lindo, los corazones.
(Sing and do not weep, pretty creature,
For singing makes the heart glad.)

I have schools in some of the old historical towns. In Santa Cruz de la Cañada, for example, one of the first four missions in the state, destroyed by the rebellion of the Indians against Spanish rule in 1680, and rebuilt during the reconquest in 1695. A school in Glorieta and Cañoncito, both situated at the entrance to Apache Canyon, called the Front Door of the East, on the old Santa Fe trail leading from Missouri to Santa Fe. At La Cueva (the cave); at La Joya (the jewel); in Chimayo, where the famous old *Sanctuario* is located—a place made famous by the purported appearance of the Blessed Virgin.

As I have told you, my people are a simple people. There are no complexities which harass us. We live—we love—we die. We laugh in joy and weep in sadness. We are superficial? Indeed, no. But there is an acceptance, a resignation, a logic, I might say, in our attitude toward life and living. An instance of this last occurred when I recently visited a home in Tesuque where a little child, one of my school children, was very ill. The doctor and nurse had reported a severe illness. I went early the next morning to inquire after the child, and the father met me at the door, not in grief, but in complete resignation. I asked,

FELIPE

By B. J. O. Nordfeldt

"How is Teresita to-day?"

"Señora, my little girl is well now. She no longer suffers. God has taken her."

These and their kind then are the Spanish-American people of New Mexico who have found peace and contentment in the canyons and the mountain tops. A vigorous people with a background of culture, of loyalty. A sensitive people with high ideals, loving the solitude of the wilderness and fearing no danger. Whether it is in defense of America or war with Spain, we respond. We are avowedly citizens of the United States. There is no shirking of our suffrage responsibility. In times of national and state elections we go eagerly to the polls, for we love the political game. What, then, is to be the trend of education in New Mexico? Is it not a question of our gradual merging, of our assimilation, into this great nation, but at the same time of conserving our distinctive contribution through the preservation of the customs, traditions, the arts and crafts of the Spanish Southwest?

The Spanish era is probably the most colorful in the history of the United States, and I am wondering, as I write this, if this progressive and advanced republic has still time and patience for charm?

An appreciation of this charm in shown by the large and increasing numbers of *Anglos* who have come to New Mexico to live and who have learned to love it. I do not believe there is an *Anglo* who does not feel that unless he takes this country and the people to his heart—loving it, scars and all—that he is every happy among us. The moment he begins to resent any aspect of his life, we still remain foreign to him.

El sol va bajando sobre mi patria, pero ningun dia muere sin el mejor entendimiento de mi gente. (The sun is setting over my country, but no day dies without a better understanding of my people.)

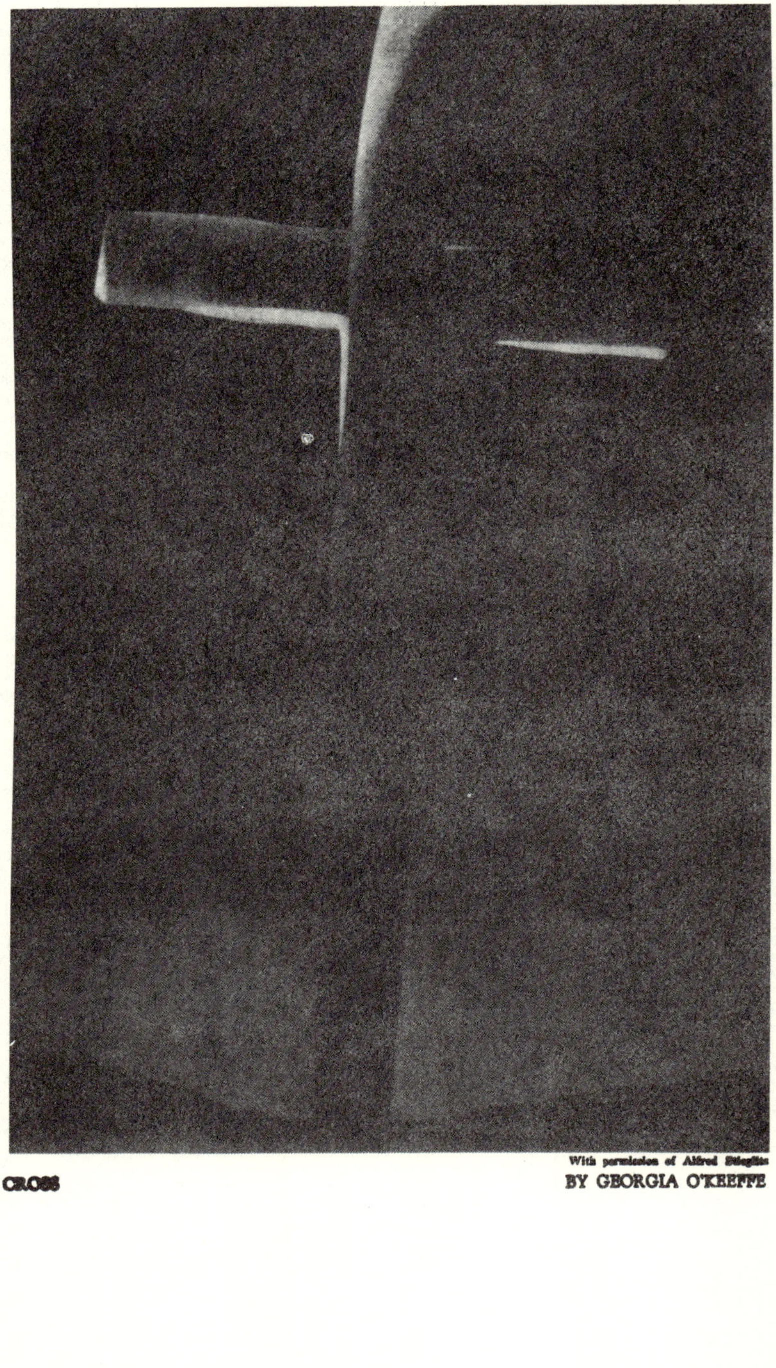

With permission of Alfred Stieglitz

CROSS

BY GEORGIA O'KEEFFE

New Mexico

By D. H. LAWRENCE

SUPERFICIALLY, the world has become small and known. Poor little globe of earth, the tourist trots around you as easily as they trot round the Bois or round Central Park. There is no mystery left, we've been there, we've seen it, we know all about it. We've done the globe, and the globe is done.

This is quite true, superficially. On the superficies, horizontally, we've been everywhere, and done everything, we know all about it. Yet the more we know, superficially, the less we penetrate, vertically. It's all very well skimming across the surface of the ocean, and saying you know all about the sea. There still remain the terrifying under-deeps, of which we have utterly no experience.

The same is true of land travel. We skim along, we get there, we see it all, we've done it all. And, as a rule, we never once go through the curious film which railroads, ships, motor-cars and hotels stretch over the surface of the whole earth. Pekin is just the same as New York, with a few different things to look at; rather more Chinese about, etc. Poor creatures that we are, we crave for experience, yet we are like flies that crawl on the pure and transparent mucous-paper in which the world, like a bon-bon, is wrapped so carefully that we can never get at it, though we see it there all the time as we move about it, apparently in contact, yet actually as far removed as if it were the moon.

As a matter of fact, our great-grandfathers, who never went anywhere, in actuality had more experience of the world than we have, who have seen everything. When they listened to a lecture with lantern-slides, they really held their breath before the unknown, as they sat in the village school-room. We, bowling along in a rickshaw in Ceylon, say to ourselves: It's very much what you'd expect: we really know it all.

We are mistaken. The know-it-all state of mind is just the result of being outside the mucous-paper wrapping of civilization. Underneath is everything we don't know and are afraid of knowing.

I realized this with shattering force when I went to New Mexico. New Mexico, one of the United States, part of the U. S. A. New Mexico, the picturesque reservation and playground of the Eastern States, very romantic, old Spanish, Red Indian, desert-mesas, pueblos, cow-boys, penitentes, all that film-stuff. Very nice, the great Southwest; put on a sombrero and knot a red kerchief round your neck, to go out in the great free spaces!

That is New Mexico wrapped in the absolutely hygienic and shiny mucous-paper of our trite civilization. That is the New Mexico known to most of the Americans who know all about it. But break through the shiny sterilized wrapping, and actually *touch* the country, and you will never be the same again.

I think New Mexico was the greatest experience from the outside world that I have ever had. It certainly changed me for ever. Curious as it may sound, it was New Mexico that liberated me from the present era of civilization, the great era of material and mechanical development. Months spent in holy Kandy, in Ceylon, the holy of holies of southern Buddhism, had not touched the great psyche of materialism and idealism which dominated me. And years, even, in the exquisite beauty of Sicily, right among the old Greek paganism that still lives there, had not shattered the essential Christianity on which my character was established. Australia was a sort of dream or trance, like being under a spell, the self remaining unchanged, so long as the trance did not last too long. Tahiti, in a mere glimpse, repelled me; and so did California, after a stay of a few weeks. There seemed a strange brutality in the spirit of the western coast, and I felt: Oh, let me get away!

BUT the moment I saw the brilliant, proud morning shine high up over the deserts of Santa Fe, something stood still in my soul, and I started to attend. There was a certain magnificence in the high-up day, a certain eagle-like royalty, so different from the equally pure, equally pristine and lovely morning of Australia, which is so soft, so utterly pure in its softness, and betrayed by green parrots flying. But in the lovely morning of Australia one went into a dream. In the magnificent fierce morning of New Mexico one sprang awake, a new part of the soul woke up suddenly, and the old world gave way to a new.

There are all kinds of beauty in the world, thank God, though ugliness is homogeneous. How lovely is Sicily, with Calabria across the sea like an opal, and Etna with her snow in a world above and beyond! How lovely is Tuscany, with little red tulips wild among the corn; or bluebells at dusk in England, or mimosa in clouds of pure yellow among the grey-green dun foliage of Australia, under a soft, blue, unbreathed sky! But for a *greatness* of beauty I have never experienced anything like New Mexico. All those mornings when I went with a hoe along the ditch to the canyon, at the ranch, and stood, in the fierce, proud silence of the Rockies, on their foot-hills, to look far over the desert to the blue mountains away in Arizona, blue as chalcedony, with the sage-brush desert sweeping grey-blue in between, dotted with tiny cube-crystals of

Back of desert, the mountain; back of American and Spaniard, the Indian and the elemental life of his cosmos; "mountain-life, cloud-life, thunder-life, air-life, earth-life, sun-life."—It remained for Lawrence to experience religion in New Mexico; it liberated him from the "era of materialism and mechanical developments." And this article, written by the novelist for Survey Graphic shortly before his death, carries his critique of modern civilization as it comes in contact with the Indians of our Southwest and confronts native cultures re-emerging below the Rio Grande.

houses: the vast amphitheatre of lofty, indomitable desert, sweeping round to the ponderous Sangre de Cristo Mountains on the east, and coming up flush at the pine-dotted foot-hills of the Rockies! What splendor! Only the tawny eagle could really sail out into the splendor of it all. Leo Stein once wrote to me: "It is the most aesthetically-satisfying landscape I know."—To me it was much more than that. It had a splendid, silent terror, and a vast, far-and-wide magnificence which made it way beyond mere aesthetic appreciation. Never is the light more pure and overweening than there, arching with a royalty almost cruel over the hollow, uptilted world. For it is curious that the land which has produced modern political democracy at its highest pitch should give one the greatest sense of overweening, terrible proudness and mercilessness: but so beautiful, God! so beautiful! Those that have spent morning after morning alone there pitched among the pines above the great proud world of desert will know, almost unbearably, how beautiful it is, how clear and unquestioned is the might of the day. Just day itself is tremendous there. It is so easy to understand that the Aztecs gave hearts of men to the sun. For the sun is not merely hot or scorching, not at all. It is of a brilliant and unchallengeable purity and haughty serenity which would make one sacrifice the heart to it. Ah, yes, in New Mexico the heart is sacrificed to the sun, and the human being is left stark, heartless, but undauntedly religious.

AND that was the second revelation out there. I had looked over all the world for something that would strike me as religious. The simple piety of some English people, the semi-pagan mystery of some Catholics in southern Italy, the intensity of some Bavarian peasants, the semi-ecstasy of Buddhists or Brahmins: all this had seemed religious all right, as far as the parties concerned were involved, but it didn't involve me. I looked on at their religiousness from the outside. For it is still harder to feel religion at will, than to love it at will.

I had seen what I felt was a hint of wild religion in the so-called devil dances of a group of naked villagers from the far-remote jungle in Ceylon, dancing at midnight under the torches, glittering wet with sweat on their dark bodies as if they had been gilded, at the celebration of the Pera-hera in Kandy, given to the Prince of Wales. And the utter dark absorption of these naked men, as they danced with their knees wide apart, suddenly affected me with a *sense* of religion, I *felt* religion for a moment. For religion is an experience, an uncontrollable, sensual experience even more so than love: I use sensual to mean an experience deep down in the senses, inexplicable and inscrutable.

But this experience was fleeting, gone in the curious turmoil of the Pera-hera, and I had no permanent feeling of religion till I came to New Mexico and penetrated into the old human race-experience there. It is curious that it should be in America, of all places, that a European should really experience religion, after touching the old Mediterranean and the East. It is curious that one should get a sense of living religion from the Red Indians, having failed to get it from Hindus or Sicilian Catholics or Cinghalese.

Let me make a reservation. I don't stand up to praise the Red Indian as he reveals himself in contact with white civilization. From that angle, I am forced to admit he *may* be thoroughly objectionable. Even my small experience knows it. But also I know he *may* be thoroughly nice, even in his dealings with white men. It's a question of individuals, a good deal, on both sides.

But in this article I don't want to deal with the everyday or superficial aspect of New Mexico, outside the mucous-paper wrapping. I *want* to go beneath the surface. And therefore the American Indian in his behavior as an American citizen doesn't really concern me. What concerns me is what he is, or what he seems to me to be, in his ancient, ancient race-self and religious self.

For the Red Indian seems to me much older than Greeks or Hindus or any European or even Egyptians. The Red Indian, as a civilized and truly religious man, civilized beyond tabu and totem, as he is in the south, is religious in perhaps the oldest sense, and deepest, of the world. That is to say, he is a remnant of the most deeply religious race still living. So it seems to me.

But again let me protect myself. The Indian who sells you baskets on Albuquerque station or who slinks around Taos plaza may be an utter waster and an indescribably low dog. Personally, he may be even less religious than a New York sneak-thief. He may have broken with his tribe, or his tribe itself may have collapsed finally from its old religious integrity, and ceased, really, to exist. Then he is only fit for rapid absorption into white civilization, which must make the best of him.

But while a tribe retains its religion and keeps up its religious practices, and while any member of the tribe shares in those practices, then there is a tribal integrity and a living tradition going back far beyond the birth of Christ, beyond the pyramids, beyond Moses. A vast old religion which once swayed the earth lingers in unbroken practice there in New Mexico, older, perhaps, than anything in the world save Australian aboriginal tabu and totem, and that is not yet religion.

You can feel it, the atmosphere of it, around the pueblos. Not, of course, when the place is crowded with sight-seers and motor-cars. But go to Taos pueblo on some brilliant snowy morning, and see the white figures on the roof: or come riding through at dusk on some windy evening, when the black skirts of the silent women blow around the white wide boots, and you will feel the old, old root of human consciousness still reaching down to depths we know nothing of: and of which, only too often, we are jealous. It seems it will not be long before the pueblos are uprooted.

BUT never shall I forget watching the dancers, the men with the fox-skin swaying down from their buttocks, file out at San Geronimo, and the women with seed-rattles following. The long, streaming, glistening black hair of the men. Even in ancient Crete long hair was sacred in a man, as it is still in the Indians. Never shall I forget the utter absorption of the dance, so quiet, so steadily, timelessly rhythmic, and silent, with the ceaseless down-tread, always to the earth's center, the very reverse of the upflow of Dionysiac or Christian ecstasy. Never shall I forget the deep singing of the men at the drum, swelling and sinking, the deepest sound I have heard in all my life, deeper than thunder, deeper than the sound of the Pacific Ocean, deeper than the roar of a deep waterfall: the wonderful deep sound of men calling to the unspeakable depths.

Never shall I forget coming into the little pueblo of San Felipe one sunny morning in spring, unexpectedly, when bloom was on the trees in the perfect little pueblo more old, more utterly peaceful and idyllic than anything in Theocritus, and seeing a little casual dance. Not impressive as a spectacle, only, to me, profoundly moving, because of the truly terrifying religious absorption of it.

Never shall I forget the Christmas dances at Taos, twilight, snow, the darkness coming over the great wintry mountains and the lonely pueblo, then suddenly, again, like dark calling dark, the deep Indian cluster-singing around the drum, wild and awful, suddenly rousing on the lost dusk as the procession starts. And then the bonfires leaping suddenly in pure spurts of high flame, columns of sudden flame forming an alley for the procession.

NEVER shall I forget the khiva of birch-trees, away in the Apache country, in Arizona this time, the teepees and flickering fires, the neighing of horses unseen under the huge dark night, and the Apaches all abroad, in their silent moccasined feet: and in the khiva, beyond a little fire, the old man reciting, reciting in the unknown Apache speech, in the strange wild Indian voice that re-echoes away back to before the Flood, reciting apparently the traditions and legends of the tribe, going on and on, while the young men, the *braves* of today, wandered in, listened, and wandered away again, overcome with the power and majesty of that utterly old tribal voice, yet uneasy with their half-adherence to the modern civilization, the two things in contact. And one of these *braves* shoved his face under my hat, in the night, and stared with his glittering eyes close to mine. He'd have killed me then and there, had he dared. He didn't dare: and I knew it: and he knew it.

Never shall I forget the Indian races, when the young men, even the boys, run naked, smeared with white earth and stuck with bits of eagle fluff for the swiftness of the heavens, and the old men brush them with eagle feathers, to give them power. And they run in the strange hurling fashion of the primitive world, hurled forward, not making speed deliberately. And the race is not for victory. It is not a contest. There is no competition. It is a great cumulative effort. The tribe this day is adding up its male energy and exerting to the utmost: for what? To get power, to get strength: to come, by sheer cumulative, hurling effort of the bodies of men, into contact with the great cosmic source of vitality which gives strength, power, energy to the men who can grasp it, energy for the year of attainment.

It was a vast old religion, greater than anything we know: more darkly and nakedly religious. There is no God, no conception of a god. All is god. But it is not the pantheism we are accustomed to, which expresses itself as "God is everywhere, god is in everything." In the oldest religion, everything was alive, not supernaturally but naturally alive. There were only deeper and deeper streams of life, vibrations of life more and more vast. So rocks were alive, but a mountain had a deeper, vaster life than a rock, and it was much harder for a man to bring his spirit, or his energy, into contact with the life of the mountain, and so draw strength from the mountain, as from a great standing well of life, than it was to come into contact with the rock. And he had to put forth a greater religious effort. For the whole life-effort of man was to get his life into direct contact with the elemental life of the cosmos, mountain-life, cloud-life, thunder-life, air-life, earth-life, sun-life. To come into immediate *felt* contact, and so derive energy, power, and a dark sort of joy. This effort into sheer naked contact, *without an intermediary or mediator,* is the real meaning of religion. And at the sacred races the runners hurled themselves in a terrible cumulative effort, through the air, to come at last into naked contact with the very life of the air, which is the life of the clouds, and so of the rain.

It was a vast and pure religion, without idols or images, even mental ones. It is the oldest religion, a cosmic religion the same for all peoples, not broken up into specific gods or saviours or systems. It is the religion which precedes the god-concept, and is therefore greater and deeper than any god-religion.

And it lingers still, for a little while, in New Mexico: but long enough to have been a revelation to me. And the Indian, however objectionable he may be on occasion, has still some of the strange beauty and pathos of the religion that brought him forth and is now shedding him away into oblivion. When Trinidad, the Indian boy, and I planted corn at the ranch, my soul paused to see his brown hands softly moving the earth over the maize in pure ritual. He was back in his old religious self, and the ages stood still. Ten minutes later he was making a fool of himself with the horses. Horses were never part of the Indian's religious life, never would be. He hasn't a tithe of the feeling for them he has for a bear, for example. So horses don't like Indians.

But there it is: the newest democracy ousting the oldest religion! And once the oldest religion is ousted, one feels the democracy and all its paraphernalia will collapse, and the oldest religion, which comes down to us from man's pre-war days, will start again. The sky-scraper will scatter on the winds like thistledown, and the genuine America, the America of New Mexico, will start on its course again. This is an interregnum.

TAOS SIGNS
Lithograph by J. Ward Lockwood

Spanish Colonial Arts

By FRANK APPLEGATE

SPANISH Colonists in New Mexico, compared with the English settlers on the Atlantic coast, were removed from their sources of supply by six months of horseback travel in addition to the sea voyage. They brought nothing with them into the Rio Grande valley that could not be carried in the square saddlebags, called *cayaxes*, or in the crude, solid wheeled *carretas* drawn by oxen. Even in the best colonial times, a year was required for the official supply train to make a round trip from Mexico to Santa Fe. The result was that the things the colonists made for themselves became, as time went on, actually more primitive in form, being largely influenced by limitations of tools and materials and by the arts and crafts of the Indians among whom they settled. Many of the articles used about their houses and their furniture were re-created from memories of those things that they had left behind them. Whatever is reminiscent of Spanish arts and crafts found among them is of early Spanish art of the 16th century.

Thrown as the Spanish colonials were on the rather scant resources of the country, they were compelled to adapt a new technique in using what materials they found there; and they had to thank the Pueblo Indians for much, for these Indians had been using these materials for centuries. From the Indians they took over the materials and technique of building their houses, adapting the pattern to their own less communal habit of living. The very wealthy could draw on Old Mexico and even Europe for some luxuries; could have the beams of his house elaborately decorated and the ends of them supported on carved corbels. Spindles, probably due to Moorish influence on Spanish arts, were used in furniture, doors, balcony and porch railings and for window bars. Earthen floors were covered with native woven carpets and the rich man could fill his house with the best furnishings that the local craftsmen could turn out.

The most numerous of still existing pieces of Spanish Colonial furniture in New Mexico are the chests, which ranged in size from the tiny *cahitas* used for holding small articles to the huge food storage chests which were often from six to eight feet long and several feet deep. This larger type was used to hold the best of the family clothing, and one of them sometimes held locked within it an image of San Antonio during the time that a member of the family might be absent on a journey, as a hostage against the safe return of the traveler. These chests were generally made of the native pine although a few were made of native tanned buffalo leather with interlacing thongs and bright Spanish flannel used as a background. The tops, sides, ends and bottoms of the wooden ones were usually made from a single board width, with all the edges carefully dovetailed and fastened together with wooden nails. Ornamental locks and hinges were produced by the local blacksmith. Most of these chests were decorated with a carved design or they were painted with gaily colored pictures of garden scenes, bull fights, gentlemen in white trousers, holding large crowned hats, bowing to ladies in hoop skirts, soldiers on horseback, people in boats and many other fantastic scenes, framed with borders of exotic looking flowers. This type usually passed from generation to generation as wedding chests.

Furniture-making practically ceased with the influx of Americans who brought in cheap and ugly machine-made articles. The early comers among them showed a vast intolerance and contempt for everything Spanish Colonial and to a great extent imparted this attitude to the natives. It is only within the past few years that there has begun a renaissance. Americans have come belatedly to see how fitting and comfortable the Spanish-colonial type of house is in its environment and climate and how well Spanish-colonial arts and crafts go with the architecture.

Weaving has always been the most important handcraft of the Spanish Colonials in New Mexico, but by the end of the eighteenth century it had so declined and was so poor in quality and so coarse that much of the wool clip was sent to Chihuahua and Sonora by the yearly caravans to be traded for Mexican goods, including blankets of Mexican weave. To avoid this disadvantageous exchange and to try and revive the industry the governor, at the end of the 18th century, engaged two expert weavers of Old Mexico to come to Santa Fe and instruct the New Mexican colonists in spinning, dyeing and weaving. These arts were carried on throughout the colony, but gradually the community of Chimayo, twenty-five miles north of Santa Fe, became the most famous center for weaving. From 1800 to 1850 Spanish Colonials employed many Navajo Indian women either as slaves or at living wages to spin and weave blankets for them. These women became in this way very proficient and carried the art back to the tribe so that ever since these Indians have been famous for their weaving. Blanket weaving is still carried on very extensively by the descendants of the Spanish colonists and many thousands of these blankets find a ready market in all parts of the United States. Chimayo is still the center so that all native New Mex-

---

A painter of distinction and a recognized authority on ceramics, Frank Applegate made himself, during his New Mexico years, master of the native arts. Closely associated with Mary Austin in the Society for the Revival of Spanish Colonial Arts in New Mexico, he had been instrumental in having these arts reinstated in the vocational training schools of the state, in establishing standards of technique and clarifying the public estimate of them. His recent death, since this article was written, is an incalculable loss. Señor Frank, as he was called, is deeply mourned by the people among whom he worked.

ican blankets whether made in Chimayo or not take their name from that community.

Much to the indignation of the Chimayo weavers, a blanket dealer in Santa Fe has within the past few years brought in blanket weavers from Mexico and employs them at low wages to imitate Chimayo blankets. These immigrants are used to a low scale of living and the Chimayo weavers find it difficult to compete with them.

The Spaniards learned the art of using fine vegetable dyes in the new country, for when the Spanish colonists entered the valley of the Rio Grande they found the Pueblo Indians using blankets and clothing made of native cotton and other vegetable fibers and using these natural dyes to color the designs on their blankets, ceremonial garments, leather, baskets and other objects.

THE fine arts reached their highest development among the Spanish Colonials of New Mexico in religious painting and carving in wood. This was natural for religion was the greatest emotional outlet of the people at that time. Their religion, however, was not entirely a concern for immortality. They felt the need of such help in getting through the daily trials of this life and they believed with implicit faith that for every need and in every emergency there was a saint that could be invoked for aid. For prayers to be efficacious, they required an image of the particular saint that had power over the situation in which they sought aid. It was proper to appeal to Saint Job in case one was covered with boils, yet he could be of no assistance if the bean crop were doing badly. In that case only San Ysidro, the farmers' saint, could be of assistance. As result representations of about one hundred different saints are to be found in the churches, missions, chapels, *penitente morados* and homes in New Mexico. This called for a fair representation of the most important of them in each place of worship, and every family possessed as many as they could afford. In filling the need for this multitude of saints the artists of the time were employed in painting and carving their images, episodes in their lives or the manner of their martyrdom. These artists were known locally as *santeros* and their paintings and carvings as *santos*. There were about twenty of them whose styles or techniques were so distinctive that their work, wherever encountered, is easily recognized. Some of the best known also painted altars and reredos.

These artists had no access to canvas or oils in devising the paintings which were known as *santo retablos*. For a background they split panels from sections of smooth grained pine logs, for there were no sawmills in the colony for sawing boards. The panels they adzed by hand. One side of a panel was then covered with a coating of calcined gypsum mixed with glue and water. This made, when dry, a smooth white surface. For paints the same Indian dyes were used that were employed for coloring the wools in blanket weaving and gave very much the same effect as fresco painting. When a painting was finished it was given a protective coating of light varnish made by dissolving *piñon* pine gum in spirits made from maize.

The statues or *santo bultos* were usually carved from the roots of cottonwood trees which were easily worked and these were then covered with the gypsum and glue preparation and colored in the same manner as the *santos retablos*. To a large extent these *santos* are portraits of Colonials. A neighbor of the artist plowing in his field became San Ysidro, the farmers' saint, while the belle of the community was represented as the Queen of Heaven. Thus the saints were created in the images of the people themselves and were therefore quite satisfying. After the arrival of the Americans and more sophisticated European priests, the making of these *santos* ceased and gaudily colored prints and unpleasant plaster casts began to take their places. It was explained to the natives by these later-comers that saints are blond and not dark complexioned like themselves, that none of the saints had worn the costumes of Spanish Colonials nor had the Queen of Heaven donned the hoop style dress of Queen Isabella of Spain.

In all the Spanish-New Mexican arts, the further the workers got from Spain, the more their work showed the influence of the Indian blood which entered into practically all except a few of the more aristocratic families of the colony. Native birds and animals played a large part in design. The Spanish lion lost his mane and acquired a long curving tail similar to the puma, the wild lion of New Mexico. Patterns of fine needlework such as the women embroidered on sheets of native cotton cloth, with the ends of blanket yarns, gradually began to resemble less the elaborate scrolls of the priest's vestments and were worked directly from motives of everyday life. One of the favorite designs called Adam and Eva, done in the later period, would convince anyone that the Garden of Eden was in New Mexico.

Many articles made of tin, such as picture frames, small boxes and candlesticks, plainly drew their designs from Indian sources, especially from the hammered gold work of the Aztecs. As the Spanish designs were lost to memory and the proportion of Indian blood increased, the workers showed extraordinary fertility of invention, and it is nearly impossible to persuade one of them today to copy an old piece exactly as it is given to him. He can never understand why he must not make alterations more to his own mind. Nor will a native craftsman make any two pieces exactly alike. He marvels at the *Americano* who wants them so.

THEY all of them take great delight in their work. And it is pathetic to see the renewal of happiness and self-respect in the older workers on finding their handicrafts, so long despised, welcomed and appreciated. Both Celso Gallegos and José Dolores Lopez, our most popular wood carvers, will reduce their prices when sales slow down, rather than be deprived of the pleasure of making new pieces. It is true that although these people have lived with the Americans for two generations, many of them never took any part in current social events until they began, a few years ago, to come forward to help the American artists in some of their undertakings. They associate the revival of their own arts—and truly—with the arrival in New Mexico of poets and painters. Sometimes the old men can be seen at the yearly Spanish Fair on De Vargas, beaming ecstatically, with tears in their eyes, at the exhibition of arts and crafts they had feared were lost forever.

Junipero Serra Museum *San Diego, California*

Bell Towers and Capitals

By WILLIAM TEMPLETON JOHNSON, A.I.A.

ONE of the most interesting characteristics in the colonial architecture of Spanish New Mexico was the bolster capital. Hewn from pine wood, roughly carved with chisel and gouge, it decorated the *portales,* and used as a corbel, supported the ceiling beams of the buildings reared by the settlers. It was the most architectural and most striking detail of their constructions of sun-dried bricks and pine timber and its origin excites our curiosity. In this case the road leads to Rome. One of the principal details of the Roman classic cornice was the acanthus leaf modillion or bracket. This modillion was a familiar motive in the Italian Renaissance, and there are rare instances in Italian architecture of the use of the bolster capital as the crowning member of columns. When the Renaissance penetrated Spain, it attained a freedom and abandon less prevalent in the Italy of classic precedent and was used in the collonades of palace after palace in the Iberian Peninsula. Following the path of exploration it crossed the Atlantic, appeared in simplified form in Mexico, then traveled northward two thousand miles with the *conquistadores* to Santa Fe where, changed from stone to wood and reduced to simple forms, it is seen today in buildings three hundred years old and is characteristic of modern adaptations of the colonial architecture.

Spanish explorers, invading Mexico early in the sixteenth century, found there and southward toward the Isthmus of Panama, the only architecture worthy of the name in North America, as expressed by the great structures of the Mayas, the Toltecs and the Aztecs. Anxious to implant the Christian religion in Mexico, the Spaniards destroyed the native temples and built churches. The land was fabulously rich in gold and silver, labor was plentiful and religious zeal fervent. By the beginning of the nineteenth century there were upwards of twelve thousand religious edifices in Mexico. The traveler today stumbles upon some village of a couple of thousand inhabitants and finds there three domed churches all of masonry and carved stone of real architectural merit. This development in Mexico followed close upon the heels of the Renaissance in Spain, the period of that country's greatest prosperity and most brilliant artistic attainment. In the new land, Aztec influence is frequently perceptible, giving a barbaric touch to the more conventional design of the old country. A hundred years of almost constant revolution have wrought much destruction in Mexico; but fortunately for lovers of good building, an enduring record of Mexican architecture was obtained in 1901 by Sylvester Baxter of Boston and published in ten portfolios of photographs with a careful explanatory text.

With the colonization of our Southwest by the Spanish from Mexico, twenty-five churches were erected in the Rio Grande Valley by 1630. The newcomers found the Indians living a communal life in buildings that they viewed in amazement, great rookeries sometimes as high as five stories and containing from five hundred to a thousand rooms. The architecture of the Indian pueblos, with its antecedents among the cliff dwellers, represented the most advanced type of aboriginal building in what is now the United States, but was nevertheless very crude. Walls were sometimes made of stone with mud joints, reinforced with small chips of stone pressed into the interstices. In the majority of cases, however, the construction was of mud, puddled between framing perhaps of wattled work or hides. As the colonists had to depend almost entirely upon Indian labor for their building enterprises, it is quite natural that what they evolved in the new region was influenced by the native product.

THE result was that even before the landing of the Pilgrims, there was born in the region of Santa Fe a style of architecture which sprang from the soil, from the excellent clay of the region and from the pine forests. A thousand miles from the nearest town in Mexico, this architectural style was like nothing else in the world. What emerged was Indian in feeling and Spanish in plan and detail, archaic, crude, picturesque and admirably suited to the needs of the people. The Spanish taught the Indians the art of making adobe bricks, bricks containing straw as in biblical times—and today adobes are still used in New Mexico and Arizona. They adopted the thick walls and roof construction of the Indians, but made their buildings usually one story high and increased the sizes of rooms, enlarged the door and window openings, and introduced typical Spanish and Mexican motives such as *portales* and *patios*. Here it was that the recessed "portal" or covered porch with pine *vigas* (beams) and wooden columns with bolster capitals became one of the most typical features of the style. Another feature always present in rooms of large area such as churches was the use of wooden corbels either single or double, and in one case known to the writer, triple, for supporting the ceiling beams.

With its flowing horizontal lines and informal plan, its simple wood lintels and inviting *portales*, the style had a flavor all its own, but the time came when its charm was not appreciated. After the American occupation in 1846, the sturdy old Palace of the Governors at Santa Fe was decorated with a Mary Ann portico. Twenty years ago people began to realize their mistake. The very attractive station of the Santa Fe railroad was built in the old manner. This was followed by the Museum of New Mexico at Santa Fe, an admirable adaptation of the old forms to new uses. The Post Office and a new hotel on the site of the old Fonda followed suit in the Santa Fe style, as it is called.

IT was in 1769, over a hundred and fifty years after the settlement of Santa Fe, that Fray Junipero Serra planted the royal standard of Spain upon California soil and founded at San Diego the Mission San Diego de Alcala, the first of a chain of mission churches constructed in rapid succession during the next forty years and reaching six hundred miles north to the Bay of San Francisco.[1] The California Indians were not builders like their brethren of the pueblos of the Rio Grande Valley, so the missions had no local precedent to influence them. The *padres'* buildings were simple structures with massive adobe walls covered with stucco. They made tiles for walls and roofs, neither of which were used in New Mexico, but the most striking difference between the two styles was the use of the Roman arch for windows and arcades. Adobe is not an enduring building material unless kept in repair, and after the American occupation in 1846, many of the missions fell in ruins. Those at San Luis Rey, San Juan Capistrano, Santa Barbara, Carmel and a few others give us picturesque glimpses of what the missions were a hundred years ago, and in 1929 there was dedicated in San Diego, the Junipero Serra Museum, built upon the spot where white civilization began in California, and designed to preserve for all time the historical data of its vicinity. It is planned in the simple style of the Franciscans but of enduring concrete. Tiles from the old Mission San Diego de Alcala, of which but little remains, were brought and laid in the entrance doorway—tiles made by hand but in perfect condition after a century and a half.

For a time "Mission" architecture, a modification of the Franciscan church forms, attained a popularity in California. The Santa Fe station hotels at Barstow and Albuquerque (N. M.), and the Mission Inn at Riverside, are prominent examples. The style, however, was heavy and difficult to adapt for types of buildings other than churches. Many horrors were committed in its name and as a style it is practically dead.

The expositions in San Francisco and San Diego in 1915, coincident to the opening of the Panama Canal, were a salutary influence in promoting the use of Mexican and Spanish design in California. At San Diego the directors retained as consulting architect Bertram G. Goodhue who in his youth had been Mr. Baxter's lieutenant in his Mexican studies, and who projected a group of structures in semi-tropical surroundings, so beautiful and so harmonious in composition that they set a new standard in exposition architecture. The building of the State of California, a permanent structure with a tiled dome and graceful campanile, is typical though in no sense a copy of the Spanish Colonial churches in Mexico. One of the temporary buildings suggests strongly the Palace of Monterey at Salamanca, Spain, another the Sanctuario of Guadalupe at Guadalajara, Mexico. The Fine Arts Gallery, built in 1925-6 replacing one of the temporary buildings, is an example of how successfully Spanish Renaissance of the sixteenth century may be blended with Mexican design of the eighteenth.

With such striking precedent for examples, contemporary architecture of California incorporates elements which are met with in Italy, Spain and Mexico. This is illustrated in the evolution of the bungalow. Twenty years ago bungalows were built of wood and their design had a strong oriental influence. This style was followed by another less artistic and quite absurd, enormous columns or piers being used to support nothing more than porch roofs. With the introduction and perfection of colored stuccoes and tiles, Spanish and Mexican motives have been emphasized. In many instances builders overloaded their creations with misplaced ornament, but today thousands of very small houses are built that are altogether charming.

The renascence of good architecture in California is nowhere more marked than in Santa Barbara. A few of the old Spanish Colonial adobe houses remained and these were saved from destruction. Using them as models and influenced too by the simple but harmonious architecture of Andalusia in southern Spain, Santa Barbara is developing a local style of its own, with many beautiful houses built by people of ample means. The Community Arts Association has through awards and competitions aroused much enthusiasm in small house design and for three years running Santa Barbara won first prize in the Better Homes in America competition. After the earthquake an architectural advisory committee was appointed which passed upon all plans for reconstruction. This committee furnished gratis to the small shop owners, who had been hard hit, appropriate plans for repairs and rebuilding and set the stamp of good design upon State Street, or Estado, as it is now called. Excellent work but with less unity is being done all over Southern California.

THE Southwest was settled by people of a pioneering spirit, seeking the end of the rainbow, the untried, the unknown. Successive migrations have brought men and women of a roving disposition ready for change, for new modes of life, new forms of building. A profound influence is the similarity of climate between Spain, Italy and southern California.

The bolster capital as we have seen traveled the long road from Rome: ceramic tiles now artistically made in California originated with the Moors. The art of juxtaposition of concentrated ornament with broad, simple wall surfaces comes from Spain. Aztec and even Mayan ornament have been used to some extent. The towers and domes of Mexico have first cousins in many a town of the Southwest. Yet the surprising thing is that the product is not Spanish, nor Italian, nor Mexican but a flourishing plant of old roots in new soil—vigorous and sometimes vulgar, but with the virility of youth which promises results of far reaching beauty.

[1] The missions at San Antonio, Texas, and Tucson, Arizona, while more florid than the California work, have many of the same characteristics.

Photograph by Tina Modotti

MEXICAN WOMAN

By JOSE CLEMENTE OROZCO

Santa Susana

By AMANDA MATHEWS CHASE

A UNITED STATES back yard had been made into a Mexican tenement court by shacks all along the fence. Where, in Old Mexico, the fountain would have splashed, here a tipsy hydrant leaned and dripped.

Doña Soledad patted *tortillas* at her kitchen table, Americanized *tortillas,* poor flabby things made from white flour instead of stone-ground corn. She was taller, whiter, and more spare than the Indian-type *señoras* dubbing away at their washboards about the hydrant.

Quite automatically she reached for the nearest dab of dough. Her splendid dark-ringed eyes were live coals of wrath still smouldering from her breakfast clash with her husband, Don Estéban, now gone to his day's labor in cement. Right there across the tabe he had sat. She saw him now —a big man and rather fair, with straight features and crisply curling black locks. He had a dashing, well-dressed way with him even in his overalls and jumper. Juan, her worshipped only child, dark, elfish, usually fearful and awestruck in the presence of his step-father, had bubbled forth a message from his teacher, about all the mothers being invited to join the Mothers' Class at school. He had begged her to come.

Then Don Estéban had growled in his throat and pounded the table until he rocked the coffee clear out of his cup. Oh yes, he had advanced his reason—his single, stalwart, and righteous reason—for all his refusals; namely, that he was a Mexican husband. Indeed, he was a super-husband of that variety.

This second marriage of Doña Soledad had closed a long, miserably skimped widowhood in Old Mexico, which had lasted since Juan, now nine, was a baby. Her brothers had families of their own. They had backed the suit of this smart worker about to return to the prosperity of the United States. His roughly passionate wooing had been a happy excitement, but—God save us—the difference between a lover and a husband! Here she was, forbidden ever to step outside the courtyard. The man was gone all day, but it seemed to her as if his will remained guarding the street gate like some invisible bulldog.

Through the open kitchen door, Doña Soledad regarded with aloof disfavor escaping billows of chemise between the nondescript waists and sloppy skirts of the washers. Yet she derived no appreciable consolation from her downward survey of her own stiffly clean bungalow apron. Don Estéban bought all her clothes according to his own egotistic and assertive taste, fetched them home and awaited her raptures, with his heavy-hitting hand ready to enforce appreciation. Nor did he ever fail to inform her that the garment was the ultimate and crowning benefaction of a model Mexican husband. In her own right, Doña Soledad was endowed with the lovely dignity of the "black shawl." That caste of exquisite Mexican womanhood wear always long-draped, dark-hued apparel, and thus hold themselves above the peon rainbow, while not aspiring to the butterfly tints of the patricians. The bungalow apron, Don Estéban's latest gift, was practically sleeveless; it showed wide bands of her detested purple stockings above her high-buttoned shoes. Its color was the crudest of pinks, plaided with the crudest of greens. The pockets were baskets holding whole bouquets of gaudy appliqué flowers. And the badge of Doña Soledad's ingratitude still dimly showed upon her face.

Yet even as she stood there, wrapping the finished *tortillas* in their cloth, she caught the admiring glances cast upon this bungalow apron by the washers at their tubs. She knew that to these women her resistances seemed not only futile but well over the border of impiety. Not that she had shared her troubles, but the shacks were crowded close together and were sound-porous, so all the neighbors must have some sketchy understanding of her situation.

Doña Soledad roused to languid interest in the peculiar tactics of Doña Amalia, her neighbor of the shack directly across the court. She was shorter, plumper, darker than Doña Soledad, yet with the same assurance of bearing which set those two somewhat above the splashing creatures at the tubs. Doña Soledad's face always betrayed the ferment of mental processes, while Doña Amalia matched this with a shrewdness of gathered wisdom wrinkling around her eyes. She, too, wore a bungalow apron, but an all-enveloping one of black sateen which Doña Soledad envied upon sight.

TODAY, however, Doña Amalia's self-assurance was evidently under some unusual strain. Doña Soledad's sombre eyes watched her neighbor come to the doorway of her shack, gaze reflectively at the washers, even set her foot outside her door and then draw back. At last, though, Doña Amalia made a real emergence, and walked resolutely to the first washer. Doña Soledad caught only an occasional word, but having already heard of the Mothers' Class at school, she made out what Doña Amalia was undertaking.

The one addressed straightened herself indignantly and waved her dripping hand to indicate the flock of pre-kindergarten infants who were alternately rolling in the mud about the faucet and the dust that bounded the mud. She resumed her washing with a plunge so vigorous that gray suds splashed the black sateen apron of Doña Amalia. That lady accepted the rebuff and the suds with a deprecating smile as really no more than she had expected and perhaps even deserved. Yet she pulled together her evidently slipping determination and stepped along to the next washer.

This one dramatically smote her forehead with her knuckles to prove how hard her head was, and passed the proposition up with a wide-mouthed laugh. Again Doña Amalia was able to evoke her meek and near-apologetic smile. For she was fracturing that unspoken non-interference code which secures whatever peace exists amid the temperamental dynamite of a Mexican court. Doña Soledad saw that Doña Amalia was now intent on nothing except decent retreat. Eagerly she called her over and ushered her into the kitchen. At least she could have the satisfaction of hearing more about this forbidden Mothers' Class.

"The teacher gives a beautiful blue cup and saucer for

bringing in a new pupil," the visitor explained in an easy equal-to-equal confession. "But it's not just the cup, it's her joyful look for a new member." And in this unexpected sun of Doña Soledad's sympathy, the visitor poured out the delights of the Mothers' Class.

Doña Soledad listened with a great and wonderful thrill. In the morning she had been angered by her husband's refusal merely as another refusal. But in her there was always this ferment of a mind, and now the Mothers' Class seemed what she had longed for since her time began. She listened and listened with all her thirsty soul.

Then her hands fell into her lap with an audible thump.

"Mi esposo es muy delicado."

In this euphonious manner did Doña Soledad state her domestic situation so that the older woman would have understood perfectly even if not previously enlightened by the common gossip of the shacks. And the visitor could not resist one gloating purr:

"Mi viejo es muy pacifico."

Then she was ashamed of having flaunted her "pacific old man" in the face of the woman with a *delicado* husband.

"At school," she began penitently, "there is a big picture of Santa Susana. She is the saint of the American women. It seems that in the older time American husbands were no better than ours. Then came Santa Susana, who walked this country crying always 'Justice for women! Justice for women!' She was reviled by men and women alike. But she went up and down from house to house and from town to town, always begging justice for women. Then American wives became brave and American husbands became gentle and now the world has no such spectacle as the kindness of the American husband. And his wife would die for him as quickly as for her son."

"Santa Susana! Santa Susana!" murmured the astonished Doña Soledad. "Why, just to speak her blessed name lends me courage. . . . I will give Juan his lunch when he comes from school. My husband works far from here. I will go to the Mothers' Class with you today. I would look upon the face of this Santa Susana!"

Two good hours before her husband was expected, Doña Soledad returned from the schoolhouse. Her face was glowing as she gaily waved *adios* to Doña Amalia and entered her own dwelling.

There sat Don Estéban, glowering in a kitchen chair, his left arm in a bloody bandage and supported from the other shoulder. He had caught the rosy radiant happiness of her before she had descried him huddled at the table. Her face blanched but she rushed to his side, setting up the wailing coronach over his injury which was his due and which indeed came spontaneously enough.

"Oh, Estéban! You are hurt! Your poor arm! Tell me what happened."

His angry eyes repelled without releasing her. His answer was a growl of wrath so deep in his throat as to be almost inarticulate.

"Where have you been? Me—to come home injured—an empty house—my deceiving wife. Who put that happiness into your ever-complaining countenance? I'll kill—"

"Only to the school," faltered the wife. "I learned—some English words—"

"You disobeyed me—your Mexican husband. I can teach you all the words you need—to address me. You have no other need of words."

He rose and moved toward her. But she had already begun desperately to heat the *frijoles* and to get the coffee on the stove. He flung himself back into his chair with a force that nearly wrecked it. She understood that he would keep the lid clamped down on his fury until supper was safely on the table, since in punishing his wife he might disable his cook.

JUAN stood in the doorway, the dark elf of a boy, who did not flourish more on the abundance of the present, along with its continuous emotional storm, than on the scantiness of the peaceful past. The boy had overheard and his eerie little face registered hate, while his fists doubled in puny threat. His mother knew that Don Estéban held the almost superstitious conviction which dictates that no man may lay hands on another man's child. But she realized also that his present temper might overleap any bounds. Hence she crowded *tortillas* into the child's hands and hastily sent him off to the street.

Doña Soledad set the food upon the table. She noted that her husband used the injured arm when he forgot and she surmised that the injury was not serious. The man ate with his hat pushed back upon his head. He signified the end of the meal by dragging it down to his bushy eyebrows. She had kept out of range of his right arm during her movements about the table and she had some hope that now, slightly pacified by food, he might not strike.

When he rose and came at her, she screamed and ran into the bed-room. He followed and, with what was luckily a glancing blow, he felled her across the bed. She lay there sobbing stormily while he strode from the house, still growling in his throat. Three women at the hydrant heard and crossed themselves. Two men coming in from work exchanged wise grins as they respectfully sidestepped the outgoing husband.

There on the bed, gasping, stinging, burning, aching, her tumbled black hair falling across the darkening bruise, Doña Soledad's sobs tore her to pieces, and the tearing brought all the relief there was. When the reaction from her *coraje* set in an hour later, she had a burned-out look, as if she were ready at any touch to go into grey-white ash and so be cooled at last.

In the quietness of her exhaustion, mental wheels went to turning once more. She knew that (*Continued on page* 190)

PORTRAIT ***By Kenneth Adams***

Drawings by N. O'Neil Ford

San Antonio

The Old Capital City of Mexican Life and Influence

By MAX SYLVIUS HANDMAN

THE center of Mexican San Antonio is filled every evening and late afternoon and particularly on Saturday and Sunday with men with big sombreros, mellow eyes and gentle expressions and with women with their heads wrapped in dark shawls, gliding along in a soft and shuffling walk. The on-coming generation, however, promenading up and down, presents a different picture. Young dandies put as much glitter in their attire as modern clothes will permit, while Mexican flappers wear the American flappers' garb of independence with more dash and grace than the originators. Here in the Mexican business district are the moving-picture theaters, the *Nacional* and the *Zaragossa,* the leading and very important Spanish paper, restaurants, bookstores of which there are many, grocery stores kept by Chinese merchants for Mexican trade, music stores emanating a constant stream of *jotas* and love songs along with the ever-present music of the military band.

In a little park, groups of Mexicans sit on the benches or squat on the ground conversing in soft tones while occasionally a reader, paid or voluntary, entertains his audience with an instalment of a perennial Monte-Christo story. Further down there is a large paved open square, used as a market-place in the daytime, but turned into a colorful outdoor eating place at night. Long tables illuminated by lanterns, red, blue and yellow, accommodate an ever-changing stream of men, women and children, eating the traditional Mexican dishes. Here and there a duet of singers and players on the guitar intone one of those endless ballads—*corridos*—dealing with the events of the life of the community or with the doings of some famous president or bandit, equally dear to their peasant hearts. The district finally shades off into more dubious types of business—fortune tellers, tattoo artists, shooting galleries and second-hand stores. But after a few more steps we are in the region of skyscrapers and American San Antonio begins.

In this American San Antonio, geography has for a long time held the whip hand and has compelled the city to come somehow to terms with a little stream which meanders lazily through it. Willy nilly the lay of the land has compelled a certain charming arrangement of unexpected turns which, striking and avoiding a number of open plazas, end in narrow pre-automobile streets which squeeze through iron bridges and lead on through a maze of tree-lined thoroughfares. San Antonio has not tried very hard to escape from this geography-given charm. Rather it has tried to contribute to it by building a municipal auditorium and setting it in a wide open space which lends dignity to the beautiful structure. But restraint as an element of beauty is something which it is hard to impress upon a community which has spent millions in an effort to be attractive in the modern manner; and so a battery of powerful lights which play on the auditorium at night deprive one of the pleasure of seeing its graceful lines and cupolas against one of those bewitching summer skies of central Texas which is one of the most unforgettable experiences.

Steel construction has struck the city which is now busy acquiring a skyline of skyscrapers, symbol of progress and high real-estate values. Yet the old quaintness still shines through this heavy covering of brick and mortar; the river still meanders lazily and one can go on some warm evening to the oldest hotel in town and eat his dinner in an open *patio*. One can still drive through streets with old houses hidden among trees and palms and can still have the colorful Mexican quarter to fall back upon, with its occasional stone dwellings covered with plaster. Their thick walls and few windows date from the days when the fear of the Indian marauder had not yet been completely extinguished. Children run in and out filling the air with a musical chatter. The porches are stacked with flower-pots; bird-cages hang in abundance; and every now and then a parrot screeches out a dubious welcome. On the empty lots there stand little shacks covered with brightly-enameled pieces of tin telling one what to drink, what to smoke, and what to chew. In these shacks diminutive stores of eatables are retailed by men full of years and dignity.

THE presence of the Mexican in San Antonio is not a recent phenomenon. He is in fact the original inhabitant. The so-called Governor's Palace, the habitation of the pre-American representative of law and order, the earliest church, the Cathedral of San Fernando, the Alamo, an early Spanish-Mexican religious establishment, now hallowed as the great monument to Texan hero-martyrs—all these attest to a direct filiation between the Mexicans who were at one time the dominating element, and the Mexicans who now, in larger number than at any time during their control, are in the main the hewers of wood and drawers of water of San Antonio's industrial civilization.

According to statistics compiled in 1929 by the municipal school authorities, 56 per cent of the children enrolled in the primary schools bore Mexican names; 22 per cent in the junior high-schools; 9 per cent in the senior highschools. These percentages give a clearer picture of the place of the Mexican population in San Antonio than could be gathered at present in any other way. That population, probably 90,000 out of a total of 265,000 (including some 30,000 colored) is in the main made up of what is called the peon class, a name which is often used to describe the manner of living of the Mexicans as well as to excuse the failure of the community to supply them with better living conditions. What strikes one forcibly who has looked into their life in San Antonio is the utter indifference of the community to their presence; it is an indifference which is palpable, almost blatant. Exceptions are the school system, the active International Institute of the Y.W.C.A., the health and social agencies, municipal and private, and the efforts of church organizations to do some work under the guise of faith. Their own natural leaders take no interest in them—the Mexican political "boss" is an Italian. The Mexican newspapers are more concerned with what is doing in old Mexico. The Mexican middle-class is busy making a living in its own way. The doctors probably take more interest in the lot of the masses than any others. When unemployed, when in trouble, when sick, when in need the Mexican turns to his own patriarchal organization, which fortunately still is strong enough in this new environment not to leave him in the lurch.

That patriarchal organization is the outstanding thing about the Mexican community of San Antonio. The large mass of Mexican humanity breaks up naturally into small groups either on the basis of family or the locality from which they come. To this must be added the relationship of *compadre* (godfather) which imposes real responsibilities upon him who accepts it. The orphaned child, and there are many of them among the Mexicans of San Antonio, is sure of a home and as good care as the other children in the home of the *compadre*.

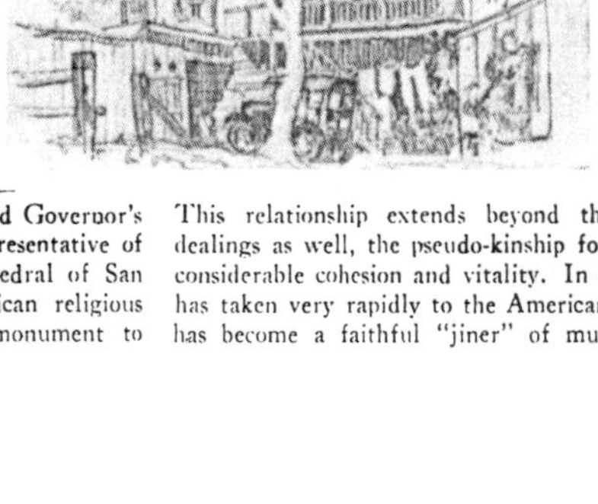

This relationship extends beyond the home to business dealings as well, the pseudo-kinship forming a sub-group of considerable cohesion and vitality. In addition the Mexican has taken very rapidly to the American lodge mores and he has become a faithful "jiner" of mutual benefit societies.

Out of his slender and sometimes all too slender means the Mexican will come readily to the assistance of his brothers in distress, the informal help relationships being far more important than the formal.

A few years ago I directed a survey which was carried out by a group of San Antonio school teachers who made a house-to-house canvass of some 1500 Mexican families. Taking the standard of a "good" house to be that of a modern-built cottage, with sewer connections, bath, toilet, sink, hot and cold water and a kitchen separate from the living quarters, our tabulations yielded exactly one Mexican family that could boast of such a home. (The situation is somewhat improved today because of the activities of certain real-estate dealers and lumber companies who have opened up additions—*colonias*—for the use of the Mexicans.) Of these houses 578 had outside and surface toilets, 159 inside toilets; in 1264 the residents were compelled to go outdoors to obtain their water supply; 39 houses had no windows; and 1141 used kerosene lamps. Half of the owners of these establishments were Americans; a third, Mexicans. As a further side-light on the same problem we found that there were 141 families having seven or more children in the family, that 51 of these had only two rooms in the house, that 28 families of seven children each had only one bed for the entire family and 82 had two beds for seven children plus the adults! It was fortunate that less than 10 per cent of the families were so blessed with offspring; and indeed 40 per cent had less than three children.

OCCUPATIONS and earnings told the same story as housing. Sixty per cent of those investigated were laborers; 25 per cent were skilled workers; 2 per cent were occupied as clerks, and over 5 per cent were engaged in keeping little stores. Half of them averaged around thirteen dollars a week, when they were employed; a fourth of them were employed irregularly even in those times of relative prosperity. The native Mexicans seem to have an all-round advantage over the immigrants—steadier jobs, higher pay and more skilled occupations. They are less inclined to let their women folk go out to work. The same sort of an advantage is found in the case of the English speaking Mexican as over against the non English speaking Mexican. The language was worth $5 a week to them on the average; and American schooling also increased their earning capacity. What modifies this picture, both favorably and unfavorably, is the fact that a very large percentage of Mexican families keep every member gainfully occupied, adding from 25 to 35 per cent to the household income. And yet the earnings per person averaged between $3.50 and $3.75 per week, —hardly enough to supply one with the bare necessities.

The explanation—not that any particular explanation is needed of how poor people with not enough to live on have always managed to live—but, in this case, the explanation is one which runs in the domain of the standard of living. They live by adjusting means which are more American to ends which are more Mexican. If it were not for their patriarchal organization and the chronic semi-starvation to which they have accustomed themselves, they certainly could not manage to exist. Much of the burden of the adjustment falls upon the women. In the main the diet and the personal demands of the Mexican population are still simple enough so that household labor can satisfy them without too great a recourse to pecuniary transactions. A Mexican child gets a *fin-de-siècle* thrill out of a piece of sugar-candy and a cold *tortilla.* An ice cream soda would be a wild and irresponsible debauch. While the food values are less unadjusted to the requirements of adults, such is not the case with children. Calcium is the greatest deficiency, due primarily to a shortage in consumption of milk. As a result, infant mortality and morbidity are high, particularly during the summer months.

All this bears on the contention of the American employer that the Mexican is undoubtedly better off here, even though he receives a most inadequate wage, than he has ever been at home: he is accustomed to little and now he has a little more. But even from the standpoint of the Mexican this position is untenable when looked at a little more closely and particularly when seen from the standpoint of the younger generation. And it is here that the rub comes and that the whole life of the Mexican community receives a different emphasis from what was true across the border.

THE adult immigrant carries into the San Antonio environment a great deal of his pueblo cultural values to which he clings with a tenacity distressing to those who realize the weakness in his position incurred by this lack of adjustment. The younger generation, on the other hand, experiences an entirely different pull. For one thing, in the school system the Mexican child is confronted with a different culture pattern, urged upon him by an almost pathetic reverence and devotion towards the teacher. A second pull comes from actually seeing that culture operate in the dominant group. Seeing it only from the outside, it looks like a shower of fabulous blessings of worldly goods; a world of romantic gorgeousness in its amusements and in its bazar-like offerings. The conflict appears early when Mexican children notice that they are dressed more poorly than some of the others. They often drop out of school in order to earn enough money to buy school supplies, a new pair of shoes, or any garment which they need or think they need. This contrast soon generates a conflict between the two culture patterns and hence between the older and the younger generations.

Under these circumstances to speak of the immigrant Mexicans as being better off than they have been at home is utterly meaningless because they are not at home, they are in America with America's standard of living and particularly with the pitilessly exigent demands of this standard of living. Not to conform very quickly brings down on one the very things from which the Mexican shrinks; and that is scorn, not because he is poor or ill-kempt, or ignorant, or unclean, but because he is a Mexican. Teachers in grade schools—not so much in highschools—have constantly to contend against these cruel ways of American children, cruel not because they are American but because they are children. More than once matters end in a quarrel and a fight—a race war if one wishes to use the terminology of the grown-ups. In schools which are made up exclusively of Mexican children, the same conflict occurs; this time between the child of the Mexican who has left the pueblo culture and has become "Americanized" and the child of him who has not done so. In terms of human suffering the problem is the same.

Of course this is not a new problem. It has confronted the American community with every wave of immigrants which has come to these shores, and it is a wonder that the argument still has to run in the same old terms, in spite of the plentiful experience which we have harvested during all these years. The immigrant comes because he wishes to improve his lot; the American community is willing to accept him because he leaves such a large margin between what is good for him and what is good for us—economically. But we are not—and fortunately we are not, satisfied to keep him in this cultural subordination. We insist that he must become "Americanized," not stopping to realize that Americanization is impossible without higher wages, or wages high enough to live like an American. Racial and national traits always and everywhere have centered mainly on outside appearances: on costume, diet, language, amusements, and social contacts. If the immigrant is to pass for an American, and that is what we mean by Americanization, he must have the things which Americans prize—and they cost money. To assume that one can go on paying low wages to a laborer because he is Mexican and at the same time expose the same laborer to all manner of stimuli forcing him to cease to be one, is certainly living in a fool's paradise.

But as yet the Mexican is docile and timid and painfully eager to conform. In the main he is well behaved. I searched carefully the records of the courts of San Antonio and Bexar County and found that the Mexican criminal does not exceed in proportion his share of the population. In the Juvenile Court he contributes far less than his share. The nature of his delinquency, while slightly different from the delinquency of the non-Mexican, is not a source of danger to law and morals. He is arrested for drunkenness because he drinks in public—there being no club for him to go to. He fights because fighting is respectable in his group. He gets arrested for traffic violations because the second-, or third- or fourth-hand car which he buys from the American dealer is no better than such cars usually are, and because he is often too poor to buy a license. He is arrested for "seduction" because he lives in common-law marriage with a young girl, socially nubile from his Mexican standpoint but not from ours; and he fights with a knife because that is the way poor men fight all over the world.

SAN ANTONIO is a permanent Mexican center. It is a large place of distribution for those who scatter all over Texas, all over the United States to do all manner of unskilled labor. It is also the place where they congregate for the winter months to consume the meager pecuniary returns which they bring with them—waiting in quiet, simple living for the next cotton season or beet season to roll around. Yet the heart of the San Antonio Mexican population is not the nomadic Mexican but the sedentary Mexican. He is an integral part of the life of the community and one wonders how long it can keep him at arm's length as a gentle and irresponsible hewer of wood and drawer of water. The Mexican is intelligent, he is alert, he is sensitive and he is ambitious. He is becoming roused into political self-consciousness by leaders more or less interested in his lot. And after that—what?

SANTA FE WAREHOUSES ETCHING BY O'NEIL FORD

A Dallas scene but in its juxtapositions typical of the outskirts of most southwestern cities

The Vaquero

Ranch Mexicans

By J. FRANK DOBIE

THE word "cowboy" is very old; in Merry England, far back in the Age of Innocence, the cowboy followed on foot the lowing herd winding slowly o'er the lea and was as gentle as the shepherds of pastoral romance. But the cowboy on a bucking bronco, the cowboy armored in leather and spurring with coiled *reata* after fierce longhorns through thickets of prickly pear and barbed *chaparral,* rounding up great herds over vast ranges and then trailing them for a thousand miles to far away markets and ranges—this cowboy is very modern. He dates only from about 1836.

In that year the Republic of Texas gained her independence from Mexico, and almost immediately after the surrender of the Mexican armies, bands of Texans began raiding down on the cattle and horses belonging to *rancheros* between the Nueces River and the Rio Grande. They already knew a little about cattle raising but after they had exchanged this captured stock in the Louisiana markets for gold they realized as never before that what was valuable enough to "lift" was also valuable enough to raise. Thus, broadly speaking, the range industry of Texas, which within forty-five years had spread to the Canadian Rockies and occupied almost the whole virgin world west of the Missouri River, was born.

The English speaking men who carried this industry forward and created a range tradition that yet flourishes learned nearly all they knew about ranching from the *rancheros* and *vaqueros.* The mustang horses that they rode and the long-horned cattle that they lived for and with were Spanish to the core. Cowboy saddle and other paraphernalia, the cowboy manner of riding, the art of roping, the *rodeo* (or roundup), the marking and branding of stock—the whole business of the range industry was taken over from Spanish-Americans. No other industry, or occupation, in the United States, not even mining, shows such a direct derivation from Spanish influences. The very language of the range is Spanish: however corrupted some of the words may have become—*rancho, rodeo, bronco,* (*mestaño*), and the rest, a language familiar to thousands of booted riders who never saw a Mexican *vaquero.* The very growth of soil, the flora, all over the Southwest is popularly known only by Spanish nomenclature, as *mesquite, nopál, chaparrál, ceniza, grama, biznaga, huisache, retama,* etc.

The *vaquero,* then, was the first range rider of North America; his brother in South America took the name of *gaucho.* In the present limits of the United States the *vaquero,* as a precursor of the cowboy, rode two great ranges. He rode in California, where his cattle were long killed for their hides and were then neglected in the mad stampede for gold. He rode on the Rio Grande, on the lower reaches of which the Texans learned from him, took even his name, and drove his cattle forth to stock an empire once occupied by only buffaloes and Indians.

AND the *vaquero* went with the Texans to serve them and teach them. Pioneer ranchmen in the border region depended almost exclusively on Mexican *vaqueros* to do their work. Great domains like the King and Kenedy ranch in southern Texas and Milton Favor's ranch on the old Chihuahua Trail down the river from El Paso employed *vaqueros* by the score. In the spacious times of trail driving that followed the Civil War *corridas* of Mexican *vaqueros* drove herds to Kansas and Wyoming and over the Pecos Trail to meet thirst and Apaches.

But unlike the "white" hands, many of whom remained in the Farwest and the Northwest to establish the traditions of the Texas cowboy, the trailing *vaqueros* generally came back to the border ranges. As time went on, however, they worked farther and farther out from the international line.

Just here it is necessary to refute a popular misconception —the idea that ranching has become a thing of the past. Over millions of acres in the Southwest and West the ranching industry still obtains. The methods of the industry have, thanks to barbed wire, windmills, improved

Fence builder of the Nueces River Country

breeds, and higher prices, changed, but the industry itself has not been supplanted. The ranch hands must often work on foot, building fences and tanks, repairing windmills, even cultivating feed stuffs, but the end of their work is to grow stock and when they work cattle they work on horseback.

IN Texas, where within the last three decades the "dry" farmer has plowed under so much good grass, the amount of land devoted to grazing still amounts to more than is devoted to agriculture. The great coastal belt and immense stretches of post oak and piney woods land are yet grazed, though east of the San Antonio River ranch labor is performed by Negroes and some "whites." The ranches left in the Texas Panhandle and southward to the Texas and Pacific Railroad, which for half a thousand miles between Fort Worth and El Paso runs through ranch country, are worked mostly by "white" cowboys—the punchers. The brushy region lying between the Nueces and the Rio Grande has been called the "nursery" of American ranges; it is still, despite development, a cow nursery, the King ranch here comprising over 1,000,000 acres, the Bill Jones holdings amounting to 500,000 acres, and many other ranches embracing from 50,000 to 300,000 acres each. Mexican *vaqueros* are depended upon to work all this range; a considerable part in two or three border counties is owned by descendants of Spanish families who received grants from the Spanish crown. From San Antonio northwest to El Paso, nearly six hundred miles, the route lies almost wholly through arid grazing lands tended largely by Mexicans. In various parts of New Mexico, Arizona, and California *vaqueros* are extensively employed; they have penetrated Wyoming and Montana also. Nowhere else, however, are they depended upon so widely as in Texas.

The ranges of New Mexico and of other states to the north and west probably employ more *pastores* (shepherds) than they do *vaqueros*.

Today on many ranches of the Southwest, particularly of Texas, one may find Mexicans doing the work that twenty-five years ago and less "white" men were doing. The *vaquero* is supplanting the cowboy. He will work for less, expect less, and often do more—so the ranchmen who employ him say. He is more willing to stay away from town and less given to spurring up automobiles.

On the smaller ranches the *vaquero* is apt to be a kind of roustabout, handy at anything. He is apt to have a family, and his children may once in a while attend the community school. On the larger ranches the *vaqueros* are still a part of something like feudal domain, getting their supplies largely from the ranch commissary, which does not overcharge, depending on other Mexicans of the ranch for human association, voting as the *mayordomo* advises, and very often regarding the ranch, in the manner that other people regard a town or a county, as a unit of citizenship. For instance, a King ranch Mexican calls himself a *Kineño*. Here on these larger ranches the *vaqueros* spend several months each year in camp, working cattle, building and repairing fences, scraping out tanks, in times of extreme drouth singeing the thorns off prickly pear so that cattle can eat it or cutting *sotol* for the same purpose.

If the ranch owner lives away, he has a "white" man for manager. The *caporál*, or foreman, under the manager may be either a Mexican or a "white" man. Frequently "white" hands work along with the Mexicans, particularly in handling cattle; in such cases, however, the *caporál* is nearly always "white" also.

Some of the *vaqueros* live with their families about the "home ranch"; some of them live far separated in remote pastures. The *pastero*, or pasture tender, leads an isolated existence, riding his fences and watching the waterings day

The Arizona vaquero singes and opens this cactus, squeezes the pulp into his cup and has good drinking water

after day, his wife sometimes going for months without seeing another woman.

The pay of the *vaquero* averages $25 or $30 a month, "grub" furnished; about $10 a month more if he furnishes himself. "White" hands receive around $10 a month more than the Mexicans. The *cocinero* (cook) draws $5 more than the *vaquero*. A *jinete* (horse breaker) also draws a premium. The best way to keep ranch Mexicans satisfied is to give them plenty of meat, whether beef or *cabra* (goat). Many ranches in southwest Texas keep herds of common Mexican goats for the purpose of supplying meat.

A Mexican will leave a $35 job on a small ranch where meat and company are scarce to work for $25 a month on a big ranch where he can be with a "crowd" and get plenty of meat.

This vaquero is getting out of the way

IN the land of the *vaquero* there is still, comparatively speaking, remoteness; there is still a kind of primitive simplicity in the ways of living and thinking. Hence the *vaquero* and *pastor* of today retain perhaps more than any other class of laborers the characteristic traits of their simple-lived forefathers. Life for them is almost as free of complexities as it was before the automobile, the radio, and labor unions were invented. Many of the young people of these pastoral families drift away, but those who remain on the ranch accept pretty much without question the stark simplicities that a life of hard labor to the soil requires—and rewards. True, the ranch Mexican now buys ready-made many of the things he used to make for himself; but the arts of weaving cinches out of horse mane, of fashioning *reatas* out of rawhide, of tanning buckskin, and of plaiting quirts and cow whips are not yet lost arts. He no longer burns cow chips to make soda, but he brews tea of the *ceniza* (a kind of sage) to cure inflammation of the chest, and tea of the San Nicolás herb affords a beverage as delectable to him as that of the Chinese herb is to any four-o'clock Englishman. He wants to sleep under a shingle roof and has become awkward at thatching with bear-grass, but he can trail a cow or any wild animal as unerringly as Comanche warrior ever trailed.

The caporál or foreman of the vaqueros. The gun is only a badge of dignity and authority

He may or may not speak English. The nearer he is to the Border and the bigger the ranch he works on the less English he hears, for the *Americanos* of the border ranches almost without exception talk Spanish, often interlarding their own language with racy Mexican idioms. These *Americanos*, being to the manner born, have, incidentally, few of the labor problems that bother newly-come farmers and tradesmen. The majority of ranch Mexicans—that is to say the men—can spell out simple print, but one who subscribes for even a weekly paper is a rare exception, and the *amo* (master) is frequently called upon to write letters for his dependents. The ranch Mexican's library is likely to be confined to an almanac, a book of dreams, and a pamphlet of testimonials and directions found wrapped around some bottle of patent medicine.

He may possess a cheap phonograph and a few records, but the best music he hears is what he and his *compañeros* make while singing in camp at night to the accompaniment of wailing coyotes. I wish I could describe the song of the *vaquero*. I cannot. It is a wail; it is, no matter what its theme, a note of sorrow, of something far, far away. It seems to go quivering up to the stars; it is wild; it is barbaric. It may be about a *ladino* (outlaw) steer roped out in the brush; it may be about a *caballo fragado* (broken down horse) that some *vaquero* has had to lead in; it may be the old and haunting *Golondrina* or the sad ballad of the *Cuatra Milpas*. Often it concerns itself with such heroes as Pancho Villa or some daring border smuggler killed by Texas rangers. The *vaquero* sings best after a big supper of fresh beef. Well filled with good meat, he must sing or bust.

He is full of stories about buried treasures, which priests

and *gachupines* are usually somehow connected with and which are guarded by white *bultos,* clanking chains, eerie lights and other mysteries. If he does not know a witch, he knows of one. If he does not fear the evil eye, he respects it. If he or any of his family become very ill, he wants a doctor, but at the same time he yearns for a *curandéro* (a kind of quack that a whole essay would be required to picture forth). He is familiar with the habits of every creature of his soil. For him every hill and hollow has a personality and a name. He regards the stars; he watches the phases of the moon. He knows the name and virtue of every bush and herb. He is a child of nature; he is truly *un hombre del campo.*

Either despite or because of his nearness to nature, he is as insensible to the sufferings of nature's progeny as nature is herself. He will run his horse into thorns and then have no thought of pulling the thorns out; he will ride a thirsty horse within fifty yards of a water hole and unless he himself is thirsty will not turn aside. He will rub sand into the eyes of a wild cow that he has roped, though in this he is no more cruel than the average old-time cowpuncher. He will sit all day in the shade of his *jacal* and never offer to carry a bucket of water for his over-worked wife. Of course this picture is of averages; there are exceptions.

For all that, the *vaquero* is kind to his family, sets no limit to his hospitality, and probably goes beyond the average human being in faithfulness. He will divide his last *tortilla* with any stranger who happens by. He will take the side of his *amo,* if he likes him, against any Mexican that tries to do his *amo* an injustice. The reputation he has somehow acquired in literature for being treacherous is, I believe, altogether undeserved. Almost the best friend, outside of my family, that I have ever had is an old Mexican *vaquero.* Once when as a result of being thrown by a horse my back was wrenched this *vaquero* nursed me alone for days, rubbing in "Volcanic oil" and applying hot prickly pear poultices; he nursed too a few poor cattle that were about to die and ruin me. Many a time "out in the pasture" I have put my lips to the same water jug that he had drunk from; at the same time neither he nor I would think of his eating at the dining table with me.

Yet if he were in want, I should go far to try to relieve him; and if I were dying and he could by going to hell save me, he would go. Once, after he had been on our place for a quarter of a century or more and after our family had been away for years, I asked him if he were going to leave also. "No," he replied, "*yo tengo raizes aqui.*" (I have roots here.) His name is Genardo del Bosque. I shall never forget him.

Clay Statuette by Hidalgo

THE *pastor,* so far as nearness to nature and simplicity of character are concerned, is very much like the *vaquero.* He is, however, of a different order. The *vaquero* looks down upon him. Years of solitude with goats and sheep are calculated to make anybody "queer." Many *pastores* are not only queer and cranky but "cracked." In Colorado, so I have heard, there is a law against an employer keeping a man out alone with sheep or goats beyond a certain duration of time. The law is calculated to prevent lunacy. Whether it has succeeded I do not know.

The *pastor* is the chief of weather prophets. Snails, snakes, coyotes, buzzards—everything that creeps, crawls, or flies can be converted by him into a favorable sign of rain. He can tell by the way nanny goats treat their kids whether the season is to be drouthy or productive of forage. If the signs are not right, he "cuts," or quarters, the sky with his staff to make it rain.

In kidding season he can stake out two hundred kids in the morning and when the nannies come in at night place each stupid one with her proper offspring, though to an outsider the nannies and the kids all look as much alike as so many peas in a pod.

Goat- and sheep-proof fences, together with the extermination of predatory animals, are now making the *pastor's* occupation unnecessary in many places, for in a well-fenced pasture free of predatory animals, sheep and goats may be turned loose to roam at will. However, on the vast unfenced domain of New Mexico and other western states these animals are still in charge of *pastores.* Here the *pastor* wanders about with his flocks, camping for a while at one watering and then at another, all his goods packed on a burro or two or in a little wagon. He cannot absent himself from his charges for even a day, except at rare times when he may be relieved. At intervals his boss or the *vaciero* (man in charge of a number of sheep camps) brings supplies to him. A saying has it that "the best way to keep a *pastor* is to keep him in debt." In regions where herders are no longer required, Mexicans do an increasing amount of the labor incident to lambing, or kidding, and to shearing.

Very often the *pastor* has one or more dogs to aid him. His way of training these shepherd dogs is to take them while they are pups and let them suck a nanny or ewe. His hissings and yellings at his charges seem to one unaccustomed to hearing them outlandish and ludicrous; but the goats and sheep appear to understand them. Sometimes he mumbles to them for company; sometimes he mumbles to himself. If he had more sense, his life would be tragic; also, if he had more sense, he would not be a *pastor.* He hears a pair of mourning doves cooing at each other and the interpretation he gives of their cooing well enough expresses his own ideals.

One dove says: "Coo-coo. *¿Qué quieres, pastor? qué quieres?*" (What do you want, pastor? what do you want?)

The answer is: *"Comer comas, comer comas."* (To eat coma berries, to eat coma berries.)

The coma is a thorned bush that bears a berry fit for birds and eaten by *pastores.* It is about the only fruit or delicacy that some *pastores* get. *Probrecitos!*

Keglar Hill

By ROBERT H. MONTGOMERY

THIS is the story of Keglar Hill. It is in process of becoming the story of the cotton belt of Texas—a large chapter in the story of the state.

Thirty years ago Keglar Hill was fair among the thousands of prosperous cotton communities in rural Texas, with its three hundred souls, predominantly Anglo-American with a small sprinkling of German and Irish among them, its Methodist congregation counting over a hundred and fifty communicants, and its three-teacher school which was the pride of Caldwell county. Its black-waxy soil was prodigiously fertile, a cotton crop of a bale-to-the-acre being a good average yield.

Today Keglar Hill lives only in a few memories. Its school-house is a hay barn; its meeting house a mule stable. Its lands are leached and gullied and over-run by Johnson grass and tie vines. They rarely produce a quarter of a bale of cotton per acre. Its fine old homes are crumbling and shapeless, inhabited by an improvident foreign tenantry. The rush of strange years has carried its sons and grandsons to new lands and unaccustomed tasks. Keglar Hill as a way of life is gone. And this is the tale.

In 1860 Joe Keglar came down from the western hill country with his flock of sheep, and moved out onto the rolling black prairie on the border between Hays and Caldwell counties. The German farmers and American cattlemen had been encroaching upon his open range in the well-watered and wooded hill country. The prairie lands were still unfenced, largely unclaimed, and offered excellent pasturage for his flock and unlimited wild game for his larder. For five years Keglar and his sheep held unmolested possession over leagues of virgin black soil. A small hillock, whose ravines supplied water for his earthen tanks, and whose live oak motts furnished wood for his campfires and brush for a crude sheep pen, became known as Keglar Hill. Then a cattle company with vast holdings in southwest Texas secured title to a huge block of land in Keglar's range. Keglar went to his Fathers, but left his name to the community that came after.

In that same year a host of ragged soldiers returned to their homes in Georgia and Alabama and Mississippi. Once prosperous farmers found their homes in ashes, their livestock gone—"stolen" by Federal or "purchased" by Confederate troops, their implements worn and rusted and rotted away, their fences down, and their fields abandoned to weeds and wild grasses. A labor force in the intoxication of a new and untried status, and a batch of worthless paper money offered slight inducement for the bitter task of rebuilding an economic order.

Under such conditions many of the younger men turned their faces toward the fabled lands of the Southwest. In 1872 two of these, from Alabama, after four years of dubious fortune in the older farming communities of Hays county, moved into the vicinity of Keglar Hill. Each purchased a hundred acres of land for one dollar an acre, cash, and two hundred acres at two dollars an acre, credit. For several years that was the established price in the locality.

For the next two years these pioneers were busy at the customary frontier tasks of building fences (cedar rails had to be hauled thirty miles, since the prairie country did not supply adequate fencing material), constructing crude houses and barns, digging wells, and clearing land for their plows.

In 1874-75 a number of families joined the Keglar Hill pioneers. Three of these newcomers were German families from the established and prosperous German communities in Comal county. Two were direct from England. One bore the singular name of O'Kelley; and a half dozen were of the same Scotch-Irish stock as the two original settlers. A count in 1880 would have shown about one hundred native white persons in the community. By 1890 this number had doubled. By 1895 it had reached its maximum of approximately three hundred, where it stood until about the close of the century, then rapidly declined.

Some of the first settlers bought large blocks of land, as much as two or three sections. But the more prevalent holdings were 160 to 320 acres. The price of land advanced very slowly during the 'seventies and 'eighties, reaching twenty dollars an acre by 1895.
(Continued on page 193)

The Receding Nordics

WHAT becomes of the displaced individuals is one of the least known phases of the displacement of American-white farmers by the tenant Mexicans. In the following table Professor Montgomery shows the occupational distribution of those now living who were residents of Keglar Hill between 1890 and 1900. A half dozen individuals could not be traced.

MEN	
Cotton farmers	13
a. In new cotton territory	10
b. In old cotton territory	3
a. Landowners	9
b. Tenants	4
Farmers, other than cotton	4
Retired farmers	6
Doctors	6
Unskilled laborers, town	5
Ranchmen	4
Merchants	4
Preachers	4
U. S. Civil Service employes	3
Lawyers	3
Insurance agents	3
Clerks	3
Salesmen, Ginners, Cotton seed breeders, Civil engineers and Carpenters (2 each)	10
Garageman, filling station operator, Hotel keeper, Editor, Music dealer, Politician, Town Mayor, Expressman, Military man, and mental incompetent (1 each)	10
Total	78

WOMEN	
Housewives, in towns and cities	39
Housewives, in country	11
Teachers	10
Boardinghouse keepers	5
Nurses	4
Clerks	3
Stenographers	1
Preachers	1
Mental incompetents	3
Total	77

THE MEXICAN COMES TO THE LAND OF GREAT TOOLS

Drawn for Survey Graphic by
DIEGO RIVERA

AND TAKES SOME OF THEM BACK HOME WITH HIM

On succeeding pages the ranking archaeologist of Spanish America, director of the great regional survey of the Valley of Teotihuacan, deals with the racial and cultural contacts between the two peoples in the light of his extensive study of Mexican immigration to the United States. His associate and translator, an American journalist, gives us at first hand the return of the Mexican immigrant to his native town.

Migration and Planning

By MANUEL GAMIO

THE old-fashioned alchemist, ignorant of the properties of elements and compounds alike, mixed his substances by chance, and exposed them indiscriminately to the action of heat, humidity or other physical agents, or subjected them to magical ceremonies. The modern chemist understands the properties and proportions of substances that must be employed to produce certain combinations, and can foretell the distinctive characteristics of their products.

An analogy exists in the contacts of peoples who are the raw materials in social chemistry. Until very recently they have mingled in an empirical manner, ignorant of their own characteristics as well as of those of resulting mixtures. The modern social sciences now permit one to know, at least in part, the distinctive characteristics of human groups. With this knowledge and by analyzing the conditions under which historical fusions have taken place, means might be found to assure more satisfactory results.

Thus, in Mexico, from the 16th century to the end of the 18th, a partial social and cultural fusion took place between Indians and Spaniards. In general these contacts were deficient for they were not harmoniously consummated, that is, not according to the best interests of both groups. They were to the detriment of the native and the advantage of the Spaniard, as was true at that time of contacts between conquering and the conquered races. After Mexico wrested her independence from Spain, the walls that had isolated her from other countries were broken down but the mixture with new racial and cultural elements did not take place in a more satisfactory manner than in Colonial times. During the last thirty years, the situation has been complicated even more by the absorption, substitution, or rejection of cultural characteristics of the American type, on the part of masses of Mexican migrants who shuttle between the two countries. Now that principles and methods of sociology, anthropology, economy and psychology are established, and permit of some expectation of success in our approach to the phenomena of social contacts, it would be very advisable for Mexicans to study the two epochs afresh from this angle.

More, Americans and Mexicans should jointly investigate the contacts resulting from Mexican immigration to the end that future contacts of their cultures might be made to take place in a manner favorable to the migratory masses as well as to the inhabitants of the regions where these go, preventing as far as possible the racial antagonisms and shocks which frequently occur between them. This would be of great importance to the peaceful relations between the two great racial groups occupying America, these of Anglo-Saxon descent and those of Indo-Iberic.

During the last thirty years the United States has played the part of a giant university in which more than a million Mexicans, for the most part poor and unschooled, have gained a free practical education of great importance; consisting not of reading and writing but of learning to live on a higher scale. In food standards, they today eat meat and milk; they have better furniture and clothing. They have learned to operate machinery and use modern tools. They have become acquainted with sports and hygienic practices. Returning to their homeland many of them have contributed a great deal to the progress the country has made in recent times.

Unfortunately the other side of the picture is less bright. These same Mexicans have suffered bitterly as a result of racial and social prejudices of which they are victims during their stay in American territory. Traditionally and deeply sensitive, they remember with satisfaction their cultural advancement, but at the same time nurse a deep resentment of the bad treatment they have otherwise received.

The American employer esteems the Mexican exclusively for his value as a workman and because he sometimes accepts low wages. The American worker is naturally hostile to the Mexicans because they are competitors. The average American (with the exception of social workers or members of churches), who is neither employer nor worker but simply an observer, generally feels an aversion toward the Mexican of the immigrant class. Proof of this was the unnecessary and inopportune Harris bill project which hurt the sensibilities of Mexico and Latin America by seeking to establish a quota in spite of the fact that, as later developments have shown, the same results can be achieved without injuring Mexican dignity. The difficult labor situation in the United States will not last forever. When conditions improve Mexican immigration will again increase because it is an economic benefit to various regions of the United States. The respective American and Mexican attitudes, if nothing is done to mollify them, will remain the same and in fact become stronger. The Mexican attitude may extend itself to the South, and lead to dangerous and unnecessary misunderstandings between Latin America and the United States.

MY belief is that if steps were taken to prevent all permanent immigration, such conflicts could be avoided. It is the indefinite residence in the United States of the Mexican immigrant that produces these inevitable racial shocks, social discriminations, and cultural antagonisms. With transitory or temporary immigration, the immigrant would be busy working in the short time he is in the United States. Cultural antagonisms would continue, not through the fault of the Mexican immigrant who absorbs many American cultural characteristics, but through the fault of the American, who through ignorance or indifference generally does not understand that the Mexican immigrant neither can, is willing to, nor should, completely and radically abandon his cultural inheritance, defective though it may be. While the culture of the Mexican immigrant is unprogressive from the American standpoint, it has certain fundamental qualities of great value, for it is an autochthonous culture, bred uninterruptedly in the course of thousands of years, by the same group of people, upon the same soil, under the same sky, and within the same natural environment. Results are the innate artistic gifts of the Mexican, spontaneously expressed in music, painting, or plastic arts, and his patience and manual skill which places a personal stamp upon whatever he does. These and many other qualities should not be ignored by the American; and if they were encouraged and stimulated instead of antagonized, the labor the Mexican performs would prove much more satisfactory.

The immigrant is uncommunicative, hermetic, and of a sad exterior aspect; his poverty may make him seem unworthy of attention. Nevertheless under this exterior exist qualities which nature has selected down the long ages, but which unfavorable life conditions, in the United States and even in Mexico, have not yet permitted to blossom and bear fruit.

Such studies of social contacts fall within the larger opportunity for research presented in Mexico, and to a degree in regions where there are Mexican immigrants. Here before they have irrevocably disappeared, we have materials of incalculable value for objective appraisal of how human civilization has developed at various stages of its evolution.

When an effort is made to investigate how the integral evolution of a civilization such as that of the United States or Europe has come about, one meets with serious difficulties because it is no longer possible to discover what the character and mechanism of the early levels of that civilization were. The level that can best be studied in any case is of course the present one in which we live, for we can observe directly and in the living individuals the biological, psychological and social processes that give rise to their cultural traits. When we turn to the historic phases of the cultural levels of these same people we can make use of architectural remains, museum objects, manuscripts and books which tell us something indirectly as to these processes. But their dynamic functioning can no longer be observed since they are no longer alive. A conception of the archeological phase of their cultural levels is still harder to gain for with but few exceptions manuscripts and books do not exist; and of prehistoric peoples we know still less since their remains consist of a few relics whose meaning we are obliged to interpret in a more or less conventional manner.

The cultural level of an existing civilization is dynamic, active, and eloquent, while past levels are static, passive, and in many cases without meaning, so that it is not only impossible to know their true characteristics, but also the interesting moments or transition-periods when humanity takes a forward step.

Among the Indo-Iberic peoples and principally in Mexico it is still possible to investigate dynamically at the present moment the evolution of human culture which in other countries took place at various epochs in the past. Certain minor Mexican social groups belong to the modern civilization or culture of the western type, the highest present cultural level of human evolution. At the other end of the scale exists another group formed by the Tarahumaras, Seris, Lacandones, who from many points of view may be considered at the most primitive levels of present-day humanity; or if you will, as prehistoric. Between these two extremes are such native groups as the Huicholes, Mixes, Yaquis, Mixtecs, Zapotecs, Tarascans, Aztecs, and others, whose cultural characteristics correspond to various archeological or historical periods of other living races. In these groups may be observed not only the cultural development which each represents, but also the transition stages by which groups rise from one to another.

The full understanding of these social processes might perhaps furnish practical means for assuring a cultural evolution, as all these groups integrate in the future, more satisfactory than the haphazard manner in which it has taken place in the past. Without falling into a paradox, it might be said that while it is impossible for obvious reasons to correct the cultural processes that have taken place in other countries at various past evolutionary stages, in Mexico these could be corrected; for although they belong culturally to a past epoch, they are chronologically modern and dynamic.

The Emigrant Comes Home

By EMMA REH STEVENSON

PETE CALOCA, Americanized and proud of it, came home from the United States not because he wanted to but because there was no work. He is one of a large number. Home was Irapuato which is in the *bajio* of Guanajuato where the best songs and the best grain come from. It is more than a fair example of the type of town which has sent many immigrants north across the Border and which is now receiving them back. It is not an especially picturesque town, does not attract tourists and its contacts with the United States have been mostly through its own nationals.

That is why I went there, and with this introduction let me pick up his story as he told it to me. After fourteen years in the States he still has a strong accent, as Mexicans do who live among their own kind, and his grammar is the usual immigrant variety.

The boy Pedro began work at the age of ten in an iron foundry on the outskirts of Irapuato, first for nothing for a period of six months, and then at twenty *centavos* a day on a ten-hour shift. It was when he was sixteen years old and had held several other jobs, that Pancho Villa came with his army to camp in Irapuato and curse General Obregon across the plains in Celaya, where later the fiercest battle in the Mexican Revolution was fought. Everybody left town that could, and when one day Villa let a train go north, Pedro was on it with the little money his family could scrape together. He went to El Paso, thence to St. Louis, where some fellow Irapuateños got him a job. In due time he sent for his brothers, and later for his parents for the revolutions in Mexico continued. At eighteen he married a Mexican girl, also from Irapuato, and when his second child was born his wife died. His children are now with his parents and brothers in Saint Louis.

Pete, as he's called today, had been back in Irapuato for a month trying to find something to do. There were no jobs to be had in the United States, he said. He found none in Irapuato. His various boyhood employers had no place for

Pete Caloca, returned immigrant, Irapuato

him. And nevertheless Irapuato is a flourishing town, for Mexico. It is a railroad center from which trains depart north, south, east and west. It has leather tanneries, shoe factories, flour mills, canning plants, an iron foundry, and a new cigarette factory. It used to have also the biggest carriage works in the entire country, but when Pancho Villa took the horses he ruined the business. When Irapuato recovered, automobiles came in. Most Irapuato industries, as in the rest of the Republic, are foreign-owned, American, English, Spanish or German. It is these that are now asked to employ the returned laborers.

Irapuato has about 20,000 inhabitants and eighteen fine large carved stone churches. The bandstand on one of its plazas was long ago replaced by an insufficient town water-tank as a mark of modern progress. Every church has its devout stream of young and aged, men and women, kneeling, confessing, and praying. For the rest, the town is almost entirely one-storied. Beauty is reserved for within, and through every doorway may be seen a stone-flagged *patio,* sunlit, and filled with pots of flowers and cages of birds. Out of the *cantinas* come the sounds of guitars, and soldiers on duty stop to listen. Windows of homes have the lower panes covered with lace through which may be seen the golden flash of the ubiquitous American brass bed—if the family is not too poor. In many cases it is used only for company, or to die on. The room has its colored prints of virgins and saints, its artificial flowers in a land of so many real ones, its candles, and generally its sewing machine. Kitchens are still very much Stone Age. There are stone *metates* for grinding corn, clay *comallis* for baking *tortillas,* homemade charcoal stoves, tall jugs of water brought from some distant fountain, and lots of lovely round brown gleaming pottery shapes baked in some village oven.

But among the Indian and Spanish wares, there is a great deal of American. Middle-class homes and hotels have cheap manufactured chairs, not nearly as good looking as the native Indian chairs with their seats of rush or colored fiber. Hardware shops have homemade tin bath tubs imitating the more expensive imported American ones, and the show-windows are full of American dishes and cutlery, of the cheaper class. The better grocery stores are almost completely stocked with American goods and one can easily imagine oneself at a Piggly Wiggly back home.

The lower-class trade is all concentrated at the native market or *puestos* that line and litter the streets facing the parochial church. Burros bring in backloads of pottery packed in hay, and water jugs for the precious water are piled three or four feet high. There are stacks of bamboo bird cages, piles of fruits and foods, stalls draped with ten-cent-store ribbons and laces from the United States (but chosen to please the Mexican color sense). There are flaring baskets for carrying loads on the back, and other long slim cylindrical ones which smeared with cowdung and baited with sugar-water, serve as bee-hives, after the manner of the Tarascans, ancient inhabitants of Irapuato. A native drug store displays hundreds of different dried herbs, seeds, nuts, flowers, roots, seashells, dried bugs, decayed birds, bones, animals' parts, and other things guaranteed to cure everything from colic to evil eye and unrequited love.

Pete was embarrassed before me by all the very Mexican things. Also Irapuato's mule-drawn street car irritated him, and gladly would he have traded every Mexican *patio* for an American front yard. In fact everything a tourist might consider picturesque or curious, he felt ashamed of. He wanted to show off his English not only to me but to his fellow townsmen. He urged me not to take snapshots of the shining pottery. The police ought to make the Indians keep those things in their yards and houses, he said, and highly recommended the new cigarette factory as a thing to photograph. As for the mule-power street car, he would—rather ride a burro.

Pete does not mean to high-hat his fellow citizens, but he does wish they would show some progress. They irritate him, and even more he them. He loves Irapuato, but with disillusioned eyes. Perhaps it loves him the same way. It calls him *gringo,* the term it uses for a Mexican who puts on American airs.

"Business is worse here than it has been in twenty years," said one American business man, established at Irapuato for more than a quarter of a century, who can be called Mr. Smith. Many Mexicans have come back to Irapuato, he said, asking him for jobs. But times are hard and he is running six-hour shifts. To his mind Mexicans are better workmen when they come back from the United States. While watching a road gang work near town, he said to the foreman, "Two of those men have been to the U. S. A."

"Yes," the foreman answered, "How do you know?"

"By the way they shovel dirt. Those two lift a shovelful, take a step forward, and throw it clear across the road. The rest do the same thing in two operations.

"You can also tell how many times a Mexican has been to the United States," Smith told me, "and mainly by the way he dresses. The first time he goes up barefooted or in *huaraches,* white cotton pajamas and straw sombrero. He comes back wearing brogans and overalls. The second time he comes back, he wears

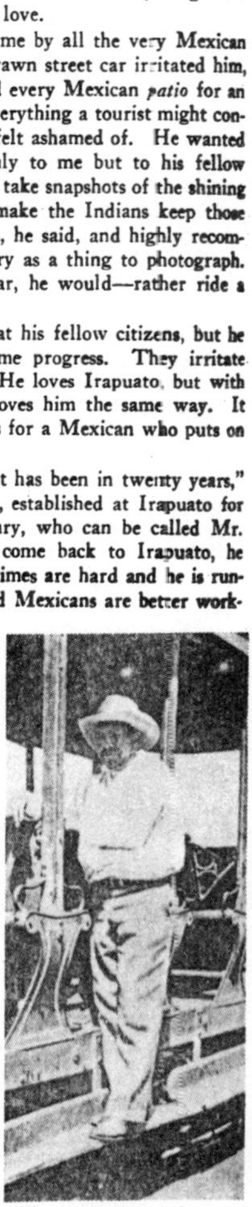

The street-car conductor

better shoes, has a cheap suit, and the straw sombrero has given way forever to a small American felt hat. After another trip he comes back a regular dude.

"They lose a lot of their Americanization after they return," he went on. "The pressure of being different gets too great to resist; but they never go back entirely to what they were. They never go barefoot again, or even wear *huaraches*.

"Every Mexican ought to go at least once to the United States," he said. "It is the best education in the world for them."

"Do you yourself hire many Mexican workers who have come back from the United States?" I asked.

"To tell you the honest truth," he answered, "I don't. I don't like to employ them once they have been there. They get too smart. They like to show off, and they talk to the other workmen and spoil them. One of my former men just came back and asked me for a job and I wouldn't give him one because he talked to me in English. I wouldn't give any Mexican a job who talked back to me in English when I address him in Spanish. I consider that a sign of disrespect. They are not like they used to be."

If a returned emigrant like Pete can not get a job in a factory, could he take up farming near his home town? A visit to several *haciendas* near Irapuato showed me what a single man on his own might be up against. The sugar cane needed rain, and the corn was in danger of parching. This was the rainy season but it had been a rainless week with a burning sun. There were two wells on one *hacienda*, deep round stone-lined holes that tapped an underground stream into ditches dug around the fields. "There is plenty of water," said the owner, explaining the geology of the distant blue ridges, "but it is all underground, and it has to be dug for." Electric wires had been strung from Irapuato's power system, expensive machinery was doing the pumping, and half a dozen peons were attending. A one-man farm trusting only to the fickle clouds that floated above seemed like an insecure proposition, and one man could not dig for water.

SO Pete wanted to go to Mexico City. He had never been to the nation's capital, and thought he would have a better chance of finding a job there. Thousands of returning emigrants think practically the same thing. He is dead broke. He says he would do anything. His eyes are a little desperate, after one month. One almost thinks of revolution on account of his eyes.

Entirely by accident Mr. Smith came by while I was talking to Pete. Pete greeted him in English, proudly. Mr. Smith almost ignored him. When he was gone the American said, "That's the fellow I was telling you about who wanted his job back."

There is another type among the returned emigrants—Jesús Delgado, for example, conductor of the mule-drawn street car that gives Pete such a pain. Jesús is older, and although he has been to the United States five different times, he is not nearly so Americanized. When he collects the five-cent fare, he touches his hat, hoping you'll have a pleasant ride. He is not a misfit. He radiates Mexican sunshine, and has a fine job. He wears good Irapuato shoes, Irapuato cotton trousers, and an American style shirt, though it may have been made at home. It is neatly buttoned at the neck, and properly tucked in at the bottom, although he was twenty-one before ever he wore his shirt tails in. However, on top of his American shirt he wears an open Mexican one, loosely linked over his ample chest by one button, and tied by the tails over his stomach in front.

Music is plentiful and water scarce in Irapuato

Jesús is proud of the gallant little mule-car that lopes over the cobbles and gets off the track at every other turn in the street. With the cooperation of the male passengers, minus Pete, he puts it lovingly back on the track when it runs off, like the Toonerville Trolley. Jesús was a little older than Pedro when he first went to the United States.

Irapuato, like similar towns in Guanajuato, Michoacan, and Jalisco, Mexican states from which the large majority of immigrants have come, has seen the tragic return of entire trainloads since the depression set in in the United States. The Mexican government gives them free rides, finding them places to sleep, and feeding them, until they get to where they think they may find a job. Most of them want to come to Mexico City, a centric movement which worries some of the officials. In the spring of 1930, the Mexican Bureau of Migrations of the Ministry of the Interior established offices at the strategic points of Irapuato, Saltillo, Monterrey, Torreon and Guadalajara, for the better handling of immigrant traffic, and for the diversion of those who through ignorance may still have illusions about entering the United States.

Americanization of Mexico by immigration has not been studied in a systematic way, but Americanization of Mexico is coming about by various channels. Most people believe that with the new international highway opening to American motor tourists, the end of Mexico as Mexican will have come. Native markets are already full of five-and-ten cent store articles where a decade ago there used only to be home-made Indian things. In the remotest corners, the American influence is felt. Even the saints are not immune. In a little Aztec town a painted wooden figure of Santiago in his old Spanish scarlet, gold, and red and blue mantle wears loud tan American shoes with bulging tips. Under his gold-braided robe American garters hold up his American socks.

Fellowship in Revolution

The Life of the People

By Diego Rivera

Photographs by Tina Modotti

These frescoes, from the series in the Public Education Building in Mexico City, stand as the great interpretation of the Revolution—of Mexico in all its phases by a man who speaks for the workers in every foot of the wall space. They are sculptural in feeling and the technique is made for the subject. There is an intense poignancy and drama in them but always subservient to the sense of form and color. The Indian strain in artist and people sets them off from interpretations of the European peasant, and there are none of the gay colors of the Russian folk dancers. These you feel to be heavy, some way a part of the soil and of the mine. It is as though the earth itself spoke. H. H.

The peon looks out at the land he hopes to possess some day

Into the mines. One of the many frescoes interpreting labor

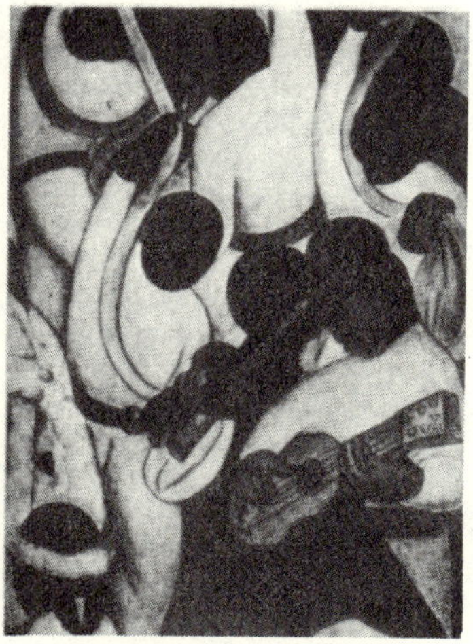

The rhythm of the peasant's song

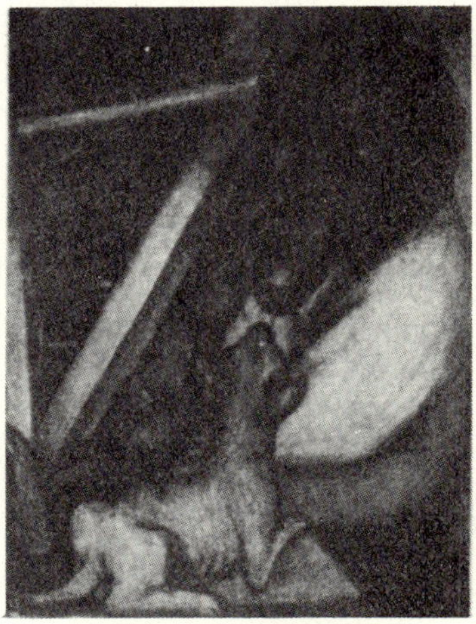

As the gargoyle to the cathedral

WHY MAKE MEXICO AN EXCEPTION?

By Chester H. Rowell

"We have adopted certain principles for our immigration policy in general. How do these apply to Mexico?" A Californian answers.

WHEN our quota law for European immigration and our exclusion laws for Asiatic immigration were passed, a vacuum was deliberately created at the bottom of our industrial system. We thereby determined either that this vacuum should remain and that industry should adjust itself to it, or that it should somehow be filled. Actually, of course, our policy since has been a hodge-podge of both principles.

Some of our industries have adjusted themselves, by labor-saving machinery and higher wages. Others have filled the vacancy with Negroes from the South—whence Harlem and De Priestville. Others, like the railway track work and hot-weather agriculture of the Southwest, have depended on Mexicans. With the pressure of economic and political conditions in Mexico and the suction of this labor vacuum in the United States, Mexican immigration was bound to continue and increase unless artificially checked. The question is whether we want this vacuum filled, and if so, from what source.

Just to get the work done, we do not have to fill it. There is no work in America which Englishmen do not do in England, Frenchmen in France and Germans in Germany, or that our fathers did not do in America. We may not want to do it, but we can. Moreover, American ingenuity devises machinery for whatever work men are too scarce or expensive to do. Our hewers of wood and drawers of water are a push-button and a faucet. The steam shovel, the drill, the carrier belt, the gangplow and the combined harvester have already replaced a whole army of laborers. For such of these tasks as may remain, there are still American Negroes available to whom unskilled industrial labor would be a promotion. The industrialization of agriculture is releasing another large body of American white labor. If we choose to adhere rigidly to the policy of not filling the place formerly supplied by immigrants from southeastern Europe, it is quite within the flexibility of American industry as a whole to adjust itself. Our problem is likely to be, not to find more workers, but to employ those we have.

Or, if we were to change that policy, there are three sources to consider—Europe, Asia and Mexico. Two of these present the race problem, which America has so far met only by the un-American institution of caste. We have limited Europeans, on political and economic grounds, and excluded Asiatics by reason of race. But in the post-war years we admitted Mexicans, almost without limit, to whom all of these objections apply!

If we are to consider the future make-up of our population, and admit only those whom we are willing to accept as co-grandfathers of our grandchildren, then the only place, if any, to relax our policy toward would be Europe. In that direction we have rightly made assimilability the test. Those who assimilate quickly, we admit as liberally as present economic conditions permit. We admit more slowly those whose assimilation is slower. But even as to these, the problem is temporary. Most of it disappears in one generation and all of it in two. If it were needed economically, we could ultimately absorb all of this immigration.

Or, if we were to ignore the human side, and measure men only as sources of profit, then the place to look would be Asia. The Chinese coolie is the ideal human mule. He will turn less food into more work, with less trouble, than any other domestic animal. He does not even plague us with his progeny. His wife and children are in China, and he returns there himself when we no longer need him. He can be rented wholesale, by the dozen or the hundred, thus eliminating the human factor. If that is what we want, China is the place to get it.

Mexican immigration is subject to both these objections. The Mexican peon is racially as alien as the Chinese coolie, and is not so good a workman. He is culturally less assimilable than the Balkan peasant, and our grandchildren will make of his grandchildren a caste apart. The Mexican peon is not a "white" man. He is an Indian. He embodies no part of that fine Latin-American culture which charms visitors to Mexico City. He is a selection downward, from the bottom of Mexican life, to fill a place below the bottom of our own. It is not a question of enriching our Anglo-Puritan tradition with a warmer Mexican spirit, as it has already been enlivened by our Irish, German and Latin elements. That is not the sort of Mexicans that our farmers and railroads want, or that Mexican poverty extrudes. It is a sort that fills no place which Chinese coolies could not fill better, and which presents, in even greater degree, the objections which led us to exclude those coolies.

IF there are exceptions to the sweepingness of this conclusion, an extension of the quota system to Mexico would more than cover them. Nobody proposes that there shall be no Mexicans in the United States. There is a considerable army of them here now, and the quota would annually let in more. The real needs of the Imperial Valley and Arizona farmers, the desert railroads, and others who need Mexicans not because they are cheaper but because they are better, could readily be met. If the quota system could include a selection upward instead of downward, it would help us judge Mexico by better representatives of its civilization. That would make for good neighborliness.

Of course the strict logic would be to include Mexico in the Asiatic and Canada in the European system, so long as we maintain the distinction between them at all, since the only excuse for the existence of two systems is racial, and Canada is on the European and Mexico on the Asiatic side of that category. However, I would be practical, and treat Canada more liberally than Europe, and Mexico more liberally than Asia, thus recognizing neighborhood as a modifying element.

If our general immigration laws are wrong, they should be changed. If they are right, our Mexican policy should be made to conform to them. The same argument in principle applies of course to much of South America, also, but it is unimportant in practice since immigration from these countries is negligible.

WITHOUT BENEFIT OF LOBBY

By Ernest Galarza

"For a moment an immigrant has the floor: and though he does not speak with authority, he speaks as one from the mill."

THE Mexican came over the Border in response to an economic urge. His cheap labor made possible a large part of the progress of the American Southwest in the last twenty years. He was cheap and he was laborious.

The small lettuce grower of Imperial Valley and the Southern Pacific Railroad were equally glad to have him. In the beet fields of Colorado in 1929 and 1930, the average earnings per family for a year were $600, many of these families having from five to seven children, all or most of whom worked in the fields. In the fruit orchards and truck gardens of the San Joaquin Valley wages for piecework have been so low at times that a ten-hour day netted an able-bodied worker seventy-five cents to a dollar and his meals, which I hope never to be compelled to eat again. In spite of the work of the California Housing Commission, housing conditions are still bad in that state. From Los Angeles to Denver and from San Diego to the Willamette, families average from five to nine persons to a room—when rooms are available. Otherwise, they average from five to nine to a tent pitched on the side of the county highway and on the leeward side of the dilapidated Ford. Water for washing, bathing, cooking and drinking comes from the irrigation canal, downstream from the watering place for the livestock. In the winter these same families crowd the poorest districts, living in condemned shacks or make-shift hovels. A typical quarter of this kind can be visited by the tourist at any time on the Yolo County side of the M Street bridge of the capital city of California. But the visitor must go with his breastplate of righteousness in place, for he is apt to see what I saw: a young woman lying on a cot in a one-room shack, a new-born infant in her arms, two babies crawling on the littered floor, the family dinner on a porcelain pan on the floor, a puppy and several dozen flies quarreling over the dinner and two more youngsters dozing in the corner. The father was out waiting for the pear picking to begin. He had been waiting six weeks.

Mexican children in the West, however, do not spend all their time dozing. Thus, ten-year-olds will do a ten-hour stretch hoeing or weeding or thinning. At twelve the boys wrestle with eighty-pound lugs or sacks or crates. At half that age both boys and girls are allowed to go into the hop fields and pull down the hot, sticky vines which their elders will pick. And since the hop season is short the youngsters go out at dawn, work until noon, return at two or shortly after and stop at five o'clock. In these varied occupations a child ten years or under will earn from ninety to one hundred and twenty dollars in a year's work.

It is about these things that the Mexican would talk if he spoke out. But he is inarticulate. And for three reasons.

He is inarticulate because he is disorganized. And he is disorganized because he is a seasonal worker. He has practically no sense of belonging to a community. His closest friends will be hundreds of miles away from one week to the next. He is a primitive unit, he and his family. Then, he dare not organize. His experience in the Imperial Valley teaches him the meaning of criminal syndicalism laws. He knows that to form a union in order to back up a demand for better wages or shorter hours in order to live more decently can be interpreted to mean "interfering with the harvesting of the melon crop."

The Mexican is inarticulate because he is discredited. He has been consistently painted as a representative of a degenerate Indian stock. Aside from the trifling fact that this Indian contributed the land upon which the Nordic now grows his beets and rears his Hoover Dam, whatever contribution he might make to contemporary life in the artistic and aesthetic fields is immediately discounted as being out of keeping with the "practical" spirit of the times.

The Mexican is inarticulate because he is disillusioned. If he came with high hope he remains with a resigned disappointment. He is without benefit of lobby; and although he does not know the meaning of the word, he does know that he has to do without that which lobbies—at least successful ones—get. He is what John Dewey might call a pathetic public with its tragic problem.

For these reasons the Mexican can not and does not speak. Occasionally he has his defenders. When Congress threatens to restrict immigration from the southern republic, those who employ him long and cheaply jump to his defence. He is pictured as *persona absolutamente grata.* He is musical—"he usually plays the guitar"; he is a family man—"he does not abuse his woman"; he is "a man, rough diamond though he be" as W. H. Kirkbride of the Southern Pacific Company put it.

BUT this in testimony serving other ends. The Mexican immigrant would look elsewhere for a statement of his case. He would look to his government; but his government is busy getting back to "normalcy." It cannot risk diplomatic complications. He might almost look to the American Federation of Labor; but its leaders in California, respectable and a little tired, have stated that the surest way of avoiding a civilization of masters and servants is to kick the Mexican out. Lastly, the Mexican would look to the social worker; and here he finds some comfort but no permanent aid. The social worker stays by the immigrant, grits her teeth and like her charge, wonders.

But the Mexican immigrant in the United States has more than just a human claim to be heard. He is needed to move thousands of crates of lettuce, melons, deciduous fruits and other perishables from the field to the box cars and thence to the markets. The biggest tribute that has been paid to his part in the economic life of the West was the panic which spread among his employers when restriction of immigration threatened. Restriction is not now an issue; restriction is here in fact if not in law. But there are hundreds of thousands of Mexicans in the United States who are producing goods and rendering services. They are maladjusted. Their problem is worthy of serious attention. Must the Mexican be satisfied with the pragmatic solution of the gang boss in a California pear orchard? To a young Mexican who had asked for a job, he said: "When we want you, we'll call you; when we don't—git."

Goodbye, Vicente!

By ROBERT N. McLEAN

In That Mexican, published in 1928, Dr. McLean interpreted Mexican immigration at the flood. He painted That Mexican as the common denominator between the United States and Mexico—told of the background of the immigrant, his problems, joys, sorrows, needs. Here he tells of the return current, as it is jamming the roads and railway stations at the Border—a swift, first-hand appraisal for Survey Graphic of the situtiion as it stood early in April—a situation of which the general American public is all but unconscious.

"*Donde vas, Vicente?*" (Where are you going, Vicente?)
"*¡Donde va la Gente!*" (I am going with the crowd!)

IT'S a handy little proverb, made in Mexico, and always used to hit off the gregarious tendencies of the Mexican people; in fact, the herd habits of *any* people. It might well have been quoted a dozen years ago when the tide of Mexican labor surged northward across the Rio Grande in answer to our frantic calls for help. And it is a proverb which may well be used now to describe the southbound movement of Mexicans: a movement which started early in the fall; swelled to mass proportions in January, and which probably has not yet reached its full crescendo. Vicente is going home!

On Monday, the sixth of April, I crossed the bridge from El Paso, Texas, into Juarez. On both sides of the street in front of the immigration office were parked the cars of homesick Mexicans; Mexicans who had picked cotton near Phoenix, melons in the Imperial Valley, grapes about Fresno. On one side of the street I counted thirteen cars, most of them battered Fords, and every car carried a California license. Loaded in the cars, upon the running boards, on racks behind, on bumpers in front, and even on the tops, was a motley and ill-arranged display of every conceivable thing which a family might collect as part of a housekeeping equipment. There were beds, bed-springs, mattresses, washtubs, cooking utensils, washboards, trunks, cots, tents, tent-poles, bedding; and a-top one of the loads was a crate of live chickens. Up at the customs house, the very courteous little Mexican stenographer with whom I chatted, told me all about the chickens. "Yes, they bring their animals!" she exclaimed, throwing up her hands in a gesture of despair. "They bring their dogs and their cats and their chickens, and yesterday a man brought a live goat. I ask them why they bring their chickens, and they say it is so they will have something to eat by the road!"

Vicente has acquired an automobile in the United States. It may not be much of a car, but it will run, and he has set his heart upon driving it over the trail that leads at last to the little town where he was born. No inconsiderable part of the movement back to Mexico is being propelled by gasoline.

It has been a long time since I heard the song, "I've reached the land of corn and wine!" But I heard it sung in Spanish in Juarez; heard it from laughing, brown-eyed children sitting upon rolls of bedding; heard it from patient wives and mothers, waiting in the cars for their husbands to conclude the tedious details of emigration; heard it from the men themselves as they tarried in their work of re-loading to tell me why they were going home. And as I talked with them, while I was pretty sure about the wine, there grew up in my mind serious doubts about the corn. But you can say this for Vicente. He hasn't had a real job for months. His children have eaten the bread of charity. He hardly knows where he is going, and he has forgotten what Mexico is like. But his heart is singing, and he is sure that everything is going to be all right.

One man had been in the United States thirteen years, and had four fine girls, all of them American-born. He had been everywhere, done everything, but now he was going home to Chihuahua; and the eyes of the little girls danced with expectation. I looked at the heavy load, and the worn tires, thinking of the rough, sandy trail that stretches through two hundred miles of stark desert—Juárez to Chihuahua! A man can forget much in thirteen years.

The man in the car near by had been listening. He gave a tug to the rope which secured a bed-spring to the running board. "No more Mexicans in the United States!" he said. "We're all going home!"

"And what are you going to do when you get there?"

"The government will give me a farm, and tools and seed, and loan me money."

"How do you know that?"

"I read it in the paper," he replied with an air of finality.

Up at the customs house, there is a large corral, where early in January more than two thousand *repatriados* camped and starved, huddled together, waiting for a kind government to provide them with transportation so that they could move on. Upon their little charcoal burners they cooked their *tortillas* and boiled their beans. Through the chilly nights they shivered because of insufficient clothing. The little Mexican stenographer told me that when it rained, the big examination rooms of the customs house were opened to them. Juárez citizens organized as best they could to provide food but there was much suffering. Women swarmed about the warehouses picking up one by one the beans which spilled through holes in the sacks. Then, late in the month, the government sent a train of thirty-three box cars—and then a second train—to take them south and scatter them over the country. Twenty-seven hundred people were thus removed from the "*Tortilla Line*" in Juárez. Now one or two cars are attached daily to the regular southbound train, by the Mexican government, and there is a normal daily movement of from thirty to fifty *repatriados* who pay their own way.

Sometimes families with automobiles camp for days in Juárez awaiting the customs-house examination. The Mexican officials seem to be doing all they can to avoid congestion, for nobody wants a repetition of what happened in January and early February. But both personnel and equipment are inadequate to handle the crowd.

Up at the station they wait also; always for the "tomorrow" when there will be room for them on the train. At the edge of the platform, I saw the *tortillas* cooking on the hot charcoal stoves, the crowd all the while milling around. Little children scampered about, as happy as though picking flowers in green meadows. And against the wall, propped up with a roll of bedding, a great hulk of a man slept noisily, oblivious to the flies crawling over his face.

THE BORDERLINE *By Angel Zarraga*

If you are out for exact figures, you can find almost anything you are looking for. If you want to prove that all of the million and three quarters Mexicans in this country are going home, you can see and hear plenty of things to back your theory. In 1930, 30,298 Mexican nationals moved southward through Laredo alone, while 2144 went through this port last January. But if you are convinced that the excess Mexican labor is simply boiling up as a result of the economic disturbance and is flowing over the edge of the "melting pot" you can find facts and figures to substantiate your view. The Mexican school enrolment in Los Angeles is just about what it was last year—around 35,000. In the Romona school of San Bernardino which is one hundred per cent Mexican there are eleven hundred children as against a thousand last year.

But before having much to say about figures, we must clarify our discussion by dividing the Mexicans who constitute the return labor movement to their own country into four groups.

First, come the deported Mexicans. This is by far the smallest group. Thousands of Mexicans are in this country illegally. Formerly it was impossible to deport many because of insufficient funds at the disposal of the immigration service. Then came the economic depression, with the resulting demand for a Mexican quota. Increased funds were provided, the border patrol was strengthened, and things began to happen. According to the estimate of the Mexican consul, between thirty and forty Mexicans a month are deported from the 31st district with headquarters at Los Angeles. The El Paso office handles about two hundred a month. The estimate for the whole country set by the Department of Labor for the fiscal year ending June 30 next is 18,500, and it is probable that the proportion of Mexicans will be somewhat more than half.

Much larger, however, is the group made up of those called "voluntary returns." These are people who are liable to deportation, but whom the immigration service for humanitarian or other reasons gives a chance to act for themselves. There are thousands of Mexicans who are being told to go, or they will be deported. It is a case of "What's your hurry, here's your hat!"

Still larger is the group made up of those who are either here legally, or whose status has never come under the scrutiny of the immigration service. Among them are many of the better class Mexicans, and they are going by sea, by train, and by automobile. Because of the new law making it a felony to come into the United States illegally, many have been living in fear for months lest some day a uniformed man call at the door, or they be stopped upon the street. For them the strain has become unbearable. As one border official has said, "The new law has put the fear of God in their hearts."

How many people belong to this group, it is difficult to say. From January 1 to April 6, the Juárez customs house checked through a total of 1169 families. Counting an average of five persons to the family this would give us an approximate total of nearly six thousand persons in a little more than three months. We have already seen that the movement through Laredo is a little larger. More Mexicans go through these two points than through any others; but we must remember that there are at least a dozen ways by which Mexicans can go home. It is interesting to note that practically all those who are going through El Paso by train are demanding "check-outs." This establishes proof of their residence in this country, and permits them to return if they so desire. Evidently Vicente is not entirely sure that Mexico will prove to be the promised land.

The fourth class is made up of indigent Mexicans whose hearts are singing the songs of Morelos, Jalisco and Michoacan, but who have not the money to return. When in January the burden of relief became particularly heavy in Los Angeles, the Mexican consul went to the Associated Charities and made the point that it would be better to pay the way of indigent Mexicans to El Paso, than to continue supporting them all winter in Los (*Continued on page* 195)

The Umbrella at Prayers

By JOHN PALMER GAVIT

UPON other occasions I have recalled the scandal committed by the little girl who brought an umbrella to the meeting called to pray for rain. Just such an episode now has all Europe by the ears—Germany and Austria proposing as between themselves to abolish customs duties; or, as the proposed "protocol for a customs' union" puts it:

> . . . the German Government and the Austrian Government have agreed to enter into negotiations for a contract to correlate the customs and trade relations of both nations.

It is expressly stated in the protocol that the absolute independence of both nations shall be preserved, as well as strict regard for existing obligations toward third nations, and both bind themselves "to negotiate with any other nation desiring to enter into a similar agreement." Perhaps with tongue in cheek the parties declare that "the contract shall serve to initiate a new order in European economic conditions by means of regional treaties."

With tongue in cheek, perhaps, because there is a grim joke in it. A joke, and grim. For all Europe, ever since the close of the war, and especially of late, has been solemnly talking about the desirability, the necessity, of exactly this thing. M. Briand, of France, has gone much further, proposing, indeed, some political federation of the states of Europe, in the interest of peace generally, and in particular of the mitigation of the cut-throat economic warfare, especially in respect of senseless tariffs, with which the nations are mutually committing suicide. He even hinted at the abandonment of the new alignments which have replaced the old balance-of-power. That was rhetorical, of course, but he went far, acknowledging repeatedly that the most important aspect of the situation was economic. At the tenth Assembly of the League of Nations, in September 1929 M. Briand said, of his proposed United States of Europe:

> I do not think we ought to have any system which would have the appearance of pitting groups against each other; but I do think that where we have a group of peoples, together geographically as we are in Europe, there ought to be some federal link between them. . . . Such a link I desire to establish, and obviously the most important component of this connecting link will be in economic agreement.

Map I. Why they are scared

Map II. The Danube—Everybody's river

WITH few if any exceptions, the replies of the other governments to the French project emphasized the economic phase of the possibility. Any kind of political merger was out of the question, as the Italian government for example was careful to point out. But economic cooperation appeared not only possible but indispensable. The Austrian reply in July last took this very seriously—so far as words go anyway:

> It is only if the governments of the different countries, realizing the urgent necessity of achieving positive results, actively encourage this economic work, hope will not be disappointed. . . . Coming generations are entitled to expect that a better and more serene future shall be prepared for them by the men of today.

Germany about the same time emphasized in her reply the fact that economic cooperation would contribute to the feeling of security upon which peace must depend:

> Closer cooperation in the economic field should not be made to depend upon the establishment of greater security. On the contrary, any understanding in the economic sphere will largely contribute to the strengthening of the feeling of union, and thereby to the sense of security as well.

But economic cooperation does not consist of the unanimous adoption of pious platitudes. It has to take some concrete form, and the nations that so fervently agreed upon the platitudes, including particularly France which fathered them, haven't been able, despite protracted foregatherings upon the subject, to agree upon any concrete forms. Especially as regards tariffs. As Professor Bonn of the Berlin Academy of Commerce says in a memorandum prepared for The Annals of the American Academy of Political and Social Science (an extraordinarily valuable symposium on Economics of World Peace), "there is a very close connection between tariff systems and nationalism." People striving towards new consciousness of separate national individuality are in the habit of using tariffs for sentimental rather than strictly economic reasons. The strongest advocates of protectionism are soldiers and writers desirous of inflaming patriotic emotions. Professor Bonn cites the pre-war exclusion of Serbian pigs from Hungary as having expressed mere political egotism on the part of the agrarian classes controlling Hungary, while the Serbs saw in it an effort to stifle (*Continued on page* 186)

Letters & Life

In which books, plays, and people are discussed

Edited by LEON WHIPPLE

The Education of Lincoln Steffens

THE AUTOBIOGRAPHY OF LINCOLN STEFFENS. *Harcourt, Brace. 2 volumes.* 884 *pp. Price* $7.50 *postpaid of Survey Graphic.*

LINCOLN STEFFENS was a reporter who made history. Driven by a demon of curiosity, bent by an interest first in philosophy, then in ethics, then morals, filled with the joy of living, and forever the good companion, he has spent two score years reporting on American government and politics. Now the great reporter—and we have none greater—covers his own story. It is front-page stuff, warm, vivid, an album of famous and infamous people from Big Bill Devery to Mussolini, rich in inside stories of trials, revolutions, scandals, movements, war and peace. Here is a text-book on journalism; a treasure-house for the historian of that wave of social idealism that shook the United States from 1900 to 1917; a case-book for the psychologist of political types. Above all it is the vivid diary of a bold and humane pilgrim who so loved his fellowmen that he has never been able to condemn them: and who after forty years of knowing everybody and seeing everything, is no tired radical but still a child among us taking notes, full of faith, hope and charity. The glory of this muckraker is that he has never found any muck!

The tale cannot be warmed over. It begins with the gay pictures of boy life in California from 1866 to 1888 where the pioneer spirit descended on "Len" Steffens from a Canadian father and an English mother—and has never departed. He finished the University of California with a low mark, but with his intellectual curiosity whetted by the astounding discovery that historians disagreed, that there was no foundation for history or ethics, that nothing was settled, either in life or academies. The world was an oyster to be opened: and Lincoln Steffens' mind had its life assignment. Four years wandering over Europe, at Heidelberg, Leipzig, Paris and way stations, gave no final answer to anything either from Wundt's psychology or Munich's beer. It did not reveal even how he came to marry Josephine Bontecou. "My marriage was none of my business. I can see through a government or a political situation, but human relations are beyond my comprehension." This seems to be true: so a defect of this book is that although the author has forever the center of the stage, he remains curiously impersonal. We see Steffens the reporter, rarely Steffens the man. Yet the sidelights show that wife and her mother were a powerful force, and the man blessed with friendships. Well, the good reporter has a right to his anonymity.

With a wife and one hundred dollars from his father, the young seeker got a job on The Evening Post in 1892 and began his career and his education covering Wall Street.. Almost at once he developed the famous technique of cultivating the men who knew, of learning the background, of putting meaning above "spot news" drama, and subtly boring after facts with the Why and How of the intellectual. With Jacob Riis he covered police, and called it a college education; he went through the Lexow investigation and learned about reformers from Parkhurst and bosses from Croker. These chapters are vastly instructive in light of the present investigation of corruption in New York City. I imagine Steffens smiles: he can learn nothing from the revival of a classic.

But he learned then, and was made city editor of the old Commercial Advertiser, an odd bird who needed help on executive matters, but inspired a queer staff of Harvard boys and literary dreamers—Norman Hapgood, Abraham Cahan, Neith Boyce—to see news with fresh eyes and human sympathy. Roosevelt comes into the picture as friend for years in spite of the Steffens gift for realistic criticism. There is the rich story of how Roosevelt persuaded himself that he had *not* called on Boss Platt when he had, and issued a denial as Steffens predicted.

THIS whole section is fat with youth, humor, thumbnail sketches of men, appraisals of character, and revelations of the close-meshed gears between big business, politics and corruption in an America that was changing hourly from agrarian to industrial. McClure's Magazine was trying to interpret the change; S. S. McClure was "the receiver of the ideas of his day." He hired Steffens as managing editor and then drove him out into the United States to learn how. This fine-tempered tool for reporting stumbled on corruption in St. Louis where Circuit Attorney Folk was fighting the gang. . . . Then came the muckrakers.

The meat of the book is in these chapters on how Lincoln Steffens discovered the shame of the cities and wrote about them. I recall the terrible impact of those grim fact-stories on my own mind. I had been reading McClure's for the tales by Kipling and Stevenson and the science articles on x-rays and liquid air (what an editor McClure was!). My faith in American democracy was deep and certain despite vague glimmerings from the Bryan-McKinley campaign of '96. Well, for me and I think all the social-minded of my generation, the Steffens articles were the end of the age of innocence. Whatever Lincoln Steffens thinks of the net results of his muckrake (and I gather he underestimates them save as garnered wisdom for his own thought) he achieved this: he taught us the facts of life. And in the face of World War and the repeated patterns of corruption and exploitation, I maintain that generation, visionary democrats and uplifters that we were, did achieve some things for women and children, for health, for labor, for liberal hopes that were beneficent and enduring.

This is the story of how Steffens educated himself to expertness in city, state, and national governments with the persistence of a laboratory scientist and exposed the "set-up" until bosses sought his opinion as a connoisseur on their machines. He found that it was not bad men but the same bad system that practically forced the business-political alliance on men who did not know what they did or why; that power and loyalty were in these bad men; that you could sometimes get them to help with their skill and power; and that to replace them by unskilled reformers or new devices of control was a stop-gap because the system was unchanged. His faith was almost answered when he organized the most diverse interests to consider the social and communal aspects of the McNamara trial. Read that chapter on applied Christianity in Los Angeles. The end of the period came when Edward A. Filene got him to come to Boston and they conceived the Boston 1915 Plan. But New England had a dual personality, the reformers could not agree, and fell into the hands of "heelers" who had not the power or the brains of the "principals" in whom Steffens puts his faith.

Boston closed his chapter on reform by politics; he took up a postgraduate course on revolution and so the rest of the book ranges from Greenwich Village radicalism through the labor dynamiters (and their goods and bads), into Mexico under Carranza, Russia under Kerenski, to the peace that was no peace, Mussolini, the failure of liberalism in Europe, with its admiration for our machine efficiency and distrust of our ideals —and so home to see this New America, bringing a new wife and a wonderful new son.

What does Steffens think of us now? He finds us a going concern, not finished as is Europe, experimental is his word, with laboratories supported by big business and new reporters (like Samuel Crowther and Garet Garrett) reporting on the New Capitalism. There are problems aplenty: the landord as ever, and the need for distribution to match our production. But business is self-conscious, and that he seems to feel means the replacing of laissez-faire with a plan. "The liberals, progressives, reformers had been beaten. Hoover, with his business conferences, not politics, defeated Smith, and represents business openly, not covertly. Bribery and corruption were over. Washington is no longer the kept woman of Wall Street. They are man and wife." The plain truth is that good business as a whole is for the common good and requires the cooperation of the people as a whole. We have learned the direction; we are spared the ancient lethargy of Europe; we shall some day take the final step that will make business social for the good life, not profits.

That is the testament of this good reporter, muckraker, seeker for right in government, and unwearied optimist. We may agree or disagree, but for this grand book, with its color, wisdom, variety and zest we owe him praise and thanks. The man had a right to be disillusioned; instead he has had the courage to relive the whole story for our instruction and entertainment. It may have omissions, restorations, changed perspectives. But as the record of a seeker for truth and a believer in human goodness it is a challenge to good hopes.

Leon Whipple

THE UMBRELLA AT PRAYERS

(*Continued from page* 184)

their own economic and national aspirations.

So when you propose to meddle with tariffs you are tampering with a thing a good deal nearer the raw than mere economics. And it works both ways. However much the proposal to abolish tariffs as between Germany and Austria might be declared, with all manner of reassurance to other nations, to be merely a step toward the highly-desirable new era in Europe, anticipating, as the Germans said, the establishment of security; it could not fail to arouse the scarcely-sleeping fears of neighbors still suffering amid the wreckage caused by the last joint exploit of Germany and Austria. Vast pains were taken in the peace treaties to keep those boys from getting together again! And here they are, taking as text and pretext M. Briand's own proposal, beating him to it. If economic cooperation is the thing we are all praying for, let's do it, beginning at an obvious point in the common interest of two peoples essentially homogeneous, and following along the outstanding line of least resistance. What could be nicer than that? Yet it has thrown Europe into hysterics, M. Briand himself apparently at the center of the uproar.

NOR is it surprising. I have roughly sketched two maps to show why they are scared. See for yourself in Map I the grim likeness to a pair of jaws about Czechoslovakia which might be constituted by Germany and Austria as an economic unit—especially if, as seems likely, Hungary should join them. See what it might mean for France, with such a unit lying across all her means of access to the East, adjoining as it does the more or less hostile Italy on the South.

There is another dangerous factor in it, in the commercial importance of the River Danube, perhaps the most truly international river in the world. It is practically navigable from Ulm in the heart of Germany to its mouth in the Black Sea, access by way of Constantinople and the Bosphorus to the open ocean.

That river runs through Germany and Austria, borders Czechoslovakia, bisects Hungary, cuts through a corner of Jugoslavia, separates Roumania and Bulgaria; and it is fed by some four hundred tributaries, main highway of the greatest grain-field of Europe. For centuries the Danube has been a bone of international contention.

On top of this comes the question of treaties according "most favored nation" treatment to the parties. What will such an agreement do by way of conferring automatically unexpected benefits and inflicting incalculable disadvantages, among nations preferring to let matters stand as they are; with the alert and highly productive Germans of the two most nearly homogeneous nations controlling the situation?

It is all very well to discuss these pious projects academically at vast length and then find that this, that or the other, or maybe all three, prevents actual doing of anything; but when the two nations that everybody thought had been hamstrung and rendered helpless for an indefinite period suddenly propose to do something concrete (incidentally very beneficial to themselves) and that along the very lines of the pious discussion—well, here are the beans spilled all over the place, and nobody knows what to do about it.

It looks almost like an "unfriendly act" against somebody. Or, it would, if the document in question did not so scrupulously throw out the latch-string to everybody else. That is the diabolical ingenuity of it. If it were exclusive as an engine of offense and defense it might conceal a threat. But there's nothing unfriendly in the familiar "Come on in, the water's fine!" Neither Germany nor Austria surrenders a whit of the independent sovereignty which in the peace treaties they guaranteed to retain intact.

IT is not the political union forbidden by the peace treaties. Austrians would like to be taken into Germany; but Germany does not want them. To add Austria's predominantly Roman Catholic vote to that of Bavaria would swamp the Protestant North and give the Clericals control in the Reichstag—a thing intolerable to both the Liberals and the Radicals. An economic alliance is something quite else. And all threat would be taken out of it if the other nations would follow suit. At this writing they are running round in circles little and big, hardly knowing which way to turn. By the time these words are published the situation may have clarified; but the fact will remain that a bluff has been called.

A thing worth noting in this connection is the vast difference in the international situation into which this episode falls, from what it would have been before the war. In the old days the world hardly would have been informed. The thing would have been consummated as routine between two military allies without a by-your-leave. Now, it seems, the protest, if any there be after all, is to be carried, not to any arbitrament of war but to the League of Nations; that failing, to the World Court.

These may have to decide whether or not the German-Austrian agreement is *lawful*. It is safe to go further and say that if they decide that it is not, it will have to be abandoned. Neither Germany nor Austria, singly or combined, is strong enough in the world public opinion. In all probability the matter will be before the Council of the League in May, about the time these remarks are published.

AS background for these events two or three recently published books may be commended, especially that of Paul Hutchinson, entitled, The United States of Europe, published by Willett, Clark & Colby, Chicago ($2.00 of Survey Graphic).

Mr. Colby well describes the dangerous situation surrounding the German-Austrian project:

. . . it happens that Europe, during the first half-dozen years after the armistice, turned itself into an economic battlefield, with twenty-seven separate states, dividing themselves off into twenty-seven different customs units surrounded with almost unscalable tariff barriers, inside which every one of the twenty-seven units scrambles desperately, trying to make itself self-sufficient and self-supporting. Of course, it couldn't be done. Clear-headed economists knew that from the first, and said so. Europe paid no attention to them. . . . A policy of suffocation. . . . The whole theory of an economic warfare between twenty-seven exclusive units was a huge delusion that could lead only to the exhaustion and poverty of all.

Another book, bearing the same title, is by Edouard Herriot, former French premier (translated by Reginald J. Dingle; Viking Press, New York; $3.50 of Survey Graphic). The striking thing about M. Herriot's book is that he, primarily a politician, is able to see clearly the momentous importance of the project from economic, social and humanitarian points of view, and appeals for it eloquently; but before the political obstacles he shrivels helplessly. Nevertheless there is no better source of information as to what M. Briand's scheme is all about.

While you are about it, you should go back to Count Coudenove-Kalergi's Pan Europe (Knopf, New York; $2.50 of Survery Graphic). He is a living embodiment of internationalism; as I wrote of him in these pages three years ago (Survey Graphic, August 1, 1928, Europe's Getting-Together):

His blood is that of all Europe and of much of Asia. He was born in 1894 in the Austrian legation at Tokio, where his father, Count Henry Coudenove-Kalergi was chargé d'affaires. The family Coudenove is Dutch; the family Kalergi is Greek; but this young man's mother was Mitsu Aoyama—Japanese. . . .

It was Coudenove-Kalergi who planted in the mind of Aristide Briand the seed of the idea, "United States of Europe," the first practical step toward the fruition of which appears now so much to frighten him. Yet it is, as Coudenove-Kalergi shrewdly indicates, the only long-run hope for France.

Anyhow, the fact remains that the umbrella has put the test to the good faith of M. Briand and his prayer-meeting.

MEXICANS AND NEW MEXICO

(Continued from page 144)

discussing, neither the Spanish nor the Indians. They never acquired the habit of receiving their education from the printed page. Much more than two or three generations is required to make any primitive group a reading people, to persuade them to take their work and behavior patterns from books. Which does not mean that these same people can not learn and learn quickly and competently through seeing and doing.

What everybody knows about Indians, what Frank Applegate wrote of the hand-craftiness of the descendants of Spanish pioneers, is proof enough that the Spanish speaking peon derives from both lines of his descent the capacity to make things requiring a high degree of artisan skill, and to make them beautifully and well. We have not only no reason in New Mexico to believe that our unskilled Spanish speaking labor could not become skilled by the proper sort of teaching, but many of us realize that they could become specialized technicians of high capacity. The educational department of Mexico has this submerged capacity of its people well in mind. Under proper tutelage the despised peon class could become the superior hand-craftsmen of the western world.

It is one of the curiosities of communism, as practiced by American Indians, that it does foster, along with the completest type of group-mindedness known, the most invincible type of individualism in hand craft. When the Indian withdraws himself from the group and works from auto-expressive impulses, he withdraws wholly, with the most absorbing personal concentration, the sort of concentration that in our kind of society is only known to the creative artist. That is why all Indian artifacts partake of that quality of expressiveness which makes works of art *(Continued on page 188)*

(*Continued from page 187*) of them. They proceed out of the profound withdrawal of the individual into the experience of the race. This applies to practically every Indian in his native culture, in the field of design, of poetry, song and ceremonial. Everybody who visits the Indian villages of our Southwest or of Mexico is familiar with the truly remarkable emergence within the past ten years, of works of pictorial art which are not surpassed by many of the American artists who have devoted all their lives to the study of art in the schools of New York and Paris under the most accomplished teachers. And I would guarantee to find in any immigrant Mexican group of railroad hands, cotton pickers, or beet-pullers, more individuals who could under reasonable circumstances produce genuine art craft than could be found among ten times as many other types of laborers.

The thing that is lacking in the Mexican is the capacity for rapid adjustment to working patterns, the motivation of which lies outside the worker's personality. Last summer I was having improvements made on my place which involved the removal of earth from one part of the garden and its redistribution in another part. To my American mind it seemed a more efficient way of working to have each barrow load, as it was taken from the place where it was not wanted, deposited at the places where it was finally to be distributed. And after half a day's effort I had to give it up. The man in charge of my work was a little more than ordinarily competent as a laborer, but he could not manage the two patterns at the same time. I had to agree to having all the dirt removed, collected in a pile as it was taken out, and then redistributed from the pile, making two distinct patterns, unrelated in anybody's mind but mine. This is the way you have to learn to work with the peon mind. But if the pattern, however complicated, originates with him, if it is a pattern which his ancestors have followed, so that its path through his subconscious has become reasonably fixed, you can confidently let him alone, undisturbed to work it out to traditional completion.

These people have the same difficulty in following the American pattern of commercial-mindedness which involves the third stronger element, the element of private profit. In the pattern which we call "business," in which the individual must be constantly aware of himself as a separate item, as he stands between the two patterns of buying and selling, your native New Mexican often fails to make the necessary private reservation. And this is precisely the difficulty of the Indian. He can not always abstract a feeling for his private gain from the situation as a whole. The necessity for so doing gives him a moral shock which is foreign to the American to whom the pattern of "business" is ancestral. In the beginning of the American Occupation the Spanish speaking New Mexican suffered this moral shock to a degree that has made him more or less distrustful of Americanos ever since.

THERE is no question that all the moral patterns of the immigrant peon have been widely disrupted. He has come to doubt, or at least to find ineffectual, his ancestral behavior patterns, without at the same time having acquired the patterns of the dominant English speaking peoples with whom he has come in contact. From both his Indian and Spanish strains he is likely to have an association of manners with morality; a kind of ceremony of virtue which suffers most in the vulgar discourtesy which characterizes American manners toward people of different customs from their own. Nor has the aboriginal *meztizo* ever quite achieved the impersonal distinctions of fact which characterize our own notions of truth. Truth to him is more directly related to the old idea of Troth, the keeping of faith, the *noblesse* of tribal sanctions. Any Indian is likely to tell you, in response to inquiry, what he thinks it will please you to hear, and this type of answer is characteristic of the peon. But once his sense of responsibility is aroused, he is also likely to be faithful unto death. Kindness is, in general, the basis of his social intercourse; and the further you get away from American influence in New Mexico, the more you are likely to meet with that simple faith which is poetically supposed to be more than Nordic blood.

Family behavior follows a pattern long a stranger to American use. A Spanish speaking New Mexican child addresses his father respectfully and defers to the judgment of his mother long after he has children of his own; family obligation is seldom denied. The poor, the unfortunate, the blind, the crippled, the "afflicted of God" are treated with great consideration. The smallest pleasure is shared, the last crust ungrudged.

In New Mexico, these people are seldom given to crimes of deliberation; bootlegging and knifing frays while intoxicated, provoked nine times out of ten by sex jealousy, are the most frequent offenses. Here too, the native under penalty of the law is likely to be docile and dependable. There have been known cases in which men under conviction have secured permission from the authorities to go home and get in a crop, or the winter wood for the family, returning punctually to serve out their appointed terms. I have not been able to discover that the misadventure of a term in the state penitentiary loses a man, otherwise acceptable to his townsmen, anything of social advantage. To get at odds with the law is a kind of natural accident which might happen to anybody. Once the score is paid, why bother?

IN New Mexico the people have never experienced the disaffection with the Church which has had so serious an influence upon old Mexico. They are for the most part cheerful and devout Catholics, not very strong on dogma, but familiar and affectionate to the Saints, several of whom have legends localized in the mountains called Blood of Christ.

There is on our side of the Border, none of that slavish subservience to the priest which non-Catholics in Mexico are fond of attributing to pious Catholics among their own people. One suspects occasionally that the parish priest in New Mexico finds his parishioners a good handful to manage, especially if he happens to be of another racial derivation than theirs. This has been unfortunately too much the case in New Mexico since the American occupation. Miss Cather when she wrote of the Archbishop to whom Death came in his New Mexican diocese, was too much intrigued by his saintly character, and perhaps a little by his French subtleties, which she racially understood, to realize that for a Spanish-Indian people such as this, the coming of the French priests was little less than a cultural calamity. The building of a French cathedral with French decoration, in a community of Spanish tradition and with the invention to their credit of the only original American type of architecture which had yet been produced, went far to inhibit the natural creativeness which was their birthright. Very much in their lives which is the natural source of cultural expression, fell into that desuetude from which it is only now being rescued. Much that is in its free state the natural rootage of literature, with all the life pressed out of it, has become superstition. It is only with the advent in the Rio Grande country of creative workers, painters and writers, capable of giving to the native temperament its due of appreciation, that this temperament is beginning to revive, and to seek its natural expression in works of creative artistry.

I have had curio dealers, who make a handsome profit on the sale of works executed by the native before the advent of Americans, complain to me that the said natives would rather sell their work to Frank Applegate than to the dealers, "even when we pay a higher price for it." This is actually the case, as it is also the case that I—a non-Catholic—was admitted to *Penitente morados* when it was supposed to be as much as an Americano's life was worth to attempt to see inside one; and that I have collected more native literature, more folk plays, than are to be found elsewhere in the whole United States. The natives sold to Frank Applegate—year after year, up to the time of his death last fall—because they recognized in him an appreciation not only of the artistry in their work, but of its human significance, and on the same ground they admit me to the means by which—however it may look to others—I realize that the divine fire is kept alive in them.

Superstition is an unsafe word to apply to an unfamiliar practice. Sometimes what is called superstition is merely a different background from which to derive explanations of unfamiliar occurrences. Last year there was a pest of grasshoppers in the Rio Grande country, and at Zuñi, where the hoppers were most pestilential, it was offered in explanation by the men of Zuñi, that the unprecedented number of the insects was owing to the pres- (*Continued on page* 190)

(*Continued from page* 189) ence of grasshopper-shaped airplanes flying about unrestrained above Zuñi land. No, not a superstition, but a logical deduction from an a priori concept of the universe as highly susceptible, likely to bring forth whatever is by suggestive mimicry impressed upon it. Recall the first airplane you ever saw and look at a grasshopper and you will see that to such a sensitive medium as the Indian assumes creative nature to be the suggestion can scarcely remain unaccepted. The suggestibility which the Indian attributes to the spirit of Nature, is, in fact characteristic of his own subconscious; he responds expressively to the suggestions made by our culture. This can be seen abundantly at the annual Indian Fair, and at the Spanish Market at Santa Fe where an appreciative atmosphere has been created for the native arts of these submerged peoples. It is just a hundred years since the degradation of Spanish Colonial Arts was begun in the contempt of the invading Americanos. Four years ago when a revival of such arts was initiated in New Mexico, there were fifteen entries for competition; the fourth year there were over two hundred articles exhibited.

The bearing of these things on Mexican immigration is explicit. If we ask from this mixed Spanish-Indian stock that they become the socially and intellectually inferior brand of standardized labor, that is what we will get. If we ask for a highly individualized artist craftsmanship, we can have that. If we demand that they become average installment-plan, subrotarian middle-class Americans, in the course of time they will become as good at that as our other remotely alien immigrants. But why ask it?

At Santa Fe we begin to perceive higher uses for our Spanish Indian contingent. They make a nucleus of warmer, more individualized—and at the same time more communal, less competitive—elements in our culture. They do actually achieve the thing we have deemed impossible in our Europeanly derived social complex, individualism without competition, complete socialization without standardization. In so doing they make a point of contact with all other American cultures. For there is no denying that other American cultures have a similar Spanish-American base. And at Santa Fe we have already begun those cultural exchanges which are suitable between neighboring, progressive nations.

In seeking to rid themselves of unassimilable Spanish elements, and to revivify the aboriginal American roots of culture, the Mexican people are already finding in the responses from Santa Fe where Spanish is understood and aboriginal Americanism not disprised, sufficient common ground for amicable adjustments. A group of interested New Mexicans, including the governor of the state, went down to Mexico City for the last presidential inaugural. At Santa Fe an Indian Art Museum for Indians is in process of erection, to house art enterprises well along toward accomplishment. A theater which will be equally devoted to American drama in both Spanish and English—and occasionally in Amerind—is being organized. Already companies of players and musicians from Mexico have been welcomed in the border towns. Such things must be reckoned with in any final determination of the whole problem of Mexican immigration.

That there may be political and economic factors in our border relations important to be taken into account by both sides is not denied. It would, however, in view of the cultural situation, be not only a pity, but a stupid loss to both nations, if the problem should be reduced to a mere factual dimension of higher or lower wages. For better or worse, Spanish and Indian elements are indissoluably entered into the American future.

It remains for us to make the most sympathetic, and therefore the happiest, and so the most effective, use of them.

SANTA SUSANA

(*Continued from page* 162)

the inward poison of the *coraje* had always made her violently ill. Herein lay her single small retaliation. Tonight Estéban would have to roll in his blanket on the kitchen floor. Tomorrow and the next day and the next she would lie in bed and glory in his clumsy movements about the kitchen as he prepared his own meals, growling meanwhile in his throat. But he would not be able to get back at her, because, while according to one article of his code as a Mexican husband, corporal discipline was necessary, by another article of the same code he never thought of striking her again until she had recovered from the *coraje* caused by his last punishment.

She raised herself higher on a fresh cool pillow and fell to thinking of the school, the long clean room, the books and blackboards, the teacher's welcoming face, the other women answering glibly in English and herself left quite unnoticed to accustom herself gradually to the newness of it all.

And then, across the school table, on the opposite wall, she saw again Santa Susana—the American women's saint! She now studied in memory that massive grand old head with low-combed white hair, the strong-featured face, sad with all the sorrows of womankind, yet with the strength to bear all their oppressions upon her soul. She recalled the white lace, hallowing neck and shoulders, the upward look pressing the carking heartaches of bondage up to the sight of heaven.

This contemplation of Santa Susana brought a certain first-aid release from the sickening personal throb. Slowly Doña Soledad swung into a larger trend of life. She grasped some dim perception of social progress from old cruel customs to new ones of gentlemen.

WHEN she dropped back into studying her own situation, she fetched with her this dawn surprise—that she was no solitary wicked rebel against sacred customs and the divine right of husbands. No! She was putting up a meritorious resistance in which Santa Susana was her ally. The saint would not side with Estéban in keeping her a prisoner during his absence. The saint knew a woman should be allowed her own taste in clothes. Above all, the saint would be for Doña Soledad's attending the Mothers' Class. Again she drifted off into mystical contemplation of that strong pitying face.

"Santa Susana!" she murmured, "I am going to be a free soul. I shall do what is right in my own eyes, and I implore you to frustrate and confound my husband. May his growl be choked back into his throat, and may his striking fist drop powerless each time he would lift it against his wife. Santa Susana, hear my plea!"

Just then Doña Amalia appeared in the doorway with the lovely blue cup and saucer in her hand.

"I want you to have this," she announced simply. Both women understood that one of them felt that the prize had cost the other too dear.

"No. Keep the cup. It is yours. I enjoyed the school. I expect to attend regularly."

Doña Amalia nearly dropped the china in her amazement.

"He—he—might kill you!" she gasped.

"I have implored the protection of Santa Susana," calmly returned the other.

Now Doña Amalia was a person of deep piety whose rosary was ever well thumbed. But no woman with so much mundane shrewdness etched into her face was going to ignore earthly weapons in arming her friend for this combat. She came closer to the bed and lowered her voice.

"Santa Susana be praised for that good American law by which a husband can be jailed for beating his wife—*just as if she were any other woman who is nothing to him.*"

Doña Soledad sat up straight in the bed in her amazement.

"Just as if she were any other women," she repeated incredulously, *"his wife—"*

Doña Amalia came still closer and spoke scarcely above a whisper.

"Yes—and more. The teacher at the school—she would go with you any minute to put in the complaint against Don Estéban. The police would come and haul him off to jail."

But here Doña Amalia, overcome by her own prefiguring, set the cup on the bureau and fled. For after all she could not conceive of any Mexican woman really working such black magic on even the blackest of Mexican husbands.

But Doña Soledad was of stronger stuff. This news that Santa Susana had a vicegerent on earth in the person of the teacher was a shot of spiritual tonic which raced through her entire being. Her feet clapped (*Continued on page* 192)

(*Continued from page* 191) down on the floor. She bathed her face and composed her hair. She crossed the kitchen rather unsteadily to a low bench. Here she sat for some time and felt the ill effects of the *coraje* subsiding and flowing out of her. Instead of dreading the coming ordeal, she drifted into the calm of one who has received extreme unction. A woman in the next shack started a folk-song as she looked over her *frijoles*. One word kept soaring clear of the rest and floating across to Doña Soledad.

"Amor . . . amor . . . amor . . ."

The listener's lips twisted into a wry smile. The love of man—just a pretense—curses and blows the reality. Yet Estéban had been in love, if ever a man was; only, so rough even then. And now, all devil, so far as she was involved. What was back of this deviltry—him a hardworking man, honest, well thought of, and kindly—except to his wife?

Again the neighbor's singing voice insisted:

"Amor . . . amor . . . amor . . ."

Could that be the answer after all? This owning and dominating and crushing—was it just a crude manifestation of love? Did Estéban really crave her love? Was this his foolish way of trying to take it by violence? Was he, in certain aspects of husbandhood, her bad rough child, needing a firm hand of motherly guidance? Was he at times her big boy, as Juan was always her little boy?

"Amor . . . amor . . . amor . . ."

This time the word mingled unheeded with her reverie, but on its wings she rose into her first understanding of a wifely love that might brook instead of cringe. She moved steadily about the kitchen. She put a white cloth on the table. She went at preparing *enchiladas* to the very top of her husband's taste.

IT was dusk when Don Estéban stood in the kitchen doorway. His wife saw that he was weak and passive from spent anger. His hurt arm sagged forlornly in its sling. He had come back to the bitter bread of the after-reaping. She noted, as his eyes fell upon her darkening bruise, a certain sickness of self-disgust at his own brutality. She had only to be passively amiable now and matters might move along rather pleasantly for days and even weeks. Shaking and dizzy as she was, Doña Soledad pushed this temptation from her. Her slight advantage of the moment must not be wasted.

"Come in," she said pleasantly, "supper is ready."

He stepped inside.

"Santa Susana!" she prayed below her breath, *"Oh, Santa Susana!"*

Aloud she addressed him with quiet even voice.

"Estéban, you must never strike me again."

He wanted no more dissension just now. He caught sight of the *enchiladas* and accepted them mentally as a peace offering from a repentant and submissive spouse. Hence he growled almost amiably:

"So long as you do not forget that I am your Mexican husband."

"You have truly been my Mexican husband," she rejoined with distant calm, "but if ever you strike me again, you will find yourself in a United States jail. *Santa Susana! Santa Susana!"*

It took half a minute for Don Estéban to grasp this declaration. Its enormity almost choked his mental swallow.

"Mujer perdida!" he roared, "You would put your Mexican husband into a United States jail?"

The man moved toward her with upraised arm and clenched fist. The outrageous affront of such a threat whipped up his flagging wrath. Doña Soledad did not cringe away like a proper wife. She actually ignored the fist and her voice came back tranquilly. . .

"You have no more right to hit me than if I were your mother or your sister or some woman who is nothing to you. (*Santa Susana! Santa Susana!*)"

Don Estéban's fist eased down, but to an accompaniment of muttered oaths. This was preposterous! You didn't reason with your own wife, *caramba!* And her even presuming to reason with you! Such follies as she was advancing! It was sacrilege even to mention a man's striking his mother, and it was not customary to chastise sisters. And of course nobody went about striking just any woman he happened to see. Such bewildering folly! And a wife claiming he had no more right in her case! *Caramba!*

But the worst of it was the way she stood there. She actually manifested the sorrowful majesty of a mother, the quiet confidence of a never-beaten sister, and even the curious aloofness of a woman who was nothing to him. Don Estéban actually had an injured sense that in putting him up against such a front she was not playing fair. He was no ruffian. He punished only on provocation and during the excitement of high passion. Here she gave him provocation enough for a felling and yet someway he could not nerve his arm with the requisite anger. But his reeling authority must be stabilized. He pumped hard at his wrath. Again he glared; again he growled in his throat: again the big fist swung in arcs before the woman's face. If she would flinch or dodge or plead—but there was just her quiet face held up to him like an open page; and on it he read only sorrow—and love—the earnest love of a woman for her husband.

The growl died away; the glare went out in blinking wonder. This time the arm dropped shakingly.

Then Doña Soledad smiled, radiant, conquering, cherishing.

"Estéban, my dear man, you will never be confined in that United States jail."

"How do you know I won't?"

There was nothing convincing in the attempted howl of derision.

"You cannot strike me ever again—beloved."

"How do you know?"

The growl was lost in its own futility.

"Because I am under the protection of Santa Susana, patron saint of American women. It was she who intervened, by a blessed miracle, so that your arm would not obey your will."

Don Estéban's face ironed itself out to a vacuity of amaze. He clicked his dropping jaw back into position. Slowly his mind stumbled through the limbo of this experience and overtook his lost self-respect. The interpenetration of the supernatural accounted honorably for his infirmity of will. It satisfied his masculine punctilio. It also cleared the future, for man must not presume to resist the saints.

Then his wife was pulling him down beside her on the bench, with due consideration for his hurt arm. She brushed his cheek with soft warm lips and snuggled her fragrant hair into the hollow of his neck.

"Angel of my life!" he muttered weakly.

Playfully she pulled open his coat and drew forth a prized possession, his beautiful long green pencil.

"Estéban, don't you want to give me this pencil? I need it to write my English lessons at school."

Fetching from himself a deeply contented sigh of total surrender, his bass voice rolled out tenderly.

"I'll sharpen it for you, *querida.*"

"Santa Susana! Santa Susana! Accept the deepest thanks of a Mexican woman's heart! Oh, my Santa Susana!"

KEGLAR HILL

(*Continued from page* 171)

During this whole period there seems to have been no case of absentee ownership. Every owner lived on his farm, and in the case of smaller owners, with the assistance of all members of his family, did all his own work. From the clearing of the very first farm, cotton was dominant. Corn, oats, and sorgums were raised to feed the farm live stock; a small amount of wheat was occasionally planted; but the only money crop was cotton. For almost thirty years this was one of the best cotton producing communities of the state. The average production was easily three times what it has been during the past ten years.

As more and more of the land was brought under cultivation, tenancy became quite general. In a few isolated cases, during the 'seventies, Negroes were employed as tenants, but after 1880 none but native whites were found in the community. The tenancy contracts were customarily of the third-and-fourth variety, under which the (*Continued on page* 194)

(*Continued from page* 193) tenant furnished his tools and teams, and gave the landowner one-third of the cotton and one-fourth of the corn and feed stuffs produced. In many cases the tenants acquired farms of their own; in a few cases their children married into the families of even the large landlords; and in all cases in church and school and community life, they were indistinguishable from the landowners.

This was the situation in 1890. The population was about equally landowners and tenants. But the tenants were of the same stock as the owners. They had the same cultural and social heritage. They entered into the affairs of community life on a basis of fundamental equality. They owned their tools and teams, their milch cows, stores of feed-stuffs, planting seeds, and meat animals. In a majority of instances they were in process of becoming landowners themselves. According to the simple frontier standards of the day, they lived well. For fifteen years cotton had sold for about forty dollars a bale. Their farms were amazingly productive. Real poverty was rare—almost unknown. In short, Keglar Hill was a community of robust, prosperous, homogeneous frontier folk.

Then came the Mexicans. At first they came only in exceptional crop years like 1887 and 1888 to pick cotton. They moved in family groups and after the harvesting season returned to their homes in the towns and country communities of southwest Texas. In 1892 two or three of these families remained, working land on the halves: the landlord furnishing tools and teams, and receiving as rent one half of all the crops produced. The next year other families came—and remained. Within five years every large landowner in the community was employing Mexican tenants. By 1900 there were no native white tenants in Keglar Hill.

Sudden and sweeping changes were wrought in the economic and social structure of the community. The landowner became a landlord. He owned all tools, teams, feed-stuffs, planting seeds, and other equipment employed in producing crops. He directed all operations of his tenants, even in such matters as when and what to plant, how to prepare the soil, and in many cases when and where to sell the crop.

The tenants were of a foreign group. They did not speak the English language, knew next to nothing of the customs and traditions of the community, they were not Methodists, and their children did not attend school. They were deplorably ignorant, and shockingly poor. Few of them owned more than an unbelievably few crude household necessities. None of them possessed milch cows. Occasionally one would own a worn out pony or a superannuated mule. They were tractable, industrious workers, willing to live in any sort of shack that might be provided, on a diet that required a minimum of cash outlay. No ridiculous notions of social prestige—no extensive home duties—no bothersome compulsory school attendance laws disturbed the even tenor of their lives, or prevented the full employment of their entire labor force in the cotton fields. Their standard of living was modestly low; their standard of work commendably high. They were ideal tenants!

BUT Keglar Hill, as a way of life, was one with Carthage and Thebes. The Nordic-American tenants, who for twenty years had tilled the farms—and bought them, had educated their children in school and church, and had contributed fairly to the building of a healthy and pleasant community were uprooted utterly. Of their scores, not one individual remained. One now drives an express wagon in Oregon. One grows wheat in the Panhandle. One raises cabbage in the Rio Grande valley. One clerks in a Fort Worth grocery store.

And, within one short span of ten years every landowner in the community had followed. The church had been moved to a nearby village. The school was abandoned. Better roads, better means of communication and transportation had tended to center social life in the villages and country towns. Children were to be educated. Standards of living were rapidly rising. The towns offered much that could not be found in the country. Absentee ownership became increasingly prevalent. The price of land rose rapidly and continuously. It would not produce more cotton—but productivity is only one of many factors affecting the price of land. Interest rates and availability of credit, improvements in transportation facilities, labor costs, and changes in technique are also factors. And these factors are not the same to all men.

The small landowner saw his land increase in value to some-one else more and faster than it did to him. His standard of living was rising more rapidly than his income. His children yearned for the fleshpots of the cities. His neighbors had set their landmarks in far places. His school was abandoned; his altars gone. There were no more camp meetings in Keglar Hill. His world had vanished. He sold his land to a large-and absentee-landlord, gathered his Household Gods, whistled to his dog, and went to the new cotton realm in West Texas—or to Oklahoma—or to town.

Of the three hundred odd white Americans who composed that robust community in 1895, not one remained in 1910.

That is the story of Keglar Hill—the story of the rural cotton community with the coming of the Mexican tenant—a large chapter in the story of Texas.

GOODBYE, VICENTE!
(*Continued from page* 183)

Angeles. The Southern Pacific Company offered to cooperate in the movement by fixing very low "charity Mexican fares." The plan had three things in its favor. It helped satisfy the ambitions of Mexico for the repatriation of her citizens; it removed human misery from the city of the angels; and it was cheap. Late in March a train load of 260 Mexicans thus had their way paid to El Paso.

Counting the movement represented by deportations, "voluntary returns," ordinary returns, and charity cases, it is estimated that about 42,000 people have returned to Mexico in the last nine months. The monthly average may be checked somewhat by the call of the crops for workers, but the movement has been going on at the rate of from fifty to sixty thousand persons a year. That looks large; but it is a question whether the stork will not run a good race with the trains and the automobiles.

JUST why is Vicente going home? He goes because of the economic depression. For months he has listened to the patter of the people who brought him, assuring him that there would soon be work for everyone. As he has hungered and waited he has seen municipality after municipality pass ordinances restricting work on public improvements to citizens. He has always known that if he became a citizen he would still be a Mexican in the eyes of everybody except his own consul, whose help and protection he would immediately lose. He has seen social pressure brought to bear upon corporations to fire Mexicans and hire Americans.

"How can you better yourself by going to Torreón?" I asked a man on the train. He looked at me a moment and then said, "If you were broke and without a job, would you rather be home, or in a foreign country?"

Said another: "In Mexico there are always beans and *tortillas*. You can eat whether you have money or not. In the United States if you have no money, you starve."

In the second place, the sensitive soul of the Mexican immigrant has been wounded by the changed immigration policy. The laws are the same; the interpretation is different. The immigration official is detective, judge, jury and prosecuting attorney. It has always been possible to refuse admission to one "liable to become a public charge." *Any* common laborer is now liable to become a public charge. As one official put it: "Two years ago if a man came with a wife and five kids and five dollars, we let him in; now if he were to come with five hundred dollars, we would turn him back." In March, fifteen native Mexicans were admitted through El Paso, and not one was a laborer. Eighty-five per cent of the applicants were refused. Once Vicente was needed, and had a welcome; now he gets the cold shoulder everywhere. His heart is sick, and he wants to go home.

But he has been wounded more than all else by the false stories which have been published in Spanish language papers from San Antonio to Los An- (*Continued on page* 196)

(*Continued from page* 195) geles, and which he has believed "to the foot of the letter." Stories of deportation have been distorted, magnified, published and copied. When the stories are investigated there is usually nothing at the end but thin air. I know, because I have worn out some shoe leather and more patience trying to investigate some of them. There are always some unfortunate circumstances in the enforcement of any unpleasant law, and deportation proceedings are not calculated to create goodwill. Border officials did not make the law; and it is my conviction that if they deviate from its strict provisions they do so on the side of mercy rather than of severity.

In the third place, Vicente is going home, drawn by the land hunger in his heart. After the Civil War there existed a firm conviction that "Uncle Sam is rich enough to give us all a farm." Each ex-slave was to have five acres and a mule. Just so, in this movement, Vicente is sure that a kind government is waiting to make him a land-owner, and to stake him to a start. Mexico, in view of her problems, the poverty of her national treasury, and her perplexities, will find it hard to care for fifty or sixty thousand repatriated citizens a year.

More than all else, of course, we are concerned with the social issues involved in this great movement of Mexican people back to their native heath.

In the first place there will inevitably come a period of stark want. As I think of that string of cars in Juarez, all moving southward over a single road, I am ready to prophesy that in two months Chihuahua will be swamped by people whose cars have broken down. Prices will soar, and hunger will stalk the streets. It will be like a gold rush without the gold. Letters are already coming back to El Paso saying, "We wish we had never come!" It is being hinted that because the repatriated people have lived in the United States, there exists an idea they are rich. So they are being charged so much that their money is soon gone. There is already need along the Border and hunger in Mexico, and unless the government accomplishes the miraculous in caring for this great horde of people, conditions will be even worse.

As a brighter side to the picture, the restrictions on Mexican immigration and the return movement are both operating to solidify the Mexican colonies remaining in this country. People are having to choose between the homeland and the adopted country; often between the homeland and their children, who have never known anything but this country and who refuse to leave. Already there has been a marked acceleration in petitions for citizenship. With the reduction in the amount of available labor, the return of better times will see employers paying better wages, and making greater efforts to keep their workers employed throughout the year, thus reducing the evils of the migratory system.

For another thing may be noted the efforts the Mexican people are now making to care for themselves. Always a Mexican family will divide its last *tortilla* with a less fortunate family. But this generosity has been indiscriminate, unorganized. Up to this time, well articulated charity has been for the Mexicans, not of them. Now the colonies are beginning to systematize their efforts for relief. Early in February, the Mexican consul in Los Angeles, Rafael de la Colina, called together some of the Mexican artists, moving picture people and business men, and organized the Comité De Beneficencia Mexicana. During the first month the committee raised $4000 among Mexicans for Mexicans, and well devised plans have been worked out for raising larger sums. Sixty per cent of the money raised goes for relief, forty per cent for repatriation. This development of an *esprit de corps* is a hopeful sign.

But while we are discussing what this movement will do to the Mexicans, it might not be out of place to consider what it will do to us. Belvedere district in Los Angeles now counts rows of empty houses on most of which money is still owed to banks. The owners have abandoned everything and gone home. At the present rate, between fifty and sixty thousand consumers are being removed from our markets in twelve months, and that at a time when we find it hard to sell what we produce. And when the cycle of depression is past, and the fields now fallow are again green, who will thin the beets, chop the lettuce pack the oranges and pick the cotton? There will again come a time when there will be work "no white man will do."

During the past decade and a half, Vicente has patiently, gladly, even sacrificially given his best in the development of the Southwest. As always happens with the common laborer, he has put much in, and taken little out. Cities have been built, railroads have pierced new territory, deserts have blossomed because Vicente has been willing to put his back into them. He has harvested the bulk of California's two hundred crops, he has tamped the ties on every mile of railroad, and as Ernest Galarza says, "he has poured his sweat into every cubic yard of concrete." Now, because there has come an industrial depression, he is being kicked out, and his job is being taken away from him that it may be given to some "American" who has just trekked into the Southwest in a second-hand car propelled from place to place by charity gasoline. I for one do not blame Vicente for going home. He has not had a square deal. During these years, he has set his roots down deep into our social and economic soil; and it is a serious thing for him to be uprooted.

My mind goes back again and again to the man who talked to me by the side of his Model T in Juárez. I can still see the household goods, and the four little girls a-top the load are still laughing in my face. Are they through the customs and on their way? They had an extra can of gasoline, but did they remember that sandy roads take much more fuel than pavements? Has one of the tires burst in the hot sand? Will the *tortillas* last till Chihuahua?

And what will Vicente do when he gets there? A man cannot live in a country thirteen years, share in her social and economic life, beget his children under her flag, and send them to her schools, without something happening to him. Will that something fit Chihuahua?

As you cross the bridge into Juárez you see a great new sign, ¡BIEN VENIDOS TODOS!—Mexico's welcome to her returning sons who have seen their muscle changed by the alchemy of trade into gold, and have then been turned out. As the cycle of business swings upward in this country, the time will come when we shall want to hang that sign on the north end of the other bridge. And I cannot help feeling that there will be a day when Vicente's eyes will see it, and his heart will be glad.

MEXICANS NORTH OF THE RIO GRANDE

(*Continued from page* 140)

discarded in repairing box-cars, or other refuse of American economic life. Generally this is but a way-station to something better. I recall one house which told plainly the story of its builder's aspirations. The first floor was patched together almost entirely of short pieces of wood from what had been packing boxes; the exterior of the second room, added later, was of drop-siding; the third room, under construction, was of stucco. When the housing of immigrant Mexicans rises to the level of that of resident American wage-earners it of course attracts less attention. As a whole, the approximation of this standard proceeds very slowly, for reasons of poverty and of difference in cultural aims. But notable improvements in individual cases and even in whole communities are significant.

Where housing is provided by employers it bears an occupational stamp. The converted box-cars which shelter railway extra-gangs, tell their own tale; so too the dismounted box-car, which is being replaced along the right of way in the Southwest by rectangular concrete or hollow tile houses which accommodate several families, each allotted two rooms. On the plantation farms of south Texas the broad fields which comprise the landscape are interrupted occasionally by groups of two-room rough lumber houses, often row upon row, one like the other, twenty, thirty, sixty of them.

In the industrial centers of the Middlewest and East, the Mexicans live where the immigrants from Europe lived before them, or still live with them. Accommodations range from basement to attic, from the poorer brick tenements and backyards of the near West Side of Chicago, to rows of frame houses whose roofs cut across the vision like saw-teeth, and on to the neat brick, single-family dwellings to which the more fortunate workers of all nationalities may attain in Gary or Indiana Harbor. Their housing reflects (*Continued on page* 200)

Traveler's Notebook

To the South of Us

AFTER the foregoing articles, particularly that of D. H. Lawrence, it seems superfluous to bespeak a visit to our Southwest, or the source of our "Mexican states." But the writer picked up some illuminating tidbits in thumbing through James T. Nichols' little volume on The New South and Old Mexico (Nichols Book and Travel Company, Des Moines). For instance, he has a ready answer to the question of why the difference in the development of the United States and Mexico; which is that one was settled for God and the other for gold. And in the march of progress, one can't help wondering whether each may wind up where the other began! (substituting, in strictly modern terms, *humanity* for *God*).

But he gives intimate pictures of Mexico, the land of flowers. There is Mexico City, with its floating gardens, its many markets, more especially the Thieves Market, where every item, from the smallest to the largest, was stolen; its interesting government-run institution, the National Pawn Shop, housing a grand collection of things, sold if not redeemed within thirty days, and marked down every thirty days until sold. Monterrey, the Pittsburgh of Mexico, with its steel works and well known Saddle Mountain. Tampico, one of the greatest oil ports. The historic city of Queretaro, where Maximilian was executed, and the scene of the fine Santa Rosa church.

One could go on and on, if space held out. You would have to visit several continents to get what you got in this one country —the whole scroll of civilization—past and present.

In the Caribbean

THE success of its annual seminar in Mexico, now in its sixth year, led the Committee on Cultural Relations with Latin America, to hold a Caribbean seminar this winter afloat on a Cunarder, to be followed in 1933 by a similar trip to South America. The fifty-eight members of the Caribbean party had a strenuous and stimulating time of it, what with four or five hours daily of lectures and discussion and visits ashore. Jacob Billikopf, director of the Federation of Jewish Charities of Philadelphia, writes us: "We felt that we had been to school, that we had worked hard, that we had our prejudices rudely and wholesomely assaulted; we had been introduced to peoples of whom we knew little in so vivid and stirring a fashion that never again would the Haitians and the Dominicans and the Porto Ricans fade away into that borderland of the unknown. We returned with no delusions as to the exactness or the scope of our knowledge, but the important point is that we had had our *introduction* to the peoples of the Caribbean, and were eager to journey further.

"The Seminar, through contact with the national leaders in each of the countries, helped us to personal appreciation. We learned to think of Porto Rico in terms of Chardon and Padin; of the Dominicans in terms of the venerable Rector of the University, Henriques y Carvajal; of the Haitians in terms of President Vincent and the Leger brothers and Edmond Lespinasse; of the Cubans in terms of some of their patriots who will be safer if their names are not printed.

"The experiences brought us up sharply to the questioning of our own national policy in the Caribbean. We learned a new unwillingness either to defend or condemn the actions of our government *in toto.* We reread together black chapters in our relations to Haiti and Santo Domingo and Cuba and Porto Rico. We found brighter chapters in the writing, and took pleasure in the vigorous and intelligent devotion of Theodore Roosevelt to the interests of the people of Porto Rico; the increasingly intelligent representation of the United States as typified by Minister Dana Munro in Haiti and Ambassador Guggenheim in Cuba."

Oberlaender Trust

MANY of our readers have a special stake in the recently announced Oberlaender Trust: a project which aims to spread interest among Americans in the endeavors of German-speaking countries in the arts and social sciences, and vice versa. The means of accomplishing this end will be by sending key people in the various fields to observe how that work is carried on across the sea. Applicants will be considered not only on the basis of their experience and what they have done, but on the opportunity they possess of making their findings known to the general public. Newspaper people, social service workers, teachers, preachers and the like are especially eligible. The Trust was created by Gustave A. Oberlaender, a retired business man, at one time connected with the Berkshire Knitting Mills of Reading, and president of the National Association of Hosiery and Underwear Manufacturers; and has been contributed to the Carl Schurz Memorial Foundation, but will be administered by a separate board of trustees, among them Dr. Haven Emerson, associate editor of Survey Graphic. It has been admirably conceived also in the fact that the entire principal of $1,000,000 and interest are to be expended within twenty-five years. For further information address Wilbur K. Thomas, 225 South 15 Street, Philadelphia.

Vacation Hints

IF YOU would "prepare" for peace, there are two Institutes of International Relations to be held by the American Friends Service Committee (225 South 15 Street, Phila.) at Haverford College, Haverford, Pa.—June 8-20 and June 22-July 3.

ARTHUR C. WATKINS, director of the National Student Forum on the Paris Pact (532—17 Street, N.W., Washington, D. C.) is on the lookout for highschool boys and girls to join their International Relations Observation Tour.

THE AMEROP TRAVEL SERVICE (132 N. La Salle Street, Chicago) is conducting an eight weeks' trip, sponsored by the Chicago Medical Society, visiting many of the leading medical centers of Europe and the Dresden exhibits of the International Hygiene Congress of last year.

UPTON CLOSE (112 East 19 Street, New York) announces an exceptionally attractive tour to Japan and China (June 24 to September 3), a special feature of which is the Rittenberg Summer School of Painting.

THE ENGLISH FOLK DANCE SOCIETY (Susan H. Gilman, 159 East 33 Street, New York) will hold a two weeks school at Amherst, Mass., in August.

THE ENGLISH SPEAKING UNION (37 Charles Street, London, W. 1) will give information to stage aspirants about the British Drama League's Vacation School, July 29-August 12.

OLYMPIA, BRADFORD, will be the scene of an Imperial Wool Fair, May 8-23.

INTERNATIONAL Town Planning and Housing, German Building, and Garage exhibitions, May 9-August 2, Berlin.

INTERNATIONAL Conference on African Children, June 22-25, Geneva.

SECOND World Conference of Workers for Crippled Children, week of June 28, at The Hague.

TRIENNIAL Congress of the Labor and Socialist International, July 25-August 1, Vienna.

TOURS

COUNTRY BOARD FOR CHILDREN

(In answering advertisements please mention THE SURVEY*)*

(*Continued from page* 197) the position the Mexicans themselves hold among the other immigrants in northern industry; it is less distinctive and less isolated than that which, as members of *la raza,* they occupy in the Southwest.

THE rapid influx of a large laboring class, migratory, prolific, with primitive standards of living, different in race and culture, is bound to disturb the social equilibrium. Whether this disturbance raises "problems" depends upon one's point of view.

Take for instance the schooling of rural Mexican children. Is their non-attendance a problem? The farmers want their labor, the parents their children's earnings, it costs money and effort to put them into school, and causes a lot of disturbance after they get there. If you think Mexican children should have the pressure of the American state behind their education, it is a "problem." If you do not, their non-attendance may mitigate local difficulties in getting the kind of farm labor you have a hard time finding anyone else to do. Said an Imperial Valley farm manager:

> If they were miserable or unhappy, I would say, "All right, Mr. Educator, do your damndest." But the Mexicans are a happy people, happier than we are; they don't want responsibility, they want just to float along, sing songs, smoke cigarettes. Education doesn't make them any happier; most of them continue the same sort of work at the same wages as if they had never attended school. It only makes them dissatisfied, and teaches them to read the wrong kind of literature (I.W.W.) and listen to the wrong kind of talk.

In the cotton belt of Texas, and the sugar-beet fields of the North, non-attendance generally is not treated as a problem; in California and in cities elsewhere, it is and Mexican children are generally checked up, and, if need be, compelled to go to school.

If Mexican children do go to school, Americans of almost all points of view see their presence as a "problem." Differences of language, culture, class, race, standards of cleanliness, rates of educational progress between the children of the Mexican laborer and those of the American farmer or townsman raise difficulties. Shall their children be educated in the same schools, or shall they be separated? If separated, shall the separation continue through four grades, eight grades, or twelve? American communities answer these questions in the light of educational and hygienic considerations, financial and administrative expediency, and racial feeling. With such a diversity of viewpoints, the resulting situations are varied as can be imagined. They range from separation through the first grade to separation through highschool; from excellent school buildings and teaching staffs to inadequate shacks inadequately equipped and staffed; while the local American schools may be operated with the aid of state money allotted to the district because of the numerical count of its Mexican children. Sometimes no school at all is provided for the Mexicans. On the other hand, notably in larger cities and in rural communities under the adult education system of California, men and women as well as children are reached by classes which are genuinely appreciated.[1]

Again, there is politics. Very few Mexican immigrants naturalize, but many men and women of Mexican blood amongst us were born in the United States and are citizens. At one extreme is political debauchery—Mexicans used as tools of American politicians—witness the elections of 1928 in Hidalgo County, Texas. At the other is Dimmit County in the same state which, to end purchase of Mexican votes by Americans, established a "white man's primary" in the name of "civic righteousness," and thus effectively eliminated the Mexican vote.

Then there are questions of social equality and race, delicate but insistent. The 1921 census of Mexico classified its population as 9.8 per cent white, 59.3 per cent *mestizo,* 29.2 per cent Indian. The great bulk of Mexican immigrants come from the *mestizo* and Indian groups, particularly *mestizos* in whom the Indian strain predominates. There are generally sufficient social and economic grounds to explain the slow educational progress of the children of Mexican *peones* without resort to the theory of race inferiority. There are many individual in-

[1] Yet the assembly of California has just passed and sent to the senate a bill permitting racial segregation of Mexican children who are of Indian blood. P. S. T. April 9, 1931.

stances of excellent educational progress among them. Not infrequently Mexican young people of working-class parentage and largely Indian ancestry, have made brilliant records in highschools and even colleges, at times ranking as valedictorians of their classes.

That many Americans in 1931 think in terms of race superiority and inferiority is itself, however, a fact of profound significance to the social and economic status of Mexicans in the United States who are of Indian or Indo-European origin. This attitude is exhibited in its cruder forms by signs in the windows of restaurants, billiard parlors and the like, reading, "White trade only," *"Se sirve solamente a raza blanca," "Este baño solamente para americanos."* The bald statement is often made in conversations that the Mexican laborers are an "inferior race," and therefore to be separated in school, in domicile, at the soda fountain, in social affairs, and in buses (but not on trains and street cars). There is the hazing and taunting in the public schools. Later on the race line occasionally bars job promotion; the shade of brown on the cheek may determine whether a man is employed in an industrial establishment, or whether a girl is accepted as a clerk or stenographer.

The Mexicans who come to the United States are hospitable and courteous. Often they possess personal charm and magnetism. Even the *peones* are sensitive to the social ostracism to which they are subjected. They may shrink in suffering like the proud old Texas *vaquero* who said to me: *"Distinción?* I feel just like if they stick me through to the other side. *Si, senorito,* we are Christians, too; we are sons of God!" Or, but rarely in the presence of Americans, they may burst out like a young Mexican machinist in the San Joaquin Valley of California: "The white race must be brought to its knees." For the most part, however, the Mexicans keep to themselves the more because of ostracism, instead of hurling themselves in defiance against it.

THE coming of the Mexicans has provided the Southwest—Texas, New Mexico, Arizona, and California—and those portions of the Middlewest and North which raise sugar beets, with an agricultural proletariat. The vast majority are laborers, not hired men who are going to become tenants and owners. California and Texas farmers are strongly anti-Japanese, because the Japanese, with lower standards of living and working their women and children were ambitious to lease or purchase land and become competitors. Those same farmers are not bothered because Mexican laborers have a low standard of living and work their women and children; rather the reverse; they use them and feel safe. As the wife of one farmer put it: "There is no danger from the Mexicans. They won't save enough to buy land."

The Mexican has at times been used as a strike-breaker and not alone in agriculture. Less well known is his role as striker. He went out from the coal mines of Colorado with the I.W.W. in 1927. In Imperial Valley in the spring of 1928 he formed a union of his own. In quaint language he appealed to the Chambers of Commerce for aid in establishing higher rates for cantaloupe picking:

> In accordance with the bad occasions we've had the past years, it makes us necessary of a better understanding of our business among the Mexican people residing as strangers in the United States. We want to keep on cooperating with our hand of labor, but we claim a more liberal wages, enough to cover our most urgent necessities of the actual situations, and we hereby propose to you gentlemen the points of our wishes.
>
> During the year we scarcely work 185 days, of which we acquire the sum of $555.00 in which we couldn't meet our expenses of alimentation, clothing, house rent, medicine, automobile, and other small exigents. . . .
>
> As you understand, with this amount above stated, we live in the most unhonorable and miserable way, in our concept. . . .

The refusal of some Mexicans to work for less than the union rates was met by a semi-hysterical outbreak from the sheriff. No strike of any extent occurred; most of the demands were granted by the growers; the Mexicans were aroused, and a union organization was launched. In 1930 the Mexicans of Imperial Valley again participated in a strike movement in which Communist leaders sought (*Continued on page* 202)

(*Continued from page* 201) to play a leading role until they were arrested, and several of them convicted under the California criminal syndicalism law.

In Colorado in 1928 a beet workers' union was formed which has spread into other areas. A Mexican editor hailed its advent with none of the courteous tones used in Imperial Valley:

> Some ranchers, individuals without morals and with the sentiments of dogs, only see in a Mexican a beast; they treat him as such, giving him wretched scraps to live on; miserable shacks much, much worse than the stables they have for their plow horses, fat hogs, and milking cows. . . . Although they live in a free country they are nothing but regular slave-drivers who see nothing in a Mexican but a beast of burden or even less than that.

The "docility" of Mexican laborers, so frequently extolled by employers who seem to have believed them racially strike-proof, is not to be taken too literally.

The migration from south of the Rio Grande is predominantly rural; the Mexican laborers live on the whole, as a class apart, maintaining a separate domicile and culture. Many factors serve to maintain the class and culture line and to prevent those contacts which might break it down. The coincidence of class, racial and cultural differences combine to maintain a social ostracism, which in turn reinforces and stabilizes the differences upon which it is based. The earlier immigration of impoverished Europeans who congregated in colonies in our large cities, was also largely a labor class movement. The Mexican migration differs in that its distribution is largely rural, and in that it involves strong consciousness of racial difference. Both these differences accentuate the domiciliary and social isolation of the Mexicans. They delay the *rapprochement* of the two cultures (or the disappearance of one), and retard the blurring of the class line.

American employers of Mexicans have welcomed them as laborers, and done all possible to obtain their admission as immigrants. They have often cared well for their needs. Yet very often they have been but slightly sensitive to low and irregular earnings, child labor with inferior schooling, and social discriminations to which the Mexicans have been subjected in their communities. Some employers have made genuine and effective efforts to meet the situation. In Colorado, for example, business men's service clubs took steps to secure the removal of discriminatory signs from the windows. Some employers, however, have contented themselves with the defense that whatever the conditions among Mexicans here, many of them are materially better off than they were in Mexico. Others have shared the view of a southwestern onion grower:

> Perhaps I'm talking to the wrong man; if you are from the North you won't understand. The Mexican is getting paid about four bits too much. He should get about $1 a day. . . . What a Mexican should be paid is just enough to live on, with maybe a dollar or two to spend. That's all he deserves. If he is paid any more he won't work so much or when we need him; he's able to wait around until we have to raise the price above what's legitimate.

The non-employing groups in the American community have often treated the Mexicans with less consideration than their direct employers. At best, their welcome has generally been as laborers, rather than as people.

THE Mexican immigrant is usually conscious of his role in the United States, but seldom faces the probability that his migration is more permanent than he had intended. The expected return to Mexico continues to recede into the future while ties to the United States become stronger.

Revolution, poverty, and the lure of economic opportunity were common factors behind the emigration. "We left Mexico," said a Mexican in the offices of the Immigrants' Protective League of Chicago, "when things got pretty bad over there, and it was very hard to get something to eat regularly. We had heard, too, that in six months we would be able to buy a car and have a piano for my little girl who likes music." The vision of wealth often turns out to be a mirage, as it did in this case. Discouragement, sentiment, resentment against the discriminations and a passionate patriotism, all urge return to Mexico. "Mexicans," began an orator addressing his compatriots gathered at Hull-House in 1928, "we are but the children of Israel who are pass- (*Continued on page* 205)

DIRECTORY OF SOCIAL AGENCIES

Aid for Travelers

NATIONAL ASSOCIATION OF TRAVELERS AID SOCIETIES—25 West 43rd Street, New York. J. Rogers Flannery, President; Sherrard Ewing, General Director; Miss Bertha McCall, Assistant Director. Represents co-operative efforts of member Societies in extending chain of service points and in improving standards of work. Supported by Societies, supplemented by gifts from interested individuals.

Association of Volunteers

ASSOCIATION OF VOLUNTEERS IN SOCIAL SERVICE—151 Fifth Avenue. Volunteer Placement, Education, Publications. Mrs. Geer, Pres., Alfreda Page, Sec'y.

Child Welfare

ASSOCIATED GUIDANCE BUREAU, INC.—One East Fifty-Third Street, New York, Telephone: Plaza 9512. A non-sectarian, non-philanthropic child guidance bureau, employing highest social work standards. Work includes consultation and home service with behavior maladjustments of children, adolescents, and young adults. For information address Jess Perlman, Director.

BIG BROTHER AND BIG SISTER FEDERATION, INC.—425 Fourth Avenue, New York, and 400 North Michigan Avenue, Chicago. A league of eleemosynary organizations of Catholics, Jews and Protestants in United States and Canada rendering personal, individual and intensive service to children in preventing delinquency. George MacDonald, President, Rowland C. Sheldon and Herbert D. Williams, Ph.D., Executives.

THE INTERNATIONAL SOCIETY FOR CRIPPLED CHILDREN, INC. — An Association of agencies interested in the solution of the problem of the cripple. Edgar F. Allen, Pres.; Harry H. Howett, Sec., Elyria, Ohio.

NATIONAL CHILD LABOR COMMITTEE— Courtenay Dinwiddie, General Secretary, 331 Fourth Avenue, New York. To improve child labor legislation; to conduct investigation in local communities; to advise on administration; to furnish information. Annual membership, $2, $5, $10, $25 and $100 includes monthly publication. "The American Child."

Community Chests

ASSOCIATION OF COMMUNITY CHESTS AND COUNCILS —
1815 Graybar Building,
43rd Street and Lexington Avenue
New York City.
Allen T. Burns, Executive Director.

Education

ART EXTENSION SOCIETY—The Art Center, 65 East 56th Street, New York City. Purpose—to promote art interest and appreciation by means of the publication of books and reproductions. Membership from $2.00 to $50.00 per annum.

Foundations

AMERICAN FOUNDATION FOR THE BLIND, INC.— 125 East 46th Street, New York. Promotes the creation of new agencies for the blind and assists established organizations to expand their activities. Conducts studies in such fields as education, employment and relief of the blind. Supported by voluntary contributions. M. C. Migel, President; Robert B. Irwin, Executive Director; Charles B. Hayes, Field Director.

RUSSELL SAGE FOUNDATION—For the Improvement of Living Conditions—John M. Glenn, dir.; 130 E. 22nd St., New York. Departments: Charity Organization, Delinquency and Penology, Industrial Studies, Library, Recreation, Remedial Loans, Statistics, Surveys and Exhibits. The publications of the Russell Sage Foundation offer to the public in practical and inexpensive form some of the most important results of its work. Catalogue sent upon request.

Health

AMERICAN BIRTH CONTROL LEAGUE, INC.—Mrs. F. Robertson Jones, President, 152 Madison Avenue, New York City. Purpose: To teach the need for birth control to prevent destitution, disease and social deterioration; to amend laws adverse to birth control; to render safe, reliable contraceptive information accessible to all married persons. Annual membership, $2.00 to $500.00. Birth Control Review (monthly), $2.00 per year.

AMERICAN CHILD HEALTH ASSOCIATION—370 Seventh Ave., New York. Herbert Hoover, Honorary President; Philip Van Ingen, M.D., Secretary; S. J. Crumbine, M.D., General Executive. Objects: Sound promotion of child health, especially in co-operation with the official health and education agencies.

AMERICAN FEDERATION OF ORGANIZATIONS FOR THE HARD OF HEARING, INC.—Promotes the cause of the hard of hearing; assists in forming organizations. Pres., Harvey Fletcher, Ph.D., New York City; Executive Secretary, Betty C. Wright, 1537—35th St., N.W., Washington, D. C.

AMERICAN SOCIAL HYGIENE ASSOCIATION—370 Seventh Ave., New York. To provide a better understanding of the social hygiene movement; to advance sound sex education, to combat prostitution and sex delinquency; to aid public authorities in the campaign against the venereal diseases; to advise in organization of state and local social-hygiene programs. Annual membership dues $2.00 including monthly journal.

THE NATIONAL COMMITTEE FOR MENTAL HYGIENE, INC.—Dr. William H. Welch, honorary president; Dr. Charles P. Emerson, president; Dr. C. M. Hincks, general director; Clifford W. Beers, secretary; 370 Seventh Avenue, New York City. Pamphlets on mental hygiene, child guidance, mental disease, mental defect, psychiatric social work and other related topics. Catalogue of publications sent on request. "Mental Hygiene," quarterly, $3.00 a year; "Mental Hygiene Bulletin," monthly, $1.00 a year.

Pamphlets and Periodicals

Inexpensive literature which, however, important, does not warrant costly advertising, may be advertised to advantage in the Pamphlets and Periodicals column of Survey Graphic and Midmonthly.

RATES:—75c a line (actual) for four insertions.

Health

NATIONAL SOCIETY FOR THE PREVENTION OF BLINDNESS—Lewis H. Carris, Managing Director; Mrs. Winifred Hathaway, Associate Director; B. Franklin Royer, M.D., Medical Director; Eleanor P. Brown, Secretary, 370 Seventh Avenue, New York. Studies scientific advance in medical and pedagogical knowledge and disseminates practical information as to ways of preventing blindness and conserving sight. Literature, exhibits, lantern slides, lectures, charts and co-operation in sight-saving projects available on request.

Home Economics

AMERICAN HOME ECONOMICS ASSOCIATION—Alice L. Edwards, executive secretary, 620 Mills Bldg., Washington, D. C. Organized for betterment of conditions on home, school, institution and community. Publishes monthly Journal of Home Economics; office of editor, 620 Mills Bldg., Washington, D. C.; of business manager, 101 East 20th St., Baltimore, Md.

Industrial Democracy

LEAGUE FOR INDUSTRIAL DEMOCRACY—Promotes a better understanding of problems of democracy in industry through its pamphlet, research and lecture services and organization of college and city groups. Executive Directors, Harry W. Laidler and Norman Thomas, 112 East 19 Street, New York City.

National Conference

NATIONAL CONFERENCE OF SOCIAL WORK—Richard C. Cabot, president, Boston; Howard R. Knight, secretary, 277 E. Long St., Columbus, Ohio. The Conference is an organization to discuss the principles of humanitarian effort and to increase the efficiency of social service agencies. Each year it holds an annual meeting, publishes in permanent form the Proceedings of the meeting, and issues a quarterly Bulletin. The fifty-eighth annual convention of the Conference will be held in Minneapolis, June 14-20, 1931. Proceedings are sent free of charge to all members upon payment of a membership fee of five dollars.

Racial Cooperation

COMMISSION ON INTERRACIAL CO-OPERATION—409 Palmer Bldg., Atlanta, Ga.; Will W. Alexander, Director. Seeks improvement of interracial attitudes and conditions through conference, cooperation, and popular education. Correspondence invited.

NATIONAL URBAN LEAGUE—For social service among Negroes. L. Hollingsworth Wood, pres.; Eugene Kinckle Jones, exec. sec'y; 17 Madison Ave., New York. Establishes committees of white and colored people to work out community problems. Trains Negro social workers. Publishes "Opportunity"—a "journal of Negro life."

DIRECTORY RATES

Graphic: 30c per (actual) line (12 insertions a year)

Graphic and Midmonthly } 28c per (actual) line (24 insertions a year)

(*Continued from page* 202) ing through our Egypt here in the United States, doing the onerous labors, swallowing our pride, bracing up under the indignities heaped upon us here."

Other attractions to residence in the United States are discovered. We were told, for example, that although it often is disliked by the men, "the women find out the freedom of the United States is pretty good for them." For the children there are schools and social agencies. "I like the United States," said a Mexican mother in Chicago. "If my babies are sick the Welfare takes care of them. I can go to the dispensary. The nurses and doctor come, and when there is no money we don't pay. It is better than in Mexico." Even the sting of discrimination is forgotten in the presence of friendliness and help:

> We heard of this Hull-House even as far as South Chicago, and they speak of it in the railroad camps outside the city. We remember those things more than the taunts of ignorant Americans. . . .

But it is the young people whose attachments to the United States become the strongest anchors against return. The movement to establish Mexican schools where Mexican culture and patriotism can be inculcated is a conscious effort to resist "de-Mexicanization" of the children, who, their parents sometimes remark regretfully, learn of Washington and Lincoln instead of Hidalgo and Benito Juarez, and say "father" instead of *"mi padre."* But very few Mexicans realize until it is too late that their bonds to the mother country have become tenuous, while at the same time they have failed to establish close cultural contacts with Americans. Fleeing as they so many of them did from ferment and poverty, they have obtained greater security and material benefit at the price of cutting themselves off from the cultural renaissance of their own people at home. Meanwhile they occupy in the United States a role of isolation often stigmatized with inferiority.

THE epoch of Mexican mass migration to the United States is now closed. As a result of increasing political pressure for quota limitation and the desire of the Department of State to forestall such statutes which might be regarded by Latin-American countries as discriminatory, the federal government has diminished the flow of Mexican immigrants to a trickle. Without legislation, but by more stringent enforcement of old legal provisions barring the admission of illiterates, of alien contract laborers, and of persons liable to become public charges, the issuance of immigration visas to natives of Mexico by consular offices has been cut from a monthly average of 4848 for the fiscal year 1927-28 to only 281 for the seven months ending January 31, 1931. The Department of Labor at the same time has effectively increased its efforts to return to Mexico persons illegally in the United States and to strengthen its defenses against surreptitious entry.

The uprooting and return to Mexico of persons already in the United States naturally causes personal hardship which is of course not mitigated by any legal flaws in the right to be here. Therefore it has aroused protests both from Americans (usually employers concerned primarily over the loss of laborers) and from Mexicans, who charge that the immigration officers "persecute systematically with exasperating passion," and by their methods of enforcement themselves "violate the same immigration laws." It is fairly apparent that the hardships now visited on Mexicans are in considerable measure due to the present efforts of officials, stimulated both by the imminence of quota legislation and by widespread unemployment, to undo the effects of previous weak enforcement of the immigration laws.

The economic depression in the United States has in turn caused the return to Mexico of many immigrants, just as it did in 1921. It will be recalled that when business picked up in 1922 and 1923 a new tide set in. Following this depression, however, thousands whose right hitherto to be in the United States rested upon an entry of dubious legality or clear illegality, or whose period of permitted absence from the country will have been overstayed in Mexico, will be unable to qualify for return to the United States under the new standards of law enforcement.

We may well recognize, therefore, the end of the tidal wave of immigration across our southern border. But we need not expect the Mexican population in this country to melt like the snow, as some have thought. The net balance of repatriations to Mexico of 45,000 in 1930 reported by the Department of State upon advices from Mexican sources is much less than a similar balance of 97,000 in 1921. Even if year after year such a balance should be maintained, and assuming neither births nor deaths among the Mexicans in the United States, it would require a quarter of a century (and how much longer we shall know only when the 1930 census is published) to return our Mexican population to Mexico. No such exodus is probable. The representatives of our two cultures will remain in juxtaposition in large and widespread areas of the United States, with contacts of varying types and degrees of intensity. The stamp of the Mexican migration will be visible for generations.

Inter-American Education

Occasional Papers, I

First Regional Conference
on
The Education of Spanish-Speaking People in the Southwest

(Held at The University of Texas on December 13–14–15, 1945)

GEORGE I. SÁNCHEZ
Editor

THE UNIVERSITY OF TEXAS PRESS
Austin

March 1946

FOREWORD

With this issue of the *Occasional Papers* of *Inter-American Education* we hope to inaugurate a series which will serve as a vehicle for making available to interested students and agencies those reports, researches, and other similar materials in the broad field of inter-American education which are deemed worthy of wide distribution. The immediate motive for this publication is to be found in one of the recommendations of the conference reported herein. That recommendation called for a journal or news-letter which would disseminate worthwhile professional information among the students of the problems confronting Spanish-speaking people in the United States. It is to be hoped that, until such a time as a more formal journal may be established in response to the recommendation, that purpose will be served through the publication of such information in the *Occasional Papers* of this series.

The education of Spanish-speaking people in the United States is a phase—a very important phase—of inter-American education. Not only is it a significant part of intercultural education in the United States, involving as it does one of the most prominent minorities in the nation, but it is a keystone in the structure of cultural relations between the United States and the other American republics. Therefore, while the education of these people is an integral part of American education, it is also proper to think of it as inter-American education.

The following report represents an important milestone in this field of education. It is eminently fitting that it should inaugurate the *Inter-American Education* series.

G.I.S.

CONTENTS

INTRODUCTION

There are in the Southwest more than two million people whose cultural heritage is, broadly speaking, Spanish-Mexican. These people do not constitute a homogeneous group, however. Biologically, they range over all the possible combinations of, first, their heterogeneous Spanish antecedents and, then, of the *mestizaje* resulting from the crossing of Spaniards and various indigenous peoples of Mexico and of the Southwest. Historically, they are both old and new to this region—some came with Oñate in 1598, others with missionaries of the eighteenth century; some were a part of the gold-rush of '49, others came to build railroads a few decades later; many came as contract-labor during World War I. Culturally, reflecting their varied biological and historical background, they are many peoples—the *californios,* the *hispanos,* the *méxico-tejanos,* and the numerous other cultural personalities produced by the range of their antecedents and their environments, by their occupations, by their culture-contacts.

These people, of whom only a minority are citizens of Mexico, are most often referred to as "Mexicans." Their mother tongue, their vernacular, is usually Spanish—though every conceivable variation of that tongue obtains, in terms of all phases of both quantity and quality. In fact, for some the home-language is English; for others a part-English, part-Spanish vernacular is the rule.

These Spanish-Mexican Americans of the Southwest, then, defy categorical classification as a group and no term or phrase adequately describes them. Since the Spanish language is the most common denominator among them (with the exceptions and with the variations referred to above), the awkward designation "Spanish-speaking people" is the one which comes closest to having general application as a name for this heterogeneous group.

The assimilation of the Spanish-speaking people of the Southwest, the inevitable cultural contacts and conflicts that occur among them and between them and other groups in this area, and a complex of many other issues and problems constitute a situation that should be of serious concern to all. As a matter of fact, however, these issues and problems have not been made the subject of attack upon a large scale by any agency or institution. While a number of individuals have distinguished themselves as students of these problems, and while some passing attention has been given to narrow phases of some segment of the situation by several private and governmental agencies, this minority population has been an orphan group insofar as effective, organized sponsorship is concerned. Even so, significant strides have been taken in the study of the educational problems of Spanish-speaking people. This has been the result of the efforts of a few individuals who, as teachers or as members of departments of education, have sought to encourage the scientific study of the problems and to apply the remedial measures dictated by sound pedagogy. These efforts have been aided from time to time through the financial assistance granted by a few organizations with an interest in these matters. Notable among these organizations are the General Education Board and the office of the Coördinator of Inter-American Affairs.*

The progress that has been made in this field has served to emphasize that there is great need for coördinated effort in the study of the problems and issues of the region and for concerted support for professional endeavor. It has been particularly evident for many years that there is great need in the Southwest for some organization or program which, at regular intervals, would bring together, in both state and regional meetings, those professional leaders who are especially concerned in the education of Spanish-speaking people. It is clear that many worthwhile results are possible from such meetings and, without question, such a continuous examination of educational problems would prove of great benefit throughout the region. The past lack of such continuous collaboration has been one of the most serious handicaps to an effective attack upon the educational issues raised by this sector of the population.

With this in mind, The University of Texas recently sought and obtained assistance from the General Education Board to finance the first regional conference on the education of Spanish-speaking people in the Southwest. Leaders in the field from over the region were invited and the conference took place at the University during December 13–15. The list of delegates who attended the meetings is given on pages 10–11.

The fundamental object of this first conference was that of obtaining a free exchange of views on the part of the experts in this field. With this object in view, all the sessions of the conference were of the round-table, discussion type. At the initial session, the delegates were introduced and Dr. B. F. Pittenger welcomed them to the University. An informal discussion of conference plans and program at this session prepared the delegates for the tasks ahead.

Since prepared papers were purposely avoided, it was deemed desirable to use another procedure to point up the discussions. For this purpose, panels of delegates were selected to give special thought to the topics of the conference and to take leadership in the discussion. The reports presented herein were prepared by the respective panels and are summarized versions of the exchange of views that took place among all members of the conference on each of the selected topics under leadership of the various panels of delegates. These reports, therefore, may be regarded as an expression of the views of all the delegates.

Members of the panels were selected at separate sessions held by the delegates from each state. The topics to be considered by the conference were discussed at those state sessions and there was an exchange of views as to

*Later the Office of Inter-American Affairs. The work with the Spanish-speaking minority carried on by that office has recently been taken over by the Institute of Ethnic Affairs, Inc., with headquarters at 1719 K Street, Northwest, Washington 6, D.C. The Los Angeles, Denver, and Austin field offices of the old program are being continued by the Institute.

the significance of those topics to each state group. In addition, each state group elected a representative to serve on the executive committee. The executive committee that was named is composed as follows:

Dr. Stuart Cuthbertson, University of Colorado, Boulder.

Mrs. Marie Hughes of the Public Schools of Los Angeles County, California.

Dr. John L. McMahon of Our Lady of The Lake College in San Antonio, Texas.

Dr. Joaquín Ortega of the University of New Mexico, Albuquerque.

Dr. Irma Wilson of the Arizona State Teachers College at Tempe.

This executive committee served, under the chairmanship of Dr. H. T. Manuel, as the panel which led the discussion on the topic of "Regional Planning." It is planned that this committee will meet again this spring to formulate a program for the future. The meeting is tentatively scheduled for May, in Santa Fe, New Mexico, in connection with the statewide conference on the problems of the education of Spanish-speaking people in that state.

The regional conference ended on a note of enthusiasm and optimism at a banquet session of which Dr. J. G. Flowers was the presiding officer. In addition to all the official delegates, the wives of the out-of-state delegates as well as several local educational and social welfare leaders were special guests of the conference at the banquet. Brief addresses were made by Miss Flora M. Rhind and Mr. Fred McCuistion, both of the General Education Board, and by Señor Gustavo Ortiz Hernán, Consul General of Mexico (San Antonio, Texas).

The conference was, in the opinion of all, highly successful and a remarkably pleasant one. The give-and-take spirit apparent in the discussion of differences of opinion, and the good-fellowship which prevailed generally, augured well for future collaboration among the members of the conference. It is a matter of regret that, for reasons beyond their control, several of the specialists who were invited as delegates were unable to attend the conference. It is hoped that, at future meetings, those individuals as well as other regional and national leaders in this field will be able to join in this program of collaboration. This writer, who, for the time being, serves as the coördinator for the regional organization, solicits the coöperation of all and welcomes all suggestions that will lead towards a more effective program. Attention is called to the fact that such suggestions will have particular pertinence if they can be considered by the executive committee at its first meeting (May).

Geo. I. Sánchez.

ROSTER OF DELEGATES

As indicated before, some of the specialists invited to come to the conference as delegates were unable to attend for reasons beyond their control. The following is the list of official delegates who were present:

Arizona

Dr. Max L. Basemann,
Chairman, Department of Languages,
Arizona State College,
Flagstaff

Dr. Victor H. Kelley,
Professor of Education,
University of Arizona,
Tucson

Dr. Irma Wilson,
Professor of Education,
Arizona State Teachers College,
Tempe

California

Mrs. Marie Hughes,
Curriculum Coördinator and Specialist,
in Education of Minority Groups,
Public Schools, County of Los Angeles,
Los Angeles

Dr. Welty Lefever,
Professor of Eduction,
University of Southern California,
University Park, Los Angeles

Colorado

Miss Prudence Bostwick,
Supervising Teacher,
Denver Public Schools,
Denver

Dr. Stuart Cuthbertson,
Professor of Romance Languages,
University of Colorado,
Boulder

Dr. Wilhelmina Hill,
Associate Professor of Education and
Director of Inter-American Education,
Denmonstration Center,
University of Denver,
Denver

Mr. John C. Unger, Director
of Secondary Education and Curricula,
State Department of Education,
Denver

New Mexico

Dr. A. L. Campa,
Professor of Romance Languages
University of New Mexico,
Albuquerque

Dr. Edward Eyring,
President, N. Mex. Highlands University,
Las Vegas

Miss Carmen Espinosa,
State Department of Education,
Santa Fe

Dr. Joaquín Ortega, Director,
School of Inter-American Affairs,
University of New Mexico,
Albuquerque

Mrs. Mary Watson,
State Department of Education,
Santa Fe

Texas

Rev. John L. Birch,
Executive Secretary, Bishops' Committee
for the Spanish-Speaking,
Bedell Building, 113 Broadway,
San Antonio

Mr. R. C. Eckhardt,
Office of Inter-American Affairs,
Scarbrough Building,
Austin

Dr. J. G. Flowers,
President, Southwest Texas State
Teachers College,
San Marcos

Dr. E. N. Jones,
President, Texas College of Arts
and Industries,
Kingsville

Dr. J. O. Loftin,
President, San Antonio Junior College,
San Antonio

Dr. H. T. Manuel,
Professor of Educational Psychology,
The University of Texas,
Austin

Dr. John L. McMahon,
President, Our Lady of the Lake College,
San Antonio

Dr. Henry J. Otto,
Professor of Elementary Education,
The University of Texas,
Austin

Dr. B. F. Pittenger,
Dean, College of Education,
The University of Texas,
Austin

Dr. Geo. I. Sánchez,
Professor of Latin-American Education,
The University of Texas,
Austin

Dr. R. L. Sutherland,
Professor of Sociology and
Director of Hogg Foundation,
The University of Texas,
Austin

Miss Myrtle Tanner,
Director, Information and Statistics
and Inter-American Relations Education,
State Department of Education,
Austin

Dr. L. A. Woods,
State Supt. of Public Instruction,
Austin

General Education Board

Mr. Fred McCuistion,
Assistant Director,
General Education Board,
49 West 49th Street,
New York, N.Y.

Miss Flora M. Rhind,
Assistant Director,
General Education Board,
49 West 49th Street,
New York, N.Y.

STATEMENT OF THE PROBLEM

JOHN L. MCMAHON, *Chairman*

Miss Prudence Bostwick
Edward Eyring
Mrs. Marie Hughes
George I. Sánchez
Miss Irma Wilson

The first panel discussion of the conference properly dealt with the basic problems confronting each of the represented states in the education of Spanish-speaking people. The discussion of the individual reports tended to show that the problem is regional in character rather than locally isolated. Furthermore, although there are important variances in the problems of the individual states, such as those that relate to the character of the population, whether urban or rural, original settler or newly-arrived immigrant, essentially the problem is one and it is a serious one throughout the region.

All members of the panel were in agreement that the basic need in each of the states, and therefore the region, is for a socio-economic survey which would supplement and coördinate the information that now we have. This survey would provide needed information about all such important factors in the lives of the Spanish-speaking as employment, wages, housing, health, migratory labor, language problems, and the like without which an intelligent and sustained attack upon the problem is impossible. Odum's *Southern Regions* was taken as an example of the type of survey that was desirable and should be made. Pending such a comprehensive analysis, spot surveys and coördination of research in this field in the graduate schools of the region should be given special encouragement.

Some of the reports emphasized that, since the resources available to some of the states are insufficient to meet the existing need, federal aid is necessary to the solution of some of the problems in this field. New Mexico, it was reported, although spending more money on education than any other state in proportion to its resources is, nevertheless, measured by its accomplishment in meeting the problem of illiteracy, the fifth or sixth lowest ranking state in the nation. This condition has been brought about in part by the inequitable application of appropriations and by the tremendous scope of the problem.

There was unanimity on the part of the panel members that there existed in each of the states patterns of segregation, isolation, and discrimination which operated against the welfare of both the Spanish-speaking people and the entire community where such patterns exist. Community coöperation between English- and Spanish-speaking peoples and agencies for the study and solution of these problems have been initiated in some areas. Such organizations as the Institute on Community Relations conducted by Los Angeles County, the Colorado Corporation on Inter-American Field Service, the Denver Unity Council, and the institute of leaders of both groups sponsored in

Texas with aid from the Office of Inter-American Affairs* have rendered valuable service. Important as such community coöperation is, the undeniable fact remains that these patterns of segregation continue to exist and that segregation is a moral and social evil, inimicable to national welfare.

To aid further in the solution of this and other problems facing the Spanish-speaking of the region, it was recognized that increasingly and to the fullest extent of their ability, the Spanish-speaking people must assume responsibility for their own development. The program carried out by the School of Inter-American Affairs of the University of New Mexico in aiding the Spanish-speaking to see their own problems, in assisting in their solution and, more importantly, in the training of leaders was recognized as one important means by which the Spanish-speaking people themselves might accomplish this end. More Spanish-speaking doctors, lawyers, social workers, teachers, and members of other professions would aid in the promotion of individual and group welfare.

Some of the reports stressed the necessity of increased state industrialization to provide employment opportunities for seasonal or marginal workers. Others, notably California, emphasized that the rapid industrialization that occurred there during the war has resulted in totally inadequate school facilities for the Spanish-speaking. School statistics there and in other states showed that, whereas as much as thirty per cent of the enrollment in the elementary grades was Spanish-speaking, this figure dropped to below eight per cent in the secondary school and became practically non-existent at the college level.

Other problems delineated by the panel members included the language handicap which constitutes an ever-present and powerful barrier to full participation in civic life; the necessity for well-developed programs of adult education, which will meet the individual and group needs of the people; and a sound program of teacher education and training to provide not only able and sympathetic classroom teachers but community leaders.

---

*As noted before, activities of this sort that were formerly sponsored by that Office have been taken over by the Institute of Ethnic Affairs, Inc. (1719 K Street, Northwest, Washington 6, D.C.).

CRUCIAL EDUCATION ISSUES

EDWARD EYRING, *Chairman*

Victor H. Kelley
Welty Lefever
Miss Myrtle Tanner
John C. Unger
Mrs. Mary Watson

Special emphasis was placed upon the problem of bilingualism, both as regards the teaching of English and the teaching of Spanish. It was a matter of general agreement that the teaching of English to Spanish-speaking students is one of the crucial educational issues throughout the Southwest. It was brought out that, in a large number of cases, the child does not have sufficient opportunity to learn English; first, because of the time limitations in classroom instruction and, secondly, because he often has little chance to hear English outside of the classroom. While, undoubtedly, much progress has been made in improving the teaching of English to these children, much more attention to the problem is still warranted in every respect—teacher education, curricular reforms, research, texts, etc. It was emphasized that, in teaching English to Spanish-speaking children, association with English-speaking students is most helpful, and that segregation militates against the learning of English by Spanish-speaking children as well as against other even more fundamental aspects of their education.

Discussion on the teaching of Spanish to Spanish-speaking children in the elementary schools indicated that this is a desirable practice having various worthwhile results. Larger demonstrations and more experimentation in this program should be undertaken. To this end, attention should be given to the preparation of teachers and to the development of suitable instructional materials and methods. It was agreed that, in the elementary grades, the greatest value to all concerned would result from teaching Spanish to mixed classes of Spanish-speaking and English-speaking children. Since the goals are different in the last year or two of senior high school and in college, this mixed-group procedure is not necessarily desirable at those levels—rather, homogeneous grouping in terms of proficiency in Spanish being the most highly recommended plan. It was suggested that, in the elementary school, teaching of Spanish is very helpful in the development of proficiency in English. A caution was offered to the effect that Spanish-speaking children are, in truth, Spanish-speaking in varying degrees in terms of both quantity and quality.

It was emphatically pointed out that school segregation is pedagogically unsound, socially dangerous, and unquestionably un-American. This matter of segregation is a crucial education issue and should be attacked with all the intelligence and insight possible. Numerous illustrations were cited which served to condemn segregation and which demonstrated the desirability of its elimination—in the interest of both the English-speaking child and the Spanish-speaking child.

The other crucial problem to which particular attention was given was that of school attendance and progress. Numerous factors were cited as contributing to delinquency in this regard: health and economic conditions of the people, unattractive school plants and programs, indifference on the part of school administrators, poor teaching, seasonal labor, and the opposition of vested interests. There was agreement to the effect that more attractive school plants and programs, by themselves, would go a long way toward correcting present lack of attendance and school progress. In addition, it was apparent that, as strongly contributing factors to current unsatisfactory conditions, much of the blame can be paid to inadequate and inequitable school financing. Along with other defects, the absence of satisfactory programs of vocational training and vocational guidance was pointed out. The group was well aware that many vital factors, economic and cultural as well as strictly educational, lie in the background of the symptoms or phenomena which we call "school attendance" and "school progress." Therefore, it insisted that much study and planning are certainly needed in this important area.

REMEDIAL MEASURES

MRS. MARIE HUGHES, *Chairman*

Max L. Basemann
A. L. Campa
J. G. Flowers
Miss Wilhelmina Hill

The extended need to improve the educational program of the Spanish-speaking people in the Southwest has been set forth above. The special problems presented by conditions in the Southwest have likewise been considered. Even the most cursory analysis of needs and problems identifies the low socio-economic status, inferior health conditions, inferior educational opportunities, the language handicap, and the isolation of the Spanish-speaking group from the larger community. Several of these problems are directly within the province of educational workers. Others need the coöperation of state and regional organizations to effect improvement. Whether or not the educational workers can directly effect improvement, they are obliged to secure accurate and comprehensive information regarding the problem within the school district and the larger community.

Inferior educational opportunities caused by inadequate financial structure can be improved through the coöperation of state and regional groups who believe in equality of educational opportunity for all the children.

The problem of segregated schools, that is, those schools attended exclusively by the Spanish-speaking children, is one of great concern. In many cases these schools are out-and-out segregated schools. Sometimes the children attending them even pass by the school attended by Anglo-American children. In few instances are these segregated schools maintained on the same standards of physical building and equipment and teacher efficiency. These schools represent discriminatory practice. A variety of approaches of doing away with such schools is necessary. A court decision oftentimes clarifies the issues involved. Such a decision has been sought in California and other areas should urge court decisions on this question. Such decisions may serve as a stimulus to school boards who need, or think they need, such outside authority in changing the policy of the district.

A second approach involves a general education program for the entire community, a program which points out the langers in segregation and the unwholesome effect on community life. Another argument, useful with lay people and educators alike, shows how impossible it is for children to learn the ways of American living when they are not in contact with people who live in that manner. This applies particularly to language and the more subtle forms of social intercourse. Administrators should become informed as to the ill effects of segregation.

Intermediary steps may be used, which open up the way to complete elimination of the segregated school. Such intermediary steps as moving the seventh and eighth grades or the kindergarten to the "Anglo" school, assemblies, play days, picnics, musical participation, and other forms of inter-communication among schools, which will accustom Anglo parents and children to being with Mexican-American children, and likewise accustom Mexican-American parents and children to being with Anglo-Americans. Still another form of action involves work with the minority groups so that they may do away with some of the obvious differences which create distinctions between themselves and the Anglo-American group.

Segregated schools and discriminatory practices stand as a direct impediment to the improvement of our relations with Spanish-speaking people in international affairs. When communities begin to realize that these practices are undemocratic, that they prevent American citizens from becoming responsible participants in the community, they cannot continue them. The present need for new buildings and existence of distinct boundaries make it a peculiarly propitious time to begin progressive campaigns against the unfriendly and undemocratic institute of segregated schools.

A problem for which educators should assume the larger responsibility is that of poor school attendance on the part of Mexican-American youngsters. Among the factors which contribute to poor attendance are inadequate curriculum, poor promotion and placement policies, and the lack of understanding by teachers of the Mexican-American pupils. It should be pointed out that special attention to curriculum and to improvement in the relation between teachers and pupils has resulted in improvement of daily attendance of Spanish-speaking children.

The whole area of curriculum, with special attention to community arts and skills, merits the attention of educators. It may be stated categorically that most schools do not really teach English because they are listening schools and provide little opportunity or motive for talking. Moreover, the activities and experiences offered within the school are so limited that a proper English vocabulary could not possibly be acquired. It is necessary to rethink the program of teaching English and to make the opportunities for children to talk with a purpose; to provide an increasing range of experiences so that a truly functional vocabulary may be acquired. The English should be given for all the activities of living, which are common in the life of the child and of the adult within the community. Such a vocabulary, supplemented by reading and the child's own insight, gives him the skill whereby he may continue to increase his speaking and listening vocabulary. Successful demonstration centers where teachers can be trained and where teachers may go to see effective language instruction is an imperative.

The curriculum should be built so that it is community and child centered. Any differences in good curriculum for "other" children and for Spanish-speaking children are only those of degree. Children cannot gain proper meanings through the use of vicarious materials. Meanings must be built through first-hand experiences. The community provides those first-hand experiences. The problems and needs which the children feel also have their basis in the community life. The materials developed under the Sloan Foundation in Kentucky, Florida, and Vermont are suggestive of the kinds desirable for children of the Southwest region.

Teacher education is continuous. The pre-service training needs to be redrawn and public school systems need to forward an in-service training program. Both programs require demonstration centers dealing with situations common within the region. Among the skills and attitudes which teachers should possess are:

1. Understanding and devotion to democratic ideals and a conviction that they can be achieved if we will work toward them.
2. Undertsanding of the social and psychological problems involved in minority-group and lower-class status.
3. Skills in studying the community and in analyzing pupil needs and in bringing the two together.
4. Skills in the preparation of reading and language materials.
5. Appreciation, interest, and development of skills in working with community organizations.

The problem of vocational education is directly related to the guidance program, which means that the opportunities for improvement within the area served should be well known and the ability to stimulate young people to prepare for further work should be cultivated.

Another point expressed by this panel group includes the total community in any effort to improve the education of Spanish-speaking children. There fore, the need for educational and community education was reiterated. Methods of achieving this are through the traditional forms—parent, teacher, and other adult organizations. For the Mexican-American, much more personal contact is needed and in many cases the setting up of opportunities which do not now exist in the community are necessary.

REGIONAL PLANNING

H. T. MANUEL, *Chairman*

Stuart Cuthbertson
Mrs. Marie Hughes
John L. McMahon
Joaquín Ortega
Miss Irma Wilson

The basic problem of education in the Southwest, as in the world at large, is that of building an effective democracy in which every person will enjoy his inalienable rights to life, liberty, and the pursuit of happiness, and will participate effectively with his fellows in the orderly processes of self-government. The problem in the Southwest is made more difficult than in some other areas by the fact that our people speak different languages, come from somewhat different cultural backgrounds, and include large numbers of people of extremely unfavorable socio-economic status. The Southwest presents, however, a peculiar opportunity to observe and study the integrating of three cultures—the Spanish, the Indian, and the Anglo-Saxon. Since the Anglo-Saxon tradition is the norm for the region, and since the Indian is the object of attention by special agencies such as the U.S. Office of Indian Affairs, special attention should be given to the seriously neglected special problem of the Spanish-speaking group. This group has cultural traditions of its own to contribute to the advance of civilization and, in both numbers and potentialities, constitutes a significant human resource.

The problems of education for this group are extremely complicated and must be attacked from many angles. They are indeed parts of the larger problems of coöperative living and are intimately bound up with them. Though recognizing these larger implications, this committee's statement is restricted to issues of more immediate concern to educators.

As educators we have four main responsibilities: (1) to furnish leadership to the public in providing adequate educational facilities for children and adults and in seeing that our people take advantage of them; (2) to conduct the processes of education with the greatest possible efficiency; (3) to advance knowledge through research; and (4) to develop a consumers' market for knowledge and for factual and factorial information so that majority thinking may coincide with the best thinking.

With respect to these responsibilities, the public needs to know that large numbers of our children from Spanish-speaking homes are out of school; that in many communities adequate provisions for their education are lacking; that in some communities an unwise policy of separating them from English-speaking children delays their language development and hinders the processes of democratic living; that programs of education for Spanish-speaking adults are generally inadequate; and that provisions for bringing English-speaking and Spanish-speaking peoples into effective coöperation are usually lacking.

In planning remedial measures we need first of all a comprehensive statement of the basic facts. To prepare such a statement will require additional research. This research should include a socio-economic survey of the Spanish-speaking people in the Southwest. The panel recommends that planning for such a survey should constitute an important phase of the next meeting of the executive committee. For immediate action, however, and as a recommendation to all state departments of education in the region, it is proposed that state departments of education make surveys of the Spanish-speaking school population—census, enrollment, attendance, age-grade status and progress, etc. Special attention is called to the desirability of determining facts of this nature for children of migratory laborers, and of determining the extent of the mobility of migratory families.

The panel discussed the need for Spanish radio programs, periodicals, and other reading materials with useful information for the people whose sole means of communication is Spanish; the advantages of offering intensive institutes for the training of community leaders; the advisability of introducing into teacher training programs courses dealing with the socio-economic facts of the area, so that teachers may be better prepared to make of the school a more effective factor in community betterment; and the utilization of expert journalists and writers for adequate presentation of the facts of the situation to the public at large.

All these proposals, though, would necessitate more elaborate consideration in successive meetings of the state organizations and of the executive committee.

For immediate concern we strongly recommend that the regional organization try to establish a professional news letter or journal, which would serve as a medium for the exchange of ideas of those actively working in this field, thus insuring continuity and coördination in their efforts.

A specific effort needs to be made to attract more students into the field of teaching Spanish-speaking people. The panel feels that this field should prove attractive to a superior type of student and that institutions of higher learning should provide attractive but realistic courses to train such students. In our discussions the hope was expressed that a greater number of superior students might be attracted into work with the Spanish-speaking peoples by integrating courses in our institutions of higher education with actual field work in communities. Committees of students (economics, sociology, nursing, dietetics, history, English, Spanish) could be formed for many communities which will represent laboratories for the application of classroom theory. Each community might thus develop a nucleus of potential leaders.

We have given careful attention to a proposal (see Addendum) for a textbook for teachers of Spanish-speaking children. It is believed that such a textbook is urgently needed. The executive committee approved the project, subject to modification of details. The conference as a whole received the proposal with enthusiasm, placing it by motion unanimously adopted on the agenda of the executive committee with high priority.

In the initial preparation of teachers and in their in-service training, demonstration centers are of paramount importance. These centers may be maintained by county boards, state departments, institutions for the education of teachers, or other agencies. They should demonstrate the best known practices and carry on needed experimentation.

We have given particular attention to the question of state and regional organization. All agree that state and regional organization should be undertaken at the earliest possible moment. It is recommended that this organization not limit itself to the strictly pedagogical phases of this field of interest but that it encompass all phases of the acculturation of Spanish-speaking people. Both the executive committee and the conference as a whole went on record favoring the establishment of the state and regional organizations, with a regional executive committee and a regional office to serve as the clearing-house, planning, and coördinating agency of the groups. With this in mind it was agreed that the executive committee of this conference was to function as the regional executive committee, and plans were made for a meeting of the executive committee some time in the first half of 1946. It was agreed that the regional office, under the direction of a regional coördinator, should serve as the clearing-house for the distribution of information, the undertaking of surveys, the examination of projects, etc. The above general proposals with reference to state and regional organizations were embodied in a motion which was unanimoulsy accepted.

* * * * * *

Addendum:

Proposal

for a

Textbook for Teachers of Spanish-Speaking Children

I. *Purpose:* To provide basic reading materials (including carefully annotated bibliographical references) for teachers and prospective teachers of Spanish-speaking children in the United States.

There is no such text at present. On the contrary, the materials are widely scattered. Indeed, there is as yet no general understanding of what these materials should be.

II. *Production of Materials:* Probably the best plan for producing the materials is to organize the work under an editor-in-chief and an editorial board, and to allot the work of production to contributors chosen for their special competence in their respective fields.

It is doubtful whether any one individual can be found who has the information necessary or who will be willing to devote the time necessary to prepare such a book alone. Besides, there would be obvious advantages in having various points of view represented, provided all are integrated in a usable volume.

III. *Specifications:* A book of standard textbook construction of about 750 pages, subsidized so that it can be sold for about $2.00. It should present the materials now available and represent the best scholarship that can be brought to bear upon it. Its tone should be factual and scientific—not in any sense devoted to propaganda or reform. It should be eclectic rather than restricted to a particular point of view. It should be constructive.

IV. *Plan of Construction and Calendar:*

1. Approval by this conference, December 15, 1945.
2. Appointment of editor-in-chief by executive committee.
3. Appeal för funds.
4. Appointment of editorial staff by editor-in-chief and executive committee, March 1, 1946.
5. Meeting of editorial staff to plan volume in detail and to select contributors for the several chapters, June, 1946.
6. Production of materials—first draft submitted to editor-in-chief by June 30, 1947.
7. Criticism of materials by other specialists.
8. Rewriting and editing of materials—final copy ready October 31, 1947.
9. Publication, April 30, 1948.

V. *Possible Contents* (actual contents would be determined by editorial Board):

1. Introduction—purpose, point of view, plan, etc.
2. Objectives—democracy, hemispheric solidarity, etc.
3. Geographical considerations—nature of area, distribution of population, etc.
4. Historical background.
5. Cultural characteristics and socio-economic status.
6. Psychological considerations.
7. Provisions for education.
8. Enrollment and attendance.
9. Types of schools.
10. Curriculum.
11. The language problem.
12. Materials and methods.
13. Sources of assistance.

VI. *Cost* (a very tentative estimate):

1. Meeting of editorial board	$ 2,500
2. Salary of editor-in-chief (Part time for several months)	2,500
3. Honoraria for editors and contributors	5,000
4. Stenographic and other assistance	5,000
5. Materials and supplies	1,500
6. Postage, telegrams, express, etc	1,000
7. Travel	5,000
8. Printing	7,500
Total	$30,000

WITHIN
These Borders

) Spanish-Speaking Peoples in the U.S.A. (

WITHIN
These Borders

by JOHN R. SCOTFORD

FRIENDSHIP PRESS — NEW YORK

LIBRARY OF CONGRESS CATALOG CARD NUMBER: 53-9345

Printed in the United States of America

To you, my Mexican and Puerto Rican friends, in the hope that this volume may lead others to enjoy you as much as I have

Contents

Foreword

The following pages provide only glimpses of a notable part of the population of the United States. No matter how expert and sensitive the reporter nor how large the book, one treatment cannot possibly do justice to Spanish Americans. There are a million of them in Texas, 760,000 in California, 250,000 in New Mexico, 25,000 in both Arizona and Colorado, 37,000 in New York, plus a scattered half million of illegal entrants. Add to these the Cubans in Tampa and visiting students from every Latin American country. Such figures merely illustrate the weakness of arithmetic to bring a sense of reality to the description of a people.

Something of Spanish culture and its contributions to life in the United States is found in these pages. But again, describing Spanish art, music, and architecture fails to reveal to the remote reader the warmth and vitality of the people. Surveys might tabulate the exact number of Spanish Protestant Christians, the number of ministers who serve them, and the value in dollars of their churches. Such information would serve only to overload the brain without producing a clarifying vision.

To appreciate any people one must communicate with them personally and so arrive at an understanding derived from experience. Without such personal contact, the best we can do is to feel vicariously the attitudes of those who do know them. Such are the Christian workers who for Christ's sake have devoted their lives to sharing the fruit of the gospel with them.

A characteristic common to those who are in "Spanish-speaking work" is a vibrant enthusiasm for their parishioners and co-workers. This grows from an appreciation of the values that develop in the soul when Christ has wrought his gracious change. If those workers could speak to us in our churches they would strive above all else to communicate to us their own radiant enthusiasm. "Here are people for whom Christ died," they would say. "These are our brothers redeemed, living new, victorious lives in him." Are we their keepers? The answer surely is "No! We are called by Christ to be their brothers."

These pages also show examples of Christian work in evangelism and education and social service. How may we see the full Christian program throughout the states and so appreciate its importance? The visiting missionary can make us respond to his conviction of a great missionary opportunity. The majority of Americans of Spanish heritage know Christianity only in a cultural sense. Without an effective ministry they have resorted to superstition, but their response to Christian love is both ready and profound.

Missionaries have a harvest to show for the planting. Their stories tell of broken lives made new, immoral people made holy, and untaught children brought to glad graduation. Behold the little cotton picker now a Christian nurse. Hear of the staunch elder whose back still bears a cross of scars inflicted by the whips of the Penitente orgy. Wonder at the bandit who once rode with Pancho Villa, now, by God's grace, a Christian pastor. Theirs are dramatic, moving stories and necessarily so, for how can miracles be reported in cold blood?

Within the limits imposed by modesty, the missionary could portray the Christian program as being good—as good as resources of leadership and equipment will allow. True enough, many chapels and churches are humble, since the little congregations are poor. But supporting friends can do a great deal to make these centers of worship and education more nearly adequate. Surely we will not blame the missionaries for conditions caused by weak support.

It is also true that many Spanish pastors need more and better training. This lack, however, need be no reflection upon their devotion nor upon their ability to evoke from their people a fervent allegiance. There is plenty of room for both pastors and people to grow, and they hope to occupy additional space.

Christian workers among Spanish people in the United States believe the field is ready for harvest and appeal for more workers to do the reaping. They hope that God will raise us up to become wholehearted participants in the redemptive endeavor that is their lifework. Their supreme trust is in the Lord of the harvest.

Hardheaded citizens may ask what practical good comes from Protestant mission work. Some may be comforted with school and hospital statistics, others with success stories of people helped to "make good." Christian workers, though, would prefer to speak of the needs felt by citizens of Spanish culture and point to the values they themselves discover in Christian experience.

Although Spanish people may be locally numerous in some places, nationally they are a minority. Like other minorities they need friendship in a new land. Where better can friendship be found than in

Christ and in the fellowship of his people? Spanish Christians know how to return friendship in unstinted measure, for they are poets at heart. Spanish friendship, however, is so tinctured with courtesy that it may tax the sense of efficiency of some North Americans.

Another need felt by a minority group is for justice—a fair chance to make a living and build a life. This does not mean asking favors, for Spanish citizens accept heavy duties that the average North American would refuse to bear. A young Puerto Rican mother raising four little ones in a Brooklyn apartment works all day in a candy factory, prepares the next day's meals at night, and shows the eldest daughter how to care for the younger ones until her return in the late afternoon. When asked if she found this life difficult, she replied in surprise, "But no. It is my work. Why should I think it hard?" This mother keeps the apartment and tries to keep up with her children's interests. She asks for work at a fair wage and a chance for the children to grow. May she expect her church to be a champion of justice?

Minorities are like majorities in one respect; all the people who comprise them need a Saviour. Surely the yearning love of God demonstrated in the world mission of the church seeks to embrace Spanish-speaking Americans.

A teen-age Puerto Rican boy in Brooklyn was one among eight school children recognized for outstanding citizenship. Though he had been in the United States only three years, he had become his teacher's interpreter. In answer to a letter from a mission board secretary he replied, "You encourage me to go ahead by the Golden Rule. I say I do, I will, I promise, not only to you, or to my parents or teachers, but to myself and my God. You also want to know from where did I learn the Golden Rule. I'll answer, from my mother, from my teachers, from the ministers of God. Who knows? I'm sure all of them had planted a little bit on my soul."

Many Spanish Americans with cultivated souls are contributing increasingly to the richness of life in the United States. Some have taken places of top leadership in business and politics. Increasingly they are found as professors in colleges and universities. In the realm of drama consider such names as José Ferrer, Diosa Costella, Olga San Juan, and Juano Hernandez. In music few stars shine brighter than pianist Jesús María Sanroma, composer and orchestra leader Noro Morales, and the coloratura soprano of the Metropolitan Opera, Graciela Rivera. Many other areas of endeavor find Spanish names among the leaders, including major league baseball, with Ruben Gomez pitching for the New York Giants. Will anyone blame the missionary for believing that what a few have already done, large numbers will do in the future by God's grace?

A graduate student in New York University came from humble circumstances in Puerto Rico. She had no money nor influential friends as a young girl, but she made the most of real ability and a burning ambition to learn. A mission college in the United States offered her a chance to earn a higher education.

Recently she appeared before a church audience to tell her experience. Those present saw a vivacious young miss, head tied in a silk scarf with saucy ends lying on her left shoulder, step to the speaker's stand. Sensing the kindness of the Christian friends before her, she discarded her notes, and told eloquently of her life.

"How real! How refreshing!" her listeners commented. They were captivated by her natural exuberance as she spoke with unfeigned gratitude of her development as a child of their common Saviour.

All of us in North America need that Spanish exuberance of spirit. Christians of Spanish culture may well bring such refreshment to American Christendom.

LESLIE C. SAYRE

Courtesy, Migration Division, Department of Labor, Puerto Rico

José Ferrer, brilliant actor-director. He holds honorary degrees from Princeton and the University of Puerto Rico.

) CHAPTER 1 (

Spanish—But Not from Spain

AMONG the four or five million Spanish-speaking Americans are the descendants of some of the oldest settlers within our boundaries and also the newest arrivals on the shores of continental United States.

At one extreme are the Old Spanish who have been living in the remote valleys of New Mexico for nearly three and a half centuries; at the other are the plane loads of Puerto Ricans who drop down out of the air to throng the streets of New York city. Other old-timers are the descendants of the original settlers of California, Texas, and Florida—a very select and hard to identify company. Other newcomers are the Mexicans who have been swarming back and forth across our southern border for the past half century.

The composition of these groups is varied. The earliest settlers probably had the purest Spanish blood, but three to four centuries away from Spain have brought an inevitable dilution. The Spaniards conquered the Indians of Mexico, and then the Indians absorbed the Spaniards. In Puerto Rico three principal strains have mingled: Spanish, Indian, and Negro, and in the process the Indian elements have disappeared. The Spanish strain appears to be dominant, but it is far removed from Spain and much mingled with the other two.

The tie that binds Spanish-speaking Americans together is the culture that the conquering Spaniard bestowed upon them, not blood. In many ways these intrepid sons of Spain were remarkable teachers. They are dead, but their language, their culture, and their religion flourish in most of the New World.

The attitude of the Spanish-speaking peoples of the Americas toward Spain is most curious. They have no apparent interest in Spain. Their lines of travel run to Paris and New York rather than Madrid. Mexicans, Puerto Ricans, and the other peoples of Central and South America use the means of communication and the ways of life that the Spaniards taught them, and yet are in no sense Spanish themselves.

This lack of attachment shows particularly in their attitude toward their language. Spanish is a great tongue. It has rare beauty. It is the most logical of languages. It is rich in humor. Yet the millions in America who use it seem to regard it primarily as a convenience. The children of Spanish-speaking parents are so eager to learn English in their new homeland that they are loathe to admit that they even understand Spanish. The writer has repeatedly tried to engage boys and girls of Mexican descent in conversation in Spanish, but his usual reward is a frown. The Spanish language is a flimsy barrier to Americanization. This is unfortunate. Spanish culture deserves to be preserved.

Individualism is one of the striking aspects of Spanish culture. This is well described by President Samuel Nelson of the Spanish American Baptist Seminary in Los Angeles: "The typical Spanish American tends to be individualistic and to think in terms of personality rather than organization. Loyalty to country has never been to the Latin American as significant as the attraction of a strong individual leader. At best this trait manifests itself in a larger concern for the interests and ideals of humanity than for loyalty to an institution or to the state. It has its disadvantage in making it difficult at times for him to cede personal interests and sovereignty for the welfare of the group."[1] This individualism makes for personal touchiness and has a connection with the lack of strong social and other organizations among Spanish-speaking people. Their interests center in the home. And yet their individualism is not as ingrained as it appears. Labor unions have had considerable success among Mexicans, while the Puerto Ricans of New York city are among the most loyal supporters of the garment trades' and hotel workers' organizations. To quote a Denver observer again, "Mexicans will not organize just for the sake of an organization, as Americans often do. They must have a strong purpose before they will combine their efforts. Given that and they work together splendidly!"

This same trait is found in their attitude toward the Roman Catholic Church. They are in it but not a part of it. Here again we will quote President Samuel Nelson: "Of little significance for 90 per cent of the Spanish American people as a faith to live by, it still forms the foundation of their culture. While the faith of Roman Catholicism has never in reality possessed the Spanish heart, as a social and cultural framework its control has been tremendous. Historically its genius has been adaptation. Among Spanish-speaking peoples it has adapted itself to their individualistic and independent temper by permitting each man to possess his own heart while controlling his mind and way of life through the mysterious beauty of its sacraments and its material power."

[1] The quotations from President Nelson are from an article to be published by the American Baptist Home Missionary Society. Used by permission.

The Roman Catholic Church has a remarkable talent for appealing to the imagination of its people without laying too great a burden upon their will. In Mexico the church buildings are always dramatic, even though they may lack much in the way of beauty. They are often in striking contrast to the homes of the people. The appeal is to the heart rather than to the head.

Neither the Mexicans nor the Puerto Ricans have brought the Roman Catholic Church with them in the way that other immigrant groups have done. In the mill towns of New England one will often find an Irish, a French, and a Polish Roman Catholic church, each standing as a monument to the devotion of an immigrant group, and each served by priests of the appropriate nationality. Spanish-speaking immigrants have not followed this pattern at all. There are six Spanish Roman Catholic churches in New York city, but they are run by monastic orders for Spaniards from Spain and have little to do with the thousands of supposed Roman Catholics who are pouring in from Puerto Rico.

As far as we have been able to discover, there are no Roman Catholic churches in this country that have been built by immigrants from Mexico or Puerto Rico. A rather typical situation is that in Detroit, where a church that was built by Irish immigrants sixty or seventy years ago now serves a colony from the Isle of Man and a group of Mexicans and Puerto Rican newcomers under the leadership of an Irish priest. Here the policy of the diocese is to speed assimilation by having new national groups move in with established parishes. This has some advantages, but it is not conducive to making the newcomer in a new land feel at home.

In its ministries to Spanish-speaking Americans the Roman Catholic Church suffers from two handicaps.

The first is the poverty of the newcomers. They have the poorest paying jobs, they live in the least desirable neighborhoods, and they have little money for church support. This is aggravated by the fact that they had had no training in systematic church support in the places whence they came. The usual pattern in the Roman Catholic Church is for each parish to pay its own way, with the priest looking to his parishioners for support. This has often been impossible with the newly arrived Mexicans and Puerto Ricans. Such a situation can be met in two ways. One is to bring additional revenue into a parish by making it a shrine. This has been done with the two churches in Chicago that avowedly minister to Mexicans. The other procedure is to turn a parish over to a monastic order, which is able to supplement the parish revenues. This has been done in a number of instances in New York city.

The second and greater source of weakness of the Roman Catholic Church is the lack of Puerto Rican and Mexican priests. As a sacerdotal church it judges its success by the measure in which it makes the sacraments available to the people. The priest stands at the center of the Roman Catholic religion. We have already mentioned how the loyalties of those trained in the Spanish tradition are personal rather than institutional. Mexicans and Puerto Ricans will go to both confession and the altar with much more willingness if the priest to whom they go is one of their own people. Yet there are no Puerto Rican priests and few if any Mexican ones in this country! Probably the reason for this is that there are very few vocations for the priesthood in either country. According to John Considine, in *Call for Forty Thousand*,[2] it would take 40,000 additional priests to supply the people living south of the Rio Grande with the same sort of ministry to which the Roman Catholics of the United States are accustomed.

The Mexican or Puerto Rican coming to the United States to live is exposed to two contradictory impulses. As a stranger in a strange

[2] New York, Longmans, Green and Co., 1946.

land there is the natural tendency to cling to that which is old and familiar. Our land is dotted with language churches built by the immigrants of previous years. Over against this is the impulse to follow the dictum "when in Rome do as the Romans do." The breaking of old social and cultural ties may make it easier to break religious ties as well.

Apparently the Mexicans are more inclined to cling to the old and the Puerto Ricans to conform to the new—at least it is reported that the Puerto Ricans are more receptive to Protestantism in New York than they are at home. We suspect that this goes back to two other things. In Mexico the Roman Catholic Church was purged by persecution under the Calles regime and in recent years has been enjoying a spiritual renaissance that is being felt to some extent north of the border, while under the American flag the Roman Catholic Church in Puerto Rico has been neither harassed nor helped but has had to stand on its own. Also the transition that the Mexican experiences in crossing the Rio Grande is not nearly so dramatic as that which befalls the Puerto Rican when he flies from San Juan to New York city. The change in total environment may make the latter a bit more willing to shift his religious allegiance.

Where does Protestantism fit into this picture?

In some ways it is the reverse of Roman Catholicism. It lacks the imposing framework of massive buildings, institutions, and ecclesiastical officials. It does not shape the culture of Spanish-speaking lands. On the other hand, at its best it speaks with power to the heart of the individual. It lacks the support of "everybody is doing it," and yet it has transforming power over human life.

Protestantism is not alien to the Spanish way of life. It is not something that is solely associated with the Anglo-Americans. Even in Spain there are Protestants who are holding to their faith in the face of persecution. In Mexico the total Protestant community includes between 250,000 and 400,000 people. Many individual Protestants are widely respected. In Puerto Rico Protestantism has penetrated into every corner of the island, and leadership is being assumed by the Puerto Ricans themselves. Protestantism is not something bearing the brand "Made in the United States."

In striking contrast to the Roman Catholic Church, Protestantism has been able to produce an indigenous leadership for its churches. It is quite unusual for an American to serve as pastor of a Spanish-speaking church; most of the ministers share the life and background of their congregations. This makes for understanding and sincere friendliness. It is a priceless asset.

The individual looms large in Protestantism. All souls are important in the eyes of God, and every man, woman, and child has significance in the life of a congregation. This builds self-respect, which is greatly needed by most newcomers to our land. Even though one is poor and pushed about, he becomes aware that he is a son of God when he enters a Protestant church.

But these advantages are simply the foreshadowing of the fundamental truth of Protestantism, that we have the right of free access to our Heavenly Father through Jesus Christ. Ours is a personal faith in a personal God. This has a strong appeal to Spanish Americans, only they do not respond in the same way as Anglo-Americans. As President Nelson puts it, "While many are won to Christ in the Spanish American churches their membership remains small. The typical Anglo-American can scarcely conceive of his faith apart from the institution that sustains it and gives it expression. Many a Spanish American sees little point in joining an organization when his needs are so fully satisfied by a personal faith in Christ as Saviour and Lord. The eagerness with which he responds to the appeal of Christ is so great as to be almost pathetic. But to make a public stand means breaking with his culture, cutting social and often family relationships, and in many ways making a radical change in his way of life. This requires great faith and more courage than many of us would possess. Only with difficulty is the Spanish American of Catholic background brought to the place of being an active, baptized member of an evangelical church."

Its practical helpfulness is one aspect of Protestantism that is greatly appreciated by Spanish-speaking Americans. Nearly all feel themselves to be strangers in a strange land. They are naturally suspicious of an environment that they do not fully understand. Problems of all sorts confront them: difficulties with the law, troubles in business, and matters of ill health. Their great need is for an understanding friend. This is the role of the Protestant pastor and of the workers in the Homes of Friendly Service that are maintained by home mission agencies in many communities—and under a variety of names.

Protestant helpfulness is usually related to the practical needs of the people. When the foods to which one has been accustomed are hard to get, and when the stove is a very different contraption from what one had back in Zamora, preparing meals for the family becomes a problem—and a cooking class is most welcome. Spanish-speaking women desire to look well and have an eye for style, but they do not have the money with which to buy American clothes. But if someone will teach them to sew, their fingers are nimble, their taste good, and the results are often remarkable. To get what one wants in this country one must speak English, which is a baffling tongue to those who were not born to it. Learning a strange language is an embarrassing business. The greatest possible help is a teacher who is friendly, understanding, and truly a Christian. Many of our customs need interpretation. Why should one consult the doctor about an expected baby, or go to a hospital? If the priest refuses to marry or to bury, what do you do?

And then there are the children. In many Spanish-speaking families it is necessary for the mother as well as the father to work if there is to be enough for everybody to eat. But what are the children to do after school? And if something goes wrong, to whom can they turn? Here the Protestant community center is often the answer. As the children grow older they enter into a world about which their parents know little or nothing. Father and Mother may mean well, but Benito and Margarita are loath to listen to them. Much suffering on both sides can be avoided if there is a friend who understands American life and who can diminish the fears of the older generation and at the same time give some guidance to the younger. The needs of the people carry them past the distrust in which they have been reared to accept the services that Protestantism has to offer.

Protestantism, when it is true to its genius, is an applied religion. It takes much thought for people, all sorts of people. Protestant home missions is far more concerned with helpfulness than with indoctrination. It seeks to lead people to Christ by revealing the spirit of Christ in daily life. On that basis it is both needed and welcome everywhere.

Methodist Prints—Rickaby

Alberto Rembao, international Christian educator and writer. Since 1931 he has been editor of *La Nueva Democracia.*

) CHAPTER 2 (

The Spaniards Came First

THE FIRST Europeans to make their way into widespread areas of our country came from Spain. Between 1539 and 1542 DeSoto ranged northward from Florida into the Carolinas, and then westward to the Mississippi. There he died, but his followers made their way down the river and back to Mexico. In 1606 the flag of Spain was carried northward from Mexico to the site of the present city of Santa Fe on the high plateau of the Rockies. This was a year before the English made their first permanent settlement at highly accessible Jamestown on the Virginia coast. Albuquerque had its beginnings in 1706, San Antonio in 1718. While the thirteen colonies were proclaiming their independence, the Spanish were establishing themselves in San Francisco Bay. In 1781 Los Angeles was a little town with a big name (El Pueblo de Nuestra Señora La Reina de los Angeles de Porciuncula) while the site of what is now Chicago was nothing but a swamp.

Courage, perhaps inspired by the love of gold, was the first characteristic of these Spanish pioneers. They delighted in going where men had never been before. They had great physical stamina, else they would not have survived. They got themselves across rivers and over mountains in a way that commands our admiration. Even with all modern conveniences it is a bit difficult to get to some of the spots where they set up crosses and unfurled their flags. And how did they manage to find something to eat? And how did they set their course through the wilderness so as to get back to where they had started? They were often cruel and frequently quarrelsome, but their sheer valor compels our admiration.

In much of our country they left little save their footprints as a possible guide to later comers. They gave us Saint Augustine as our oldest settlement, but until the railroad arrived it developed little. In California they built missions that still delight the tourists, they established land titles on a semimonopolistic basis, they supplied the basis for many colorful but highly synthetic local celebrations. Nobody seems to know what has become of the descendants of the first settlers in Florida. In California some of them became wealthy by selling their real estate, but nothing indicates that any of them have multiplied greatly.

The one place where the old stock has thrived is in the mountains of what is now New Mexico. Here is to be found both the oldest and the purest Spanish blood in the United States. Old World customs were superimposed on Indian traditions and the two blended into a distinctive whole. The encircling mountains isolated the colony from the other Spanish dependencies, and Spanish officials lowered a virtual iron curtain to keep out influences from the north. For three centuries these people kept company with the past; only in the last few years has modern life caught up with them.

Dr. J. T. Reid writes:

And a remarkable people they are in many respects, remarkable not only for their tenacious racial qualities and customs, but for their unique history as well. For more than two centuries they were a "lost people," isolated in the hinterlands of New Spain, forgotten by warring Mother Spain in the seventeenth and eighteenth centuries, neglected by Mexico with its newly won independence after 1821, and finally all but ignored for three quarters of a century after we had gobbled them up in 1848.

When the English settlers on the eastern coast of this continent were founding Jamestown and beating their way into the wilderness of the Ohio Valley and stampeding into the open places of the "wild west," these Spanish settlers of the Rio Grande Basin were conquering hostile Indians, working mines, establishing huge ranches of sheep and cattle, raising crops on the right valley lands, setting up schools and churches, and otherwise adapting their European culture to the emergencies of a frontier land that had only so much to offer.

Under the medieval system by which they lived, with *ricos* and *hacendados* ruling, more or less independently, over vast grants of land and hundreds of slaves and servants, these Spanish pioneers developed an economy that fitted the soil and took care of their needs. They were a proud and self-reliant people.

Then in the latter part of the nineteenth century came the squatters and the cattlemen and the outlaws from the states, and competition and exploitation. Progress plodded its inevitable, stubborn way. A militant, forceful, reckless race of men met a proud, lost remnant of landed barons grown soft with easy living. In less than fifty years much of the land and other property had changed hands. The Spanish settlers were ill-equipped to meet the issue, for many reasons—the type of decadent life they had fallen into, lack of a driving response to the challenge of an expanding frontier, limited resources and credit for new enterprises, lack of functional education, and others.

The result has been a gradual increase of poverty with its attendant ills.

There are in the Southwest some two million of these Spanish-speaking citizens of the United States, who are proud of their allegiance to the Stars and Stripes, who fought valiantly for this country in its two recent wars, and who have contributed much of intrinsic value to the culture and growth of this their native land.

But they are a linguistic minority. Most of them speak Spanish as a native tongue, hold ardently to traditional customs inherited from the past, and find it difficult to make a cultural transition to the American way of life. The education provided in the public schools, though consistent with general practice elsewhere in the country, has been inadequate and ill-suited to their needs, resulting in a lowered educational status and the disadvantages that such a condition brings.

They live among their peaks with their handicaps—poverty, sickness, superstitions and ignorance.[1]

This issue the Protestant churches sought to meet with a classic example of pioneer missionary work. In the second half of the nineteenth century word got around that here was a group of people living under our flag who had no schools. Various denominations heard the call and sent schoolteachers to these remote villages that are known as "plazas" (although often they have no plaza, or square) to gather the children together and teach them to read. By so doing they achieved far more than just introducing book learning. These mission schools were the forerunners of the public schools. The Protestant churches nudged first the territorial and later the state governments toward their duty in the field of public education. More than this, these schools broke the unquestioned control of the pattern of life that the Roman Catholic Church had enjoyed for two and a half centuries. Some of the teachers were also preachers. All of them were the exponents of a vigorous evangelical faith. In New Mexico the Protestant church was built beside the mission school. The combination meant a more abundant life for the people. The teacher and/or the preacher brought some knowledge of hygiene and often a more effective way of tilling the soil. Wholesome recreation came to the young people. Life grew cleaner and brighter.

Meanwhile the world was creeping up on the mountains. First came

[1] *It Happened in Taos,* by J. T. Reid. Albuquerque, University of New Mexico Press, 1946. Used by permission.

the railroad, which thundered on past to the Pacific Coast. In its wake followed the automobile with its much higher power of penetration into what the state automobile tags proclaim to be "The Land of Enchantment." The Governor's Palace in Santa Fe became a museum and the town a show place for California-bound motorists. The artists discovered and embellished Taos. Albuquerque grew from a railroad town to a city of considerable distinction, with the University of New Mexico becoming a cultural center with a strong interest in the people and customs of the hinterland.

The new highways and the people who traveled over them affected the secluded villages in several ways. They created a market for their handicrafts, such as the Chimayo blankets. Jobs developed along the roadsides in filling stations and overnight accommodations. The highways were arrows pointing toward the cities, with Albuquerque the immediate destination. Here the large Spanish-speaking population has not come from south of the border to any considerable degree but has moved in from the surrounding valley.

Then came the atomic bomb. It was in New Mexico that the first bomb was detonated, and it is in New Mexico that it has probably had its greatest local effect. All atomic centers are places apart, hard to get into and operated by people from afar. Los Alamos, however, has profoundly affected the countryside for a hundred miles around. To the descendants of the ancient Spanish settlers Los Alamos has offered jobs, and the jobs have paid real money. Workers, not necessarily on the bomb itself but in the settlements growing out of the bomb, have been recruited from far back in the mountains. Housing being scarce in all the new settlements, these people live at home and work where work is to be had, either in Los Alamos or the other booming towns about it. Instead of changing from one mode of life to another they have both retained the old and added the new. They still live in their ancestral homes, tilling their fields and tending their animals as of old. But every working day the more able-bodied and ambitious drive off to do their part in the life of the mid-century. The immediate result is that they come home with far more money than they have ever known before. The long range effect will probably be to weaken their traditional way of living, but as yet that is not too apparent. For the moment the big change is in their financial status.

But the new day has its shadows. The same forces that have brought prosperity to these Spanish-speaking villages have also drawn into the same region those who do not appreciate their traditions and who are inclined to look askance at their dark Spanish features. The transferred workers and the footloose from everywhere have come to the mountains to work on the bomb, and they have brought with them prejudices that flower into discrimination against the people who have lived here for three centuries. For these long-time residents an injured pride has been part of the price that they have paid for pockets overflowing with dollars. Prosperity has threatened their self-esteem. As yet the surface changes have been too new and dazzling for these deeper implications to be too troublesome, but some unhappy days may lie ahead.

Another element in the picture is the ex-GI. The draft took thousands of boys from the mountains, put them into uniforms, and sent them out to the ends of the earth. Many never came back. They found work and greater opportunities elsewhere. Some returned quite unchanged. As one observer put it, "The chief difference is that now they drive to their Penitente meetings in Cadillac cars." A third group are those who have tried to adjust to life in the larger world but who have been unable to do so. They have drifted back to the mountains because there was nowhere else for them to go. They are defeated men and no asset to their communities.

Over against these new elements certain old facts continue. Forty per cent of the people of New Mexico are Spanish-speaking. Ability to use the Castilian tongue is most helpful to office seekers. Spanish is still a legal language in New Mexico. The people who speak Spanish have a larger proportion of the votes than anywhere else in our country. They feel that "We are the people." This very pride creates difficulties. The old families feel no pressing obligation to master English, and yet without a good command of English their children cannot make their way in the present day world.

The changing scene has brought changes in Protestant missionary activity. Where the state and local communities have accepted the responsibility for education, and where the public schools can be carried on without garbed sisters on the faculties and Roman Catholic domination of school boards, mission schools have usually been withdrawn. Those that have been continued, which are a minority of those once operated, are maintained for a number of reasons. In some instances public schools are still not accessible to isolated families. In other instances the public schools may be of poor quality or under Roman Catholic control. On the positive side, the mission schools have trained the ministers and lay leaders of the Protestant churches, and may be expected to continue to do so in future. They are closely related to local churches. Often they bring to the community a needed health service. They pioneer in kindergartens for children and education for adults. They serve their communities in many ways.

Mission schools are maintained in New Mexico by the Presbyterian Church, U.S.A., the Woman's Division of Christian Service of the Methodist Church, and the Evangelical United Brethren Church. They serve what has been described as a double minority: first, a group that has been set apart from the rest of the nation by blood and language; second, the Protestant minority within the Spanish-speaking population. These schools are a means of maintaining the dignity and increasing the competence of both minorities. In addition to the common problems of education they face unusual tasks in the areas of language, diet, and social adjustment.

Some parents of the young people who attend these schools have had little education, and consequently they speak a colloquial or archaic form of their native tongue. "One of our great needs is for someone who can teach our pupils good Spanish," we were told at one school. The lack of grammatical training and a hazy notion of the meanings of words make the mastery of English even more difficult than it would ordinarily be.

Dinner, or the midday lunch, can be quite an educational opportunity. "These young people have been brought up on beans and bread," as one dietitian put it. "Our job is to introduce them to salads and to develop in them an appetite for other vegetables, which is really quite a chore." Health begins with a wholesome diet.

The Presbyterian Church, U.S.A., operates a complete educational system. At one time or another it has had fifty village schools. Of these, six are still functioning. Three are on main highways, two are a bit remote, while the one at Truchas is on a mountain plateau at an elevation of 9,000 feet and is difficult to reach when the dirt road is wet. These schools send their students on to Allison-James, a coeducational junior high boarding school on a spacious campus at Santa Fe. From here they go to Menaul, a senior high boarding school on the outskirts of Albuquerque. Graduates of the school can continue to live there and earn at least a part of their room and board while attending the University of New Mexico. Usually there are about fifteen young people in this group. Thus a clear road is kept open from the first grade in a mountain valley to the university in New Mexico's largest city. Over this Christian highway of learning have traveled many who are now ministers and teachers, business and professional people, leaders in the churches. The aim of this comprehensive system of education is to make a personal faith in Jesus Christ the eventual experience of every pupil.

The Evangelical United Brethren Church has a similar system, which centers in the tiny village of Santa Cruz—a truly rural setting. Here is located the McCurdy School, which has all the grades plus a four year boarding high school. Associated with it are three village schools that send their graduates on to it. Here the evangelical influence is strong. Half of the 204 members of the McCurdy Church are students, and of these 30 have decided to devote their lives to Christian service. Twenty-two who had previously become Life Work Recruits are now attending college. In the local county are 47 public schoolteachers who were trained at McCurdy.

Harwood Girls' School in Albuquerque is conducted by the Woman's Division of Christian Service of the Methodist Church for girls who lack good school facilities at home, or who have no real homes. In addition to the Spanish-speaking girls, there are those of Italian, Syrian, Russian, and Japanese parentage. The modest tuition fees can be paid in farm produce or by the labor of the girl herself. The teachers and students conduct a community center and also run a church vacation school in the Mexican town of Cabezon. A Harwood girl writes, "I have learned that not only preachers, missionaries, and Christian workers can be good Christians, but that we in our simple lives can also follow the Christ-like way. Not everybody has the privilege of hearing Dorothy Maynor, the Negro soprano, in person or of seeing Yehudi Menuhin produce sounds from his violin which lift you up to heaven. Harwood has made it possible for me to see and hear these artists as well as many others."

The Protestant churches have responded to the health needs of New Mexico by establishing two hospitals.

On the highway between Santa Fe and Taos the Presbyterian Church, U.S.A., has a grade A hospital at Embudo at the foot of a steep reddish-brown hillside looking over open fields and a big highway to another ridge of striking formation thrust up sharply from the sloping fields. It is a twenty-five bed hospital, specializing in the care of women and children, although men patients are also received. It includes, in addition to the one-story hospital building, a nurses' residence, a doctors' house, and several small buildings. Dr. Sarah Bowen, with few intervals of relief, was the only doctor on the staff for a number of years, though a second doctor has now been appointed. Seven nurses, six ward aides, a dietitian, and laboratory and office workers complete the total staff.

This small hospital, with the dispensary and out-clinics, cares for as many as 4,500 patients a year. Sometimes a woman whose first four or five children were born in her plaza home with neighbors to help comes somewhat distrustfully for the sixth to the hospital, and afterwards wonders why she waited so long. Others come for the first and all others. Children are brought in who are undernourished. However, there is definite improvement in general health conditions, as county and state health agencies, the Red Cross, and the public schools, as well as the mission forces, all have their part in raising the level.

Daily evangelistic services, a Bible and a hymnal in Spanish beside each bed, the Christian quality of the staff members, the frequent visits of the pastor from nearby Dixon, the whole atmosphere of service in the name of Christ, make Embudo Hospital one of the strong Christian influences of the region.

Two years ago, it became apparent that the village of Truchas was suffering from a lack of consistent medical care, and the people banded together to put up the adobe building that now houses a regular clinic. Some contributed time to make adobe blocks; men and women alike worked at building the walls of the clinic. Village men made the wooden beams, and the women plastered over the adobe bricks with mud, as is the customary practice. Inside, the clinic is provided with examining tables, sterilizer, supplies of modern drugs. The medical staff from Embudo Hospital (about 25 miles away) goes once a week for consultation. In between, the registered nurse attached to the mission school, capable and conscientious Miss Frances Sanchez, looks after minor and emergency ills and makes needed referrals to the medical staff.

A companion story to Truchas is that of Penasco. Here there has been no Protestant school. Years ago, when medical work was first instituted in the plaza country, a Presbyterian doctor was attacked and almost killed. More recently the Embudo Hospital staff has carried on periodic clinics in makeshift quarters. When word of the clinic at Truchas got around, the people of Penasco, Roman Catholic and Protestant alike, joined in a request for a similar building in which both a clinic and a community program are carried on.

In May, 1948, the Evangelical United Brethren Church dedicated a new hospital where abundant sunlight shines through large, modern windows upon the newest in equipment. It has a staff of thirty-five members from several states and two Canadian provinces whose missionary zeal has brought them to New Mexico. It is located on a hill overlooking the town of Española through which multitudes of workers on the atomic bomb pass daily on their way to Los Alamos. During its first three years this hospital was the scene of almost a thousand births, besides taking care of over five thousand other patients. One of the doctors spends half his time conducting clinics in surrounding towns in cooperation with a full-time visiting nurse. Together they penetrate into the mountains to communities that are not reached by either private physicians or the state health service.

The church is the most widespread Protestant institution in New Mexico. Many congregations are the outgrowth of mission schools that have now given way to public schools. Their first achievement was to break the religious monopoly that had long been enjoyed by the Roman Catholic Church. They have also been effective in prodding that institution toward a better service to its people. But the function of Protestantism is only incidentally competitive.

The following statement is in the Findings of the National Home Missions Congress of 1950: "We recognize our Protestant responsibility for Christian nurture and evangelism among the non-Christian and the nominal Christian groups in our country. A large part of the Spanish-speaking population is unchurched and without Christ. Most of them claim allegiance to the Roman Catholic Church, but very many have actually neglected the faith of their fathers and many more are not even nominal Catholics, much less Christian. They are the so-called 'liberals' but really 'Pagans'."

Although the response to Protestant religious teaching is not startling, particularly numerically, it does have power. This is shown in two churches that we visited.

In Santa Fe we found a church that in a year and a half had grown from five to fifty members and that was in process of erecting a building. The pastor was born in Mexico of Roman Catholic family. He came to this country as a youngster, and was converted by reading the Bible in a hospital. He earned his way while getting an education by taking care of a church, running an elevator, and painting houses. Finally he achieved a master's degree.

The possibilities of the self-supporting Spanish-speaking church are illustrated by the Methodist church of El Buen Samaritano in Albuquerque, which has a good building on a prominent location in the center of the city. Here we found a number of lay people at work in the evening improving its already excellent facilities. The young pastor was born in the Rio Grande Valley of Texas on land that his family had originally secured as a grant from the King of Spain. He was converted at the age of eighteen and attended the Lydia Patterson Institute in El Paso and Trinity University in San Antonio. He confessed that in Texas he had been proud of his Mexican ancestry, but that in Albuquerque he found it wise to say little about it.

His church has been self-supporting since 1943, and with a membership of 500 is raising a budget of $11,000. Three men are giving $5.00 a week to the support of the church, while others are contributing $4.00 and $3.50 weekly. The congregation uses 125 sets of pledge envelopes. Among the members of the church are the assistant to the superintendent of schools, the secretary to Senator Chavez, three public accountants, a school principal, the head of the Spanish department in the schools, some union leaders, several teachers, and twelve university students.

Many churches like this one are attaining maturity in program and self support. They are also producing leadership of quality able to direct and extend their own affairs.

Thus are the descendants of the Spanish settlers of three centuries emerging into the American life of the day. Of these people, it is said that they did not pass over the border, but that the border passed over them. In the coming years they need to become increasingly adjusted to the national life. Protestant missions have opened to them the door of educational opportunity. For today and tomorrow we should help them to adjust spiritually to the world in which they are now living. This is a difficult and demanding task.

Brooke Baldwin

The citizen of Mexican antecedents is eager to make his full contribution to the life of his community.

) CHAPTER 3 (

Mexico in Texas

IN TEXAS the restless, land-hungry, westward surging tide of American settlers first encountered the more easygoing landholding Mexicans. Here they met, mingled, and then fought at the much remembered Alamo. Some months later the Americans won the Battle of San Jacinto, which established the independence of Texas.

These unfortunate beginnings have somewhat colored the relations of the two groups ever since. Although more people of Mexican extraction live in Texas than in any other state, there has also been more fear and ill will between them and their American neighbors than elsewhere. Fortunately, this situation is beginning to change. Intelligent efforts are being made to improve Mexican-Anglo relations in Texas. Yet our largest state does not change easily. Nowhere are Americans and Mexicans more of a problem to each other.

Geography explains much of what has happened in Texas. The state has no natural Eastern boundary. When the frontier of American settlement got to western Louisiana, there was nothing to stop it from going farther. The land was good, and it could be bought for little money from those who had been given their titles by the King of Spain. Such an illusory and utterly invisible thing as an international boundary line could not restrain the American pioneer stock. During the early decades of the nineteenth century they wandered west and south into this promising land until they outnumbered the Mexicans who had originally possessed it.

A second significant fact is that Texas is a thousand miles from the seat of Mexican rule in Mexico City and that the first two hundred miles south of the Rio Grande is unprepossessing desert. In the 1830's Texas was on the far periphery of Mexican power—and that power was exceedingly weak. The most astonishing fact about the Battle of San Jacinto is that the Mexican General—and President—was able to get something that looked like an army that far from home. Santa Anna deserves credit for that achievement, and it will be cheerfully granted by anyone who has been through the country over which he had to make his way.

On the other hand, the arid region beyond the Rio Grande has been the political salvation of our southern neighbor. The reason that American occupation stopped at its northern bank is that settlers from the north and east could see no conceivable reason for crossing over to the southern bank. Her northern deserts have been Mexico's real protection against American settlers.

The nature of the Rio Grande has also had its effect upon Texas. This river is one of the most significant boundaries in the world. It makes a lot of difference which bank one lives on. Here two civilizations meet. To the south the Indian dominates; to the north the Anglos[1] hold power. To the south the laws, religion, and culture came from

[1] Popular term for "Anglo-Americans."

Spain; to the north they are European. To the south poverty and ignorance have prevailed through most of the years for most of the people; to the north every man is supposed to get ahead and every child to have an education. In few parts of the world does an international boundary line mean so much.

Between these two utterly dissimilar countries lies the Rio Grande, one of the world's strangest rivers. Its name means "big river," but its distinction lies in its length rather than in its depth. From source to mouth it is 1,800 miles, of which half lies between Texas and Mexico, but it is a rare drop of water that ever gets from the mountains of Colorado to the Gulf of Mexico. It flows through arid regions where the sun takes away more moisture than the clouds bestow. In recent years what little water there was has been eagerly diverted into irrigation ditches. During much of the year most of the river is a dry bed, with possibly a brook-like stream meandering down the middle. The Rio Grande peters out rather completely long before it gets to Brownsville.

The international boundary line between the United States and Mexico can properly be described as porous. It operates like a one-way sieve. For reasons already stated, it has served to keep the North Americans out of Mexico, but it has been far less successful in keeping the Mexicans out of the United States. With so many disadvantages to the southward and so many seemingly glistening opportunities to the northward it was inevitable that the more venturesome Mexicans would cross over into what looks and sounds like a modern Promised Land, even if it does not flow with milk and honey. From 1910 to 1920 this movement was accentuated by the disorders of that revolutionary decade in Mexico. As we will see later, there have been many times when influential forces north of the border were eager to have Mexicans cross over, legally or illegally, to help them.

Although the Mexican population immediately south of the border is relatively scant, the Mexicans are a mobile people. While migrants may come a long way to get to the boundary line, it takes only a step to get them across. This has had two curious results. In Texas, the area to a hundred miles north of the Rio Grande is usually far more Mexican than American in population. Those who drive down the Pan-American highway really meet Mexico as soon as they leave San Antonio, judging by road signs, language, and people. The second strange fact is that the Mexican population is much heavier on the north bank of the Rio Grande than on the south bank. As a barrier between nations, the river is a dismal failure!

Behind the present situation along the Rio Grande lies a long story. Putting it in a sentence, the Mexicans first retired before the incoming tide of American settlers and then slowly returned in what have now become overwhelming numbers. For these movements of population there have been several reasons.

In the negotiations of the Treaty of Guadalupe Hidalgo that finally brought peace between the two countries, the Mexican Government was more concerned about the rights of their people who were passing under the sovereignty of the United States than it was with the details of the boundary. Those who did not claim Mexican citizenship within a limited time became citizens of the United States automatically, and theoretically at least enjoyed all the rights of such. The Spanish land titles were confirmed.

A few Mexicans shared actively in the government of the Republic of Texas, and one of the first senators that the state of Texas sent to Washington was of Spanish-speaking ancestry. Some families of wealth and position entered heartily into the new regime. More, however, sold their lands to Americans for what now appear to be pitiful sums, although these were much higher than the prices they had paid for them. In general, the Mexican population of Texas receded into the background for at least fifty years after its incorporation into the United States. And when they "came back," it was not as landowners, but as the humblest of workers.

The original occupation of the Mexicans in Texas was the care of livestock. The American cowboy is indebted to them for his skills, his equipment, and most of his lingo. "Cowboy" is a literal translation of the Spanish term *vaquero* and was first used in Texas in 1836. The terms ranch, bronco, lasso, burro, quirt, stampede, vamoose, mesa, canyon, rodeo, corral, sombrero, loco, all come from the Spanish language by way of Texas. Along with them came much know-how in the handling of cows, the breeding and breaking of horses, and the tending of sheep. Men of Mexican descent still follow these lines of work in Texas and in the Southwest generally. The Spanish term for sheepherder is "pastor." As a worker with livestock the Mexican has a splendid reputation for pastoral reliability and faithfulness. Animals worth many thousands of dollars are entrusted to his care for long periods of time with complete confidence. Many years ago a South Texas farmer told the writer, "A Mexican will work better if you don't watch him than if you do!" At the higher levels of skill, the system of branding cattle is Mexican in its origins, while Mexicans still shine in the demanding but relatively well paid trade of sheepshearing.

The change from cattle raising to farming has greatly increased the demand for Mexican labor in Texas but has drastically lowered its status.

Over the years the reign of King Cotton has been dependent in an increasing degree for its success upon the backbreaking exertions of the lowly Mexican with his wife and children toiling beside him. At the close of the War between the States, Texas' 182,000 slaves constituted one-third of the population. For the most part they became sharecroppers raising cotton. Not until 1890 did the Mexicans begin to enter the cotton fields. They did not come as sharecroppers or as tenants, but as cotton pickers following the season from place to place. Two circumstances sounded the knell of cotton tenancy: the rise in the price of land, which began about 1920; and the advent of the tractor. The family-sized cotton patch became uneconomic under these conditions. Thousands of both Negroes and whites were "tractored off" the soil in the manner so unforgettably described in the opening pages of *The Grapes of Wrath.* Between 1930 and 1940 the number of sharecroppers in Texas declined from 205,122 to 39,821, while the average acreage in a cotton farm went up from 251.7 to 329.4 in the same period.[2] Cotton also moved west and northward toward the Panhandle, with great cattle ranges being turned into cotton fields. The cultivation was done with tractors and the picking by migrant workers imported for a short period in the fall.

The mechanization and expansion of cotton cultivation in Texas would have been impossible without large quantities of cheap Mexican labor. As far back as 1926 a Texan told the House Committee on Immigration and Naturalization:

> Mr. Chairman, here is the whole situation in a nutshell. Farming is not a profitable industry in this country, and in order to make money out of it, you have to have cheap labor. In order to allow landowners to make a profit off their farms, they want to get the cheapest labor that they can find, and if they get the Mexican labor, it enables them to make a profit. That is the way it is along the border, and I imagine that is the way it is anywhere else.

For the most part, cotton has offered the Mexican seasonal and migratory employment. The usual pattern begins with cotton picking in the lower Rio Grande Valley in early summer, north to Corpus

[2] *Latin Americans in Texas,* by Pauline R. Kibbe, p. 170. Albuquerque, University of New Mexico Press, 1948.

Christi in July and August, then north to the central part of the state and then westward on to the great plains for October, November, and December, and then back to the Rio Grande Valley. According to the Texas Employment Service, 1937 was the peak year for participation in this great trek on the part of Latin Americans, with somewhere between 250,000 and 400,000 men, women, and little children making at least part of this circuit.

The mechanization of cotton has carried over from the method of cultivation to its human relations.

> Generally speaking, the Latin American migratory worker going into west Texas is regarded as a necessary evil, nothing more nor less than an unavoidable adjunct to the harvest season. Judging by the treatment that has been accorded him in that section of the state, one might assume that he is not a human being at all, but a species of farm implement that comes mysteriously and spontaneously into being coincident with the maturing of the cotton, that requires no upkeep or special consideration during the period of its usefulness, needs no protection from the elements, and when the crop has been harvested, vanishes into the limbo of forgotten things—until the next harvest season rolls around. He has no past, no future, only a brief and anonymous present.[3]

A third development that has drawn hundreds of thousands of Mexicans across the Rio Grande has been the transformation of the lower Rio Grande Valley from an arid desert raising nothing but brush to a winter garden supplying the nation with citrus fruits and a great variety of vegetables.

This has been made possible by irrigation. The word itself is of Latin origin and we are indebted to our southern neighbors for the laws by which it is administered, for the techniques by which it works, and for the labor that has made it possible.

Large scale irrigation became possible in 1902 when Congress passed the Reclamation Act. The railroad got to Brownsville in 1904. At this

[3] *Ibid.*, page 176. Used by permission.

time the standard of living of our nation was rising rapidly. More varied and more nutritious foods were in demand, while the refrigerator car and the tin can were bringing increasing quantities of fruits and vegetables to the dining rooms of America. At the same time the native-born Americans were no longer willing to do hard physical work. Labor saving machinery was still in its infancy. Even today it is less adapted to the production of fruits and vegetables than any other large scale activity. It has been the muscle and sweat of Mexicans that has dug many of the ditches, cleared away the omnipresent brush, and made the soil ready for cultivation.

It was not alone the strength of his arm, but the Mexican's readiness to live on little, that brought about one of the most astonishing agricultural developments of recent years. Irrigation is by nature expensive. The irrigated land of the Rio Grande Valley was greatly overcapitalized. The long haul by fast freight to the cities of the North cost money. The one cheap item was Mexican labor. Without it these other developments would have been long delayed. Astonishing are the wonders that have been wrought.

A Northern visitor driving into the Lower Rio Grande Valley would experience the illusion

> . . . of moving into a modern version of the Garden of Eden. As he drove along the Valley's Main Street, a 65-mile highway, he would see stately palms and green citrus-fruit trees laden with golden orange fruit; bougainvillea vines in full bloom; bright green papaya plants. . . . And when he came to the level, rich fields he would see bronze-skinned people by the thousands harvesting vegetables—red beets with their green tops, white and purple turnips with their green tops, golden carrots with their green tops—everything green. He might see other laborers harvesting cabbage, broccoli, endive, peppers, beans, tomatoes, new potatoes, peas, anise, cauliflower, or squash.[4]

[4] Hart Stilwell, quoted in *North from Mexico,* by Carey McWilliams, pp. 175-76. Philadelphia, J. B. Lippincott Co., 1949. Used by permission.

The value of these crops runs to $100,000,000 a year—of which the men who do the work receive a rather pitiable proportion.

When Texas achieved her independence, 5,000 Mexicans formed one sixth of her population. By 1900 the Mexican population had increased to 70,000. Thirty years later it had jumped to 683,000, and at present it is well over a million—still a sixth of the people of the state.

However, the Spanish-speaking population is unevenly distributed over Texas. Some are found in fabulous Houston and booming Dallas. In El Paso and San Antonio they constitute more than half of the population. Most of the Mexicans in the Lone Star State live south of a line drawn through El Paso and San Antonio and then extended eastward to the gulf at a point somewhat south and west of Galveston. This is the part of Texas that is least attractive to fortune seekers from other parts of the world. Few industries are found here and only two cities of over 100,000 population.

The distribution of Mexicans in Texas is significant in another way. They are more rural than urban; more live in the open country and the small towns than in the cities—a fact that has hindered their progress in several ways, as will be pointed out shortly.

In America the business success and social approval of any group is largely dependent upon fluent use of the English language and adequate education. This cultural hurdle all non-Anglos must negotiate. This has been most difficult for the Spanish-speaking people of Texas, because they have never had a good opportunity to learn the language. This is due to their concentration in certain areas, usually in the small towns and the country, and their employment in tasks in which they work as a group with the minimum of contact with their English-speaking over-bosses. Each gang is recruited by a *capitán* or *jefe* who speaks English. He gets his orders and then tells his workers, in Spanish, what to do.

The pathway from the Mexican home to the American public school is long and hazardous. The home may be a jalopy rattling around from cotton field to cotton field, or even going on some of the longer excursions that will be described later. Any school board finds it difficult to provide facilities for children who are really birds of passage. It is the exceptional schoolteacher who has a cordial welcome for a pupil who is here today and somewhere else tomorrow.

Even though the home be firmly anchored in one spot, there are difficulties. Often the struggle to keep alive is so intense that even the hands of the seven-year-old are needed if the family is to have its daily minimum of *frijoles*. Even beans come hard to the poor. Suitable clothes may be lacking. The way to school may be so long and the child so poorly nourished that he can learn but little when he gets there. The pathway itself is strange. His parents have never traveled it in many cases. Uneducated parents, who have had few agreeable contacts with educated people, do not see value in schooling for their children. They doubt if book learning will materially improve their lot in life. Some may not send them at all, or they may send them only when it is convenient and there is nothing else for them to do.

Other troubles beset the Spanish-speaking child when he passes through the door of the schoolhouse. To him this is a very strange place. To the American child the first grade teacher is a mother substitute to whom he can turn with some assurance of being understood. With the Spanish-speaking child this usually does not work. The teacher may not understand his language. She is alien to him, and he does not trust her. Oftentimes a most unfortunate attitude toward the school is developed by the Spanish-speaking child on his first encounter with it. He does not feel at home. This is not his natural world, and therefore he resists that which it offers. Too often this becomes the habit of his later days.

Then there are other difficulties. The teacher may be lukewarm in her welcome, the other children scornful if not antagonistic. The Spanish-speaking child's clothes or even his lunch may be the object of derision. These things hurt when you are small, and the child of the lowly Mexican has no defenses.

The work of the school may be both difficult and uninteresting. The language must be learned, as well as the usual lessons. Almost inevitably little Benito and his sister Carmencita are retarded. They may be kept in first grade for two or three years, becoming increasingly bored with their lessons and sensitive to their growing height and age in comparison with the other pupils.

Here the picture is complicated by some features peculiar to Texas. Education was not made compulsory in the state until 1916, and the responsibility for its enforcement is wholly local. Because of the lands that she has retained, Texas has the largest state fund for the aid of schools to be found in the Union. For many years this was distributed on the basis of the children enumerated in each school district rather than on the basis of school enrollment or attendance. From the point of view of the school, every child who could be discovered meant dollars from the state, regardless of whether the child had ever even seen the schoolhouse. The way this worked in the smaller communities was that the fewer the Spanish-speaking children who got to school, the more money there was to spend on the English-speaking children. This meant either a better school or a lightened load for the taxpayer. Here was a temptation that many communities could not resist. To state the matter mildly, they did not overexert themselves in their efforts to persuade Mexican children to go to school. Fortunately this has now been corrected by the passage of the Gilmer-Aiken Bill, which requires that state funds be distributed on the basis of actual attendance, but the effects of the former arrangement are still felt.

There has also been a tendency on the part of some local administrations to apply the pattern of segregation to the Mexicans, both in the schools and elsewhere. The linguistic difficulties of the Mexican child and also his alleged lack of cleanliness have been used to justify segregation. Sometimes there have been separate buildings and sometimes separate rooms in the same building. The root motive has been "social customs," which is another name for prejudice. The result has been to set the Spanish-speaking child apart from the other children and to give him a sense of inferiority. Fortunately, there is no legal basis for this segregation, and the United States District Court for the Western District of Texas has ruled that it violates the Fourteenth Amendment to the Constitution.

> Honesty demands that full credit and recognition be given to those Texas teachers, principals, and superintendents who through the years have pioneered in giving adequate and equal educational advantages to children of Mexican descent. Their number is large, even though they do constitute a small minority among the thousands of public schoolteachers in Texas. Bucking administrative apathy—even antagonism at times—and confronting more frequently the opposition presented by some Anglo parents who are prompted only by unreasoning and unfounded prejudice, these educators have stuck to their guns, winning out in the end.[5]

Fortunately this tendency to segregation does not go all the way up. Often it stops at the third grade; never does it persist into high school, although there the child of Mexican antecedents may encounter some forms of social ostracism. The colleges of Texas are wide open to sons and daughters of her Spanish-speaking citizens.

The Spanish-speaking child in Texas can have an education if he wants it enough to make somewhat more of an effort than is required of the Anglo child. In the cities, the young people from the more prosperous Mexican homes are nearly on a par with the other boys and girls of the community. While most Spanish-speaking children are

[5] Kibbe, *op. cit.*, p. 103. Used by permission.

under a handicap, which varies with where they live and with their economic position, some of them are climbing all the way to the top.

The state is taking measures to improve conditions.[6] In 1943 the State Department of Education issued a two-point statement of policy, the first of which proposed that the courses of study used in Texas schools be revised so as to give all the children a better appreciation of Latin American history and culture. The second point stated flatly, "Any administrative or curricular practices which isolate, or tend to isolate, the Latin American children solely on the basis of such descent, through physical separation or inequitable educational offerings, are deemed pedagogically unsound, contrary to state and national policy, and inimical to the best interests of both those groups of children." With the financial assistance of the Office of the Coordinator of Inter-American Affairs in Washington a number of conferences and workshops were held under the auspices of the colleges of the state to study the situation and to seek ways of improving it, particularly by training elementary teachers in the use of Spanish and in promoting better community relations. The Governor appointed a Good Neighbor Commission, with offices in the state capitol, which had among its objectives:

> To educate our present adult Anglo-American population in the history and culture of Mexico, on inter-American relations, and on the problems faced by Latin Americans in Mexico.
>
> To study the economic and educational opportunities of the Latin American residents of the community, as well as their housing and health conditions, with a view to effecting improvements.
>
> To promote friendship, understanding, and respect between Anglo-Americans and Latin Americans of the community, thereby insuring the continuance of cordial relations between Texas and Mexico.
>
> To investigate fully, in case problems in human relations arise between Anglo-Americans and Latin Americans in the community, and adjust such

[6] *Ibid.*, p. 104.

difficulties with justice to both sides, to the end that strife may be avoided and understanding promoted.

None of these aims has as yet been fully achieved, but officially the power of the state and the influence of its educational institutions is on the side of affording better educational opportunities and social treatment to its Spanish-speaking population.

Now let us look briefly at the economic and social position of the Americans of Spanish-speaking ancestry in Texas.

On the lowest level are the agricultural workers, who may be here legally or illegally and who may be settled or migrant. A large proportion of the recent arrivals from Mexico are in this classification. Here are the families that have a minimum acquaintance with the English language, and whose children have few contacts with our schools.

The Spanish-speaking people of the towns are better off than the agricultural workers. Most of them can speak some English. Their range of employment expands to include all sorts of humble but necessary tasks. The children go to school. The boys get jobs and the girls may clerk in stores.

In the cities, Spanish-speaking Latin Americans are spread over a wide gamut both economically and socially. In El Paso and San Antonio are considerable slums occupied by Spanish-speaking people; in Dallas there is a remnant of such a deteriorated neighborhood. However, the slum is not the usual dwelling place of the urban Latin Americans of Texas. As fast as they can, they get themselves bungalows in better and better neighborhoods. Owing to informal agreements among real estate interests, it would not be fair to say that they enjoy entirely free choice as to where they will live, but they have some chance to pick and choose, particularly in the lower price levels.

The cities offer a wide range of employment in the service trades, industry, business, and the professions, with the women at some levels doing better than the men. The women have quick fingers and excel in the needle trades, and may become department heads in the garment factories that are developing in Dallas.

In the cities many of the young people graduate from high school, many of the boys becoming bank clerks and the girls stenographers. Public health nursing is open to those who can go further, and the professions generally. Many are active in government and politics, some having been elected to high state and national offices.

On the business side, the natural starting point is the small neighborhood grocery store, known as a *bodega,* specializing in Spanish foods—and language. A further step up is the barbershop, which may serve the Anglo trade. The Mexican eating place is taking on distinction, first as an atmospheric spot appealing to adventurous Anglos, and then simply as a good restaurant where anybody is glad to go. One of the most popular eating places in the best residential section of Dallas is owned and operated by a Mexican. Dallas also boasts six tortilla factories under Mexican ownership and management.

In Texas the social acceptance of a Mexican depends largely on his clothes, the way he carries himself, his use of English, and the amount of money that he has in his pocket. Agricultural workers are discriminated against early and often. The smaller the community the higher the social barriers. "Most instances of refusal of service occur in towns and villages of less than 5,000 population, and those most frequently refused service are in the lower income brackets."[7] A man who has spent his life working with Mexicans put it this way, "If a Mexican is well dressed and enters one of the better eating places with a confident manner and is not heard to speak Spanish, he will be served practically anywhere in Texas." My friend stressed the importance of avoiding the

[7] *Ibid.*, page 217. Used by permission.

use of Spanish in public places in the smaller communities; the sound of a strange language seems to frighten the rural Anglo-Americans! Although they suffer from certain disabilities as a group, it is not difficult for an individual to extricate himself from the discriminations practiced against his fellows. In every social situation there is some sort of an escape hatch.

Most Spanish-speaking Americans of Texas are nominally Roman Catholic. When possible, they desire to be baptized, married, and buried by their traditional church. How much further this affiliation goes depends upon circumstances. The agricultural workers have scant if any contact with the Roman Catholic Church. On the other hand, in cities such as El Paso and San Antonio, Roman Catholic institutions, including the parochial school, enjoy considerable Mexican patronage.

In Texas the investment of Protestant missionary dollars among the Spanish-speaking people has not been at all in proportion to their need. For this there are several reasons. This is not one of the long established mission fields of the church. Most of the Spanish-speaking population of Texas has entered this country during the past twenty-five years. This is a period when our churches have been concerned with the problems growing out of the depression and the greatest of all wars. Upheavals nearer home have kept our attention from such a remote spot as the Rio Grande Valley.

The influx from Mexico has had more of the aspects of a flood than of an ordered migration. Workers came and went and came again as far as the international boundary was concerned. In the local communities north of the border they were distinctly transient. Their low economic status and their roving habits made it difficult to do anything with them or for them—and so little has been attempted.

A successful contact between Protestantism and Mexican newcomers in Texas has been through the Migrant Service of the Division of Home

Missions of the National Council of Churches, which has sent a succession of young people into the lower Rio Grande Valley to do what could be done with the Mexicans who were gathering the vegetables with which to enrich the winter diet of our country. I have seen a graduate of Yale Divinity School teaching English to a group of adult Mexicans by lantern light in the crudest of settlements—and have returned after two hours to find him still holding the attention of his class. I have seen a nurse representing cooperative Protestantism examining the babies of unbelievably young Mexican mothers. I learned that the churches of one of the valley communities had agreed to give $1,000 toward making life tolerable for the Mexicans in their fields.

Like the workers, this work has been highly mobile, with trailers used for living quarters by some of the staff. There has been neither the time nor a favorable situation for thoroughgoing religious instruction. The migrants have been given help that they needed, and in the name and spirit of Christ. Equally important, the local communities have been awakened to some sense of responsibility for these people who toil in their fields when needed and then disappear. In the eyes of some of the local church people, they have moved up from the status of "hands" to that of human beings.

Somewhat similar, but with a bit more local rootage, is the work camp that the Methodists launched at Pharr in the summer of 1950. Here eighteen young people of the Anglo, Mexican, and Negro groups, all with some college training, lived and worked together for six weeks, with "work" running the gamut from ditch-digging to teaching in vacation schools and even preaching. Their devotion shone in such contrasting ventures as painting churches and conducting evenings of hilarious recreation. The result was improved work by the local leaders in the churches and church schools of the Rio Grande Valley in helping newcomers from across the border to make a hopeful adjustment.

The Protestant churches can never ignore the conditions under which people live. The Spanish-speaking people of Texas have been an invitation to humanitarian endeavor. The Mexican Christian Institute that is maintained by the United Christian Missionary Society of the Disciples of Christ in San Antonio illustrates the purposes of a number of similar institutions maintained by various denominations. Mr. E. G. Luna, the head of the institute, was born in Mexico in 1906 and originally came to this country to study for the Mexican consular service, taking degrees at Texas Christian University and the University of Texas. He became head of the institute in 1944.

This is a missionary institution that is addressing its Christian idealism toward the practical goal of improving the conditions among the Mexican people and helping them to find their proper place in the community. It serves 4,000 people a year. Its program starts with health. It has a maternity clinic and campaigns against diarrhea and tuberculosis. It stresses the need for a better diet, plugging for cod liver oil and pablum, and helps the women with their canning, particularly tomatoes and apricots. It asks, "Why be a migrant?" inviting everybody to take a bath, urging the men to wear coats and ties, and helping the women to make better clothes for less money for themselves and their children. The result is increased personal pride, better job opportunities, a higher type of home.

The institute is troubled because only 15,000 out of 150,000 Mexicans in San Antonio care enough about the duties of citizenship to pay the $1.75 poll tax and vote, and because 30,000 Mexicans in the city have failed to secure their naturalization papers. It takes pride in the recent bond issue of $9,000,000 to be used to improve the schools in the Mexican areas.

Mr. Luna states, "The Mexicans can and should solve their own problems. Signs of hope are the 1,700 Mexican young people who finish high school each year in Texas, the many hundreds who are attending college in Texas, and those who are doing graduate work." Although the gospel that he preaches majors on adults learning to read and write, parents sending their children to school regularly, and everybody saving money, this is rated as quite "Protestant" by the Roman Catholic authorities—but "that does not keep the people from coming to us," reports Mr. Luna.

A vacation school conducted by two students from the University of San Antonio in 1937 has led to the establishment of a community center at Ozona, Texas, in the heart of the sheep and goat ranches. It is sponsored by a board representing three denominations and serves a Spanish-speaking population of 1,200 under the direction of two Methodist deaconesses. The Methodist minister reports, "The initiative of these people shows their growth in character. The men built the sidewalk, driveway, and garage at the center, while the women bought the piano, silver, dishes, cooking utensils, linoleum for the kitchen, and curtains for the stage." Through the center better relations have been established with the community, and this has brought more jobs for the young people and an increasing mutual respect.

In Texas conditions have led Protestant home missions to reverse their usual pattern. For the ambitious young person of Spanish-speaking ancestry the doors of the colleges and universities are wide open, which obviates the need for missionary colleges. At the high school level instruction is readily available. The real problem is at the bottom of the educational ladder. The time when the Spanish-speaking child most needs help is when he first starts to school. That is the crucial moment.

Mrs. Alfredo Nanez, wife of the director of religious education for the Rio Grande Conference of Mexican Methodist churches, puts it this way, "Did you ever take two or three courses or even a major in

Spanish and then find yourself in a group of Spanish-speaking people where you could neither speak nor understand the language? Then you may have some idea of how a six-year-old from a Spanish home feels when he first goes to the public school."

The Woman's Division of Christian Service has maintained three kindergartens along the Rio Grande border since 1947. Mrs. Nanez describes their work: "These kindergartens give the child a year or two of language development, which enables him to feel at home in school and thus avoid the problem of retardation. He learns to get along with other children in a free but supervised program. Through play he learns right attitudes toward children of other races and toward his environment."

Interestingly, the church schools that have been established have been aimed at the south bank of the Rio Grande almost as much as at the north bank.

What is popularly known as Pres-Mex (the Presbyterian School for Mexican Girls) is an institution maintained by the Presbyterian Church in the U. S. at Taft, Texas, near Corpus Christi. Its purpose is to train Mexican young women for Christian service. The girls live on their own campus but attend the local high school along with the Anglo boys and girls of the community. The state takes care of their academic training, while the church agency teaches housekeeping and cooperative living. Pres-Mex takes pride in the ministers' and teachers' wives that it has produced.

The big brother to Pres-Mex is Tex-Mex, or more formally the Texas Mexican Industrial Institute at Kingsville, to the south of Corpus Christi. This is also supported by the Presbyterian Church in the U. S. It has 700 acres of what was originally mesquite brush that has been turned into a productive farm and adorned with numerous attractive buildings by the labor of generations of Mexican boys who have been working their way through school and thereby making their way up in the world. Practical training is given in printing, woodworking, welding, plumbing, and other trades, but Christian character is its major aim.

The Lydia Patterson Institute is in the heart of the Mexican section of El Paso and almost in sight of the Mexican boundary. Its students, to the number of 500, come from both sides of the international line. It is supported by the Methodist Church. In addition to offering a good high school education it has a Department of Ministerial Training, with a dozen or so candidates for the ministry distributed through the grades, the high school, and the first year of college. These men are given practical experience along with their school training. Those who are high school graduates attend the Western College of the University of Texas, which is located in El Paso, but live at the institute. From here ministerial students are sent to the Southern Methodist University at Dallas, where there are sixty Latin Americans among the undergraduates and four in the Perkins School of Theology. The Reverend Ben O. Hill, who has spent his life working with Latin Americans of Texas, looks after these Spanish-speaking students.

Another border school is Holding Institute at Laredo, Texas, which attracts boys and girls from as far south as Mexico City and as far north as Chicago. They come from both isolated areas and broken homes. About half of the students are from Roman Catholic homes. A graduate testifies, "I owe Holding for all my schooling through the grades and four years of high school. There I accepted Christ as my personal Saviour under the preaching of Dr. Onderdonk. In my efforts to live the Christian life I have been helped by both the precepts and the example of the teachers at Holding." As high as 50 per cent of the graduates go on to college.

At San Juan, in the heart of the lower Rio Grande Valley, the American Lutheran Church maintains a Bible school for the training of workers with the Mexicans.

The local Protestant church is the place where most Mexicans are most likely to find that which they need. Here it is that they can learn to know and trust a God who cares for them. Here it is that their self-respect is first awakened and then nourished. Here they learn to work with other people. In the church are the springs of eternal life. Through the church the individual can achieve an increasing measure of favor with both God and man.

The local church is the most permanent of missionary institutions. In education the state in the end offers the church impossible competition. In social welfare the local community ultimately assumes its responsibilities. But nothing supersedes the church.

But the local church is also the most difficult of institutions both to found and foster. The reason is simple. Schools and other institutions can be financed and managed from outside, but a church can only succeed in proportion as the people to whom it ministers assume responsibility for it. The church is perhaps the most intimate of human institutions. People must give themselves to it before it can do much for them. For this very reason the Spanish-speaking church has had a hard time and has often made a disappointing record.

The people of Mexico have never been trained in the sort of teamwork that is essential to a successful church. In their local communities they have had few responsibilities. The Roman Catholic Church has decided all religious matters for them. The Spanish tradition is one of individualism rather than cooperation. Where its culture prevails there are few voluntary organizations, and it is an axiom that "committees rarely commit." The spirit of the New England town meeting is utterly alien.

Most of the Spanish-speaking people of the United States are poor.

They have little money with which to support a church and no training whatever in giving.

As we have stressed repeatedly, most of them have few permanent roots in the soil of the United States. A Protestant church presupposes a settled, continuing constituency, and not one that moves around with the crops.

These conditions have made it difficult to recruit and train effective pastors. Here the church faces an almost impossible alternative. If a minister lacks education and is compelled to live on a pittance, he can rarely lead his people far. On the other hand, if he has received college and seminary training and is guaranteed a living wage by his mission board, he is in danger of becoming separated from the people whom he is supposed to serve, and may not be able to lead them at all! A man's effectiveness does not depend upon what he knows, but upon the intimacy of the ties that unite him to his people. For this reason the man with less training may sometimes outshine the man with more training. Against this is raised the question, "Unless a minister knows something, how can he teach his people anything?"

Three policies are followed by the various denominations. The first is to insist upon full college and seminary training for all pastors. The second is to profess this ideal in theory, but not to hold to it too strictly in practice. The third is to take ministers where you can find them and then do what may be possible for them. The last policy seems to achieve the most immediate practical results.

This ministerial supply problem is matched by another similar one in the life of the churches. The people who most need the stimulation that the Protestant church usually brings are the poor, the uneducated, the underprivileged, but as soon as they become a part of the church they proceed to dress up, work their way up in the world, send their children to high school and college, and move away into a better neighborhood. Should a church stay on the job for which it was originally intended, or should it follow its constituency? And unless a church keeps up with the prosperous segment of its constituency, these people, or at least their children, will move over into an Anglo church.

Facing the same problem from another angle, should the educated, privileged person of Latin ancestry continue in a Spanish-speaking church, with its more or less inevitable limitations, or should he slip over into an English-speaking congregation? The argument for staying is that his money and his leadership are needed by his old friends. The argument for moving over is that by so doing he breaks down prejudices that many Anglos carry and commends his people as a group to his new friends. He gives his children a more favorable social setting, and may keep them from deserting the church by so doing. In theory, at least, the sooner we develop unsegregated churches in which several racial groups worship together, the better. The church rarely promotes segregation willingly, but it often finds itself working among segregated people. The appeal of assimilation is great, but it has a dismal sound to the ear of the Spanish-speaking minister who needs both liberal contributors to his budget and people with the education and self-confidence to exercise effective leadership.

Interesting signs of the times in San Antonio are the decision of the son of a Texas-Mexican minister to prepare himself to serve Anglo churches, and the building of an attractive church in a good neighborhood with a retired banker as the pastor, for the avowed purpose of saving to the church the carriage trade that has developed among the Spanish-speaking people of this city. The more a foreign-language church does for its people, the more of them is it likely to lose to English-speaking congregations. In one sense it should live to die, but that takes an abundance of Christian grace and is never an easy assignment.

The Rio Grande Conference of the Methodist Church is the largest Spanish-speaking ecclesiastical organization in the United States. It has three district superintendents, sixty-five pastoral charges, of which eight are in New Mexico, and just under 10,000 members. The conference raises $60,000 a year for local expenses and has 18 self-supporting congregations. Next to poverty, the greatest problem of these churches is the way their people come and go. On the other hand, they minister to youth to a remarkable degree. The families are large and the young people responsive. From 60 to 80 per cent of the people are under thirty-five years of age. Sunday school attendance is large in proportion to membership. Both are growing. Church and Sunday school attendance have doubled in the past fifteen years.

The Methodists and the Presbyterians are the best organized and the largest groups of Spanish-speaking Protestant churches in Texas—but there are many more sponsored by various denominations and by no denomination.

Protestantism has a firm rootage among the Latin Americans of Texas. Spectacular growth is not to be expected, but healthy development is assured. As Protestant people obtain a firmer economic foothold and their children secure a better education, they are certain to increase in influence, probably out of all proportion to their numbers. The over-all situation calls for leadership that will put responsibility upon the people in the churches and yet at the same time inspire them to exercise it in wise ways. Probably the greatest single need is for ministers who combine an education with the common touch, who can meet the standards that our communities set for Protestant pastors but who at the same time can keep the confidence of humble people who labor with their hands and who have little if any education. Where such ministers are found, they are most fruitful both in human good and in the enlargement of the church.

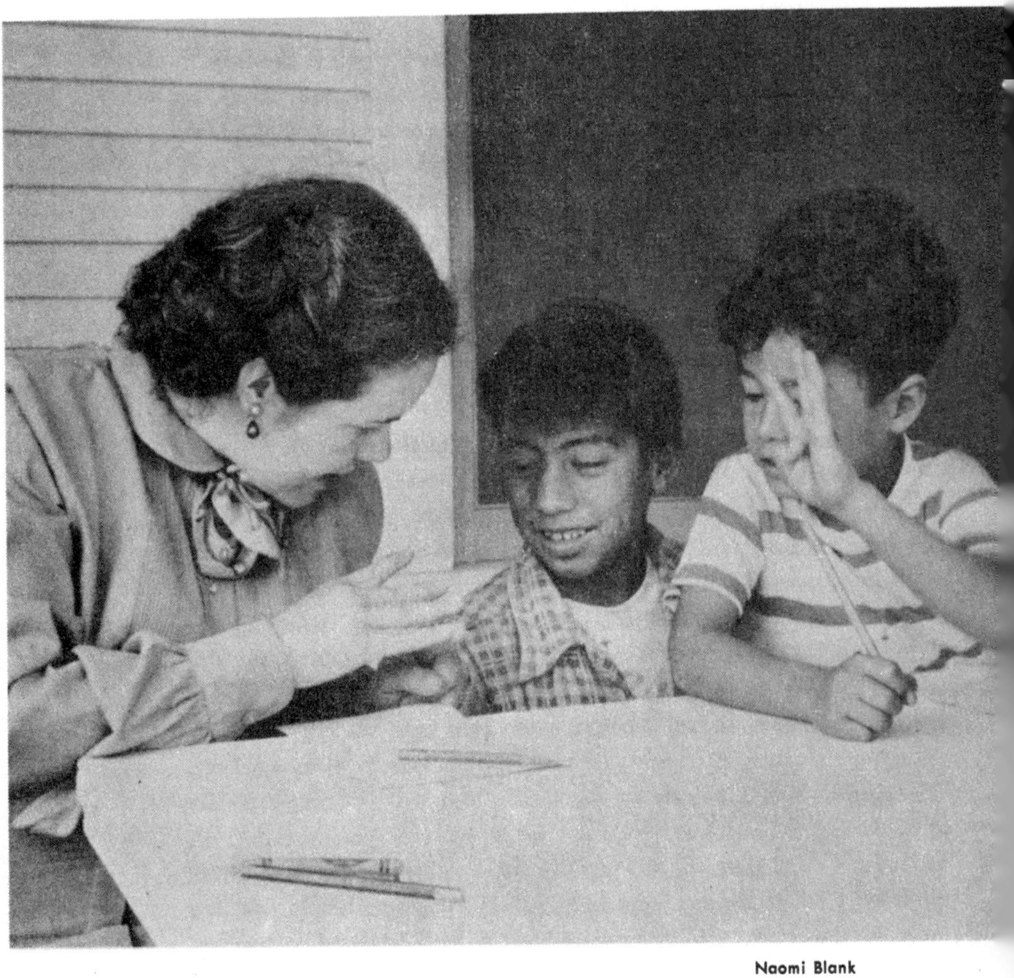

Naomi Blank

Pedro learns quickly when the home missions teacher gives him a chance and a good friend lends encouragement.

) CHAPTER 4 (

Mexicans in Wonderland

TO THE imagination of Mexicans on either side of the border, California seems to be a Promised Land. Here Mexico's discredited politicians take refuge. The late President Plutarco Elías Calles, Mexico's last strong man in the old tradition, spent five years in retirement in San Diego during a period when he was out of political favor at home. In Denver we were told by a Mexican pastor, "When my people take a trip they don't go to Mexico, but to California. That is where they have connections, and that is where their eyes are pointed!" Los Angeles claims to be second only to Mexico City as a center of Mexican population and life.

Yet California is not easily accessible from the populated centers of Mexico. The border is near at hand, but there is nothing south of it save resorts such as Tijuana—where Americans can indulge in more or less illicit pleasures—and great open spaces. The total population of Lower California would soon be lost on the streets of Los Angeles.

There is no connection by rail or highway with the rest of Mexico. The nearest port of entry through which much immigration flows is Nogales, Arizona, which is 572 miles from Los Angeles. Mexicans cannot drift into California in the casual way that they do into Texas. They do not arrive by accident; it takes real effort for them to get to California.

In southern California the Mexicans have played a minor role in one of the great dramas of modern times. They have been behind the scenes in the creation of a new center of world population. Their lowly labor has added much to the splendor of the nation's fourth and fastest growing city, and to the wondrous region round about.

Carey McWilliams has aptly described southern California as an "island on the land." It is surrounded by the ocean, mountains, and deserts. It is not a natural center for either commerce or culture. Southern California's original asset was sunshine, and it is still a basic attraction. Here is a land where people can live out of doors the year around.

Southern California has shown a remarkable ability to find new economic opportunities for the sunshine lovers who have flocked to her. First came the citrus industry, then tourists and health seekers, then the movie industry. Recent years have brought the manufacture of sports clothes, the fabrication of airplanes, and the work of roaring steel mills.

Each development has attracted a new flood of settlers. As Carey McWilliams points out, each tide of population has come a shorter distance and has brought less money with it. First came New England capitalists to invest considerable sums in the growing of citrus fruits. They were followed by the retired Iowa farmers, who at least had enough to live on without too much work. The stream of Mexicans began to flow in 1911, but first stopped and then reversed during the thirties. During the depression years the Okies and the Arkies chugged into the state in their ancient jalopies. And then came the Mexicans.

Although there have always been Spanish-speaking people in California, the large-scale migration from south of the border is a relatively recent development.

In southern California the Mexican immigrant has found a ready-made role awaiting him. He falls into a pattern that is a century old. In the days of the Gold Rush the Chinese appeared to wash the clothes and cook for those who were striving to get rich in a minimum of time. They stayed on to do the hard work in the pioneer settlements. As they saved their money and prospered, they became unpopular, and the Japanese were brought in to take their place. These, in turn, worked hard, bought land, and were discriminated against on a variety of alleged grounds. This pattern was repeated again and again until the Mexicans took over the hard, back-breaking jobs that nobody wanted. Along with their employment, they inherited the prejudices under which their predecessors had suffered.

There are several circumstances that have conspired to keep the Mexican newcomers from entering into the main stream of California life.

The original land grants made by the kings of Spain and confirmed by the Treaty of Guadalupe Hidalgo have been the basis of land tenure in California ever since. Instead of being homesteaded in quarter sections by humble people, as was the case in much of the West, most of the good soil of California has been held in vast tracts by the fortunate few. The uses to which it was put—first cattle and then fruit—were conducive to large scale operations. The result has been what Carey McWilliams has described as "factories in the field"—production line techniques applied to agriculture.

The Mexican stepped into this picture not as an individual but as a "hand," a member of a gang taking orders from a Spanish-speaking boss. The rule in southern California has been to hire a lot of Mexicans or none at all. Chances of promotion are scant and the contacts with American workers almost non-existent.

Along with segregation in work has gone segregation in living quarters. Poor pay has meant poor homes. The traditional pattern has been the *colonia,* a small cluster of substandard huts on the wrong side of something—a railroad, river, *arroyo,* highway, or hill—restricted solely to Mexicans. Such settlements are characteristic of southern California, although usually tucked away in such a fashion as not to attract the notice of the traveler. There is said to be such a community within a mile and a half of Los Angeles' ornate Civic Center. Usually the lines are sharply drawn about such groups. Poorer class Mexicans have few if any American neighbors. Their contacts are with their own people.

This separateness has been further accentuated by the attitudes of the people whose places they have taken in the economic scheme of things. The rapid growth of southern California has brought together a lot of people in a hurry. Many have sought its sunshine because they were not doing too well in the places from which they came. This has been particularly true of the large migration from the Southern states to Los Angeles. These people are rootless and insecure. They have many new neighbors but few old friends. Their church ties are tenuous. They are eager for emotional outlets, and have fallen an easy prey to political charlatans and fake messiahs. They are looking for someone to look down on, and are predisposed to hate. The Mexicans, being on a lower rung of the ladder than they, have been an easy target for their prejudices. These were manifested in the zoot suit riots and other similar occurrences.

Inevitably, this situation has had an unhappy effect upon the Mexicans who have newly come to this country. They find themselves in a strange and dazzling land, but their jobs are usually seasonal and their living quarters unsatisfactory. Insecurity faces them on every side.

They distrust employers, landlords, and anyone in authority, having had little experience with friendly public officials and no knowledge of social agencies such as are found in American cities. The Mexican immigrant withdraws from the larger life about him. His interests center in his own countrymen and pre-eminently in his family.

How to feed himself and his children is the problem that constantly confronts him. Not knowing the language, with his strong arms and nimble fingers as his chief asset, having no knowledge or experience with either industrial or agricultural machinery, he is compelled to take the jobs that nobody else wants. Much of this is "stoop labor." At the end of the day he is too exhausted with his arduous toil to be concerned about much more than something to eat and a place to sleep.

His numerous children are the ultimate salvation of many a Mexican, in that they help him to adjust to American life as does nothing else, but they are an immediate economic burden. The Mexican consul in a Midwestern city put it this way: "If an American gets only three thousand dollars a year, he has just one child. When he gets a raise to four thousand, he has a second, and when his pay goes to five thousand he may have a third. But a Mexican does not do it that way. If he loses his job, he is likely to have two children more to add to those already on hand!" Just getting enough to feed the family is the first concern of most Mexicans during their early years north of the border.

Yet from these lowly beginnings the Mexicans and their children are going far in southern California. The disabilities from which they suffer are temporary rather than permanent, and there appear to be no hurdles that some young American of Mexican ancestry cannot get over.

The very newness of southern California helps. In the long established steel mills of South Chicago the Poles have pre-empted the good jobs, leaving the hottest and dirtiest work for the Mexicans. In the new steel mills of southern California there are no such vested interests, and the Mexicans have a better chance for the work that pays real money. Truck driving is another new field where they are getting a good foothold. As the children go through high school and the more ambitious boys and girls manage to go on to college, they spread out into all manner of occupations and callings. Real estate and law are two areas where they are conspicuously present. The children of Mexican immigrants have traveled far from the place where they started.

This is reflected in where they live. Some Mexicans live in all but the most expensive areas of Los Angeles, but the chief concentration is in East Los Angeles. Part of this area is outside the city limits and therefore lacks some of the usual urban services, such as pavements, street cleaning, libraries, etc. Most of the buildings are forty years old. The prevailing type of house is the one-story bungalow that was particularly beloved by young American couples who were not too well off in the years before the first world war. The people who built these humble homes have prospered and moved elsewhere; the Mexicans have inherited them. The property has not deteriorated as much with the years as one might expect. Many homes are well kept without and immaculate within.

The principle that largely governs where the Mexicans live in southern California is the amount of money in their pockets. They get the best homes that they can pay for. This means rent to begin with, but ownership later in many cases. When they get more money, they will live in better houses. It is as simple as that. Also, these finer abodes will be scattered over the city. The present concentrations of Mexicans are not due to inherent clannishness, but to their common poverty. Since the world began poor people, whatever their nationality, have had to live together. As they escape from the limitations imposed by the lack of coin of the realm, they will mingle more with the larger community.

Mounting prosperity is multiplying the contacts between the Mexicans of southern California and the Roman Catholic Church.

In Los Angeles the Mexicans are achieving an economic level at which church support is possible. When poor people get money, among their first luxuries are elaborate church weddings.

The parochial school has long enrolled Mexican children in Los Angeles and in the other cities with a sizable Mexican population. The pastor of a Mexican Methodist church reported the arguments being used to persuade Mexican parents to send their children to parochial schools: "Public schoolteachers smoke, they drink, they run around at night and sometimes arrive at school the next morning weary and unprepared. The nuns who teach in the parochial schools lead orderly lives. At night they study their lessons for the next day, say their prayers, go to bed early, get up, pray some more, and arrive in the schoolroom with refreshed bodies, clear heads, and well prepared lessons ready to teach your children." For Mexican fathers and mothers who are distrustful of American life and ways, this is a convincing line of reasoning, which may be reinforced with allusions to sin and purgatory.

In the Los Angeles area the variety of Protestant churches ministering to Mexicans is most impressive. Their constituencies run the gamut from the minority who are hungry and homeless to the majority who are on their way up economically. In the western portion of the city there is at least one well built, well maintained church catering to a well-to-do congregation. In East Los Angeles some of the buildings have been inherited from English-speaking congregations. In addition, there are a number of stucco and wood buildings designed for their present occupants.

The range of emphasis is equally wide. A social worker in a church-supported center stated, "Language is the greatest handicap under which these young people suffer; one of our big jobs is to teach them to speak good English." We met a pastor who felt that part of his mission was to keep alive the Spanish language and the culture that it represents. We found churches where athletic games were going on outdoors while the women learned to cook and sew indoors. Underlying all programs of useful activities was the Christian appeal to the personal. Some churches express it in mass meetings and some through personal visitation and counseling, but all seek to exalt Jesus Christ as the one altogether worthy of the highest loyalty, the all-sufficient Saviour.

In evaluating the work of these social centers, Dr. Glenn W. Moore writes:

With older people not using the English language easily, with uncertain economic basis, with prejudice against Protestant churches, and with fear of persons prying into personal affairs, it is often difficult to establish contact with Mexican families. But a program of storytelling, of crafts, of games, and a friendly worker can soon establish confidence and friendship with children. Attitudes of cooperation, sociability, and confidence soon are developed. Christian workers can find many ways to tell the Christian story and awaken an interest.

The doors of homes otherwise closed are soon opened to the visitor who is a friend of the children in the household. Mothers are invited to visit the House of Neighborly Service and find help in their problems. A nurse helps when sickness comes. Soon many homes know that the House of Neighborly Service is a place of friendship and help. It is then found that this place exists because the people who operate it are Christians and are therefore interested in the welfare of the people of the neighborhood.

Some fine Christian homes may now be witnessed, established by young people first touched by the church in this way.

A church is found next to each House. The minister of at least one of these is himself the product of the House that he went to as a boy seeking companionship. Other former young people are now teachers, social workers, housewives, and elders in churches. Community Chests have recognized the value of the service and have supported these enterprises. This has been another way of ministering in the name of Christ.

When we approached the El Salvador Baptist Church, members of an interracial Mexican-Negro Sunday school were leaving the building. The advent of a housing project adjoining the church property had led the congregation to establish an English-speaking Sunday school in which the teachers were Mexicans but most of the pupils Negroes. Inside the church, we found that the regular Spanish-speaking Sunday school was still in session. The transition from it to the church service was not marked by anybody going out or coming in but by the superintendent leaving the platform and the pastor taking his place. It happened to be Fathers' Day. As part of the observance, all the fathers present, to the number of about twenty, were lined up across the front of the church and asked, first, how many children they had and, second, where they were. One father reported twelve and another eight and the rest less impressive figures. A few had some of their children with them; the rest reported that they were scattered from Korea to the Atlantic Coast. The atmosphere was informal and folksy; the congregation shared lustily in all of the proceedings. One could see how such a church service might compensate for a week of humble and not too much appreciated toil.

At another Mexican Baptist church, the service was more formal, although at one time all newcomers were asked what denomination they belonged to. The preaching was eloquent and the attention close. The first church was an expression of the group life; the second church was an agency for evangelizing men. Both are needed, and both are powerful. In both instances the people were present in good numbers.

In the Los Angeles area there are four notable Protestant institutions.

The Plaza Community Center stands at the heart of Old Los Angeles. Here the Spanish built their first adobe huts—a strange beginning for the present far-flung metropolis. In the years before the second world war this was the center of Japanese life. Today it is a strange mixture of old and new, a spot where all sorts and conditions of men meet and mingle. Facing the old square is the Plaza Community Center, which is first of all a Methodist church with 600 members drawn from all over the city and second a five-story, glistening white building dedicated to all manner of good works. It operates a clinic, employs a welfare worker, carries on many classes and much shop work, sends 80 boys and girls to camp every summer, and operates a children's home in Sierra Madre. The total budget is $56,000 a year, much of it drawn from home missionary sources. This is a dramatic Protestant approach to the Spanish-speaking Americans of the Southwest.

Mexican young people are offered the experience of living in a happy Christian atmosphere while attending school by other Methodist institutions, including the Spanish American Institute for boys at Gardena and the Frances DePauw School for girls, in Los Angeles. Both began as schools, but both now send their young people to the public schools, adding to this training a Christian home life and many extracurricular activities. The girls learn to keep house, to enjoy music, to teach English to those who need it, while the boys at Gardena look after sixty of the finest cows in the Los Angeles area. For hundreds of young people of Mexican parentage who have known little of well established homes, these institutions have opened the door upon a new way of living together.

Although located in East Los Angeles, the work and influence of the Spanish American Baptist Seminary extends far beyond California. It is the only college grade school for the training of ministers in continental United States in which Spanish is the language of instruction. In a recent year it enrolled students from California, Arizona, Missouri, Michigan, Illinois, Indiana, Kansas, and New York, not to mention Mexico, Puerto Rico, Guatemala, Cuba, and Colombia. Young women constitute about a fifth of the student body. Work is of college level, but with a five year course. The school is supported by the American Baptist Home Missionary Society.

Graduates of this seminary have gone out to serve faithfully and effectively wherever Spanish is spoken. Some have attained distinction as professors and writers. One of them is the present national director of the American Baptist Spanish work.

An international school such as this attracts unusual characters. One such, whose father was a prosperous business man in Mexico, left home at eighteen "to see the world," and was disinherited. After much wandering, he went to live with his sister in Tijuana, where she was a member of the Baptist church. She persuaded him to go with her to church, with the result that he was baptized. Shortly thereafter two Mexican Baptist ministers became martyrs at the hands of a mob. He decided to devote his life to taking the place of one of these men—and so he has made the strange transition from Tijuana to the Baptist Seminary in Los Angeles.

Almost as interesting is the story of another student at the seminary. He was born in Puerto Rico, the oldest of a large family. At the age of fourteen the family moved to New York city, where he became a member of the Second Spanish Baptist Church. He graduated from high school in New York. His mother has a good position, and he had every reason to believe that he could do well in business—but he felt a call to the ministry, and so he crossed the continent that he might learn to preach in the Spanish language.

Arizona is in many ways becoming an extension of southern California, as both citrus fruits and winter visitors bring increasing prosperity. It has the smallest Spanish-speaking population of any of the border states—and the least current immigration from Mexico. In general the picture is the same as for southern California, with the mines and the railroads as among the largest employers of Mexicans.

In Nogales, Arizona has the largest port of entry into Mexico west of El Paso, with Laredo, Texas, its only other rival as a gateway between the two nations. In Nogales has taken place one of the brightest stories of Christian service in the annals of modern home missions.

O. A. Smith started his ministry in the United Brethren Church in Michigan, but for reasons of health he found it necessary to move west, and in the process he became a Congregationalist. In 1920 he was sent to the little home missionary church in Nogales, and has been there ever since. In those days the international boundary line ran down the middle of a wide and dusty street that had one curb in Mexico and the other in the United States. This has since been replaced by a high wire fence through which one can peer from one country into the other. Mr. Smith arrived just as Mexico was subsiding into order after ten years of active revolution. Until the appointment of Dwight Morrow as ambassador to Mexico in 1927 the relations between the two countries were marked by mutual suspicions and ill will. During the decade of turmoil each had repeatedly exasperated the other. At the border this meant that all sorts of people got into all sorts of trouble with both governments.

Mr. Smith was concerned with people rather than with international relations. People sensed that his heart was good and that he might be their "friend in need." Both Americans and Mexicans sought him out with their various difficulties. His patience, his good sense, and his incorrigible smile enabled him to straighten matters out—especially as the officials on both sides of the line soon came to trust him. Under his leadership a social service bureau was set up to take care of the "situations" of human distress that were continually arising. This was financed locally, and for many years was headed by this home missionary pastor.

As the years have gone by, Nogales, Arizona, has had fewer and fewer Anglo citizens and more and more Mexican residents. Mr. Smith has continued to be everybody's friend, and is now pastor of the combined Congregational and Methodist churches, which makes him the one Protestant Anglo minister of the city. This important link in the international boundary is a more human, happier place because of his ministry. By way of recognition, some years ago the government of Mexico invited O. A. Smith, Protestant home missionary, to attend the inauguration of a president of the republic as its guest and at its expense. At Nogales, home missionary effort has achieved international recognition.

Many Protestant agencies sponsor work among Spanish-speaking people. To consolidate these efforts the Interdenominational Council on Spanish-speaking Work was organized in 1911. It is representative of both field workers and boards of missions. It has helped provide a community spirit among the Protestant churches serving Spanish-speaking people.

The council has fostered cooperative leadership training, religious education, and youth work. A strong program of women's work is sponsored by the General Department of United Church Women.

Should the council try to develop a strong group consciousness among Spanish-speaking churches, or should it lead toward the full integration of all Protestant work? To develop a strong group consciousness might bring a distinctiveness amounting to segregation. Integration might mean a needy field would be lost to sight. Here is an unsolved dilemma.

However, the council must continue to provide a channel for cooperation until Christian united fellowship becomes a reality.

Standard Oil of New Jersey

Picking pecks of peppers is a back breaker as well as a tongue twister. This is "stoop" labor.

) CHAPTER 5 (

Mexicans on Wheels

ANCIENT jalopies with black haired, dark faced drivers and overloaded with both children and household goods have been a common sight on our Western highways. The most recent role of the Mexican on the American scene has been that of a migrant agricultural laborer flitting from crop to crop. In this capacity he has taken from the ground or plucked from the tree much food that has entered American mouths. He has also scattered himself far and wide over our country. In many places the visits of Mexican migrants have been the prelude to the establishment of a Mexican settlement.

Mexicans do not rattle about from place to place because they enjoy traveling. Their instincts are not at all nomadic. For boys even to think about running away from home is contrary to their traditions. Mexicans move about from necessity.

In this large-scale movement of Mexican workers there is both a push and a pull, with the former probably a bit stronger than the latter.

Two facts of life in Mexico explain both the source of this flood of humanity and the forces that have set it in motion. The population of Mexico has increased from 16.5 million in 1930 to 25.5 million in 1950, with a 30 per cent gain during the past decade. The simple fact is that the resources of the country have not expanded sufficiently to take care of the extra mouths to be fed. This basic situation has been further aggravated by inflation, which has been twice as severe as in this country. Taking 1939 as a base line (or 100) the cost of living in Mexico City was 354 by June of 1950, as compared with 171 in the United States for the same period.

Over against these facts should be put another. In 1949 the per capita income in the United States was $1,453; in Mexico it was $114. The greater the disparity of income and opportunity between the two sides of a boundary line, the greater the pressure to which that line will be exposed. Stories and pictures of the opulence of this country inspire the hungry, tattered Mexican with a great desire to push on across the line and help himself to some of our much advertised wealth.

But there is also a pull from this side. American agriculture, shifting to a large-scale mechanical operation, produces more food and fiber with relatively fewer workers. The year round employment of hired workers on our farms is decreasing. This same process has accentuated the need for part-time workers, particularly during the harvest. Plowing, planting, cultivating have been mechanized far more easily and quickly than cotton picking or the getting of sugar beets out of the ground. When it comes to the picking of cherries and strawberries, it would be hard to find anything to take the place of human fingers.

This situation has been aggravated by the long-time practice of using cheap labor for these processes. In some areas human hands are still cheaper than machines. As long as people can be had to work for little, the farmer is not likely to offer them more. But in recent years it has become increasingly difficult to enlist what is known as "stoop labor." The better wages offered in industry have drawn off many of those who once worked on farms. Why torture oneself bending over all day when more money can be had at jobs that are both less exhausting and much steadier? Inevitably farmers have turned their eyes southward across the border in their quest for cheap help. All along the boundary the argument is heard, "For many years we have had willing workers at a low wage from Mexico. Our farms have been developed on this basis. Are we not entitled to it now?"

Mexican migrant workers in this country fall into three groups: "wetbacks" who have entered the country illegally, contract workers brought in under an agreement between the two countries, and Mexicans who have become permanent and legal residents of this country. We will describe them in this order.

By common usage "wetback" means any Mexican who has gotten into the country without interviewing the immigration authorities. With the vast extent of the boundary, most of it running through very sparsely settled country, and with the very scant numbers of the border patrol, this is not a difficult matter. The term "wetback" is a fine sample of Western humor of the tall tale variety. Except in flood times, it is rarely necessary to get wet above the knees to cross the Rio Grande River.

As to the extent of this movement, the President's Commission on Migratory Labor reports:

> The magnitude of the wetback traffic has reached entirely new levels in the past seven years. The number of deportations and voluntary departures has continuously mounted each year from 29,000 in 1944 to 565,000 in 1950. In its newly achieved proportions it is virtually an invasion. It is estimated that at least 400,000 of our migratory farm labor force of one million in 1949 were wetbacks.

The same report describes how this movement operates.

The hub of the wetback traffic is in the plazas of the Mexican towns and cities immediately below the border. Here, or in sections around the railroad which serve the same purpose, the wetback seeks information about jobs in the United States and how to get them. His urgent need of food and money makes him an easy mark for the smuggler, the labor contractor, or the agent of the farm employer. He is eager when any of these approach him and whisper that there is a way to get out of the vast mob, all looking for a job, and a chance to get into the United States where jobs seem plentiful and wages seem high.

Although the smuggling of wetbacks is widespread, the majority of wetbacks apparently enter alone or in small groups without a smuggler's assistance. In a group moving without the aid of a smuggler there usually is one who has made the trip before and who is willing to show the way. Not infrequently the same individual knows the farm to which the group intends to go and sometimes he has made advance arrangements with the farm employer to return at an appointed date with his group. Such wetbacks stream into the United States by the thousands through the deserts near El Paso and Calexico or across the Rio Grande between Rio Grande City and Brownsville. When employment on the farms adjacent to the border is filled, the wetbacks push northward into new areas following rumor or promise of employment.

Often the wetbacks entering alone or in small groups have written to farm employers or friends and have made arrangements to be met at some crossroad, gate, or other well known place within a night's walk of the border. Some make two or three separate entries within a season, after having been apprehended, and head for the place where they were formerly employed.

If the wetback makes a deal to be guided or escorted across the Rio Grande or some section of the land border, everything which he is able to pay is usually extracted from him in return for the service, which may be no more than being guided around the fence or being given a boat ride across the Rio Grande. Wetbacks who are without funds to pay the smuggler for bringing them in or to pay the trucker-contractor who furnishes transportation or direction from the boundary to the farm are frequently "sold" from one exploiter to the next. For example, the smuggler will offer to bring a specified number of wetbacks across the river for such an amount as $10 or $15 per man. The smuggler or boatman with his party in tow will be met by the trucker-contractor who will then "buy" the wetback party by paying off the smuggler. This trucker-contractor, in turn, will have a deal to deliver workers to employers at an agreed-upon price per head.

Once on the United States side of the border and on the farm, numerous devices are employed to keep the wetback on the job. Basic to these devices is the fact that the wetback is a person of legal disability who is under jeopardy of immediate deportation if caught. He is told that if he leaves the farm, he will be reported to the Immigration Service or that, equally unfortunate for him, the Immigration Service will surely find him if he ventures into town or out onto the roads. To assure that he will stay until his services are no longer needed, his pay, or some portion thereof, frequently is held back. Sometimes he is deliberately kept indebted to the farmer's store or commissary until the end of the season, at which time he may be given enough to buy shoes or clothing and encouraged to return the following season.

The wetback is a hungry human being. His need of food and clothing is immediate and pressing. He is a fugitive and it is as a fugitive that he lives. Under the constant threat of apprehension and deportation, he cannot protest or appeal no matter how unjustly he is treated. Law operates against him but not for him. Those who capitalize on the legal disability of the wetbacks are numerous and their devices are many and various.

During the last two or three years the wetback has received much publicity, and efforts have been made by the government and others to have something effective done about his plight, but as yet the results have been meager. Deportation is often futile, as he comes back in a day or two. It is said that the Immigration Service tried flying repatriated wetbacks far into Mexico, but that they return just the same. The man who profits by the wetback is his employer, and as yet no real penalties have been invoked against him.

Inevitably such a fly-by-night person as the wetback can have little contact with churches, either Roman Catholic or Protestant. He may be in the United States for some months, but he is not of it. The effect of the wetback upon the position of his fellow Mexicans in this country will be discussed in connection with the other phases of agricultural migrancy.

A second group of migrant workers are the Mexicans brought into the United States under contract on the basis of an agreement between our government and that of Mexico. This arrangement began during the first world war as an emergency measure to assure help in harvesting. Between 1917 and 1921, 73,000 Mexicans were brought into this country on a temporary basis. This practice was revived in 1943 and extended to include workers from Jamaica, the Bahama Islands, and elsewhere. Between 1942 and 1947 our government brought 219,500 Mexicans into this country at public expense. The agreement with Mexico has been repeatedly extended, with the result that over 100,000 Mexicans were imported in 1949 and just over 90,000 in 1950.

To secure Mexicans under contract, it is necessary for farmers to certify that they are unable to obtain the labor needed from American sources and to agree to pay the prevailing wage to these workers, as well as to meet certain other conditions that we will mention later. Necessarily this statement of need must be filed some time before the harvest, and therefore is somewhat hypothetical. The most that the farmer can do is to state that he "expects" a shortage. Harvests are at best brief. The farmer wants to have enough workers on hand to get the crop gathered in a short period of time. His view of what constitutes a shortage is quite different from that of the workers.

The prevailing wage is also somewhat hypothetical. At the beginning of the season the farmers set a figure at which they hope they can secure sufficient workers to serve their ends. If workers prove scarce, this figure may be boosted. The effect of importing Mexicans is to make labor abundant and thus to make the prevailing wage rather less than would have been the case if it had been necessary for the farmers to bid for workers from a lesser number of possible harvesters.

On the other hand, the Mexicans who come in under contract enjoy certain advantages that are denied to American workers—such as health care, a reasonable standard for both the transportation and the housing provided them, and the assurance that they will be returned to the place where they started. In case the terms of the agreement are violated by the employer, the employee has the privilege of appealing to the Mexican consul. During his employment the Mexican under contract has a security that those who live here all year do not know.

Both the wetbacks and the Mexicans under contract are resented by the migratory workers who have permanent residence in this country—both those of American and those of Mexican descent. They feel that citizens of this country should have the same guarantees that are given to aliens. More important, they feel that the ability of the farmers to secure both illegal and contract labor has enabled them to keep wages at a lower level than would otherwise have been the case. This is substantiated by the President's Commission on Migratory Labor, which states bluntly, "We find that alien labor has depressed farm wages and, therefore, has been detrimental to domestic labor."

In the early months of 1943 the writer visited a number of the migrant labor camps that were being maintained at that time by the government in Florida and Texas. The men in charge of these camps did not believe that there was any need for the importation of alien labor but that with proper adjustments as to wages, period of work, and housing accommodations enough laborers could be found in this country to take care of agricultural needs. The President's Commission is of the same mind. It reports:

> Since 1945 more hired workers are being employed to do continuously less work. Many imperfections in the employment structure of American agriculture result in poor use of our labor resources. Notwithstanding these imperfections and obstacles to effective use of labor, we are convinced

that, by the better recruitment and placement of domestic labor, we would have eliminated most if not all the occasion for the certifications of labor shortage during the years 1947 to 1950.

That is, if American agriculture attacked this problem with energy, resourcefulness, and ingenuity, we could get along without either the wetbacks or the legally imported labor of Mexico—and our agricultural workers would be better off.

The President's Commission states the matter rather poignantly:

> Migrants are children of misfortune. They are the rejects of those sectors of agriculture and of other industries undergoing change. We depend upon misfortune to build up our force of migratory workers and when the supply is low because there is not enough misfortune at home, we rely on misfortune abroad to replenish the supply.

During the war years, Mexico refused to send contract labor to Texas because of the discriminations practiced against Mexicans, with the result that most of the legally imported workers during that period went to California and the Pacific Northwest. Since the war, Mexico has lifted the ban against Texas, with the result that in recent years most of the contract labor has gone to Texas, New Mexico, and Arkansas. Although these men (no families are brought in under contract) have been relatively well cared for, they have had few real contacts with American life, particularly the churches.

We now come to the third group—the Mexicans who came to this country legally and who regard themselves as permanent residents.

It should be stressed that this is not too difficult a status to attain. Unlike most parts of the world, Mexico does not have an immigration quota. There are no limits to the number who may be legally admitted to residence in the United States during a given year. The barriers, such as they are, are administrative and technical. Any reasonably persistent Mexican who is not afraid of paper work can secure admission.

Such an immigrant needs to secure permission from the Mexican Government to leave and permission from a United States consul to enter. He must meet the requirements as to health and moral character. He must either produce one hundred dollars in cash at the border or have letters promising support from friends or relatives already in the country. To get a friend in, a Mexican living in this country needs such things as letters from his banker and employer, possibly from some church, a tax receipt if possible, and so on. These are undoubtedly burdensome requirements to unlettered people, but they are not impossible.

There is another and rather interesting way that a Mexican can stay in this country, or even return to it. Every child born in this country whose parents do not claim citizenship for him elsewhere is by that very fact a citizen of the United States. Except when they come in as contract laborers. Mexicans commonly bring their families with them—and frequently give birth to American citizens. Any baby for whom somebody will claim the right can stay in the United States or even return to it. Now to separate a baby or a small child from its parents would cause distress to all concerned. To prevent such distress any Mexicans who can prove that their child was born beneath our flag can remain in the United States. After a person has resided here legally for seven years he achieves the "right of residence" and cannot ordinarily be deported. Thus it is far easier for Mexicans to enter the United States legally than for people of most of the other nations. However, we have a suspicion that the person who can meet the requirements for residence is not the sort of person who is likely to become a migrant agricultural worker after he gets here.

It is plain hunger that brings the Mexican farm worker into the United States either legally or illegally. It is his inability to earn a living in one place that compels the American of Mexican descent to take to the road, as shown by the following testimony before the Senate subcommittee on migratory farm labor:

> My name is Jacinto Cota, Jr. I do all kinds of farm work in the fields. Right now I am loading carrots. All my life I have lived in the Imperial Valley. All my friends and I have worked with the wetbacks and the nationals and we know these conditions that we are talking about. They have pushed out our local people because they will do any kind of work on farms for low wages. The ranchers tell them in old Mexico that they are going to get different good wages. They promise good houses. . . . The labor contractors gyp the nationals. They make them pay high prices for food, blankets, and medicine. All the local people will have to leave the valley if they keep bringing in nationals and wetbacks.

Obviously few Mexicans who have established themselves on this side of the border voluntarily choose to become migrants. The hunger and want of Mexico pushes her people across the international boundary and deprives those already here of at least a part of their employment. In order to maintain the standard of living they have attained, they take to the road. Here they find life unsatisfactory for many reasons, chief of which are irregular employment and low wages.

According to a survey made by the United States Department of Agriculture, in 1949 the average migratory farm worker got 70 days of farm work and 31 days of non-farm work, making a total for the year of 101 days with annual earnings averaging $514. These figures included everybody over fourteen years of age for both sexes. Almost a third of the workers were women, while between one-fourth and one-fifth of the workers were between the ages of fourteen and seventeen. Everybody must help. The larger the family, the larger the income, but even then two thousand dollars a year is unusual. On the other hand, for the actual time they work migratory workers make a little more than non-migratory workers—but this is more than offset by the irregularity of their employment and the cost of getting around.

The President's Commission reports:

> Although migratory farm workers travel long distances to get employment, very few of them use the bus or train. In the ordinary sense of the word, they do not travel; most of them are hauled.
>
> Whether supplied by contractors or employers, the trucks used too frequently are old and dilapidated and generally unfit for carrying people. There have been many accidents which would not have happened had the driver not been exhausted from continuous driving or if the truck had been in proper mechanical repair. In many cases no rest stops are made though the trip requires thirty-six hours or more. One reason why trucks come straight through from points of origin to points of destination is that there are no accommodations for rest stops en route. A survey in Indiana reveals that the most frequent suggestion of workers from Texas was the need for "rest camps along the route at which they might stop to clean up, rest, and cook."

At this point Mexican contract workers fare better than American citizens:

> The Mexican worker's contract provides for transportation by common carrier or in approved equipment. Conditions which must be met include: insurance to protect the workers against injury en route; fixed seats and covering against inclement weather; hours of travel limited to twelve per day, not to commence before four A. M. and not to continue after eight P. M.; ten minute rest stops every two hours with half hour stops for meals; provision of overnight accommodation; an experienced, licensed driver who agrees to observe the safety regulations of common carriers.

Next to modes of travel, the housing or lack thereof is the greatest hardship for migratory workers. The shorter their stay, the scantier the provision for their needs. The President's Commission states:

> On job, housing consists of barracks, cabins, trailers, tents, rooming houses, auto-court cabins, shack houses, and depreciated standard housing. Ownership may be by employers' associations, local housing authorities, labor contractors, or private commercial groups.
>
> "Good" housing for a family of four, five, or six members might consist

of an unpainted cabin, 9 by 12 feet, one in a row of such cabins, with one or perhaps two screened windows (though not necessarily with glass) and with unfinished interior walls. The cabin would be equipped with bunks, chairs, and table. It would be fairly clean and free from vermin. The cabin might possibly, but probably would not, have electricity. It could have running water, but this would be unusual. Characteristically, water suitable for drinking would be obtained from centrally located faucets. Cooking facilities, if existent, would probably be central. (We have seen a dozen stoves, each assigned to a different family, all in one big room.) Sanitary facilities would be central and clean. In exceptional cases, there would be flush toilets; more often, there would be privies. Central shower facilities would be equipped with hot and cold water. In the better camps there would be facilities for laundering and receptacles for garbage which would be regularly emptied. There would probably be no trees about the cabins, so that during the summer months they would be fully exposed to the sun.

To be "good" a camp is not required to have any provisions for recreation, but it might be located within walking distance of a community center. If, by chance, a school was nearby, the children could attend. If it was not so located, no alternative arrangements would be made for schooling. No arrangements would exist for the care of the small children. Since both parents often work, the children would be left to their own devices or would join their parents in the field. If, as is usual, the camp is located beyond the reach of medical and health facilities, it would be unusual if arrangements existed for regular visits of a nurse or physician.

A series of such "good" camps, or a single such camp, might, if the migrant were fortunate, be his home for four to six months of the year. If so, he would be one of a minority, because even in those states that officially inspect and rate their camps, less than one half of the inspected camps are found to be "good."

The work of the migrant is terribly impersonal. He rarely sees and hardly ever knows his employer. He is a "hand" rather than a human being, and works for a crop rather than a person. This is reflected in his use of words. He works "in cotton," "in beets," "in carrots," "in cherries." His labor is wholly without personal recognition. Often no payroll is kept; the worker brings in the fruit or vegetables or cotton that he has picked and is paid for his work by the basket or other container.

Mexican migrants have two points of departure: southern California and Texas.

The "swing" of the Mexican migrants in California is relatively short, with a range of about 500 miles. However, the work is remarkably varied, as shown by testimony before the President's Commission:

> We start about in late April. The Valencia orange season starts in Tulare County. That lasts pretty well, usually up until June. Around the first of July, I leave there and go to the Sacramento River and work in the pear houses. The pear harvest in that area is the first pears that ripen in California. That usually lasts about three weeks. There is usually also a time right in there in Lake County—a week or so—and then pears start in other places —Tulare County, Santa Clara County. The pear harvest will last pretty well into September, and then the walnuts start. And then I return home in October, and the olive crop is about to start. Early in November we have another orange crop season. That usually carries through until the middle of January.

With the exception of "some little pruning in citrus and grapes in March" the witness usually has no work from mid-January to late April. He reported his earnings for the year to be between $1,800 and $2,000.

The Texas-Mexicans are a more traveled lot. In our chapter on Texas we told how they follow the cotton crop within the state. There is also the great migration from the Rio Grande Valley and San Antonio to the Yakima Valley in Washington for apples and hops, to Montana, Colorado, Nebraska, and Kansas for sugar beets, and to central Michigan for sugar beets and fruits. A glance at the map will show that the distances involved are terrific.

Sugar beets are the crop most intimately associated with Mexicans—probably because it involves really violent labor. In Montana I have

Top, Division of Foreign Missions, NCCC; bottom, Ray Drap

seen a Mexican girl who could hardly have been twenty years old pu beets out of the ground, knock them together to shake off the dir and toss them to one side at a speed that made picture taking mo difficult. In Michigan I have seen Mexican men swishing off the tops beets with a rapidity that taxed the eye. This is exhausting work—an yet the Mexicans manage to stick at it for hours.

In the western areas German-speaking immigrants from Russia were the original beet workers. At the opening of the century they did the work that the Mexicans now do; today they "own the beets." Will the Mexicans follow their example? It is not impossible.

Some years back stories were current of non-stop "standing room only" truck rides for Mexicans from San Antonio to the area north of Lansing, Michigan, but we believe that this is of the past. In its handling of migrant labor, Michigan has led the other states. Before he leaves Texas, the worker is commonly given both a medical examination and a contract. Also the growers in Michigan have gone further than elsewhere in providing continuous employment by shifting the workers around from crop to crop and place to place. Between the thinning and the harvesting of the sugar beets, employment may be had in cherries or peas, or the workers may be shipped to Wisconsin or even Minnesota, at the employers' expense, to assist in crops there. Michigan is fortunate in having a variety of fruit and vegetable crops, often in the same areas, but it has also demonstrated what can be done when an effort is made to provide continuous employment even in the face of seasonal conditions.

There are reasons to believe that the Mexicans who have permanently established themselves in this country will become less migratory as the years go by.

Mechanization is taking place in the two crops that have employed the largest numbers of migrants: cotton and sugar beets.

The rise of the cotton picking machine is shown by these figures from the San Joaquin Valley, where cotton is a major crop. In 1945 less than one per cent of the crop was picked by machines, but by 1949, 17 per cent was handled in this way, with a 1950 estimate of 35 per cent and with a lively expectation that very shortly 90 per cent of the crop will be gathered mechanically.

From the Arizona Cotton Cooperative Growers' Association comes some interesting testimony:

> We believe that we can see the time in the very near future when cotton picking machines will eliminate most of the problems caused by migrant labor in Arizona. At the present time we have in the state enough machines to pick approximately 25 per cent of the crop if they are used full time. The machines must have skillful operators, and they cannot be trained overnight. They are taking over the biggest part of the total. The grower will gain more economical harvesting of his cotton at a time when he wants to do it, making it unnecessary for him to worry much about the labor supply. However, machines will never replace all of the labor. Early in the season cotton must be picked by hand.

The mechanization of the sugar beet harvest is already far advanced in California, where between 85 and 90 per cent of the work is now done by machines. Michigan is less advanced but is on its way. The work of thinning the beets remains, but this is being reduced by changes in the seeds and in better planting practices. A mechanical beet thinner has been proved practical and may soon be on the market. Apparently it is only a matter of time until the human back and the human arm will be excused from the arduous task of getting sugar beets out of the ground.

Progress is in prospect on other fronts. A spokesman for the California citrus fruit industry has stated, "We have in the research laboratories machines which will eventually take care of the need for additional labor in the citrus industry. Given another three or four years, assuming we can go along using the inventive skill that we have, I don't think that the citrus industry will be in need of migrant labor."

There is even hope for such a tender thing as asparagus. Two years ago the secretary of the California Asparagus Growers' Association said, "We have a machine in the field this year. It is the second year of research into the development of mechanical harvesting. We feel that eventually we will develop a harvester that will handle the harvesting of asparagus."

This does not mean that the need for migratory workers will disappear overnight. The day when cherries, strawberries, blueberries, peaches, and other fruits will be picked by machines is not imminent. But increasingly the hardest tasks will be done mechanically rather than by human muscles. It is also true that the higher the wage paid for human energy, and the better the care required for human machines, the more rapidly will they be superseded. On the other hand, the cheaper the labor available, the less the enthusiasm for machines. Mechanization is not a live issue in those areas where wetbacks can be had. Agriculture is not immune from the principle that has made American industry great: the higher wages go, the greater the incentive to devise machines to do the work.

A second reason why we may expect migrancy among Mexicans to decline is their own desire to settle down. No group has ever remained permanently migratory. Mexicans will grasp at any straw that promises them permanency. When they get to a place where there is a good roof over their heads, they do their best to stay. The farmers and farming communities are anxious that the people who gather their crops should go back to where they came from as soon as the harvest is over. One of the attractions of the wetbacks and the Mexican contract workers is that they are easy to get rid of.

An interesting development is that wherever Mexicans have been, a permanent settlement of Mexicans usually grows up. In spite of the anonymity of their work and the impersonal nature of their employment, here and there a Mexican will sell himself to the boss as a good worker who might be a year around asset. They have considerable skill in managing irrigation. Many of them have "green fingers" when it comes to handling growing plants. They have brains as well as brawn—and terrific energy when they see a chance to better themselves. In our next chapter we will discuss these clusters of Mexicans scattered about the country, which may prove to be the finest fruit of their toilsome years as agricultural migrants.

The religious organization most successful in making contacts with Mexican migratory workers has been the Division of Home Missions of the National Council of Churches.

About thirty years ago the former Council of Women for Home Missions discovered the agricultural migrants. Their hearts were touched by the plight of these workers, and they undertook to do something about it. This began by employing young women to tend the babies while their mothers worked in the fields—a task of almost pure humanitarianism. Out of these nurseries came centers that gradually provided the equivalent of Daily Vacation Bible Schools for the older children, recreation for the young people, some measure of health care for everybody, and, in some instances, religious services. In addition to college students of both sexes, venturesome schoolteachers were employed for the vacation period, with finally a year-around staff who followed the migrants from the Rio Grande Valley to Minnesota and Michigan, by way of the strawberry patches of Louisiana and Arkansas. In the early years, the migrants served were largely of Anglo-Saxon ancestry, but recently more attention has been paid to the Negroes and the Mexicans. Ordained ministers from both groups have been employed for full-time work among their people.

This Protestant agency has had contacts with Mexican migrants in California, the Rio Grande Valley, and elsewhere in Texas, Arizona, Colorado, Minnesota, and Michigan. Its efforts have been twofold: to serve the needs of these people but at the same time to lead the communities in which they labor to accept some responsibility for them. This has begun with local financial support for the centers but has developed into cooperation in the use of schools and churches and some community contacts with the Mexicans. The ultimate aim is to have the Mexicans recognized as human beings rather than as a cheap substitute for machines. The amount of religious instruction has varied with circumstances. The Okies and Arkies and the Negroes are far readier to attend religious services than are the Mexicans, both for reasons of language and because of their traditions.

The migrant centers have reached their highest development in Michigan, thanks to the cooperation of state and county councils of churches and, in some instances, of the school authorities. A large degree of financial responsibility has been accepted locally. In some instances, the women of the neighboring churches take turns in supplying the noon lunch. Vacation schools and local church groups visit the centers and join in games with the migrant children. Unused schoolhouses, and some that are modern and regularly used, have been made available for migrant centers.

I visited a lovely example of community cooperation at Mt. Pleasant, Michigan, where the State Teachers' College was operating an experimental summer school for both English-speaking and Mexican children. The equipment was that of a model school. The children came equally from the two groups. They were playing together, doing art work together, and studying both English and Spanish together, with teachers of both national backgrounds. The Home Missions Council—as it was then called—was cooperating by assigning a worker to visit in the Mexican homes to interpret the school and encourage the children's attendance.

Probably the greatest service that organized Protestantism has rendered the agricultural migrants has been to publicize them and their needs. Before the appearance of *The Grapes of Wrath*, the American people were hardly aware of their existence. It was the women of the churches who got the word "migrant" into the language. It was the pioneering of the church that stirred the state to action.

Today the Western Area of the Division of Home Missions has a year-around staff of eight working with agricultural migrants, most of whom are Mexicans. This is supplemented with a considerable number of college students, who may be supported by their denominations, their local churches, or work on a volunteer basis. Here are some of their reports for the summer of 1952:

From Colorado: The summer program began in mid-June with the arrival of the summer staff for the two-day Training Institute. With excellent crops all over Colorado, many migratory workers were used, including 200-300 Navajo Indians on the Western Slope; several hundred Spanish Americans, Sioux Indians, and Mexicans in the Arkansas Valley, and scattered families in the San Luis Valley and northern Colorado.

The special unit of study was the Christian Home and Family Life, chosen by the staff and offering an excellent opportunity to get acquainted with families and the children. Before many days the community center took on a new look with pictures, scrapbooks, spatter prints, miniature houses, cutouts of family groups, and dioramas of homes of many lands.

Fun Night brought folks from all directions to Palisade, some to take part, some to watch. The highlight at Fort Lupton was the two performances for parents and friends staged by the children. One was a portrayal in a succession of tableaux of nursery rhymes while the other was the Parade of the Months. The children were simply thrilled at the thought of dressing up and going behind the footlights. The teachers struggled and sweat. They felt that they had both lost and won—lost a perfect production, but won a memorable experience for the children. Just try to keep excited, eager children from peering over the backdrop to see every other child take his part, and you will understand!

From Washington: The Mobile Chapel on Wheels has again been visiting the migrant camps. The children look forward to the beginning of the vacation schools, and the time of departure to a new camp brings with it some rather sorrowful good-bys.

The visual aid equipment and the portable organ make even more attractive and effective the work of the Chapel on Wheels. And these wheels roll a good many thousand miles during the course of a season, for reliable statistics indicate that this year there were over 21,000 migrant laborers in the state, not including members of the family who did not work.

Edith Mason, a summer worker, reports: The missionary story had come to an end. Immediately the picture of little children of various races gathered around the friendly figure of Jesus became the center of attraction. "Teacher, is it really like belonging to one family?" a child asked.

Before the teacher could answer, a five-year-old piped up, "In God's way it is."

Among the little children of this camp that phrase soon became a common expression. "We mustn't fight—in God's way we're all brothers and sisters."

"Let's ask Estrellita to come to our Bible school, too. In God's way she is our sister." Estrellita belonged to a new family that had just moved into the camp and she spoke a different language and her skin was a different color.

How different was the attitude of the schools nearby, where the migrant children were made to feel unwanted. How different was the attitude of the town toward the teenagers and the young people, where they were discriminated against because of their address.

Godliness and cleanliness go together, as revealed in this report: The child was bathing. Not in a big enamel bathtub, but in a wash tray in the camp laundry house. Not in hot, soapy water, but in cold water. It was all she had.

A staff member asked why she was taking a bath in the middle of the day. The child replied in Spanish, "I like to be clean because God loves clean children better than dirty ones, and I want him to love me. You and the other girls are always clean and neat, and I want to look pretty, too."

Opal Beymer, a staff member in California, writes: Those of us who stay on through the winter months get intimations of what our work has meant to the boys and girls.

There was eight-year-old Rachel who was in one of those out-of-the-way winter cotton camps. When the staff worker introduced a new song, she suddenly clapped her hands and danced all over the tent floor. "I know that song!" she cried with delight. "I learned it from my teacher when we were in Merced in the figs."

Eleven-year-old Mary—also in a winter camp—told over and over about the good times she had enjoyed in the summer school in a fruit camp where she had lived two summers before. Lovingly she brought out some of the articles that she had made and had carefully kept for two years.

Billy one day taught the group how to play a new game that "we learned when we were in a camp in Oregon."

Katherine Schaeffer, a summer camp worker, composed what she calls "A Migrant Mother's Prayer":

Lord, give us a house that's clean and neat,
And a refrigerator to keep our meat;
A small fenced yard with grass so green,
With children playing nice and clean.

A little house in town, dear Lord,
Where we may shop at a neighborhood store;
And have close friends on either side
And never have to say good-by.

A place where we'll be welcomed
By friends that we will make—
At church, at school, at play, dear Lord,
I pray for my children's sake.

Just a little house, dear Lord,
With pictures on the wall;
And help us grow in Christian love,
And happiness for all.

Miss Edith Lowry, executive secretary of the Division of Home Missions, sums up the interdenominational service to migrants that she directs by saying, "We want people to think of the migrant not as a problem, but as a person. In any situation we enter, we try to build cooperation and reconcile tension, rather than going in as a pressure group."

An observer comments, "This approach probably accounts for their success. For both growers and processors, on the one hand, and migrants, on the other, are likely to receive the division's first overtures with considerable skepticism. The grower or processor has the job of harvesting X tons of crops for Y dollars, and is afraid the division's efforts will alter this ratio."[1]

The home mission workers with migrants seek to reconcile the laborers and their families with one another and with God. There is also the job of building understanding and appreciation between employers and the labor force. Christian hope may be born, children and adults may be started on the path of education, but one thing more must be done. To save migrants from being itinerant strangers, someone must bridge the gap between them and the communities they visit. This, too, is the work of the Division of Home Missions, aided by local churches sensitive to the opportunity to practice Christianity in human relations.

The agricultural migrations of Mexicans in this country are probably passing their peak. Movements are on foot that will severely limit if not outlaw the wetback traffic. When that is stopped, there will be less occasion for the importation of Mexicans under contract, in part because the "prevailing wage" will then rise. Ultimately the employers of migrant labor will be compelled by economic necessity to do two things: to use the available labor more intelligently and economically, as is being done in Michigan and other Northern states at present, and to substitute machinery for men in the more arduous and backbreaking tasks.

Undoubtedly some will ask the questions: Will not the wetbacks get even hungrier if they are kept out of this country? What will happen to those legally here when they are displaced by machines?

To this there are several answers. The more fundamental one is that

[1] "The Ladies Had an Answer," by Paul Marcus, in *The Saturday Evening Post,* October 4, 1952. Used by permission.

we are never doing people a favor by employing them at starvation wages. Just keeping people alive is no help to progress, but impedes it. The Mexican Government is aware of this and has little enthusiasm for this traffic. Mexico's problem of poverty cannot be solved by sending workers across the border to lower the standards of those already here.

The sweatshop situation in this country at the beginning of the century is a close parallel to the one that we are discussing. The employment of men, women, and children for long hours under unsanitary conditions at miserable wages was abolished. What became of the victims of this situation? They did not starve; when they had to, they found something better to do. Neither did their employers go broke. With much machinery, good working conditions, and high wages the garment industry is in far better shape than it was fifty years ago. Much the same future can be expected for the Mexican migrants and the men who employ them. If they will apply the same intelligence to their problems that industry has done, American agriculture can be transformed into a self-respecting and profitable activity for both the workers and the owners. As for the Mexicans, they can evolve a better solution to their problems than rushing from crop to crop to earn a pittance.

Indirectly migratory labor has rendered the Mexicans a real service by distributing them over the country in a fashion that would probably have been impossible without it. If they are to live in the United States, they should become a part of our national life. As long as the Mexicans are massed along the Rio Grande Valley and in the Imperial Valley and similar sections of California their adjustment to American life is bound to be partial. Both their language and their employment encourages them to keep to themselves. The experience of other immigrant groups is that it is only as they scatter out that they become a true part of the American scene. How their experience as migrants has opened many doors of opportunity to them will be the theme of our next chapter.

Brooke Baldwin

With hopeful persistence, Mexicans are establishing little beachheads in hundreds of communities.

) CHAPTER 6 (

Mexican Beachheads in the North

THE SECOND world war taught the American people that beachheads are difficult to establish and precarious to hold; that of and in themselves they do not amount to much, but if properly exploited they can lead almost anywhere.

Scattered across our country are little clumps of Mexicans who help to open doors into American life for their fellow countrymen. Their experience parallels that of soldiers landing on an alien shore. For soldiers, the first night is the worst; for the Mexican the first winter. It takes courage for a family to face the prospect of cold and snow for the first time, and usually with inadequate shelter. At the next point our analogy falls down. A military expeditionary force gets too much attention; a new Mexican family in town probably gets too little. They are rarely esteemed to be important. They are neither welcomed nor rebuffed because of their obvious harmlessness. But if a Mexican family remains in a community, it is almost certain to increase, both biologically and by the arrival of relatives and friends. As the children grow up and go to school, the way will finally open for them to become a part of the community.

In most Western and Northern communities this is far in the future. Usually the well-to-do element hardly know that their Mexican neighbors exist. We asked an intelligent and socially conscious minister who had served for nine years in a Montana sugar beet town what contacts and experiences he had had with the Mexicans who lived there. He looked blank and then replied, "None whatever." We suspect that he is quite typical.

Three types of employment have led to the establishment of Mexican settlements away from the border: the railroads, sugar beets, and steel.

In much of the West the Mexican laborer has inherited the pick and shovel with which first the Irish and then a long succession of European immigrants have done the necessary track work for our railroads. During the second world war, it was the Mexicans who kept our transcontinental lines in operation.

From the nature of the case the railroads distribute their employees widely. The remarkable feature of the Mexicans is the way they keep out of sight. The only time the traveler notices them is when he sees a string of freight cars marked "Maintenance of Way" and obviously overflowing with inhabitants sequestered on some siding. This is the first step, and obviously a transient one. The next is a house near the railroad, which may be its property and therefore is painted in its proprietary colors. As the prosperity of the Mexican increases, he acquires a better home.

The Mexicans have their share of bright boys, and some of them are bound to rise in the world. From the fixing of the track on which the trains run it is not too great a step to tinkering with the engines that pull the trains. In Gallup, New Mexico, we were told that a man of

Spanish-speaking ancestry was foreman of the roundhouse, and we heard of a similar instance elsewhere. From their humble position beside the tracks the children of these track men will both move into town and make their way upward in the railroad hierarchy, probably on the mechanical side to begin with.

As we have seen, it was originally expected that the Mexicans who came north to cultivate and pull the sugar beets would all be back in Texas by Hallowe'en at least. Apparently somebody usually managed to miss the return trip. Wherever you find beets, you find year-around Mexicans. The first step was to spend the winter in the barracks that the sugar company had built for what is locally known as "the campaign"—when the beets come out of the ground and are transformed into sugar. From the company houses they branched out into something a bit better for themselves. This has been the story in Montana, Colorado, Nebraska, Kansas, Iowa, Minnesota, and other states. The Mexicans live unobtrusively somewhere near the sugar factory. Their children go to school, and speak the English language habitually. A public health nurse in Montana told me that she found the Mexicans most cooperative. Nowhere have I heard complaints about them. They may not be accepted, but neither are they rejected.

In Michigan the pattern is somewhat different. Here the Mexicans have worked in various fruits as well as beets. Instead of clustering around the sugar beet refineries, the Mexicans have had their first homes on farms and then moved into town. Also, Michigan has many small and some large cities that have been growing rapidly in recent years and have attracted Mexicans. There appears to be considerable traffic back and forth between the cities and the harvest fields. We once encountered a Mexican who claimed to be a meat cutter in Muskegon, giving himself and his wife a bit of variety with a few weeks in the beets. In the summer of 1952 some forty or more Mexican families who were thrown out of work in Detroit by the steel strike improved their enforced vacation by going to the country to pick cherries.

Denver owes her 20,000 or more people of Spanish-speaking ancestry to two sources: beet workers moving to town, old Spanish working north from the plaza towns of New Mexico. The Mexican consul stated that there were only 1,500 Mexican citizens in the city—and that he could do nothing about the troubles in which American-born or naturalized Mexicans might become involved. He thought that there was some discrimination against Mexicans in Denver but that conditions were better than in many other places.

Many lines of employment seem to be open to Spanish-speaking people in Denver. Although a majority are laborers, there are also stenographers, clerks, teachers, and professional people. As seemed to be true in all cities, the Spanish-speaking people are spreading out. Once most of them had lived in the quite undesirable area north of the business center, but now many of them are moving to the west, which is "on the other side of the tracks," but which is nevertheless a moderately attractive residential area in which there is a considerable Jewish element. Bethel Presbyterian Church, which is Spanish-speaking, has recently moved into this area but reports no opposition whatever from its Jewish and other neighbors.

Conrad Pyle, boys' worker on the staff of the Epworth Methodist Church, which serves a mixed parish in connection with the Good Will Industries, reported that he had found the Spanish-speaking boys entirely trustworthy and that he had never seen anything that looked like a gang fight, although the boys regarded it as a matter of personal pride to hit back whenever anyone hit them. Somewhat less than half of his boys attend parochial grammar schools, but they all go to public high schools. After that the emphasis is on getting a job.

Spanish-speaking Protestants in Denver number approximately 2,000.

Three well established churches serve them. The Presbyterians have a new church in a good neighborhood, as we have mentioned, and also a House of Neighborly Service in the old Spanish section. There are Baptist churches and a community center here also.

The First Spanish Methodist Church has a prominent location about a mile from the business section. The building is an ancient monument to the piety of the eighteen-eighties that was assigned to a Spanish-speaking congregation during the twenties. Worship services and the church school are held on the ground floor; what was once the church proper now serves for basketball and dinners. The congregation once numbered 700 members, but during the depression half of these people either went back to Mexico or moved elsewhere, and the present membership is a little under four hundred.

The pastor, Hector Franco, was born in Mexico City and baptized a Roman Catholic. His father was an army man, his mother died when he was quite young, and so the three children of the family were sent to El Paso for safety. There he attended the Lydia Patterson Institute and later graduated from the Harwood Boys' School in Albuquerque. While attending these schools he was converted and began to study for the ministry. He has served six Spanish-speaking churches, and in each of them his people had a different type of employment. In Emporia, Kansas, they were railroad workers; in Lyons, Kansas, they toiled in the salt mines; in Garden City, Kansas, they worked "in beets"; in Kansas City, Kansas, they were employed in the railroad roundhouses and in the packing plants; in Wichita, Kansas, they did "city work," which means personal service with some store and office jobs, and were also employed at the Boeing airplane plant; in Denver it was "city work" again. He said, "The more our people are in a minority, the greater are the opportunities for the individual to branch out in new lines of work and to get ahead generally."

The third movement of Mexicans to the North and East is industrial, and quite different from the other two that we have described. Both as railroad workers and as agricultural migrants the Mexicans were employed as groups rather than as individuals. They came in numbers, ordinarily bringing their families with them. They lived apart from the general community. Ultimately individuals separated themselves from the mass, usually by remaining behind when the tide of humanity flowed back toward the border again. As we look farther east the migration becomes increasingly individualistic.

This is reflected in a recent complaint from South Chicago about an influx of *solos,* which means men unaccompanied by their families. They are quite unpopular among other Mexicans, largely because of the competition that they offer for women who have already been spoken for by the local Mexican males.

This industrial migration has its roots in the same general situation as that which has drawn agricultural workers north. Some jobs are either so unpleasant or so poorly paid (or both) that no one who has been long on the American scene will take them. European immigration largely ceased at the time of the first world war. Only two sources of cheap labor remained: Negroes and Mexicans. Both were enlisted in large numbers during and after the war. When the dark days of the twenties arrived nothing cold be done about the surplus Negro population other than to put it on relief. The Mexicans were more vulnerable, as many of them were not American citizens, and so could be deported. With the second world war the tide flowed northward again, and this time it appears to be here to stay. Most of the Mexicans in the North have become American citizens. As we will see, they are gradually getting their roots further and further into the life of Northern communities.

Chicago not only has the largest Mexican population of any Northern city, but what has happened there will be repeated on a smaller scale elsewhere.

The first Mexicans to come to Chicago were railroad track workers. A leader among them reports, "Only the old men who know nothing else and the young ones fresh from Mexico or the Southwest are now tamping ties."

The stockyards were a second field of employment. Here the avenues of advancement are said to be more open than in steel, but the proportion of Mexicans is declining.

The largest employers of Mexican labor in the Chicago areas have been the steel mills in South Chicago and Indiana Harbor. As "chippers" they did the hottest and dirtiest work. They also joined the unions, although they are not particularly active in union affairs, and have enjoyed the economic prosperity that has been the lot of steel workers in recent years. Many of their leaders do not feel that their advancement has been as rapid or has gone as far as it should. Their predecessors in the mills were the Poles, and the Poles have managed to hang on to the really good jobs. It is also said, by Mexicans, that they have not been as alert and as self-confident in their quest for promotion as they might have been. Apparently they are in steel to stay, at least for the foreseeable future.

The hotels are a relatively new field of work. In the past hotels have been designed and operated on the assumption that much cheap labor could be had. As other sources of willing workers at low pay dried up, Mexicans were employed in increasing numbers. They began as dishwashers, chambermaids, bus boys. Here, too, they have both joined the union and worked their way up. One page of the paper gotten out by the hotel workers' union is printed in Spanish. As for advancement, Mexicans are now working as waiters, headwaiters, chefs, stewards—and one of their number is chief steward of the Palmer House. In the meantime, hotel work is becoming less physically exhausting and much better remunerated.

From these basic occupations the Mexicans are gradually branching out into many lines of employment. According to a social worker in Chicago, more of the girls than the boys go to high school—and graduate into office work.

The increasing prosperity of the Mexicans in Chicago is reflected in the places where they don't live. Apparently they are departing from the deteriorated sections and are scattering out over the city into the neighborhoods where other people of similar incomes live. They move wherever they can get homes that they can afford to rent or buy.

In the North, Mexicans have always lived in porous rather than compact communities. That is, they do not bunch up solidly as the Italians have commonly done, or as the Jews and the Negroes have been compelled to do, but live intermingled with other nationalities.

The original Mexican colony in Chicago was around Halsted Street on the near West Side. However, in the long history of this section the Mexicans promise to be just one more in the procession of nationalities that have passed through. They were preceded by the Italians, and it looks as though they would be followed by the Negroes. Mexicans mingle in the neighborhood with Italians, Greeks, Lithuanians, and Negroes. Both the Methodist and Presbyterian churches for Mexicans are in this area.

Two social institutions have large Mexican contacts, although these are not intended exclusively for them. The South Chicago Community Center occupies what was originally the Bird Memorial Church. It is supported one-third by the Chicago Congregational Union and two-thirds by the Community Fund. Its strong points are its nursery school and its youth activities. An interesting feature is the "V" (for volunteer) Staff consisting of Mexican young people who share responsibility with the paid workers. Bright and lively are the adjectives that best describe both the building and the people in it.

Hull House has more dignity and suffers somewhat from its ancient architecture and the gloom of its surroundings, but appears to be as well worn as ever. The present head resident has had much of his social experience with Mexicans. The telephone operators and other helpers are Mexican.

At Hull House is the office of the Mexican American Council of Chicago. The preamble of its constitution reads:

> We, the Mexican Americans of the Chicago area, are determined: To affirm faith in human rights and the dignity and worth of all men and women, and for these ends to practice justice and live in peace, and have resolved to organize our strength and hereby establish an organization to be called the Mexican American Council of Chicago. The purpose of the council is the better integration of the Mexican American in the life of the community, promotion of the welfare and aiding the development of all Mexican Americans in the Chicago area. The council shall be non-sectarian and non-partisan.

Just before my visit, the council had presented a program of Mexican music and dances in Thorne Hall of Northwestern University, with an accompanying talk on "Contributions of the Mexican People to Our American Heritage," by Dr. Louis Leal.

The Mexicans were first brought to Detroit in 1918 to work in the automobile factories. Their numbers climbed to 16,000 during the twenties and then dropped to half of that during the thirties. Detroit being a city of new industries, the employment opportunities have been varied. Most of the men came without their families, with the result that there has been more intermarriage with other groups than elsewhere.

There appear to be ties between the Mexicans of Detroit and those who "work in brass" in Port Huron and also with the settlements that have sprung up around the beet fields and orchards farther north.

Apparently some of the Mexicans in Detroit combine industry and agriculture; at least a considerable group were off picking cherries when we visited the city.

In Detroit we were given some insight into the problems of young people of Mexican ancestry, which are similar to those found in many other youth groups. If they go to college it is their decision and not that of their parents, and they are likely to go to a school where they already have a friend. They resent the crowding in many of their homes and also the inclination of many parents to tell them when they should come home. Often they meet the situation by moving out and living with someone else. This is not "running away from home," for the mother knows where the boy or girl is living, but a convenient way out of a situation that can be mutually embarrassing.

A steel mill brought 1,500 Mexicans to Lorain, Ohio, from Texas in 1923. This colony has been further recruited both from Texas and from the beet fields of Michigan. At first the people lived in the box cars in which they had arrived, but they have gradually moved up in the world without discarding many Mexican characteristics. According to Robert O. O'Brien, "American radios are covered with *serapes* and bits of Indian pottery. Stone hand mills grind our corn, which is cooked on gas and even electric stoves. American phonographs play South American tangos and Mexican marches. Mexican trunks (which are likely to be iron bound and forbidding) contain a mixture of objects, from new Sunday clothes to old country *sombreros.* Portable typewriters in vivid colors compete for space with bits of cactus from the Southwest. Bottles of medicine from Lorain doctors vie with patent medicines or Mexican 'teas' for position on the bathroom shelf. . . . American canned food is supplemented by *enchiladas, chile verde,* and *tamales.*"

The Spanish-speaking population of Lorain, which was formerly wholly Mexican, is now being enlarged by an influx of Puerto Ricans.

On a much smaller scale the same sort of thing is happening in Detroit and Chicago. An interested minister writes:

> The Puerto Ricans, like the Mexicans, live largely in South Lorain. There is no strict segregation and both Mexicans and Puerto Ricans can be found throughout the city. The first 500 Puerto Rican men were brought to the city by the National Tube Company as contract labor in 1946. Since then their brothers and sisters, fathers and mothers and cousins by the dozens have followed them in a never-ending stream, until there are close to 4,000 here now. The majority work at "the Tube" or at Freuhauf, or on the railroads, but a number have found their way into other jobs. There are a number of Protestants among them and a few have found their way into established churches, chiefly the Presbyterian, which is the one most available. The language creates a problem, as only two Protestant ministers in the county speak Spanish, and neither are very fluent.

Here we see the beginning of a new cycle, but one quite similar to that through which the Mexicans are passing.

These Northern beachheads will probably go through a two-fold process of both growth and absorption. These *colonias* will multiply in number and increase in population simply because they will offer ambitious young Mexican Americans a chance to escape from the discriminations that they suffer along the border and to better themselves economically. Yet the more these isolated groups of Mexicans prosper the less Mexican will they become. In all likelihood it will be in the North and not on the border that Mexicans will be most completely made a part of the nation's life.

Fotomasters

Rafael Palacios, former resident of Puerto Rico, now a New York free-lance artist specializing in book jackets and maps.

) CHAPTER 7 (

The Puerto Ricans Fly to New York

NEXT to Mexico, Puerto Rico offers the United States its most available source of cheap labor. Puerto Rico is a small island, three times the size of the state of Rhode Island, twice that of Long Island, somewhat smaller than the state of Connecticut. It is one of the most densely populated areas in the world, and from the economic angle is entitled to hang out a "standing room only" sign. New York is becoming the largest Puerto Rican city in the world, with a Puerto Rican population equal to 15 per cent of that of the island from which they came.

The Puerto Ricans are citizens of the United States, "with all the rights and privileges thereto pertaining." Some time ago I arrived in New York on a boat from Venezuela, thinking myself the only United States citizen on the passenger list. The immigration inspector looked at me and announced, "I will take the citizen first," at which a Puerto Rican stepped up and presented his papers. United States citizenship does for the Puerto Ricans something similar to what Roman citizenship did for the Apostle Paul. It is a great help in getting around.

The Puerto Ricans come far, but fast. The island's nearest point in continental United States is Key West, which is a bit farther from San Juan than Chicago is from New York. The trip to New York is 1,500 miles, which is approximately the distance from New York to Omaha. Today the quickest and cheapest way to make the trip is by air. Since the war the fare has been as low as $75 on the regular lines and $35 on non-scheduled flights. Instead of going through Ellis Island, the Puerto Ricans land at Idlewild Airport. This is the world's first large scale movement of population by air.

For this recent spurt in immigration there are three reasons. Puerto Rico is overcrowded. By exporting workers she increases the available jobs and food for those who remain. The mainland is suffering from a labor shortage, especially in employment where the work is muscle-taxing and the pay low. The development of mass air travel has made the trip fast and painless. Sometimes only five hours elapse between departure from San Juan and arrival in New York.

The vast majority of the migrants had jobs in Puerto Rico, and fairly good jobs judged by local standards. According to a careful investigation the first job in New York averages double the wage of the last job in Puerto Rico, with a jump from $20 a week on the island to $40 a week in the United States not at all unusual.[1]

The lure of New York, where over 80 per cent of the Puerto Ricans settle, is more than a matter of dollars. Pretty pictures put out by the airlines do not attract them so much as the letters of friends and relatives and the stories told by Puerto Ricans who have come home to

[1] Most of the data in this chapter is from *The Puerto Rican Journey*, by C. Wright Mills, Clarence Senior, and Rose Kohn Goldsen. New York, Harper and Brothers, 1950.

visit—and to brag about their new estate. Even though they may share in it in only a slight way, the life and movement of New York appeal to them—the picture shows, the beaches, even the subway. Compared to Manhattan Island, San Juan, one of the brightest of Latin American cities, is a drab place.

On a hot summer's night I discovered six rides ranging from a merry-go-round to a Ferris wheel and an aerial torpedo, which appeared to turn one upside down only really didn't, going full blast on a vacant lot in the Puerto Rican section of the Bronx. Everything was running at capacity, and everybody seemed to be having a wonderful time. It was reminiscent of the early years of this century, when Americans hung on open streetcars like iron-filings on a magnet to get to amusement parks where they could be swished through the air in strange ways. Most of the people "doing the rides" that night in the Bronx probably had not yet achieved automobiles.

Curiously, few Puerto Ricans appear to be disillusioned by New York. They have heard about snow storms and six-story walk-ups on the island. They are accustomed to living close to other people, and rather like crowds. As for noise, they delight in it. Despite the problems that confront them, the Puerto Ricans of New York strongly prefer where they are to where they were.

Most of the immigrants are in the middle years of life, ranging from young people ready to look for their first jobs to parents with a couple of children. Both old people and teen-agers are scarce. The venturesome years are the migrating years. Most of the families come from the cities of San Juan and Ponce, few from the country. They are already city-wise. Both their education and their pay is above that of the island as a whole. Their background is industrial rather than rural, which may explain why they are not disappointed with life in New York.

Although the two sexes are numerically equal in Puerto Rico, over a third more women than men have come to New York. In addition to the normal number of housewives, there have been many whose marriages have been ended by death, divorce, or desertion. In Spanish lands, the unattached mature woman has had a difficult role. If she lived with her family she was likely to be dominated by it; if she lived by herself she was regarded with disapproval. For these women New York has meant a larger degree of personal freedom to earn their own living and make their own way. New York is a city of refuge for those who have been overdominated by their families. There women of all nationalities are free to be themselves with the minimum of attention from onlookers, who are busy with their own affairs.

Ever since the United States took over Puerto Rico in 1898 her people have been coming to this country. Puerto Ricans have been a part of New York, and New York has figured prominently in the life of the island for a good many years. The new factor is the volume of this migration; what was once a trickle is now a fast flowing stream. Few came during the war, but in 1945, 13,000 more people traveled from the island to the mainland than journeyed in the opposite direction. The next year this figure jumped to 39,000, then dropped slightly, but for 1951 it was 49,000. In New York city there are somewhere between 300,000 and 350,000 Puerto Ricans and the children of Puerto Ricans. There is no apparent slackening in this flow of humanity.

Why do 80 per cent of the Puerto Ricans remain in New York city? Probably for much the same reasons that many of their predecessors, particularly the Irish, the Jews, the Italians, have lingered for some years in the metropolis before venturing into the hinterland. All immigrants have heard about New York city as a place where there is lots of money and people can get rich quick. In New York they have friends and relatives who speak their language and who will look after them.

New York is accustomed to people who speak strange tongues and eat strange foods. It is, from necessity, a tolerant town. Actually in New York the minorities are in a majority. It also offers a larger market for unskilled and semiskilled labor than any other American city. Except for clothing, New York is not a manufacturing center. It requires relatively few skilled craftsmen. It does not create, but rather distributes. It is also a place where millions come for personal services. What New York needs is a lot of people who are willing to perform relatively simple operations. For centuries this has been the lot of the last to arrive, who at present are the Puerto Ricans.

From necessity, most immigrants begin on the bottom rung of the ladder. As far as their status and the significance of their jobs are concerned, most Puerto Ricans step down rather than up when they come to New York. This is due primarily to difficulty with the language and to the lack of the skills that are highly rewarded in this country. As we have seen, the new job pays better in dollars than the old one but is likely to detract from rather than add to one's self respect. New York offers money in the pocket rather than nourishment for one's ego. And there is evidence that many of the Puerto Rican immigrants do not rise far above the place where they start in this country, although their children do.

The first group of Puerto Ricans to come to New York were stevedores who worked on the Brooklyn docks and lived nearby. More recently the starting occupations have been in restaurants and hotels for men, in the garment trades for women. A Roman Catholic priest oversimplified the matter when he said, "The men wash dishes; the women sew," but this is a vivid way of describing what happens to many of the newcomers.

The Puerto Ricans have no particular aptitude for restaurant and hotel work but have entered these fields because the jobs were there.

They have not done at all badly. The Waldorf-Astoria employs 300 Puerto Ricans, which is 12 per cent of its labor force. The men work as bus boys, waiters, coffee and salad men, ice cream makers, pastry cooks, and chefs, and the women as chambermaids. The personnel manager rates them as equal to the other employees in cleanliness, productivity, and punctuality.

Many Puerto Rican men and some women are found in assembly work and in processing. One establishment in the Bronx employs 400 Puerto Ricans as punch pressers, cutters, spot welders, and on assembly lines and in packaging. Several of the foremen are Puerto Ricans.

Puerto Rican women have always distinguished themselves in needlework. They bring with them to New York sharp eyes and nimble fingers. Signs such as this are common, *"Operadoras con experiencia en blusas. Trabajo por sección,"* which means that piecework is available for women with experience on blouses. Contrary to the sweatshop traditions of the past, the garment industry in New York has excellent employment conditions, while the two unions, the International Ladies' Garment Workers and the Amalgamated Clothing Workers, are famous for their cooperation with the employers to improve conditions in the industry and for the educational and social programs that they offer their members.

The Puerto Ricans do not come to this country to undercut those who are already here. Although they are not "joiners" by tradition, they go into labor unions quickly and apparently unanimously. The unions in the hotel and garment industry have Spanish-speaking locals and print part of their papers in Spanish.

Although the mass of the Puerto Ricans have humble employment, individuals have gone far. Puerto Rican stenographers are both common and popular in New York. In Spanish-speaking neighborhoods the smaller stores are commonly Puerto Rican owned. The children of the early comers are doing well in the professions and in business. Given time, it is reasonable to expect that the Puerto Ricans will prosper as have other immigrant groups before them.

As the last comers, the Puerto Ricans have been compelled to take such living accommodations as they could get. From the point of view of housing they have arrived at a peculiarly inopportune time, when even those with financial resources and powerful connections have had a hard time finding a place to live. On top of this, the Puerto Ricans have frequently found themselves right in the path of large-scale building and housing developments. Their original place of residence in Brooklyn simply isn't there any more!

To find living quarters that no one else wanted for a rent that they could afford to pay has been most difficult. The more recently arrived Puerto Ricans live under the worst conditions to be found in New York city. The first step is to move in with somebody else, usually a relative newcomer. The "port of entry" for many if not most Puerto Ricans is East Harlem. Here the prevailing type of building is the six-story walk-up cold water flat.

The Jews, the Italians, the Russians, the Negroes have come and also largely gone. The procession of many feet has worn the steps, multitudinous voices in assorted tongues have echoed in the hallways, families have come from many quarters of the globe and then moved on to better things, but the old foundations and the ancient walls still stand to welcome yet another influx from afar.

However, it is possible to exaggerate tenement conditions. We have passed through dingy hallways to tidy rooms, and we have heard of irate housewives vainly pursuing cockroaches over immaculate floors. It should be said that Puerto Ricans are accustomed to living in close quarters and that the per square foot population may not be any greater in Harlem than in San Juan. A large factor of difference is the sun. On the island it purifies and cleanses. The garbage that the birds of the air do not take care of is sterilized by natural heat. In New York the sun is less powerful and has less chance to neutralize filth. The cold weather is also a new experience and one in which ancient housing does not help.

Like the Mexicans, and for the same reasons, the Puerto Ricans live in mixed neighborhoods. Rarely do they constitute more than 50 per cent of the population of a given area, and the longer they are here and the better their incomes the more they mingle with the general population. In East Harlem they have Italians and Negroes for neighbors.

The first step up from East Harlem is likely to be the southeast section of the Bronx. Here the housing is better, the streets wider, and the sun more effective. The neighbors are Jews and Negroes. From here the Puerto Ricans scatter out to lower Manhattan, to Brooklyn, to the West Side, to Washington Heights, almost anywhere. Two-thirds of the public schools of the city have some Puerto Rican children. The long term prospect points toward a general diffusion of the Puerto Ricans among the population.

In this process there is one catch. The Puerto Rican whose complexion is light can rent or buy almost anywhere that he can afford to live. His problem is almost wholly economic. But the Puerto Rican who is of darker complexion does not fare so well. For him East Harlem and the Bronx are likely to be more permanent places of residence. Curiously, there is just one way that he can escape from being classified as a Negro, and that is to retain his Spanish speech and to pose as a newcomer from overseas. New York extends rather better treatment to the foreign Negro than to the American Negro. If one's face is dark, there is profit in professing the Moslem faith and aspiring to being taken as a Moor!

New York can frighten anyone. We once employed a most self-confident girl from Minneapolis who insisted on being thoroughly briefed on where she was going before she would venture onto the sidewalks of New York. The newly arrived Puerto Rican is likely to be overwhelmed by the sights and sounds around him. The only people with whom he feels safe are his fellow countrymen. New York assumes that everybody can read English. Ten-car subway trains are manned by a crew of three. If one can neither read nor speak English, he is in a bad way, and is not likely to venture far alone. Puerto Rican women sometimes walk for a mile or two to get to a hospital or some other destination simply because they feel far more sure of themselves on foot than in a subway or on a bus.

During the first years, the life of a Puerto Rican family moves in a small circle. Most social contacts are "on the block." Groceries are purchased near at hand, preferably from small stores in which Spanish is spoken. Rice, beans, and plantains are the chief items of diet and the frying pan the chief kitchen utensil. If there are neighbors in New York who have also been neighbors in Puerto Rico, that is a comforting circumstance and gives one a sense of security. The first job is likely to be where fellow Puerto Ricans are employed and where the boss speaks Spanish. What looks to be a plunge into the alien life of New York turns out to be a dip into a Puerto Rican pool in a secluded corner of the metropolis. But so has it ever been with immigrants.

Adjustments come gradually, with the younger members of the family leading. The children are very shy at first, but gradually become as fresh as the other urchins of New York. Ultimately even the women achieve a sense of freedom. A Puerto Rican student reports that they "hop around much more freely at parties" in New York than back home.

Competent social observers believe Puerto Ricans will make an exceptionally quick adjustment to American life. Favoring circumstances

Black Star

are their United States citizenship and their disposition to scatter out into the American community as soon as they master the language and acquire the financial resources for such a move.

The concentration of the Puerto Rican population in New York city is probably temporary. It can be argued that New York is not America and that no group can become integrated into the national life until it gets away from the banks of the Hudson. Already 20 per cent of the Puerto Rican migrants are going elsewhere, and in a way that is both interesting and significant. The Government of Puerto Rico is undertaking to direct the migration of its people and to aid them in adjusting to life on the mainland. This is something new under the sun. It is an endeavor to relieve the overcrowding on the island by discovering employment opportunities for Puerto Ricans in all the states of the union.

During the war years Bahamians and Jamaicans were brought into this country under contract for the harvesting of crops, particularly sugar beets and various fruits. Although they were available, Puerto Ricans were not used in this way. The reason was given by the president of a Florida growers' association: "The vast difference between Bahama Island labor and the domestic, including the Puerto Rican, is that (it) . . . can be diverted and sent home if it does not work." In other words, Puerto Ricans could not be deported at the end of the season. Since the war, however, Puerto Ricans have been brought to the mainland under contract in increasing numbers.

The Report of the President's Commission on Migratory Labor states:

> Beginning in a small scale in 1946 and 1947, Puerto Ricans have been drawn increasingly into the domestic seasonal labor force, reaching a peak in 1950, the last year covered by the report, of 8,500 or more. Before 1950 the Puerto Rican contract workers were located mainly in the Northeast; in the year 1950 some 5,300 were contracted for sugar beet work in Michigan. Technically, the movement of Puerto Ricans, either seasonal or permanent, does not require negotiation of work contracts or prior certification of labor shortage. Nevertheless, in its desire to protect its citizens as much as possible, the Puerto Rican Government has insisted on both work contracts and certification of labor need before approving recruitment of its people.

As contract laborers, the Puerto Ricans enjoy both the rights that have been secured for Mexicans, Bahamians, and others, and the rights that are theirs as American citizens. They are guaranteed 150 hours of work for each four week period covered by the contract at the prevailing rate, but with an agreed upon minimum that must be paid, and are protected as to travel, housing, and discrimination. Until quite recently, no American migrants have had such assurances as this. But, also, as an American citizen the Puerto Rican cannot be deported. If he chooses to remain in the community after his contract period is up, that is his privilege. And that is exactly what happens. As the Mexicans are establishing beachhead settlements where they first came as migrants, so are the Puerto Ricans. In the preceding chapter, we noted how this is happening in Lorain, Ohio.

The circumstances for this air-borne agricultural migration are most fortunate in that the slack season on sugar cane cultivation in Puerto Rico comes at the same time as the busy season in sugar beets on the mainland, so that the same people can cultivate cane sugar in Puerto Rico and beet sugar in Michigan. Quick transport makes possible an economical use of labor in both places.

The Government of Puerto Rico is also looking for permanent employment for its people in the states. It has gotten out a most attractive brochure announcing, "Capable hands can be flown to your plant from Puerto Rico, U.S.A." This states, "In Bridgeport, Connecticut, there are around 3,000 Puerto Rican industrial workers. In Philadelphia and Camden, around 4,000. Close to 1,500 men and women from Puerto Rico work in Cleveland, between 6,000 and 7,000 in Chicago. Between 400 and 500 of Milwaukee's foundry workers are from Puerto Rico, U.S.A." This publication also contains pictures of Puerto Ricans happily at work and testimonials from satisfied employers. Wabash Frozen Foods in Chicago reports that they are "superior in punctuality, cleanliness, and productivity to previous workers on the same jobs." The superintendent of employment at National Tube, Lorain, Ohio, is most enthusiastic: "They're tops. Many of them served in the U.S. fighting forces during the recent war. Most have had at least a grade school education. Many have high school certificates, and the University of Puerto Rico is pretty well represented." The only drawback to Puerto

Rican labor is that rather more time is needed to break them in than is true of groups that have become adjusted to industrial work. The Art Steel Company "rates Puerto Ricans equal in productivity and punctuality to others, although some of them take slightly longer in learning machine operations, due to deficient English."

Until quite recently there have been few industries in Puerto Rico, with the result that few Puerto Ricans have had the type of training in machine work that is needed on the mainland. Puerto Rico is endeavoring to remedy this situation by developing eleven vocational schools that will take care of 6,000 students. One school alone has an enrollment of 3,000 students at the present time and offers training in 21 basic fields.

In the meantime, the problem is to direct unskilled and semi-skilled workers to the places where they are most needed. To this end the Government of Puerto Rico maintains labor offices in New York, Chicago, and Los Angeles. The New York Office is a large and busy place, serving three functions. It issues certificates of citizenship to Puerto Ricans who are entitled to them, which is a great aid in securing employment. Puerto Ricans who desire work are interviewed in Spanish and then referred, along with the appropriate information, to the state and federal employment services, which have few Spanish-speaking workers, or directly to employers. Any Puerto Rican who has a problem is interviewed in Spanish and then referred to the New York social agency best equipped to handle it.

As an exhibition of human thoughtfulness, this office compels admiration. As American citizens, Puerto Ricans are entitled to go to the state and national employment service and to social agencies, but as strangers in New York speaking little if any English, they are not likely to do so. They feel free to talk in Spanish with the representatives of their own government, and these in turn direct them to the right places. Anyone acquainted with the complexities of the social agencies of a great city will appreciate what this means.

But the Puerto Rican Government is going even further; it is seeking to interpret its people to their fellow citizens of the mainland. It has published a most attractive picture booklet of 64 pages entitled "Know Your Fellow American Citizen from Puerto Rico." The foreword states, "This booklet has been prepared as an aid to understanding the background of the relatively small migration of Puerto Ricans to the U. S. mainland. As American citizens most of them have come to the States in search of jobs, schooling, or commercial opportunities. As American citizens they must struggle for a livelihood and for acceptance in much the same way that their mainland neighbors do. It is hoped that this booklet will be helpful to neighbors, social workers, writers, teachers, clergymen, and men of good will who are helping these newcomers adjust properly to the opportunities and expectations of their adopted communities."[2]

Obviously this industrial migration is relatively new, which means that jobs may not have been thoroughly mastered and in many instances the families have not been sent for. The major significance of this movement lies in the future. Puerto Ricans will be used increasingly to meet the labor shortages that may develop in our industrial centers. They will be better and better prepared for their tasks and will ultimately work as individuals instead of as groups as at present. It is quite likely that in a few years the Puerto Ricans will be as well integrated into the total life of the nation as their predecessors are now—the Irish, the Germans, and the Scandinavians.

When several hundred thousand people migrate from an island to a continent, changing their mode of livelihood and modifying their

[2] This may be obtained without charge by writing to the Office of the Government of Puerto Rico, 1026 Seventeenth St., N. W., Washington, D. C.

way of life, their religious life will not go unaffected. Other groups have met this situation in one of two ways. The Irish, the Germans, the Poles have been even more loyal to their ancestral faith in the new home than in the old. They have brought the church with them. The Chinese, Japanese, Mexicans, and, to a large extent, the Jews, have left their church behind them. The small proportion of Puerto Ricans who are Protestants have brought their church and their ministers with them, while the 85 per cent who are nominally Roman Catholic have for the most part left their church behind them. Unlike many other immigrant groups, Puerto Rican Catholics have established no parishes of their own in this country.

The Roman Catholic Church enjoyed a religious monopoly in Puerto Rico for four centuries. It was then disestablished without being persecuted. Instead of facing persecution it was called on to meet competition, which crept up on it in an unspectacular way.

The attitude of the Puerto Ricans toward the Roman Catholic Church has two sides. Outwardly they conform. They use the church for baptisms, weddings (when they can afford it), and funerals. They enjoy church festivals. The church is a place where they see their friends and are seen by their neighbors. Underneath, however, there is much resentment toward the church. They use it but do not love it. They feel that the church is in some ways alien to themselves and that it has imposed upon them.

A Roman Catholic priest gave me a clue as to why this might be so. He said, "The Germans are loyal to the church as an institution, but the Irish and the Latins give their loyalty more to the priest as a person." Organizations as such mean little; personal ties are all powerful.

We have found no explanation of why the Roman Catholic Church cannot recruit priests in a land where the population has outrun the employment possibilities. For some reason, the clerical life does not appeal to Puerto Rican boys. The Roman Catholic Church cannot export priests from the island to the United States simply because it has none to spare.

The reverse situation prevails among Puerto Rican Protestants. Although the most that they can claim is a membership of 200,000 in a population of 2,200,000, they do not lack for native leadership. Even the theological seminary that trains ministers for the major denominations now has a Puerto Rican president with the Puerto Ricans a majority on its faculty. Only a handful of North Americans serve the mission boards on the island; from the point of view of the common man, Protestantism is more indigenous and much closer to the people than is the foreign-dominated Roman Catholic Church. As a consequence, it is natural for Puerto Rican young men to enter the ministry—and enough of them do so to take care of the Protestant churches on the island and also to minister to the Puerto Rican congregations on the mainland. It is heartening to see how splendidly the close relationship between the Protestant clergy and the laity is paying off at this point.

Puerto Rican Protestantism has the further virtue of practical ecumenicity. The various denominational mission boards arrived on the island simultaneously at the time of the American occupation. Instead of competing with one another, the major groups divided the island between them on a geographical basis. They have trained their ministers together and published a common paper. For years it has been assumed that when a Protestant moved from *el campo Metodista* (the country of the Methodists) to *el campo Presbyteriano* (the country of the Presbyterians) he would shift his denominational affiliations accordingly. This type of loyalty has proved invaluable in the present migration. Instead of hunting for their own brand of Protestantism, the Puerto Ricans have been ready to accept what was offered them, asking only that it be Protestant.

Turning our attention to the mainland, according to the best estimates available, based on research sponsored by Columbia University, the Puerto Rican population of New York city is 83 per cent nominally Roman Catholic, 9 per cent Protestant, 5 per cent adherents of Pentecostal sects that are graphically described by the Puerto Ricans as *los aleluyas,* and 2 per cent spiritualist. These figures are on the basis of adherents rather than active or actual members. The New York City Missionary Society has been able to discover 62 Puerto Rican Protestant churches that reported a membership of 7,856 in 1949, with a slightly smaller number enrolled in Sunday school. The number of churches, membership, and Sunday school enrollment have increased steadily since then. The multiplicity of Protestant congregations has in it elements of both strength and weakness, as we will see.

Protestantism in Puerto Rican New York is kaleidoscopic in its range and color—as we have seen demonstrated on successive Sundays.

On an August Sunday afternoon we visited La Iglesia Cristiana del Valle (The Christian Church in the Valley) in the Bronx. At first we thought that we would have either to stand up or sit in a front pew, which might be embarrassing, but a thoughtful soul pointed to a folding chair, which we placed in the aisle, inwardly hoping that the Fire Department would not look in that afternoon. Some 150 people had been in session for at least half an hour before we arrived, and probably continued long after the forty-five minutes that we spent with them. The range of age was from three on up. When we came in a woman was singing a solo, with the help of a loud-speaker. While we were there, she and two men "presided" in succession. The meeting was a mingling of songs, some without either announcement or books; prayer, more or less in concert; and sheer ecstasy. At times the congregation clapped their hands with a powerful rhythm. As the meeting progressed, several women left their seats to move down the aisle with a revolving step that was a sort of slow whirl. There was no discoverable intellectual content to the service. The people were expressing their emotions even more freely than they might have done at the nearby Yankee Stadium. For many of them it must have been the high spot of the week. Here drab lives were rising above themselves through the emotional escape of religious ecstasy. In this the Puerto Ricans are not alone; similar services can be found among other groups.

Of a similar but much milder nature were the three street meetings within half a mile of one another that we discovered at dusk on a Sunday night, and the services of two small groups that were huddled together in earnest prayer in garage-sized rooms on the same night. At least here Puerto Ricans were responding to one type of Puerto Rican leadership.

In striking contrast to this was the Sunday morning service that we attended in the same neighborhood at La Luterana Iglesia España (The Spanish Lutheran Church). Here was both order and reverence. The service began with the singing of the tune "Ein Feste Burg" in full-throated Spanish and proceeded heartily in accordance with a Spanish version of the prayer book of the United Lutheran Church. But the formality was well tinctured with friendliness. After the sermon the minister spoke more casually, calling on another minister in the congregation to say a few words, which were followed by some remarks from a layman. The congregation appeared both friendly and prosperous.

About a score of Protestant churches minister to the Puerto Ricans of New York. Among these are the four Spanish churches sponsored by the New York City Mission Society, an interdenominational organization that has also given general leadership through careful study of the

Spanish-speaking population and the effort to meet new needs. Two common procedures with foreign language groups have not worked at all well with the Puerto Ricans. One is for the foreign-speaking group to use an English-speaking church for Sunday afternoon or other meetings. The social gap between the newly arrived Puerto Ricans and the old established congregations has made this difficult. We discovered a Puerto Rican congregation meeting in the building of a Lutheran Church of German antecedents on East 119th Street on Sunday afternoon, but without benefit of a sign! Another procedure has been for the incoming population to take over the churches or synagogues of the departing population. Unfortunately, the Puerto Ricans have settled in two areas of New York that are almost totally devoid of religious structures of any sort. Their immediate predecessors have been Jews, and apparently rather irreligious Jews. To find meeting places for Protestant congregations both in East Harlem and in the southeast Bronx has been most difficult, while to clear away existing structures and build a church in New York is terribly expensive. The result has been to give Protestantism a rather lower degree of visibility in the Puerto Rican neighborhoods than it really deserves.

As the Puerto Ricans scatter out, they face the choice of either returning to distinctly Puerto Rican churches or of affiliating themselves with local English-speaking congregations. No marked trend in either direction has as yet developed. So far as the city itself is concerned, well dressed Puerto Ricans who speak English would be welcome in practically any church.

The East Harlem Protestant Parish was born of the conviction on the part of some students in Union Theological Seminary that Protestantism should do something for East Harlem, in many ways the most neglected section of the city. These students have lived among the people. Accepting the "live-in-the-block" custom, they have started three store front churches whose general crudity matches that of the general surroundings. They found both the Negroes and the Puerto Ricans of East Harlem eager to find someone who would listen to their woes. They also found that much could be done to help these people, particularly by standing up for them and with them as against landlords, city officials, and the police. The last named have often been careless and even brutal in their dealings with the boys of the neighborhood. Now when the police round up a group they ask them where they go to church, and if they reply "East Harlem Protestant Parish" they are quite likely to let them go!

Probably the greatest lesson of the East Harlem Parish is that these people are more or less lost in a new world and that their supreme need is for a sense of personal security. They will support a church that supports them. And here is a place where the church has much to do on every level—from inspiring a cleanup campaign to agitating against the use of narcotics, from tending babies to conducting meaningful worship.

Presbyterian Labor Temple, in a crowded downtown section of New York, carries on a varied ministry among all nationalities and faiths that its leaders call "symphony in a democracy." A Puerto Rican minister, the Reverend Salvador Bernart, is assigned to this staff to help Puerto Ricans in the neighborhood in their orientation to living in New York. This is done through job counsel, lessons in English, and invitations to participate in the fellowship. The Governor of Puerto Rico, the Honorable Luis Muñoz Marin, has written to Labor Temple in appreciation of their help.

The Puerto Ricans appear to be more susceptible to the appeal of Protestantism in New York than in San Juan. They are groping for something that Protestantism possesses—a sense of both religious and social security.

Protestantism when it is true to itself is always evangelical. It proclaims a God who is concerned about men, and who will enter intimately into their lives if given the chance. The Roman Catholic God is awe-inspiring but remote. The Protestant God need not lack grandeur and is never far away. The genius of Protestantism is the closeness of the ties between God and man.

Even more effective than its religious teaching is the social aspect of Protestantism. The church is something to which you definitely belong. It is not a vague conception; it is a company of people who care for one another. Here the individual is always important. Whatever his workaday lot, in the church he has status in the eyes of both God and man. Here is a basis for emotional security, a rock to which one may anchor. The bewildering immensity of a city such as New York and the individual helplessness of those who have come to it from another land accentuate the need for religious fellowship. And this is what gives power to many little groups whose expression of religion may seem most bizarre.

The principles that we have been trying to state are well illustrated in the true story of Gustavo and Carmen, to whom we will give the fictitious name of Blanco. The fact that they are Cubans rather than Puerto Ricans rather improves the drama.

Gustavo worked for the railroad as a ticket-seller and minor accountant. He was a nominal Roman Catholic. Carmen's father had broken with the church, and had advised his children to seek their own religion. Carmen had a sister who was married and living in Yonkers. When Gustavo had some time off, they came to the States for a visit. Being pregnant, Carmen consulted a doctor, who urged her not to risk the trip back to Havana, but to have her child here. As Carmen was not averse to giving birth to an American citizen, this was done.

Returning to Cuba, they found that the declining business of the railroad did not offer much of a future for Gustavo, and so they decided to take advantage of the baby's citizenship and return to New York, perhaps permanently. They flew to Miami and then took a bus to New York, "so we could see the country," Carmen explained.

Looking for work was not too happy an experience for Gustavo. His English is not fluent, and he is temperamentally shy. Instead of working with figures and books he has had to adjust himself to operating a machine. He began at $37.50 a week but has now worked up to $42 a week, a good wage in Cuba but not in New York. He and Carmen have a three room apartment on upper Columbus Avenue "with the bathtub in the kitchen," and the rent is $38 a month.

"I love the United States—but *this* is not the United States!" Carmen frequently exclaims. "We must get out into the country, the real country!" But that is not easy. Her immediate problem is to improve Gustavo's English—her own is rather good. Fortunately he is employed where there are no other Spanish-speaking workers, and so must use English. He tried night school but felt that it was not giving him what he needed. At present Carmen is working with him diligently every night. The baby is now two, and before long may take a hand with his father's education.

Carmen has been afraid of her neighbors and somewhat afraid of New York. She dreads the idea of her boy growing up "on the street." In her insecurity she has turned toward religion. She went to Mass. The Roman Catholic Church seemed far away and remote from her problems. She sampled *los aleluyas,* but her intelligence rebelled. Then she stumbled upon the Lutherans. Carmen realized that at last she had found the faith that could answer her needs. She says, "They have the same atmosphere of reverence as the Catholic Church, but they know what they believe—and they are friendly."

Here was what Carmen and Gustavo needed—faith and fellowship.

Carmen studied the catechism and was confirmed, and Gustavo followed her example. Last summer she helped with a Vacation Bible School, and when the minister went on his vacation the Blancos moved into the parsonage to look after things until he returned. What has happened to Gustavo and Carmen happens to thousands of others like them. They have deep needs to which only Protestantism has a satisfactory answer.

But Puerto Ricans have much to give as well as to receive. This is shown in the story of Elba Arias, now Mrs. Paul Benson. She grew up in the Presbyterian church in Lares, Puerto Rico, and attended the Polytechnic Institute at San Germán, a school that was established by the Presbyterians and that still, even though it has become a private enterprise, has a majority of Presbyterian trustees. For two years she worked on the Presbyterian rural life project at El Guacio, where she met a worker from the states, Paul Benson, who was a Lutheran of missionary parentage. After completing her term at El Guacio, she followed her family to Lorain, Ohio, where her father owns a grocery store and her brother-in-law has a restaurant. She found employment as a nurses' aide at St. Mary's Hospital. She and Paul were married in the summer of 1951. While he was completing his course at the Augustana Theological Seminary in Rock Island, Illinois, she took another year of college. In June, 1952, they left for South America, where they will be permanently stationed in either Uruguay or Chile as missionaries representing a combined venture on the part of several Lutheran bodies. Thus the evangelical seed that was planted in Puerto Rico and nourished in Lorain, Ohio, will bear abundant fruit in South America.

Whiteeve Studios

Youthful leaders in training with the Division of Home Missions, NCCC, before beginning their work among migrants.

) CHAPTER 8 (

The Lesser Streams

SO FAR we have considered three groups of Spanish-speaking Americans: those whose ancestors had already established themselves in the West before it passed under the sovereignty of the United States; those who have crossed over from Mexico; and those who have flown over from Puerto Rico, arriving with the full rights of citizenship. We will now meet a fourth group, those who have come here from the other countries of Latin America. Although their numbers are relatively few, they exert a considerable influence on our relations to the countries to the south of us.

The most numerous of these are the Cubans. During the latter part of the nineteenth century the making of "Havana" cigars moved over from Cuba to Florida. A large colony of men whose deft fingers rolled the then popular cigar established themselves first at Key West and later at Tampa. The advent of cigar making machinery and the rise of the cigarette have reduced the number employed in this skilled trade to relatively small numbers, but the children of the original cigar makers have entered other occupations and have prospered generally. Today Tampa is the most cosmopolitan and industrialized city of Florida. Approximately one-third of its people speak Spanish.

The Cubans have followed a pattern of settlement quite different from that of the Mexicans and Puerto Ricans. In the portion of Tampa known as Ybor City they have established a distinctly Latin cultural center of their own, which has been reinforced by immigration direct from Spain and from Italy. The dominant social influences are the Cuban and Spanish clubs, which have ornate buildings and which provide many services for their members, including medical care for a monthly fee. Children do not ordinarily learn English until they enter the public schools. Girls are carefully chaperoned. Restaurants serving Spanish and Italian food attract the winter tourist. Here is a bit of authentic Latin atmosphere in the midst of America.

Only 10 per cent of the people of Ybor City attend the Roman Catholic Church. The attitudes of the rest range from indifference to positive antagonism, with the latter predominant. Many have broken with the church completely and even bury their dead without benefit of priest, minister, or prayer.

Various approaches have been made to the 50,000 Cubans, Spaniards, and Italians of the Tampa area by various groups, including the Methodists and the Evangelical United Brethren. A most successful venture has been the Ybor City Presbyterian Mission, where the Reverend Walter B. Passiglia has labored since 1935. Here is a trilingual church with a trilingual pastor. The largest service of the week is on Sunday morning and in English, but there is also a Spanish service on Wednesday night and one in Italian on Thursday night. The pastor, a Sicilian, as are most Italians in Tampa, is a graduate of Union Theological Seminary, Richmond, Virginia, a Southern Presbyterian school.

The greatest evidence of the success of this mission is its achievements in the area where the Roman Catholic Church has been pitiably weak in its work with Spanish-speaking people—the recruiting of the ministry. It has sent three of its boys and their well trained wives into the ministry, and two of its girls into Christian vocations. Its faith is catching; its concept of the ministry as a life of service is alluring.

Around New York city are a considerable number of Cubans and also of people from the Dominican Republic and the Central and South American republics, but they appear to have no group consciousness nor organizations. The Cubans and Dominicans in particular have been lost in the flood of Puerto Ricans who have swept into the city, and follow the same pattern of moving up the economic ladder and out from the more congested areas as soon as they can afford it.

The students who are coming to our colleges and universities from Latin America number approximately 10,000. They may be most significant from the point of view of international relations.

The role of the student in Latin America is far different from that of students in this country. Here nobody takes the political views of students very seriously. Their vote is not large enough to excite our politicians. In the republics to the south of us, student attitudes often decide the fate of a government. I traveled in South America with a passport in which I was described as a "student." The British laughed at this designation, but the South American officials took it seriously and treated me with more courtesy than would be the lot of a Spanish-speaking student in this country. However, when I came to a country where the students had unsuccessfully tried to throw the dictator out, I registered in the hotel as a "professor," but the management had trouble with my writing and told the police I was a *petrolero,* or oil man, the safest occupation for an American in that country.

There are several reasons for the political importance of students in

Latin America. They are a small and rather intimate group. Their parents are the people of power. The result is that the students feel a sense of responsibility for their country such as no group could know in the United States. When they start to this country to attend school, they leave home as important people. They are accustomed to being taken seriously. Too often that illusion perishes when they reach our shores. In Colombia I traveled for some days with a well dressed and charming student who was endeavoring to master English against his arrival in the United States. I have always wondered what happened to him when he landed in New Orleans. His face was quite dark.

We are likely to misunderstand the motives and attitudes of these students. For one thing, Latin America has nothing in the nature of the American liberal arts college. There are numerous *colegios*, many run by our mission boards, but in Spanish *colegio* does not mean "college" in our sense, but just "school." The Latin American student gets his *bachillerato* at the end of what we would call high school, and then proceeds immediately to the professional school of the university. Higher education is not thought of in terms of personal development but as a means for entering a profession that will give one both social prestige and a means of earning a good living. Possibly they are simply more frank about their aims than students in this country.

This attitude is reinforced by the expectations with which students look toward this country. They rate us tops in everything mechanical. They love our automobiles, our electric refrigerators, and all our gadgets. They admire our engineers and are convinced that our dentists are the best in the world. Unfortunately, they see this side of American life in such a clear light that our other characteristics are lost in the shadows. Before leaving home they have been indoctrinated with the stereotype that North Americans are by nature uncultured, unmannerly, unphilosophical, and utterly materialistic. They welcome our machinery, but they discount our ideals. On the basis of the movies that they have seen and the Americans whom they have met, this is not as unfair a generalization as it might seem.

What happens to these students after they reach our shores may be important to future relations between their country and ours.

In Buenos Aires I called upon Dr. Alfredo Palacios, who was at that time the fountainhead of anti-Americanism in Latin America. I found a proud man who had much prestige, particularly with the students of the South American countries. I learned that he had once visited New York for a few days. The one friend whom he had in this country could not be found. Dr. Palacios spoke no English, and had a horrible time. One can imagine his experience with taxi drivers, subway employees, police, and waiters. He has hated our country ever since.

In Chile I met Graciela Mandijano, who had spent a year or more in New York, living in the settlement house connected with the Spring Street Presbyterian Church. She was lyrical in her description of the experience. "It was in New York that I found myself. In Chile people had come to see me because I was somebody's daughter or niece or cousin. In New York they came to see me, not because of my connections, but because I was I!" She had been received as an individual, and there was no doubt as to her attitude toward our country.

The Spanish-speaking students in this country below the university level often attend Roman Catholic schools; graduates favor our technical and professional schools rather than the liberal arts departments of the universities. Both of these circumstances make it difficult for them to come into contact with the Protestant churches and the more characteristic aspects in American life. However, we have met Spanish-speaking students in the home of a local pastor. They are delightful to have about. Their great need is hospitality and personal friendliness. Great is our reward when we extend it to them.

Spanish American Baptist Seminary, Los Angeles

This divinity student is representative of scores of Spanish young men who are training for the Christian ministry.

) CHAPTER 9 (

What Shall We Do?

WE HAVE endeavored to portray the vast panorama of the life of the Spanish-speaking people of our country from the hidden valleys of New Mexico to the enforced intimacies of the New York subway. Now we come to the questions: What difference should these people make to us? What can we do as Christians, as Protestants, as church members, to include them more fully in the richer aspects of American life?

We can help to rid ourselves and others of several commonly accepted stereotypes concerning Spanish-speaking Americans.

Once I tried to tell a group of Y.M.C.A. boys in Nebraska about Latin American attitudes toward life, but I could not get them beyond the idea that every Mexican has a knife concealed upon his person that he is most anxious to plunge into somebody's back. On the evidence of movies, pulp magazines, and comic books the boys were sure that I was wrong and that they were right. It did no good to tell them that I had traveled in many parts of Mexico, at all hours, and usually alone, and that I have never had the least occasion to be afraid. Their picture could not be changed by my testimony. I fear that there are many like them. Actually, except in times of revolution, Mexico is a peaceful place. The chief knives carried by Mexicans are big *machetes,* manufactured in Connecticut, which are most useful for harvesting crops or in cutting one's way through underbrush and which are certainly not in the concealed weapons classification. The Mexican workers in this country have a remarkable reputation for harmlessness. It is time that our story writers cast them in another and more truthful role.

Many people assume that Mexicans in the United States are lazy. Their chief evidence seems to be pictures of men taking noonday naps. For the climate of Mexico the noonday siesta is probably a good idea, and one of the virtues of the Mexican people that we might well emulate is their ability to relax. But when it comes to work, real work, hard, exhausting work, we are the lazy ones and not the Mexicans. When a Mexican is free from disease, when he has enough food in his stomach to make his body go, and when he is sure that he will be paid, he is a fiend for work. For sheer energy the boys who offer their services to tourists as guides and general helpers are the world's wonder. And their brains are just as active as their hands and feet. They're a nuisance until you hire them; after that they will do anything for you. In this country there are no complaints by employers of slothfulness on the part of Mexican workers. No one who knows them will dub them "lazy."

A persistent libel around New York is that the Puerto Ricans fly in from Puerto Rico only to get on relief. Actually Puerto Ricans have a fear of both government officials and welfare workers that discourages them from seeking assistance from these sources. As the last to be hired they are commonly the first to be fired, which means that their employment follows the minor fluctuations of business. In recent years the proportion of Puerto Ricans on relief has varied from 6 to 10 per cent, and most of these have been mothers with small children who cannot work because they cannot find day care for their children. As with other groups, the number of Puerto Ricans on welfare depends upon business conditions.

Many people assume that the only people who are really clean are those who have white skins and that therefore the large number of Spanish-speaking Americans whose skins are darker must be dirty. Actually the cleanliness of a people largely depends upon the climate and the availability of bathing facilities. In the tropics water is usually abundant and bathing a pleasant experience. Employers testify to the exceptional cleanliness of the Puerto Ricans.

The background of the Mexicans is quite different. The interior of Mexico is high, cold, and singularly destitute of rivers, while such as do exist only run part of the time. The areas to which they have come in the United States are quite similar. According to the boast of a southern Californian, their rivers are so smart that they get their work done in three months out of the year and stand by in a fine state of emptiness the rest of the time. When one considers that Mexicans quite literally do the dirty work wherever they are, and that water is usually difficult to come by, the degree of cleanliness to which they commonly attain is to be wondered at. Yet from all sorts of hovels, shacks, and tenements, Mexican young people manage to emerge all spick and span, in well pressed and immaculate clothes. The price that they must pay in effort for personal cleanliness is often high, and yet they manage to meet it. For this they deserve far more honor than they commonly receive.

All that any group of people can ask is to be judged on a retail rather than a wholesale basis. Instead of being plastered with a label because of their language or their complexion, they ask for an individual appraisal. It can be pointed out that there are shiftless and dirty Anglo-Americans, but we would not think it fair for our nation to be judged by them. All that other peoples can ask is the courtesy of a similar discrimination.

To approach Spanish-speaking Americans sympathetically we need a finer appreciation of their background.

Behind the Spanish-speaking people of our country lies a great artistic tradition, and one that is surprisingly accessible to us. On the Spanish side, the Sorolla Room in the Hispanic Museum in New York city is one of the most thrilling spots in this country. The eye is overwhelmed by the brilliance of the color and the seeming liveliness of the movement. Spain becomes a flashing reality. On the Indian side, the work of Rivera and Orozco may be seen in the Detroit Art Museum, at Dartmouth College, and in the New School of Social Research in New York. Modern Mexico has given American art its most recent and arresting inspiration.

As thousands of American women and some men have discovered, Mexico is a shoppers' paradise. For this there are three reasons. The products on sale are always interesting and often beautiful, and the range is wide: art work, blankets, leatherwork, glassware, pottery, jewelry. Each object is a new creation and neither matches nor "nests" with anything else. It is fun buying them; salesmanship in Mexico is a form of sport. The price is usually low, particularly if one penetrates below the border.

Mexican products are quite generally available in the United States. We once acquired what we thought was a good set of blue glass in a factory in Guadalajara for only $3.50 our money. As breakage has cut down the set and as we have desired to expand it we have picked up additional pieces from the same factory, but for a much higher price, in all sorts of places in this country. There are also stores that handle only Mexican handiwork.

Mexicans and Puerto Ricans are primarily people with the same hopes and fears as the rest of us. They are just as much the children of God as are we. Our duty and our opportunity is to accept them as such. All they ask is that they be accepted as individuals on the basis of their individual worth, rather than being classified as members of a peculiar group on the basis of fanciful misconceptions. To think in terms of the members of a crowd rather than of the crowd as a whole is not easy, but it is always the Christian thing to do. In the case of Spanish-speaking Americans, there are many barriers to acquaintance and understanding—language, occupation, place of residence.

The easiest contacts are through educational institutions. We visited one of the state supported colleges of Texas where the dean claimed that there were no distinctions between young people of Spanish-speaking ancestry and Anglos, and we were told by a faculty member that pressure was being put on the sororities to persuade them to pledge at least one girl for each chapter from the Mexican students. We suspect that some of this was window dressing in response to pressures that have been put upon the school, but it was wholesome even to have the issue raised.

A special program of service to foreign students, including those of Spanish-speaking background, is offered by the Committee on Friendly Relations among Foreign Students. It was founded to study the needs of these students, to expand the opportunities open to them, and to stimulate communities to share in the experience of international relations. Many individuals and private organizations, such as church boards, the Ford Foundation, the Y. M. and Y. W. C. A., are giving their support to the committee.

The committee's program is varied. The Port of Entry Services

Methodist Prints

are particularly significant. "Foreign Student Advisers," wearing blue armbands so that they may easily be spotted, meet the ships and planes of incoming students. The bewildered newcomers are helped to get through the multitudinous details of their entry with the least possible embarrassment and stress.

Throughout the year the committee helps and advises with the institution of campus and community programs designed to help integrate the students into their environment and to acquaint others with the rich contributions they can make to campus and community life. Counseling, information, and program services are included in the plan to promote mutual understanding and appreciation.

The committee has definite suggestions for church groups, other organizations, and individuals who sincerely want to extend the hand of friendship to these students. Most of the suggestions are based on two principles: take an intelligent interest in the student as a human being, trying to understand his thoughts and feelings; share your own everyday interests with him in a simple, natural way. Churches are cautioned not to regard these students simply as resource speakers to be whisked into a meeting to fill a place on the program and promptly forgotten when it is over.

Possibly the staff would consider the following statement by a student from Paraguay as representing one fine initial approach to friendship with foreign students:

"I cannot forget K. K., a boy with whom I got so well acquainted as to consider him my brother, and I know he feels the same about me. He took me home for Christmas, giving me a wonderful chance to see life in a small community and a typical farm family. He helped me in everything I needed and was so eager to learn about my country that right now he knows just about as much as I do."[1]

Two Spanish-speaking students were invited into a church home in New Jersey, after having met the family through a church group meeting. The several small children in the home were delighted with their visitors and asked them innumerable questions. The students seemed to respond with pleasure and soon were asking questions themselves, about the garden, the hobby room, and at last—timidly—about the recipes the hostess had used in preparing the meal. Before they left, the students had promised to come back and cook a genuine Spanish meal as a special treat for the children!

If you live in a college or university community, it is a simple matter to find out if there are students of Spanish-speaking American background or from Latin American countries, and then to include them in

[1] *The Unofficial Ambassadors,* Report of the Committee on Friendly Relations among Foreign Students, 1952, p. 3.

church or personal social occasions. They are likely to be most attractive, as the Spanish tradition stresses the social graces. To arrive in an institution of higher learning is also evidence of either unusual ability or ambition. Students of Spanish-speaking antecedents are not just ordinary young people. They are interesting to meet and well worth knowing.

Probably the most natural relations between Anglos and Spanish-speaking Americans are to be found in the high schools of the Southwest. Here day-by-day contacts lay the basis for real friendships. The home can encourage or discourage such relationships. The church can promote them. To do so is to be fair with young people who face rather more difficulties than the average and at the same time to strengthen the unity of our nation.

Perhaps the most discouraging discovery in connection with the preparation of this book has been the obliviousness of many of our communities to the very existence of the Mexican in their midst. In the sugar beet country the people who attend Protestant churches may have seen the Mexicans about, but they regard them as part of the scenery rather than as human beings. Even the ministers appear to have no contacts whatever with them.

We hope that this book will inspire some of its readers to take thought for their forgotten neighbors, at least to the point of being conscious of their existence. As is usually the case, the best contacts are through the children. If there is a migrant center maintained by the state council of churches or by the National Council of Churches in your vicinity, your Sunday school class or young people's group would undoubtedly enjoy visiting it, and perhaps playing with the young people whom it found there. If you are conducting a vacation church school and there are Mexican children about, why not invite them to participate?

The Puerto Ricans are our newest comers, and offer an unusual opportunity. Outside of New York city, their movements are being directed to a considerable degree by the Government of Puerto Rico, largely on a group basis. If a group of Puerto Ricans should come to your town or city it is because some industry asked for them, the state employment office was convinced that they were needed, and the Government of Puerto Rico has approved of their coming. This is far different from the haphazard, unguided migrations of the past. The Puerto Ricans are American citizens. The community is in some measure responsible for their coming. This being so, it would be a lovely and most American gesture for the churches to make them welcome. They are strangers in a strange land; they need help in all sorts of adjustments, but most of all they need a sense of belonging. Here is a chance for some inspired Christian helpfulness.

No one who has come to know our Spanish-speaking Americans has failed to like them. They are a friendly, cordial people, with rather more and better manners than the rest of us. They have much to add to our American life not only through their physical vigor but through their feeling for the beautiful and the liveliness of their imaginations. They have an excellent capacity for religious understanding and expression. They can bring a new vigor to our churches. It should be our ambition to include them more fully in both our community and our church life.

A Short Reading List

The purpose of this list is to suggest recent and available books to provide background for the study of Americans of Spanish heritage. The views expressed in the several books are not necessarily in harmony with those of the author and the publishers of this volume.

Leaders of groups using *Within These Borders* as a text for study and action may secure supplementary material by applying to their own denominational literature headquarters. From these sources and from book stores they may order *The Adult Guide on Spanish-speaking Americans,* by Edwin F. Tewksbury. Price 50 cents.

Accent on Liberty, edited by Mabel M. Sheibley. Contains several dramatic stories of Spanish Americans. New York, Friendship Press, 1952. Paper $1.25; cloth $2.00.

American Me, by Beatrice Griffith. Boston, Houghton Mifflin Co., 1948. $3.50.

Beyond Good Friday, by Edith J. Agnew. A one-act play about Spanish-speaking Americans in the Southwest. New York, Friendship Press, 1953. 35 cents.

Forgotten People; a study of New Mexicans, by George Isidore Sánchez. A university professor of Spanish-speaking ancestry analyzes the life of his people. Albuquerque, University of New Mexico Press, 1940. $2.00.

Fun and Festival among America's Peoples, by Katherine Ferris Rohrbough. A treasure house of suggestions for those responsible for planning programs and parties. New York, Friendship Press, 1943. 50 cents.

It Happened in Taos, by Jesse Taylor Reid. The story of a successful social experiment in a Spanish-speaking community in the mountains of New Mexico. Albuquerque, University of New Mexico Press, 1946. $2.50.

Know Your Fellow American Citizen from Puerto Rico, picture pamphlet. An appeal by the Government of Puerto Rico for fair treatment for her citizens as they come to the mainland. The Office of the Government of Puerto Rico, 1026 Seventeenth St., N. W., Washington, D. C., 1952. Free.

Latin Americans in Texas, by Pauline R. Kibbe. How the Government of Texas has endeavored to improve the relations between her Spanish-speaking and her other residents. Albuquerque, University of New Mexico Press, 1946. $3.50.

Migratory Labor in American Agriculture. Report of the President's Commission on Migratory Labor. Washington, D. C., Government Printing Office, 1951. 75 cents.

North from Mexico; the Spanish-speaking people of the United States, by Carey McWilliams. A current report on the status, economic and otherwise, of those of Mexican descent in this country. Philadelphia, J. B. Lippincott Co., 1949. $4.00.

Papi, by Eleanor Hull. New York, Friendship Press, 1953. Paper $1.25; cloth $2.00.

Puerto Rican Journey; New York's newest migrants, by Charles Wright Mills, Clarence Senior, and Rose Kohn Goldsen. The results of a recent study of Puerto Rican immigration to New York. New York, Harper and Brothers, 1950. $3.00.

Southern California Country; an island on the land, by Carey McWilliams. Although this deals with Spanish-speaking Americans only indirectly, it gives an excellent analysis of the forces that have molded Southern California. New York, Duell, Sloan and Pearce, 1946. $3.75.

Strangers—and Neighbors; the story of our Puerto Rican Citizens, by Clarence Senior. A popular interpretation of the Puerto Ricans in our midst. New York, Anti-defamation League of B'nai B'rith, 1953. 25 cents.

The Secret Suitcase, by Dorothy W. Andrews and Louise B. Scott. New York, Friendship Press, 1953. Paper $1.25; cloth $2.00.

Who? Spanish-speaking Americans in the U. S. A., edited by Mae Hurley Ashworth. New York, Friendship Press, 1953. 50 cents.

THE AUTHOR

JOHN R. SCOTFORD was born and raised in Chicago and received his education first at Dartmouth College and later at Union Theological Seminary. After holding several Congregational pastorates in Texas, Oklahoma, and Ohio, he joined the staff of the *Missionary Herald,* where he took on a great many assignments involving extended travel. During those years he became more and more familiar with the status and problems of Spanish-speaking Americans in the U.S.A., an area of knowledge he had been exploring since his early pastorates in the Southwest.

After twelve years with the *Missionary Herald* he was invited to the editorship of *Advance,* a post he occupied until 1950. During the past three years, in addition to writing many articles, he has traveled even more extensively through areas in which Spanish-speaking Americans are concentrated, investigating closely, and in person, many Mexican settlements in this country, as well as a great many communities in which Puerto Ricans, Cubans, and others, have largely located.

Dr. Scotford has written several books and pictorial presentations, including *Spanning a Continent, Together We Build America,* and *The Church Beautiful.* In addition to his journalistic activities, he is also a well-known figure in the field of church architecture, and is today a member of the board of managers of the Bureau of Church Building of the National Council of Churches.

THE FORMAT

The text of this book is set in Caledonia on the linotype by Ruttle, Shaw & Wetherill, Inc., of Philadelphia, Pennsylvania. It was printed by offset lithography by General Offset Company, Inc., of New York. It was bound in paper by F. M. Charlton Company, Inc., and in cloth by Charles H. Bohn and Company, both of New York.

Typographic design by Patricia Birdwood
Jacket and paper cover designed by Rafael Palacios
Binding by Louise E. Jefferson

The Mexican-American Market In the United States

Market Characteristics
From a Personal-Interview Survey in Spanish,
City and County Populations
From the U.S. Census

By
BELDEN ASSOCIATES
Dallas

ABOUT BELDEN ASSOCIATES

Established in 1940, Belden Associates is the oldest and largest research firm of its kind in the Southwest. In 1947 the company also founded the first independent marketing research firm in Mexico, what is now International Research Associates, S.A. de C.V.

Belden Associates offers complete research and counseling services in marketing and public affairs. It has acquired specialized knowledge in Spanish-language research from numerous studies in the Southwest, Far West, New York City, and Mexico for manufacturers, advertising agencies, and media.

In 1962 a nation-wide study of the Spanish and Negro markets made by Belden Associates received first prize for quantitative research in the annual Los Angeles Advertising Women Achievement Awards. The citation was given to Irene DeNoyer of the Carnation Company, which sponsored the study.

Joe Belden, president of Belden Associates and himself a bilingual, has become one of the country's few experts in Spanish-language research by virtue of his two decades of experience in the Southwest and fourteen years of residence in Mexico and Central America.

CONTENTS

TO HELP YOU INTERPRET THIS REPORT

OBJECTIVES

This report has been compiled to meet the need for reliable marketing data on the Spanish-language, Mexican-American population of the United States. The study covers the states containing the great majority of Mexican-Americans, more than 3,600,000: Arizona, California, Colorado, New Mexico, and Texas.

Market characteristics have been measured by means of a personal-interview survey, in Spanish, with a sampling of housewives covering the twelve most important urban concentrations of Mexican-Americans. City and county populations reported are from the 1960 Census count of persons of Spanish surname. We have adjusted these figures to reflect total Mexican-Americans, for not all Spanish-speaking people of Latin origin have Spanish surnames. We have identified this market as "Mexican-Americans" because by far the greatest portion of it is Mexican in ancestry and in many ways clings to Mexican culture.

SPONSORSHIP

The study was originated and executed by Belden Associates as an independent research firm. It has been financed in part by the sale of copies of the report and by a manufacturer who used a portion of the survey questionnaire for other market research. Belden Associates has itself contributed to the cost in the interest of furthering its own knowledge of this market.

METHODS

A description of the population data and the projection to total Mexican-Americans appears on page B-1. The discussion below applies to the survey conducted to measure the market characteristics reported in the yellow pages that follow.

The data were gathered through interviews in a sample of homes designed to be representative of the entire population surveyed. The universe or total population to be represented in the survey was defined as Spanish-speaking households of Latin origin in certain communities in the five states where the U. S. Census makes a count of Spanish surnames. An examination was made of the Census Spanish-name counts for 1950 and 1960 for all urban places in these states containing at least 2,500 persons of Spanish surname. Twelve areas emerged as the most important in size in both censuses; so the criterion was established that the survey should include all urban places (as defined by the Census) which in 1960 had a projected Mexican-American population of at least 40,000 (see green section of this report).

Below are the urban places thus selected, showing the distribution of the interviews proportionate to their Mexican-American populations. The total population in the twelve areas is 1,214,576, or about 33 per cent of all Mexican-Americans in the five states.

Phoenix, Arizona	3.5%
Los Angeles, California	22.7
San Diego, California	3.3
San Francisco Bay Area, California (San Francisco, Oakland, and San Jose)	9.1
Denver, Colorado	3.8
Albuquerque, New Mexico	3.8
Corpus Christi, Texas	5.2
El Paso, Texas	11.0
Houston, Texas	5.5
Laredo, Texas	4.3
San Antonio, Texas	21.2
Lower Rio Grande Valley of Texas (Brownsville, Harlingen, and McAllen)	6.6
Total	100.0%

Five hundred interviews were made. While the actual distribution of interviews was extremely close to the above percentages, it was not exact; to render it exact, the sample was weighted. The weighted sample was of 621 cases, and it is on this base that the percentages are actually computed; in the report, however, we show the true base of 500. Recomputations of percentages should be made using 621 (the corresponding weighted bases for sub-samples of less than 500 shown in the tables will be furnished on request).

In each of the twelve cities we first designated areas where Mexican-Americans are concentrated. This designation was based on previous studies using probability samplings and from listings of Spanish surnames in telephone directories. In these areas we made a random selection of one hundred starting points, to which the interviewers were directed.

Beginning at the precise location designated, each interviewer then called at every home, following a systematic routing, interviewing only where she found Spanish-speaking Latin Americans. A total of five interviews was made for each starting point. The respondent was designated as the housewife, the person most likely to be able to answer the greatest number of questions on the questionnaire.

Provision was made to represent in the sample the people not found at home when the interviewers called. This was done by asking everyone whether she had been at home at the same time as the time of the interview during the past three days. With such data it is possible to determine the degree of "stay-at-homeness" of the respondents, and to adjust the results for those missed. An analysis of the results in this manner indicated that the usual weighting method based on "stay-at-homeness" degrees -- or making call-backs -- would not significantly affect the results. The results were therefore not weighted for this factor. Many of our studies of Mexican-Americans have revealed the highly homogeneous nature of this population group; thus the usual call-back requirements for people not at home assume less importance.

All interviews were made in Spanish by bilingual interviewers who were themselves Mexican-Americans. Full written specifications were furnished to the interviewers. They used a questionnaire which was originally written in Spanish. The questions in English that appear in this report are translations and may therefore appear slightly stilted in places. The word "plural" after "you" in these questions indicates that the plural form of the pronoun, ustedes, was used, referring to the family in general rather than to the respondent alone. The questionnaire is available on request.

The interviews were conducted in the spring of 1962, mostly in April.

A total shown adding to more than 100 per cent indicates that some respondents gave more than one reply. All percentages are rounded to the nearest whole number, and a hyphen is used to indicate less than one-half of 1 per cent.

The number of interviews, or base, on which percentages are computed is given at the foot of each table. This base must be borne in mind in evaluating the stability of each result -- for all samplings produce results subject to plus-or-minus tolerances ranging from a fraction to several percentage points. As a rule of thumb, the larger the sample on which a percentage is based, the more accurate the percentage (results on the total sample of 500 are therefore more reliable than those based on portions of the sample); the further a percentage is from 50, in either direction, the more accurate it is. Small differences between percentages are seldom significant.

HOME OWNERSHIP; PURCHASED NEW OR USED

Question: "Do you pay rent here, or do you own the house?"

Pay rent	47%
Own home	53
Total	100%
Base - all interviews	500

Question: "When you moved here, was it a new house or not?" (Asked of home owners.)

Home purchased new	31%
Home purchased used	60
Don't know or no answer	9
Total	100%
Base - home owners	275

RADIO AND TELEVISION SET OWNERSHIP

Question: "Is there a radio here in your home? Is it in working order or not?"

Question: "How many radio sets do you have in the house?"

Radio sets in working order:

One	59%
Two	21
Three or more	8
Total homes with radio	88%
Homes with no radio or not in working order	12
Total	100%
Base - all interviews	500

Question: "Do you have television here at home? Is it in working order or not?"

Homes with television	87%
Homes with no television or not in working order	13
Total	100%
Base - all interviews	500

Question: "Does your family have a car or truck?"

Have car or truck	75%
Have no car or truck	25
Total	100%
Base - all interviews	500

Question: "Is there a radio in the car (or truck)?"

Car or truck has radio.	72%*
Car or truck has no radio	26
Unreported	2
Total	100%
Base - car or truck owners	385

*Among all families, 67 per cent have a car or truck with radio.

Question: "Do you have an electric or gas refrigerator, or do you have an ice box?"

Have electric refrigerator	94%
Have gas refrigerator	1
Have ice box	1
Have no refrigeration	4
Total	100%
Base - all interviews	500

Question: "Do you have a clothes washing machine? Is it automatic or not?"

Have automatic washer	38%
Have regular washer	47
Have no washer	15
Total	100%
Base - all interviews	500

Question: "Do you have a telephone in the house?"

Have telephone	56%
Have no telephone	44
Total	100%
Base - all interviews	500

Question: "Do you have an air conditioner in the house? Is it the kind that uses water (evaporative cooler) or the refrigerated air kind?"

Have evaporative cooler	20%
Have refrigerated air conditioning	6
Have neither	74
Total	100%
Base - all interviews	500

NUMBER OF EARNERS IN THE FAMILY

Question: "Now I'd like to ask you how many persons in your family, including youths, work full-time, and how many work less than a full day (part-time jobs)."

a. "How many men and how many women work full-time?"

	Men	Women	Total Per family
One	72%	19%	67%
Two	7	1	17
Three or more	1	1	3
None	20	79	13
Total	100%	100%	100%
Base - all interviews	500	500	500

b. "And how many men and how many women work part-time?"

	Men	Women	Total Per family
One	9%	8%	14%
Two or more	1	1	4
None	90	91	82
Total	100%	100%	100%
Base - all interviews	500	500	500

FAMILY INCOME

Income is something that can vary widely by part of the country, and even from one city to the next. The figures below present the average picture for the markets covered in this study and should not be applied to any one specific market.

Question: "Please tell me approximately in which of these groups the total income of all your family falls." (A card was shown to the respondent listing the income classifications shown below.)

Less than $30 per week (Less than $1,500 per year)	11%
$30 to $39 per week (From $1,500 to $1,999 per year)	9
$40 to $58 per week (From $2,000 to $2,999 per year).	19
$59 to $77 per week (From $3,000 to $3,999 per year).	20
$78 to $96 per week (From $4,000 to $4,999 per year).	14
$97 to $135 per week (From $5,000 to $6,999 per year)	16
$136 to $192 per week (From $7,000 to $9,999 per year)	5
$193 or more per week ($10,000 or more per year)	1
Don't know or refused	5
Total	100%
Base - all interviews	500

Question: "Does someone in the family have an account in a bank to pay for purchases by check?"

Family has bank checking account	26%
No bank checking account	65
Don't know	9
Total	100%
Base - all interviews	500

Question: "And does someone in the family have a savings account in a bank or some other place?"

Family has savings account	33%
No savings account	56
Don't know	11
Total	100%
Base - all interviews	500

Question: "Does your family make all its purchases for cash, or do you pay for some things in installments?"

Make cash purchases only.	38%
Make installment purchases	63
Don't know or no answer	6
Total	107%
Base - all interviews	500

Question: "Does someone in your family have an account in a store where you may make purchases and pay the bill each month?"

Have store charge account	26%
Have no charge account	65
Don't know or no answer	9
Total	100%
Base - all interviews	500

Question: "Here in your home, at what times does the family usually arise in the morning?"

Before 5:00 AM	7%
5:00 - 5:59 AM	15
6:00 - 6:59 AM	46
7:00 - 7:59 AM	26
8:00 AM or later	5
Varies or no answer	1
Total	100%
Base - all interviews	500

Question: "And at what time do you (plural) usually retire at night?"

Before 9:00 PM	7%
9:00 - 9:59 PM	23
10:00 - 10:59 PM	46
11:00 - 11:59 PM	13
Midnight or later	10
Varies or no answer	1
Total	100%
Base - all interviews	500

Question: "At what time does the head of the family leave the house to go to work?"

Before 5:00 AM	3%
5:00 - 5:59 AM	4
6:00 - 6:59 AM	21
7:00 - 7:59 AM	35
8:00 - 8:59 AM	10
9:00 AM to noon	3
After noon or evening	6
Varies, does not work, or no answer	18
Total	100%
Base - all interviews	500

VACATIONS

Question: "During the last twelve months, did you (plural) go out of the city on a vacation or did you spend your vacation here?"

Left the city for vacation	22%
Took vacation in city	33
Did not take a vacation	31
Don't know or no answer	14
Total	100%
Base - all interviews	500

MIGRATION HABITS OF THE FAMILY

The belief is sometimes expressed that a characteristic of Mexican-American families is that they are migratory, following the crops from one place to another. While this may be true among some whose livelihood is farm labor, it does not necessarily apply to residents of cities. The following questions were asked to determine the extent of migration among Mexican-Americans residing in urban centers in the spring of the year.

Question: "During the last twelve months, that is, since April of last year, did someone in your family leave the city to go to work temporarily some other place?"

Yes, someone in family left city	11%
No one left	86
Don't know or no answer	3
Total	100%
Base - all interviews	500

Question: (Asked of those who left city) "Did all of you in the family leave, or did someone remain at home during that time?" (The percentages below combine replies to this and the preceding question to show net number of homes where no one was present during the absence.)

All members of family left city	3%
Someone remained at home	93
Don't know or no answer	4
Total	100%
Base - all interviews	500

Question: "What do you (plural) speak most at home, English or Spanish?"

English	24%*
Spanish	40
Both the same	36
Undecided or no answer	-
Total	100%
Base - all interviews	500

Question: "Which is the radio station that you (plural) listen to more than any (at home or any other place)? Are the majority of the programs that you (plural) listen to on that station in English or Spanish?"

Listen mostly to stations broadcasting mostly in English	31%
Listen mostly to stations broadcasting mostly in Spanish	52*
Do not listen, or don't recall station	17
Total	100%
Base - all interviews	500

Question: "Which is the television station that you (plural) view more than any other (at home or any other place?) Are the majority of the programs that you (plural) see on that station in English or Spanish?"

View mostly stations telecasting mostly in English	76%
View mostly stations telecasting mostly in Spanish	8*
Do not listen, or don't recall station	16
Total	100%
Base - all interviews	500

*All the respondents spoke Spanish.

NEWSPAPER AND MAGAZINE READING, LANGUAGE PREFERRED

Question: "Do you or some other person in the family read a daily newspaper?"

Read a daily newspaper	69%
Do not read a daily newspaper	31
Total	100%
Base - all interviews	500

Question: "Do you (plural) read more newspapers in English or Spanish?"

Read mostly English newspaper	78%*
Read mostly Spanish newspapers	12
Read both about the same	9
Don't know or no answer	1
Total	100%
Base - newspaper reading homes	343

Question: "Do you or some other person in the family read any magazines?"

Read magazines	64%
Do not read magazines	36
Total	100%
Base - all interviews	500

Question: "Do you (plural) read more magazines in English or Spanish?"

Read mostly English magazines	73%*
Read mostly Spanish magazines	15
Read both about the same	11
Don't know or no answer	1
Total	100%
Base - magazine reading families	316

*All the respondents spoke Spanish.

MOVIE GOING

Question: "Do you or someone in your family ever go to the movies, or do you never go?"

Go to movies	69%
Never go to movies	31
Total	100%
Base - all interviews	500

Question: "Do you (plural) see more films in English or Spanish?"

See more films in English	47% *
See more films in Spanish	16
Both the same	35
Don't know or no answer	2
Total	100%
Base - families that go to movies	338

*All the respondents spoke Spanish.

Question: "How many adults and how many children of your family live here?"

	Adults	Children	All
One	9%	16%	2%
Two	65	17	10
Three	17	15	14
Four	6	12	16
Five	1	9	18
Six	1	6	14
Seven or more	1	8	26
None	-	17	-
Total	100%	100%	100%
Base - all interviews	500	500	500
Average per family (arithmetic mean)	2.3	2.9	5.2

Among families with children, the average number of children is 3.5.

Question: "What are the ages of the children?"

Under 6 years	60%
6 to 12 years	67
13 to 19 years	40
Total	167%
Base - families with children	415

Question: "What is the age of the head of the family?"

29 or younger	16%
30 - 39 years	32
40 - 49 years	22
50 - 59 years	13
60 - 69 years	8
70 - 79 years	2
80 or older	1
Don't know or no answer	6
Total	100%
Base	500

EDUCATION, OCCUPATION OF HEAD OF FAMILY

Question: "What was the last year of school the head of the family attended?"

No schooling	11%
Went to grade school, did not finish	27
Finished grade school	16
Went to high school, did not finish	19
Finished high school	12
Went to college, did not graduate	3
Graduated from college	2
Don't know or no answer	10
Total	100%
Base - all interviews	500

Question: "What is the occupation of the head of the family?"

Professional and technical	4%
Farmers, ranchers	-
Clerical and kindred workers, sales workers	8
Craftsmen, skilled workers, operatives, laborers	58
Service workers	13
Unemployed	6
Housewife, widow	4
Student	-
Retired, on pension	4
Armed forces	1
No answer, refused	2
Total	100%
Base - all interviews	500

NATIVITY OF MEXICAN-AMERICAN HOUSEWIVES

Question: "In what country were you born?"

U. S. A.	70%
Mexico	27
Other country	2
No answer	1
Total	100%
Base - all interviews	500

CITY AND COUNTY POPULATIONS -- DESCRIPTION

The population figures in the following section represent the 1960 U. S. Census count of Spanish surnames in Arizona, California, Colorado, New Mexico, and Texas -- the only states where such an analysis has been made. These data are the most extensive and only uniform population count of this group across the United States.

Beginning in 1930, the Census has attempted various definitions involving "Mexicans," "Spanish mother tongue," and "Spanish surname" in classifying the population of Spanish-American and Mexican-American descent. Probably Spanish surname comes closest to providing a total count, and this was the criterion used both in 1950 and 1960.

Admittedly, however, a count of Spanish surnames alone omits some people of non-Spanish names who are nevertheless Spanish-speaking and of Latin origin. Using Census data and our own research, we have arrived at an adjustment factor to correct, at least to a great extent, for this deflation. In the third column, "Total Mexican-Americans," in the following tables we have provided these projections, amounting to 5.8 per cent over the Spanish surname count. We have tested this factor empirically; that is, by actual field studies we have determined the proportion of persons who are Spanish-speaking and of Latin origin, but who do not have Spanish surnames. This has been done in the course of surveys in four different Southwestern cities in which samplings of Latin-appearing respondents were all interviewed in Spanish and had their names recorded; a count of non-Spanish names then revealed the adjustment necessary. (While it is true that there are some non-Latin people with Spanish surnames, our conclusion has been that this is a negligible factor.) The adjustment has been applied uniformly to all cities and counties, in the absence of more detailed data by locality.

We have called this projected population "Mexican-American" because the vast majority undoubtedly is of Mexican origin, whether from recent migration from Mexico or dating back to the Spanish-Colonial era. In addition to past Census data and years of first-hand observation, a clue to this origin is provided on page A-18: 27 per cent of the housewives interviewed said they had been born in Mexico, and only 2 per cent gave another foreign country.

From a marketing point of view, it is these five Southwestern states that contain most of the Mexican-Americans in the U. S., thus presenting a certain market homogeneity in background, language peculiarities, and geographical concentration. Other Spanish-speaking populations, such as Puerto Rican and Cuban, residing mostly in other areas of the country, have not been a part of this analysis. Neither has there been any attempt to represent the annual swelling of this market by the temporary entry of Mexican aliens as farm laborers.

The total Mexican-American population of these five states for 1960 has been projected to 3,666,278. The Census has reported an increase of 51.3 per cent between 1950 and 1960 in the number of persons of Spanish surname in this area. By states, this has been the increase:

	1960	1950	Increase
Arizona.	194,356	128,318	51.5%
California	1,426,538	760,453	87.6%
Colorado	157,173	118,131	33.0%
New Mexico	269,122	248,880	8.1%
Texas	1,417,811	1,033,768	37.1%

Growth has undoubtedly continued in most areas since 1960 (between 1950 and 1960 the rate was about 4 per cent per year for the over-all five-state Spanish surname population).

Cities bordering Mexico should be viewed in relation to the population on both sides of the border, all of the portion on the Mexican side, of course, being Spanish-speaking. Such cities as Brownsville, Laredo, El Paso, and San Diego usually serve economies considerably larger than their U. S. populations indicate. Many residents of Mexico work and shop daily on the U. S. side.

The Spanish surname count is a projection by the Census from its 25 per cent sampling used to determine all population characteristics; therefore, the figures are not intended as exact head counts, and neither are our projections to total Mexican-Americans. The adequacy of a Spanish surname count as a measure of this population has been verified in a number of our marketing studies. We have made probability samplings of all households in several cities containing large numbers of Mexican-Americans. In every instance the proportion of Mexican-Americans produced by the samplings has been very close to the proportion our Mexican-American population projection is of total population.

The definitions used by the U. S. Census have been adopted here for "standard statistical metropolitan area" and "urban place."

	1960 U.S. Census		Total
	Total Population	Spanish Surnames	Mexican-Americans
The State	1,302,161	194,356	205,646
Standard Metropolitan Statistical Areas			
Phoenix	663,510	78,996	83,585
Tucson	265,660	44,481	47,065
Urban Places of 10,000 or More With 2,500 or More of Spanish Surname			
Douglas	11,925	6,652	7,038
Flagstaff	18,214	3,308	3,500
Mesa	33,772	2,773	2,934
Phoenix	439,170	40,241	42,579
Tucson	212,892	35,722	37,797
Yuma	23,976	4,522	4,785
Counties			
Apache	30,438	960	1,016
Cochise	55,039	13,764	14,564
Coconino	41,857	4,341	4,593
Gila	25,745	5,633	5,960
Graham	14,045	2,433	2,574
Greenlee	11,509	5,238	5,542
Maricopa	663,510	78,996	83,585
Mohave	7,736	565	598
Navajo	37,994	2,604	2,755
Pima	265,660	44,481	47,065
Pinal	62,673	17,343	18,351
Santa Cruz	10,808	6,222	6,583
Yavapai	28,912	2,463	2,606
Yuma	46,235	9,313	9,854

	1960 U.S. Census		Total
	Total Population	Spanish Surnames	Mexican-Americans
The State	15,717,204	1,426,538	1,509,404
Standard Metropolitan Statistical Areas			
Bakersfield	291,984	29,219	30,916
Fresno	365,945	61,418	64,986
Los Angeles - Long Beach	6,742,696	629,292	665,847
Sacramento	502,778	30,078	31,825
San Bernardino - Riverside - Ontario	809,782	96,401	102,001
San Diego	1,033,011	64,810	68,575
San Francisco - Oakland	2,783,359	177,239	187,535
San Jose	642,315	77,755	82,272
Santa Barbara	168,962	22,267	23,560
Stockton	249,989	30,585	32,362
Urban Places of 10,000 or More With 2,500 or More of Spanish Surname			
Alameda	63,855	2,840	3,005
Alhambra	54,807	3,153	3,336
Anaheim	104,184	5,315	5,624
Bakersfield	56,848	4,422	4,679
Baldwin Park	33,951	3,340	3,534
Berkeley	111,268	3,759	3,977
Brawley	12,703	4,731	5,006
Buena Park	46,401	3,149	3,332
Burbank	90,155	2,868	3,035
Compton	71,812	6,495	6,872
Daly City	44,791	2,912	3,081
Downey	82,505	3,722	3,938
El Centro	16,811	3,296	3,487
Fremont	43,790	5,147	5,446
Fresno	133,929	13,669	14,463
Fullerton	56,180	3,271	3,461

Urban Places of 10,000 or More With 2,500 or More of Spanish Surname Continued	1960 U. S. Census Total Population	Spanish Surnames	Total Mexican-Americans
Glendale	119,442	3,595	3,804
Hanford	10,133	2,672	2,827
Hayward	72,700	8,243	8,722
Long Beach	334,168	7,857	8,313
Los Angeles	2,479,015	260,389	275,515
Madera	14,430	3,513	3,717
Merced	20,068	3,339	3,533
Montebello	32,097	7,019	7,427
Monterey Park	37,821	4,944	5,231
Mountain View	30,889	3,591	3,800
National City	32,771	4,150	4,391
Norwalk	88,739	13,321	14,095
Oakland	367,548	23,729	25,107
Ontario	46,617	4,266	4,514
Oxnard	40,265	12,793	13,536
Pasadena	116,407	5,188	5,489
Pico Rivera	49,150	14,596	15,444
Pomona	67,157	6,161	6,519
Redlands	26,829	3,244	3,432
Redondo Beach	46,986	2,831	2,995
Richmond	71,854	5,050	5,343
Riverside	84,332	7,199	7,617
Sacramento	191,667	14,651	15,502
Salinas	28,957	3,501	3,704
San Bernardino	91,922	16,460	17,416
San Diego	573,224	38,043	40,253
San Francisco	740,316	51,602	54,600
San Jose	204,196	28,596	30,257
San Leandro	65,962	6,036	6,387
Santa Ana	100,350	15,372	16,265
Santa Barbara	58,768	8,616	9,116
Santa Clara	58,880	7,048	7,457
Santa Monica	83,249	5,145	5,444
Santa Paula	13,279	4,404	4,660

Urban Places of 10,000 or More With 2,500 or More of Spanish Surname Continued	1960 U. S. Census Total Population	Spanish Surnames	Total Mexican-Americans
South San Francisco	39,418	3,428	3,627
Stockton	86,321	12,017	12,715
Sunnyvale	59,898	4,808	5,087
Torrance	100,991	4,808	4,325
Alisal	16,473	2,581	2,731
Carson	38,059	3,377	3,573
East Los Angeles	104,270	70,802	74,915
Florence - Graham	38,164	10,964	11,601
South Sacramento - Fruitridge	16,443	3,923	4,151
Counties			
Alameda	905,670	67,866	71,808
Alpine	397	-	-
Amador	9,990	612	647
Butte	82,030	2,179	2,306
Calaveras	10,289	468	495
Colusa	12,075	1,152	1,219
Contra Costa	409,030	24,854	26,298
Del Norte	17,771	245	259
El Dorado	29,390	696	736
Fresno	365,945	61,418	64,986
Glenn	17,245	1,128	1,193
Humboldt	104,892	2,268	2,400
Imperial	72,105	23,850	25,235
Inyo	11,684	414	438
Kern	291,984	29,219	30,916
Kings	49,954	11,656	12,333
Lake	13,786	358	379
Lassen	13,597	1,009	1,068
Los Angeles	6,038,771	576,716	610,217
Madera	40,468	6,225	6,587
Marin	146,820	5,634	5,961
Mariposa	5,064	116	123

Counties Continued	1960 U. S. Census Total Population	Spanish Surnames	Total Mexican-Americans
Mendocino	51,059	1,201	1,271
Merced	90,446	13,429	14,209
Modoc	8,308	166	176
Mono	2,213	32	34
Monterey	198,351	23,118	24,461
Napa	65,890	2,715	2,873
Nevada	20,911	508	537
Orange	703,925	52,576	55,630
Placer	56,998	3,729	3,946
Plumas	11,620	305	323
Riverside	306,191	36,224	38,328
Sacramento	502,778	30,078	31,825
San Benito	15,396	4,642	4,912
San Bernardino	503,591	60,177	63,673
San Diego	1,033,011	64,810	68,575
San Francisco	742,855	51,602	54,599
San Joaquin	249,989	30,585	32,362
San Luis Obispo	81,044	5,788	6,124
San Mateo	444,387	19,722	20,868
Santa Barbara	168,962	22,267	23,560
Santa Clara	642,315	77,755	82,272
Santa Cruz	84,219	5,774	6,109
Shasta	59,468	1,202	1,272
Sierra	2,247	125	132
Siskiyou	32,885	1,363	1,442
Solano	134,597	7,561	8,000
Sonoma	147,375	5,196	5,498
Stanislaus	157,294	11,866	12,555
Sutter	33,380	1,747	1,848
Tehama	25,305	931	985
Trinity	9,706	48	51
Tulare	168,403	27,387	28,978
Tuolumne	14,404	766	810
Ventura	199,138	33,980	35,954
Yola	65,727	7,757	8,208
Yuba	33,859	1,323	1,400

	1960 U.S. Census		Total
	Total Population	Spanish Surnames	Mexican-Americans
The State	1,753,947	157,173	166,303
Standard Metropolitan Statistical Areas			
Denver	929,383	60,294	63,796
Colorado Springs	143,742	6,135	6,491
Pueblo	118,707	25,437	26,915
Urban Places of 10,000 or More With 2,500 or More of Spanish Surname			
Colorado Springs	70,194	3,471	3,673
Denver	493,887	43,147	45,653
Pueblo	91,181	16,036	16,968
Trinidad	10,691	3,688	3,902
Counties			
Adams	120,296	8,542	9,038
Alamosa	10,000	2,494	2,639
Arapahoe	113,426	2,987	3,161
Archuleta	2,629	953	1,008
Baca	6,310	172	182
Bent	7,419	1,454	1,539
Boulder	74,254	3,103	3,283
Chaffee	8,298	732	775
Cheyenne	2,789	8	9
Clear Creek	2,793	17	18
Conejos	8,428	4,476	4,736
Costilla	4,219	3,065	3,243
Crowley	3,978	1,023	1,083
Custer	1,305	93	98
Delta	15,602	1,173	1,241
Denver	493,887	43,147	45,653

Counties Continued	1960 U. S. Census Total Population	1960 U. S. Census Spanish Surnames	Total Mexican-Americans
Dolores	2,196	3	3
Douglas	4,816	191	202
Eagle	4,677	1,187	1,256
Elbert	3,708	62	66
El Paso	143,742	6,135	6,491
Fremont	20,196	1,798	1,902
Garfield	12,017	285	302
Gilpin	685	75	79
Grand	3,557	91	96
Gunnison	5,477	142	150
Hinsdale	208	3	3
Huerfano	7,867	3,608	3,818
Jackson	1,758	58	61
Jefferson	127,520	2,515	2,661
Kiowa	2,425	17	18
Kit Carson	6,957	69	73
Lake	7,101	901	953
La Plata	19,225	2,346	2,482
Larimer	53,343	2,160	2,286
Las Animas	19,983	7,443	7,875
Lincoln	5,310	58	61
Logan	20,302	839	888
Mesa	50,715	2,612	2,764
Mineral	424	3	3
Moffat	7,061	207	219
Montezuma	14,024	901	953
Montrose	18,286	1,291	1,366
Morgan	21,192	1,642	1,737
Otero	24,128	5,328	5,638
Ouray	1,601	217	230
Park	1,822	39	41
Phillips	4,440	31	33
Pitkin	2,381	4	4
Prowers	13,296	1,424	1,507

Counties Continued	1960 U.S. Census Total Population	1960 U.S. Census Spanish Surnames	Total Mexican-Americans
Pueblo	118,707	25,437	26,915
Rio Blanco	5,150	32	34
Rio Grande	11,160	3,477	3,679
Routt	5,900	99	105
Saguache	4,473	1,411	1,493
San Juan	849	145	153
San Miguel	2,944	132	140
Sedgwick	4,242	322	341
Summit	2,073	22	23
Teller	2,495	20	21
Washington	6,625	46	49
Weld	72,344	8,831	9,344
Yuma	8,912	75	79

POPULATION -- NEW MEXICO

	1960 U. S. Census Total Population	1960 U. S. Census Spanish Surnames	Total Mexican-Americans
The State	961,023	269,122	284,755
Standard Metropolitan Statistical Area			
Albuquerque	262,199	68,101	72,057
Urban Places of 10,000 or More With 2,500 or More of Spanish Surname			
Alamogordo	21,723	3,497	3,700
Albuquerque	201,189	43,790	46,334
Artesia	12,000	2,803	2,966
Carlsbad	25,541	4,317	4,568
Clovis	23,713	3,103	3,283
Gallup	14,089	4,404	4,660
Grants	10,274	3,022	3,198
Las Cruces	29,367	10,244	10,839
Roswell	39,593	5,628	5,955
Santa Fe	34,676	17,635	18,659
Counties			
Bernalillo	262,199	68,101	72,057
Catron	2,773	755	799
Chaves	57,649	7,784	8,236
Colfax	13,806	5,535	5,857
Curry	32,691	3,676	3,890
De Baca	2,991	748	791
Dona Ana	59,948	25,214	26,679
Eddy	50,783	11,224	11,876
Grant	18,700	8,820	9,332
Guadalupe	5,610	4,068	4,304
Harding	1,874	497	526
Hidalgo	4,961	2,013	2,130

Counties Continued	1960 U. S. Census Total Population	1960 U. S. Census Spanish Surnames	Total Mexican-Americans
Lea	53,429	2,555	2,703
Lincoln	7,744	2,240	2,370
Los Alamos	13,037	1,463	1,548
Luna	9,839	3,388	3,585
McKinley	37,209	4,521	4,784
Mora	6,028	5,148	5,447
Otero	36,976	5,891	6,233
Quay	12,279	3,604	3,813
Rio Arriba	24,193	16,835	17,813
Roosevelt	16,198	1,024	1,083
Sandoval	14,201	4,538	4,802
San Juan	53,306	3,645	3,857
San Miguel	23,468	16,077	17,011
Santa Fe	44,970	24,400	25,817
Sierra	6,409	1,382	1,462
Socorro	10,168	4,761	5,038
Taos	15,934	11,015	11,655
Torrance	6,497	2,710	2,867
Union	6,068	1,472	1,558
Valencia	39,085	14,018	14,832

	1960 U. S. Census Total Population	1960 U. S. Census Spanish Surnames	Total Mexican-Americans
The State	9,579,677	1,417,811	1,500,170
Standard Metropolitan Statistical Areas Of 250,000 or More With 25,000 or More Of Spanish Surname			
Dallas	1,083,601	36,990	39,139
El Paso	314,070	136,993	144,951
Houston	1,243,158	75,013	79,370
San Antonio	687,151	257,090	272,024
Standard Metropolitan Statistical Areas Of Less than 250,000 With 2,500 or More Of Spanish Surname			
Abilene	120,377	6,676	7,064
Amarillo	149,493	3,717	3,933
Austin	212,136	26,072	27,586
Brownsville - Harlingen - San Benito	151,098	96,744	102,364
Corpus Christi	221,573	84,386	89,288
Galveston - Texas City	140,364	11,872	12,562
Laredo	64,791	51,784	54,792
Lubbock	156,271	17,003	17,991
Midland	67,717	4,004	4,237
Odessa	90,995	7,000	7,407
San Angelo	64,630	8,876	9,392
Waco	150,091	7,801	8,254
Wichita Falls	129,638	3,494	3,697
Urban Places of 10,000 or More With 2,500 or More of Spanish Surname			
Abilene	90,368	4,568	4,833
Alice	20,861	11,086	11,730
Amarillo	137,969	3,717	3,933

Urban Places of 10,000 or More With 2,500 or More of Spanish Surname Continued	1960 U.S. Census Total Population	1960 U.S. Census Spanish Surnames	Total Mexican-Americans
Austin	186,545	23,872	25,259
Beeville	13,811	6,181	6,540
Big Spring	31,230	3,251	3,440
Brownsville	48,040	35,440	37,499
Bryan	27,542	2,861	3,027
Corpus Christi	167,690	59,859	63,336
Dallas	679,684	29,464	31,176
Del Rio	18,612	10,237	10,832
Eagle Pass	12,094	10,404	11,008
Edinburg	18,706	13,441	14,222
El Paso	276,687	125,745	133,049
Fort Worth	356,268	16,322	17,270
Galveston	67,175	7,997	8,462
Harlingen	41,207	20,309	21,489
Houston	938,219	63,372	67,053
Kingsville	25,297	10,929	11,564
Laredo	60,678	49,819	52,713
Lubbock	128,691	11,672	12,350
McAllen	32,728	20,187	21,360
Mercedes	10,943	9,161	9,693
Midland	62,625	4,004	4,237
Mission	14,081	10,029	10,612
New Braunfels	15,631	4,880	5,163
Odessa	80,338	6,144	6,501
Pecos	12,728	4,180	4,423
Pharr	14,106	10,054	10,638
Port Arthur	66,767	3,227	3,414
San Angelo	58,815	8,211	8,688
San Antonio	587,718	243,627	257,779
San Benito	16,422	11,857	12,546
San Marcos	12,713	5,424	5,739
Seguin	14,299	4,620	4,888
Uvalde	10,293	5,222	5,525
Victoria	33,047	7,160	7,576

Urban Places of 10,000 or More With 2,500 or More of Spanish Surname Continued	1960 U. S. Census Total Population	Spanish Surnames	Total Mexican-Americans
Waco	97,808	5,632	5,959
Weslaco	15,649	12,114	12,818
Wichita Falls	101,724	3,244	3,432
Counties			
Anderson	28,162	397	420
Andrews	13,450	525	556
Angelina	39,814	530	561
Aransas	7,006	1,368	1,447
Archer	6,110	50	53
Armstrong	1,966	21	22
Atascosa	18,828	8,545	9,041
Austin	13,777	240	254
Bailey	9,090	1,129	1,195
Bandera	3,892	262	277
Bastrop	16,925	1,819	1,925
Baylor	5,893	132	140
Bee	23,755	8,580	9,078
Bell	94,097	6,332	6,700
Bexar	687,151	257,090	272,024
Blanco	3,657	235	249
Borden	1,076	-	-
Bosque	10,809	235	249
Bowie	59,971	652	690
Brazoria	76,204	5,172	5,472
Brazos	44,895	3,572	3,780
Brewster	6,434	2,743	2,902
Briscoe	3,577	396	419
Brooks	8,609	5,928	6,272
Brown	24,728	1,346	1,424
Burleson	11,177	765	809
Burnet	9,265	756	800
Caldwell	17,222	4,905	5,190

Counties Continued	1960 U. S. Census Total Population	1960 U. S. Census Spanish Surnames	Total Mexican-Americans
Calhoun	16,592	4,170	4,412
Callahan	7,929	190	201
Cameron	151,098	96,744	102,364
Camp	7,849	91	96
Carson	7,781	359	380
Cass	23,496	94	100
Castro	8,923	1,368	1,448
Chambers	10,379	185	196
Cherokee	33,120	503	532
Childress	8,421	277	293
Clay	8,351	110	116
Cochran	6,417	1,274	1,348
Coke	3,589	244	258
Coleman	12,458	591	625
Collin	41,247	1,132	1,198
Collingsworth	6,276	259	274
Colorado	18,463	1,181	1,250
Comal	19,844	5,431	5,747
Comanche	11,865	239	253
Concho	3,672	738	781
Cooke	22,560	429	454
Coryell	23,961	1,040	1,100
Cottle	4,207	495	524
Crane	4,699	119	126
Crockett	4,209	1,098	1,162
Crosby	10,347	2,084	2,205
Culberson	2,794	1,075	1,138
Dallam	6,302	437	462
Dallas	951,527	32,741	34,643
Dawson	19,185	4,569	4,834
Deaf Smith	13,187	2,468	2,611
Delta	5,860	8	8
Denton	47,432	885	936
DeWitt	20,683	3,928	4,156
Dickens	4,963	383	405

Counties Continued	1960 U. S. Census Total Population	Spanish Surnames	Total Mexican-Americans
Dimmit	10,095	6,760	7,153
Donley	4,449	42	44
Duval	13,398	9,788	10,356
Eastland	19,526	814	861
Ector	90,995	7,000	7,407
Edwards	2,317	764	808
Ellis	43,395	2,232	2,362
El Paso	314,070	136,993	144,951
Erath	16,236	147	155
Falls	21,263	1,783	1,886
Fannin	23,880	273	289
Fayette	20,384	423	448
Fisher	7,865	1,138	1,204
Floyd	12,369	1,965	2,079
Foard	3,125	157	166
Fort Bend	40,527	9,972	10,551
Franklin	5,101	11	12
Freestone	12,525	28	30
Frio	10,112	6,250	6,613
Gaines	12,267	1,003	1,061
Galveston	140,364	11,872	12,562
Garza	6,611	907	960
Gillespie	10,048	379	401
Glasscock	1,118	100	106
Goliad	5,429	1,900	2,010
Gonzales	17,845	3,594	3,803
Gray	31,535	168	178
Grayson	73,043	1,275	1,349
Gregg	69,436	258	273
Grimes	12,709	545	577
Guadalupe	29,017	6,871	7,270
Hale	36,798	6,504	6,882
Hall	7,322	321	340
Hamilton	8,488	193	204
Hansford	6,208	70	74

Counties Continued	1960 U. S. Census Total Population	Spanish Surnames	Total Mexican-Americans
Hardeman	8,275	382	404
Hardin	24,629	256	271
Harris	1,243,158	75,013	79,370
Harrison	45,594	250	265
Hartley	2,171	95	100
Haskell	11,174	1,155	1,222
Hays	19,934	7,208	7,627
Hemphill	3,185	84	89
Henderson	21,786	67	71
Hidalgo	180,904	129,092	136,591
Hill	23,650	843	892
Hockley	22,340	3,537	3,742
Hood	5,443	96	102
Hopkins	18,594	282	298
Houston	19,376	526	557
Howard	40,139	4,091	4,329
Hudspeth	3,343	982	1,039
Hunt	39,399	217	230
Hutchinson	34,419	379	401
Irion	1,183	198	209
Jack	7,418	59	62
Jackson	14,040	1,929	2,041
Jasper	22,100	170	180
Jeff Davis	1,582	887	939
Jefferson	245,659	6,571	6,953
Jim Hogg	5,022	3,861	4,085
Jim Wells	34,548	18,848	19,943
Johnson	34,720	593	627
Jones	19,299	1,644	1,739
Karnes	14,995	5,595	5,920
Kaufman	29,931	323	342
Kendall	5,889	698	739
Kenedy	884	712	753
Kent	1,727	23	24
Kerr	16,800	1,920	2,032

Counties Continued	1960 U. S. Census Total Population	1960 U. S. Census Spanish Surnames	Total Mexican-Americans
Kimble	3,943	533	564
King	640	13	14
Kinney	2,452	1,166	1,234
Kleberg	30,052	12,514	13,241
Knox	7,857	709	750
Lamar	34,234	66	70
Lamb	21,896	3,562	3,769
Lampasas	9,418	702	743
LaSalle	5,972	3,832	4,055
Lavaca	20,174	933	987
Lee	8,949	247	261
Leon	9,951	52	55
Liberty	31,595	251	266
Limestone	20,413	432	457
Lipscomb	3,406	26	27
Live Oak	7,846	2,686	2,842
Llano	5,240	205	217
Loving	226	-	-
Lubbock	156,271	17,003	17,991
Lynn	10,914	2,092	2,213
McCulloch	8,815	1,308	1,384
McLennan	150,091	7,801	8,254
McMullen	1,116	314	332
Madison	6,749	52	55
Marion	8,049	21	22
Martin	5,068	787	833
Mason	3,780	323	342
Matagorda	25,744	3,582	3,790
Maverick	14,508	11,253	11,907
Medina	18,904	6,998	7,404
Menard	2,964	694	734
Midland	67,717	4,423	4,680
Milam	22,263	1,262	1,335
Mills	4,467	98	104
Mitchell	11,255	1,870	1,979

Counties Continued	1960 U. S. Census Total Population	1960 U. S. Census Spanish Surnames	Total Mexican-Americans
Montague	14,893	120	127
Montgomery	26,839	414	438
Moore	14,773	321	340
Morris	12,576	136	144
Motley	2,870	142	150
Nacogdoches	28,046	566	599
Navarro	34,423	584	618
Newton	10,372	50	53
Nolan	18,963	1,726	1,826
Nueces	221,573	84,386	89,288
Ochiltree	9,380	131	139
Oldham	1,928	10	11
Orange	60,357	1,548	1,638
Palo Pinto	20,516	852	901
Panola	16,870	140	148
Parker	22,880	471	498
Parmer	9,583	981	1,038
Pecos	11,957	3,708	3,923
Polk	13,861	157	166
Potter	115,580	3,668	3,881
Presidio	5,460	2,700	2,857
Rains	2,993	-	-
Randall	33,913	336	356
Reagan	3,782	512	542
Real	2,079	402	425
Red River	15,682	34	36
Reeves	17,644	7,128	7,542
Refugio	10,975	3,484	3,686
Roberts	1,075	-	-
Robertson	16,157	1,084	1,147
Rockwall	5,878	230	243
Runnels	15,016	1,698	1,797
Rusk	36,421	125	132
Sabine	7,302	16	17
San Augustine	7,722	26	27

Counties Continued	1960 U. S. Census Total Population	1960 U. S. Census Spanish Surnames	Total Mexican-Americans
San Jacinto	6,153	32	34
San Patricio	45,021	22,239	23,531
San Saba	6,381	582	616
Schleicher	2,791	579	613
Scurry	20,369	1,730	1,830
Shackelford	3,990	16	17
Shelby	20,479	-	-
Sherman	2,605	52	55
Smith	86,350	613	649
Somervell	2,577	51	54
Starr	17,137	15,196	16,079
Stephens	8,885	194	205
Sterling	1,177	154	163
Stonewall	3,017	22	23
Sutton	3,738	1,476	1,562
Swisher	10,607	999	1,057
Tarrant	538,495	19,373	20,498
Taylor	101,078	5,032	5,324
Terrell	2,600	1,128	1,194
Terry	16,286	2,460	2,603
Throckmorton	2,767	86	91
Titus	16,785	46	49
Tom Green	64,630	8,876	9,392
Travis	212,136	26,072	27,586
Trinity	7,539	-	-
Tyler	10,666	53	56
Upshur	19,793	20	21
Upton	6,239	776	821
Uvalde	16,814	8,002	8,467
Val Verde	24,461	10,814	11,442
Van Zandt	19,091	155	164
Victoria	46,475	10,767	11,393
Walker	21,475	584	618
Waller	12,071	331	350
Ward	14,917	1,792	1,896

Counties Continued	1960 U. S. Census Total Population	1960 U. S. Census Spanish Surnames	Total Mexican-Americans
Washington	19,145	106	112
Webb	64,791	51,784	54,792
Wharton	38,152	5,664	5,993
Wheeler	7,947	47	50
Wichita	123,528	3,444	3,644
Wilbarger	17,748	583	617
Willacy	20,084	13,734	14,532
Williamson	35,044	5,284	5,591
Wilson	13,267	4,911	5,196
Winkler	13,652	917	970
Wise	17,012	237	251
Wood	17,653	59	62
Yoakum	8,032	360	381
Young	17,254	208	220
Zapata	4,393	3,285	3,476
Zavala	12,696	9,440	9,988

THE VAQUERO

Nicholas S. Firfires

THE VAQUERO

by

ARNOLD R. ROJAS

Illustrated by

NICHOLAS S. FIRFIRES

McNally and Loftin, Publishers
Charlotte / Santa Barbara

Library of Congress Catalog Card Number 64-17234

PRINTED IN THE UNITED STATES OF AMERICA
BY HERITAGE PRINTERS, INC., CHARLOTTE, N. C.

To Billy Polkinhorn,
my friend and pupil,
who loves the lore
of the California vaquero.

Preface

With the publication of this book, *Vaquero,* A. R. Rojas completes the demolition of a mountain of apocrypha hitherto burying the truth about western horsemen and horses. Mr. Rojas' three earlier books, a trilogy of notable literary achievement, were successful precursors of this final definitive volume. I believe him to be the foremost authority on the tradition and history of the western horseman. *Vaquero* gives more information about the genesis of the western horse and the western horseman than any other book within my experience.

There is so much fiction, so great a mass of erroneous matter in connection with the vaquero and that misnomer, the "cowboy," that it is a fine thing a genuine vaquero of fifty years in the saddle—for such is Rojas—has been at pains to set down the facts. It is a particularly happy circumstance, one of those fortuitous things we encounter in life, that Mr. Rojas, a man of practically no formal education as a writer, has the talent of being able to write well. He has a delightful style reminiscent of the late Cunningham-Graham, and he is that very rare man indeed, a natural story teller.

Mr. Rojas is a master of the "conte" form of writing, a brief story of cleverly selected details and single, strong impact. In this book are a number of such charming stories embellishing the history of the horse in the West and the Spanish tradition of its rider.

It will be a very useful publication indeed, for it will set the record straight for those perceptive enough to read it with respect to the "boloney" perpetuated by "western" movies produced in a rigid pattern of literary cliché at almost complete odds with the western horseman as he really existed since the origin of western horsemen with the Spanish Conquest and the end of it in the 1920's when cattle handling was changed on the great ranches.

J. F. M. (Jim) Day
Managing Editor
Bakersfield *Californian*

Contents

Introduction

The vaquero, as I knew him, was the embodiment of all the heroes that I had read of in books.

In the years since Miller and Lux and other great cattle outfits passed out of existence, millions of words have been written about the West, but little about the real vaquero or buckaroo.

Much valuable history has been lost because of the inability of the vaquero, under the handicaps of language, lack of schooling, or indifference on the part of those who could have written them, to get his experiences into print.

I have managed to salvage some of the lore, although I met the vaquero, as my friend Arthur Woodward says, "at the tag end of a great era in California history." I managed to make contact with some of the men who had lived during the Gold Rush period, and who remembered the tales their great-grandfathers and grandfathers had told them. They were natural story-tellers whose talents went back many generations to the Arabs, the fathers transmitting it to the sons from one generation to another. The *viejos*, the old men, I knew had a gift for capturing the mood of the vaquero, his joy and his grief, his humor and his sorrow, his nostalgia and his pride. I have no individual heroes or heroines. I but tell of things as they were and of men as they were—of simple men who toiled, hungered, froze, or scorched in doing a job which required skill and courage.

It has been said that we learn more of history from fiction than from our schoolbooks, that fiction has a wider influence than generally accepted historical accounts. This may hold true in one respect, that is in the influence of fiction on the reader, but it is not true that it teaches facts. He who writes of incidents as they happened has no need of fiction.

If this narrative had been a work of fiction, I could have followed the rule of the "Western" writer and shaped it in a different fashion, but in dealing with facts we cannot let our imagination run roughshod over truth.

In undertaking this work I hope to right a common misunderstanding. I saw that the vaquero was almost universally confused with the cowboy, and that the actual Westerner, the vaquero or buckaroo, was not given his rightful place in history. Having shared his tobacco, I must out of loyalty defend him. No one can expect to portray the whole pattern of the vaquero's life. In a factual book such as this there can be little continuity; the events did not happen so. At best the sketches must be short. The events described here are true as they were told to me, and as accurate as I can make them. Whoever reads this will know that this is the way it was in the old days.

Some of the men who told me stories have risen to wealth or high station, but having once been vaqueros or buckaroos, they must, in memory at least, remain vaqueros all their lives.

The stories of bandits and the legends, many of which had their origin in Spain, were so much a part of the vaquero's life that his story would not be complete without them. They may be history, legend, or tradition; they are tales which changed in name and locale with each telling.

This book is not an attempt at history. It is just one man's picture of a time which has passed and will never come again. It is a picture of the men with whom I worked, talked, and lived. It is an effort to bring to the printed page old California in an era full of epic heroism, of which the heroes were totally unaware.

Little of what I write here was learned from books. I write of what I have learned on the range, at the campfire, in the dust of the corral, and the reader can trust what he reads in this book, because this is the only way these incidents could have happened.

Vaquero is, in part, the story of the men who herded cattle in the Far West, of the men who rode far and hard and suffered many hardships in making their living. But hardships, however painful to endure, are pleasant to look back upon, and old buckaroos have told these stories with a fond retrospective chuckle. Time rubs off the sharp edges, and even the roughest experiences on the cattle ranges are remembered with the strongest interest and nostalgia—and sometimes exaggeration.

The horse lore comes from men who have studied the history of the horse in Spain and Spanish America, from students of hippology who have pored over many old records from throughout the Spanish speaking world to find a thread of truth in a mesh of fable. The lore has been traced through words written in English, Spanish, and Portuguese.

Much has come from Spain, Argentina, Mexico, Brazil, Portugal, and from men who have studied the actual history of the West. Besides the good people in Europe and Latin America who have supplied me with information, I am indebted to Irving "Bob" Robertson of Carson City, Nevada, and to the vaqueros and buckaroos who worked in Nevada, Oregon, Montana, and Arizona. I am indebted to Mrs. Bernice Harrell Chipman, Walter Kane, Jim Day, and Ralph Kreiser of the *Bakersfield Californian*, without whose help, constant friendship, and encouragement this book would never have come into being.

ARNOLD R. ROJAS

Calexico, California
January 28, 1964

THE VAQUERO

Cowboy *Vaquero*

Loyalty

Although the terms "cowboy," "vaquero," and "buckaroo" have in the past been used interchangeably and indiscriminately, to do so is not, as a matter of fact, wholly accurate. They are not actually synonymous, because there is a vast difference between the cowboy and the vaquero or buckaroo.

This may sound contradictory to those who are not familiar with the terms used in the actual West. To explain the difference in terminology we must go back into early history. In the United States there are two systems or styles of working cattle, or, rather, two kinds of herdsmen. One, the vaquero, is Hispanic in origin; the other, the cowboy, is African in origin. The herdsman of the North is a composite of the two styles.

By vaquero or buckaroo is meant the original rider—Spaniard, Mexican, Indian, or Anglo—who herded cattle in the far western states and the territory of Hawaii, that is to say, in California, Nevada, Oregon, Arizona, Utah, and Washington, and in parts of Idaho, Montana, Wyoming, and British Columbia.

By cowboy is meant the Negroes and whites who herded cattle in the southern states, from the Atlantic seaboard to the eastern base of the Rocky Mountains, and from the Gulf of Mexico to Canada.

The vaquero or buckaroo is a Westerner in fact. The cowboy is a Southerner, however people may call his territory the "West." The rider of the northern states, like the buckaroo of the Pacific slope, is of Yankee stock. Although there was a great Irish migration into the Northwest, the culture of the real or actual Westerner is entirely Yankee.

The cowboy's territory is east of the Rockies; the vaquero's is west of this great barrier. The vaquero or buckaroo is unlike the cowboy in many ways: their racial background, lingo, character, methods of working cattle, and conception of what a horseman should be are different, even when the vaquero, buckaroo, or cowboy happen to be Anglo, Negro, Spaniard, Mexican, or Indian.

Vaqueros, buckaroos, and cowboys drove the same Spanish cattle, rode the same Spanish mustang, met the same dangers and difficulties in their work. They ate the same kind of food, suffered the same hardships, yet were as far apart as East and West.

The vaquero's pride was in having a bridle hand; the cowboy had to have a horse that knew more about working cattle than its rider. That is to say, the horse worked cattle of its own accord, without the guidance of its rider. This instinct, however, is common in all horses that work cattle, from Tierra del Fuego to Canada.

The difference was that the vaquero's and buckaroo's horse, besides having *amor al ganado*, love for cattle, as this instinct is called in California, also had a trigger rein and could be turned against his instinct to close with a grizzly bear. Lassoing bears was a common enough vaquero sport.

The vaquero has had some influence on the cowboy—especially the northern one—but the cowboy has never had any influence on the vaquero or buckaroo, regardless of what "western" writers may say on the subject. These writers have confused the terms "cowboy," "vaquero," and "buckaroo" either from ignorance of their subject, chauvinism, disregard for truth, or plain malice. Most motion pictures, television shows, and popular books on the West have served only to obliterate the truth.

The vaquero or buckaroo, the real Westerner, was a cultural force that writers have ignored. He never had a true history written about him while, on the other hand, the Gulf Coast rider or cowboy has had his chroniclers by the score.

The buckaroo who drove the Oregon cattle into Montana, with his long reata, and single-rig, center-fire saddle, has been immortalized on canvas by the great artist, Charles M. Russell. But there has been little worthwhile prose published on the subject of vaqueros or buckaroos.

Will James, in his *Cowboys North and South* is highly readable—but all wrong. There are only western and eastern herdsmen. James split it the wrong way.

Jo Mora in his *Trail Dust and Saddle Leather* made a great and sincere effort, and his illustrations were authentic. But in his effort to translate vaquero terms into English he used the lingo of the Gulf Coast which was not typical of the West Coast. In other respects he had great merit as a historian. Neither Will James nor Jo Mora was a vaquero and neither of them knew the craft at first hand.

It is not my intention to prove that one system or style is better, or which herdsman is superior. But in justice to the men who developed the cattle industry in the far West before the "cowboy" was ever heard of, I must correct some errors that have marred the true story for years. I speak as a vaquero—and I know whereof I speak.

As nature segregates and forms distinct groups from creatures of a common stock, so the Californiano developed into a type of his own differing from those of his background in Spain. To understand who and what the vaquero or buckaroo actually was, and why he was found with a distinct culture differing from that of any other herdsman, even from those who spoke the same language and were neighbors—English in the United States and Spanish in Mexico—we must go back to Cristóbal Colón, to the fifteenth century Spain of Fernando and Isabela.

Since the Castilian Isabela either financed or permitted Colón to make his expedition of discovery (we do not know since accounts and legends differ) only the subjects of the Castilian crown were permitted to go to those regions where gold was to be found. Thus it was that the Castilian, Andalusian, Extremaduran, Basque, and Portuguese had a free hand in pillaging the fabulous El Dorado of the New World. The subjects of Don Fernando—the Aragonese, Catalans, Valencians, Murcians, and southern Italians—had to stay at home, being refused the opportunity to share in carving up the golden pie.

By the time northern New Spain (what is now western United States) was colonized, however, some of the stay-at-homes could come to America, and the men who guarded the first colonists on the journey across the desert into Alta California were Catalonians.

These Catalonians brought the art of *La Jineta* from Spain and transplanted it in California. There the system of riding was much modified from La Jineta of the fifteenth century Andalusian which prevailed in central Mexico. We thus find the California rider distinct not only in costume, custom, speech and character, but also in nature, from the other riders or herdsmen of the New World, including those of central Mexico, even before the gringo came to the West Coast or went to the Gulf Coast states.

The central Mexico rider is a leverage-bit man. His steel curb-chain is still the iron-ring curb of the Moors. On the other hand, the Californiano is a palate-bit man. He uses a leather curb-strap. He does not depend on leverage so much as on the signal of the port touching the palate. The only thing the central Mexico vaquero and the California vaquero or buckaroo have in common is that they both wrap the rope around the horn of the saddle to hold a beef when they lasso it.

The California vaquero was born when Don Juan Bautista de Anza led his colonists across the desert into California in 1776. These Catalans had centuries of hand-to-hand combat on horseback in their background; and when they hung up their *chaquetas de cuero*, their leather jackets, to settle on the ranchos and raise cattle they kept alive their pride in an ages-long tradition of horsemanship. The Indians they trained as vaqueros became converts and disciples of the same proud tradition and often exceeded their masters. Some of the very best reinsmen were Indians.

From the beginning the vaquero followed a pattern furnished him by his ancestry in the Old World. He never subordinated his conception of a gentleman on horseback to that of a herder of cattle—a precept which all vaqueros, no matter of what race, have followed religiously in California. And to this day the art of riding is affected by the ancient military tradition, although it has passed through successive modifications.

The vaquero's horse was trained first as a cavalryman's horse, and as a cattle horse afterwards, even though the vaquero's worst enemy was usually nothing more than a maddened bull or an enraged grizzly. That the vaquero's horse was trained for war was proved at San Pasqual in 1846, when the Californians (the majority of those who fought that battle were Sonorans, however) made a brave defense, with reatas and lances, against a seasoned regiment of United States troops.

When the Yankees came around the Horn in sailing ships to California, the *paisano*, the native, called them *marineros*, or mariners. They were of the best Anglo stock and became pupils of the hard riding Californians. To their credit let it be said that they loyally adopted the Spanish tradition. They called themselves vaqueros, pronounced it *bukeras*, and later corrupted it to buckaroos.

When the paisano put the New England sea-dog on horseback and taught him the vaquero's trade and the Spanish style of horsemanship, this gringo became the first buckaroo, and while adapting the sober, prosaic Yankee to the Spanish tradition, the paisano took him out of character enough to imbue him with a touch of Don Quixote. The transplanted sea-dog absorbed his teaching so well that he often carried the passion for decorating himself and his horse with silver trappings to further extremes than the proverbially ostentatious paisano. Observe any parade in any western town.

The gringo immigration began in the 1830's and in time these Yankees and their sons and grandsons spread the longhorned Spanish cattle of California from the Mexican border to British Columbia, and from the Pacific to the continental divide.

Their cult of Spanish horsemanship was, as late as 1910, as clean as it was when the first cavalrymen rode into Alta California, and its influence has been so all-prevailing that as long as men ride horses with curb-bits and drive cattle in North America they are paying tribute to the Spainards.

Draw a line on the map of North America, starting in Old Mexico at the southern tip of the peninsula of Baja California. Draw the line a little south of Culiacan in Sinaloa to the Sierra Madre Occidental, then north through this sierra to the border of the United States where Arizona and New Mexico meet, then along this border to that of Utah and north to the corner of Wyoming. From here follow the western base of the Rocky Mountains into Canada. This is the American West, the territory of the vaquero and buckaroo. Of course the vaquero drove cattle over more territory; but to be specific we will say three states and one territory in Mexico—Sinaloa, Sonora and Baja California (the state and the territory), and California, Nevada, Oregon, Washington, Arizona, Utah, and parts of Idaho, Wyoming, and Montana in the United States. Or, roughly, the part of North America lying west of the Rocky Mountains, and the part of Mexico lying west of the Sierra Madre, from the Tropic of Cancer to Canada.

The vaquero and his counterpart, the buckaroo, plied their trade from the Hawaiian Islands to the prairies of central North America, where he was taken to rope buffalo. *A palate-bit man first, last, and forever, while pursuing his calling, he never forgot, wherever he found himself, that merit lay not only in what he did, but also in how he did it.*

Those who wrote of early California are unanimous in saying that the vaquero's skill was marvelous, and although this subject does not come within the scope of this work—nor does the author feel qualified to expatiate on the general history of California—it must be said in passing that, unfortunately, these same writers copy each other in saying that the Californian lost his lands and cattle to the gringos as a consequence of his love for ease and gambling. This is an unjust slander. There is no truth in it.

When the gringo took over the land, the paisano—if he did not migrate to Mexico, Chile, or Spain—gathered what few cattle were left to him and disappeared into the most distant and isolated places he could find in the West, as far away from the marauding bands of gringos as he could get. Where is he now? Ask the lonely canyons and deserts of the far places. They could tell if they could talk.

So much for the vaquero; let us return to the cowboy.

The cowboy still exists. He can be found at any of the numerous "rodeos" staged in many cities and towns of the United States. This rodeo is not a "gathering of cattle." That was the original meaning of the word. The rodeo is now a stylized performance to which admission is charged. Bucking horses and Brahman bulls are ridden and calves and steers are roped against

time in this rodeo by men who are called "cowboys."

These cowboys are not herders of cattle, they are rodeo followers. They have more the character of performers than of herdsmen. Some of these cowboys may have come originally from a ranch, but more often than not they have never worked on one.

Although the rodeo had its birth in the southern states, modern rodeo performers come from every state in the Union. One top performer learned to ride bucking horses on a dude ranch in the Adirondacks of New York.

These men are an aberration. Their calling serves no useful

purpose and is more brutal than that of the bullfighter. However, in justice to the rodeo cowboy, it must be said that he can ride anything that wears hair, the worst bucking horses and the meanest Brahman bulls, and he is afraid of nothing but an ambulance. Although conversationally the present day rider does not compare with the "old time" rider, the records and the size of today's horses prove the reverse.

This cowboy is indebted to the Negro for his culture. The African was a herdsman in his native habitat. The African status symbol was cattle. It still is in many parts of Africa. The Negro handled great herds of cattle and made a virtue of necessity to develop methods of handling cattle without a horse. Some of the practices of today's rodeo come directly from Africa and are in use there to this day.

The original cowboy came from the Atlantic seaboard and was frequently a Negro or poor white who was not always supplied with a horse by his cavalier master. As a result, the system of bulldogging, flanking, working cattle in closepens and chutes—and the sports of the rodeo arena—were developed. The fastidious vaquero or buckaroo called this "wallowing in manure."

When the United States took possession of the vast territory east of New Mexico and north of the Rio Grande, the Anglo from the South (as always in our reference, this is a loose term, since there was a heavy Scotch and German migration into that part of the Union) found himself in possession of vast herds of cattle which he could have for the taking.

When he came to work these cattle, some writers would have us believe, he would not adopt the Mexican's way of working because of his hatred of Mexicans. Actually he adopted all he could, the two-cinch saddle of central Mexico, the lazo, and the curb-bit.

The bondsman dumped from the English convict ships was a snaffle-bit man; he tied his rope, not because of a disregard for consequences, but because he had to have two hands to guide his horse. He could never learn to take turns around the horn to hold a beef. The truth of the matter is that the cowboy adopted the methods he used, not from choice, but from the pressure of circumstances.

The first cowboy was poorly mounted. The horse he rode, contrary to tall tales of wild white stallions, was never more than a pony. The assertion of Will James that the horses of the Pacific Northwest were the best mustangs in North America is true. And it is also true that the mustangs of Texas, New Mexico, and the Mexican states that border the United States were the poorest.

When the first herds of cattle were driven from the Gulf Coast into the Pacific Northwest, it was found that the horses often gained as much as two or three hundred pounds of growth after a year or two there. This was so even when they had, presumably, reached their full growth in Mexico or Texas. Grass and water can do wonders.

While it is treason to depart from the incredible pattern of the "western" yarn immortalized in so much printed matter, it is nevertheles true that the cowboy waving a sixshooter did not win the West. The cowboy never got to the actual geographic West. If anyone is to have the credit for the winning of the West, it should be the United States Army private.

The cowboy got as far west as central Arizona. There he met the buckaroo. There the two systems—one Spanish, the other African—clashed.

It was in the nature of things that when the West Coast rider met the Gulf Coast rider there would be friction. The buckaroo looked down on the man who would dismount and wrestle cattle afoot while his horse stood around with its reins dragging in the dirt.

Ironically, it was the Anglo rider representing each system who upheld the superiority of his way of working cattle and handling a horse; this to the great astonishment of the tolerant paisano.

The West Coast rider abhorred the plain equipment of the Gulf Coast rider; in it he found no silver, no beauty, no pride in possession or profession. The Afro-Anglo idiom jarred with the Hispanic-Anglo terms. Besides, the low port bits favored by the cowboy spoiled horses' mouths.

The buckaroo and the cowboy quarreled and quite often fought. The excuse was that one used a single-cinch saddle and the other used a double-cinch saddle, or that one used a high-port bit and the other used a low-port bit.

It makes a man stop and think about the actual history of our West when he pictures two men fighting, one Anglo fighting another Anglo, one for a culture he got from the Spaniard, and the other for a culture he got from the Negro. These clashes did not occur on the Gulf Coast or on the Pacific Coast, but in Arizona, Nevada, and Montana. And it is a fact that the many fights and quarrels which resulted from these differences of opinion were not fought by the Hispanic Californian on the one hand and the Negro on the other; the contending Anglo riders were descended from Yankee stock on the one hand and from Southerners on the other. However, this was the general case. There were all sorts of exceptions to the rule. The men who were on one side of the fence or the other were not all descendants of Yankees or Southerners. And one fine old gentleman, to whom I am indebted for much of this material—a staunch old buckaroo whose lip still curls at the sight of a "rimmy," a two-cinch saddle —is a grandson of Tenneseeans.

Just remember that the environment of the old time cattle ranch was a close one. It bred strong loyalties.

Vaquero

I do not come from an "Old Spanish Family." Old Spanish families are an invention of the gringos. They are a myth which the paisanos have come to believe themselves, as Sancho did his enchantment of Dulcinea in *Don Quixote*. My father was of Sonoran stock and of clerical people, that is to say, there had been priests and nuns in his family. He had enough education to act as interpreter in court, as he was sometimes asked to do. He was a skilled craftsman who made silver mounted bits and spurs for the trade in his own shop. Besides that source of income the financier Lucky Baldwin paid him one hundred dollars a month to make the plates for and to shoe his favorite race horses at Santa Anita Rancho.

My mother's mother, Rita Ruiz, was born in Los Angeles and had come to Rancho San Pasqual (which is now the city of Pasadena) after the gringos had disposessed her. That was before my mother was born and when Tia Concepcion, Aunt Concepcion, the second child in my mother's family, was yet a babe in arms. Tia Concia, as we called her, in later years told a story of having been driven away from home by gringos, and of her and my grandmother being without food or shelter when Vasquez, the bandit, found them and fed the mother and child. My grandmother's parents had come from the old colonial town of Alamos, Sonora, while Don Pablo Sola, the last Spanish governor of California, was still in office.

There were two Spaniards from Extremadura, and two Yaqui women on my father's side of the family, two Catalans and two Mayo women on my mother's side. So if I now and then take a dig at the Spaniards or at the Indians, I am exercising an inalienable right. I am speaking about my own family.

Mother, having been born after the gringos took California, could speak English, though she could not read or write. Although we spoke Spanish at home, the Yankee schoolmarm was already an influence, because we brothers and sisters spoke English among ourselves and had a leaning toward the gringos. My first actual contact with them was at the Garfield School on California Street in Pasadena. The teachers were kind and from that childhood impression I have had a high regard for the gringo teacher.

Mother died when I was a child, and as a result we were all five small children sent to orphanages. I spent four years in one, then ran away and was never caught. I was in the third grade then and have never gone to school since. Although I was subsequently sent to other orphanages, the authorities were never able to keep me in one for more than a few weeks at a time.

I lived with my aunt Concia in Pasadena, but never liked it. Perhaps I would have vegetated there and never known about vaqueros if it had not been for my uncle Jim McFall. He came to Pasadena to visit my grandmother, and when he went back to his ranch in Soledad Canyon I went with him. Uncle Jim was my mother's oldest brother. When ten years old he had gone on a trail drive which crossed half the continent. Grandmother told us that he had run away from home in 1860 and did not return to southern California until he was middle-aged.

He had joined a company of gringos—though Aunt Concia said that it was Vasquez with whom he had left—who were driving horses east into a middle-western state. Grandma could not tell us the name of the state. Perhaps she could not pronounce it. All she knew was that it was a land of *chubascos*, blizzards, *muy lejos, donde había puros gringos*—far away where there are only gringos. It was most probably Nebraska. It was during the late 1850's and early 1860's when the vast herds were driven out of California into the eastern states, after the members of the best families in California had emigrated to other lands and left their herds and ranchos to be despoiled by the gringos.

My uncle Jim was a neighbor of Don Leonardo Ruiz who was a relative of my grandmother, Rita Ruiz. Don Leonardo had lost his property on the coast and had come to Soledad to grub out a living. He was a kindly old man, and because he never scolded me as my uncle Jim did, I went to live with him.

It was on his *ranchito* that I stumbled, so to speak, on the trade I was to follow throughout my lifetime. It was to be my work, my hobby, my study. Don Leonardo had a fine background, both practical and historical, in Spanish horsemanship, even if he was too old to practice it. He opened a new world for me. From him I learned that we had a Spanish tradition of horsemanship, the antique Arabic-Moorish Hispanic art of La Jineta. *Cosas de muy lejos atrás*, things of the distant past, as he expressed it.

I shall always cherish the memories of the long winter nights on the little ranch, when the wind howled out of the Mojave and we sat by the fire of black *chamiso* roots which burn like coal, and listened as Don Leonardo told of *garañones Guzmanes y Valenzuelas*, stallions of Guzman and Valenzuela breeding, from which descended the Carthusian chargers which the breeders of Jerez and Sevilla cherished. From these war stallions came the Isabellas (palominos and buckskins) of Andalusia from which the mustangs that ran wild in the New World were descended. These *destriers* were bred and trained by priests and monks in Carthusian monasteries, and took the name of that order. They were sometimes called the "monk's horse" or "monastery horse." The equestrian monks and priests who came to the New World and taught the ancient Hispano-Arabic hippology of which they were masters were probably Carthusians.

I have often pondered on the perversity of fate which sent Don Leonardo, such a fine old gentleman, to that lonely, sterile desert canyon, so aptly called La Soledad—the Solitude. He was so out of place there. Perhaps I have given Don Leonardo attributes he did not possess, but this he did for me: He taught me the value of things which link us to a bygone day, and placed before me a cavalcade of horsemen which has been passing now for fifty years.

It was there on the ranchito that I began to worship the men who rode horses and to envy them their bowed legs. There I decided never to go back to the town of my birth. I would seek out a ranch where there were vaqueros and I would learn to ride. True, it was poorly paid work, and there were many risks and dangers incident to the life of a vaquero, many hardships to be endured. But at least I would be on horseback and would not be looked down upon.

The great ranches were in the San Joaquin Valley, so I decided to go there and see Don Jesús Lopez, manager of the Tejon Ranch. Don Leonardo gave me the old hump-backed, hip-shot pinto mare and the saddle with the broken tree. It was all he had to give.

I shall always remember my first interview with Don Jesús Lopez at the vaquero camp on Tejon Ranch. After I had told him I had come to the ranch to look for work, he looked for a long time at the hump-backed mare, then at the saddle, then at the bit. Then he turned to me and asked the question which has made many good men hesitate to answer, "*Y tú, hijo, eres vaquero?*" And you, son, are a vaquero?

Young as I was I had sense enough to answer, "*No, pero puedo aprender.*" No, but I can learn.

The next question was another which many good vaqueros have been loath to answer: "*Y si un caballo repara, hijo, te tumba? Aqui hay caballos muy malcriados.*" And if a horse should buck, son, would he throw you? There are horses here that are very rude.

"*Pues,*" I answered, "*depende en los reparos.*" Well, it depends on the bucking.

Don Jesús turned and looked again for a long minute at the hump-backed mare, at the old saddle, then at the skinny kid before him. He assumed a very serious expression, and said, "*Bueno, como buen paisano te voy a dar trabajo. Pero yo no quiero muchachos que maltratan y estrujan caballos. Todo que te pido es que cuides tus caballos, pobrecitos.*" Well, as a good fellow townsman (he was from Los Angeles) I am going to give you work. But I will not have boys who mistreat and abuse horses. All I ask of you is that you take care of your horses, poor things.

The horses Don Jesús gave me were Chocolate, a gray; Kelly, a sorrell; White Stockings, a stocking-legged sorrell; Smokey, a brown; and Horcado, a gray. They were the best horses I have had the good fortune to ride.

The Spanish California Dialect

In these stories I use the Spanish of the vaquero, who is now gone forever, even if the dialect does not conform to the best Castilian. The reader will, no doubt, search through Spanish dictionaries for some of the words. He will either fail to find them or they will have definitions which do not agree with those in the text; because of that circumstance, some explanations are in order.

The Spanish spoken in California was a dialect of old Castilian which was brought by the Catalonian soldiers who accompanied the missionaries into this part of New Spain. Even today the paisano counts his money in *reales*. Often the vaquero adopted terms to suit the occasion or circumstance. The word *nuqueador*—one who slaughtered cattle by stabbing them at the base of the neck, the *nuca*—is an example.

Many of the words used here had gone out of use in Spain long before the gringos came in 1846. From that time the paisano's language began to die out in California. Few of the old people could read or write, but spoke a clean, simple Spanish; and it was not until the gringos erected schools and the paisano sent his children to them that the young ones began to interlard their speech with English words. Those who retain fragments of Spanish today speak it with a Yankee accent.

The children did not have a chance. In the hands of that peerless civilizer, the Yankee schoolmarm, they were taught the three R's—and to think in English. It is safe to say that the school, more than the barbed-wire fence or the plowing up of the range, was responsible for the decline of the vaquero.

It is not true that many Indian words were used, as some writers assert. About the only Indian word (said to be derived from the Yaqui—and that is debatable) is *pochi* or *pocho*, lopped off or bob-tailed. A bob-tailed horse was called "El Mocho" by Californians, and "El Pocho" by Sonorans. Californians became "pochos" or "pochis" when Alta California was severed from Mexico.

Another word of doubtful etymology is *coche* or *cochi*. In Spain it means coach, in Mexico an automobile, but in California it meant hog.

The word *bravo* is often translated as brave in English. In California it was used in the sense of fierce. A *toro bravo* was a fierce bull, not necessarily a brave one. The word also meant sharp or keen. A knife with a fine edge was said to be *brava*, barbs on fence wire were *alambre bravo*, rock which cut up a horse's feet was *piedra brava*, and an awl with a fine point was *brava*. Anything that drew blood or would attack, as a wildcat, was *brava*. Even chili, when extra peppery, was *chili bravo*.

The best interpretation of the term *bravo* I have ever heard was given by Russell Hill, who spoke Spanish fluently.

A rodeo was in progress at the old fairgrounds in Bakersfield. One of Russell's vaqueros was standing under the grandstand. He was holding a lady's hand and looking into her eyes, probably telling her she was beautiful and that he couldn't live without her. Russell, mounted on one of his fine Morgan horses, rode by, and seeing the soulful little tableau, said, warningly, "*Muncho cuidado, es muy bravo el marido*." Look out! The husband is very fierce.

Whether the lady had a husband, we do not know. It is very probable that Russell was joking.

The vaquero never used the proper *mucho*, much. He said *muncho*.

The cowboy expression "broke in two" may very well have been derived from the vaquero's *se mocho*, meaning a horse bucked, and similarly, the phrase "part out," to separate cattle, came from *apartar*.

Whenever a vaquero plunged after a runaway beef, or raced after an animal to lasso it, it was said he *arrebato una res*, assailed a beef. The same term arrebato was used when one person attacked another.

Quite often the vaquero, when at a loss for a word, called a thing he had no name for by an unchaste name, as people call a thing that has no name a "doohickey" or a "hootenanny."

The *Californiano*—writers on California to the contrary—called himself a *Sonoreño*. I have heard third or fourth generation descendants of members of the De Anza expedition (Don José Jesús Lopez for one) say, "*Nosotros somos Sonoreños. Sonora es nuestra tierra*." We are Sonorans. Sonora is our motherland.

This prideful distinction stemmed from having descended from the actual colonists, not from the convicts who were introduced in subsequent expeditions.

The gringo vaqueros—by gringo vaqueros I mean the Anglos, sons of Yankee parents, who could handle a sixty-foot reata and a full spade bit, and there were many who could—interlarded their speech with Spanish words, and more often than not used them correctly.

Whenever they became loosened in the saddle and they were forced to grab the saddle horn, as sometimes happened, the gringo vaqueros would say that they had "grabbed the apple." The paisano's equivalent for this term was, "*agarrar la comadre*," clutch the comadre. Perhaps they called the horn "comadre" because the word means literally co-mother. The comadre is the woman who sponsors one's child when it is baptized. Since a comadre or *compadre* would never fail one in time of emergency, it was quite logical that the saddle horn should be called "la comadre."

There were many stout youngsters on the ranches who could rake a bucking horse from shoulder to flank with their spurs, and hit him with their hat at every jump, but it was no disgrace to clutch the horn when the rider felt himself getting loosened in the saddle, because he "had bought the horn when he bought the saddle." Sometimes, however, a rider did not have time to grab the horn. He often found himself on the ground twenty feet away, with a handful of dirt.

Every now and then in some musty old Spanish book one meets with the word *jinete*. In Spain and Latin America jinete means simply a man on horseback, but in the language of the vaquero it has much more significance. To us a jinete is an expert rider of bucking horses. No ordinary rider who just managed to stay on a bucking horse was called a jinete in California; such a person was merely a *travieso*, a mischievous one, a rapscallion.

Used in the sense of a verb, *jinetiar* meant to ride a bucking horse.

At the vaquero camp on Tejon Ranch one day many years ago, the following conversation took place between Don Jesús Lopez, the mayordomo, and Don Porfirio Valencia, the *caporal,* or foreman. The object of their discussion was a new vaquero who was as yet untried.

Don Jesús: "*Y ese vaquero, podrá andar en El Canelo?*" And that vaquero, will he be able to ride the Roan?

Don Porfirio (By the way, Don Porfirio lisped.): "*Pues, el dice que es jinete y amansa caballos.*" Well, he says that he is a bucking horse rider and tames horses.

Don Jesús: "*Bueno, bueno. Vamos a ver.*" Good, good. We shall see.

Don Porfirio: "*Adolfo dice que está enfada de andar en ese caballo.*" Adolfo says he is fed up with riding that horse.

Don Jesús: "*Sí, sí. Pobre muchacho.*" Yes, yes. Poor boy.

The outcome of this conversation was that the new vaquero was given the Roan, and in the course of events was thrown "as high as a kite."

The Indian Vaquero

When a vaquero was especially skilled, and he was asked how he had reached such a degree of proficiency, his answer would invariably be: "*Me crié entre los Indios.*" I was raised among the Indians. Or when some vaquero had performed his work with great skill, the other men would look at each other, smile approvingly, and say, "*Se crió entre los Indios pues.*" Well, he was brought up among the Indians.

Contrary to a lot of false statements, a man took pride in calling himself "Indio." The Indian vaquero was highly respected for his skill and good qualities—that is, by those who knew him. And the proof is that very few of the men who have ridden on the Tejon stayed there any length of time without becoming "*Indios del Tejon,*" Tejon Indians, whatever their true race may have been.

At night around the fire a note of awe would creep into the old man's voice, as he told of hard riding Indian vaqueros who had roped grizzly bears and led wild cattle out of the Sierra, men who had become legends on the Tejon Ranch.

Cattle ranching was the Californiano's preferred—his sole—occupation for the first hundred years after the state was founded. Indeed, from 1769 until the turn of the present century, cattle raising was the most important industry in California.

In the beginning the ranches were Spanish and Mexican land

grants. After California became a part of the United States, big cattle companies formed the greatest cattle ranches in North America. The Tejon, Kern County Land Company, and Miller and Lux are examples of these huge ranches.

It was boasted, in his many bunkhouses in California, Nevada, and Oregon, that Henry Miller could ride from the Mexican border to British Columbia and sleep on his own land every night, change horses every day from his own *caponeras* (a *caponera* is a band of horses, usually geldings, kept for the use of the vaqueros) and eat beef from his own herds on the entire journey. Of course this was an exaggeration, but nevertheless the Miller and Lux holdings were enormous.

One might say that cattle ranching in California did not lose its paramount importance until after 1927, when Miller and Lux started selling out their land. The Kern County Land Company with its three and three-quarter million acres is still the largest producer of range beef in North America.

The vaquero or buckaroo who herded the cattle on the ranches of California was sometimes a Cahuilla, a Piute, a Mission Indian, or a member of one of the numerous tribes which populated California. Sometimes he was a Sonoreño, that is to say, a native of the state of Sonora in Old Mexico, or a descendant of Sonoreños born in California. Sometimes he was a Californian of pioneer colonial stock, like Don Jesús Lopez. At other times he was from Baja California like Frederico Lamas, and sometimes he was a gringo. Once in a while a Chilean was met among the vaquero crews.

The vaquero of California was the North American counterpart of the Argentine *gaucho*, the Brazilian *vaquiero*, and Chilean *huaso*. But our histories have ignored him. This rider was called a "vaquero," a word derived from *vaca*, cow. He was never called a "cowboy." In fact, the Anglo rider of the West (if an Irishman can be called an "Anglo") particularly of California,

Nevada, and Oregon, so disliked the word "cowboy" that he coined the term "buckaroo" from vaquero, and by this he was known.

Perhaps this Hispanicization came from the padres who were the vaquero's teachers. They were almost invariably good horsemen and could balance a lance or throw a *lazo*, a lasso, with the best leather jacket soldier. Indeed, they sometimes solved the problem of bringing their neophytes into the fold by lassoing them. Often some recalcitrant Indian, who later became a good vaquero of the mission herds, got his first object lesson in throwing the lazo when a zealous padre rode after him and roped him, thus literally leading him into the bosom of Mother Church.

It is doubtful whether the first padres brought vaqueros with them from Velicata. The first cattle were probably driven into Alta California by *harrieros*, muleteers, and cavalrymen. The padres trained native Indians as vaqueros as the herds increased, despite the Laws of the Indies which forbade Indians, on penalty of death, to ride horses. The Spaniards feared the Indians would become warriors like the Apaches. Subsequent events proved that the Spaniards were not wrong. The padres were good teachers. A few years after the arrival of the first cattle there were a number of good Indian vaqueros at Monterey.

The *rancheros*, the ranchers, of the old Spanish and Mexican grants used Indian vaqueros almost exclusively until the Gold Rush period. Then Sonoreños who had migrated to California to seek gold began to take over the herding of cattle. Some ranches, however, use Indian vaqueros to this day, as do the Tejon Ranch and the Paubo Ranch. The Santa Margarita used them until it became Camp Pendleton. The vaqueros who drove the first great herds out of California in 1836, when Ewing Young began supplying the Oregon ranchers with cattle, were probably Californians and Indians, but when Pete French and John Devine stocked the eastern Oregon and western Nevada ranges with California cattle their vaqueros were Sonoreños.

The gringo came into the vaquero picture in numbers after the 1850's and from his advent the crews became mixed. These riders were, for the most part, sons of immigrants or small ranch owners. These gringos had been reared with Spanish speaking children and, more often than not, spoke Spanish. All riders, no matter of what racial background, used the same type of equipment—spade or half-breed bit, rawhide reata, "shotgun" or "wooly" chaps, and flat, hard-brimmed hat.

It would be unjust to say that men of one racial group were better at the work than those of another racial group. There were good Indian vaqueros, good Mexican vaqueros, good Californian vaqueros, and good gringo vaqueros, and the only Negro vaquero this writer ever knew was a good one too. He would ride any of the other vaquero's broncos for ten cents. If that price was too high, he would ride the bronco for a sack of Bull Durham tobacco which cost only a nickel, and few if any horses could buck him off.

It is only when they have ridden together stirrup to stirrup, and depended on each other in the thousand emergencies which arise when working wild cattle or riding bronco horses that men really know each other. Differences in race are forgotten as they learn each other's worth.

Contrary to the "western" writers who have written so much of hatred between the Anglo and the Latin peoples of California, the relations between the gringo and the paisano, as far as the vaquero and buckaroo were concerned, were good. The skilled men of any race were respected and usually had a large following. Such men were Juan Olivera, Lupe Ortiz, Juan Gomez, and many others. By the same token the Bowers, the Hathaways, the Brunks, the Roses, and the Pascoes were respected as first-class buckaroos. As a matter of fact, a man took more pride in calling himself *Indio* than in calling himself anything else. Regardless of what malicious writers may say, the Indians were liked, by those who knew them, for their good qualities. The Indian vaqueros

Carlos Valenzuela, Bill Nichols, Vic Cordero, Nacho Montes, and many others earned the respect of all men.

The Indian vaquero was sparing in speech, and serene under all circumstances. He was pithy in all his expressions and often spoke in metaphor or ironically. One would have to be well acquainted with him to know his meanings. He had a knack for giving names which never failed to correspond to something risible in their owners. His nicknames told the characteristics of the victim. There was a man in Bakersfield who every year managed the Frontier Days parade. He had a long, thin, straight nose and little blue eyes. He would have filled the description of Ichabod Crane in *The Legend of Sleepy Hollow.* Agustin Hinio named him *El Pájaro Carpintero,* the Woodpecker. A vaquero stationed at Fort Tejon liked to ride up and down Highway 99 so that the people could admire his figure on horseback. The other vaqueros named him "Highway Bill."

To a man whose color approached that of roasted coffee, the Indians would apply the term *El Guerro,* the Blond, or *El Gringo,* the Gringo. Or if the luckless one happened to be of Yaqui extraction, which was quite often the case, he would be named, *El Yori,* the White Man. To a man on Tejon who rode humped up over his horse the other men applied the name *El Tacuachi,* the Possum. They would say of a man who showed much Indian blood in his makeup, *Ése no le debe ni los Buenos Días a los Españoles*—that one doesn't owe even a "good day" to the Spaniards. Or if person's hair was stiff, they would say, *Ése lo tienen que peinar a martillasos*—that one has to be combed with a hammer.

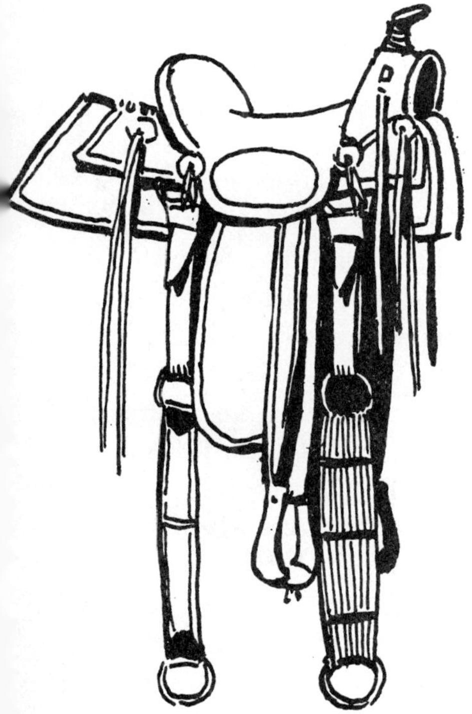

Double Rig

Center Fire

The Vaquero's Saddle

The Iberian invaders from Andalusia and Extremadura brought the high-peaked Moorish saddle of which the big-horned saddle of central and southern Mexico is a modification. The Spaniards from every part of Spain who settled in Mexico over a period of three centuries had very little in common with the first *conquistadores* in respect to styles of riding and horse equipment. As a result, "Mexican" saddles, bits, and spurs vary in type, style, and period.

The California vaquero's saddle is not adapted from the

Moorish saddle. It is a modification of the Persian saddle which was brought to the New World in later years. However, Moorish, Persian, and "Mexican" saddles are basically the same. They have the same side-bars, high fork, and steep, high cantle, and the stirrups hang at the same angle.

The Persian saddle was adapted for use in hot country. It was a skeleton tree with a detachable housing called a *mochilla* in Alta California and a *cojinillo* in Baja California, Sonora, and parts of Sinaloa. It was the saddle that the Spaniards, who went to the Hawaiian Islands in 1808, took and introduced there. This saddle is still used on Hawaii's Parker Ranch.

In Alta California it went through succeeding modifications. The detachable mochilla and cojinillo were discarded and a permanent cover was put on the tree. This original tree was the model for the Visalia, Taylor, and Ledesma trees which spread over the West in the last century. It was the best saddle in the world for practical use.

Here we must digress to explain why the vaquero abhorred the two-cinch or double-rig (rimfire) saddle and despised the man who rode one. The double-rig originated in Mexico in the days of the colony. It was in use there until by brutal trial and error it was found that it inflicted unnecessary pain on the horse and was inefficient besides; the vaquero discarded it.

The early vaquero was an observant man. In the course of his work he found that the forering on the double-rig saddle was so placed that it acted as a pivot between the cinch and the fork. When a rope was attached to the horn and a pull was exerted, the fork of the saddle would tilt forward, and the sharp ends of the side bars would be driven into the horse's shoulders. The mechanical principle was the same as that of a plow. Indeed it had the same effect as a plowshare. The back cinch, being loose, served only to hurt the horse's belly muscles.

On the other hand, the center-fire, single-cinch saddle had the ring placed in the center of the tree. When a pull was exerted on the horn, the pull would be equal from front and back of the saddle and, as a result, the saddle would not tilt. However, the center-fire had one bad feature. It had a tendency to slide forward and needed constant attention. This constant "fixing" had its benefits. The fixing kept the saddle from bearing too long on one spot, and thus prevented many a sore back.

Back at the turn of the century the "rimmys" started coming out of the south and often there were mixed crews on the roundups in Montana and Arizona. Men who rode double-rigs were on roundups with men who rode single-rigs. The foreman, when he had assembled the crew before sending them out to gather cattle, would say, "All you buckaroos riding center-fires get off and fix your saddles. All you lazy sons of bitches riding rimfires can stay on your horses."

This riding in mixed crews made the vaquero and buckaroo cleave all the more to the center-fire. Those riders who had wandered away from the home range to ride in other climes came back to California and told around the campfire of the customs and methods of the rimfire men.

"Those cowboys," they would say, "never got off to fix their saddles. When they pulled them off in the evening, they took off half the horse's hide with the saddle. The reason they had to have so many of those little horses in their strings was that the horses had to have time between saddlings for their backs to heal."

In like manner the old-timer clove to the slick-fork. The swell fork, sometimes eighteen inches across the swell, "beat a man to death" when a horse bucked, and the swells were in the way when a rider leaned down to avoid obstacles such as tree branches.

So the vaquero used the California saddle with single rigging, that is to say, one cinch. The ring extends from the center of the saddle. The single-rig is better from a humane and from a practical standpoint, because a horse, in order to move in comfort, must have freedom at the shoulders, and anything that binds that part of the animal's body, as the double-rig does, will interfere with the animal's movements. The single-rig saddle also came to the United States from Mexico, where both styles were used until the double-rig was discarded.

Another advantage of the single-rig over the double-rig is that the stirrups hang slightly forward, and thus the weight of the rider and the pressure of the stirrups equalize the load on the horse's back. The length, width, and shape of the bars distribute the load over the horse's back; a tree that is too long is better than a tree that is too short.

Because no two backs were alike, each horse in the vaquero's string presented a different problem. There were high and low withers, broad and wide backs, long and thin backs, "hump" or "hog" backs. The hog back and high-withered back were anathema to the vaquero. Kidney sores result from hog backs, caused by the side-bars digging into the back when the vaquero rode too much on the cantle. Low, sloping cantles, much in use today, were scorned by the old-time vaquero. He knew their evil. The straight, high, broad cantle had a purpose; it kept the rider where he belonged in the saddle. The muscles which propel the horse press against the ends of the bars, and a thin horse will bruise more easily than a fat one.

But of all sizes and shapes of horses' backs, the low-withered back was the bane to the life of the man who had to keep a saddle on it. The low-withered horse required a cinch to be kept excessively tight. Of late years saddle makers have come out with a contraption they call a "quarter-horse-tree"; this, however, does not solve the problem of low withers.

Another troublesome type of horse was the "one-gutted" animal. A one-gutted horse had flanks so narrow that they let the cinch slip or drop back. Such a horse could hardly be ridden without a breast-collar and was such a "poor keeper" that his rider "would have to tie a knot in his tail to keep him from going through the cinch" before the day's ride was over, as the gringo buckaroos expressed it.

Careless cinching was cause of galled horses. Riders differ in their methods of cinching. Some cinch loosely, then tighten up after the horse has traveled a while and warmed up. Others cinch up tightly when they first saddle up. Some horses fall over backwards when cinched up the first time in the morning. The belief was common among riders that a "cinchbinder," as the gringos call a horse that falls over backwards, would never have acquired the vice if he had been cinched up tightly from the beginning of his training or breaking. Horses that have been broken with a loose cinch invariably buck or fall over backwards when they are cinched up tightly.

Good vaqueros never failed, when the opportunity presented itself, to dismount, loosen the cinch, raise the saddle and blankets and let the air pass over the horse's sweaty back for a few moments. But they never removed the saddle from the horse's back until the animal was cool, believing that a horse would chill if its wet back were exposed to the wind. They never turned a saddle blanket over once it was shaped to a horse's back; nor would they ever wring out a wet blanket. Wringing broke the threads.

Ranchers who kept the same breed of stallions and mares over a period of time were not troubled with back problems so much as were the ranchers who bought their saddle stock wherever they could get it. Ranchers who bred their own saddle horses could breed for certain type and breed out faults in conformation. Each ranch bred for a certain type; in the days of great ranches in California, a person could determine where a vaquero rode by the appearance of his horse. At a gathering of vaqueros or at a rodeo, a Kern County Land Company horse could be easily distinguished from a Miller and Lux horse. And a Tejon horse could be distinguished from as far as the eye could see it; and, for that matter, so could a Roland Hill Morgan.

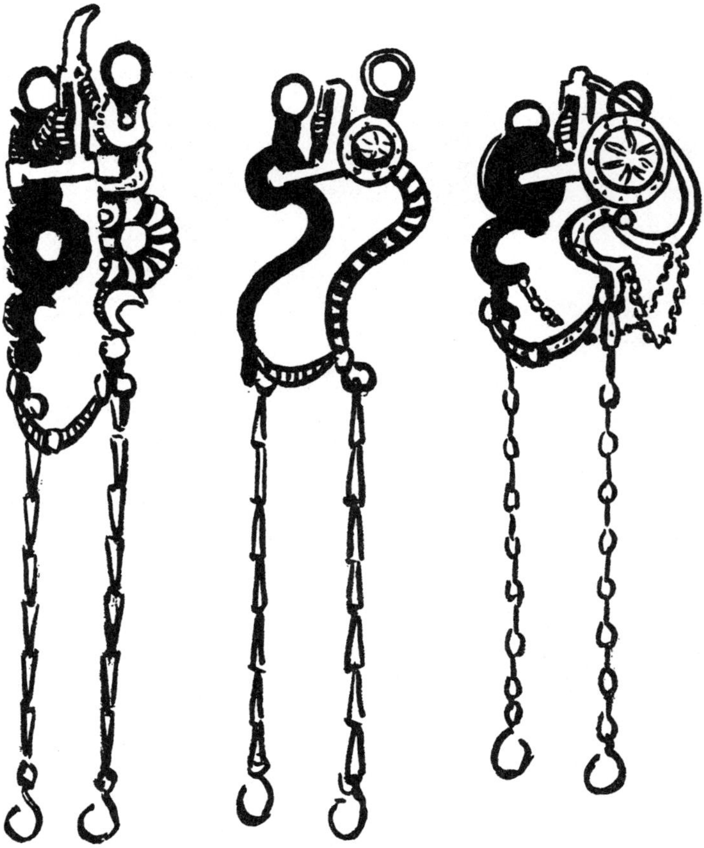

The Vaquero's Bridle Bit

The bridle-bit was the most important piece of equipment in the vaquero's outfit. Without a good bit he could not work a horse properly, and unless a vaquero had a good bit a mayordomo worthy of the name would not hire him. It was as simple as that. And it was just as important that the vaquero know bits and their function.

The California vaquero never used a low-port (grazer) bit, nor one with abnormally long shanks or jaws. He learned very early that such bits would spoil a horse's mouth. The curve in the mouthpiece of the low-port grazer clamped a horse's tongue, and the animal learned to ball its tongue and brace its jaw in self-defense. The grazer was deficient in leverage and as a consequence the horse learned to bear on it and thus became hard mouthed.

The long shanked bit with "enough leverage to lift a boxcar," as the gringos expressed it, either pulled a horse's head up too high or pulled it down into his chest. In any case, a long shanked bit was sure to cut a horse's tongue.

For these reasons the vaquero used the high port bit, either the spade or half-breed. However, the bit did not make the horse. The horse was made before a bit was ever put in its mouth. No bit in the world can make a mouth. The horse was made with the *jáquima*, or hackamore, a band put around its nose in order to school the animal. The jáquima saved the mouth because it accustomed the horse to obey the rein without hurting it as would be the case if it were to be pulled with a bit in its mouth. The jáquima was not removed until the horse could stop, turn, and back perfectly. The bit was then used to maintain the condition into which the jáquima had put the horse.

In the old days vaqueros never started to break a horse until it was five years old. The reason was that a vaquero never liked to put a bit in a horse's mouth until it had its "bridle teeth," the canines. Vaqueros believe that a horse cannot be bitted successfully until it has all its permanent teeth. A colt changing teeth will not pay attention to the pull on the rein because of the pain. Another reason vaqueros would not put a bit in a horse's mouth until the animal had adjusted to carrying a load on its back was that a colt will stumble and have to be pulled, or will shy and have to be doubled. If the colt were wearing a bit, doubling and pulling would hurt its mouth.

Most old-timers who had colts in their strings rarely rode them more than two or three times a month. Actually it was only a short period that a colt was ridden with a jáquima. During much of this period it was ridden with double reins, with both bit and jáquima. The reins of the bit were not pulled, however.

From this practice, no doubt, has come the myth current among dudes and aficionados of the spade bit and "California style" of today that the old Californianos rode a colt two and three years with a jáquima. These people never take into account that a horse is a creature of habit, that the longer one wears a jáquima the more habituated to it the animal will become. As a consequence it will be just so much harder to accustom to a bit.

The mouthpiece, of whatever form, has nothing to do with the severity of a bit. The length of the shanks or jaws of a bit decides the amount of its leverage or severity. Actually, however, the weight of the rider's hand decides whether any kind of bit is mild or severe. The leverage or curb bit is actually a lever. The mouthpiece is the fulcrum or prop, the shanks or jaws are the lever lifting against the chin or curb strap. It operates on a principle of mechanics. Originally the spade bit (in Spanish *paleta*, diminutive of *pala*, spade) had only two or two and a half inches of leverage. When bit makers lengthened its shanks and made a leverage bit of it, they spoiled it for the purpose for which it was designed.

To be effective in the function for which it was designed, the port of the spade bit must be at an angle where it will signal the horse just as the curb tightens. Careful adjustment of the curb strap is very important. The Californiano never used a curb chain on a spade bit. He believed that a chain calloused the chin-groove and as a result the horse lost the sense of feel in that part of its anatomy. The vaquero used a leather curb strap. The secret of the spade bit is that a horse never learns to lean or brace on it and as a result never has a hard mouth. Contrary to present day opinion, spade bits were not intended for nor used on hard mouthed horses. The old-timers often said that a spade bit was the only bit that fit a horse's mouth, and that the braces were responsible for this result. Contrary to those who exhibit ideas about bits nowadays, not all vaqueros were enthusiastically dedicated to the use of the spade bit. Many of them preferred a half-breed bit, yet the fact remains that they too rode good horses.

Good spade bit men were rare, even in that era of good reinsmen. Those who were outstanding were men who devoted themselves to putting a trigger rein on a horse. This bit was for those men who prided themselves on having a "bridle hand." Someone once asked Juan Olivera why he used a spade bit when the horse Juan rode would have obeyed with a silk string in his mouth to control him. Juan retorted that it was not a matter of strength, but a matter of pride in having a bridle hand. However, many old vaqueros had no bridle hand, and perhaps that is the reason the Creator imbued the mustang with *amor al ganado* or what buckaroos call "cow sense." The horse taught himself to herd cattle. There is an old saying, born of Spanish equitation, that "*El caballo de rienda: no se hace; él nace.*" The reined horse is not made; he is born.

Of late years there have been many tirades against the spade bit, and by the same token, many encomiums bestowed on it. But those who censure or praise it don't know what they are talking about. The men who could handle a spade bit died out long ago.

The teeth have much to do with the way a horse obeys the rein. Horses that slobber, throw their heads, pull to one side, or go frantic when ridden with a tight rein, do so for no reason other than their teeth are sharp on the outside edges. The horse's upper jaw is wider than the lower, and after the animal is five years old, the upper grinders wear to a razor edge on the outside. In using a curb bit with a curb strap the pull on the reins presses the bit against the side of the horse's mouth. This in turn squeezes the flesh against the sharp points on the teeth, cutting gashes into the flesh. Riders often blame the bit for the horse's erratic behavior when it is the teeth that are causing the trouble. Horses with mouths that have been neglected never fail to have old scars in the mouth where they have been cut. The contraption called the "hackamore bit" which exerts a squeeze on the horse's nose and jaw seems to have been designed to slice the side of the horse's mouth.

Love of Craft

More often than not the vaquero and his gringo counterpart, the buckaroo, stood the long hours, bad food, extreme heat and cold incident to his calling because of his love for horses. Surely in the southern San Joaquin Valley of fifty years ago there were jobs that paid more money and were much less strenuous. The oil fields were booming; even the farmer paid better wages than the cattleman. But the vaquero was a romantic. He liked to make his living riding a horse even if it entailed hardship and suffering.

Moreover, he was a perfectionist. His way of life was passing, but he still tried to perfect himself in his work. Though the ranch management frowned on the practice, he would put his rope on anything that walked and often with dramatic results. Many of the most comical situations the vaquero found himself in came from his penchant for experimentation. He would rope a grizzly bear, wild horse, wild cow, buffalo, wild hog, elk—even ostriches on the Tejon and Tracy ranches—and work out the problem of extricating himself as best he was able. He roped wherever he could, whenever he could, whatever he could with a serene disregard for consequences. The results were seldom if ever tragic. There is a providence that protects children, drunkards, vaqueros, and buckaroos.

Coyotes were the hardest of the wild animals to rope and the man who caught one was respected far and wide as a *lazador*, a roper. But when a vaquero snared one, while he took justifiable pride in the feat, he would say with becoming modesty, "*Ése fué un sapo*"—that was a lucky throw.

Whenever the vaqueros caught a coyote they would mark it in some way. Once a coyote was caught on the plains west of Los Baños by Miller and Lux vaqueros. This time the vaqueros branded it with the S Wrench, bobbed its tail, and put the Miller mark in its ears. This coyote was caught in a trap two years later on the Tejon Ranch by Jerky Johnson, who was trapping for Tejon that year. The distance from where the coyote was caught and branded to the place where it was trapped is well over a hundred miles.

Once it came to the attention of Henry Miller that his men were chasing coyotes. He waited until they were all together. Then he stormed into their camp and at the top of his voice, screamed that he was not raising horses for buckaroos to stove up chasing coyotes. But the men would never stop trying to improve their skills. There has never been, in the history of the world, a man who took more seriously the skills of his craft than the vaquero; and though the range rider has been depicted as a man of violence, that is far from the reality of the true vaquero.

The vaquero spent hours in preparing his reata, stretching and smoothing it with loving care. He knew that the condition of the rope would decide whether the throw would be accomplished successfully. There are several ways to throw a reata. The whirling of the rope overhead, horizontally or vertically decides where the loop will meet its target. *Mangana,* from *manos,* hands, is the skill of lassoing an animal by the forefeet, and *pial,* from *pies,* feet, is the skill of catching one by the hind feet. These, of course, were in addition to the skill of catching an animal by the horns.

But all this must be done gracefully. A vaquero was proud of being able to lasso his animal without undue haste. To the vaquero it was undignified to throw a rope hurriedly. The loop could be thrown crossways, from the left, from the right, underhand, overhand, or backwards, but it must be done without hurting the animal roped or the vaquero's horse. This to the vaquero was of the utmost importance.

Although he often did not know it, the vaquero's beliefs, myths, and superstitions about horses came from the Arabs and their influence was predominant in all the vaquero's relations with his mount.

The Arab's belief, shared by the vaquero, was that a horse had more than forty whorls or verticils—circlets of hair radiating from an axis, that is, spots on the horse's coat where the hair is in spiral form or pattern—and that of those forty, twenty-eight were lucky and the rest were unlucky, depending on where on the horse's body they appeared.

If he came upon a horse that had more lucky spirals than unlucky ones he would try to get that horse in his string. Unlucky spirals are found just above the cheek, on the hip, beside the tail, and on the inside of the leg. Fortunately, there are more lucky spirals than unlucky ones. Those that are on the ears, neck, belly, and flanks are all lucky.

Another Arab tradition the vaquero believed in was the worth of certain colors in horses. Dark shades were preferred to light ones. Light colored horses were distrusted. The old Arab prejudice against the spotted or yellow horse with white mane and tail prevailed among the vaqueros, although pseudo-Hispanophiles, in writing of the early history of California, disseminated the myth that Californianos preferred the palomino. The California vaquero preferred the chestnut, *alasan tostado,* above all other colors in horses. The black came next, then the gray. However, the tradition that no Arab chief would ride a yellow horse or allow one to remain in his stable overnight, was unknown in California.

This third-hand belief—from Arab to Spaniard to Californiano

—that it was a despicable act to ride a yellow horse with white mane and tail was not widely accepted in California, perhaps because the Spaniards that came to California were not Moorish Spaniards, but Catalans. The stamina of the yellow horse with black mane and tail, the buckskin or *bayo*, was proverbial among vaqueros.

A horse of solid color without a trace of white was a prize, indeed. Though Arab traditions and myths are not pertinent yet it still holds that there is no bad color on a good horse and that a perfect horse is hard to find.

White feet meant white hoofs, which are inferior to black hoofs. The Arabs believed that a horse with one white forefoot and one white hind foot was a lucky horse, since they could mount on a white (good) omen and dismount on one. A horse with white hind feet was preferred to one with white forefeet.

The vaquero, like the Arab, believed that a horse had three ages: the first seven years of the animal's life was the period in which it could be left with the trainer. A horse is never fully developed before the age of seven. The second seven are the best or prime years of the animal's life, and then the owner should use it. According to the Arabs, the horse should be lent to an enemy the third seven years, if he can be prevailed upon to accept it.

But if the horse had a good mouth, it could be of any color and have only three legs for all the vaquero cared. A good mouth was the vaquero's greatest pride. A horse that would not turn, stop, or back at the slightest twist of the rider's wrist was worthless in the vaquero's eyes.

However, in judging the vaquero's horse we must take into consideration the fact that the vaquero and his horse had been together over a long period of time and in many a tight squeeze. Through association the horse had learned every mood and quirk of its rider and could, to a large extent, read its rider's mind and from the rider's movements anticipate his slightest wish. This affinity between horse and rider was what made good horsemen. It also was the reason a vaquero stayed on a ranch year after year. He did not want to leave a string of good horses.

This applied only when each rider used certain horses exclusively. The old adage that two of the best riders will spoil the best horse is true in the sense that the horse will be confused by different signals, since no two men signal a horse in the same way.

To slide to a stop, back at a trot, and spin to the right or left without opening its mouth or throwing its head was the test of a good horse. And all this with only a slight pull on the reins—an open mouth indicates a hard tug on the reins.

Here we must digress to speak of open mouths on horses that are ridden with a bit that has a high port. A high port does not necessarily make a horse open its mouth. A hard pull on any bit will do the same thing. This writer has many pictures taken over all the world showing horses being pulled, and it seems that horses that are ridden or driven with straight or snaffle bits seem to brace their jaws and open their mouths even more with bits that have no ports at all.

We shall not undertake in this work to give instructions on how to stop and pull a horse. That has been covered by experts in many other books and it would be superflous to include it here. The good Lord did not make two sand grains on the seashore alike so it follows that there are no two horses alike. This circumstance renders all these instructions useless and the books worthless, since the writer of such books cannot set down the dispositions and characters of the horses the trainer will meet.

Of course, being human, a vaquero would be more skilled in one thing than in another. One was better at riding bucking horses, another was better at throwing the lazo, or at teaching horses to rein; but this does not mean that they were specialists. They could handle all the skills of the trade with more or less expertness. It has often been said that a *jinete,* a bucking horse rider, was good for nothing else; but that is not altogether true. There were good reinsmen on the ranches that a good bucking horse would have trouble in throwing.

One of the skills of the vaquero, that of throwing a beef by a pull on its tail, though common in early California, had gone out of practice at the turn of the century. Although old vaqueros speak of it as often done on the ranches, the last time this writer saw it attempted was on the Tejon Ranch in 1920. The attempt was a failure. When the vaquero, Mike Tapia, bent down to grasp the beef's tail, his horse, El Machucado, lit into bucking. The rider straightened up and grabbed the saddle horn to stay aboard. Nepomuseno Cordero, who did not like Mike, for a long time afterwards would give us instructions on how to tail a beef. He would wait until Mike could not avoid seeing him and then go through the exact motions Mike had gone through. This made Mike angry but there was nothing he could do but *pelar los ojos* —show the whites of his eyes—at Nepomuseno.

George Hoskings, who worked for the Kern County Land Company at Bellevue and at San Emideo, was very skilled at doing this trick, and often gave proof of his ability by turning some refractory beef heels over head. The skill had its risks. If the tailer did not have a hazer he had to crowd the beef. If he permitted his horse to lag, the beef could cross in front and cause a pile-up. Perhaps the introduction of modern beef, tamer but much heavier than the Spanish cattle, made it risky to continue the practice. Hereford and Durham cattle did not need the rough treatment the Spanish cattle got. Besides, they were too valuable.

Of late years the San Joaquin Valley has become a cotton producing country. The farmers of the Buttonwillow area have brought in large flocks of geese to eat the weeds which grow in the cotton. So my friend Buford Fox acquired a large flock of geese. True to the western tradition, he looked around for someone to herd them. He went into Bakersfield and there ran into the old vaquero Adolfo Encinas, and offered him the job of herding the geese. Adolfo's daughter, Carmen, somewhat dubious about her father's being able to cope with the new job, warned Buford, saying, "My father doesn't know about geese. All he knows is herding cattle and breaking horses."

But Buford put Adolfo's bed in the pickup and took him out to Buttonwillow. Buford raised Arabian horses then (he has quarter horses now), so he mounted Adolfo on one of his Arabs and turned the geese over to him.

I learned about Adolfo's new job one day and was surprised to run into him the next day, back in town. So I asked, "How come?" Adolfo is a good raconteur but this time he would not talk. All he would say was, "*Esos gansos estaban locos.* Those geese were crazy. They would run here and there like sheep. I couldn't drive them."

And that was the end of his goose buckarooing.

ORIGINS OF THE VAQUERO

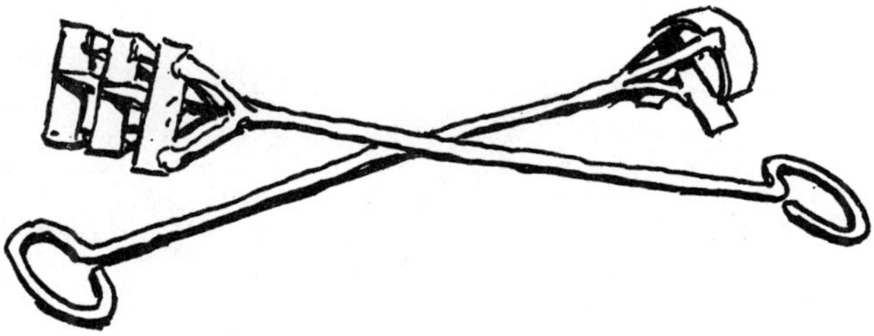

Origins of the Vaquero

The legend that the native-born vaquero developed the bit, spur, saddle, and method of riding used in the Americas after the arrival of the Spaniards is an old one. But, alas, it is only a legend.

The riding equipment and the method of guiding a horse by pressure on the neck were centuries old before Colón ever sailed from the port of Palos in Spain. The Crusaders had met with this style of riding in the tenth century when they fought the Saracens.

The hero gods in Hindu mythology roped the wild Cebu cattle; the ancient Persians used the lazo as a military weapon; the Spaniards were adept at using the running noose, which was one of the classic uses of La Jineta, long before the rape of the Aztec empire. The word jinete is said to come from the blue-eyed Berber tribe that supported Abderaman in his struggle for the Caliphate of Cordova.

The saddle used here was adapted from the one in use in the Egyptian Sudan which originally came from Persia; and for that matter, so was the spade bit. Spade bits are found over all Sonora, parts of Chihuahua, Sinaloa, and Baja California. Many have been dug up in the ruins of towns and buildings which the Yaquis destroyed long before Gaspar de Portolá ever brought the first riders and horses into California.

Two styles of riding existed in Spain at the time of the Conquest, La Jineta and La Brida. Bernal Díaz says, "The Conquest was made *a La Jineta*." The two styles were diametrically opposed. Differences were in the bits, spurs, and saddles, but the chief one was in the length of the stirrups. Since the vaquero's style of riding was adapted from La Jineta, and since La Brida had no influence whatever on the Latin-American rider, we will speak no more of it.

True, in later years the New World rider lengthened his stirrups, but that was because he had let his charger run wild and multiply. He could not mount a bronco with the short stirrups of La Jineta. So by the time the Spaniards came to California they rode with long stirrups. Those old horsemen were toe riders and prided themselves on the extreme length of their stirrups.

The guiding of the animal by holding the reins in the left hand, that is to say, by pressure of the rein on the neck, was the swordsman's way of riding, and the use of the rider's feet as an aid in the control was conducive to the maximum speed and dexterity in turning, which was vital in individual combat. Indeed, this starting and stopping the horse and the speed in the dashes and starts decided the outcome of battle.

When the first Spaniards came to America their horses' speed, dexterity, and aptitude for racing was noted faithfully in Díaz's *Historia Verdadera*. Díaz called such a horse "*revuelto*"—well-turned or well-reined. In the kingdoms of Castile, Valencia, and Aragon since ancient times—probably before Hannibal brought his Numidian cavalry across the straits—short races called *cosos*, from the Latin word *cursus*, were popular. One may well say that the original Spanish horse was a "short-distance" racer, or that the original "quarter-mile" horse was a Spanish horse.

The term La Jineta was applied to the equipment used in this style of riding. There were Jineta spurs, saddles, bits, and other articles. From them came the vaquero's equipment, and, for that matter, that of the *huaso* of Chile, the *gaucho* of Argentina, the *vaquiero* of Brazil, the *charro* of Mexico, and to some extent, of the cowboy of the Gulf Coast, and the *panieola* of Hawaii.

The Jineta saddle was square, strongly made, with both high pommel and high cantle. The rider was literally boxed in without much risk of being ejected during the violent movements of racing, bull-fighting, or skirmishes with the Moors, from whom the Spaniards had adopted this type of fighting. The height of the pommel and cantle permitted the rider to stand in his stirrups and wield sword and lance without danger of falling out. The broad flat stirrups supported the feet firmly, which was a help in wielding the sword.

The influence of La Jineta spread into the far Northwest. Charles M. Russell, that peerless observer (who, incidently, never painted a cowboy, only buckaroos) speaks of those old center-fire, slickfork, spade bit, rawhide reata men as watching their shadows as they rode along, admiring their figure in the saddle.

The horseman's seat was like the light cavalryman's. It was called the "hunting seat" in Europe, which is simply what is being introduced today as the "forward seat" or "balanced seat." It was the jockey seat before Tod Sloan invented the "monkey on a stick" seat used by the present-day race rider. It is the seat which the Arabs, Moors, Tartars, and Cossacks, all natural horsemen, use; it permits the ball of the foot to absorb the shock. It was used for centuries among horsebreeding peoples, and developed through generations of living in the saddle. It was what a buckaroo would call "riding one's stirrups."

In La Jineta the *alludas*, the aids, such as the use of the feet and legs, or shifting of the body, were used to change pace or action, as the present-day *rejoneadores* do in the bull ring.

The La Jineta and La Brida schools of riding were so distinct that the old Jesuits, in listing church property, were careful to place each item in its respective category. There are still extant in musty church records long lists of articles such as a Jineta spur, a La Brida stirrup, a Jineta saddle. The *fiador*—theodore to the gringos—was another Arab, Moor, and Persian piece of equipment which the vaquero inherited.

Oddly enough, the *Tira de Bocado*—indispensable to the Argentine gaucho and called *barbuquejo* in California—was a piece of La Jineta equipment never adopted here, though the Plains Indians used it exclusively in place of a bridle. It is a strip of cloth, a strap, a string of rawhide, or a cord tied around the horse's lower jaw. The reins are attached to this and it is used in place of the bit until the colt is broken.

The Plains Indians acquired horses soon after the Conquest and learned to use the lazo after the classic style of La Jineta. This was long before the vaquero had cast aside the *bastón*, or cane used to place the loop over an animal's head, and learned to whirl and throw his lazo as the present-day riders do. The northwestern tribes who met the vaquero driving cattle north out of California in the 1830's learned from them the art of throwing the lazo.

Another heritage of La Jineta was the prejudice extant among *caballeros Ibericos*, the Iberian gentlemen, of the sixteenth century that made them consider it *altamente deshonroso montar en yegua*—highly dishonorable to ride a mare. This prejudice has endured in California to the present day. Perhaps this is why the vaquero referred to the bands of horses from which he drew his string as *La Caponera*, from capon or gelding.

An ancient book on the classic uses of La Jineta says, "The reins must be carried in the left hand. Over the shoulder of the same side as the lance the jinete should wear the cape, the hood snug. The knees tight against the saddle; the feet parallel to the horse's body; the heels down. The spurs should be buckled firmly to hang below the stirrups. This article, in the conception of the author, should be heavy."

The La Jineta bit called *freno de candado* had a high port, fixed bottom bar, very short shanks curved in the form of an S. The shanks of the bit are the two parallel bars of metal which terminate in rings in which the headstall and reins are attached. Forged to the mouthpiece, the shanks make up the sides of the bit, and act as levers when the reins are pulled.

A small wheel, the roller or cricket, placed in the port, turned on a pin at the movement of the horse's tongue (from habit showing either pleasure or displeasure). The noise made is proportionate to the size of the silver conchos which amplify the sound. This in some Latin-American countries is called *freno de buen eco*—bit of a good echo. These bits were so extensively used in all Latin America that manufacturers in France, Belgium, and England produced them for the American trade. The type was called in California *freno Chileno* ("Mexican ring" by the gringos), and *freno de argolla*, or ring bit. Its original name, however, was *freno de la Jineta*. In Mexico today one can still find stacks of old worn-out ring bits, which proves how extensively this bit was used.

Bits as depicted in the paintings of Velasquez and other Spanish painters are so like many of the present-day ones that they seem to have been forged by the same hand, though they are centuries apart. They are *frenos forjados por muy capaces maestros*—bits forged by very capable masters—and those painted by Walker and Russell could well have been forged by the same hand as those depicted by the old Spanish masters.

The Jineta spur had no rowels. It was a gaff in the shape of a sparrow beak, a *pico de gorrión*, sometimes called *asicates*. The use of the rowel became universal in New Spain soon after the arrival of the Spaniards. The *asicate del Moro*, or Moorish gaff, was a long spur without rowels. Later the pico de gorrión had a small rowel. The spurs the conquistadores used had no rowels.

One page in an ancient Spanish book has this to say about spurs: "Spurs are a necessary aid to the *lazador* (roper), and to all who work on horseback. He who uses them wisely will not have to trade off his horse. He who rides without them commits a fault; for him they are as shackles to a prisoner."

The same old author remarks further, "The vaquero though rustic had the innate courtesy acquired from Spanish ancestors to remove his spurs before entering a house." Then he added as an afterthought, "Besides, the large rowels scoured the earth or dirt floors."

Bits and saddles, as time passed, were adapted to the climate, terrain, or to the type of horse the vaquero rode.

The spade bit came with the first Spaniards to northern New Spain. Like the original freno de la Jineta it had but one or two inches of shank or leverage. However, this bit had a four- or five-inch port.

The spade bits dug up in old adobe ruins in Mexico never had more than two inches of shank. These were made before Alta California was colonized. The bits that came to California later had the same measurements from side to side, from the bottom of the port to the top, and from the bottom of the mouthpiece to the bottom of the shank. Later the bit makers in California, perhaps because of the change in the type of horses the vaquero rode, made the spade into a leverage bit and spoiled it for the purpose for which it was originally intended.

During the nineteenth century the mines of Sonora prospered, and the saddlers and bit makers produced much fine work. Finely carved saddles and elaborate bits found a ready sale. For that reason many of the old bits found there show skilled workmanship.

Most of the saddlers and bit makers in Alta California were from Sonora, a few from Baja California. They came to work in the mines or to take up their trade here. Marteral and Herrera came to seek gold. They found riches in the saddles they manufactured for the men outfitting for the gold fields and cattle drives out of California to the East and Northwest. When the great cattle ranches were set up in the San Joaquin Valley they moved there. But by that time the miner and would-be miner had scattered the California tree over half a continent. Ladesma, Moreno, Wilson, Walker, Brydon, García, Alberto Cuen, (brother of Rafael Cuen, the Miller cattle boss) were some of the old-time saddlers.

Famous bit makers included Tapia, David and Abran Rojas, Gutierrez, Figueroa, Amistosa, Espinosa, Madueño, Bob Pini, Harry Malone, and A. B. Hunt, who was a pupil of Madueño. Hunt was still making bits a year or two ago. Tapia, in this writer's opinion, was the best workman of them all and Madueño was the poorest. When this writer came on the vaquero scene about 1910, and began to take an interest in bits and pore over saddlery catalogs, García and Sterns produced the best work. Later Manuel and Pasquel Gil, brothers from the old colonial town of Alamos, Sonora, were the best in the country. Bit makers worked for different saddleries at different times, so as a result, the quality of the work varied. But G. S. García in Elko, Nevada, always had good workmen.

Though of late years his bits have become collectors' items, Madueño always made his bits too short above the mouthpiece. They required a very tight chin-strap to keep them from rocking. He hammered out a piece of iron and bent it upward in a half circle to form the shank. He probably was unique in using this method; but the assertion that he invented the spade bit is preposterous. The shanks of his bits were always beveled. The most useful bit he ever made was owned by Emiliano Cordova and is now in the possession of a man in Vista, California.

David Rojas made bits in San Luis Rey from 1888 until 1900 when he went to Elko, Nevada, to open García's shop. He died in 1902. He and his brother Abran made light, thin, narrow shanks. But Tapia did the most beautiful work of them all. The bits could be identified by the class of silver and the engraving.

While to riders of other climes a bit was just a bit, the California rider laid much stress on his bit; he demanded, and would be satisfied with nothing but the best.

In speaking of the origins of the vaquero we must not forget to mention in passing the first horses to come from Spain. They came with the first Armada, and were such faithful, heroic horses and played so important, though innocent, a part in the conquest, that a list of them should be included in all books of the American horse. There were sixteen mares and stallions, mostly grays and sorrels, in the original conquest of the New World.

Bernal Díaz gives their colors and the names of the most outstanding. Two were of the famed Valenzuela breed of Spain. There were *El Harriero*, the Driver; *Motilla*, Little Tuft; *El Romo*, the Roman Nosed One; *La Rabona*, the Rat-tailed One (she was the "good gray mare" of Velasquez de Leon). *La Rabona* was probably an appaloosa because the rat, or stub tail, is a characteristic of that type of horse, and prevails on the appaloosa from Tierra del Fuego through South America, Mexico and western United States to Canada. Díaz called her a gray; but there are many shades of gray and some of the appaloosas are a mottled color which closely approaches, or is, gray. The "blunt old soldier" says of *La Rabona*, "when the battle was going against the Spaniards and the men were weakening, Velasquez de Leon would appear on his good gray mare, and the men would take courage."

The Indians' belief that man and horse were one (the centaur myth) was true in the sense that there existed a perfect affinity between horse and rider. This affinity has never been better exemplified than in the Conquest, where man and horse made one terrible creature.

The fabulous amount of gold which the Spaniards took from the New World had at least one benefit to posterity. It brought to America the finest horseflesh to be found in Europe. These horses were shipped to New Spain and in time sired the great-hearted mustang, the vaquero's horse. True, before the vaquero went out of existence he rode horses of many breeds and mixtures, but the mustang was the perfect horse for working cattle—sure-footed, utterly loyal, tireless, patient and brave. He was the welder of two continents, a worthy descendant of the Andalusian barb.

The vaquero while working cattle rode hard and was hard on horses, but he never abused them to make a spectacle. The way the vaquero went about taming a horse was not always gentle, but he was not deliberately cruel. He had applied his military riding to the herding of cattle and the roping of grizzly bears, Tule elk, and wild hogs. He never overestimated the intelligence of his mustang, and had studied the degree to which a horse could be taught. He had learned that patience and repetition were the only means to success in teaching the horse. He never asked the animal to do more than could be expected of it.

The blood of caballeros, bullfighters, Jews, Moors, Basques, and Indian heros ran in the vaquero's veins. He was a strange mixture of races. He admired his Iberian father, but sided and sympathized with his raped Indian mother. If food was short he fed his horse before he fed his wife. Though often a strange contradiction, he was, without doubt, the most interesting man in the New World.

He was a descendant of the old conquerors, and retained the language of Spain. In living the free life of the nomad he imitated the Spaniard in the trappings of his horse, and the Indian in his abode. He spent his wealth on silver-mounted bits and spurs and often left his home destitute of necessities. He slept on the ground, but rode a silver-mounted saddle. He may not have combed his hair, but his horse's mane was trimmed, with one tuft for a colt and two for a bridle horse. He was named after the saint's day on which he was born; it was often Jesús who was the most proficient in stealing cattle.

The vaquero would lie on the ground with his saddle for a

pillow even though the rain was falling, and sleep without a word of complaint, yet he would grumble when his saddle-blankets got wet. Wet saddle-blankets make a horse's back sore.

The vaquero's way of life gave him virtues which do not exist in this modern day, and at this distant time no man can judge a man of that era. His life was hard. He would stand shivering in the early morning cold, holding a cup of coffee in his shaking hand, then sit a horse all day in the driving sleet, chilled to the bone. He would ride from dawn to dusk in a cloud of alkali dust, his tongue parched and swollen, with rippling water in a mirage shimmering in the distance, with visions of all the water he had ever drunk or seen wasted haunting his memory, for memory plays queer, cruel tricks. The want of water was the vaquero's greatest hardship in the burning heat of a San Joaquin Valley summer. He often rode in a daze with visions of springs of cool water bubbling out of the pine-scented Sierra, of canals of water from which he had never bothered to drink. And when he came to drink it would more than likely be out of a reeking waterhole that contained the putrid remains of some animal.

But there was another side. A matchless sky overhead. An expanse of wild flowers that spread over the great valley like a purple carpet, so vast that a day's ride would take one only to the middle of it. The bold, brooding Sierra standing in grim outline that stretched away to the northern horizon. A wild chase down a mountainside in the fall when the air is like wine and life is good. The feel of a good horse between one's knees as he sweeps and wheels around a herd of restless cattle. The evening campfire when men broil *costillas,* ribs, on chamiso root coals, and gather around to tell tales of long ago, of Murrieta, Vasquez, and García.

Colors of Horses

Some quaint and curious beliefs regarding the colors of horses have come down to us from medieval Spain, and the vaquero still puts faith in them.

One of the old beliefs is that the color and markings indicate the horse's temperament, that the horse of solid color, without a touch of white, is bad tempered and treacherous. Such a horse never fails to have a bad mouth. However, now and then, one found a chestnut of solid color that was well reined and useful. Chestnut horses are more spirited than those of other colors. The redder the color the more pronounced this characteristic becomes.

The bay is spirited in proportion to the amount of black in his color scheme. The blacker the markings, the better his temperament. On the other hand, the black with no white markings is seldom other than quiet and gloomy.

Another belief, not quite so widespread, is that all creatures are composed of the four elements earth, air, fire, and water, and that a horse's characteristics are decided by the proportions of these elements contained in its body.

Spanish horses were of all the colors of the rainbow, yet many old vaqueros held to the belief that there were thirty-five colors of horses, each of which had four or five different shades. I have yet to find a vaquero who could name all thirty-five colors.

Whenever I have asked one of them to name all the colors, he would tell me that there was only one man in the two Californias who knew them all, and there came a day when even he failed to name a certain color. This vaquero was much sought after when horses changed hands. He named the color that was put down on the bill of sale. One day he was hired to attend a sale where a large band was being sold. For hours, one after another, the mayordomo, the manager, parted out broncos, and the man called out each one's particular hue.

The band had dwindled down to a few head when a horse of a very original shade was parted out. The man who knew all the colors was at a loss to name this particular one. Never in either of the two Californias had such a shade been seen. The horse was of none of the known colors; yet he was of all of them.

Immediately the work stopped. The mayordomo waited. The vaqueros gathered around the odd-colored bronco. This man said he was of one color, that man said he was of another. None agreed. The mayordomo called a consultation of the oldest vaqueros. They could not agree.

So the bronco was turned back into the manada, and the expert on colors, *con mucha verguenza*—covered with shame—rode home.

I had been thinking of that story. So I went to Francisco (Chico) Urrea and asked him to tell me what were the colors of the horses that he had ridden back in the last century, when the greatest cattle outfits in the world were operating in the San Joaquin Valley. Chico is one of the old-school vaqueros, one of the last three left alive in the Great Valley, and perhaps in all of California. He said that the Miller and Lux horses which were ridden by the vaqueros on the southern division were all S-Wrench mustangs, and they came from the White Horse Ranch in Nevada and from the Malheur and Harney ranches of Miller and Lux in Oregon.

These mustangs are not to be confused with the southern range ponies which the gringos called "broomtails." The Oregon and

Nevada horses were of the best Spanish stock, the best range horses in the West.

Among them, Francisco says, were *bayo*, buckskin; *rusbayo*, light buckskin; *bayo Zebruno*, zebra stripped buckskin; and *grullo*, crane colored, or slate gray (these never failed to have a black line down the back). Palominos were scarce, though *jilotes*, flaxen-maned sorrels, were frequently found among those mustangs. There were many variations of roan: *canelos, rosillos, sabinos*—cinnamon, rose red, strawberry. Grays predominated: *moros*, iron grays; *tordillos*, light grays; *moros obscuros*, dark grays; *moros claros*, blue grays; *tordillos dorados*, dappled grays; and *tordillos manchados*, fleabitten grays.

When a horse turned white with age, he did not become a *blanco*, a white; he remained a tordillo. Vaqueros from Lower California called a fleabitten gray an *escarchado*. Why? I do not know. *Escarcha* means frost. Perhaps they meant hoary with age. *Quién sabe?* Who knows?

The term blanco was applied to a horse with a white skin, whether its eyes were white (albino) or dark. An albino horse was called *guerro*, blond. *Zaino* means bay in California, Lower California, and Sonora, whether the horse has white markings or not, though this term is used for a horse of any solid color in some parts of Mexico and Latin America.

Retinto, brown, also had several shades. When a black horse faded out in the summer he became a *retinto quemado*, a burnt brown, or *prieto quemado*, burnt black. *Prieto*, jet black that did not fade out, was very rare. *Alasan*, sorrel or chestnut, had many variations in shade: *alasan tostado*, toasted or liver chestnut, was by far the most popular among vaqueros, and there were few of them who did not know the centuries-old verse

> Caballo alasan tostado
> Muere antes que ser cansado.

Which was to the effect that a horse of chestnut color expires before he tires. A sentiment no doubt inherited from the Moors.

There were also *alasanes obscuros* and *alasanes claros*, dark and light sorrels. *Castaño* is another term for chestnut, but it was used only by Spaniards in Spain, never in California. The Californiano clung to the Moorish alasan for sorrel.

A spotted horse was called a *pinto* whether he was skewbald or piebald or whether the spots were large or small or any color of the rainbow. The odd colored appaloosa, though often met with, had no special name; he was a pinto here, though there are other terms for that color in Mexico and Spanish America.

A *lucero* had a star in the forehead; a *cara blanca* had a bald face and a *pico blanco* a white muzzle. An *un-albo* had one white stocking or sock; a *dos-albo,* two; a *tres-albo,* three; and a *cuatro-albo* had four.

The *caballo alasan cuatro-albo* or four stocking-foot sorrel, was very popular among the younger, flashier *vaqueritos.* "Vaquerito" is a term applied to a young fellow who has not quite acquired all the skills of a full-fledged vaquero. To call a boy a good vaquerito was a compliment; but to call him a vaquero was to give him the accolade. He had won his spurs.

Chico Urrea says that when Miller and Lux took possession of the Spanish Ranch in the Cuyama Valley about the turn of the century, the company bought all the horses and cattle the ranch carried. Among the horses acquired were two little black *chinos, muy buenos caballitos*—very good little horses. There were also a very good gray and a very good sorrel in this manada. *Chino*, in the dialect spoken in California, means curly; a curly-headed person is a chino, and so is a curly horse. The chino horse was often met with among the mustangs, but now seems to be extinct. The last chino horse this writer remembers was a leggy brown on Tejon Ranch along about 1919 or 1920. The horse, at that time, was ridden by a man we called *El Molacho*, the Toothless One. The chino's hair had a pronounced curl and would never lie flat, not even in the summer when the hair was short. The mane and tail had a curl or wave, sometimes so perfectly marceled that a woman could well have envied it. The chino was a distinct type like the appaloosa and was never found among the horses descended from those brought by the gringos. This type occurred in horses of Spanish strain only. Like the alasanes, bayos, and grullos, the chino had a reputation among vaqueros for being *muy guapo*, very tough, either in the sense of being tireless on long hard rides, or in bucking long and hard.

"One day," Chico says, "I was riding the gray at Salt Slough. I lassoed a very fierce Chihuahua bull. I had to throw that bull about ten times before he would stay down long enough for me to take my reata off his horns. He seemed to be made of rubber. He was the toughest bull I ever put a lazo over. I would hold my horse and let the bull charge toward me, when he had two or three feet over the reata I would take a run and throw him. But he would bounce up again.

"But the little horse never failed me. He never got tired. *Ah! qué buen caballito era*–Ah! what a good little horse he was."

A *caballo romo* was a roman-nosed horse or ram-headed horse. This horse was also considered to be muy guapo. Like the mean horse, the roman-nosed horse was obstinately tough.

Blooded Horses

Writers on the West for many years have been in the habit of calling the range rider's horse a "pony." This term may hold true in southern or prairie states; but in the far West the rider, vaquero or buckaroo, never rode a pony.

True, in the southern or Gulf Coast states the horses were little better than ponies, and were so small that each man had to have ten or twelve in his string and changed mounts two or three times a day. These were little horses that disappeared under the bulk of saddles which often weighed over forty pounds. The riders believed that the bulk of the saddle was a benefit to the horse, that on long journeys the ease of the saddle compensated for the added weight, and that large saddles distributed the weight of the rider over a larger portion of the horse's back. As a consequence of this practice and belief, when working cattle the ponies had to be changed two or three times a day, depending on the class of work.

In California, Oregon, Nevada, and Washington the range riders were mounted on horses, never on ponies.

California has always had the best of Spanish horses. For over a hundred years men who wrote of this state have praised the California mustang. As early as 1840 blooded horses were coming to the West over the Oregon trail. In the southern San Joaquin Valley J. B. Haggin and Bill Carr established the Kern County Land Company. They brought thoroughbreds from Kentucky, and at one time had as many as six hundred brood mares. The vaqueros rode horses culled from this stock.

Men from Argentina and Chile have come to the Carr and Haggin breeding farm to buy horses. Lucky Baldwin acquired horses at this farm, horses which made the name of Santa Anita famous over the world.

Roland Hill of the Tehachepi Cattle Company for many years bred more Morgan horses than any other breeder. His vaqueros rode the best of the Morgan breed.

Miller and Lux, with its control over millions of acres in three states, needed thousands of horses to mount the hundreds of riders in its employ. Henry Miller imported the finest coach stallions to be found in Europe, and these bred to Oregon and Nevada mares produced good saddle stock.

On some of the ranches, Buttonwillow for one, there were as many as five hundred saddle horses, and the roar of their pounding hoofs as they were driven into the corral in the morning was an unforgettable sound that never failed to bring the vaqueros out of their blankets. It would have awakened the dead.

The Tejon Ranch, after the passing of the Barileño mustang, bought seventeen mares and three stallions of Carr and Haggin breeding from Charlie Kerr. These stallions and mares produced the saddle stock on the Tejon until the ranch management imported an Arabian stallion, one of the first in the southern San Joaquin.

In the southern part of the state ranchers were using fine stallions to breed saddle horses as early as 1849.

One of the factors responsible for the skill of the vaquero was the breeding of the horses he rode. The quality of the horse made the vaquero famous as a reinsman over the land.

Ahijar

Abu Khalil, the blue eyed Arab, spoke perfect Spanish. He had lived in Spain, Morocco, and Egypt. He was an old man and in poor circumstances when I met him, but friendly and genial. Every now and then I would invite him to eat with me.

It was not altogether hospitality which prompted me, however. I wanted to ask him questions in respect to the etymology of Arabic words which the Spaniards had inherited from the Moors, words which are still used in California although they were brought from Spain centuries ago, and which have been adopted into the gringo buckaroo's vocabulary.

Such words are *moro*, gray; *cincho*, cinch; *alasan*, sorrel or chestnut; *jáquima*, anglicized into "hackamore" by the gringos; and *barbiquejo* or *barbuquejo*, the string which goes around the chin to hold a hat in place and the thong which is tied around the horse's lower jaw to serve as a bridle. This was the Plains Indian's method of bridling, which like the practice of using a cane or pole to place the loop over the head of the animal to be roped, as the present-day Mongols do, was one of the classic usages of La Jineta. It was adopted from the earliest Spaniards, probably from Coronado or his contemporaries, long before the method of swinging and throwing the loop was developed in the New World.

Abu Khalil said that the old proverb we have already quoted, *Caballo alasan tostado muere antes que ser cansado*, the horse of dark chestnut color dies before he tires, had its equivalent in Arabic. This accounts, in some measure, for the veneration the paisano had for certain colors of horses. It was a survival of an ancient hippology which had its roots far back in Central Asia.

The gray color must have predominated in the horses the Moors rode into Spain, and the Spaniards associated the color with the rider and *Moro,* Moor, became a synonym for gray.

Cincho still remains "cinch" in the gringo's vocabulary for all the influence of the Anglo-Saxon and his girths.

Abu Khalil said that *ahijar,* the practice of engrafting a dog onto a goat, so that the dog would grow up and stay with the flock and protect it from coyotes, wolves, and other predators, was as old as Father Abraham and his son Ishmael. This system of inducing a dog to adopt a goat as its mother was the same in old California as in Arabia. The Spaniards brought it to the New World.

"In order to accomplish this task one must wait until the bitch has a litter of pups. Then one must search for a goat which has had a kid on the same day as the bitch. Then one must take a pup before its eyes are open and put it to suckling the doe. But first one must take care that the milk of the goat has the same richness and fat content as that of the dog; otherwise the pup will not thrive."

But how the ancient herdsmen decided this question without instruments, Abu Khalil did not tell me.

Spanish Bits

It was a time of great riches in Spain. The *escudero harto pobre y humilde* had come back to Spain, loaded down with the gold of the Aztecs. Adventurers without a centavo in their ragged pockets but with larceny in their hearts were eager to sail for the New World where Cortez had found a cacique from whom he had squeezed a room full of gold.

In hopes of finding another Montezuma or Atahualpa, hordes of avaricious men set out with expeditions in which they had sunk every centavo they possesed or could borrow. Many of these expeditions met with failure, and thus much of the blood-stained gold brought to Spain went into ships and armaments which were lost or destroyed in the New World. The legend of El Dorado died with the last conquistadores and dreams of gold soon vanished before the greedy and sinful eyes of rude soldiers. Men fought like tigers not for freedom, nor for any noble end, but to free themselves of penury in Spain.

Though some of these robber groups reached their objective, there never was another golden Mexico or Peru. The later arrivals came to guard the mines already established. In many localities Europeans were needed because the local Indians the Spaniards recruited as soldiers were no match for warlike Yaquis, Apaches, or others.

The Spaniard who led the expedition that brought the spade bit to the New World must have come directly to Northern New Spain, because the spade bit is not found south of Sinaloa. He must have recruited his soldiers in some isolated part of Spain close to the Basque country. From the evidence we must assume that he was probably one of the soldiers of Urdaide or Ybarra.

This man's name is unknown to history. Perhaps he was some out-at-elbows relative or younger son of a noble house, made bold by poverty, but sharp enough to grasp and hold his share of golden loot after the disaster which befell Pizzaro. Or perhaps he was one of the few who were too smart to be cheated by the sly Cortez as were many of his followers such as Bernal Díaz del Castillo. He was, no doubt, a black-bearded rascal with olive skin and Moorish eyes, but a horseman to the very *tutano,* the very marrow.

The First Cattle Drive

Ewing Young may well be called the father of the great cattle migrations over the American West. The first cattle drive in the history of the West started from San Jose, California, in 1836. These cattle were driven to the Willamette Valley in Oregon. Young had contracted to supply the ranchers there with breeding stock. This was thirty years before the Texas trail herds are claimed to have started moving north.

This herd from San Jose was the first of the large scale movements in which thousands of head of cattle were handled. Subsequent trail drivers over all the West learned to handle big herds from those pioneer cattle drivers.

These men rode for months in an endless monotony of landscapes, of swaying backs, tramp of hoofs, clash of horns; of bawls, smells, dust; of footsore horses, footsore cattle, or exhausted animals left to be devoured by wolves; an endless monotony of solitude, of herds of elk, antelope, deer, and great gray bears.

There were no towns or villages on that trail from San Jose to the Willamette Valley, only tribes of stolid Indians who stared at these gaudy riders whose ornate trappings filled the red men with wonder.

But these men had no quarrel with the Indians, rendering it necessary to take their lives. On the contrary whenever the riders met the Indians, the vaqueros curried their friendship and with presents of meat averted hostility. The vaqueros respected the Indian's right to human dignity, and as a result records show that there were few if any differences with them.

These vaqueros were always on the alert, never sleeping their fill, only dozing with one eye open for crawling things whose bite was fatal, dozing with the ever present dread of the wild stampede sweeping over them. They were afraid to die in this savage land lest they be buried in unhallowed ground like a heathen, far from the prayer of mother or sister.

At night the vaqueros crawled into damp blankets to dream of fiestas and fandangoes in a sunnier clime, before suffering had made those old scenes so remote as to be almost forgotten. These vaqueros, born in the serene South, were to know the howl of blizzards, the pelt of hail, the chill of snow, and in the North the endless, cold, clammy mist that was almost, but never quite, a rain, that hung on day after day and wet the riders through and through.

Riding day after day, in the chill of dawn or blaze of noon, riding through pitch black nights or glaring days, riding in wet weather or in dry these men helped make possible the settlement of the West.

BEWARE THE APACHES

Alamos, Mother of California

After hearing Mass on September 29, 1775, there left from San Miguel de Horcasitas the expedition commanded by Don Juan Bautista de Anza, who had drawn *un buen contingente*, a good company, of colonists from El Fuerte, Ures, San Miguel de Horcasitas, and Alamos. Alamos contributed twelve families, making forty-nine persons in all. On leaving Horcasitas the men waved their sombreros and the women their mantillas, saying "Adios" to the residents who had followed them to the edge of town, calling the usual warning of the time:

"*Cuidado con los Apaches.*" Beware the Apaches.

Brave Alamos, who from behind her grilled windows and blank walls bore the onslaught of fierce warriors and yet sent her sons through the gantlet of Seri, Yaqui, and Apache to carry the banner of Castille and Leon over half a continent.

Colonial Alamos, priceles legacy of the Moor and Goth, where the whispering spirits of long departed conquistadores haunt the narrow, lonesome streets and stir restlessly at the hollow ring of footsteps. Here is the same oriental atmosphere that clings to the somber old missions of California.

The soul of Alamos abides in her ruins, and one comes very close to the spirit of old mother Spain in her empty patios. The forlorn *portales*, roofed porches, fall in ruin. They bespeak the fate of the Moor; but the old stone church stands firm against the ravages of time, as a grim Gothic warrior faced the hosts of Islam. The proud, haughty spirit of northern Spain still lives in the buttressed old pile. Unyielding as the mountaineers that built her, she stares at the empty houses and the people who shuffle to and fro across the plaza, where the world of today is the world of yesterday.

In contrast, the portales were fashioned by no hand other than one fresh from the building of such as the Alhambra. The fine old buildings of Alamos are empty and dilapidated. The inhabitants have drifted into a currentless backwater of life and are probably unaware that from here rode forth, "all fire and threadbare velvet, the finest horsemen in the world" to make the tradition of the West. Men still ride mules and horses with high-horned, center-fire saddles along the narrow, cobbled, old-world streets between blank, windowless Arab houses.

Señor Palomares showed me an old spade bit that had belonged to his father's grandfather. Don Romulo Feliz had another antique bit.

"*Son cosas de los viejos*," things of the old people, he said of the silver mounted, well made article.

"*Desgraciadamente*, unfortunately, this fine inlaid work is not made here any more. Nobody has the money to pay for it."

The crumbling tombstones in the ancient Campo Santo are inscribed with old names such as were brought to California by the *fundadores*, the founders. They are commemorated in the towns and streets which bear the names of those colonists: Palomares, Feliz, Cantua, Valencia, Ibarra, Vasquez, Ruiz, Chavez, perhaps the very brothers of those who lie at rest there. They tell the story of a people who carried the embers of European culture from one frontier presidio to another across the New World to Alamos which was the outpost of civilization, and from Alamos, Padres Kino, Salvatierra, Garces, and other pioneer priests pushed their missions and "little cattle ranches" into the frontier.

Though poverty and distress remain where pride and pomp once reigned, Alamos in her decline is still an enchantress. She still casts her spell across the far reaching deserts to the great cities in California of which she is the mother.

The Devil's Highroad

In the northwest corner of Old Mexico, in the state of Sonora bordering the Gulf of California, lies a vast, forbidding desert. It is a land of contrasting landscapes, of odd and varied aspects. Its topography in part is made up of great level plains covered with loose sand where a horse sinks to its fetlocks. Here the winds blow the sand into dense yellow clouds, drift it about, and finally lay it in dunes and long, twisted ridges like snowdrifts.

Some plains are covered with *cholla*, a growth of stunted, twisted cactus, and brush. There are other plains where the land is bare and covered with glaring white alkali. Here the mirages can lure an unwary traveler to his death. Immense areas are covered with black lava which at some remote period was spewed from the bowels of the earth. There are chains of bare, burnt mountains with ridges that suggest the scaly legs of some giant sleeping lizard. These *cordilleras* extend across the desert for interminable miles, with their peaks standing clearcut against a flawless sky. Down from these mountains come great *cañones* and *barrancas*, canyons and ravines, deep and awful to behold, cut out by torrents in some prehistoric age.

There are solitary hills, buttes, pinnacles, and flat-topped mesas which stand apart in lonely grandeur and rise abruptly out of the flat plain.

There is a dusty, tortured, lonely road that crawls across this land from Sonoita to the Colorado River and beyond into far California. Men risked their lives to cross this desert, and the demon of thirst has strewn the white bones of hapless travelers along the stretch from the little village of Sonoita to the Sierra of California. In two hundred miles there was but one water hole.

The road has been called *El Camino del Diablo*, the Devil's Highroad, since friendly Indians led Padre Garces over its route. It was this far-ranging explorer who mapped it for Sonora's greatest son, that intrepid *hombre de buena cepa*, man of good family, Juan Bautista de Anza, who led the way across it in the first overland journey into California.

This inhospitable land had its denizens. They were the Papago and Cucapa tribes, and on its far western edge, where the waters of the Gulf lap its shores, lived a remnant of the once warlike Seris. These Indians traverse this land in small groups, subsisting on scanty roots, seeds, rodents, reptiles. Food gleaned from the desert is scarce at best.

There was another Indian, distinct from those mentioned, who also ventured into this land. This was the Apache warrior. As the wayfarer plodded over the Camino, the warning, *Cuidado con los Apaches*, which he had heard at every stop on his way across Sonora, rang ceaselessly in his ears.

Many men have come over the Devil's Highroad—priests,

soldiers, colonists, and gold seekers—but the most outstanding was the martyred Padre Francisco Garces. Though he laid down his life more than a century ago, he is still honored. Along the great highway that runs north through the central valley of California a statue of the pathfinder has been erected where travelers may see him gazing down into the heart of Bakersfield.

The Little Band

They had opened the route overland to California across the burning sands. And now, the "Little Band" stood on the banks of the Colorado, to find that after the perils of the waterless desert, they had fallen *de las llamas al brasero*, from the flames into the brazier.

Between them and the life-giving water stood a host of Indians, eager to spill the blood of these strange white men, to learn if the blood of the man in the torn, threadbare robe was of the same color as that of the captain in the plumed hat, he who rode the fine horse and carried the ornate sword.

Don Juan Bautista de Anza and Padre Francisco Garces, the leaders of the Little Band, were pre-eminent among the daring men in an age of great adventure. They bade their soldiers stand firm and wait. Men of that era had great faith, and these were confident of yet finding a way out of this new peril.

A veteran of many a pitched battle, the captain carefully scanned the enemy, noting his arms and numbers. De Anza and Padre Garces noticed that for all their enmity the Indians seemed hesitant to attack. In looking for an explanation for this attitude, the Spaniards saw that among the Indians a number of men carried *cruzitas de carriso,* little crosses made of reeds. So the Little Band knew that this adventure would end well for them. The Cross planted years before by the far ranging Padre Kino had borne fruit in this barren desert.

It is many years since "el hombre de buena cepa" opened the route into California. But every now and then the shifting sands to this day uncover the whitened bones of some long-dead animal, with those of his luckless rider lying close by. They are mute evidence that men stayed alive on the Devil's Highroad only as long as their mounts lived.

"When the mule one rides over the Camino becomes mad with thirst and fights to turn back to the last place it had water, let it go," the men who traveled its burning length said. "One will find only death on the road back. The animal will come to the end of its strength, and lie down and die long before it reaches its last watering place."

From necessity and from experience, the king's soldiers and their descendants turned to the long-eared hybrid as best suited to the conditions of the desert. Here the mule survived long after the Andalusian horse was dead. Many weary miles of cactus and sand would never have been covered in early days if it had not been for the stamina of that unsung hero, the perverse, intractable mule.

Though a prolific mother, Sonora, due to its geographic location, is often cursed with drought. The poverty of moisture brings hunger to her children. As a result, they have drifted periodically, a stream of woebegone humanity and animals, down the barren tableland to seek sustenance in the great valleys or coastal regions to the northwest. They ran a great risk of death from thirst and from the arrows of the world's greatest warrior, the Apache, to reach California far across the sand dunes.

While they accompanied the Cross, they brought cattle and brood mares through the desert, ever on the alert for the menace of the Apache that dogged their footsteps. They would end one thirsty *jornada*, or stage, to begin another at the same monotonous two-mile-an-hour gait, day after day, months on end, over half a continent, in oven-like heat or bitter cold and always in suffocating dust. It was an epic of dauntless men and brave animals of immense vitality who brought the cattle industry to California and the western United States. They were humble, resolute men who took danger as it came and savage, sudden death as it found them.

The Last Ride

As we have seen, beginning in 1774 and continuing for more than a hundred years, Sonoreños traveled on horses, mules, and burros over the Camino del Diablo into California. The knowledge that many thousands of travelers lost their lives on that *Jornada del Muerto*, that Route of Death, never deterred others from venturing over it. However, since the beginning of this migration there have been but few who have not yearned to return to Sonora when they had come near the end of their days.

This urge was so strong that when an old man felt that his time was near, he would leave everything he owned—his house, his herds, his children—to return to his homeland to die.

Alfredo Bohorques and I were talking of the old days and of old-timers, those iron-willed men who crossed wastes of burning, shifting sands and lived when mules and burros died. And Alfredo said:

"There was an old man of my acquaintance who had spent his youth searching for gold in the placers of the Sierra Nevada. He had managed to accumulate enough of the elusive metal to establish a little ranch and to stock it with animals. He specialized in the breeding of saddle mules. The mules he bred had a reputation for being mean and hard to handle, but they were not entirely without virtue. Their reputation for meanness was compensated by their excellence under the saddle and their endurance on long, hard roads.

"The old man had five strapping sons, every one capable of handling the mules his father raised.

"One morning the old man awoke with the feeling that his life was coming to its end, and that it was time for him to prepare for his journey into the next world. He decided to go back to his birthplace to die. He informed his sons of his intention. They remonstrated, but to no avail. He was determined to make the journey.

"He ordered them to comb the manadas of mules and find an animal strong enough to carry him across the desert which stretched for many miles between the ranch in California and his destination in Sonora.

"The only animal stout enough to survive on that terrible road was an eight-year-old bronco mule which had escaped from the ranch and had been running with wild mustangs on the desert. The old man's sons had but recently captured it.

"The sons lassoed and threw the mule, and after much struggling strapped a saddle on its back, put a jáquima around its nose, and blinds over its eyes.

"The old man strapped his belongings to the saddle. These consisted of a blanket, an *anfora* or *bota*—a leathern water bottle—a sack of *pinole*, which is made of either wheat, corn, acorns, or even mesquite beans, toasted and ground into a meal, and mounted while the mule was still on the ground.

"The mule got to its feet bawling and bucking, pawing at the jáquima around its nose, and biting at its rider's legs. But the old man weathered the storm. When the mule at last assumed a horizontal position, the old man got it into a run and headed it south. The last the sons saw of their parent and his recalcitrant mount was their forms disappearing in a cloud of dust.

"Some weeks later the sons received a letter which told them that their father had arrived in the town of his birth, and that he had died a few days after his arrival; that the mule was thoroughly broken-in and had become so attached to its old master that it had refused to eat and had brayed forlornly for days after the old man's death.

"The sons were convinced that the old man had willed Death away for as long as he had to stay on the back of that wild mule, crossing the Camino del Diablo."

Joaquin Murrieta

The old stone church in Alamos, Sonora, faces the plaza and frowns down on the boys and girls who, serenely indifferent to its disapproval, walk round and round the brave little cluster of vegetation that serves as a park.

The girls chatter as they walk arm in arm. Each girl carries a flower. The girls walk counterclockwise, the boys walk clockwise to face the girls. Each boy also carries a flower.

When a boy meets a girl who pleases him, he offers her his flower, which the girl never refuses to accept. If the boy is to her liking, she will keep the flower and give him hers. On the other hand, if he does not please her, on the next turn around the plaza she will return his flower, and in this delicate way close the matter between them.

It was in the momentous year of 1849 in this oldest pueblo in northwestern New Spain that Joaquin Murrieta humbly offered his flower to Rosita, and was accepted. The records of the old church attest to their marriage before its altar.

Shortly after this important event in their lives Joaquin and Rosita set out to seek their fortune in the gold fields of California. They crossed the Devil's Highroad, and after weeks of travel arrived in the gold fields. They found riches, nuggets of gold, but they also found disgrace and death.

Joaquin had gone to work on his placer claim, leaving his young bride alone. Thirteen gringos came to the cabin. The thirteen men found Rosita without a defender. They must have beaten her into submission before each one of the thirteen ravished the poor little-girl bride. Joaquin came on the scene in time to find them robbing his house and his wife breathing her last. He fought, but to no avail. The thirteen men beat him until he no longer moved. Then they left him there for dead.

But Murrieta did not die. While the desperadoes were beating him, he had kept his senses long enough to impress on his memory the features of every one of his wife's murderers. He would recognize each one again whenever he should meet him.

He lived from then on for revenge. When, after many days, he could ride again, he set out to do the task for which he thenceforth lived. For many weary, desperate years he hunted down his wife's ravishers. He searched from one mining camp to another until, one by one, he found them all, and the last of the thirteen died begging for mercy.

Murrieta, his work done, went back to Sonora to live out his broken life, not with gold, a wife, children, happiness, but with bitter memories.

How long he lived in Cucurpe after his return from California, we do not know. When he died the compassionate people of the town laid him to rest in the old cemetery with a prayer that this much abused man might now sleep in peace after a ruined life.

But it was not to be. The gringos who had never been sure whether they had actually killed the nemesis of California's gold rush days, or an innocent man, learned of his death and burial. Still in keeping with their earlier acts of barbarism, they denied him, to the very last, the right to human dignity. They committed the last indignity by an act of desecration of the dead. They dug up his bones to measure his cranium!

Murrieta, after a hundred years, still remains a legendary figure, and as long as the Spanish tongue remains in California, his tragedy will be remembered.

Among the men who followed Murrieta out of the Sierras,

over the desert, and across the Colorado were Avilez, Pinto, Arbiso, Sesenia, and Duarte. There was a substantial amount of gold among the articles carried in the *alforjas*, the pack saddles, with which the mules were loaded. Murrieta divided it among the men who had followed him. There on the east bank of the Colorado the men disbanded, each to go his separate way and lose himself in the many villages and hamlets of Sonora, never to be heard of again, except for the tales which rose over the length and breadth of Sonora as the smoke rises from its many hearthfires.

Only Manuel García, also called Three Fingered Jack, was ever heard from again. That desperado came to the violent end of his bloody trail, perverse and unrepentant to the last. He looked into the muzzle of the revolver which was to take his life and scoffed:

"You may shoot me, but I still have the best of the bargain. My one poor life is but poor pay for the many I have taken."

California Herb Medicines

A good vaquero "never had time to get sick." Few if any germs had effect on his weatherbeaten body, and except for the knocks, bruises and cuts which were so much a part of his day's work he seldom was ill. However, he had his nostrums.

Gavino García wore buckskin *armitas,* a sort of apron which takes the place of chaps, he said, because buckskin would cure his rheumatism.

José Dominguez, whose mother had been a sister of the bandit Tiburcio Vasquez, would turn his shoes upside down and cover them when he went to bed. This procedure was supposed to prevent them from "catching cold."

In the infrequent times he needed medicine the vaquero used herbs, which grew everywhere and could be had for the taking. Some had been used for centuries in the Old World. The first Spaniards found herbs which they had used in Spain growing abundantly in America.

We read in Cervantes of the shepherd using *Romero,* or Rose Mary, common in California, to heal the torn ear of Don Quixote, after that mad gentleman's fight with the Biscayan.

The vaquero's *Esteafeate* (Artemisia Mexicana) was the *Ixtahuatl* of the Aztecs, and was used by them to treat bowel disorders.

Saffron, the Arab's *zafaran* and the Spaniard's *Azafran,* was used to flavor food. It was also used in bath water to cure rheumatism.

Rosa de Castilla (Castilian Rose) was used as a purgative for infants.

Yerba Buena, literally Good Herb (Mentha Piperita) common mint, was a universal tea. It was the first herb planted whenever the paisano established a new home. It would grow wherever the ground was kept moist and when crushed had a very pleasing odor. It was used to flavor food, and gave *menudo,* a tripe stew, a distinctive flavor.

Ruda (Ruta Graveolens) was picked, crushed, and applied locally to relieve pain.

Cilantro (coriander) was another plant which was used for food and for medicine.

Hojasen (Florrencia Cernica) was used as a physic.

Sauco (elder blossoms) were gathered in the spring. When they were steeped into a tea, they were used in cases of fever and to treat children who had measles.

In speaking of the many herb remedies used and relied upon by the paisano, Dan Castro says that *Yerba del Pasmo* (Waltheria Americana), *Canutilla* (squaw tea or Ephedra Californica), *te de Aliso* (tea made from the bark of the sycamore tree), and *Yerba Mansa* (literally Tame Herb, Anemopis Californica) were the favorites. Yerba del Pasmo was a universal poultice.

Canutilla, Dan says, would make a man as skinny as a rail if taken over a period of time. The herb was brewed into a tea.

Te de Aliso was purple in color. It was used as a specific in the treatment of blood ailments. Paisanos drank it to enrich their blood.

Yerba Mansa was found in all creek bottoms. It was chewed to relieve colds. Some vaqueros said it would cure tuberculosis. It was brewed into a tea and used to bathe wounds. Vaqueros tied a piece of the root to the mouthpiece of their horse's bridle-bit to prevent the animal from becoming wind-broken or to cure that condition—whether this practice had the desired effect, I do not know. Yerba Mansa had a very astringent effect and would pucker the mouth.

IN OLD MEXICO

Baja California Vaquero

There is a legend to the effect that when Don Gaspar de Portolá saw Baja California for the first time he wept because Spaniards had to live in so desolate a land.

Father Francisco Palou complained that the mules which had been taken by Father Junípero Serra on the expedition to Monterey were badly needed at Loreto and that the raising of cattle in Baja was hardly worth the effort, since beef did not bring in enough money to pay the vaquero's wages. Brush and cactus grow so thickly there that there is hardly room for grass.

Baja California is, however, a fertile ground for the student of the history of the far West, for it is part of the territory where the spade bit and Spanish spur were used. It cannot be ignored by the historian who seeks to establish the exact limits of territory over which that type of bit and spur were used in Mexico and the United States. Much of the Baja vaquero's equipment in use today is like that which was brought to Alta California in 1769.

The Baja vaquero is an anachronism. His saddle has not changed in two centuries. He wears a *cuera*, a tunic of buckskin, that is no different in design from those worn by the *soldado de cuera*, the leather-jacket soldier, who guarded Padre Serra. The Baja vaquero wears the same *bota* they wore. This bota is a sort of legging which he wraps around the calves of his legs to protect them from thorns. He wears a hat made of buckskin. He puts a heavy leather housing over his saddle tree, and folds it back over his legs. He calls this housing *armas*, or armor.

But the Baja California vaquero is worthy of respect for he is the granddaddy of the Western American vaquero and buckaroo; moreover, he is a skilled workman. The Baja vaquero is of necessity a "brush popper"; for there is no rougher terrain or denser vegetation on this continent than on the peninsula of Baja California. It is actually a mountain range sticking up out of the water. Everything that grows there has thorns: cholla, ocotilla (palo adan), brasil, mesquite, cacachila, unia de gato (cat claw), palo zorilla, palo blanco, palo verde, long boy, to name a few. This "long boy" was named by the English pirates or buccaneers who waited along the coast for the Spanish galleons in order to rob them.

The Baja vaquero's horse must of necessity be small, a pony in fact, for he must be able to follow the cattle into any hole through the brush the pursued beef makes. The Baja vaquero does not carry his rope fastened to his saddle. It would be torn off before he got well started. In fact he has no use for a long rope. He does not have the time nor room to rope a beef as the vaquero farther north does. He carries an eighteen-foot rope fastened around his waist and so adjusted that he can release it in an instant. If he can rope a beef before it gets into the brush, well and good; otherwise he follows the beef into the brush and when he is close enough, he reaches over the horse's ears, grasps the beef's tail, raises his leg to clear the horn, and slides down the horse's neck to the ground. With a quick jerk he throws the beef to the ground and ties it. The vaquero's little horse or mule is trained to follow his master when he dismounts so that in the event the vaquero fails to throw the beef and it escapes, he can mount the horse and take up the chase again.

El Barroso

I met him in the *bosque,* the backwoods, of Baja California, almost at the end of the peninsula. He popped out of the brush and cactus, leading a wild cow.

Cattle are shipped out of Baja by boat. They are led into the surf and herders in a rowboat tow them, swimming, to the ship. There they are hoisted out by a crane and lowered into the hold.

This was the last beef to go on the ship, so when it had disappeared into the hold, he invited me to his camp. His camp consisted of a *ramada,* a sort of arbor made of brush, under which was a table and a bench. A circle of stones served for a stove and the cooking utensils consisted of a coffee pot and another pot which contained beans.

He made a fire and put the coffee pot on to heat. Then he cut some slices of meat, sprinkled them with salt and pepper, and wrapped them in a cloth. When the coffee was boiling he took it off the fire. There was a fine bed of coals left on which he put the meat to broil. When it was done he dug up some tortillas which he had stored away safe from animals. The tortillas were fresh, which meant that some woman had made them for him in the last day or two. They were not the large-as-a-hat, thin-as-paper tortillas of Sonora, but the small, thick *gordas,* or fat ones, of Baja California. He placed the food before me and said, "*Coma.*" Eat.

The meat was fat, juicy, delicious. I ate one of the best meals I have had in years.

In my travels I always carry two or three cartons of American cigarettes for just such occasions as this, when it would be an insult to hospitality to offer money and when words are inadequate to express one's appreciation for courteous treatment. I opened one of the packages and offered him one. After he had lit it I gave him the carton and said:

"*Éstos son para usted.*" These are for you.

He filled his mouth with smoke, expelled it through his nostrils, and said, "*Ah, tobaco Americano, qué sab roso.*" Ah, American tobacco, how flavorful.

He put the carton of cigarettes away, then sat down again to talk. This is the story he told me as we sat under the ramada and waited for the tide so the ship could sail.

"The Spaniards, like the slave holders of the American South, bred their own slaves. My father was a Spaniard, my mother was the daughter of a vaquero on the rancho, so I became a *pistolero,* a gunman.

"The Spaniards had many illegitimate sons, and while the fathers never recognized them legally, the sons knew who their fathers were. When such offspring grew up, the Spaniards took advantage of this relationship and used the sons as their personal bodyguards.

"I was twelve years old when I went into the service of Don Fermin, the owner of half the valley. Don Fermin was the last of the old-school dons. He was a hard master but he was just. When we did anything well we were paid, either in money or in praise, which is at times worth more. Don Fermin could ride as well or better than any of his vaqueros, and would never hesitate to show us how to throw the lazo on the wildest bull, or how to mount and ride the wildest mustang. In a word, he would never ask a man to do a thing that he would not do himself. He rode just as hard and just as far as his toughest vaquero.

"In time I acquired a measure of fame as a bull rider and the name of 'Barroso' which means clay-colored [*barro* means clay] in this way. One day a young Spaniard from a neighboring estate came to visit our patron. He was riding with us on the morning that a wild, clay-colored bull followed a heifer into a big stone corral. Don Fermin ordered us to ride into the corral and to close the gate so the bull would not escape. When we were all inside, Don Fermin said, 'Two of you throw a lazo on that bull and stretch him out so that José may ride him.'

"The bull was soon roped and stretched out on the ground where I mounted him. He was very active. He bucked across the corral and when he came to the stone wall, he jumped it and carried me across a field and under a tree where I caught hold of a branch and pulled myself off his back. I stayed in the tree until the vaqueros drove a couple of *cabestros*, lead oxen, up and led the barroso bull away. When I got back to the corral, Don Fermin and the young Spaniard both gave me a present of money.

"The young Spaniard stayed some weeks and rode with us every day. He seemed to have taken a liking to me because he always chose me for a partner whenever the vaqueros roped in pairs. One day in speaking of me to Don Fermin he referred to me as 'El Barroso.'

" '*El Barroso, cual el Barroso?*' Don Fermin asked. El Barroso, which El Barroso?

" '*El muchacho del toro barroso,*' the Spaniard replied. The boy of the clay-colored bull.

" '*Ah!*' Don Fermin exclaimed, '*José. Sí, sí. José.*' Ah, José. Yes, yes. José.

"From that time on I was known as El Barroso.

"Many years after I had left that ranch, I returned for a visit. Don Fermin had long since gone back to Spain. The place had changed owners. The vaqueros were working cattle in the corrals, so I took my place near the gate. I had been standing there a few minutes when someone called, 'Barroso!'

"I turned to answer the call when to my surprise a young fellow also answered. There was another Barroso on the ranch. I had a *tocayo,* a namesake.

"Just then an old man came up to me and said, 'I know you. You are the old Barroso, the pistolero.' He had spoken so loudly that the vaqueros crowded around us to see who I was. The old man—he was the caporal—turned to the vaqueros and said:

" 'This is the original Barroso. He was a great *jinete de toros,* rider of bulls, and a man who could be trusted to guard a man's back in a fight.'

"The boy who was called Barroso came up to greet me. He had wild, yellow eyes and a lanky, cat-hammed *cuerpo de jinete,* horseman's body.

" '*Este muchacho es tu tocayo,*' the caporal said. '*Lo nombramos Barroso porque es muy horqueta.*' This lad is your namesake. We named him Barroso because he is a good rider.

"Just then the patron came up to see who I was and the caporal introduced me to him. The patron told me that I was welcome back to the ranch, that I could work there if I wished, and that I could stay as long as I liked.

"But I did not stay there long; for as you know when a man has a reputation there are always young men who will test him to see if what is said of him is true. And if a man stays too long in one place he is sure to get into a fight and kill somebody."

The Yaqui Warrior

I was attracted to him the moment he came aboard the train in Guadalajara; and as he stood in the aisle, a short, broad figure, I noted every detail of his appearance. I saw at once that he was a Yaqui, and from his erect carriage and square shoulders that he was an old soldier.

His eyes were those of a man who had never flinched; they were the eyes of a man who has no imagination, that is to say, no fear; for fear is but imagination.

One might say that his face was grim, but by no means stolid. He had those features which proclaim unsullied Toltec blood: the straight nose, thin lips, and square chin of the pure-blooded Yaqui.

He found a place in the rear of the car and sat down. Every little while I would turn around and stare at him, until at last I decided that I must talk to this old warrior. I sensed that there was a story behind his resolute, inflexible, impassive air. I got up, walked back to his seat and sat down beside him.

He had been expecting me. He greeted me with a wide grin which reminded me of another Yaqui, Mariano Sanchez, the friend of my boyhood; he had grinned like this old man.

Perhaps it was some atavistic urge which attracted me to this man, for we had nothing in common. He had been born in the wild reaches of the Sierra del Bacatete, had let a primitive life, and had known bitter, unrelenting struggle to survive racial extermination, while I had been born in a city in comparative comfort. All I had had to worry about during my boyhood had been getting enough to eat, which in the United States, at any rate the part I was born in, was no great problem.

All the Indians I had known heretofore had been of a peaceful race. All I knew of Indian strife was what I had read in books, and I only half believed what I had read.

As the train crawled across the barrancas and through the mountains of Jalisco and Nayarit, en route to the States, I listened to the saga of the reluctant warrior who had wanted to live in peace and had spent a lifetime fighting. For this was Exciquio Chavez, the Yaqui who rose from peon to brigadier general against his will. I listened attentively and respectfully; this man was of a race which had defied the Aztec, set limits for Spanish territorial expansion, and fought Spaniards, gringos, and Mexicans for generations.

In good but curt and simple Spanish which ran in typical Indian monotones, he began the following recital:

"When the Yaquis *se alzaron,* rose against the government—or, to use an American term, 'went on the warpath'—I was sixteen years old. I did not want to fight. That I might live in peace I left the town of my birth and went to Ures, Sonora. There I found work as a peon on an hacienda.

"I had been there only a few days, when as I was busy shelling corn a squad of soldiers came and suddenly siezed me. I asked them why I was being arrested and the *cabo,* the corporal, answered, 'We are making prisoners of all the Yaquis alzados.' [An *alzado* is an Indian on the warpath.] 'They are to be hanged or sent to Yucatán.' A Yaqui sent to Yucatán was sent to his death. Few Yaquis born on the uplands or in the mountains of Sonora could survive, for very long, the tropical climate of that peninsula.

"I protested that I was a working man, that I earned my living honestly, and that I had never taken up arms against anyone, much less the government. But it was to no avail. I was marched to the *comandancia*, the office of the district, and before an officer who said, 'You are an alzado, if you will tell me where you have hidden your arms, you shall not be hanged. You shall be sent to Yucatán instead.'

"I protested again that I had hidden no arms, and that I had never been an alzado.

"The comandante said. 'Bueno! If you will not tell you shall be hanged as soon as we can find a tree high enough to raise you off the ground.' "

Here the old Yaqui grinned broadly and went on with his tale.

"I was sixteen years old and *muy tonto*, very stupid. So I answered him with, '*Ah ----- me van a matar!*' Ah ---- you are going to kill me!

"My remark made the comandante laugh uproariously, but I was marched away nevertheless. I was put into a group of other captives.

"Of course the only crime these men were guilty of was that they were Yaquis. Many of them had not been alzados at all. We were herded out of town and traveled half the morning before we came to trees which could serve as gallows.

"When we finally arrived at this forest the soldiers wasted no time. They pulled a man out of the group of captives, adjusted a loop around his neck, threw the end of the reata over a limb and pulled him kicking and struggling into the air, as we watched. They left him hanging for what seemed a long time, then they suddenly released the rope and dropped him to the ground.

"When he had quit gasping and had recovered his breath and could talk, the cabo asked where he had hidden his arms. But like all Yaquis he was *cate monte*, he would not speak.

"The soldiers strung the man up again and left him hanging, then pulled another man out of the group. They used the same routine with all the captives, but none told where they had hidden their arms—that is, if they had ever had any.

"Because I was a boy, I was left for the last. When all the other captives were hanging from the trees, the cabo came to me and said, 'Now, alzado, it is your turn.'

"I had two pesos secreted in my clothes. I pulled them out and said to the cabo. 'Here are two pesos, I will give them to you if you will give me something to eat. I do not want to die hungry.'

"The man accepted the money and laughed. Then he said, 'We will not take time to hang you now; you may go back with us. You shall be sent to Yucatán instead.' "

The old man paused in his narrative to chuckle, then continued.

"Whether it was consideration for my youth, or the two pesos, or whether it was for the lack of a reata with which to hang me, I do not know, but I went away from that grove of trees alive.

"Back in Ures I was held in a *corralon,* an inner courtyard, and after more Indians had been brought in, I was taken with them to Hermosillo, the capital of the state.

"In Hermosillo I was taken before the comandante of that district. After he had asked me some questions, he said, 'I do not believe that you, muchacho, have been an alzado, therefore I am not going to send you to Yucatán. You may stay here and work on the prison we are building.'

"The men brought in with me were put to work on the prison. I worked there for two years, and when the building was completed, I was released.

"I found work in a flour mill in Hermosillo. My mother came to keep house for me. But I was not to live in peace, much as I desired it. One day a cabo came to me and said, 'You are ordered to report for duty at the *cuartel,* the barracks, as a soldier of the revolution.'

"I was content with the work I was doing and did not want

to leave it. I ignored the cabo's orders and went on working at the mill.

"Two days later I was returning home from an errand for my mother when three men accosted me. They were Yaquis and each carried a rifle. They told me to go with them. I was taken to a house near by and one of my captors said, 'We are going to kill you for not obeying orders. Why did you not go to the barracks?' Luckily, I had the order from the comandante for my release from work at the prison in one of my pockets. I pulled it out and showed it to my captors. I said, 'Here is the reason why I did not report.'

"The Yaquis could not read, but they were impressed. One of them said, 'Bueno, compadre.'

" '*Compadre,*' in the vernacular, is the equivalent of comrade, so I was safe for the time being, anyhow. After some more questions the man said, 'You may go.' My mother asked me what had kept me so long. I told her I had been visiting a compadre.

"A week later the same three men came to my house, and the one who had acted as spokesman before said, 'Compadre Chavez, you have been chosen to gather the tribesmen to fight the enemies of the revolution. You shall take ten men and provisions and bring in the warriors.'

"Two days later I left for the Yaqui country. There I was so successful that I returned to Hermosillo some weeks later with five hundred men. I delivered them to a cabo and went home. The next morning I went back to my work at the mill, hoping that I was done with military life. The comandante awoke the next morning to find his army of the revolution swelled by five hundred fighting men. When he was told who had brought them in, he sent for me. He thanked me for my help, and I told him that I hoped he would find a man to put in charge of them because I was needed at the mill. With that I went back to work.

"But the men I had brought in would have no other leader

than me. They said that I had brought them and that I was the one who should lead them. The consequence was that, very much against my will, I was made a captain.

"My men were such good fighters that in the very first battle we engaged in, we defeated the enemy and took a huge store of arms and horses.

"Pancho Villa with four thousand men attacked us. I had four companies of Yaquis. We dug in on a hill, and when the battle was over the 'Centaur of the North,' as he has been called, was defeated and in retreat.

"General Obregon in gratitude for the services they had rendered his cause ordered that all Yaquis who had been banished to Yucatán during the Diaz dictatorship should be brought back to their original home. I was ordered to go to Yucatán and invite all the tribesmen there to return to Sonora. In Merida we found that the governor there had recruited two companies of Yaquis. He had equipped, trained, and armed them, and was using them as palace guards. They were well disciplined, first-class soldiers.

"Two officers and three men had come with me. We presented General Obregon's orders to the governor. He promised to turn over the command of the Yaquis the next morning. He assigned us to quarters in an old hotel near the palace.

"We were preparing for bed that night when two Yaqui women married to two of the governor's guards came to us and told us that the governor did not want us to take his guards away, and that he was going to have us shot when we went to take over the command of the Yaqui soldiers. After the women left we talked over our predicament. We resolved to fight for as long as we could. We supposed that the Yaquis would take the part of the governor.

"Early the next morning we loaded our guns, set up a barricade in the vestibule of the hotel and walked out and stood facing the street. Soon we heard the sound of marching men and the guard came into view in formation. Three officers were in the lead. The soldiers wheeled and came to a halt in front of us. Just as one of the officers raised his sword, we fired. Our volley killed the three officers.

"We retreated into the *saguan* and knelt behind and waited. As the first Yaqui entered we held our fire. He advanced until he saw us behind the barricade, halted and called out, '*Que cham alea compa?*' How are you comrade? Then we knew that the Yaquis were not going to attack us. More came in and they too were soon greeting us.

"The people of that town barricaded their doors and stayed in their houses until I had gathered all the other Yaquis living there, commandeered a train and took my tribesmen back to Mexico City, and finally to Sonora."

Little Bay Horse

He was a chunky little bay mustang. The strain of the original Spanish horse could be discerned in the set of his "sheep" head, little pin ears, and coyote hips. He was blindfolded; and when the Judas on his back reined him into the path of the charging bull, he obeyed the rein. As the horns struck, he braced his legs and never gave an inch. Here was an "honest" horse, a dream horse which a range rider always seeks, but seldom finds.

When he turned into the path of the bull, he was obeying an instinct inherited from generations of ancestors that had been reined into Aztec spears by Spaniards, and into herds of countless buffalo by Indians through the centuries since the first horse came to America. He was faithfully going to his death in this dilapidated bull ring.

When the picador turned him around, we saw that his hip was covered with brands. How many times he had changed hands for better or for worse only he could have told, and now he faced an ignominious end to a useful life.

He was draped with the mattress-like padding which protects the horses from the bull's horns. His stubby, hairy legs gave him the appearance of a robust man in shorts, wearing a kitchen apron.

When the bull charged the second time, he pricked his ears forward at the sound of the pounding hoofs and braced himself. We hoped fervently that he would come out of that slaughter pen without being gored—bulls sometimes lower their heads and get under the padding to gore a horse. And luck was with him. When the crowd filed out after the fight, he was still on his feet.

It took us two days to find his owner and one more to find a man who could buy him for us for what he was worth. His price was one hundred pesos.

The little bay horse is safe now from the sharp horns of fighting bulls. Now he has a home on a ranch where a baby boy rides him around and around the yard. When the little boy slides to one side of his fat back, the little horse stops and waits until the lad is astraddle again. Then he starts walking around the yard once more, pricking his ears forward and setting his feet down carefully lest he jar the child he is carrying.

IN THE
SAN JOAQUIN VALLEY

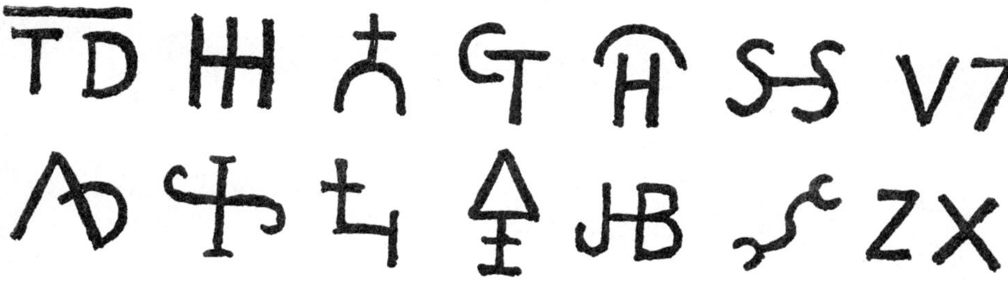

Old San Joaquin Brands

Gringo brands in the southern San Joaquin, with but few exceptions, date from 1849. Of the many hundreds of brands in California the Tejon's Cross and Crescent is the oldest. It has been in use over a hundred years. It is made up of the oldest religious symbols to come out of Asia, the cross of the Christian Spaniards and the crescent of the Moslem Moors.

In the early days Tejon Ranch vaqueros held their rodeos over four counties and ran cattle over a range of two hundred miles. They would start their rodeo where the present town of Palmdale stands in Los Angeles County, and end up on the San Joaquin River in Merced County. The Tejon vaqueros gathered cattle on the Mojave Desert, in the Sierra Nevada, and on the plains of the central San Joaquin.

J. B. Haggin and Bill Carr, who organized the Kern County Land Company, used Haggin's initials JBH for a brand in California only. They had several different irons: the Diamond A in New Mexico, the ZX in Oregon, the Wagon Rod in Old Mexico before the Madero revolution.

Harrell's brand, the Shoe Sole, was a "forty-niner" brand, and so, for that matter, was the JF of John Fancher. He brought the first red Durham cattle into the southern San Joaquin.

Francisco Temple was ranching as early as 1840. He ran his Diamond P iron on Spanish cattle on the San Emideo.

Jack Sutherland ran his Scissors brand in both Kern and Tulare counties.

The Cross C of George Crossmore and the Wine Glass of John Montgomery were worn on the hips of cattle from the Kern River to the San Joaquin River.

R. L. Stockton's CT was a pioneer brand; so was Roland Hill's Circle H. Roland, however, was better known for his breeding of Morgan horses than for his cattle ranching operations. Although he pioneered the baby beef feed-lot operation in California, he was twenty years too early. People were not quite ready for baby beef in the early twenties.

Jesús García ran his JG on the Carrizo Plains. His ranch was called the Saucito.

Goode and Peacock, another pioneer outfit, ran their V 7 near Cholame in San Luis Obispo County, though they were a Kern County firm.

But Miller and Lux was the greatest of them all. Their brands H H connected and S Wrench were worn by more cattle and horses than any other brand in North America, even if we include the enormous herds of Don Luis Terrazas in northern Mexico.

Cattle King

We were talking of the old days, when Henry Miller controlled fourteen million acres in California.

Catarino Reese, as a young man, was for a number of years in the employ of Miller and Lux, and, as a result, had many opportunities to study the Cattle King's singular character. He has many vivid recollections of the old man's eccentricities.

Miller was a far cry from the novelist's characterization of a cattle baron.

"He was cranky," Catarino said, "and gave a man hell for no reason that I could see. I guess he did it to let the man know who was boss and to keep him under control. I don't know what else he did it for. Both Miller and his foreman, Rafael Cuen, had one thing in common. Neither one had any use for a man who did not talk back.

"One time a vaquero told Miller to go to hell. Miller raised his wages. At another time he said to a man, 'You are a teef.'

" 'If I were as big a thief as you are,' the man retorted, 'I would have a lot of cattle.' Miller walked off chuckling.

"Rafael and Miller quarreled all the time, but Rafael was loyal and Miller trusted him implicitly. When a superintendent (over Rafael) was incompetent, Rafael would get Miller to fire him. This is the way Rafael would go about it: The superintendent would give certain orders about the cattle. Rafael would obey them to the letter. When the cattle would arrive at Los Baños,

Miller would see them. He would immediately go to Buttonwillow and jump Rafael, but that worthy would be ready. He would say that he had followed orders, so there would be nothing left for Miller to do but to fire the superintendent.

"This roundabout way of doing things could have been solved by simply making Rafael superintendent. But that was out of the question. Rafael could neither read nor write."

"One day," Catarino went on, "the vaqueros were branding cattle on one of the numerous camps or ranches which made up the vast Buttonwillow Ranch when Miller drove up in his buckboard.

"He was evidently in very bad humor because he got out of the buckboard and went up to the fire, which was made on the bank of a ditch filled with water, and stood looking down at the branding-irons which were heating.

"Suddenly he started kicking, and kicked the burning logs and irons into the water. The men who had been tailing the calves as they were dragged up to the fire, stopped working and grouped around the remains of it. The vaqueros who had been doing the roping coiled their lassos and waited. Miller suddenly realized that the men were idle and that he was losing money. There was a Japanese kid working as wrangler. Miller ordered him to retrieve the irons. The boy waded into the ditch and fished them out. Miller then turned around, walked to his buckboard and drove away muttering."

The old Dutchman must have let off a lot of steam by kicking things around. Being a Cattle King must not have been all fun, and even what appeared to others as simple little matters just might cause an explosion when viewed through the eyes of one such as Henry Miller.

For more than two hundred miles north and one hundred miles west, and over millions of acres, cattle with the Double-H-connected brand of Miller and Lux ranged and multiplied.

The three chuck wagons that covered the Southern Division

of Miller and Lux ranches had made camp at Salt Slough, where they were lined up in a row.

One morning the three wagon bosses, Tom McRaff, Bill Stubblefield, and Rafael Cuen, had stayed in camp; they had sent their respective crews out under Catarino Reese to make a rodeo.

Catarino was far out on the west side of the valley and had already sent out all the men but one. They were spread out in an immense circle and were driving the cattle within it into the rodeo ground, when Catarino saw Henry Miller in his buckboard driving toward him.

All of Catarino's meetings with the Cattle King had been disagreeable—Miller had scolded each time the vaquero had been unlucky enough to meet him. Once started on his tirade Miller would not let up until Catarino would become angry and tell him to see the bosses about the matter, and not him—he was only a hired hand. Whereupon the Cattle King would walk away mumbling to himself.

Seeking to avoid him this time, Catarino rode into a draw, but Miller cut across and intercepted him.

"Vot you do me mit the cattle?" he asked, as he drove up. Catarino explained that he had orders to gather cattle and hold the rodeo at Salt Slough where the wagon bosses were waiting.

Miller ordered him to send the men back to camp. The one vaquero who remained with Catarino was sent out to inform the men of the changed orders. Miller, with Catarino riding beside the buckboard, went back to Salt Slough.

Since there were three crews, there were three cooking fires, one behind each wagon. Miller went from one fire to another, lifting the lid off each pot and examining the contents. When he had peered into each of the pots, he went to the wagons one after the other, and looked through the supplies of food carried in them.

After he had looked into every corner of the wagons, he turned to one of the cooks and asked, "Where is the meat?"

The cook pointed to the side of a wagon, where a greasy gunny sack hung from a nail. Miller jerked the sack off the nail and peered into it. There were four scrawny, dried up strips of jerky in it. Miller threw the sack on the ground, then gave it a kick. The sack sailed through the air and landed in the dust. The Cattle King followed after it, and he kept kicking it until the jerky fell out and he was clear of camp.

All through this proceeding he kept muttering, "No meat in camp. No meat in camp." Still muttering, he walked to where the three bosses were lying on their beds and said, "Go bring a cow for meat." Rafael Cuen mounted his horse and beckoned to Catarino who was still on his horse. The two were riding away, when Miller called to them and said, "Take six men, take six men."

When the cow (of course it was an old one, a heifer would never have been slaughtered while the Cattle King was in camp) had been brought in and butchered, Henry Miller got into his buckboard and drove away.

The Tejon Ranch

The Tejon Ranch lies in a corner of the San Joaquin Valley, and spreads across the Sierra Nevada and into the Mojave Desert. It is made up of four ranchos granted by the governors of California during the period of Mexican rule–Rancho Castaic, Rancho Tejon, Rancho la Liebre, and Rancho Alamos y Agua Caliente.

The vastness of its area covers various types of climate. On the south side lies the high arid plain, where a forest of giant cacti, relic of some prehistoric age, raises its grotesque limbs like arms in pain or supplication. Antelope once abounded here and horses of purest Andalusian strain roamed its vast expanse.

On the northwest side of the ranch is the great valley of the Tulares (San Joaquin), and between the desert and valley the Tehachepi Mountains stand as a barrier. There is a pass over these mountains. It is the southern gate into the San Joaquin Valley, and many adventurous men, priests, scalp hunters, trappers, colonists, and soldiers, have passed over it.

Much of the ranch is occupied by the massive Sierra Nevada, with its frowning peaks and its sides covered with pine and oak trees. The great *Oso Pardo*, the California grizzly, once roamed in vast numbers through its meadows, and Indian tribes fought each other to the death for possession of the fruit of the mighty oaks.

Along the western base of the Sierra are the foothills where once the redmen drove the Tule Elk into canyons and slaughtered them with reed arrows shot from elderwood bows.

To the northwest lie the great plains where the streams flowing out of the mountains sink into marshes in the floor of the valley.

In the year 1772 Don Carlos II ruled in far-away Spain and George III sat on the throne of England. On the eastern coast of North America men were dreaming of a free land released from the yoke of the motherland. In Virginia a man named George Washington was gathering fame as a leader.

From the Asiatic mainland the Russian Bear had reached across the Bering Strait and laid his huge paw on the opposite shore; already new Russian blockhouses were being built farther south along the Pacific coast. Far to the south, across the drifting sand dunes, De Anza was fighting Apaches and waiting to fulfill his destiny by crossing the Devil's Highroad and founding the great city by the Golden Gate.

In this same year a travel-worn Spanish captain paused on the crest of the Tehachepis and gazed down on the oak groves and *cienegas*, meadows, in the little valley below him. He was the first man of European blood to set foot on Tejon Ranch.

He had come a long way in the service of Spain, from Barcelona in his native Catalonia to Mexico and now to California. He had traveled thousands of miles over bleak highlands, through lush tropic jungles, warm seas, and forbidding deserts.

The long arm of Spanish authority in the person of the Catalan, Don Pedro Fages, had reached out across the Colorado desert, over the San Bernardinos, through Cajon Pass and across the edge of the Mojave. He was searching for deserters, and now here he was, at last, in the mountains where the fugitives had taken refuge among the Indians. Whether the Spaniard found the men he was seeking in that time so far away, we do not know; but he was the first white man on record to gaze on the San Joaquin Valley.

Four years later one of the greatest trail blazers in the history of the New World, Padre Francisco Garces, came. He was the second white man to cross over the Tejon Ranch. He was at his everlasting task of searching out and mapping the route for the colonists sent out by Spain to hold the frontier against "The Bear Who Walks Like a Man."

We do not know how long the rancho has had a name, but as early as 1820 Padre Mariano Payeras recommended "the place we call Tejon" as suitable for a mission.

The Tejon Pass was already well known before Edward Fitzgerald Beale, "the lord of all he surveyed," as Lincoln was said to have called him, came to the Ranch of the Badger.

There are many Spanish names listed in the records of the ranchos which make the present Tejon. José María Covarrubias was granted Rancho Castaic. A member of his family, Don Nicolás, won fame as the finest horseman in the Pueblo de los Angeles. Ignacio del Valle, listed as one of the fundadores of California, had come over the Camino del Diablo with Juan Bautista de Anza. With José Angel Aguirre he was granted Rancho el Tejon. Pio Pico, last Mexican governor of California, granted Rancho la Liebre to José María Flores.

Rancho Alamos y Agua Caliente was the property in part of Francisco Lopez. Don Chico brought the first Spanish horses to Antelope Valley. They were called *Barileños*—mustangs. Elizabeth Lake was then known as Laguna de Chico Lopez. Don Chico had the distinction of having discovered the first gold in California, in Placeritas Canyon while he was pulling *cacomites*, wild onions, out of the ground.

Cummings

California's pioneers came from every part of the globe. One youngster, still in his teens, left his native Austria and embarked on a sailing ship bound for California by way of Cape Horn. When he found he could not enter the country without a guardian, the captain of the ship adopted him, and bestowed his own name, George Cummings, on the Austrian lad.

Young Cummings spent some time in the gold fields, and in the late 1850's he drifted into southern California. There he found the dons with enormous herds of cattle, but no market for them.

Some five hundred miles north lay the city of San Francisco. Its thousands of miners needed beef, so Cummings became a dealer in cattle. He married the daughter of the mayordomo of San Fernando Mission, Don Francisco (Chico) Lopez.

Cummings bought his steers in southern California and drove them north through the San Fernando Valley, over Frémont Pass, up San Francisquito Canyon to Elizabeth Lake, and across the desert to Willow Springs. From there he drove over Oak Creek Pass, through the valley that bears his name and down into the San Joaquin Valley, skirting tule marshes for hundreds of miles before he came to the end of his drive in San Francisco or at one of the mining camps in the Sierra north and east of Sacramento.

How and when the forty-niner chose the site of the present Cummings Ranch we do not know, but we can easily see why. The ranch sits at the foot of majestic Cummings Mountain, with the valley, which is also named after the pioneer, spread below and Bear Mountain towering in the background, a panorama which can hardly be excelled in all of California.

The Cummings Ranch never grew to the size of some of the ranches of that period which were larger, in some instances, than European principalities. It remained a small ranch, yet it was well known, perhaps more so than many of the larger ones. And that was because every homeless person who came into the Tehachepi country could find hospitality at the Cummings Ranch.

Throughout the years Cummings and his son Ed made welcome everyone who came to their door, though their kindness has often been abused and they have been paid in *mala moneda*, bad coin, as the old people say.

Ed Cummings, the pioneer's son, is well past eighty. He was born on the ranch in Cummings Valley. A white-haired old man with the air of a benign patriarch about him, his sense of humor is still keen, his memory still bright. He remembers many laughprovoking inconsistencies of the early day Angeleños.

Vasquez the bandit, he says, was a crack shot. The men who made up the posses which periodically chased him out of Los Angeles were very careful to stay back out of range of the bandit's rifle. They would stop whenever Vasquez stopped to fix his saddle or to breathe his horse. They were also careful to wait until he was well on his way before they took up the chase again. This lack of enterprise in the face of danger, when revealed by some irresponsible babbler, never failed to provoke laughter in the City of the Angels.

The posses always turned back when the bandit reached Laguna de Chico Lopez (Elizabeth Lake), allowing him to ride unmolested into the Sierras. They would show the same lack of determination whenever the Indians, who rode into southern California to take horses away from the ranchers, reached the lake with the horses. The posses never followed them past that point. It was Indian country from there on.

Tehachepi was so tough a town that Ed's mother, in constant fear because of the shootings and brawls, was driven to leave the ranch and return to Los Angeles to live.

"Don Jesús Lopez, manager of the Tejon Ranch, was my second cousin, but I called him '*tío*,' uncle. You see," Ed said, chuckling, "he had money."

In the wintertime Ed's cattle would drift down out of the mountains into the Tejon Ranch's range, so Ed attended the rodeos on that ranch when the vaqueros worked the country adjoining the Cummings Ranch.

Ed could never get used to going without eating from four in the morning until eight at night and sometimes later. So one morning he asked Santos Montaño the *cocinero,* the cook, for a lunch. The lunch consisted of three strips of *tasajo,* jerky, and a couple of *semitas,* unleavened biscuits, which he tied behind him on his saddle.

The Tejon vaqueros eyed the package tied to Ed's saddle,

looked at each other, grinned, but said nothing. They knew what it contained. At twelve o'clock they gathered around Ed and asked, "*Onde está el lonche, pues?*" Well, where is the lunch?

Ed untied the package, opened it and hospitably passed it around to the self-invited guests. By the time the three strips of jerky and the two biscuits had made the round of the assembled company, there was hardly a morsel left for the reluctant host.

After this experience, whenever he carried a lunch while riding with the vaqueros on Tejon Ranch, he ate it before he got to where the vaqueros were gathered.

Ed's son, who is known as Buddy (he was a football star at Santa Clara) tells of the time when he, too, attended the rodeos on Tejon Ranch, and of the hard work tailing calves that were to be branded. Tailing calves fell to the lot of the boys on the crew, while the easier job of lassoing was left to the old men.

This was rather an injustice to the youngsters, because the old men, after a lifetime of using the reata, were good ropers, while on the other hand, the boys needed the practice.

On Tejon Ranch calves were roped by the hind legs and dragged up to the fire. One of the boys, who was tailing, would take hold of the calf's tail, give a pull and throw the calf. The man on the horse, who had roped the calf, would ride his horse away from the calf to help the man tailing throw it. Then the man tailing would bring the calf's tail between its legs, hold it close to the flank, kneel on the animal's side and grasp a foreleg to hold it while it was being branded, earmarked, and if a male, altered.

The man on the horse, meanwhile, had brought his horse up close to the calf, and taking his turns around the horn, would hold the calf with the rope around the hind legs.

The man who roped could help the man who tailed by pulling with his horse away from the calf. Or he could let the rope slacken, making it hard or impractical to throw the calf. It was exhausting work under the best conditions.

Buddy remembers very vividly Sutah Coway's stoical behavior under pain and injury. Sutah was a native Indian and one of the best ropers on the Tejon. One day he was roping and Buddy was tailing calves. Buddy had caught a calf by the tail and pulled to throw him, when the rope went slack. He looked up to remonstrate with the roper, and saw blood streaming from Sutah's hand. His thumb had been cut off.

The Indian dismounted leisurely, tied his horse to the corral bars, then slowly, as if he had all the time in the world, gathered some foxtail grass and made a little pile of it. He then asked Buddy for a match and lit the grass. When it had burned down to ashes he gathered them and applied them to the stub of his thumb. He did this to stop the flow of blood. Sutah then wrapped his hand in a red bandanna kercheif, got on his horse, and went on roping.

"My Gosh!" Buddy exclaims. "No antiseptic, no doctor, no medicine, no nothing!"

Haunted House

Over on the west side of the Great Valley, against the foothills which buttress the vast expanse of the Carrizo Plains, close to a spring of brackish water, stand the walls of an old adobe. The house stood beside the Old Road to Los Angeles—*El Camino Viejo a Los Angeles* as the paisanos, who often gave fanciful but otherwise pertinent names to places, called it.

One night forty years ago when we were holding rodeos on the Carrizo Plains, I mentioned the ancient adobe as we sat around the campfire. And this is the tale an old vaquero told about it.

"The rains have all but washed away the walls of that old house; it was deserted during my grandfather's time. It was during his boyhood that the old man who lived there alone and who never spoke to anyone, was found dead in his bed. It has been haunted ever since, and because of the sad circumstances connected with it no one would ever live in it again. It has deteriorated as empty houses that have lost their souls do.

"Ethnographers never have pieced together the scanty scraps of information in the records which the old padres left. They know that many groups made up the colonists who came to California: crossbreeds of Moor, Berber, Catalan, Basque, Celt, Arab, and Jew; Yaqui, Mayo, Opata, Piute, and Mission Indians. Suffice it to say that this particular ranchero's name was Martinez, an old Castilian name if ever there was one. He was one of those hardy herdsmen who prefer the perils incident to the life of a cattleman, one of those souls who hover on the fringes of civilization, never at ease in towns.

"His cattle ranged into the tulares of the Great Valley that geographical history tells us was, in the time of my grandfather, an immense swamp; that an unbelievable luxuriance of grass and flowers grew during the wet seasons; and that it was a desert spotted with leprous alkali patches during the seasons of drouth, where heaps of bones marked the deaths of thousands of animals, victims of thirst and hunger. It was a place into which cattlemen did not venture too far, for fever lurked in its tule swamps.

"The ranchero lived with his two sons, having lost his wife when the boys were mere children. The wants of this little family were met by the sale of his cattle which he drove to market in the mission town of San Luis Obispo. But as time passed an enterprising Prussian came into the Great Valley and drained the tule swamps. The town of Bakersfield came into being. The town thrived from the very beginning, not only in point of population but in the number of homicides. Not even the fabled Bisbee, Tombstone, Abilene, or Dodge City of the western writer's imagination could compare with Bakersfield as it actually was. It was said that men never rode under a tree near Bakersfield lest their heads strike the feet of the bodies hanging from its branches. Bakersfield was a roaring cowtown and groups of gunmen—and just plain cattle and horse thieves—employed by the big cattle companies swaggered through its red-light district which covered six solid blocks. But, fortunately, California historians, unlike those of other states, have seen no glory in the departures from decency of the state's early citizens, and have tried to play down the more lurid history of our state.

"In time Bakersfield became a market for cattle and Martinez sold his beef to a buyer from there. The buyer brought his vaqueros and Martinez went along with the drive to collect his pay for the cattle. There were no incidents other than those met in driving and moving cattle. He arrived in the town and was paid in gold coins. Martinez then bought a few presents for his sons, consisting of clothing which could be carried tied to the saddle strings. He started back home.

"He had kept his business secret and so when night came he camped along the road and slept soundly. The next day he had traveled about three hours and was looking forward to seeing his own roof when suddenly his horse shied violently, almost unseating him. Two men wearing masks jumped out of a ravine and leveled guns at him, demanding his money. Martinez thought quickly and moved slowly. He untied the bags which were fastened to the saddle horn. Then he took a bag in each hand and tossed them on the ground in front of the robbers. The shiny gold pieces were spilled and the robbers, showing their inexperience, took their eyes off their victim and stooped to gather up the money. Martinez, who had his revolver stuck in his waist, drew it, and with two quick shots killed both assailants.

"He dismounted and went up to the first robber and uncovered his face. He must have given a deep cry of pain, for looking up at him was the dead face of his younger son. With a great dread in his heart he walked to the other body and uncovered the face. It was his elder son.

"Two vaqueros riding toward the coast found the old man bent over the bodies of his offspring and babbling over and over again, '*Aqui está el dinero si lo quieres. Aqui está. Aqui está.*' Here is the money if you want it. Here it is. Here it is."

Cookee

Fifty years ago the cooks found on the camps and ranches of the southern San Joaquin Valley were, for the most part, Chinese. The chuck-wagon cooks, however, were always of some other racial stock because a "Chinaman" could never be found who could drive four mules, the chief requirement in a chuck-wagon cook.

The Chinaman was a reliable employee. He seldom went off on a drunk, and he would stay on the job year in and year out without missing a day's work. His meals were always on time. But that was a far as his virtue went. The Chinese camp or ranch cook was a copyist, a creature of habit and routine. He had no originality; his food was dreary and monotonous. He cooked each thing in just one way and every time he cooked it he would cook it exactly as he had the first time. He never varied in the smallest pinch of salt or drop of flavoring. His purpose was to duplicate.

After one had eaten a Chinaman's cooking for a week, one would know what he would get for breakfast, for dinner, and for supper each day of the week, of the month, and of the year. Day in, day out the food would taste the same, smell the same, and look the same.

A good Chinaman was a blessing to the ranch housewife during the busy season. He was a cheerful worker and more often than not possessed a sense of humor. His remarks were always sing-song laconisms, full of wit.

I remember a Chinaman who came to work for Dick Brite one summer. This cook asked Mrs. Brite to bring out some food article from town. She either forgot it, or it was too high priced for her purse.

I was standing in the doorway when the cook asked her if she had brought the article. When she answered that she had not, the Chinaman, in a high-pitched sing-song entirely devoid of passion, but without hesitation said, "You son-a-bitch, you too stinch [stingy]."

Of course Dick had to fire him. But I think he did it regretfully.

Bedroll

The buckaroo called his roll of blankets a bed, but it was his wardrobe, suitcase, and safe-deposit box rolled into one. It consisted of blankets and quilts wrapped in a heavy canvas. A mattress was rarely used by the buckaroo; it made the roll too cumbersome for use in camp life. Some bosses like Rafael Cuen, however, by virtue of their position, sometimes included a mattress in their roll. A big bedroll took up too much space in the wagon and caused the cook and horse-wrangler to grumble when they had to lift it into the wagon when camp was moved.

Besides the blankets and quilts, the roll contained the buckaroo's extra clothing and a sack "warbag," as the gringos called it, in which was packed a razor, soap, towel, and his supply of tobacco, which was more often than not a carton of Bull Durham. Odd pieces of equipment such as bits, spurs, and ropes were also wrapped up in the bed. Sometimes a book or a magazine was carried. The book, though, was usually a saddlery catalog.

The bedroll was the safest place to store anything of value or that was fragile. Rolled up in the blankets the article could never drop out even over the roughest roads, and the thickness of the bedding protected it from breakage.

A sheet of eight-ounce canvas sixteen feet long and six wide was used as an outer covering for the roll. This canvas shed water and kept the rider's "forty years gathering," as he called his possessions, dry. It also kept out much of the cold.

When the bed was spread out on the ground, one half of the sheet was on the bottom to keep out the dampness of the ground and the other half was folded over the top. The sides, which were equipped with snaps and rings, were folded over and the snaps fastened into the rings. The buckaroo thus would be snug for the night.

The canvas was the rider's most important piece of equipment, and was one of the first considerations when buying an outfit. A man could not work efficiently without a dry bed. When there was snow, sleet, or rain the buckaroo would prop up the top sheet with a stick so it would shed water. On such nights he could build a big fire and stand as close to it as he could, for as long as he could stand the intense heat. When his clothing was steaming or scorching, as the case might be, he could run to his bed and crawl in. In this way he would not have to lie and shiver until his body heat overcame the cold, if it ever did on a freezing night.

The buckaroo's preparation for sleeping consisted in taking off his boots and putting them under the warbag which he used for a pillow. This was to keep them dry and to prevent packrats or other night prowlers from carrying them off, and to eliminate the possibility of rattlesnakes, scorpions, or centipedes crawling into them.

Every morning the buckaroo rolled up his bed so that it could be loaded on the wagon which took it to the next camp.

Glennville: A Pilgrimage

I have gathered the names of vaqueros and buckaroos who rode the ranges of the southern San Joaquin and its surrounding sierra, and though the list exceeds five hundred names, it is not now, nor will it ever be, complete. The list goes as far back as the memory of the oldest old-timer, Francisco Urrea, and includes the names of men active in the trade to about 1930. The old-time vaquero and buckaroo has just about passed out of the picture since then. My "census" included only professional vaqueros and buckaroos who had worked for the big cattle companies with headquarters in the valley.

Up in the Sierras there were men who owned small herds of cattle, to whom cattle ranching was not a full time occupation, and who held their rodeos in the spring and fall on a community basis. But for all that, they were no whit less salty than the professional riders. As a matter of fact, it took an extra good valley man to stay in their dust in rough mountain country. Quite a few of these mountain boys had reputations as vaqueros and buckaroos which many valley men might well have envied.

A listing of vaqueros and buckaroos without the names of the mountain men would be entirely too narrow. The place to go to gather their names was Glennville, because, through the years, it has remained a cowtown. There the old-timers congregate once a year for the town's annual rodeo, to spend a day renewing old friendships, and go away in the evening smiling and looking forward to next year's celebration. Glennville is still an old western town where the spirit of neighborliness has not died, where the word neighbor is still used in its older, truer, honest sense. This spirit is a survival of pioneer days when neighbors shared joys and sorrows, famine and plenty, when a man, called in the hour of need, never failed to go to the aid of his neighbor.

The road to Glennville winds from Bakersfield up out of the floor of the valley, over rocky hills into the Sierra, and on into the little town nestling in a draw between pine covered mountains.

On the road I met Remick Albitre. Here was a man who was qualified to give me the names of mountain riders. His father, Bautiste Albitre, had come into the mountains in the early days, and had been R. L. Stockton's foreman. But the Albitres go back much further than the last century. When Padre Junípero Serra left his little token mission of San Diego de Alcala to go to Monterey in 1769, he left four rickety, scurvy-stricken soldiers to guard it. One of these soldiers was Bautiste Albitre, ancestor of Remick, and the first Albitre in California.

Remick has attended every rodeo in the Greenhorn Mountains since he was a boy. (By this "rodeo" I mean a gathering of cattle, not a wild west show which is also called "rodeo.") He promised to meet me later in the day, and I drove on into the town. At the little church I met Superior Court Judge Warren Stockton, who had once been my boss when he was running cattle near Buttonwillow. Reminiscing of the days when he was a rancher, Judge Stockton mentioned old Bruno Contreras, who lived to be well over a hundred years old and was an active rider up until the time of his death. In his youth Bruno had been a vaquero for Pio Pico, last Mexican governor of California. Old Bruno, the Judge said, would never speak English to a man. If a gringo spoke to him, it would have to be in Spanish, but whenever the old man had to speak to a woman or child who did not know Spanish, he would relax his rigid idiosyncrasy and courteously use English.

The Judge said further that all the vaqueros and buckaroos

who had worked for him or his father, R. L. Stockton, had one characteristic in common: They were never anything but loyal to the man who paid their wages. He added, too, but somewhat mournfully, that he could never get any practice lassoing calves because he was the boss and had to stay afoot and mark, alter, and brand the calves while someone else did the lassoing. (The old-time gringo in California always said "lasso," he never said "rope.")

I found Remick at the rodeo grounds. Jesse Stockton, the Judge's brother, had come along to help him in remembering names for my list. I wondered what the Kern County Superintendent of Schools had to do with the names of vaqueros and buckaroos. I was in for a very big surprise. For a time the names came thick and fast, as Jesse wrote them down. I soon learned how good the vaquero or buckaroo was, or had been, by Remick's grin. The better the vaquero or buckaroo, the wider the grin.

It seemed to me that as a name came up, Remick's memory would flash back to some incident in the past when the rider mentioned had ridden some hard-bucking horse or lassoed some wild outlaw steer on a rough mountainside. Jesse would suggest a name tentatively. If the man mentioned was only fair, Remick would give a hesitant, "Yes." If the man was not up to his standards of what constituted a vaquero or buckaroo, he would put his chin in his hand, frown deeply, study a while, then very reluctantly say, "Well."

What was surprising was that Jesse, who has spent so many years as an educator, could remember as many names as Remick, who has spent his lifetime among the riders of the Sierras.

Cow Horns

In the old days before the coming of the Hereford to California, vaqueros in gathering their herds would, in certain localities, come upon cattle which had horns of abnormal length while others of the same Spanish breed on neighboring ranges would have normal horns. This curious circumstance caused some controversy among the riders. Some vaqueros contended that these conditions were not the result of breeding but of certain substances contained in the grass the animals ate or in the water they drank which promoted the extraordinary length of horn. Others believed that the continual friction against the branches and limbs of underbrush as the cattle forced their way through heavy growth was responsible for this development. However, the latter contention does not hold true in tropical country where cattle in heavy jungle do not grow horns of unusual length.

The occurrence of long horns in herds of cattle ranging in areas widely separated was not limited to the western United States but was common to all Latin America. The elements which were responsible for these abnormalities seemed to be most abundant in the grasses or water in the State of Chihuahua in old Mexico. The cattle which made the longhorn famous in song and story were brought from that part of Mexico.

OLD VAQUEROS SPEAK

Juan Bravo

"Every man" said Lupe, "who ever worked on the Tejon Ranch and rode colts during the course of his stay there, got thrown from a horse, no matter how good a rider. Juan Bravo, the jinete, came up from Chihuahua about 1900. He was a relative of Terrazas and came with a shipment of longhorn cattle from one of their ranches. *Hay! como eran malditos.* My! how mean those cattle were. I was caporal when the cattle arrived and when they were unloaded Juan asked me for a job. I took him to Don Jesús who said, 'If you can ride bronco horses I will give you a job.' Juan assured him that he could do this. In fact, he was a very good jinete, but like every other man who ever rode on the Tejon Ranch, he too was bucked off.

"One day we were holding rodeos in a territory which had many wild cattle that had escaped the rodeo for several years. Don Porfirio ordered Juan and me to stay with the *puestos,* the men posted to stop and hold the cattle that are driven down out of the mountains by other members of the crew. 'If any wild cattle come down,' he said, 'don't let them get away.' Juan and I promised that none should escape.

"While we were waiting two wild cows came down together in one of the bunches. When they got to the *parada,* the herd, they went through it and struck out for the mountains. Juan and I were ready. I took after one and he the other. I lassoed mine and tied her. Juan roped his but she proved to be very active. He would throw her but she would bounce up on her feet before he could get her tied. He was riding a colt which he was breaking for Dick Dougherty. The horse got tired of being jerked around and lit into bucking and Juan was thrown. The cow got away with his reata. I chased her and lassoed her just before she got into the deep brush. By that time she was pretty tired so I had but little trouble tying her. When I got back to where I had left Juan he had caught his horse and was mounted. 'Where is the cow?' he asked. 'Didn't you catch her?' Just for fun I said, 'No, and you will be fined five dollars to buy whiskey for the men for letting the cow take your reata away from you.' Juan said disgustedly, '*Qué vaqueritos de cincuenta pesos estos.*' What little fifty-dollar vaqueros these are.

"By that time the rest of the crew had all come in with their cattle and I said to Don Porfirio, 'There is a wild cow in the brush tied up with Juan's reata.' Juan, who was near, said eagerly, '*Onde? Onde?*' Where? Where? We rode over and led the cow back to the herd.

"Some time later, when we got back to Lebec, Juan bought a gallon of whiskey and treated the crew because he had lost his reata."

Jack Leiva told another story of Juan Bravo.

"He was a famous bronco buster in his day. He had a deep bass voice and was always threatening someone with death, but he never hurt anyone. His bark was worse than his bite. When Juan came to work he was assigned a room in the bunkhouse. The rooms were shared by two men, but Juan had this one all to himself, for reasons which will be explained later on in the course of this story. He rode through the spring and fall rodeos and stayed that winter. In the spring he left the Tejon to go to Walla Walla, Washington, to break army horses.

"In all the time he had slept in the room he had never swept it out. When the next man to occupy it opened the door and saw its condition he was appalled. Vaqueros do not have access to laundries, nor do they have wardrobes, so Juan had worn his clothes until he could wear them no longer. When he took them off and put on new ones, the possibility of soap and water having any effect on them was so remote that the vaquero threw them in a corner. The old clothes could stand upright. They had been so molded to the vaquero's body from having been slept in and worn in the rain, that a sculptor could have modeled an exact likeness of their owner from a study of his cast-off clothes.

"During the winter Juan had tracked mud mixed with manure into the room and a layer of it covered the floor. Bunches of hair he had scraped off rawhide strings, and strips of unused rawhide, buckskin, and leather left from the reins and reatas Juan had made and repaired during the winter were strewn over the floor.

"In a corner was a pile of 'long-handled' underwear, socks, and pants he had discarded as he had acquired new ones. The degrees and color of the dirt on the clothing could have told how long the vaquero had been out on rodeos and on which part of the ranch, as the age of a tree can be told by its rings.

"Into another corner had been thrown old saddle blankets, burlap sacks, an old hat, and worn-out boots with their tops cut off—the tops were cut off and made into a bag in which was carried a hammer and staples. This bag was tied to the saddle and carried when the vaquero was sent out to ride fence. But, strangely enough, Juan seldom if ever used up the staples. He could never find a broken place in the fence which could be fixed on horseback. If the boots had no stitching, as those made by Buckingham and Hecht, the tops were cut into strings and made into bridle reins.

"To get back to Juan and the room, the new man called the other members of the crew. They came to the door and looked in, then looked at each other. One of the riders stood looking into the room for a while, then he turned and went out. He had been struck with an idea. He returned in a few minutes with a box, a rake, a scoop shovel, and a broom. Then he got some newspapers and lined the box. He then proceeded to sweep and rake up the room. One of the vaqueros asked him if he was going to preserve the trash, and he answered, 'Juan will be lonesome for this stuff so I am going to send it to him.'

"The rest of the men immediately went to work to help him. They picked up every bit of litter and put it in the box. They swept up every bit of dirt and put that in the box. When the room had been cleaned and all the litter carefully packed, they nailed a cover on the box and shipped it C.O.D. to Juan in Walla Walla, Washington. The charges came to sixteen dollars and some cents.

"When Juan came back to the Tejon the following year, he tried to find out who had played the joke on him, so, as he said, he could kill him. But everybody just looked innocent and went about their work.

" 'Sure was a *dirty* trick,' they sympathized."

Catarino

In the more than fifty years in which Catarino Reese has been foreman for the Kern County Land Company, he has taught many kids their trade. There also have been several superintendents who are indebted to him for whatever knowledge of beef they may have, however little they acknowledge the debt.

The kids who learned to be buckaroos under him called him "Pop," because he always had their interests at heart. Though the older members of the crew often disapproved of his actions, he would put a kid to doing some job which was usually reserved for an experienced older man. Catarino would order some green kid into the herd to part out beef, telling the kid to not be afraid to bring out whatever beef he thought was fat. "I will tell you whether the steer is good or not," he would say.

One day Catarino, riding a green colt, along with another vaquero on a green colt and a boy riding a gentle, well-broke horse, came upon a wild Chihuahua cow that had got out of a pasture. The wild cow would not drive back through the gate into the pasture, so it became necessary to lead her back.

Catarino turned to the kid and said, "You have a good, gentle horse, so you will have to lasso her. First get off your horse and tighten your cinch."

When this had been done, Catarino said, "Now you are going to rope that cow, and if you follow directions, you will not have any trouble. I will yell directions so you won't have to look up. Now when you throw your rope, throw it good and hard. When the loop is around the horns, jerk it up tight, then take three turns around the horn and let it run just a little. Don't let it slack because if the cow steps over it she will be tripped and will fall. Do not look at the cow, but keep your eyes on the gate that you are going to lead the cow through."

The boy threw his lasso around the cow's horns and took his turns as directed.

Then Catarino yelled, "Turn your horse toward the gate." The boy did so.

Catarino yelled again, "I am going to get off my horse and start the cow. When she starts, head for the gate, and don't stop."

Catarino rode off a little way and dismounted. He pulled the blinds down over his horse's eyes and walked toward the cow. He put himself between the cow and the kid who had her roped. The cow charged him.

"Get going," he yelled to the boy.

Before the cow could reach him the boy put spurs to his horse and pulled her through the gate. She passed within two feet of Catarino.

Catarino mounted his colt again and rode through the gate to where the cow and boy had stopped.

He said to the kid, "Throw your rope behind her and go on past her." The boy did as directed and threw the cow.

Catarino dismounted and blindfolded his colt again.

"Now," he said, "I will get hold of her tail and hold her down while I take the rope off her horns and put it around her hind legs."

After he had caught her tail and placed the rope around her hind legs, he said, "Bring your horse up close to the cow, so that when she moves the horse will back up to keep from being kicked and will hold her."

Catarino mounted his horse again and said, "Now slack your rope suddenly, so that the cow will rise free from it."

The boy obeyed and the cow got up. By that time the vaqueros had ridden away and left her to join the other cattle in the field.

The Impenitent Penitent

This tale came from Sonora, and was told to me by my friend, Alfredo Bojorques. The name Bojorques is included in the list of fundadores of California. A member of Alfredo's family came with De Anza in 1776.

There was once a timid man who suffered so much from the depredations of one of his neighbors that in desperation he went to a compadre for advice on how to deal with his problem.

The compadre was a man of little patience. When told of the circumstances he said, "The next time you find one of your calves branded with his iron, following one of your cows, kill him—the neighbor, of course, not the calf."

The timid man was horrified at the thought of using such stern measures, and said, "Oh! I could never bring myself to do so violent a deed."

"Well," the compadre answered, "if you are afraid to do it yourself you can very easily find a man who will do it for you for a hundred reales."

The timid man hesitated before he asked, "But where could I find such a man? That would be hard indeed."

The compadre snorted. "Bah," he said, "that is very simple. Go to the church in the morning and look for the man who is praying the loudest. He will be the man who has committed the greatest crimes and the one most willing to execute your commission."

Accordingly the timid man went to the church the next morning. After listening to the various moans and lamentations he located a man who was scourging himself with a bundle of nettles, wearing a necklace of cactus, and crawling down the aisle on his knees.

"Surely," the timid man thought, "this man has sinned greatly. He is the man for my purpose."

He waited until the man was outside the church and then approached him on the matter of eliminating his rapacious neighbor.

The compadre had been right on the matter of finding a man for the job in a church, but wrong on the price he would demand for his services.

After much haggling the price was set at five hundred reales, half the amount to be paid in advance. The timid man paid the amount demanded and went on his way.

"Now," he thought, "my troubles will be over." His property would henceforth be safe from his rascally neighbor. He ate a big supper and went to bed.

But "conscience is a hungry dog that gnaws and gnaws." He could not sleep. He asked himself many questions. What would become of the neighbor's family? If he were killed his children would be orphans and his wife a widow. They would starve without a father to protect them.

True, the timid man would not do the actual killing, but since he was having it done, he would be guilty of it. He would be just as guilty of the crime as his hireling.

The next morning, anxious and sleepless, he arose and went to the church to find his man, his hireling, repenting louder even than on the day before.

The timid man rushed to him and said, "I have changed my mind. I don't want my neighbor killed. His wife and children will suffer if they lose him. You may keep the money I have paid, but please don't kill him."

But to the timid man's consternation, the hireling said, "I am indeed very sorry, but I cannot do as you ask. Even if you don't want him killed now I must go through with it. You see, I have just finished doing penance for killing him."

Martinez

"Francisco (Chico) Martinez," said Lupe Gomez, "was the son of old '*Cachcuero*' (Teodoro Martinez). He was one of the best vaqueros on the Tejon ranch, and for many years was the *amansador,* the trainer, there. Some of the colts he broke were ridden five times, others were ridden ten times, and yet others had to be ridden by the amansador for months before they could be turned over to some vaquero as properly broke.

"When broke these horses were supposed to have no vices; however, they often displayed whims and vagaries. Every morning we paid them the compliment of assuming that they could buck us off. We rode out in the gray dawn with a firm hold on our reins and with all the slack out of them.

"One of the first lessons Martinez gave a colt was to rope a beef on it. However, the fact that Martinez could rope on a horse did not mean that just any other vaquero could do so. Once in a while one of the horses would buck his rider off. If

Don Jesús Lopez, the mayordomo, happened to be present and witnessed the incident, he would hurry to the fallen man, help him to his feet, brush off his clothes, and ask in a surprised voice, '*Pero qué tiene ese caballo, hijo? Martinez lazaba en él!*' But what is the matter with that horse, son? Martinez lassoed on him.

"All the horses on the ranch bucked now and then, even the old ones. But we would have ridden no others, for we knew their virtues. That little tendency to 'break in two' did not prevent them from being faultless vaquero horses. They were the best horses that I have ever had the good fortune to ride. Sure-footed, tireless, loyal, they would race down slopes of the Sierra where one would not dare go afoot.

"The Tejon was known from one end of the state to the other for its good horses, and the reason they were good was that the vaqueros and buckaroos were always good men. Taken as a whole—gringos, native Californians, Sonorans, and native Indians —they were as good as any in the West.

"I don't know what it is that transmits the instinct for working cattle from one mustang to another, but this amor al ganado is common in all horses that work cattle. It is much stronger in some, however, than in others.

"On cold mornings our horses would all leave camp with a hump in their backs, looking for an excuse to buck. Some young fellow would be riding an old reprobate that had had a bad reputation in his colt days. He would be going along with his ears laid back, *pelando los ojos*—showing the whites of his eyes—as if daring his rider to slacken the rein.

"One of the other riders would say, '*Afloja le la rienda, vale.*' Slacken the rein, pal. But the man on the old reprobate would do no such thing. Instead he would hold his hand palm upward, bring the tips of his fingers together, back and forth, in a repeated motion and say, '*La familia no me deje,*' which could be translated as 'The thought of my family will not let me.' But it meant that he had no faith in his ability to stay on that old reprobate, because the horses *eran muy enchilosos*, were very peppery.

"The best horses on Tejon, during the years I spent there, were *El Mostela*, the Weasel; *El Español*, the Spaniard, who would start bucking the instant his rider put his weight in the stirrup to mount him; *El Jabalín*, the Peccary, who was untrustworthy; *El Clavo*, the Nail, who bucked with Chamale Montes and threw him; *El Naranjo*, the Orange—no doubt because of his color; *El Gallineta*, the Guinea Hen—Why? *Quién sabe?; El Patas Coloradas*, Red Legs; and *El Mira Lejos*, He Sees Far, because he carried his head stretched forward, as if he were looking at something in the far distance.

"There were also *El Membrillo*, the Quince; *El Soldado*, the Soldier; and *El Censontli*, the Mocking Bird. Don Toribio, the caporal, was one day racing after a beef on Censontli. The horse stepped into a squirrel hole and fell. Don Toribio's hip was broken in the accident.

"Our horses had to be good in those days. The Tejon had fifty thousand head of cattle; besides those which strayed onto the ranch from Walker's Basin, from the Miller and Lux and the Kern County Land Company ranches, and from ranches in the Tehachepi Mountains, the Coast Range, and the Sierra Nevada. Riders from three counties met at the Tejon rodeos. As a result we had a lot of fun—fun meaning seeing a horse break in two with its rider.

"When one horse lit into bucking there would be a chain reaction. Three or four others would follow the first one's lead and go into action. Then there would be horses without their riders going in all directions. Of course we would have to lasso them, and that was fun too."

Aficionado

"Sometimes a man will carry his *aficion,* his special enthusiasm, even past the grave." said José Juan. "There was a man who liked horse racing so well that he took his passion for that sport into the next world.

"When he arrived at the gates of Heaven and knocked for admission, Saint Peter opened the gate a crack, looked out and said, 'There is no room for you; the place is filled with horse race enthusiasts like yourself.'

"The *difunto,* the deceased, peered in through the crack and studied the great crowd. He recognized some of his old cronies, so after a few moments he turned to the Saint and said, 'If I get rid of most of them will you let me in?'

" 'I most certainly will,' Saint Peter replied.

"The difunto announced in a loud voice for all to hear, 'There is to be a great race down in the Other Place, and all of you who miss it will have cause for regret.'

"As he had forseen, there was an immediate rush out of the Pearly Gates down into the Other Place.

"When the last of the aficionados had passed out, Saint Peter said, 'Now there is plenty of room and you may come in.'

"But to the Saint's surprise the difunto did not enter. He stood staring at the disappearing crowd of aficionados rushing down to the Pit. Then he turned to the Saint and said, 'That race may be as good as I said it would be.' And without even saying 'Adios' he hurried after the crowd."

El Chiquito

The colt was clumsy, big-footed, and awkward. We sat, backs against the shed, and watched the kid who was breaking him. He would gallop the colt from one corner of the corral to the other, where he would stop him against the bars and try to lift him in a spin backwards.

Mariano, who had been watching the longest, shook his head at the kid's efforts and said disgustedly, "It is useless to try with such a dunce. It is hard to teach even a good horse; and one must search long and hard for a colt that will take a good rein, for they are precious few.

"This reminds me of a *cuento,* a story, which is apropos of the matter in hand. It is about the fatherless Chico, his burro El Chiquito, and the bars of silver.

"Chico lived with his mother and sister. He managed to support them by hauling wood and charcoal with the burro and selling it from door to door. He never overloaded or beat the little animal and so, because of the good treatment, the *burrito* stayed fat and sleek and free of saddle galls.

"As he was very timid, El Chiquito soon learned to run to his master for protection from the fiercer members of his breed. Since all animals ran at large about the town, he was often chased home by one of the other burros.

"In those days, the gringos had not yet brought screens to California; so in hot weather the doors were left open, and niños, chickens, goats, and calves went in and out at will.

"One day El Chiquito ran home, chased by a big black burro. As El Chiquito approached the house, his master failed to come to his rescue and drive off his assailant, so he ran into the house. His pursuer, who was nipping at his fat rump, followed through the door and hemmed him against the *hornilla,* the oven. There he spun around and was showering a rain of kicks against El Chiquito's ribs when the women, who had been away gossipping, returned and drove off the pursuer.

"When Chico returned home he was met by the scolding women who told him that there would be no supper until the hornilla, which the burros had demolished, was repaired. Being very hungry, the boy set about fixing the stove.

"He picked up a brick which, oddly enough, had not been broken, and on examination found that it was black and of solid metal. He carried it outside and showed it to his mother. She took one look at it, and grasping his arm, led him back into the house.

"Safe from prying eyes and ears, she said, '*Santo Niño bendito!* It is silver. It is an *entierro,* a buried treasure. An old entierro.'

"They uncovered a small fortune in silver bars. The old house had once been occupied, so it was said, by the lady friend of an old-time bandit.

"The little family knew that it would not have the silver long if the officials of the town learned of the find, so the mother went to Don Fermin who had a shop and lent money at usurious rates. She told him about the bars of silver. Don Fermin rubbed his hands, and with a greedy gleam in his eyes he said, 'Bring me the silver and I will exchange it secretly; no one will know. Bring me the boy and I will send him to school and make him a partner in my shop.'

"So Chico went to school and his mother and sister were doled out enough money to barely keep body and soul together. The boy was kept at his books and became an expert at accounting. El Chiquito, the burro, gained the most from all this because he was never loaded again and lived, fat and sleek, to a ripe old age.

"When Don Fermin died his heirs denied any knowledge of the silver, and because Chico persisted in his claims, they turned him out without a cent. From this reverse of fortune Chico became mad and the butt of those who had envied him in the past. However, he never lost his knack with figures, and whenever he passed a band of sheep or herd of cattle he looked each animal over carefully.

"He would then estimate the weight of each animal and compute the gain each one would make when fed so much for so many days, for such and such a price. When his figures were completed, he would write below them, 'In order to make this gain they must be sold for cash.'

"So, by the same token," finished Mariano, "to make a reined horse, you must first find a colt that has the capacity to learn."

Overheated Cattle

"One day," said Catarino Reese, the old Land Company foreman, "the vaqueros from Bellevue Ranch were ordered to ride toward Goose Lake and meet the vaqueros from Poso Ranch who were driving a herd of steers from the lake. The Bellevue riders were to take over the cattle when they met the other crew. The cattle were to go to Buena Vista Ranch.

"It was a very hot day even for the southern San Joaquin, so you who have spent forty summers here can imagine how hot it was.

"About half-way between Goose Lake and Buena Vista we met the men driving the steers from Poso. It was still early in the day. In fact, it was far too early for them to have covered as much distance as they had. But when I reached the herd I saw why they had made such good time. The cattle had been driven too fast.

"Francisco Urrea was in charge of those riders and cattle, and I don't know why a man of his experience could have let them get into that condition.

"I took one look at them and I said to Urrea, 'These cattle are overheated. You drove them too hard; and I will not be responsible for the ones that are lost.'

"The vaqueros from Poso turned their horses and went back to Poso, leaving us with our problem.

"First we tried to let the steers stop and spread out, so they could cool off; but they would only crowd together and bawl. Then we tried to move them at a slow walk. But they would not start out at a walk. When they moved at all it was at a run.

"A steer would be standing still; then, all of a sudden, he would throw up his head and run. He would run about a hundred yards or so, then drop dead. The cattle were terribly frightened and in a panic. We lost ten head before they cooled off, and it was late evening before we could move with them at all."

Old Bronco Riders

I asked Lupe Gomez if it was true that *Cachecuero*, "Rawhide Sheath," as old Teodoro Martinez was called, rode bad horses after he was ninety years old.

"*Pues*," Lupe answered, "*en 1900 estaba muy viejo y todavía amansaba caballos.*" Well, in 1900 he was very old and he still broke horses.

"One day Don Jesús, an impish look on his lean old hawk face, approached Cachecuero and said, '*Te voy a dar otro caballo para que no estes apie.*' I am going to give you another horse so that you will not be afoot.

"Now being *apie*, afoot, did not mean that a man was walking. It was an ironical term that meant that a vaquero's horse was old, lame, poor, or sore-footed, or had a sore back. A man could be mounted and still be 'afoot.' When some man was riding a 'poor keeper' the other men would remark that he would be 'afoot by noon.' It meant that the horse would gaunt up so much that the rider would be laughed at on account of his horse's condition.

"To get back to Cachecuero. Don Jesús gave him a mean horse. A big bay which we had named *El Toro*, the Bull. Cachecuero wrapped his *ramal*, his rein end, around the horn of his saddle and using this for a hand-hold, he rode the horse. El Toro just couldn't shake him loose.

"All those old men could ride a bucking horse. The fact that the horse was mean did not bother them in the least.

"Don Luis Lopez had a horse in his string that we called *El Catrin*, the Elegant One. El Catrin bucked every time the old man mounted him. This, of course, never deterred Don Luis.

El Catrin got ridden whenever the old man decided to throw a saddle on him."

There were lots of old men among the vaqueros who could put the youngsters to shame. Old Don Antonio Leiva rode with his stirrups so long he could barely touch them with his toes. It was the style of riding peculiar to the old Californians, and Don Antonio, being of that race, would never shorten them no matter where, what, or how he had to ride.

The young men on the ranch, who had not known him in his youth, often wondered what the old gentleman would do if a horse were to buck with him. Don Antonio one day put their minds at ease in respect to this.

Even the old horses on Tejon Ranch would buck on occasion, and Don Antonio had one in his string that would hump his back every morning. The old vaquero would ride out holding his rein tight until the horse's back was warm. The younger vaqueros would watch the performance and look at each other and grin.

One morning Don Antonio woke up with his *santo ladiado.* In the vernacular this means he got up on the wrong side of the bed. He saddled and mounted.

One of the vaqueros said, "*Cuidado, Don Antonio, se va mochar ese caballo.*" Look out, Don Antonio, that horse will break in two.

Don Antonio snorted an unprintable reply and slacked the rein.

The horse lit into bucking. The old man stood up in his stirrups and rode the animal to a standstill. During the bucking, the bridle slipped off the horse's head, and with the headstall around his chest and his head between his legs he was free of any restraint. But Don Antonio, in spite of that, weathered the storm.

When he dismounted later, he came to the surprised and awed youngsters. "Muchachos," he smiled, "he is merely a horse—and am I not a vaquero?"

Vaqueros Buenos

Lupe Gomez can well be proud of the title of vaquero. He has ridden wild range horses and tamed them, and has lassoed wild cattle on the steep, rocky slopes of the Sierra, led them out and yoked them to oxen.

He was telling of the times back in the last century when he was young and thousands of cattle ran wild in the mountains.

"There were five head of *cabestros*, lead oxen, on Tejon when I went there as a boy. They were kept in a little pasture near the vaquero camp.

"In the morning, when we were all mounted and in a group waiting for orders, Don Jesús Lopez would say, '*Muchachos, vamos a bajar ganado bronco de la sierra ahora. Lleben los cabestros.*' Boys, we are going to bring wild cattle down out of the mountains today. Take the oxen.

"We obeyed orders with alacrity, because we were sure to have a lot of fun that day running in the Sierra. We would drive the oxen to a spot as near to the wild cattle as we could, and leave them there. They never strayed away, and when some vaquero led a steer out they would be there waiting to be yoked to the wild one.

"*Pero los vaqueros buenos eran contados.* But the good vaqueros were few. The men on the vaquero crew who could, and would, venture to lasso and tie a wild steer in the rough terrain of the Sierra Nevada could be counted on the fingers of one hand, even on the Tejon which was known far and wide for its good vaqueros. *Porque les hacía cinco.*" This is an untranslatable term which means that some of the men were afraid. Here Lupe turned his hand palm upward and brought his five fingers together in the vaquero's age-old manual sign for fear.

"Did you tie your reata to the saddle-horn when you dismounted to tie a steer?" I asked.

"Of course not," Lupe snorted, "I never tied a reata to the horn in my life. That was a despicable thing to do, because if the steer should get up with the reata tied, the horse would be at the mercy of the steer. The rider could get to safety while the poor horse was being gored, tangled up in the rope, or at least jerked around.

"Whenever a vaquero lassoed a steer, and it was *patas arriba*, legs in the air, he would drop his reata on the horse's neck, dismount and tie the beef. He usually had plenty of time. In the event that the steer got to its feet before the vaquero could reach it and get its tail between its legs to hold it, he could mount his horse, pursue and tail it, or pick up his rope and throw it again. But a vaquero *never* tied his reata," he ended emphatically.

"Tying the hind feet was enough; the beef could not get away with its hind feet tied. Sometimes an active beef would have to be thrown two or three times before it would lie still long enough for the vaquero to dismount and tie it.

"*Juan Viejo,* Old Juan Leivas, taught me to lasso and tie wild cattle in the Sierra. '*No tengas miedo apiarte,*' don't be afraid to get off your horse, he would say.

"Don Luis Lopez would also help me. He would say, '*Pon*

cuidado como hasen los viejos.' Heed the old men's methods. '*Mirando los viejos se apriende.*' One learns by watching the old men.

"In those days any vaquero could tail a steer and it was often done to stop a runaway or to take the starch out of a mean one. But the hardest part of the chore of capturing wild cattle in the mountains was not the roping and tying, but that of leading them out to where the oxen were waiting. If the oxen were too far away, one could tie them to a tree and let them fight the rope until they got sore around the base of the horns. If one undertook to lead one that hadn't been treated in this manner, it would sit back on the rope and refuse to lead.

"One day we were at Los Lobos when Ed Conley, the cattle buyer, borrowed El Naranjo from Don Luis Lopez. Ed and I rode out of camp together. In the course of our ride we came upon a bull *sestiando*, or drowsing, under a tree.

"Ed, who spoke perfect Spanish, said, '*Vale, vamos coliando ese toro.*' Pal, lets tail that steer.

"I answered, '*Bueno, pero primero compon tu silla.*' Good, but first fix your saddle.–El Naranjo was a 'one gutted' horse.

"In his excitement, Ed disregarded my advice. He at once got his horse into a run after the bull, which had awakened on our approach and was making off. The cattle buyer's horse was in a fast run when he overtook the bull. Ed leaned over and grasped the tail; as he went to straighten up, the saddle turned. Of course, Ed was thrown. He landed on his head and El Naranjo ran off kicking at the saddle hanging under his belly."

VAQUERO TALES

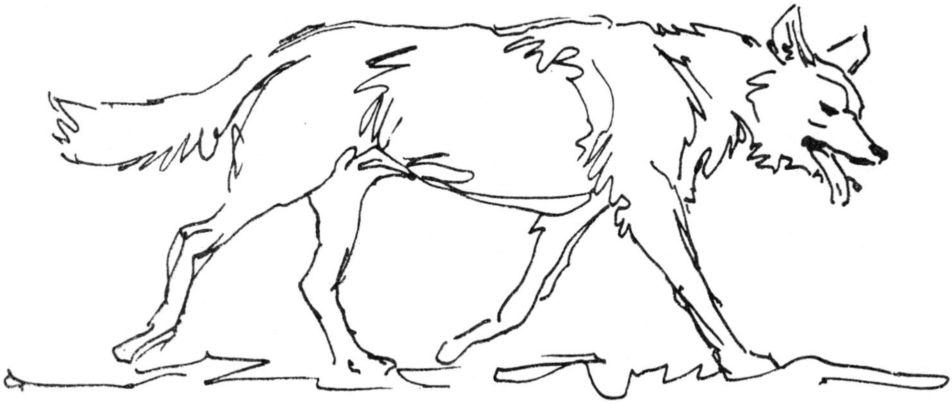

El Molacho

El Molacho, the Toothless One, told many entertaining tales of incredible doings which had happened only in his fertile imagination, or he attributed to himself the more interesting incidents which had befallen other people. No one can say with certainty whether he believed them himself, but that did not matter. His tales never hurt anyone; he had no malice. He told them to prove the fertility of his imagination and theatrical instincts, because he had nothing else to do to relieve monotony, or just for the hell of it. His repertoire of yarns was quite ample, to say the least, and covered every subject under the sun.

He told the following tale as we sat throughout the day at Commanche waiting for the sun to go down so we could move on to the next camp with the beef we were driving to the railroad.

"Everyone knows," he began, "that rattlesnake meat, ground and sprinkled over a leper's food, will cure him of the disease. The same is true of buzzard meat. I once cured a man with a broth made of buzzard, though the treatment was very severe.

"The lepers in the old days, when their disease began to be obvious, would take up their abode in the town's cemetery. If they did not go there voluntarily they would be stoned out of town.

"When a boy of my acquaintance contracted the disease, a friend and I undertook to cure him. First we set about catching a buzzard. We got a fishhook and baited it with a piece of meat, then set it out in the sun to ripen. In a few days the buzzards were attracted to it, so we threw it out to them as bait. A big fellow grabbed it. When he had swallowed it hook and all we pulled him in and tied him securely.

"We went in search of a pot with a tight cover. When we had found the pot we filled it with water. Then we made a fire and set the pot to heat over it.

"We put the buzzard into the pot, feathers and all, and sealed the cover on the pot with dough so that the steam would not escape.

"We let the pot boil until we thought that the buzzard was dissolved. Then we took the pot off the fire, uncovered it, and looked into it. The buzzard had boiled down into a broth of about a cupful and had turned a dark green. We strained it through a screen and put it in a cup. Then we squeezed enough lemons to make a cupful of juice. This, with a cupful of sugar, we set near us ready to hand.

"We found the boy in the cemetery sitting on a tombstone.

" 'Come with us,' I said. 'We have a medicine that will cure you.'

" 'No,' he answered, 'leave me to die in peace.'

"My companion took hold of him and held him firmly while I pried his mouth open with a stick. I poured the broth down his throat, and so that he couldn't spit it out, I worked his tongue as one does when one drenches a horse.

"When he had at last forced all the green stuff down his throat, we poured the lemon juice into his mouth. When this was down we poured in the sugar for dessert. He rolled his eyes around, shuddered, and passed out. We left him there and rode away.

"Four days later we rode by. We found him sitting on a tombstone and strumming a guitar. In two weeks he was back in town, to all appearances a healthy man."

"Speaking of rattlesnakes," El Molacho went on, "one day I was following another boy through some bushes when he suddenly jumped into the air and screamed, '*Me pico una vibora,*' a rattlesnake bit me. I ran after the snake, and as I passed it I made a wide sweep around it and met it coming toward me. I faced it because a snake can strike backwards much faster than it can forward. I killed it and went to see if I could help the boy, who had sat down in the trail.

"Just as I reached him, a man appeared around a bend in the trail. He was carrying a mattock. I told him what had happened and he said, 'Quick, we must bury the bitten leg in the ground. Help me dig a hole!'

"We found a soft spot of ground and quickly dug a hole about three feet deep. We put the boy's bitten leg into the hole, filled the hole with dirt, and with a stick tamped the dirt around the leg.

" 'There,' the man said, 'let him stay there for four hours.'

"He went on his way, and I stayed with the boy. In a little while he quit moaning, but it was late in the evening before I dug his leg out of the hole. The pain and swelling were gone, and he was able to walk home."

However, I liked El Molacho's stories about *diableros*, men possessed of the devil, and about witchcraft much more than I did the ones about his nostrums. They were not as gruesome.

"*El Guerro Rosalio*, Blonde Rosalio, had strange powers, for he had sold his soul to the devil. He could throw a bull by simply lifting it by the tail. He would stand in the middle of the round corral and ask us to drive the broncos around the corral in a fast run. One moment we would see him standing there and the next we would see him astride one of them. We could never understand how he did it. He would ride this wild horse out of the corral without saddle or bridle and work cattle with it. In a day or two he would turn this horse over to us thoroughly broke. He never ate meat. He never cooked food. He would go to one of the many women on the ranch and ask her for tortillas and beans from the pot. That is, beans that have not been fried. Or he would ask for salt and sprinkle it on the tortilla, roll it up, and eat it. He never slept in a house. He built a nest in a tree and slept there, away from the other people on the ranch.

"El Guerro Rosalio would catch fish without a hook and line. One day a woman asked him to catch one for her. He went to a puddle by the horse trough and pulled an enormous trout out of it. The woman was afraid to take it. She said it was a devil. But one of the vaqueros, who was afraid of nothing, took the fish to another woman, who fried it for him. He ate it with great gusto.

"El Guerro Rosalio would disappear for days at a time. He would turn himself into a coyote and run with the packs. No one dared shoot at the coyotes seen on the ranch for fear that one of them might be Rosalio.

"When he died we laid him out on a bed made of rawhide strings laced lengthwise. When our work was finished we all went a short distance away and made coffee. We were sitting around the embers of our fire when we saw one corner of the house in which the body of Rosalio lay catch fire. Then the flames jumped to the next corner and burned there. Then they jumped to the next, then the next. The house burned to the ground in two hours.

"When the fire had died down enough for us to approach it we went to where the body lay. To our surprise, the bed on which the body lay was not even scorched. The blanket which covered it did not have ashes on it.

"We went back to our fire to wait for morning. When it came we approached the bed to carry the body to the cemetery. But El Guerro Rosalio's body was gone. It had been spirited away from under our very noses. We never found a trace of it again."

The best tale Molacho told was the one about the bucking bull.

"I once tamed a bull," he began, "that bucked so long and so far that I would have starved to death if the vaqueros in the crew hadn't taken pity on me.

"A wild *barroso,* a clay colored bull, had followed a heifer into the corrals at the home ranch. We knew he came from a wild band because he bore no brand and had never been seen by any of the vaqueros on the ranch.

"The boss ordered the men to lasso him, and when he was down we branded and earmarked him. I jumped on his back as the men let him up. But I was to wish that I had stayed off. He bawled and bucked across the corral and when he came to the bars he did not stop. He jumped them and struck out across the valley.

"He would buck for a while, then he would run for a while until, bucking and running, he had crossed the valley and got into the mountains. I clung to his back and thought he would never stop. At last when he had reached the desert and had run under a number of Joshua trees in an effort to brush me off his back, he turned back toward the home ranch again.

"I had now been on his back five days and was beginning to get a little hungry. As the bull raced along I suddenly espied a package hanging from the limb of a tree. I snatched it as the bull tore by, and when I opened it I found it contained *burros* of meat and *frijoles.* [A *burro* is beans, meat, or other food wrapped or rolled in a *tortilla.*] I had finished devouring them when I saw an *amfora,* a water bottle, hanging from another tree. I managed to get hold of it, too, and drink the water it contained. The vaqueros from the ranch had followed the bull's tracks into the mountains, and there lost them. They had then hung the packages of food on the trees on the chance that I would see them.

"Some weeks later when I rode that bull back to the home ranch he was thoroughly tame. He became the pet of the children who fed him *panocha,* brown sugar."

The Lost Bull Pup

Whenever I pass through the town of Tehachepi I stop for a chat with Jack Leiva, who is in business there. He never fails to tell me a story of his old vaquero days on Tejon Ranch, when Don Jesús was manager of the ranch.

Jack is a good story teller and like the other old vaqueros remembers the humorous incidents of earlier days on the Tejon. With something of nostalgia, he says:

"Oh, if only those days when Don Jesús Lopez was the boss could have lasted forever! Those were the happy days." There is always a chuckle in his stories, though it stems frequently not from the sense of the comic but rather of the ironic.

"One day," he once told me, "we were riding on the plains near Rose Station when one of the boys saw a small animal, about the size of a rabbit, under a bush. The vaquero saw at once that it was not a wild animal, so we rode over to investigate. We found, of all things, an English bull pup. To all appearances it was a purebred dog and we were at a loss to determine how it happened to be on the plains of Tejon Ranch, far from any human habitation or people who would own such a dog.

"We sat there on our horses looking at the forlorn little creature, when suddenly Chico Martinez said, '*Mira, hay está el Dyner*.' Look, there is Dyner. Curiously enough, the name stuck. From then on the pup was known as Dyner.

"My father—Don Antonio Leiva, the caporal—dismounted, picked up the pup, put it inside his shirt, and mounted again. He carried it in his shirt all the way back to the vaquero camp. Every little while on the way back he would pull the puppy out of his shirt, talk to it, pet it, and then put it back in his shirt again.

"On our way we were conjecturing on how the pup had got to the place where we had found him, when we came upon some wagon tracks. We saw in the distance a number of Gypsy wagons moving in the direction of Bakersfield. The pup had evidently fallen from one of the wagons.

"The pup grew up at the vaquero camp and was a favorite with everyone. He was always as fat as a seal because everyone at the camp would take meat from the table and feed him.

"At that time a number of greyhounds were kept at the ranch. We used them to run the numerous coyotes. The bull pup would run with the hounds, but of course he could never keep up with them. He would arrive at the kill panting for breath and long after the coyote was dead. He would immediately attack it, growling fiercely, much to the amusement of the vaqueros.

"Of the men in the crew, Willie Husband was the dog's favorite. Willie would take the dog to his camp where he let him sleep in the house. On some nights Willie would quarrel with the dog and put him out, but the pup would create such a racket that Willie would let him in again. Men riding by the camp late at night would hear Willie arguing with the pup, and think that Willie had another man in the house with him.

"The bull pup was full grown, and had been running with the hounds all the time he had been on the ranch, when one day they all turned on him and killed him. We could never figure out why.

"We had a lot of fun with those hounds. The water from Tejon Creek would spread out into ponds when it reached the floor of the valley. A dense growth of cockleburs would grow in those wet spots. The coyotes would hide in them as they afforded the only cover on the bare plains. We never failed to scare up one of the predators there.

"One day I was alone with the hounds, following at some distance behind them. They were chasing a coyote, when it suddenly disappeared. The hounds stopped and stood about in a circle, barking. When I rode up to them I saw that the coyote had fallen into an abandoned well which had been filled with trash and dirt to within six feet of the surface of the ground.

"I dismounted and went to the edge and looked down. The coyote was huddled against one side of the hole trying to avoid the five rattlesnakes that were striking at him. So far none had reached him.

"I took my reata, dropped a loop around his neck, and hauled him out to the surface where the hounds immediately attacked him. They worried him until he lay still, then they left him and went to the trough and lay down in the water from the trough's overflow, leaving the coyote stretched on the ground with my reata around its neck. While the hounds were cooling off I looked around and found an old shovel. I was busy chopping up rattlesnakes with it when I happened to look up and saw the coyote making off with my reata still around his neck. He had been playing possum.

"I called to the dogs, and at long last one of them saw him and gave chase. When the dogs caught the coyote the second time, I made sure that he was dead and that my reata was off his neck before I went to exterminating rattlesnakes again."

In speaking of the stoical, dauntless old vaqueros he knew, Jack said, "I do not believe my father ever feared anything in his life, judging from the stories I have heard of him and from my own observations. The only time he ever showed emotion was on the day I left to join the Army in the First World War. He was afraid I would not come back."

Chuckles on the Ranch

One day, on San Emideo Ranch, the buckaroos were butchering a steer. Ernest Brunk was sitting on his horse, a brown called *Boracho,* Drunkard, watching the men work when he should have been helping. He had a rope in his hand and every time one of the boys bent over at his work, Ernest would hit him across the posterior.

Alfred Frago got tired of Ernest's playing. He cut a piece of the beef's liver, and turning around slapped it on Boracho's nose. Boracho had not earned his name for nothing—he bucked in a weaving, staggering way. He snorted, reared and pawed at the liver sticking to his nose, then spun around and bucked off across the field, bellowing and pawing. Of course Ernest got bucked off.

* * *

Joe Nicholson was tall and skinny. He brought to mind the story of Ichabod Crane, especially so when he was on horseback. His feet were so big that he had to shop for extra large stirrups.

Joe was riding down the trail into Pleito camp on San Emideo Ranch when Alfred Frago, whom we called Frager, saw him. Joe was some distance off and Frager had time to hide in a thicket of pomegranates which lined the trail. Joe was riding a mule named Tony. Tony was as gentle as a lamb, but like all mules he would sometimes shy and "swap ends," as the buckaroos say.

Just as Joe on the mule passed him, Frager let out a war whoop and jumped out of the bushes. Tony "swapped ends" and Joe's feet went through the stirrups. He grabbed the saddle horn with both hands and as Tony stampeded toward the corral where the other men were working, Joe yelled, "Help me, help me, help me!" When Tony reached the corral the men caught him and extricated Joe from the stirrups.

Frager made himself scarce until Joe had got over his fright and anger a little, and when Joe did finally find him, Joe said in a hurt, complaining voice, "You son of a bitch, you could have got me killed."

* * *

"Whenever," Catarino said, "I told some rider to be careful, or that the horse he was riding would buck him off before the day was over, my prediction never failed to come true.

"One day Ramón, who thought he was a great horseman, was riding a brown colt. When he had mounted that morning, the colt had given a few crow hops, and Ramón was grinning around at the men as if he had made a great ride.

"I did not want my horses spoiled so I said to him, 'Don't think that horse can't buck. If he does really turn it on he will throw you so high the birds will build nests in your ears before you come down!'

"Sure enough, about the middle of the morning, the horse broke in two with Ramón and bucked him off so hard that we lost an hour waiting for him to get up off the ground.

"That night he quit because, he said, I had put a curse on him and caused the horse to buck him off. But the truth of the matter was simply that Ramón was not as good as he thought he was."

* * *

The mishaps his vaqueros suffered often made Don Jesús Lopez laugh despite the seriousness of the situation.

One day Campas, a vaquero, was hung in the stirrup when his

horse fell with him. The horse ran off across the plains dragging poor Campas over brush and cactus.

Don Jesús was sitting his horse, talking to Don Porfirio Valencia, the caporal. As he watched the horse running and kicking at the dragging Campas, he turned to the caporal and said, "*Mira, Porfirio, este Campas ha de querer mucho a ese caballo, porque no lo quiere soltar.*" Look, Porfirio, this Campas must love that horse very much because he does not want to leave him.

* * *

Henry (Hank) Hoskings asked Salvador Carmelo for a chew of tobacco. Salvador handed him the plug. Henry put it between his teeth and was pressing down on it when a rope, on a cow they were doctoring, got under his horse's tail. Bill, the horse, clapped his tail down on the rope and went bucking off across the field with Salvador riding behind, yelling, "Bite it off, Hank, bite it off." But Hank, in one of Bill's hard jumps, had swallowed the plug, and was sick afterwards.

* * *

Juan Bravo was a crack shot. One day he was sitting in the shade of a grape arbor. A rooster came by. Juan drew his gun and shot the rooster's head off. The noise the rooster's body made jumping around brought a woman to the door. She asked how the rooster got that way. Juan drew his gun, shot the head off another and said, "This way."

On another occasion Juan was out on the range with two other men. They had been riding since dawn without food and one of the men complained. Now the vaquero never likes to hear one say he is hungry when there is no food to eat. It goes against his grain to hear useless complaints.

So when in the course of the ride the men came upon a snake, Juan shot it. He got off his horse, made a fire, skinned the snake and roasted it.

When it was done to a turn he told the man who had complained to eat. The man refused. Whereupon Juan pulled out his gun and told the man to eat it or he would die on the spot. The man ate the snake. He never complained in Juan's presence again.

* * *

The smell of garlic never fails to remind me of the day, back in the early twenties, when Henry Hoskings, Bert Hobbs, Uel Matthews, and I rode to Salt Creek Camp near Tecuya.

We had dinner with Joe Nicholson, who was stationed there. The dinner consisted of enormous steaks which Joe had smeared with garlic. While we were eating, Henry, who was the foreman on San Emideo then, never ceased complimenting Joe on his skill as a cook. That individual, very pleased, grinned from ear to ear and boasted, "I never took a back seat for any man when it comes to cooking."

After dinner we started back to San Emideo. We had traveled about five miles when the garlic began its work and we became sick and remained so all the way back to the ranch.

As we made our woeful way along belching garlic, Uel Matthews, whom we called Booger Red, would say every little while, "And Hank said Joe is a darn good cook," imitating Hank's voice and trying to spit the taste of stale garlic out of his mouth.

Elk and Coyotes

Old vaqueros never liked to run their horses. They never got them out of a walk unless it was absolutely necessary. They saved them as much as they could. Those who did like to *correr como los muchachos,* to run about like boys, were looked upon as being not quite grown up.

No doubt this practice of saving the horse for some untoward emergency was a survival from the days of the Apache, when it was certain death to be surprised by an enemy when one's horse was tired or jaded.

For many generations, since the coming of Father Kino, Sonorans have fought Indians. Even today the word Apache is imbedded in the vaquero's vocabulary. It is often used as a synonym for implacability. A fighting, striking, kicking, squealing bronco would, quite often, be named El Apache.

Whenever a beef had to be roped in an open field, an older man would hold his horse in and wait until some young blood took after it. When the youngster had thrown his loop and, of course, missed, the older man would cut across into the beef's path and lasso it. This was not conducive to good humor in the vaquero who had missed, but it saved horses.

Catarino Reese always starts his stories with, "It tickled ta hell out of me." He was telling of his days as foreman for the Kern County Land Company, in whose employ he spent fifty-four years. During this time he never wore a ten-gallon hat, or wore or fired a revolver in the line of duty.

However, he had many and varied experiences; all his tales have a touch of humor. It is to be remarked that all old-time vaqueros and buckaroos had a good measure of this quality in their makeup.

"One day," he began, "we were riding along on our way to work some cattle, when we came on a herd of about five hundred elk. There were about eight men in my crew, and all of them became excited and started chasing the elk.

"I was riding ahead of the crew when I heard the commotion behind me—the elk running, the buckaroos yelling and swinging their ropes.

"There was a boy riding along with me. He was very willing and always obeyed orders promptly, so I turned to him and said, 'I will stop those darn fools from raising hell. You get on one side and I will get on the other, so the elk will run between us.'

"The boy did as I directed, and as the elk passed I threw my loop on a big bull and pulled him out of the herd's path. I then waited for those darn fools to come up.

"The elk fighting at the end of my rope stopped the crew. They left off chasing the herd and turned to help me take my rope off the big bull. It took some time to do that little chore, but it got their minds off chasing elk and running their horses down, and back to the job on hand.

"Although a buckaroo, whenever he saw an elk, would chase it, an elk was very seldom lassoed by overtaking it. It was too fast. When pursued by a mounted man the elk seemed to be going at a slow lope, but the pursuer would have his horse in a dead run, spurring and whipping in an effort to close in for a throw. If the horse was fast enough to close in, which was seldom the case, the elk would lengthen his stride just a little and easily draw away from the horse just as if the horse were standing still.

"This does not mean that we rode slow horses. We rode some of the finest horses in the country. Sometimes when I was riding one of Willie Tevis's polo ponies, and all conditions were in my favor, I would overtake an elk. But that was seldom."

Catarino chuckled again. "One day a buckaroo was chasing an elk. He was nowhere near it and the chances of his catching it were hopeless. He was losing ground at every stride.

"I got in the elk's path—they always run in a straight line—and as it passed I lassoed it. The buckaroo was very angry with me. He felt that I had cheated him out of the glory of lassoing an elk.

" 'Did you really expect to catch that elk on that horse?' I asked him.

" 'Yes,' he answered. Some fellas never learn." Catarino chuckled at the memory.

Coyotes are as hard to catch as elk. One day Catarino was riding on the range west of the Company fence when he saw a kid on a pot-bellied mare chasing a coyote. He was a long way off, but approaching rapidly. Catarino took down his reata and waited for him to approach.

"I expected the coyote to run away from the mare. But to my surprise, as the chase wore on, the mare closed in on the coyote. She was crowding it when I threw my loop and caught it.

"The coyote was played out but the mare was not even panting. She was breathing as if she had not run a yard! I asked the boy how he expected to catch the coyote without a rope. He said that he didn't need a rope; that he often killed coyotes by running them down on the pot-bellied mare; that when she had overtaken one she would paw it to death."

This time Catarino's laugh exploded loud enough to break up our quiet conversation about the good old vaquero days.

Jake

Around 1918 there were thirty or more dogs of every mixture and breed on San Emidio Ranch. There were two Russian wolfhounds, several greyhounds, an airedale or two, and some bird dogs. The only one worth anything was Shorty, half English bulldog and half great Dane or St. Bernard or some other big breed, because Shorty was a big dog. His usefulness consisted in catching a steer by the nose and hanging on until it was exhausted. Sometimes he would throw the steer. He could never be persuaded to let go.

There were many more cats on the ranch than there were dogs. At noon when the men gathered at the cookhouse to wait for the bell which announced that the meal was ready, the dogs and cats would gather there, too. The reason the animals did this was that some of the men would adopt one of them and take food from the table to feed it.

The instant the bell rang the thirty or more dogs would start barking. Then each dog chose a cat and chased it up a tree or into the grape arbor. This cat and dog routine was performed every noon.

One day the ranch management decided to cut down on the number of cats. Two men were delegated to do away with them. When they were through they piled, Ed Norton told me, seventy-five cats in the wagon used by Jake the stable buck. Jake's last name was Smith or Schmidt. He was a Dutchman and couldn't read or write. He had been stable buck on San Emidio for twenty years and the wagon was the vehicle used to haul away the manure and trash from the stable and corral. Before he came to San Emidio Jake had been a prospector in Arizona and had left a partner there to whom he sent a grubstake every payday. Once a month, just before payday, this partner sent a sample of ore which Jake would forward to an assayer in Los Angeles. Of course the sample would have no trace of precious metal.

The men on the ranch said that the old Dutchman was being swindled, but Jake never lost faith and through all the years he spent on the ranch he never failed to send his partner money after every payday. If I remember rightly, it was twenty dollars which he sent. At that time such an amount was almost enough to keep a family in food for a month, so the partner had a very good thing of it.

To any man willing to act as secretary Jake would dictate a letter to the assayer. The wording never changed. The letter always read like this: "I am sending a sample of ore for you to assay. I am sending five dollars. If it is not enough let me know. If it is too much have a drink on me. Jake Smith."

On payday Jake took a bath. There were two bath tubs for the men to use. After filling a tub with water, he took all the clothes he had worn for the month–socks, long handled underwear (worn winter and summer), overalls (bib variety)–into the tub with him. As he sat in the tub he washed the clothes and himself, using a sock for a wash cloth. Jake affected loud colored socks and with the red underwear the resulting laundry was streaked with several colors and never failed to have more than a trace of tattle-tale gray.

Riding Colts

Contrary to general belief, there were many good vaqueros and buckaroos who couldn't ride a bucking horse, that is to say, one that bucked hard. As a result, they would try their best to keep one from bucking. This caution was common not only among poor bronco-riders. There were many vaqueros whom "it took a good horse to buck off" that did not like to have a horse buck because it spoiled the animal. They, too, tried everything in the book to keep a horse from bucking.

On the other hand, there were men who welcomed strife and liked to have a horse buck; but those riders spoiled horses. It was seldom that a *jinete*, a bucking horse rider, turned out a good vaquero horse. Most of them spoiled everything they rode. All they taught a horse was bad habits. On the other hand, the men who were not combative, those who never let their colts buck, turned out the best working horses, and that is the mark of the good vaquero.

"When we rode colts out in the early morning," Lupe Gomez said, "we would sit up stiff and straight in our saddles, with one rein shorter than the other, so that we could double our colts if they were to 'break in two.' Our eyes were glued to the colt's ears, because the position of the ears indicate the horse's mood.

"The colts would travel with their ears laid back flat against their head, *pelando los ojos,* showing the whites of their eyes, the very picture of malice and bad humor, as if daring their riders to give them an excuse to buck.

"It is the first jump the bronco makes that is the hardest. If the buckaroo stays after the first one, he will most probably weather the storm.

"After we had traveled two or three miles, the colts' backs would begin to get warm and the humps would settle down to normal. Their ears would start moving back and forth, an indication that they were in good humor at last. The vaqueros would relax, slacken their reins, and start rolling cigarettes and telling lies."

They had got through the critical period of the morning without having to ride through an equine earthquake.

Penance

The fat cattle we gathered during the summer and fall were held in a pasture near the vaquero camp until the buyer came and parted out his choice of the beef. When a number were ready for shipment, we drove them to the corrals at Caliente and loaded them on the cars.

When we were through with the work of shipping, Don Jesús would invite us all to the one saloon in town for a drink. One round of drinks was all he would buy, no matter how much we hinted for him to buy another round. Immediately after we had finished our one drink he would order us to mount our horses and go back to the camp at Los Lobos.

On one occasion José María Velasquez and Nacho Montes disobeyed orders. They stayed in Caliente and went on drinking. When they finally started back to Los Lobos their horses somehow got away from them and they arrived at camp on foot. José María's horse made his way back to the ranch in good order, but Nacho's was bleeding from a deep gash across the chest. He had been caught in barbwire.

Some days later, when we had got back to headquarters, and the men were all gathered at the corral to catch their horses, Don Jesús arrived and ordered the caporal to catch a certain *tordillo* (gray). When the *tordillo* had been led up Don Jesús turned to Nacho, who was still *muy crudo*. To be *muy crudo*, very raw, is to have a bad hangover. "*Ahora, por boracho, me amansas este caballo,*" said Don Jesús. Now, for being a drunkard, you will break this horse for me.

The gray was *muy maldito*, very mean, and Nacho, though he was one of the best Indian vaqueros on Tejon, had a lot of trouble with him. The horse was very tall and Nacho very short, so he had difficulty in mounting. Perhaps Don Jesús had taken that circumstance into consideration when he gave Nacho the penance.

Burro Meat

Rawley Duntley and I were discussing the merits of beef, venison, pork, and even–ugh!–mutton. After all had been passed upon, he said, "Do you know that burro sometimes makes good eating?"

"One year we were preparing for our annual barbecue," he went on, "and when everything else was ready for our celebration, we found that beef was not available at any price. Rather than disappoint a lot of people, I sent some boys out on the desert to shoot a number of burros.

"They shot four nice fat ones, dressed them out, and brought them home. The lads meant well, but in dressing the carcasses they cut them up crosswise, as one would chop up a snake.

"However, they barbecued well, and when served on the day of the celebration, a woman came up to me and said:

" 'Oh, Mr. Duntley, this meat is so delicious!'

" 'Yes,' I answered, "burro makes good eating.'

" 'Burro!' she said, 'Do you mean to say that this is burro meat?'

" 'Of course,' I said, pointing to a chunk of meat on the table, 'can't you see the prints of hobnails on that piece where the prospector kicked it?' "

Querencia

The homing instinct that draws all dumb creatures back to the place of their birth is so pronounced in some cases that it is a cause for men to marvel. An animal left to itself more often than not will return to its home pasture no matter how many miles away it may be. Paisanos call this instinct *querencia* from the verb *querer*, to love, and have so much faith in its power that, when lost or unsure of their route, they will leave the finding of the way home to their mount.

That the swallows return to the mission of San Juan Capistrano on St. Joseph's Day every year has long been known to all the world, and is one of the most interesting features of that mission. However, the *golondrinas* are not the only creatures that have developed an intense love for that particular part of California. There was a sorrel horse that escaped his groom three times and each time made his way from San Francisco back to his home pasture at San Juan—a distance of nearly five hundred miles.

For many years over the seven western states, the sorrel horses bred by Don Chico Forster of San Juan Capistrano were known for their superior qualities. The sorrel color predominated because at one time the Forsters had acquired a fine stallion and he had stamped most of his descendants with his color. The cavalrymen who pursued the Apache chieftains, Victorio and Mangas Coloradas, over the desolate plains and hills of Arizona were, for the most part, mounted on horses bred by Don Chico Forster.

The Army remount buyers were not the only ones who appreciated the good qualities of these horses. Among those who sought the best in horseflesh were the purchasing agents of the city of San Francisco. They bought horses from the Forsters for the renowned mounted police of that city.

One day an order for a select number of colts was received from the bay city and the vaqueros combed the bands for the best. They were justifiably proud of the record their horses had made with the mounted police. Among the colts parted out was an outstanding sorrel. He stepped higher, moved faster, and carried his head more proudly than any of the others. He also fought the rope harder and bucked higher and longer. One of the sweating, swearing vaqueros struggling with him remarked, "*Este alazan está bueno para el capitán.*" This sorrel will do for the chief. And as chance sayings often take root, the horse became known as *El Caballo del Capitán*, the Chief's Horse.

The horses were sent to San Francisco and the sorrel entered into the intensive and intricate training required of a police horse. Nor did he escape the chief's discerning eye as later on he lived up to his name and in reality became the Chief's Horse.

Winter passed, spring came and went, the golondrinas had long since returned to Capistrano when one morning a four-year-old niece of Don Chico awoke and got out of bed. She walked to a front window and looked out. There, standing at the front gate, was the Chief's Horse. His *querencia* had brought him back. How he had escaped his grooms in the bay area and avoided capture on the five hundred miles of road home, no one will ever know. But here he was.

In that era when horses could often be had for the asking, an animal's only value was the time spent in its training. A police horse, because of a long and complicated schooling, was a valuable animal. The same applied to his contemporary, the fire horse.

The sorrel was sent back to San Francisco and affairs at San Juan resumed their usual routine until the horse appeared at the

Forster Ranch again. How he had escaped his grooms a second time is a matter of conjecture. He had completed his training for police work so there was nothing to do but send him back despite whatever feeling Don Chico and his vaqueros might have had in the matter.

Time passed. One season came and went, then another. It was late fall and the rodeos were over in Southern California. Don Chico's vaqueros had pointed the beef herd north to market and had them strung out in a long line, traveling freely, when the vaquero on the point saw a riderless horse coming toward him. When it had come near enough to be recognized the men saw that it was the Chief's Horse. He had escaped for the third time and was making his way back home again. We do not know, but perhaps Don Chico prevailed upon the police chief to let the horse stay at San Juan. This is a reasonable assumption as men who know and ride horses never fail to have that streak of sentiment which makes them all kin.

One summer during the Old Spanish Days in Santa Barbara, Jimmy Rogers and I were sitting in the grandstand and talking of the range rider's sense of humor and of campfire tales in general when Mr. Beale, who was present, told us the story of the Chief's Horse as he had heard it in San Juan. So one day while passing through the town I stopped at the Tom Forster Ranch. Mr. Forster informed me that the little girl who had seen the horse from the window had been his aunt, the late Mrs. McFadden. Mr. Forster and I talked of vaqueros and horses, of stories and story tellers. He told me this tale about Juan Manriquez, one of his father's vaqueros. Juan was entrusted with the messages sent from the ranch and made many trips to Los Angeles. He was very popular with the children on the ranch and on his return from a trip they would crowd around him; for he always had an interesting story to tell of his adventures while away from home. These adventures came out of a fertile imagination and the children were fascinated with the tales.

"Ustedes no van a creer lo que les voy a platicar de lo que me paso; pero es la pura verdad." You won't believe the things I am going to relate; but it is the purest truth, was always the prelude to one of Juan's stories. Here is one of them:

"As you know, the patron sent me to the *pueblo,* to Los Angeles, the other day on a very important mission. I started at a gallop and my horse, El Liston, ate up the leagues. I had covered almost all the distance and it was not yet daylight when I came to the Rosa de Castilla hills near Los Angeles. There my horse went lame. After I had examined him I saw that he could never reach the pueblo, so I started looking for a horse that I might rope to carry me the rest of the way. There are many range horses in that part of the country so after urging my limping mount only a little farther along, I came upon a flat where I saw a little horse moving across the trail. He was short and round, had a sharp pointed muzzle and little pin ears. I thought he was an odd looking horse. He traveled in an awkward shuffling gait and I said to myself, 'I am lucky to have chanced upon *el caballo para ir a traer el cura,* the horse on which to bring the priest.' "

Here we must digress to explain to the gringos who are not of the initiated the meaning of this term. A *caballo para ir a traer el cura* is a pacer. Pacers originally came from Spain and according to the old people were the palfreys one reads about in old books. Vaqueros never liked to ride them because their feet were always in the wrong position when one went to turn them. Anglo vaqueros called them "side wheelers." Pacers were called *generoso* by the paisanos and before the gringos brought buggies to California they were ridden by women because of their easy gait. On those occasions when some paisano was on his deathbed the caballo generoso was used to mount the padre who was brought to the rancho to help the dying man prepare for the next world. Not that all padres were poor riders. But they lacked practice and it was not fitting that they should ride a hard-gaited horse. Now, to get back to Juan and his tale . . .

"I threw the lazo around his forelegs and threw him. While he lay there I fitted the jáquima around his nose and put the *tapa-ojos*, the blinds, over his eyes, then let him get to his feet. While I was saddling him I noticed that he had short, stiff hair and that someone had hogged his mane, no doubt to make a hair rope. His owner had not intended to ride him. No one would ever think of cutting off a horse's mane if he intended to ride him because, as you know, a horse's mane, like a woman's hair, is its crowning glory.

"Before mounting I tied a stout limb of a tree across the saddle next to the fork as we all do when we ride a bronco. This was to keep my leg from being broken or pinned under the saddle in case the bronco threw himself and tried to roll. I mounted, but instead of bucking, the animal turned and bit my leg and growled. This surprised me very much since I had never heard a bronco growl before. I kicked his head around and got him into his peculiar shuffle and rode on. It was broad daylight when I reached the *plazita* and as I passed the Church of Nuestra Señora the people who were going to mass stared at me. This surprised me as men riding wild broncos in the City of the Angels were a common sight. But the more people I passed the more surprised they appeared so at last I looked down at my mount and saw that I was riding a grizzly bear!"

Mr. Forster says that Juan would get up and walk away immediately after he had finished his yarn and before the children had recovered enough from the sensational details to start questioning the truth of it.

Epilogue

It is a matchless summer day in beautiful Santa Barbara, California.

The bright warm sun beams down on the groups of people who are massed for the Old Spanish Days parade. They are all in costume, and though there may be some incongruities in their dress, they make up in enthusiasm for whatever they may lack in conformity to period, for it is fiesta time, that week in August when the *Barbareño* gracefully lets the present slip back into the past to pay tribute to the fundadores of California.

The marchers are taking up their positions for the parade when an old vaquero, on an ancient sorrel horse, rides up and takes his place in the line of march. He is a man out of the past, a figure of legend. He stares straight ahead, seemingly indifferent to the many eyes that are upon him. This old vaquero represents the horsemen of an era that is past. And today Santa Barbara, and in spirit all California, pays tribute to a tradition of horsemanship which his ancestors brought from Spain—a superb art which every man, be he Spaniard, Mexican, Indian, Anglo, who has taken it for his own, has cherished and been faithful to.

The old vaquero's saddle, bit, spurs, reins, and hair rope are old, but well made. The silver on the bit, spurs, conchas is fine, white. The saddle has acquired that mellow tint which only loving care and pure castile soap can impart to California oak-tanned leather.

But the old vaquero's hat, shirt, denim pants, and boots are new, unfortunately. The clothing which would have been in keeping with the old equipment went out of style fifty years ago and has not been manufactured since.

The band begins to play; the five flags which have flown over California move up the street. Spanish Santa Barbara is passing in review. The old vaquero, his reins nipped delicately in the fingers of his left hand, moves them ever so slightly, and the sorrel, good vaquero horse that he is, takes the signal. He senses the old man's pride, and perfectly in keeping with his rider's mood, arches his neck and, stepping as if he were walking on eggs, struts up the street, spinning the cricket in the bit for all the world to know that he is content under the hand of his old master.

The old vaquero rides on up the flag-lined street and out of sight. He is lost in the groups of riders that follow him. All too soon the pageant is over. Santa Barbara has come back into the present and the old vaquero has ridden back into history. Perhaps, *con el favor de Dios,* if its pleases God, we shall see him again an another such beautiful August day during Old Spanish Days next year, when the spirit of old mother Spain returns to hover for a few brief hours like a benediction over Santa Barbara.

We shall scan the groups of riders in search of the old vaquero, for he is a symbol of a time which will never come again. And though there may be "cowboys" in this speed-mad world, the vaquero is gone forever from the soil of California.

THE CHICANO HERITAGE

An Arno Press Collection

Adams, Emma H. **To and Fro in Southern California.** 1887

Anderson, Henry P. **The Bracero Program in California.** 1961

Aviña, Rose Hollenbaugh. **Spanish and Mexican Land Grants in California.** 1976

Barker, Ruth Laughlin. **Caballeros.** 1932

Bell, Horace. **On the Old West Coast.** 1930

Biberman, Herbert. **Salt of the Earth.** 1965

Casteñeda, Carlos E., trans. **The Mexican Side of the Texas Revolution (1836).** 1928

Casteñeda, Carlos E. **Our Catholic Heritage in Texas, 1519-1936.** Seven volumes. 1936-1958

Colton, Walter. **Three Years in California.** 1850

Cooke, Philip St. George. **The Conquest of New Mexico and California.** 1878

Cue Canovas, Agustin. **Los Estados Unidos Y El Mexico Olvidado.** 1970

Curtin, L. S. M. **Healing Herbs of the Upper Rio Grande.** 1947

Fergusson, Harvey. **The Blood of the Conquerors.** 1921

Fernandez, Jose. **Cuarenta Años de Legislador:** Biografia del Senador Casimiro Barela. 1911

Francis, Jessie Davies. **An Economic and Social History of Mexican California** (1822-1846). Volume I: Chiefly Economic. Two vols. in one. 1976

Getty, Harry T. **Interethnic Relationships in the Community of Tucson.** 1976

Guzman, Ralph C. **The Political Socialization of the Mexican American People.** 1976

Harding, George L. **Don Agustin V. Zamorano.** 1934

Hayes, Benjamin. **Pioneer Notes from the Diaries of Judge Benjamin Hayes, 1849-1875.** 1929

Herrick, Robert. **Waste.** 1924

Jamieson, Stuart. **Labor Unionism in American Agriculture.** 1945

Landolt, Robert Garland. **The Mexican-American Workers of San Antonio, Texas.** 1976

Lane, Jr., John Hart. **Voluntary Associations Among Mexican Americans in San Antonio, Texas.** 1976

Livermore, Abiel Abbot. **The War with Mexico Reviewed.** 1850

Loyola, Mary. **The American Occupation of New Mexico, 1821-1852.** 1939

Macklin, Barbara June. **Structural Stability and Culture Change in a Mexican-American Community.** 1976

McWilliams, Carey. **Ill Fares the Land:** Migrants and Migratory Labor in the United States. 1942

Murray, Winifred. **A Socio-Cultural Study of 118 Mexican Families Living in a Low-Rent Public Housing Project in San Antonio, Texas.** 1954

Niggli, Josephina. **Mexican Folk Plays.** 1938

Parigi, Sam Frank. **A Case Study of Latin American Unionization in Austin, Texas.** 1976

Poldervaart, Arie W. **Black-Robed Justice.** 1948

Rayburn, John C. and Virginia Kemp Rayburn, eds. **Century of Conflict, 1821-1913.** Incidents in the Lives of William Neale and William A. Neale, Early Settlers in South Texas. 1966

Read, Benjamin. **Illustrated History of New Mexico.** 1912

Rodriguez, Jr., Eugene. **Henry B. Gonzalez.** 1976

Sanchez, Nellie Van de Grift. **Spanish and Indian Place Names of California.** 1930

Sanchez, Nellie Van de Grift. **Spanish Arcadia.** 1929

Shulman, Irving. **The Square Trap.** 1953

Tireman, L. S. **Teaching Spanish-Speaking Children.** 1948

Tireman, L. S. and Mary Watson. **A Community School in a Spanish-Speaking Village.** 1948

Twitchell, Ralph Emerson. **The History of the Military Occupation of the Territory of New Mexico.** 1909

Twitchell, Ralph Emerson. **The Spanish Archives of New Mexico.** Two vols. 1914

U. S. House of Representatives. **California and New Mexico:** Message from the President of the United States, January 21, 1850. 1850

Valdes y Tapia, Daniel. **Hispanos and American Politics.** 1976

West, Stanley A. **The Mexican Aztec Society.** 1976

Woods, Frances Jerome. **Mexican Ethnic Leadership in San Antonio, Texas.** 1949

Aspects of the Mexican American Experience. 1976

Mexicans in California After the U. S. Conquest. 1976

Hispanic Folklore Studies of Arthur L. Campa. 1976

Hispano Culture of New Mexico. 1976

Mexican California. 1976

The Mexican Experience in Arizona. 1976

The Mexican Experience in Texas. 1976

Mexican Migration to the United States. 1976

The United States Conquest of California. 1976

Northern Mexico On the Eve of the United States Invasion: Rare Imprints Concerning California, Arizona, New Mexico, and Texas, 1821-1846. Edited by David J. Weber. 1976